U. S. TRADE DEFICIT ISSUES

U. S. TRADE DEFICIT ISSUES

CARL T. YANKOVICH
EDITOR

Nova Science Publishers, Inc.
New York

LIBRARY OF CONGRESS CATALOGING-IN-PUBLICATION DATA

Available Upon Request

ISBN: 978-1-60692-090-9

Published by Nova Science Publishers, Inc. + New York

CONTENTS

PREFACE

The U.S. trade deficit has risen more or less steadily since 1992. In 2006, the trade imbalance reached $811.5 billion, an increase of $20 billion over the 2005 deficit, and a total increase of about $765 billion since 1992. The trade deficit's growth in 2006 was largely the consequence of increase of import purchases of nearly $210 billion, a slight deceleration from import growth in 2005. Exports in 2006 increased a smaller $162 billion, but this was an acceleration over the 2005 results. As a percentage of GNP, the trade deficit in 2006 was 6.1%, a decrease from 6.3% in 2005. The investment income component of the trade balance moved from a surplus of $10.3 billion in 2005 up to a surplus of $36.6 billion in 2006. The large and growing size of U.S. foreign indebtedness caused by successive trade deficits suggests that the investment income surplus is likely to soon be pushed toward deficit.

The size of the U.S. trade deficit is ultimately rooted in macroeconomic conditions at home and abroad. U.S. saving falls short of what is sought to finance U.S. investment. Many foreign economies are in the opposite circumstances, with domestic saving exceeding domestic opportunities for investment. This difference of wants will tend to be reconciled by international capital flows. The shortfall in domestic saving relative to investment tends to draw an inflow of relatively abundant foreign savings seeking to maximize returns and, in turn, the saving inflow makes a higher level of investment possible. For the United States, a net financial inflow also leads to a like-sized net inflow of foreign goods — a trade deficit. Absent a major shift in the underlying domestic and foreign macroeconomic determinants, most forecasts predict the continued widening of the U.S. trade deficit in 2007, but the rate of increase of the trade deficit is expected to slow.

The benefit of the trade deficit is that it allows the United States to spend now beyond current income. In recent years that spending has largely been for investment in productive capital. The cost of the trade deficit is a deterioration of the U.S. investment-income balance, as the payment on what the United States has borrowed from foreigners grows with its rising indebtedness. Borrowing from abroad allows the United States to live better today, but the payback must mean some decrement to the rate of advance of U.S. living standards in the future. U.S. trade deficits do not now substantially raise the risk of economic instability, but they do impose burdens on trade sensitive sectors of the economy.

Policy action to reduce the overall trade deficit is problematic. Standard trade policy tools (e.g., tariffs, quotas, and subsidies) do not work. Macroeconomic policy tools can work, but recent and prospective government budget deficits will reduce domestic saving and most likely tend to increase the trade deficit. Most economists believe that, in time, the trade deficit will most likely correct itself, without crisis, under the pressures of normal market forces. But the risk of a more calamitous outcome can not be completely discounted.

Chapter 1 - This report provides an overview of the current status, trends, and forecasts for U.S. international trade. The purpose of this report is to provide current data and brief explanations for the various types of trade flows, particularly U.S. exports, along with a short discussion of particular trends and points of contention related to trade policy.

The United States is now running record deficits in its trade with other nations. In 2006 the U.S. merchandise trade deficit reached $838 billion on a balance-of-payments (BoP) basis and $817 billion on a Census basis. A surplus in services trade of $80 billion resulted in a deficit of $759 billion on goods and services for the year — up $44 billion or 6.2% from the $714 billion deficit in 2005. While U.S. exports are highly competitive in world markets, these sales abroad are overshadowed by the huge demand by Americans for imported products. In 2006, U.S. exports of goods and services totaled $1,446 billion, while U.S. imports reached $2,204 billion. Since 1976, the United States has incurred continual merchandise trade deficits with annual amounts fluctuating around an upward trend.

Trade deficits are a concern for Congress because they may generate trade friction and pressures for the government to do more to open foreign markets, to shield U.S. producers from foreign competition, or to assist U.S. industries to become more competitive. As the deficit increases, the risk also rises of a precipitous drop in the value of the dollar and disruption in financial markets. Compared to a Federal Reserve index of currencies weighted by importance to U.S. trade, the dollar has lost a third of its value since 2002. In 2007, the dollar has fallen against major currencies such as the euro, yen, British pound, Australian dollar, and Canadian dollar.

Overall U.S. trade deficits reflect excess spending (a shortage of savings) in the domestic economy and a reliance on capital imports to finance that shortfall. Capital inflows serve to offset the outflow of dollars used to pay for imports. Movements in the exchange rate help to balance trade. The rising trade deficit (when not matched by capital inflows) places downward pressure on the value of the dollar which, in turn, helps to shrink the deficit by making U.S. exports cheaper and imports more expensive. Central banks in countries such as China, however, have intervened in foreign exchange markets to keep the value of their currencies stable.

The broadest measure of U.S. international economic transactions is the balance on current account. In addition to merchandise trade, it includes trade in services and unilateral transfers. In 2006, the deficit on current account rose to a revised $811.5 billion from a revised $754.8 billion in 2005. In trade in advanced technology products, the U.S. balance improved slightly from a deficit of $44 billion in 2005 to a deficit of $38 billion in 2006. In trade in motor vehicles and parts, the $145 billion U.S. deficit in 2006 was mainly with Canada, Japan, Mexico, Germany, United Kingdom, and South Korea. In crude oil, major sources of the $225 billion in imports were Canada, Mexico, Saudi Arabia, Venezuela, and Nigeria. This report will be updated periodically.

Chapter 2 - The U.S. trade deficit has risen more or less steadily since 1992. In 2006, the trade imbalance reached $811.5 billion, an increase of $20 billion over the 2005 deficit, and a total increase of about $765 billion since 1992. The trade deficit's growth in 2006 was largely the consequence of increase of import purchases of nearly $210 billion, a slight deceleration from import growth in 2005. Exports in 2006 increased a smaller $162 billion, but this was an acceleration over the 2005 results. As a percentage of GNP, the trade deficit in 2006 was 6.1%, a decrease from 6.3% in 2005. The investment income component of the trade balance moved from a surplus of $10.3 billion in 2005 up to a surplus of $36.6 billion in 2006. The large and growing size of U.S. foreign indebtedness caused by successive trade deficits suggests that the investment income surplus is likely to soon be pushed toward deficit.

The size of the U.S. trade deficit is ultimately rooted in macroeconomic conditions at home and abroad. U.S. saving falls short of what is sought to finance U.S. investment. Many foreign economies are in the opposite circumstances, with domestic saving exceeding domestic opportunities for investment. This difference of wants will tend to be reconciled by international capital flows. The shortfall in domestic saving relative to investment tends to draw an inflow of relatively abundant foreign savings seeking to maximize returns and, in turn, the saving inflow makes a higher level of investment possible. For the United States, a net financial inflow also leads to a like-sized net inflow of foreign goods — a trade deficit. Absent a major shift in the underlying domestic and foreign macroeconomic determinants, most forecasts predict the continued widening of the U.S. trade deficit in 2007, but the rate of increase of the trade deficit is expected to slow.

The benefit of the trade deficit is that it allows the United States to spend now beyond current income. In recent years that spending has largely been for investment in productive capital. The cost of the trade deficit is a deterioration of the U.S. investment-income balance, as the payment on what the United States has borrowed from foreigners grows with its rising indebtedness. Borrowing from abroad allows the United States to live better today, but the payback must mean some decrement to the rate of advance of U.S. living standards in the future. U.S. trade deficits do not now substantially raise the risk of economic instability, but they do impose burdens on trade sensitive sectors of the economy.

Policy action to reduce the overall trade deficit is problematic. Standard trade policy tools (e.g., tariffs, quotas, and subsidies) do not work. Macroeconomic policy tools can work, but recent and prospective government budget deficits will reduce domestic saving and most likely tend to *increase* the trade deficit. Most economists believe that, in time, the trade deficit will most likely correct itself, without crisis, under the pressures of normal market forces. But the risk of a more calamitous outcome can not be completely discounted. This report will be updated annually.

Chapter 3 - The U.S. trade deficit is equal to net foreign capital inflows. Because U.S. investment rates exceed U.S. saving rates, the gap must be financed by foreign borrowing. Net capital inflows have grown over recent years to a record 6.6% of gross domestic product (GDP) in 2006. Economists have long argued that the low U.S. saving rate, which is much lower than most foreign countries, is the underlying cause of the trade deficit and that policies aimed at reducing the trade deficit should focus on boosting national saving. The most straightforward policy would be to reduce the budget deficit, which directly increases national saving.

In an often-cited speech in early 2005, Ben Bernanke, now the chairman of the Federal Reserve, argued that the underlying cause of the trade deficit was not insufficient domestic saving, but rather a "global saving glut." He argued that there was too much saving worldwide and not enough investment demand, and that the United States was the natural destination for this excess saving. As a result of the global saving glut, the trade deficit increased, interest rates remained low, demand for capital and residential investment rose, and the incentive to save decreased in the United States. He argued that because the trade deficit was not "made in the U.S.A.," policy steps to reduce the budget deficit or raise private saving were unlikely to significantly reduce the trade deficit until the global saving glut ended.

The conventional view and the global saving glut view are not necessarily mutually exclusive. To an extent, the difference between the two is tautological — the conventional view stresses that U.S. saving is too low relative to foreign saving, and the global saving glut view stresses that foreign saving is too high relative to U.S. saving. It is important to acknowledge foreign causes for international capital movements, but in doing so, changes in domestic conditions should not be neglected. Although neither view leads to any hard conclusions about whether the trade deficit is good or bad, the global saving glut implies that reducing it is largely out of American hands.

Contrary to the global saving glut hypothesis, data show that world saving is close to its lowest level in decades. However, low interest rates (although not unusually low by historical standards) suggest that worldwide investment demand is probably low as well. Data also show that the rise in saving in the developing world (notably among oil producers and East Asian countries) over the past few years has gone hand-in-hand with the significant accumulation of official foreign exchange reserves. At the same time, there has been a decrease in government saving in the United States since the 1990s. In recent years, a large fraction of U.S. net capital inflows have been the result of foreign reserve accumulation by other countries rather than coming from private sources, which suggests that global imbalances are not primarily the result of decisions by private investors and that (because of the fall in U.S. government saving) the trade deficit to a great extent may indeed have been "made in the U.S.A."

Chapter 4 - The U.S. merchandise trade deficit is a part of the overall U.S. balance of payments, a summary statement of all economic transactions between the residents of the United States and the rest of the world, during a given period of time. Some Members of Congress and other observers have grown concerned over the magnitude of the growing U.S. merchandise trade deficit and the associated increase in U.S. dollar-denominated assets owned by foreigners. This report provides an overview of the U.S. balance of payments, an explanation of the broader role of capital flows in the U.S. economy, an explanation of how the country finances its trade deficit or a trade surplus, and the implications for Congress and the country of the large inflows of capital from abroad. The major observations indicate that:

Foreign private investors sharply increased their purchases of U.S. Treasury securities in 2007 as they reduced their purchases of U.S. corporate bonds. At the same time, foreign official purchases of U.S. Treasury securities plummeted in 2007 as foreign governments curtailed their purchases of such securities.

The inflow of capital from abroad supplements domestic sources of capital and likely allows the United States to maintain its current level of economic activity at interest rates that are below the level they likely would be without the capital inflows.

Foreign official and private acquisitions of dollar-denominated assets likely will generate a stream of returns to overseas investors that would have stayed in the U.S. economy and supplemented other domestic sources of capital had the assets not been acquired by foreign investors.

Chapter 5 - Petroleum prices have risen sharply since early 2005. At the same time the average monthly volume of imports of energy-related petroleum products has fallen slightly. The combination of sharply rising prices and a slightly lower level of imports of energy-related petroleum products translates into an escalating cost for those imports. This rising cost added an estimated $70 billion to the nation's trade deficit in 2005 and $50 billion in 2006. Imported energy prices moderated in early 2007, before rising again through the summer and more sharply in the fall, following a pattern of rising energy import prices in the spring and summer. This report provides an estimate of the initial impact of the rising oil prices on the nation's merchandise trade deficit.

In: United States Trade Deficit Issues
Editor: Carl T. Yankovich

ISBN: 978-1-60692-090-9

Chapter 1

UNITED STATES INTERNATIONAL TRADE: TRENDS AND FORECASTS*

***Dick K. Nanto*[1], *Shayerah Ilias*[2] *and J. Michael Donnelly*[3]**

[1]Specialist in Industry and Trade Foreign Affairs, Defense, and Trade Division

[2]Analyst in Industry and Trade Foreign Affairs, Defense, and Trade Division

[3]Information Research Specialist, Knowledge Services Group

SUMMARY

This report provides an overview of the current status, trends, and forecasts for U.S. international trade. The purpose of this report is to provide current data and brief explanations for the various types of trade flows, particularly U.S. exports, along with a short discussion of particular trends and points of contention related to trade policy.

The United States is now running record deficits in its trade with other nations. In 2006 the U.S. merchandise trade deficit reached $838 billion on a balance-of-payments (BoP) basis and $817 billion on a Census basis. A surplus in services trade of $80 billion resulted in a deficit of $759 billion on

---

* This is an edited, reformatted and augmented version of a CRS Report for Congress publication dated January 2008.

goods and services for the year — up $44 billion or 6.2% from the $714 billion deficit in 2005. While U.S. exports are highly competitive in world markets, these sales abroad are overshadowed by the huge demand by Americans for imported products. In 2006, U.S. exports of goods and services totaled $1,446 billion, while U.S. imports reached $2,204 billion. Since 1976, the United States has incurred continual merchandise trade deficits with annual amounts fluctuating around an upward trend.

Trade deficits are a concern for Congress because they may generate trade friction and pressures for the government to do more to open foreign markets, to shield U.S. producers from foreign competition, or to assist U.S. industries to become more competitive. As the deficit increases, the risk also rises of a precipitous drop in the value of the dollar and disruption in financial markets. Compared to a Federal Reserve index of currencies weighted by importance to U.S. trade, the dollar has lost a third of its value since 2002. In 2007, the dollar has fallen against major currencies such as the euro, yen, British pound, Australian dollar, and Canadian dollar.

Overall U.S. trade deficits reflect excess spending (a shortage of savings) in the domestic economy and a reliance on capital imports to finance that shortfall. Capital inflows serve to offset the outflow of dollars used to pay for imports. Movements in the exchange rate help to balance trade. The rising trade deficit (when not matched by capital inflows) places downward pressure on the value of the dollar which, in turn, helps to shrink the deficit by making U.S. exports cheaper and imports more expensive. Central banks in countries such as China, however, have intervened in foreign exchange markets to keep the value of their currencies stable.

The broadest measure of U.S. international economic transactions is the balance on current account. In addition to merchandise trade, it includes trade in services and unilateral transfers. In 2006, the deficit on current account rose to a revised $811.5 billion from a revised $754.8 billion in 2005. In trade in advanced technology products, the U.S. balance improved slightly from a deficit of $44 billion in 2005 to a deficit of $38 billion in 2006. In trade in motor vehicles and parts, the $145 billion U.S. deficit in 2006 was mainly with Canada, Japan, Mexico, Germany, United Kingdom, and South Korea. In crude oil, major sources of the $225 billion in imports were Canada, Mexico, Saudi Arabia, Venezuela, and Nigeria. This report will be updated periodically.

MOST RECENT DEVELOPMENTS

In 2006, the **trade deficit in goods** reached a record $838.3 billion (balance of payments [BoP] basis), up $51.1 billion from $787.1 billion in 2005. The 2006 deficit on merchandise trade with China was $232.6 billion (Census basis), with the European Union (EU-27) was $117.2 billion, with Japan was $88.6 billion, with Canada was $71.8 billion, with Mexico was $64.3 billion, and with the Asian Newly Industrialized Countries (Hong Kong, South Korea, Singapore, and Taiwan) was $11.8 billion. **Imports of goods** of $1,861.4 billion increased by $179.6 billion (10.7%) over 2005. Increases in imports by sector were: crude oil up $40.9 billion, capital goods except automotive up $38.9 billion, automotive vehicles and parts up $17.2 billion, and consumer goods up $35.4 billion. **Exports of goods** of $1,023.1 billion rose by $128.5 billion (14%), particularly of industrial supplies (up $43 billion), capital goods except automotive (up $51.6 billion), automotive vehicles and parts (up $8.6 billion), and consumer goods (up $13.9 billion). Exports grew faster than imports, but this was not enough to narrow the trade deficit.

Figure 1 shows the latest monthly balance data for both goods trade and services trade. The services balance remains positive for the entire period. The goods trade balance fluctuates each month. For January and February 2007 the deficit on goods trade was less in 2007 than the corresponding months in 2006. This reversal of the previous trend of steadily increasing trade deficits began in August, 2006. In March 2007, however, the deficit level exceeded that in March 2006, but again receded in April through September 2007. The October 2007 deficit in goods exceeded the deficit for a year earlier. In goods and services, total imports in October 2007 of $199.5 billion were the highest in the year and in U.S. history. Also in October 2007, total exports of goods and services of $141.7 billion were the highest in the year and U.S. history. This produced a deficit on goods and services for that month of $57.8 billion, below the record high set in August 2006 of $67.6 billion. For July through October 2007, the trade deficit remained below the $60 billion monthly level. Although U.S. imports increased by 9.2% from September to October 2007, exports increased by an even greater amount of 13.7%. At $141.7 billion, U.S. good and services exports for October set a record high for 2007.

In services, as shown in **Figure 1**, the U.S. surplus in 2006 increased by about $2 billion from the beginning to the end of the year, reaching $8.3 billion in December. The trade surplus in services for January through October of 2007 was greater than over the corresponding months in 2006. Service imports reached $31.7 billion for October 2007 and exports totaled $40.6 billion, yielding a services surplus of $8.9 billion.[1]

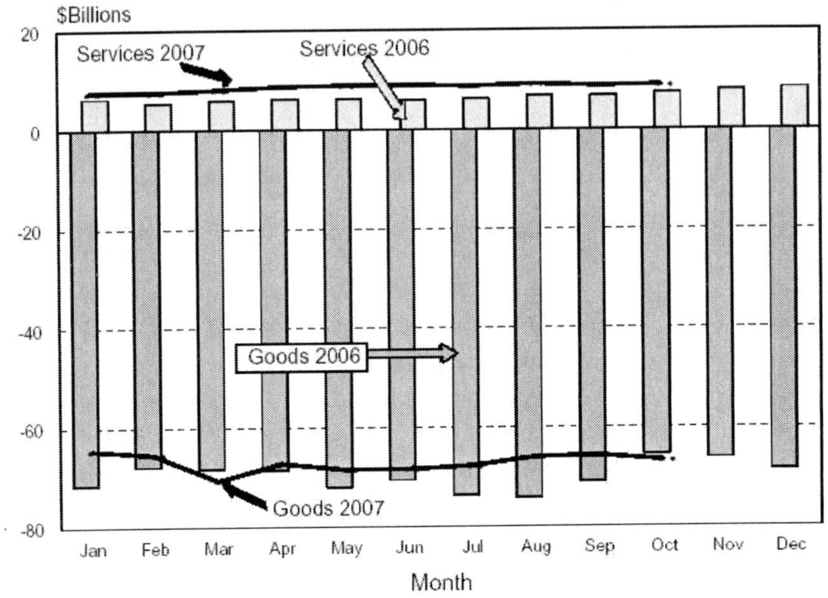

Source: CRS with Data from the U.S. Department of Commerce

Figure 1. Monthly U.S. Balances of Trade in Goods and Services, 2006 and 2007 (in Current Dollars)

For 2006, the trade deficit on goods and services reached a record $758.5 billion or 5.7% of U.S. gross domestic product (GDP, $13.2 trillion in 2005), up slightly from 2005. U.S. consumer demand remains strong and continues to pull in imports at a rapid pace. For 2007, it appears that the trade deficit will decline slightly from that in 2006. Preliminary statistics for 2007 will be released on February 14, 2008.

The U.S. Deficit in International Trade

International trade in goods and services along with flows of financial capital affect virtually every person living in the United States. Whether buying imported clothes, gasoline, computers or cars, or working in an industry that competes with imports, or sells products abroad, the influence of international trade on economic activity is ubiquitous.

The United States in now running record deficits in its trade with other nations. In 2006 the U.S. merchandise trade deficit reached $817.3 billion on a Census basis and $838.3 billion on a balance-of-payments basis (BoP). A surplus in services trade of $79.7 billion produced a deficit of $758.5 billion on goods and services for the year — up $146.4 billion or 23.9% from the $612.1 billion deficit in 2004. While U.S. exports are highly competitive in world markets, U.S. sales abroad are overshadowed by the huge demand by Americans for imported products. In 2006, U.S. exports of goods and services totaled $1.446 trillion, while U.S. imports reached $2.204 trillion (BoP). Since 1976, the United States has incurred continual merchandise trade deficits with annual amounts fluctuating around an upward trend.

For the Congress, the trade deficit and other aspects of international trade enter into public policy considerations through many portals. At the macroeconomic level, trade deficits are a concern because they affect U.S. economic growth, interest rates, labor, and the debt load of the economy. As the trade deficit rises relative to the total economy, the risk increases that the dollar will weaken, raise prices, disrupt financial markets, and reduce the economic well being of the population. On the strategic level, trade ties often lead to a deepening of bilateral relations with other nations that can develop into formal free trade agreements or political and security arrangements. Trade also can be used as a tool to accomplish strategic objectives — particularly through providing preferential trading arrangements or by imposing trade sanctions.

On the microeconomic side, imports of specific products can generate trade friction and pressures from constituent interests for the government to shield U.S. producers from foreign competition, provide adjustment assistance, open foreign markets, or assist U.S. industries to become more competitive.

This report provides an overview of the current status, trends, and forecasts for U.S. import and export flows as well as certain balances. The purpose of this report is to provide current data and brief explanations for the various types of trade flows along with a brief discussion of trends that may require attention or point to the need for policy changes. The use of trade policy as an economic or strategic tool is beyond the scope of this report but can be found in various other CRS reports.[2] Further detail on trade in specific commodities, with particular countries or regions, or for different time periods, can be obtained from the Department of Commerce,[3] U.S. International Trade Commission,[4] or by contacting the authors of this report.

Savings Shortfalls and the Trade Deficit

Overall U.S. trade deficits reflect a shortage of savings in the domestic economy and a reliance on capital imports to finance that shortfall. A savings shortfall is the analogue of excessive spending that is financed by borrowing. Households borrow for consumption; businesses borrow to invest; and the government borrows to cover its budget deficit. At the international transaction level, the savings shortfall is manifest when the United States imports capital to pay for its excess of imports (trade deficit).

Whether this foreign borrowing is beneficial for the U.S. economy depends on how the imports of capital are used. If they are used to finance investments that generate a future return at a sufficiently high rate (they raise future output and productivity), then they may increase the well being of current and future generations. However, if the imports are used only for current consumption, the net effect of the borrowing will be to shift the burden of repayment to future generations without a corresponding benefit to them.

Implications of the Trade Deficit

U.S. trade balances are macroeconomic variables that may or may not indicate underlying problems with the competitiveness of particular industries or what some refer to as the competitiveness of a nation. The reason is that overall trade flows are determined, within the framework of institutional barriers to trade and the activities of individual industries, primarily by macroeconomic factors such as rates of growth, savings and investment behavior (including government budget deficits/surpluses), international capital flows, and exchange rates.[5]

Increases in trade deficits may diminish economic growth, since net exports (exports minus imports) are a component of gross domestic product. In the late 1980s and early 1990s, export growth was an important element in overall U.S. economic growth. In 2006, merchandise exports accounted for about 7.7% of GDP, compared with 5.9% in 1990. Recently, however, rising trade deficits have reduced total domestic demand in the economy, but the weakness in the trade sector has been offset by strong consumer, business, and government demand.

Many economists fear that the rising U.S. trade and current account[6] deficits could lead to a large drop in the value of the U.S. dollar. The current account deficit now exceeds 6% of GDP and is placing downward pressure on the dollar. A weakened dollar boosts exports by making them cheaper, narrowing the U.S. trade deficit. Compared to a Federal Reserve index of major currencies weighted by importance to U.S. trade, the dollar has lost a third of its value since 2002 (see **Figure 2**). The dollar has fallen against the euro, yen, British pound, Australian dollar, and Canadian dollar. In fact, the U.S. dollar fell to parity with the Canadian loonie in September 2007 for the first time in thirty years, and remains roughly in that range. The dollar's decline was exacerbated when the Federal Reserve lowered interest rates on September 18, 2007.

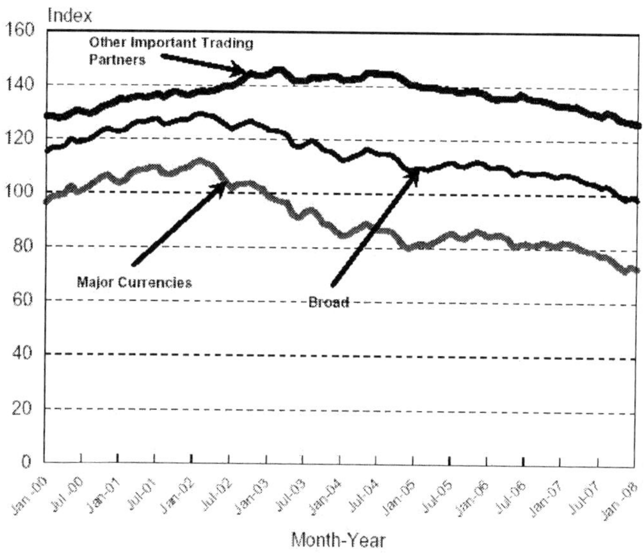

Source: Federal Reserve Bank of St. Louis, [http://www.federalreserve.gov/releases/h1 0/Summary/].

Notes: **Broad Index (January 1997 = 100):** Euro Area, Canada, Japan, Mexico, China, United Kingdom, Taiwan, Korea, Singapore, Hong Kong, Malaysia, Brazil, Switzerland, Thailand, Philippines, Australia, Indonesia, India, Israel, Saudi Arabia, Russia, Sweden, Argentina, Venezuela,Chile and Colombia.

Major Currencies Index (January 1993 = 100): Euro Area, Canada, Japan, United Kingdom, Switzerland, Australia, and Sweden.

Other Important Trade Partners Index (January 1997 = 100): Mexico, China, Taiwan, Korea, Singapore, Hong Kong, Malaysia, Brazil, Thailand, Philippines, Indonesia, India, Israel, Saudi Arabia, Russia, Argentina, Venezuela, Chile and Colombia.

Figure 2. Month-End Trade-Weighted U.S. Dollar Against Broad, Major Currencies, and Other Important Trading Partner Indices, January 2000-January 2008

Although a weakened dollar helps to reduce U.S. trade imbalances, it also may reduce the dollar's attractiveness to foreign investors. If foreign investors stop offsetting the deficit by buying dollar-denominated assets, the value of the dollar could drop — possibly precipitously. In that case, U.S. interest rates would have to rise to attract more foreign investment; financial markets could be disrupted; and inflationary pressures could increase. In the International Monetary Fund's May 2006 consultation with the United States, for example, its directors reiterated their long-standing concerns about the large U.S. current account deficit. They stated that "there is broad agreement that the large U.S. current account deficit ... cannot be sustained indefinitely. Although a gradual adjustment is the most likely outcome, delaying progress increases the risk of fanning protectionist sentiment or disorderly foreign exchange market conditions."[7]

Currently, foreign investment in dollar assets along with purchases of securities by central banks of countries, such China and Japan, have been sufficient to keep the value of the dollar from falling too far. These central banks have intervened in currency markets to keep their exchange rates relatively stable with respect to the dollar, although Japan claims not to have intervened since spring of 2004. This intervention adds to the foreign currency reserves held by these countries. Japan's central bank held $946 billion in foreign currency reserves (end of November 2007),[8] and the Bank of China held $1,434 billion (end of September 2007).[9] In U.S. Treasury securities, as of October 2007, Japan held $592 billion and China $388 billion.[10] On July 21, 2005, China announced a 2.1% revaluation of its currency, but the value of the renminbi has appreciated only a few more percentage points since then (indicating that China may still be intervening in currency markets).[11]

A recent development in foreign country holdings of dollars and other reserve currencies is that some are turning toward creating sovereign wealth funds. These are funds owned by governments that are invested in stocks, bonds, property, and other financial instruments denominated in dollars, euros, or other hard currency. For China, Japan, South Korea, Russia, and oil-exporting nations, the source of capital for these funds is coming from governmental holdings of foreign exchange. For China and Japan, for example, foreign exchange reserves have traditionally been invested by their respective central banks primarily in low-yielding but low-risk government bonds, i.e., U.S. Treasury securities. The purpose of sovereign wealth funds is to diversify investments and to earn a higher rate of return. China, for example, is creating a fund of more than $200 billion that already has bought a 10% ($3 billion) share (non-voting) of the initial public offering of the

Blackstone Group, a U.S. private equity group. Morgan Stanley research estimates that such sovereign wealth funds could hold up to $12 trillion by 2015.[12] Depending on how these funds are managed and what leverage they acquire, they could affect U.S. interest rates (foreign purchases of U.S. Treasury securities tend to reduce U.S. interest rates), corporate activities (if funds buy significant voting shares of companies), and foreign access to technology and raw materials. The U.S. trade deficit provides some of the foreign exchange that goes to finance these sovereign wealth funds.

How long can the United States keep running trade deficits? U.S. deficits in trade can continue for as long as foreign investors are willing to buy and hold U.S. assets, particularly government securities and other financial assets.[13] Their willingness depends on a complicated array of factors including the perception of the United States as a safe haven for capital, relative rates of return on investments, interest rates on U.S. financial assets, actions by foreign central banks, and the savings and investment decisions of businesses, governments, and households. The policy levers that influence these factors that affect the trade deficit are held by the Federal Reserve[14] (interest rates) as well as both Congress and the Administration (government budget deficits and trade policy), and their counterpart institutions abroad.

In the 110th Congress, legislation directed at the trade deficit is taking several strategies. Some address trade barriers by particular countries, particularly China. Others are aimed at preventing manipulation of exchange rates or at imposing import duties to compensate for the arguably undervalued Chinese currency.[15] Other bills seek to find domestic substitutes for imported oil, or require the President or a policy group to take certain actions if the trade deficit exceeded a threshold amount (for instance, a bilateral trade deficit of $10 billion or 2% of GDP). Legislation is tracked in other CRS reports dealing with trade.

Types of Trade Data

The U.S. government compiles trade data in four different ways. The data on goods trade are first compiled on a Census basis. Bilateral and sectoral data are reported only on a Census basis. The Census numbers are then adjusted and reported monthly on a balance of payments (BoP) basis that includes adjustments for valuation, coverage, and timing and excludes military transactions. The data are finally reported in terms of national income and product accounts (NIPA). The NIPA data also can be further adjusted to include correcting for inflation to gauge movement in trade volumes as distinct from trade values. Conceptually, this procedure is analogous to adjusting macroeconomic data from nominal to real values.

The Census Bureau also reports imports on a c.i.f. (cost, insurance, and freight) basis which includes the value of insurance, international shipping, and other charges incurred in bringing merchandise to U.S. ports of entry. The customs (or f.a.s. — free alongside ship) data do not include these supplementary costs. U.S. import data are reported on a customs basis with insurance and freight charges counted in U.S. services trade. Other countries, however, commonly report merchandise import figures that include insurance and freight charges. This tends to overstate their imports and understate their trade surpluses with the United States.

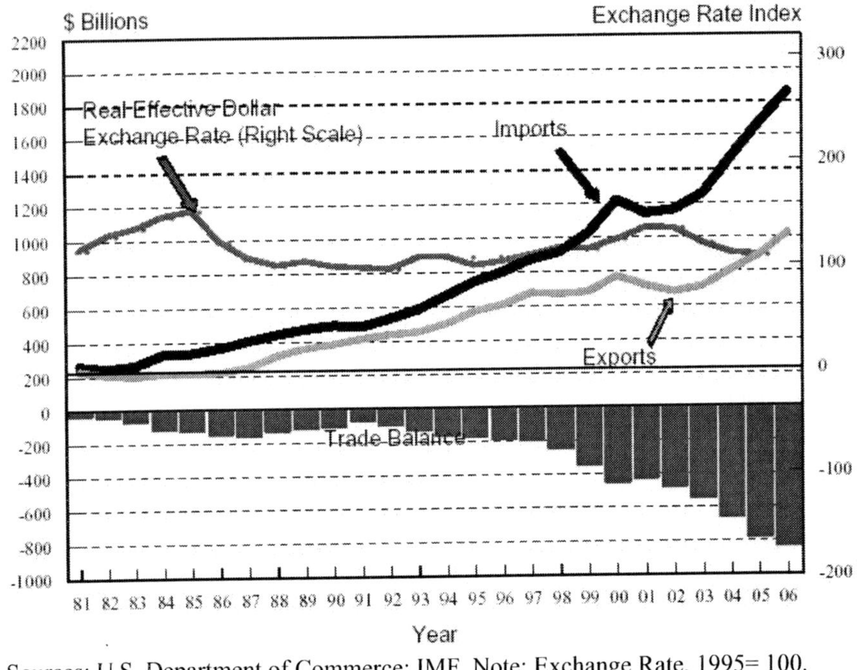

Sources: U.S. Department of Commerce; IMF. Note: Exchange Rate, 1995= 100.

Figure 3. U.S. Merchandise Exports, Imports, Trade Balance, and Real Effective Dollar Exchange Rate Index, 1982-2006

U.S. MERCHANDISE TRADE BALANCE

The merchandise (goods) trade balance is the most widely known and frequently used indicator of U.S. international economic activity (see **Figure 3**). In 2006, total U.S. merchandise trade amounted to $2,884 billion, with exports of $1,023 billion and imports of $1,861 billion (BoP basis). The U.S. merchandise trade deficit rose 6.5% in 2006 to $838 billion following a 17.6% rise in 2005 and a 22% rise in 2004. The rate of increase in the deficit, therefore, is beginning to taper off.

Table 1. U.S. Exports, Imports, and Merchandise Trade Balances, 1982-2006 (billions of U.S. dollars)

	Census basis			Balance of payments basis		
Year	Exports (f.a.s.[a])	Imports (customs[b)])	Trade Balance	Exports (f.a.s.[a])	Imports (customs[b)])	Trade Balance
1982	212.3	243.9	-31.6	211.2	247.6	-36.4
1983	201.7	261.7	-60.0	201.8	268.9	-67.1
1984	218.7	330.5	-111.8	219.9	332.4	-112.5
1985	212.6	336.4	-123.8	215.9	338.1	-122.2
1986	226.4	365.7	-139.3	223.3	368.4	-145.1
1987	253.9	406.3	-152.4	250.2	409.8	-159.6
1988	323.3	441.9	-118.6	320.2	447.2	-127.0
1989	362.9	473.4	-110.5	359.9	477.7	-117.8
1990	392.9	495.2	-102.3	387.4	498.4	-111.0
1991	421.8	487.1	-65.3	414.1	491.0	-76.9
1992	448.2	532.6	-84.4	439.6	536.5	-96.9
1993	464.8	580.5	-115.7	456.9	589.4	-132.5
1994	512.6	663.2	-150.6	502.9	668.7	-165.8
1995	584.7	743.5	-158.8	575.2	749.4	-174.2

Table 1. (Continued)

	Census basis			Balance of payments basis		
Year	**Exports (f.a.s.[a])**	**Imports (customs [b])**	**Trade Balance**	**Exports (f.a.s.[a])**	**Imports (customs [b])**	**Trade Balance**
1996	625.1	795.3	-170.2	612.1	803.1	-191.0
1997	689.2	869.7	-180.5	678.4	876.5	-198.1
1998	682.1	911.9	-229.8	670.4	917.1	-246.7
1999	695.8	1,024.6	-328.8	684.0	1,030.0	-346.0
2000	781.9	1,218.0	-436.1	772.0	1,224.4	-452.4
2001	730.9	1,142.3	-411.4	718.7	1,145.9	-427.2
2002	693.5	1,163.6	-470.1	681.8	1,164.7	-482.9
2003	724.8	1,257.1	-532.3	713.1	1,260.7	-547.6
2004	818.8	1,469.7	-650.9	807.5	1,477.1	-669.6
2005	906.0	1,673.5	-767.5	894.6	1,681.8	-787.2
2006	1,036.	1,853.9	-817.3	1,023.1	1,861.4	-838.3

Source: U.S. Department of Commerce, Bureau of Economic Analysis, U.S. International Transactions Accounts Data.

Note: Goods on a Census basis are adjusted to a BoP basis to include changes in ownership that occur without goods passing into or out of the customs territory of the United States, to eliminate duplication, and to value transactions according to a standard definition. Export adjustments include counting military sales as services not goods, adding private gift parcels, and foreign official gold sales from U.S. private dealers. Import adjustments include adding in inland freight in Canada and foreign official gold sales to U.S. private dealers, and subtracting imports by U.S. military agencies.

a. Exports are valued on an f.a.s. basis, which refers to the free alongside ship value at the port of export and generally include inland freight, insurance, and other charges incurred in placing the goods alongside the carrier at the port of exportation.

b. Imports are valued as reported by the U.S. Customs Service, known as Customs basis, and exclude import duties, the cost of freight, insurance, and other charges incurred in bringing merchandise to the United States.

U.S. merchandise exports (as shown in **Table 1** and **Figure 4**), decreased in 2001 and 2002 in response to the global slowdown, but generally have been increasing each year. As shown in **Figure 4**, the growth of imports has also been steady, although they too fell by 4.4% in 2001 before recovering in 2002. In 2003, import growth was nearly double export growth, although in 2004, export growth almost caught up with that of imports, and in 2005, the rate of increase for both dropped slightly (11% for exports and 14% for imports). In 2006, exports grew by 14%, while imports grew by 11%. Exports grew faster than imports, but the trade deficit still increased. This is because U.S. imports are about 82% greater than U.S. exports, so exports must grow 82% faster than imports just for the deficit to remain constant.

MERCHANDISE TRADE BALANCE IN VOLUME TERMS

Like other economic variables, exports and imports, reported in terms of their values, can change merely because prices change. Trade data, therefore, can be adjusted for inflation by dividing by a chained price index (chained price indexes are weighted by two-year averages) to generate real or volume data (some trade commodities actually are reported in volume terms [e.g., tons of wheat]). The real data provide a more accurate picture of how the underlying flows of merchandise are changing. As with the nominal trade deficit, the real deficit continues to widen.

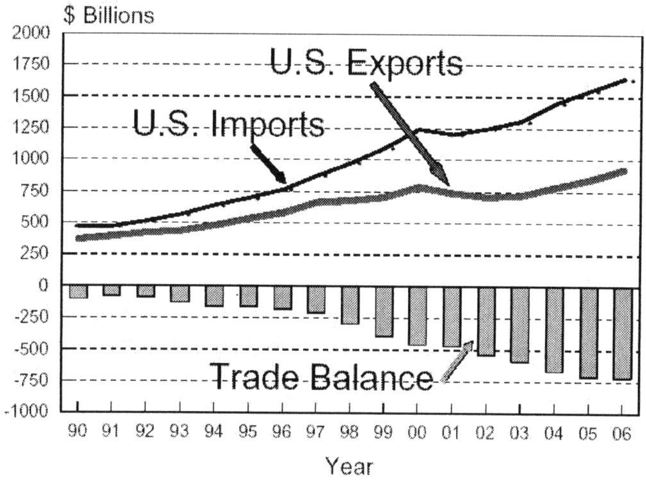

Source: CRS with data from U.S. Bureau of Economic Analysis.

Figure 4. Real U.S. Imports, Exports, and Trade Balance of Goods (chained 2000 dollars), 1990-2006

As shown in **Table 2** and **Figure 5**, the constant-dollar value, or physical volume, of merchandise exports increased by 9.9% in 2006, up from 7.5% in 2005 and 9.0% in 2004. The physical volume of imports rose by 6.0% in 2006, down from 6.6% in 2005 and 11.3% in 2004, but up from 4.9% in 2003. Because the growth of merchandise imports is higher than the growth of exports and because imports exceed exports by more than 80% on a physical volume basis, exports would have to grow more than 80% faster than imports just for the U.S. trade deficit in terms of volume to remain constant. In 2005 and 2006, export growth actually exceeded import growth, but the deficit still increased. In recent year's, the deficit in volume terms has varied relative to the deficit in value terms partly because of fluctuations in oil import prices (when oil prices rise, the deficit in value rises relative to that in volume terms).

CURRENT ACCOUNT BALANCE

The current account provides a broader measure of U.S. trade because it includes services, investment income, and unilateral transfers in addition to merchandise trade. (See **Figure 6**.) The balance on services includes travel, transportation, fees and royalties, insurance payments, and other government and private services. The balance on investment income includes income received on U.S. assets abroad minus income paid on foreign assets in the United States. Unilateral transfers are international transfers of funds for which there is no *quid pro quo*. These include private gifts, remittances, pension payments, and government grants (foreign aid). Data on the current account lag those on trade by several months.

Table 2. U.S. Merchandise Trade in Volume Terms, 2001-2006 (billions of chained 2000 dollars)

Year	Exports	Export Growth	Imports	Import Growth	Real Trade Balance
2001	736.3	-6.1	1,204.1	-3.2	-467.8
2002	707.0	-4.0	1,248.2	3.7	-541.2
2003	719.8	1.8	1,309.3	4.9	-589.5
2004	784.4	9.0	1,457.0	11.3	-672.6
2005	843.5	7.5	1,553.6	6.6	-710.1
2006	927.4	9.9	1,646.9	6.0	-719.5

Source: CRS calculations from Bureau of Economic Analysis, National Income and Products Accounts data, Table 4.2.6, [http://www.bea.gov/].

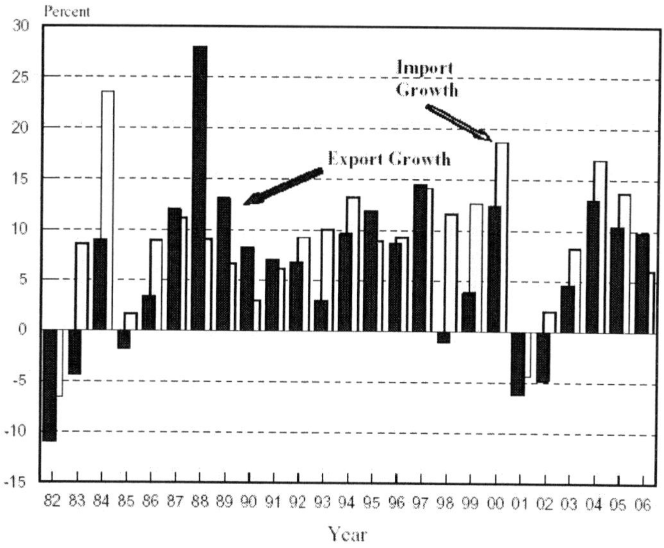

Source: Underlying data from U.S. Department of Commerce.

Figure 5. Annual Growth in U.S. Merchandise Exports and Imports, 1982-2006

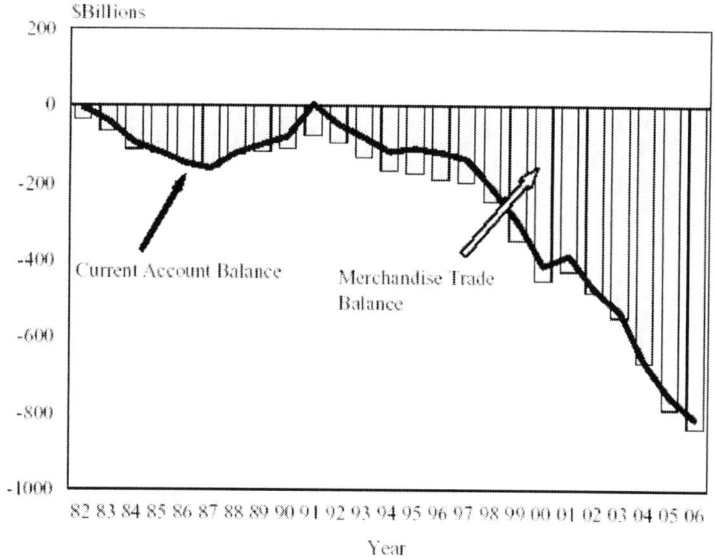

Source: CRS with data from U.S. Bureau of Economic Analysis.

Figure 6. U.S. Current Account and Merchandise Trade Balances, 1982-2006

Table 3. U.S. Current Account Balances: 1985-2006 (billions of U.S. dollars)

Calendar Year	Merchandise Trade Balance [a]	Services Balance [b]	Investment Income Balance [c]	Net Unilateral Transfers [d]	Current Account Balance [e]
1985	-122.2	0.3	25.7	-22.0	-118.2
1986	-145.1	6.5	15.5	-24.1	-147.2
1987	-159.6	7.9	14.3	-23.3	-160.7
1988	-127.0	12.4	18.7	-25.3	-121.2
1989	-117.7	24.6	19.8	-26.2	- 99.5
1990	-111.0	30.2	28.6	-26.7	-79.0
1991	-76.9	45.8	24.1	10.8	3.7
1992	-96.9	57.8	24.2	-33.1	-48.0
1993	-132.5	62.3	25.3	-37.1	-82.0
1994	-165.8	67.4	17.1	-36.8	-118.0
1995	-174.2	77.9	20.9	-34.1	-109.5
1996	-191.0	87.1	22.3	-38.6	-120.2
1997	-198.1	89.8	12.6	-45.2	-140.9
1998	-246.7	81.7	4.3	-53.2	-214.9
1999	-346.0	82.6	13.9	-50.6	-300.1
2000	-452.4	74.1	21.0	-58.8	-416.4
2001	-427.2	64.5	25.2	-51.9	-389.4
2002	-482.9	61.1	10.0	-64.0	-475.2
2003	-547.3	52.5	46.3	-71.2	-519.7
2004	-669.6	54.1	27.6	-81.6	-665.3
2005	-787.1	72.8	48.1	-88.5	-754.8
2006	-838.3	79.7	36.6	-89.6	-811.5

Source: U.S. Bureau of Economic Analysis, U.S. International Transactions. On the Internet at [http://www.bea.gov/bea/international/bp_web/list.cfm?anon=71].

a. On a BoP basis.

b. Includes travel, transportation, fees and royalties, insurance payments, other government and private services, and investment income.

c. Income receipts on U.S. assets abroad minus income payments on foreign assets in the United States.

d. International transfers of funds, such as private gifts, pension payments, and government grants for which there is no *quid pro quo*.

e. The trade balance plus the service balance plus investment income balance plus net unilateral transfers, although conceptually equal to the current account balance, may differ slightly as a result of rounding.

Table 3 summarizes the components of the U.S. current account. In 2006, the U.S. deficit on current account increased to $811.5 billion from $754.8 billion in 2005. As a share of U.S. GDP, this deficit rose to 6.2% in 2006. This is considerably above the caution level used by the International Monetary

Fund of 5%. Since the dollar is used as an international reserve currency, however, the United States can run trade deficits without the same downward pressure on the value of the dollar as other nations. Historically, the current account deficit fell from a then record-high \$160.7 billion in 1987 to \$79.0 billion in 1990, and switched to a \$3.7 billion surplus in 1991 (primarily because of payments to fund the Gulf War by Japan and other nations). However, since a slight decline in 1995, the current account deficit has been increasing significantly except for a slight dip in 2001 because of the U.S. recession.

Since the merchandise trade balance comprises the greater part of the current account, the two tend to track each other. Unlike the merchandise trade balance, however, the services account registered a \$79.7 billion surplus in 2006. Since Americans are such large investors in foreign economies, the United States traditionally also has a surplus in its investment income. The deficit in unilateral transfers (primarily dollars sent abroad by foreign workers and recent immigrants) at \$89.6 billion in 2006 continued to rise and has reached more than triple the level of the late 1980s.

FORECASTS

According to Global Insight, Inc., a leading U.S. economic forecasting firm, in 2007 the U.S. merchandise (goods) trade deficit is projected to decline to about \$820.5 billion on a balance of payments basis and to continue to decline in 2008 and 2009 before beginning to rise again in 2010 (see **Table 4** and **Figure 7**). The U.S. current account deficit likewise is projected to decline from the peak of \$811.5 billion in 2006 to \$774.1 billion in 2007. After additional dips in 2008 and 2009, the current account deficit is forecasted to increase again in 2010.

U.S. TRADE WITH SELECTED NATIONS

The overall U.S. merchandise trade balance consists of deficits or surpluses with each trading partner. Many economists view the overall figure as more significant than bilateral trade balances, since rising deficits with some nations are often offset by declining deficits or growing surpluses with others. Nonetheless, abnormally large or rapidly increasing trade deficits with particular countries are often viewed as indicators that underlying problems may exist with market access, the competitiveness of particular industries, currency misalignment, or macroeconomic adjustment. **Figure 8** and **Table 5** show U.S. trade balances with selected nations.

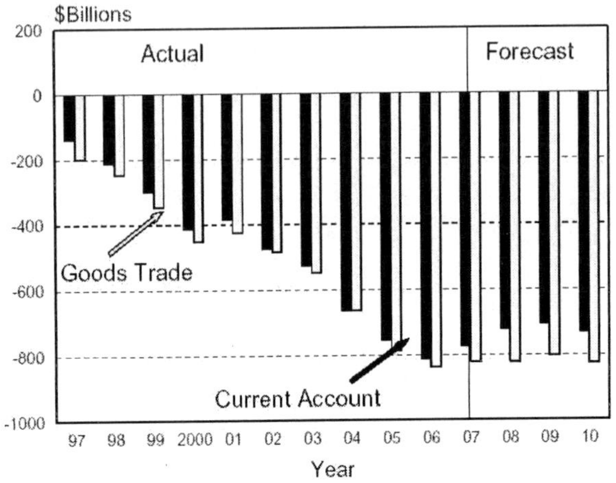

Sources: U.S. Bureau of Economic Analysis and Global Insight (BoP basis).

Figure 7. U.S. Merchandise Trade and Current Account Deficits, 1997-2009 (forecast, in current dollars)

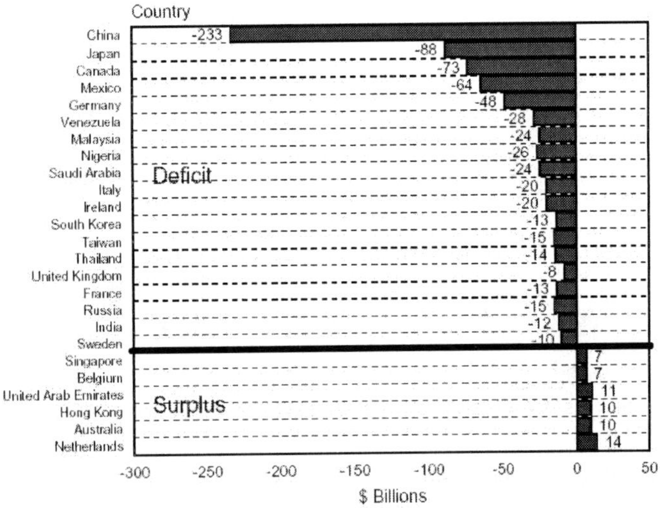

Source: CRS with data from the U.S. Department of Commerce (Census basis).

Figure 8. U.S. Merchandise Trade Balances with Selected Nations, 2006

Table 4. U.S. Merchandise and Current Account Trade, 2003 to 2010 (Forecast) (billions of U.S. dollars)

					Forecast			
	2003	2004	2005	2006	2007	2008	2009	2010
Merchandise Trade								
Exports								
Actual	713.4	807.5	894.6	1,023.1	—	—	—	—
Global Insight	—	—	—	—	1,150.5	1,290.2	1,419.7	1,527.9
Imports								
Actual	1260.7	1472.9	1,681.8	1,861.4	—	—	—	—
Global Insight	—	—	—	—	1,989.3	2,095.3	2,204.0	2,330.6
Trade Balance								
Actual	-547.3	-665.4	-787.1	-838.3	—	—	—	—
Global Insight	—	—	—	—	-820.5	-784.3	-764.1	-782.5
Services Trade Balance								
Actual	52.5	54.1	72.8	79.7	—	—	—	—
Global Insight	—	—	—	—	106.6	137.8	158.6	178.0
Current Account Balance								
Actual	-519.7	-665.3	-754.8	-811.5	—	—	—	—
Global Insight	—	—	—	—	-774.1	-686.6	-663.6	-689.7

Sources: U.S. Bureau of Economic Analysis and Global Insight (BoP basis).

Table 5. U.S. Merchandise Trade Balances with Selected Nations and Groups, 2002-2006 (millions of U.S. dollars, Census basis)

Country	2002	2003	2004	2005	2006
Total	**-468,263**	**-532,350**	**-650,930**	**-767,477**	**-817,304**
North America	-853,110	-92,319	-111,547	-128,230	-136,056
Canada	-48,165	-51,671	-66,480	-78,486	-71,782
Mexico	-37,146	-40,648	-45,067	-49,744	-64,274
Europe	-93,355	-105,603	-119,907	-132,269	-123,016
European Union 27	-86,377	-98,521	-109,999	-123,123	-117,216
United Kingdom	-7,540	-8,967	-10,274	-12,445	-8,103
Germany	-35,876	-39,281	-45,850	-50,567	-47,763
France	-9,224	-12,166	-10,342	-11,432	-12,822
Italy	-14,164	-14,854	-17,413	-19,485	-20,109
Netherlands	8,462	9,742	11,839	11,623	13,787
Russia	-4,473	-6,171	-8,930	-11,344	-15,127
Pacific Rim Countries	-310,170	331,869	405,298	-469,223	-513,662
Japan	-69,979	-66,032	-75,562	-82,519	-88,568
China	-103,065	-124,068	-161,938	-201,545	-232,589
Newly Industrialized Countries (NICS)	-22,080	-21,217	-21,883	-15,782	-11,783
Singapore	1,416	1,422	4,238	5,532	6,916
Hong Kong	3,266	4,669	6,513	7,459	9,829
Taiwan	-13,766	-14,152	-12,879	-12,757	-15,165
Republic of Korea	-12,996	-13,157	-19,755	-16,016	-13,362
South/Central American Countries	-17,952	-26,883	-37,183	-50,460	-44,706
Argentina	-1,602	-732	-357	-462	797
Brazil	-3,405	-6,699	-7,263	-9,064	-7,136
Colombia	-2,022	-2,629	-2,751	-3,387	-2,557
OPEC	-34,433	-51,064	-71,843	-92,867	-105,289
Venezuela	-10,664	-14,305	-20,153	-27,557	-28,131
Indonesia	-7,087	-6,999	-8,139	-8,960	-10,346
Saudi Arabia	-8,369	-13,473	-15,702	-20,380	-24,049
Nigeria	-4,888	-9,377	-14,694	-22,618	-25,630

Sources: United States Census Bureau, Foreign Trade Statistics. For other countries and further detail, see U.S. International Trade in Goods and Services Annual Revision for 2006, FT 900 (07-04), released June 8, 2007.

Note: Trade Balance equals Total Exports (f.a.s. value) minus General Imports (Customs value).

Most of the U.S. trade deficit can be accounted for by trade with China, Japan, Canada, Mexico, and Germany. Trade with the oil exporting countries, particularly Venezuela, Nigeria, and Saudi Arabia, also is in deficit. U.S. trade surpluses occur in trade with the Netherlands, Australia, Hong Kong, and the United Arab Emirates.

The U.S. trade deficit with China has soared over the past decade. From $32 billion in 1995 to $100 billion in 2000 and $233 billion in 2006, the negative net balance in trade with China has grown to account for 28% of the total U.S. trade deficit.[16] The U.S. trade deficit with China exceeded that with Japan for the first time in the year 2000 and now is more than twice as large.

China claims that its trade is less imbalanced than U.S. data indicate. Chinese trade data differ from those of the United States primarily because of the treatment of Hong Kong as an entrepot. Since Hong Kong is a separate customs area from mainland China, Beijing counts Hong Kong as the destination for its exports sent there, even though the goods may be transshipped to other markets. For example, China would count a laptop computer that is assembled in Shanghai but shipped through Hong Kong before being exported to the United States as a sale to Hong Kong. By contrast, the United States and many of China's other trading partners count Chinese exports that are transshipped through Hong Kong as products from China not Hong Kong, including goods that contain Hong Kong components or involve final packaging in Hong Kong. The United States also counts Hong Kong as the destination of U.S. products sent there, even those that are then reexported to China. However, the PRC counts many of such reexported goods as U.S. exports to China. So by U.S. figures, U.S. exports to China tend to be understated, while by Chinese figures, Chinese exports to the U.S. tend to be understated. The net result is that China's reported trade surplus with the United States at $144 billion in 2006 is about 60% of the reported U.S. deficit with China of $233 billion.

Table 6 lists the U.S. top deficit trading partners in merchandise trade, on a Census basis. In 2000, China overtook Japan as the top U.S. deficit trading partner. After, China, the next highest deficit trading partners are Japan, Canada, Mexico, Germany, and Venezuela.

As shown in **Table 7**, in 2006, Canada again was America's largest total merchandise trading partner, but China passed Mexico to take second place in the ranking. Fourth was Japan, then Germany, and the United Kingdom. South Korea ranked seventh. **Table 7** lists the United States' top trading partners ranked by trade turnover. Trade with Canada accounts for 18% of total U.S. trade. Canada is the largest supplier of U.S. imports but China is rising fast and could surpass Canada in 2007. By far, Canada is the top purchaser of U.S. exports with Mexico second, Japan third, and China fourth.

Table 6. Top U.S. Merchandise Deficit Trading Partners, 2006 (millions of U.S. dollars)

Country	Balance	U.S. Exports	U.S. Imports
China	-232,589	55,186	287,774
Japan	-88,568	59,613	148,181
Canada	-71,782	230,656	302,438
Mexico	-64,274	133,979	198,253
Germany	-47,763	41,319	89,082
Venezuela	-28,132	9,002	37,134
Nigeria	-25,630	2,234	27,863
Malaysia	-23,989	12,544	36,533
Saudi Arabia	-24,050	7,640	31,689
Ireland	-20,010	8,516	28,526
Italy	-20,109	12,546	32,655
Taiwan	-15,165	23,047	38,212
Russia	-15,127	4,701	19,828
Algeria	-14,354	1,102	15,456
Thailand	-14,320	8,147	22,466
Korea	-13,362	32,442	45,804
France	-12,822	24,217	37,040
India	-11,775	10,056	21,831
Indonesia	-10,346	3,079	13,425
Sweden	-9,745	4,126	13,870
United Kingdom	-8,103	45,410	53,513
Brazil	-7,136	19,231	26,367
Austria	-5,318	2,986	8,304
Norway	-4,691	2,394	7,085
South Africa	-3,039	4,462	7,501
Chile	-2,779	6,786	9,565
Colombia	-2,557	6,709	9,266

Source: U.S. Department of Commerce. U.S. International Trade in Goods and Services Annual Revision for 2006, FT 900 (07-04), released June 8, 2007.

Note: Data are on a Census basis. Exports are valued f.a.s.; imports are valued Customs.

Table 7. Top U.S. Trading Partners Ranked by Total Merchandise Trade in 2006 (millions of U.S. dollars)

Rank	Country	Total Trade	Balance	U.S. Exports	U.S. Import
1	Canada	533,094	-71,782	230,656	302,438
2	China	342,960	-232,589	55,186	287,774
3	Mexico	332,232	-64,274	133,979	198,253
4	Japan	207,794	-88,568	59,613	148,181
5	Germany	130,401	-47,763	41,319	89,082
6	United	98,923	-8,103	45,410	53,513
7	Korea	78,246	-13,362	32,442	45,804
8	Taiwan	61,259	-15,165	23,047	38,212
9	France	61,257	-12,822	24,217	37,040
10	Malaysia	49,077	-23,989	12,544	36,533
11	Venezuela	46,136	-28,132	9,002	37,134
12	Brazil	45,598	-7,136	19,231	26,367
13	Italy	45,201	-20,109	12,546	32,655
14	Saudi Arabia	39,329	-24,050	7,640	31,689
15	Ireland	37,042	-20,010	8,516	28,526
16	India	31,887	-11,775	10,056	21,831
17	Thailand	30,613	-14,320	8,147	22,466
18	Russia	24,529	-15,127	4,701	19,828
19	Sweden	17,996	-9,745	4,126	13,870
20	Algeria	16,558	-14,354	1,102	15,456
21	Indonesia	16,504	-10,346	3,079	13,425
22	Chile	16,351	-2,779	6,786	9,565
23	Colombia	15,975	-2,557	6,709	9,266
24	South Africa	11,963	-3,039	4,462	7,501
25	Austria	11,290	-5,318	2,986	8,304
26	Norway	9,479	-4,691	2,394	7,085

Source: U.S. Department of Commerce. *U.S. International Trade in Goods and Services Annual Revision for 2006*, FT 900 (07-04), released June 8, 2007.

Notes: Total trade = imports + exports. Data are on a Census basis. Exports are valued f.a.s.; imports are valued Customs.

Table 8 lists trade balances on goods, services, and income, net unilateral transfers and current account balances for selected U.S. trading partners. While trade in services, flows of income from investments, and remittances home by foreign workers are considerably smaller than merchandise flows, as the economy has become more globalized and service oriented, these components of the current account have become more important. In many cases, the bilateral current account balances are quite different from bilateral balances on merchandise trade only.

Table 8. U.S. Current Account Balances With Selected U.S. Trading Partners, 2006 (millions of U.S. dollars)

Country	Merchandise Trade Balance[a]	Services Balance[b]	Investment Income Balance[c]	Net Unilateral Transfers[d]	Current Account Balance[e]
All Countries	**-838.3**	**79.7**	**36.6**	**-89.6**	**-811.5**
Mexico	-67.3	7.5	0.2	-11.1	-70.7
Canada	-75.1	15.5	18.5	0.4	-40.7
Asia and Pacific	**-409.8**	**32.1**	**-38.9**	**-15.1**	**-431.7**
China	-233.1	3.6	-26.7	-2.1	-258.2
Japan	-91.0	16.5	-35.7	1.6	-108.5
S. Korea	-14.4	4.2	-0.1	-0.6	-10.9
European Union	**-120.2**	**14.3**	**1.7**	**-1.9**	**-106.2**
Germany	-48.5	-7.0	-2.4	0	-57.9
United Kingdom	-9.0	9.8	-15.5	3.6	-11.1
Latin America	**-112.6**	**12.2**	**18.9**	**-29.1**	**-110.6**
Middle East	**-36.1**	**-0.2**	**-2.5**	**-12.7**	**-51.5**

Source: U.S. Bureau of Economic Analysis, International Transactions Account Data.

a. On a BoP basis.

b. Includes travel, transportation, fees and royalties, insurance payments, other government and private services, and investment income.

c. Income receipts on U.S. assets abroad minus income payments on foreign assets in the United States.

d. International transfers of funds, such as private gifts, pension payments, and government grants for which there is no *quid pro quo*.

e. The trade balance plus the service balance plus investment income balance plus net unilateral transfers, although equal to the current account balance, may differ as a result of rounding.

For example, since Japan has invested considerable amounts in securities, equities, and in factories in the United States, the United States ran a deficit of $35.7 billion in investment income with that country in 2006. This more than offset the surplus of $16.5 billion in trade in services with Japan. As a result, the current account deficit with Japan of $108.5 billion in 2006 exceeded the bilateral merchandise trade deficit of $91 billion. Likewise with China; the U.S. deficit on investment income of $26.7 billion far overshadowed the U.S. surplus of $3.6 billion in services.

In 2006, a different situation existed with the European Union and Canada. In 2006, the United States earned a $1.7 billion surplus in investment income with the EU while the U.S. surplus in services came to $14.3 billion. These two flows offset a merchandise deficit of $120.2 billion to produce a U.S. current account deficit of $106.2. From Canada the United States received $18.5 billion in investment income plus a surplus in services trade of $15.5 billion. Hence, the current account deficit with Canada at $40.7 billion was lower than the $75.1 billion merchandise trade deficit.

The rising deficit with many countries in investment income reflects the accumulating debt relative to the world of the United States. Inflows of capital to compensate for the U.S. trade deficit and low U.S. savings rate help to maintain the value of the dollar, but interest paid and other income that accrues to that capital is often repatriated to the home countries. That means more capital must be invested in the United States or the United States must export more to compensate for the outflows of investment income. In 2006, the overall U.S. balance on investment income registered a surplus of $36.6 billion. Imbalances in investment income with certain countries have been growing and could become a problem in the future.

Advanced Technology, Autos, and Oil

Table 9 shows U.S. trade in advanced technology products. This includes about 500 commodity codes representing products whose technology is from a recognized high technology field (e.g., biotechnology) or that represent the leading technology in a field. The United States long ran a surplus in these products, but that surplus dropped sharply in 2000 and turned into a deficit in 2002. In 2003, the deficit in U.S. trade in advanced technology products jumped 65% to $27.4 billion, again rose in 2004 and in 2005, but declined in 2006 to $38.1 billion. This does not necessarily imply the United States is losing the high technology race, since many of the high technology imports are from U.S. companies (particularly electronics manufacturers) who assemble the products overseas. However, this growing deficit may warrant closer policy scrutiny.

Table 10 provides data on trade in passenger cars with major automobile producing nations for 2006. This does not include foreign cars assembled in the United States. The United States incurs the largest deficits in this trade with Japan, Mexico, Germany, Canada, and South Korea.[17]

Table 11 shows imports of crude petroleum by major country source. In 2006, the United States imported $225 billion in crude oil or 13% of all imports. Roughly half comes from the Organization of the Petroleum Exporting Countries (OPEC) with Saudi Arabia, Venezuela, and Nigeria the predominant suppliers. Imports from Iraq are recovering with $11 billion worth in 2006. Over 40% of U.S. petroleum imports come from non-OPEC sources, primarily Canada and Mexico.[18]

Table 9. U.S. Trade in Advanced Technology Products (billions of U.S. dollars)

Year	U.S. Exports	U.S. Imports	Trade Balance
1990	93.4	59.3	34.1
1995	138.4	124.8	13.6
1996	154.9	130.4	24.5
1997	179.5	147.3	32.2
1998	186.4	156.8	29.6
1999	200.3	181.2	19.1
2000	227.4	222.1	5.3
2001	200.1	195.3	4.8
2002	178.6	195.2	-16.6
2003	180.2	207.0	-26.8
2004	201.4	238.3	-36.9
2005	216.1	259.7	-43.6
2006	252.7	290.8	-38.1

Source: U.S. Bureau of the Census. *U.S. International Trade in Goods and Services*. FT-900, issued monthly.

Notes: Includes about 500 of some 22,000 commodity classification codes that meet the following criteria: (1) contains products whose technology is from a recognized high technology field (e.g., biotechnology), (2) represent leading edge technology in that field, and (3) constitute a significant part of all items covered in the selected classification code. Data are on a BoP basis.

Table 10. U.S. Trade in Motor Vehicles and Parts by Selected Countries, 2006 (millions of U.S. dollars)

Trading Partner	U.S. Exports	U.S. Imports	Trade Balance
Total World	**109,177**	**254,167**	**-144,990**
Japan	2,291	60,212	-57,921
Mexico	17,065	48,976	-31,911
Germany	6,818	26,594	-19,776
Canada	57,079	68,982	-11,903
Korea	750	12,369	-11,619
United Kingdom	1,983	6,788	-4,805

Source: U.S. Bureau of the Census, *U.S. International Trade in Goods and Services*, FT-900, issued monthly.

Some Common Perceptions

This section of the report addresses a few common perceptions about trade that can be validated by data.

Outsourcing

A common perception is that an increasing amount of U.S. imports are actually goods manufactured overseas by U.S. affiliated companies. U.S. manufacturers have moved production abroad in search of lower production costs or other economic advantages and are sending their product back to the American market.

Figure 9 shows the percentage of U.S. imported products by affiliation of the foreign producer. The total value of such imports from foreign affiliates of U.S. parent companies rose from $39.3 billion in 1982 to $209.1 billion in 2004, but the percentage of total U.S. imports accounted for by these imports has been fairly constant at around 15%. In 1982, such imports accounted for 15.9% of total imports, while in 2004 they accounted for 14.2% of the total. These are products such as American branded computers assembled in China in a subsidiary affiliated with a U.S. company.

The share of imports from foreign parent companies with affiliates in the United States has been rising somewhat — from 21.0% in 1982 to 21.7% in 2004. These reflect the growing foreign direct investment in the United States and include imports such as transmissions from a Japanese automaker for use in its assembly plant located in the United States.

Imports from unaffiliated foreigners accounts for about 60% of all imported goods. Their share has risen somewhat from 63.2% in 1982 to 64.1% in 2004. 2004 data is the latest currently available.

Table 11. U.S. Imports of Crude Oil by Selected Countries, 2006 (quantity and customs value)

Country	Quantity (Thousand barrels)	Customs Value ($million)
Total World	**3,873,914**	**225,156**
OPEC Total	**2,098,249**	**126,171**
Saudi Arabia	514,424	30,218
Venezuela	521,207	28,752
Nigeria	391,854	26,042
Algeria	186,780	12,386
Angola	181,674	11,295
Iraq	194,424	11,147
Kuwait	67,539	3,737
Other OPEC	40,345	2,595
Non-OPEC Total	**1,775,665**	**98,985**
Canada	626,054	33,031
Mexico	566,566	30,595
Ecuador	97,911	5,344
Colombia	56,728	3,456
Russia	45,449	2,985
United Kingdom	44,380	2,919
Congo	43,779	2,830
Brazil	48,045	2,809
Norway	44,071	2,506
Other Non-PEC	163,092	12,510

Sources: U.S. Census Bureau, *U.S. International Trade in Goods and Services*, FT-900, issued monthly, and World Trade Atlas, using Harmonized Schedule (HS) 270900 for crude oil.

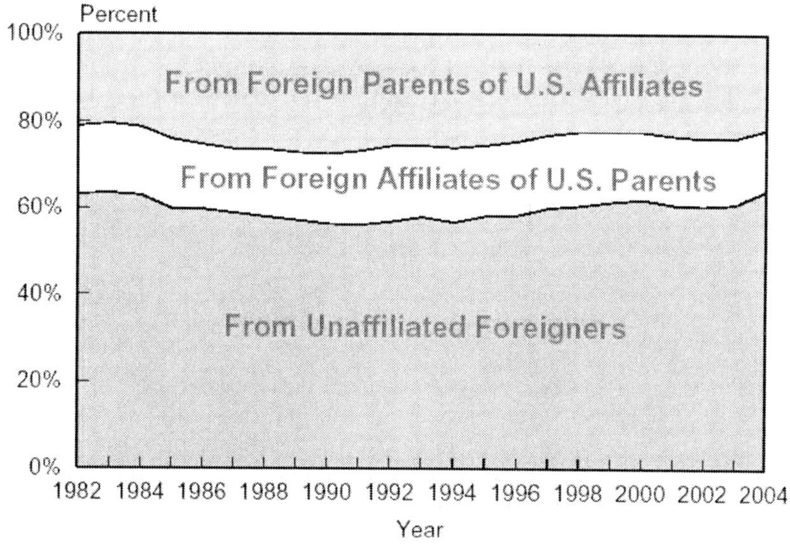

Source: CRS with Data from U.S. Bureau of Economic Analysis.
Note: 2004 data is latest available as of 11/20/07.

Figure 9. Shares of U.S. Imports of Goods by Affiliation of Foreign Producer, 1998-2004

Is the Trade Deficit at a Dangerous Level?

The International Monetary Fund has used its experience with currency and exchange rate crises to say that caution should be exercised when a nation's current account deficit reaches a level of 5% of gross domestic product. At this level, nations have difficulty borrowing to finance imports and the nation's exchange rate may come under severe downward pressure. The United States is a special case, since the dollar is a secondary medium of exchange (one can use dollars in many foreign countries without exchanging them for local currency) and dollars are used extensively as an official reserve currency by national banks. Still, the IMF has been warning that the size of the U.S. current account deficit could cause a large depreciation of the dollar and disrupt financial markets.

Figure 10 shows the U.S. current account balance as a percent of nominal U.S. gross domestic product (GDP). It grew in magnitude from near zero in 1980 to 3.4% in 1987, dropped into negative 0.1% in 1991 and rose to 6.2% in

2006 (exceeding the 5% level considered to warrant caution by the International Monetary Fund). The current account balance-GDP ratio is expected to remain above the IMF caution level for 2007. However, beginning in 2008 through 2010, it is predicted to decline to below the IMF caution level.

Is Trade with China Merely Replacing That with Southeast Asia?

Some observers claim that the rising U.S. imports from China are merely displacing those from other East Asian nations. Labor intensive industries, such as apparel, shoes, and consumer electronics, that produce for export to the United States and other industrialized nations are simply moving to China from Southeast Asian nations, including South Korea, and Taiwan. The overall level of imports from Asia is not changing. Its composition is just shifting toward China.

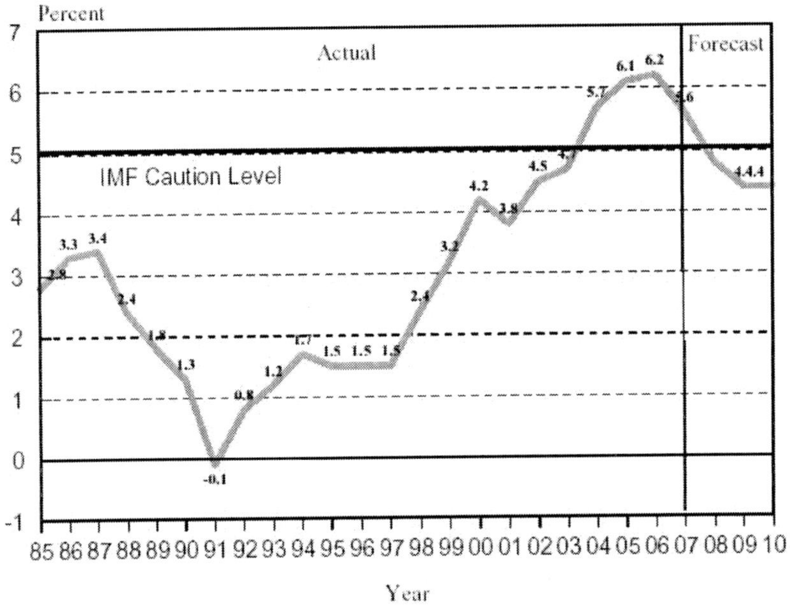

Sources: Data from U.S. Department of Commerce. Forecasts by Global Insight, Inc.

Figure 10. The U.S. Current Account Deficit as a Percent of Gross Domestic Product, 1985-2008 (forecast)

For specific industries, the shift in imports from traditional Asian exporting nations to China is clear. In woven apparel (HS 62), for example, in 1990, Hong Kong, South Korea, and Taiwan accounted for 33.4% of U.S. imports as compared to China with a 14.7% share. By 2006, China accounted for 31.3% of such imports, as compared to 4.9% for Hong Kong, South Korea, and Taiwan combined.

In terms of overall imports, however, U.S. imports from Hong Kong, Taiwan, and South Korea rose from $50.6 billion (10.2% of total U.S. imports) in 1990 to $92.0 billion (5.0% of total) in 2006, while imports from China rose from $15.2 billion (3.3% of total) in 1990 to $287.8 billion (15.5% of total) in 2006.[19] Clearly, the share of U.S. imports from Hong Kong, Taiwan, and South Korea has been falling, while the share of imports from China is rising. The value of U.S. imports from both, however, continues to rise, while the value of those from China is rising faster.

The large U.S. trade deficit with China, moreover, is not just a transfer of the deficit from other Asian nations to China. The U.S. trade deficit with Hong Kong, Taiwan, and South Korea has gone from $17.9 billion (17.5% of the total U.S. deficit) in 1990 to $18.7 billion (2.3% of the total) in 2006. U.S. trade with Hong Kong actually went from a deficit to a surplus. The U.S. trade deficit with China, meanwhile, went from $41.1 billion (10.2% of the total U.S. trade deficit) in 1990 to $232.6 billion (28.5% of the total) in 2006. What actually is happening is that the U.S. trade deficit is rising with most regions of the world, particularly with Asia, including China, and it also is rising with Canada and Mexico, the European Union, and with oil exporting countries.

International Trade Statistics Web Resources

Listed below are a list of resources available online for international trade statistics.

The single most authoritative, comprehensive, and frequently-published trade data statistical source is the monthly "FT900". Its actual title is *U.S. International Trade in Goods and Services*. The FT-900 is issued monthly by the U.S. Census Bureau and the U.S. Bureau of Economic Analysis. It provides information on the U.S. trade in goods and services (balance, exports, and imports) in specific commodities and end-use categories and with selected countries. The report also provides information on trade in advanced technology, petroleum, and motor vehicle products. The report is available from the U.S. Bureau of Economic Analysis at [http://www.bea.gov/newsreleases/rels.htm]. Under "International" click on latest news release.

Information on trade in specific commodities, with particular regions, or for different time periods also can be obtained from the U.S. International Trade Commission at [http://dataweb.usitc.gov/].

Historical and current U.S. exchange rate data are available from the Federal Reserve Bank of St. Louis at [http://research.stlouisfed.org/fred2/].

Information on foreign country holdings of U.S. Treasury securities are available at [http://www.treasury.gov/tic/].

End Notes

[1] Monthly trade data are available from the U.S. Bureau of Economic Analysis at [http://www.bea.gov/bea/di/home/trade.htm].

[2] See, for example, CRS Report RL3 1832, *The Export Administration Act: Evolution, Provisions, and Debate*, by Ian F. Fergusson; CRS Report RL33463, *Trade Negotiations During the 110th Congress*, by Ian F. Fergusson; CRS Report RL3 1356, *Free Trade Agreements: Impact on U.S. Trade and Implications for U.S. Trade Policy*, by William H. Cooper; CRS Report RL3237 1, *Trade Remedies: A Primer*, by Vivian C. Jones; CRS Report RL3 2493, *The North Korean Economy: Background and Policy Analysis*, by Dick K. Nanto and Emma Chanlett-Avery; or CRS Report RL33653, East Asian Regional Architecture: *New Economic and Security Arrangements and U.S. Policy*, by Dick K. Nanto.

[3] Commerce Department data are available at [http://www.bea.gov/].

[4] U.S. International Trade Commission data are available at [http://dataweb.usitc.gov/].

[5] For further information on trade deficits and the macroeconomy, see CRS Report RL3 1032, *The U.S. Trade Deficit: Causes, Consequences, and Cures*, by Craig K. Elwell and CRS Report RL33 186, *Is the U.S. Current Account Deficit Sustainable?*, by Marc Labonte.

[6] U.S. trade in goods and services plus net flows of investment income and remittances.

[7] IMF, 2005 Article IV Consultation with the United States of America. Concluding Statement of the IMF Mission. May 31, 2006.

[8] Statistics on Japanese international reserves are released on a monthly basis by the Japanese Ministry of Finance and available at [https://www.mof.go.jp/english/gaijun/ e1 911 .htm].

[9] Statistics on Chinese international reserves are available from the Chinability website, a non-profit website that provides Chinese economic and business data and analysis, at [http://www.chinability.com/].

[10] Statistics on foreign holdings of U.S. Treasury securities are available at [http://www.treasury.gov/tic/mfh.txt]. For further information, see CRS Report RS22331, *Foreign Holdings of Federal Debt*, by Justin Murray and Marc Labonte.

[11] For further information, see CRS Report RL32165, *China's Currency: Economic Issues and Options for U.S. Trade Policy*, by Wayne M. Morrison and Marc Labonte.

[12] Morgan Stanley, *Currencies, How Big Could Sovereign Wealth Funds Be by 2015?* Morgan Stanley Research, May 3, 2007.

[13] See Mann, Catherine L. *Is the U.S. Trade Deficit Sustainable?* Washington, Institute for International Economics, 1999. 224 p. See also: CRS Report RL33274, Financing the U.S. Trade Deficit, by James K. Jackson. CRS Report RL3 1032, The U.S. Trade Deficit: Causes, Consequences, and Cures, by Craig K. Elwell.

[14] For details, see CRS Report RS20826, *Structure and Functions of The Federal Reserve System*, by Pauline Smale.

[15] For legislation related to trade with China and the Chinese currency, see CRS Report RL33536, *China-U.S. Trade Issues*, by Wayne M. Morrison.

[16] For details and policy discussion, see CRS Report RL31403, *China's Trade with the United States and the World*, by Thomas Lum and Dick K. Nanto, or CRS Report RL33536, *China-U.S. Trade Issues*, by Wayne M. Morrison.

[17] For information on the automobile industry, see CRS Report RL32883, *U.S. Automotive Industry: Recent History and Issues*, by Stephen Cooney and Brent D. Yacobucci.

[18] For policy discussion, see CRS Report RS22204, *U.S. Trade Deficit and the Impact of Rising Oil Prices*, by James K. Jackson.

[19] The numbers are comparable for all Asian countries.

In: United States Trade Deficit Issues
Editor: Carl T. Yankovich
ISBN: 978-1-60692-090-9

Chapter 2

THE UNITED STATES TRADE DEFICIT: CAUSES, CONSEQUENCES, AND CURES*

Craig K. Elwell
Specialist in Macroeconomics
Government and Finance Division

SUMMARY

The U.S. trade deficit has risen more or less steadily since 1992. In 2006, the trade imbalance reached $811.5 billion, an increase of $20 billion over the 2005 deficit, and a total increase of about $765 billion since 1992. The trade deficit's growth in 2006 was largely the consequence of increase of import purchases of nearly $210 billion, a slight deceleration from import growth in 2005. Exports in 2006 increased a smaller $162 billion, but this was an acceleration over the 2005 results. As a percentage of GNP, the trade deficit in 2006 was 6.1%, a decrease from 6.3% in 2005. The investment income component of the trade balance moved from a surplus of $10.3 billion in 2005 up to a surplus of $36.6 billion in 2006. The large and growing size of U.S. foreign indebtedness caused by successive trade deficits suggests that the investment income surplus is likely to soon be pushed toward deficit.

---

* This is an edited, reformatted and augmented version of a CRS Report for Congress publication dated January 2008.

The size of the U.S. trade deficit is ultimately rooted in macroeconomic conditions at home and abroad. U.S. saving falls short of what is sought to finance U.S. investment. Many foreign economies are in the opposite circumstances, with domestic saving exceeding domestic opportunities for investment. This difference of wants will tend to be reconciled by international capital flows. The shortfall in domestic saving relative to investment tends to draw an inflow of relatively abundant foreign savings seeking to maximize returns and, in turn, the saving inflow makes a higher level of investment possible. For the United States, a net financial inflow also leads to a like-sized net inflow of foreign goods — a trade deficit. Absent a major shift in the underlying domestic and foreign macroeconomic determinants, most forecasts predict the continued widening of the U.S. trade deficit in 2007, but the rate of increase of the trade deficit is expected to slow.

The benefit of the trade deficit is that it allows the United States to spend now beyond current income. In recent years that spending has largely been for investment in productive capital. The cost of the trade deficit is a deterioration of the U.S. investment-income balance, as the payment on what the United States has borrowed from foreigners grows with its rising indebtedness. Borrowing from abroad allows the United States to live better today, but the payback must mean some decrement to the rate of advance of U.S. living standards in the future. U.S. trade deficits do not now substantially raise the risk of economic instability, but they do impose burdens on trade sensitive sectors of the economy.

Policy action to reduce the overall trade deficit is problematic. Standard trade policy tools (e.g., tariffs, quotas, and subsidies) do not work. Macroeconomic policy tools can work, but recent and prospective government budget deficits will reduce domestic saving and most likely tend to *increase* the trade deficit. Most economists believe that, in time, the trade deficit will most likely correct itself, without crisis, under the pressures of normal market forces. But the risk of a more calamitous outcome can not be completely discounted. This report will be updated annually.

INTRODUCTION

International trade continues to grow in importance for the world economy as well as the U.S. economy, enhancing economic well-being generally, but also imposing costs on trade sensitive sectors of national economies. The importance of trade has been well-recognized by Congress, which in recent years has paid close attention to many dimensions of U.S. international trade performance. This report examines the trade deficit, paying special attention to why it continues to widen, why it may be a problem, and what can be done to correct it.

TRADE PERFORMANCE IN 2006

The U.S. trade deficit as tallied in the *current account balance*[1] reached $811.5 billion in 2006, up from $791.5 billion in 2005.[2] As a percentage of GDP, the 2006 trade deficit stands at 6.1%, down slightly from a record share of 6.3 % in 2005. The small decrease in the trade deficits size as a percentage of GNP could indicate that a degree of stabilization of the imbalance may be occurring.

The trade deficit rose slowly and, more or less, steadily from a small surplus in 1991(a recession year) to about $135 billion in 1997. Then, as the pace of the economic expansion rapidly accelerated, the trade deficit posted particularly large increases over the next three years, reaching $413.4 billion in 2000. With recession in 2001, the trade deficit fell moderately to $389 billion. With the economic recovery in 2002, the trade deficit again began to expand along with the steady improvement in the pace of economic growth.[3] The cumulative increase in the trade deficit between 1997 and 2006 is $806 billion, with more than half of this increase occurring since 2001. **Table 1** shows the anatomy of recent trade trends.

Table 1. U.S. Current Account and Components (BOP basis, billions of dollars, annual rate)

	2001	2002	2003	2004	2005	2006
Current account balance	-389.0	-472.4	-527.5	-665.3	-791.5	-811.5
Goods balance	-427.2	-482.3	-547.3	-665.4	-782.7	-838.3
Exports	718.7	682.4	713.4	807.5	894.6	1023.1
Imports	-1145.9	-1164.7	-1260.7	-1,473.0	-1677.2	-1861.4
Services balance	64.4	61.2	52.4	54.1	66.0	79.7
Exports	286.1	292.3	302.7	344.4	380.6	422.6
Imports	-221.8	-231.0	-250.3	-290.3	-314.6	-342.8
Investment income	25.1	12.2	36.6	27.6	11.3	36.6
Transfers (net)	-51.3	-63.5	-69.2	-81.5	-86.1	-89.6

Source: U.S. Department of Commerce (Bureau of Economic Analysis) and Global Insight

Goods Trade

Goods trade is the largest component of the current account balance, and what has happened in this form of trade has been the major source of change in the overall the current account in recent years, including 2006. The deficit in goods trade increased in 2006 to $838 billion from $783 billion in 2005. Since 1992, the goods trade deficit increased a total of $739 billion. Over this period, both exports and imports generally rose, but import growth out paced export growth. In 2001, in response to slack demand across the world economy, U.S. goods exports had fallen, but the U.S. recession in 2001 also led to an even larger curtailment in the U.S. demand for imports, causing the goods deficit (and the current account deficit) to fall. In 2002, weak world demand continued to push U.S. exports down, but even a tepid U.S. economic recovery in 2002 was enough to cause goods imports to increase, and the goods deficit (and the current account deficit) was once again on the rise. In 2006, goods exports increased about $129 billion in response to the stimulating effects of earlier dollar depreciation and faster economic growth in Japan and the euro area. But accelerating U.S. economic growth in 2006 also accelerates the inflow of goods imports by about $210 billion, causing the goods deficit to increase by about $56 billion. However, this is the smallest increase of the goods deficit since 2002 and could be an indicator the trade deficit beginning to stabilize.

Services Trade

In 2006, the U.S. surplus in services trade increased to $79.7 billion from $66.0 billion in 2005. In contrast to goods, services trade had shown a slowly rising surplus through the mid-1990s. That trend ended in 1997, however, with the services surplus peaking at $91.9 billion. In 1998, the surplus fell to about $83 billion, but steadied near that level through 2000. Service exports grew more than $30 billion in this period, but with the dual effects of very rapid economic growth in the United States and the continued strength of the dollar, services imports moved apace. From 2001 through 2003, the services surplus decreased. This decline reflected the continued increase of service imports despite (1) recession and slow growth in the United States and (2) the weak service export sales because of weakness in other economies and the continued negative impact of the strong dollar (the dollar had begun to depreciate in 2002, but given the typical lags, the positive effect of that depreciation was unlikely to have been significant in 2002). In response to continued weakening of the dollar in 2003 and 2004, as well as faster economic growth abroad, the surplus in services trade began to increase again in 2004 and continued to increase in 2005 and 2006.

Investment Income Balance

In 2006, the balance in the U.S. investment income account moved up from a surplus of $11.3 billion in 2005 to a surplus of $36.6 billion. The investment income balance is a tally of what U.S. foreign investments earn against what foreign investments in the U.S. earn. This pattern of surplus seems inconsistent with the rapid growth of foreign assets in the United States relative to the stock of U.S. assets in the rest of the world. Nevertheless, since 1998, the surplus in investment income has exhibited a rising trend, even as U.S. net indebtedness to the rest of the world increased sharply. The investment income surplus reached $46.3 billion in 2003 and fell to $30.4 billion in 2004. The persistence of the U.S. investment income surplus through 2006 is the result of the interplay of several forces. First, U.S. investments abroad on average earn a higher return than foreign investments do in the United States. This differential is thought to result from a higher incidence of mature, high yielding, assets in the U.S. investment portfolio, greater risk exposure, and the special status of the dollar as the worlds reserve currency of choice. Second, the sharp fall of interest rates between 2000 and 2004 translated into a fall in the rate of return as a large portion of U.S. foreign debt is repeatedly rolled over. Third, in the period 2002 to 2006, a falling dollar, particularly against the euro, caused the foreign currency value of U.S. foreign assets and the associated earnings to rise.

In the long run, however, it is likely that the United States' large and still growing stock of net foreign indebtedness will come to dominate movement of this balance and lead to steadily larger deficits in the investment income balance.[4]

Why the Trade Deficit Widens

A rising current account deficit (or a falling surplus) over the course of a brisk economic expansion is not a remarkable event for the U.S. economy. In the 1960s, brisk economic growth steadily eroded a small current account surplus. In the 1970s, modest deficits occurred with each economic expansion. However, from the 1980s through 2006, the average size of the trade deficits steadily increased. Cyclical factors certainly have at times played some role in this phenomenon, particularly in recent years with the United States growing rapidly relative to most major trading partners. Trend forces are also at work, however, inclining the U.S. economy toward generating large trade deficits in all but recession conditions. The next section examines in more depth the fundamental determinants of the trade balance.

The trade deficit widens as the economy expands, not because of trade barriers abroad, not because of foreign dumping of exports, and not because of any inherent inferiority of the U.S. goods on the world market, but because of underlying macroeconomic spending and saving behavior at home and abroad. In the U.S. economy, there is a strong tendency to spend beyond current output, with the excess of demand met by a net inflow of foreign goods and services that results in the U.S. trade deficit.[5] Of course, the U.S. trade deficit is only possible if there are foreign economies that produce more than is absorbed by their current spending and are able to export the surplus. Trade deficits and trade surpluses are jointly determined through international capital flows that lead to a mutually favorable reconciliation of these domestic spending-production imbalances. These imbalances will be sensitive to the short-run effects of the business cycle (at home and abroad) as well as long-term effects of trends in spending and production. But, these imbalances will not be significantly changed by trade policies that try to directly alter the levels of exports or imports such as tariffs, subsidies, or quotas.

A Saving-Investment Imbalance

National spending-production imbalances are analyzed by economists from the standpoint of national saving and investment behavior. Saving is just the flip side of spending (an excess of spending essentially translates into a deficiency of savings) but focusing on saving has the analytical advantage of rooting the phenomenon in the transactions on international asset markets that are the key to understanding aggregate trade imbalances.

International Capital Flows

A large and fluid trade in assets is one of the central attributes of the current world trading system, growing from flows totaling only a few billion dollars in 1970 to $7 trillion in 2005. The United States has been a major participant in international asset markets. In 2006, it received capital inflows of \$1.9 trillion and send capital outflows to the rest of the world of \$1.1 trillion.[6]

With fluid world capital markets, domestic saving-investment imbalances will tend to cause two equivalent transfers: one, an initiating capital market transfer of real purchasing power (i.e., a loan) from the country with a surplus of saving to the country with a shortage of saving; and two, a corresponding transfer of real output (i.e., an import to the borrower and an export from the lender) through a goods market transactions.

It is an economic identity that the amount of investment undertaken by an economy will be equal to the amount of saving — that is, the portion of current income not used for consumption — that is available to finance investment. But for a nation this identity can be satisfied through the use of both domestic and *foreign saving*, or domestic and *foreign investment.* Therefore, a saving investment imbalance is a relationship between domestic saving and investment and one that can only occur if foreign saving or investment are available to satisfy the overall saving investment identity.[7] International capital flows from lender to borrower are the means by which the saving of one country can finance the investment of another. If international capital flows did not exist, domestic investment could be no larger or smaller than domestic saving.

In a relatively open world economy with reasonably fluid and well functioning international asset markets, it is possible for domestic saving-investment imbalances to be reconciled by international capital flows. With a willing lender and a willing borrower, flows of capital from a saving surplus country to a saving shortage country can achieve *overall* saving-investment balance for both nations. These asset market transactions will change the demand for and supply of national currencies needed to purchase foreign assets, causing changes in exchange rates, which, in turn, induce an equivalent sized net flow of goods (i.e., trade deficits and trade surpluses) between economies.

Interest Rates and International Capital Flows

Differences in the level interest rates between economies are the basic equilabrating mechanism that works to induce saving (income) flows between countries as investors seek out higher rates of return. A nation with a "surplus" of domestic saving over domestic investment opportunities will tend to have relatively low domestic interest rates because the domestic supply of loanable funds (i.e., saving) exceeds the domestic demand for loanable funds (i.e., investment) pushing down interest rates (i.e., the price of loanable funds). As a result this economy will also likely see some portion of domestic saving flow outward, attracted by more profitable investment opportunities abroad. This net outflow of purchasing power, which generally can only be used to purchase goods (or assets) denominated in the country's currency, will, through changes in exchange rates, induce a like-sized net outflow of real goods and services — a trade surplus. Japan is an example of a nation that in recent decades has produced large net outflows of saving to the United States and other nations.

Conversely, another nation that finds its domestic saving falling short of desired domestic investment will tend to have relatively high domestic interest rates because the domestic demand for loanable funds exceeds the domestic supply of loanable funds. As a result this economy will likely attract an inflow of foreign saving, attracted by the higher rate of return, and that inflow will help support domestic investment. Such a nation becomes a net importer of foreign saving (income), able to use the borrowed purchasing power to acquire foreign output, and leading to a like sized net inflow of foreign output — a trade deficit. That deficit augments the output available to the domestic economy, allowing the nation to invest beyond the level of domestic savings.

International asset market transactions and goods market transactions influence the demand and supply of dollars on foreign exchange markets. In most circumstances, however, there is a strong expectation that asset market transactions will tend to be dominant and ultimately dictate the exchange rate's actual direction of movement. This dominance is the result of asset market transactions occurring on a scale and at a speed that greatly exceeds what occurs with goods market transactions. Electronic exchange makes most asset transfers nearly instantaneous and, in most years, U.S. international asset transactions were two to three times as large as what would be needed to simply finance that year's trade deficit. The telling sign that asset transactions have been the determining force is that the dollar appreciated as the trade deficit grew. If goods market transactions were the determining force, the increase of the trade deficit would tend to depreciate the dollar, as rising U.S. imports cause more dollars to be exchanged for foreign currency, increasing the supply of dollars on the foreign exchange market, and pushing the dollar down. In general, the exchange rate of countries that receive a net inflow of foreign capital will tend to appreciate, whereas the exchange rate of countries that have a net capital outflow will tend to depreciate.

Other Factors That Influence International Capital Flows

Although relative levels of interest rates between countries are likely to be a strong and prevalent force directing capital flows among economies, other factors will also influence these flows. For instance, the size of the stock of assets in a particular currency held in the foreign investor's portfolio of assets can cause a change in investor preferences. Prudent investment practice counsels that one's portfolio should have an appropriate degree of *diversification*, across asset types, including the currency in which they are denominated. Diversification of holdings spreads risk across a wider spectrum of assets and reduces over exposure to any one asset. Therefore, even though dollar assets may still offer a high relative return, if the accumulation of dollar assets already in the investor's portfolios is large, at some point foreign investors, considering both risk and reward, will decide that their portfolio's share of dollar denominated assets is large enough. To improve the diversity of their portfolios, investors will slow or halt their purchase of such assets. Given that well over $8 trillion in U.S. assets are now in foreign investor portfolios, diversification may be an increasingly important factor governing the behavior of international investors toward dollar assets.

There is also likely to be a significant *safe-haven* effect behind some capital flows. This is really just another manifestation of the balancing of risk and reward by foreign investors. Some investors may be willing to give up a significant amount of return if an economy offers them a particularly low risk repository for their funds. The United States, with a long history of stable government and steady economic growth, presents a continually safe investment climate. There is likely also an important *market size effect* influencing the attractiveness of dollar assets. Not only do U.S. asset markets offer a great variety of instruments, they are also very liquid markets with the ability to handle huge sums of money with only a small impact on price. The precise size of these effects is not easy to determine, but the persistence of large capital inflows despite already large foreign holdings of dollar assets and the disproportionate share of essentially no-risk U.S. Treasury securities in foreign holdings suggests the magnitude of flows attributable to the special status of U.S. asset markets is probably substantial.

In addition to private investors, governments will, with varying frequency, also buy or sell assets on the international capital market. Such *official purchases* are seldom motivated by the factors of return and risk that typically propel private investors. Government *official purchases* can serve two objectives. One, the accumulation of a reserve of foreign exchange denominated in readily exchangeable currencies, such as the dollar, to afford a store of international liquidity that can be used for coping with periodic currency crises arising out of often volatile private capital flows. This is most often a devise used by developing economies that periodically need to finance short-run balance of payments deficits and can not fully depend on borrowing on international capital markets to offer timely finance of these deficits. Also the Asian financial crisis in the late 1990s heightened the importance for many developing economies of having very large stocks of international reserves.

Two, official purchases are used to counter the impact of capital flows that would otherwise lead to unwanted changes in the countries exchange rate. The United States and most other industrial nations, while most often allowing the value of their currencies to float on the foreign exchange market, have at times undertaken such *intervention*. This, however, is a common practice for many east Asian economies that buy and sell foreign assets to influence their currencies' exchange rate relative to the dollar and other major currencies to maintain the price attractiveness of their exports. Globally, dollar assets in official foreign exchange reserves increased $1 trillion between 2001 and 2006. Among the large industrial economies in recent years, Japan has been a highly visible practitioner of accumulating international assets so as to slow the rise of the yen relative to the dollar, accumulating dollar-denominated foreign exchange reserves in 2003 of about $117 billion. Among emerging economies, China has undertaken large scale accumulation of dollar assets to fix the value of the renminbi relative to the dollar, accumulating $260 billion dollar- denominated assets between 2001 and 2005. In most cases, however government exchange rate intervention is unlikely to be substantial enough to change the direction in which private investors are pushing the dollar. This intervention has likely slowed the fall of the dollar since early 2002, but not stopped it.

Recent Patterns of U.S. Saving and Investment Behavior

A domestic saving-investment imbalance can occur as a result of either investment rising relative to saving or saving falling relative to investment (see **Table 2**). In the 1 980s, the saving rate and the investment rate both declined, but the saving rate fell substantially faster, inducing capital inflows and a rising trade deficit. The fall of the saving rate in this period was rooted in two occurrences. The first was a substantial fall in the public saving rate caused by the run up of large federal budget deficits (which amounts to negative saving or dissaving). The second occurrence was the decline of the household component of the private saving rate. In the late 1980s, this imbalance narrowed due to increased public saving (i.e., smaller deficits) and a sharp decline in the investment rate in response to a decelerating economy headed for recession.

After recovery from the 1991 recession, the U.S. saving-investment imbalance began to increase steadily, but the form of the imbalance changed. The rates of saving and investment both rose, but the investment rate climbed faster. The turnaround in the overall saving rate in the 1990s was the consequence of a sharp change in the public saving rate, where the steady move by the federal government from budget deficits to budget surpluses increased the public saving rate from -2.5% (i.e, dissaving) in 1992 to 5.2% in 2000. Dampening the rise of the overall saving rate, however, was the continued decline in the household saving rate, falling from about 6.5% in 1992 to 0.0% in 2000. The rise of the overall saving rate in the 1990s did not bring that rate up to the magnitude that prevailed in the 1950s, 1 960s, or 1970s, and fell well short of the 1990s' briskly ascending rate of domestic investment. The predictable consequence of a widening savings-investment imbalance was a rising inflow of foreign savings to close that gap, and in turn, an ever larger trade deficit.

A substantial decrease in the rate of investment during the 2001 recession narrowed this gap and the trade deficit in that year. During the period from 2002 to 2005, the U.S. rate of investment increased and the rate of saving declined, causing the investment-saving gap to widen and the trade deficit to expand. The higher rate of investment was the result of the faster pace of economic activity in the ongoing economic expansion. The further fall of the saving rate was caused by reductions in both the household and government saving rates. The overall rate of saving in the economy in this period remained positive due to a generally steady rate of business saving. In 2006, however, with stabilization of both the saving and investment rates, the investment-saving gap stopped rising and the trade deficits advance slowed significantly.

Two questions may come to mind. One, why has the household saving rate collapsed over the past 20 years? Other factors unchanged, a higher rate of household savings would have likely meant the generation of smaller trade deficits. Two, why did U.S. investment spending boom in the 1990s? Other factors unchanged, a rate of investment at the lower level typical of other expansions would have also led to smaller trade deficits. The fall of the household saving rate has been the object of much economic research, but the reasons for the decline remain problematic. No single theory can fully account for the phenomenon, but three have considerable plausibility. First, capital gains on real estate, stocks, and other investments, particularly in the 1 990s, have greatly increased household wealth. Economic theory predicts that a rise in wealth reduces the need to save and increases the tendency to spend. Second, increased government outlays for Medicare and Social Security transfer income from a relatively high saving segment of the population to a relatively low saving segment. Third, more streamlined credit market vehicles, such as credit cards and home equity loans, have removed constraints on household liquidity and prompted increased spending (and reduced saving).[8]

The reasons for the investment boom in the late 1990s also remain somewhat unclear, but three plausible forces have been suggested. First, the wealth induced spending mentioned just above also provides a stimulus to business investment, as new plant and equipment is needed to meet the rising demand for output. Second, it is argued that recent deregulation of industry, liberalization of trade, and massive integration of ever cheaper and more powerful computers into the production process have boosted productivity and raised the profitability of investment in the United States. Third, and perhaps most plausible, pervasive economic weakness abroad, most recently in Asia, has made the United States a singularly attractive destination for foreign investment. Even the relatively slow pace of the U.S. economic recovery in 2002 and early 2003, when juxtaposed with generally weaker growth in the rest of the world made it likely that the trade deficit would expand in 2002 and 2003. In 2004 and 2005, the U.S. economic growth was brisk and outpaced that of other major economies.

Table 2. U.S. Saving-Investment Balance (percentage of GDP)

	Ann. Avg. 1975 to 1982	Ann. Avg 1983 to 1990	2000	2001	2002	2003	2004	2005	2006
Saving	19.7	17.1	18.2	16.5	14.7	13.5	13.4	13.5	14.1
Investment	20.3	19.5	21.8	19.1	18.4	18.2	19.2	19.7	20.0
Net[a] lending(+) or borrowing(-)	-0.6	-2.4	18.6	-2.6	-3.7	-4.7	-5.8	-6.2	-5.9

Source: U.S. Department of Commerce, Bureau of Economic Analysis.

a. Net lending, in concept, should equal the size of the current account balance. Statistical discrepancies prevent a precise matching, however.

A change of significance in U.S. saving behavior over the past five years is the shift in the trajectory of public saving. In 2002, the federal budget moved back into deficit and in 2004 that budget deficit had risen to $413 billion, with the prospect of similar sized budget deficits persisting into the foreseeable future. This has resulted in the federal government moving from being a net saver in 2000 at a magnitude equal to about 2.8% of GDP to being a net dissaver at a magnitude of about 2.5% of GDP in 2005. This fall in government saving exacerbates the saving-investment imbalance and, other factors constant, widens the trade deficit. In 2005, the federal budget deficit was reduced and government dis saving improved to -1.8% of GDP. The budget deficit continued to fall in 2006, down to about -1.1% of GDP. This recent reduction of the budget deficit has not been the result of any policy change, but rather the result of an unexpectedly large inflow of tax revenue largely due to record levels of corporate profits. Despite this short-term reduction, most projections see large budget deficits extending for many years into the future.

For that widening of the trade deficit to happen, however, there will also need to be foreign lenders willing to invest in the United States. If, to take one extreme position, there are no such investors then any fall in the domestic saving rate will, through higher interest rates, lead to a like sized fall in the domestic investment rate. If, at the other extreme, there are legions of investors eager to invest in the United States, the savings shortfall will be overcome with little dampening of domestic investment. More realistically, there will likely be willing foreign investors, but that willingness might have to be gained through the prospect of a higher rate of return. The higher domestic interest rates must go to attract investors to bridge the domestic saving shortfall, the more downward pressure there will be on domestic investment.

The macroeconomic forces that generate trade deficits are entirely consistent with high rates of capacity utilization and employment. Trade deficits, however, can have negative effects on output and employment in particular sectors. (The output, employment, and sectoral effects of trade deficits are discussed at greater length in a latter section of the report.) The United States has regularly been the net recipient of foreign capital inflows and regularly had trade deficits for the past 25 years. It has also regularly achieved high rates of economic growth and low rates of unemployment over this time period.[9] This is more understandable in that although a deficit in goods and services trade caused by the rise of the exchange rate tends to have a negative effect on domestic economic activity that is sensitive to international trade, there is also a positive effect on domestic economic activity because of the lower interest rates caused by the like-sized net inflow of foreign capital (saving). Therefore, the trade deficit changes the composition of domestic output, but does not change the overall level of domestic output.

It is also true that an overall trade imbalance need not be reflected in the balance with individual trading partners. Bilateral balances will reflect additional forces such as geographic proximity, scale economies, and comparative advantage. Therefore, some could be in deficit and others in surplus. Similarly, overall trade balance can be consistent with significant bilateral imbalances. For example, even if Unites States were to eliminate its trade deficit, it would likely have a sizeable trade deficit with China. Or seen the other way, a reduction of the U.S. trade deficit with China, not accompanied by a change in the U.S. economy's overall domestic saving-investment imbalance, will not lead to a reduction of the overall U.S. trade deficit. If, however, a decrease in the U.S. trade deficit with China is the result of a reduced inflow of capital (saving) from China, and there is no like-sized increase in another source of foreign saving, then the overall U.S. trade deficit will also fall, but so must domestic investment in the United States to bring it into line with the smaller pool of saving that would be available to finance domestic investment.

This overall scenario leaves three strong impressions. One, U.S. trade deficits appear to be largely (but not completely) created and propelled by macroeconomic forces in the domestic economy that influence international flows of capital. Two, those deficits must be sustained by willing foreign lenders, and substantial reduction of that willingness, other factors constant, might lead to deficit reduction on less than the most favorable terms. And three, these forces may not be easily manipulated by policy.

Sustainability of the Trade Deficit

The U.S. trade deficit is very likely to grow larger in 2007.[10] Nevertheless, an ever larger trade deficit is not likely to be sustainable indefinitely. There are automatic adjustment processes that will dampen the willingness of borrowers to borrow and of lenders to lend, and which can cause a more or less orderly reduction of the saving-investment imbalance and, in turn, the trade deficit.

Borrower's Constraint

The central issue for a borrower country like the United States is the "ability to pay," that is, the capacity to meet the interest and principal payments on the accumulated stocks of foreign debt. Such payments must come at the expense of other forms of national expenditure and, therefore, will not increase without bound. For the United States, the Net International Investment Position (NIIP) is the measure of its stock of obligations and GDP is the measure of its ability to pay. Therefore the ratio NIIP/GDP is a possible proxy of the borrower's constraint. Because the United States do not have much experience with a rising foreign debt to GDP ratio, it is difficult to judge at what value this ratio would begin to sharply deter more borrowing. Between 1992 and 2003, this ratio (expressed as a percentage) has risen from 7.3% to 21.6%, a substantial gain, but that is still below the 25% to 35% common among other high income countries, well short of the debt burden of most households.

In 2006, the debt to GNP ratio fell to 19 %. Given a $811 billion current account deficit in 2005, it may seem odd that the debt to GNP ratio did not also increase. However, the change in the total dollar value of U.S. foreign debt reflects not only current borrowing but also changes in the market value of existing assets. These "valuation effects" were particularly beneficial for the United States in 2006, slowing the rate of advance of the negative NIIP. But such strongly favorable effects are unlikely to persist over the long run. Nevertheless, it is still problematic what level of the debt to GNP ratio would begin to significantly constrain the behavior of U.S. borrowers.

An alternative measure of constraint is the ratio of the current account balance (CA) to GDP (CA/GDP). This measure lays more stress on the size of the annual flow of foreign obligations relative to GDP as an initiator of borrower behavior. The value of CA/GDP for the United States has risen from 0.8% in 1992 to 4.4% in 2000. Evidence from industrial economies indicates that, on average, when the CA/GDP ratio exceeds 4.2% the current account begins to narrow.[11] This suggests that the United States may be getting close to a point at which borrowers may begin to slow their rate of debt accumulation. However, there are special attributes of the American economy that would allow it to prudently push borrowing beyond this benchmark ratio (see below).

Lender's Constraint

The willingness to lend to a particular destination will be influenced by the risk- return profile of a borrower's assets *relative* to other available assets. A broad array of alternatives with comparable risk-return prospects would tend to reduce the willingness to lend to a single borrower. Similarly, a paucity of alternative investment opportunities would have the opposite effect. It can be expected that the array of alternatives faced would be influenced by the strength of economic conditions across the globe. In addition, the desire by investors for some degree of portfolio diversification will tend to limit their willingness to become overly saturated in assets denominated in a single currency. Beyond the willingness to invest is the issue of ability to invest. The ability to sustain a large or rising outflow of capital will be limited by the size of the lender economy and its wealth portfolio. Other economies are substantially smaller than the U.S. economy and may be unable to sustain the magnitude of outflow the United States can apparently readily absorb. Also limiting cross-border lending is the observed preference in most economies to hold a high percentage of wealth in home assets, although it is suspected that this preference is steadily being eroded by the improving efficiency of international asset markets. Finally, the holders of dollar assets, particularity shot-term portfolio investments, will be sensitive to the expected path of the dollar's exchange rate because a sizable depreciation can quickly decrease the rate of return of the dollar asset to the foreign holder. Therefore, the expectation of a depreciating dollar is likely reduce the foreign investors demand for dollar assets.

Two recent events, are likely to induce a substantial diversification of foreign investor portfolios *toward* dollar assets. One, the recent liberalization of the Japanese postal saving system, with a portfolio of $3 trillion, that had been held almost exclusively in very low yielding Japanese government bonds. And two, a large accumulation of foreign currency earnings by petroleum exporting countries looking for a preferred resting place in more liquid, hard currency assets. The sheer size and high liquidity of most U.S. markets, alone, will probably draw a large share of these funds. If U.S. assets also have a rate of return advantage then the inflow will be all the greater.

The willingness of central banks to accumulate dollar assets will be governed by different considerations then the standard profit-loss calculation that motivates private investors and can be sustainable for long periods of time. Nevertheless, there will be pressures that will work to limit such official purchases. For unless the asset accumulation is *sterilized,* the growth of official reserves will be inflationary, and since the capacity for sterilization is not likely to be infinite, particularly if the financial markets of the lending country are not well developed and have small absorptive capacity, the inflationary impulse of official lending may not be avoidable forever. In general, sustained asset accumulation through official purchases ties the monetary policy of the lending country to that of the borrowing country and the lending countries need to avoid an acceleration of inflation will make it an unsustainable policy.[12] Also, like private investors, the prospect of incurring capital losses on holdings of dollar assets due to a likely depreciation of the dollar on the foreign exchange market could dampen foreign central bank's willingness to purchase more or continue to hold the dollar assets it has.

Special Considerations for the United States

There are factors unique to the United States that may reduce the constraints on international lending or borrowing. First, more than 90% of the U.S. international borrowing is denominated in dollars.[13] This means that the pressures that other borrowing countries might face because of fluctuations in the value of debt service burden caused by volatile exchange rates are largely not an issue for the United States. Second, a large portion of foreign capital inflows to the United States is in relatively stable long-term investments. Such investments tend to be less prone to volatility caused by sudden changes in investor confidence. Third, about 50% of the investment in the United States by foreigners is in the form of equity (stock) holdings. Equity holdings tend to carry less strict payment requirements than debt holdings, working to lower the potential service payments (for a given level of NIIP), and extend the period over which the nation can prudently run current account deficits. Finally, the size, stability, and liquidity of the U.S. asset markets puts the United States in a special position as a borrower. That importance is enhanced by the dollar also being the world economy's principal reserve currency and therefore a readily held asset as well as a readily exchanged asset. In recent years, foreign central banks have greatly increased there holdings of dollar reserves.

Prospects

Where is the trade deficit headed in the period just ahead? In the analytical framework presented in this report, the answer to that question will hinge on the net direction of capital flows into and out of the American economy. At present, the United States is an international borrower receiving a net inflow of foreign capital. If that net inflow decreases, the trade deficit will also decrease. If the net inflow increases, the trade deficit will also increase. If the capital inflow remains the same, so will the trade deficit. So, what direction are capital flows likely to take?

Whether the current capital inflow gets bigger, smaller, or remains the same will most likely be determined by the resolution of two contenting forces: risk and reward. If, on balance, foreign investors see further investment in the United States as a far more riskier undertaking, other factors equal, the capital inflow will ebb and bring the trade deficit down with it. On the other hand, if the relative rate of return from investment in U.S. assets grows more attractive the net capital inflow could expand and bring the trade deficit up with it.

The important risk factor currently is the adequacy of *diversification* in investor portfolios. Large dollar balances have been accumulated in recent years. A survey by *The Economist* magazine shows that American assets make up 53% of the typical foreign investors equity portfolio and 44% of the typical bond portfolio. As recently as the mid-1990s, these percentages where only about 30%. It has also been estimated that the average investor in recent years has allocated about 80% of his increased wealth to dollar assets and would have to continue at this rate or higher to sustain the U.S. trade deficit for the next few years.[14] This is possible, but it is fair to doubt that it is probable, as standard investment practice increasingly suggests that investors move away from dollar assets. Such a shift was likely part of the cause of the dollar's depreciation from early 2002 through 2004. In 2002, almost all foreign capital inflows were from private sources. But in 2004, only about 75% of that inflow was from private sources. The difference has been a sharp increase in official purchases by foreign central banks, rising from about $42 billion in 2000 to a peak of about $395 billion in 2004 and a still substantial $235 billion in 2005. For the period 2001- 2006, holdings of dollar denominated foreign exchange reserves by foreign central banks grew from $28 billion to $440 billion.

The dollar changed course and appreciated in 2005, reflecting some re-shifting of private foreign investor preferences toward dollar assets. Two factors are probably the principal reasons for this rise. One, bourgeoning petroleum earnings looking for a safe and liquid resting place have moved toward dollar assets. And two, a significant nudging up of short-term interest rates by the Fed has made short-term dollar assets more attractive to all investors. The dollar was fairly steady through most of 2006, but began to weaken significantly at year-end. This may be the market's response to the Fed putting a halt to rate increases, and it also may reflect some softening of the demand for dollar assets by some oil exporting countries. In the period ahead, will the private foreign investor move away from or toward dollar assets? Will foreign central banks continue to increase there holdings of dollar assets?

For the private foreign investor, a relatively high *rate of return* is likely to continue to be a powerful incentive for holding an asset, and there are reasons to believe that for the immediate future, there will be some more attractive alternatives to dollar assets on the world market. In 2007, economic growth in the United States appears to be slowing and to avert recession monetary policy has lowered interest rates to provide added stimulus to economic activity. In contrast, economic growth in the euro area seems to have finally taken hold and the economic expansion in Japan continues. Improved relative profitability in both these areas may attract investors who had previously channeled their investments toward dollar assets.

There is likely to be some degree of uncertainty in forecasting the U.S. trade deficit's path. Nevertheless, the trade deficits rate of increase slowed markedly in 2006 and through the first three quarters of 2007 real net exports have been in surplus. This could be evidence that the deficit has at least bottomed out or perhaps begun to decline. This could reflect a willingness of foreign investors to continue their accumulation of dollar assets, but at a steadily slowing rate, due to concerns about higher risk attached to U.S. assets and broader opportunities for alternative investment destinations broaden.[15]

IS THE TRADE DEFICIT A PROBLEM?

A trade deficit is not necessarily undesirable. It confers benefits and carries some costs, and the former may exceed the latter. Trade deficits are a vehicle for extending the gains from trade, where lending and borrowing among nations can lead to a more efficient allocation of saving and a preferred pattern of consumption over time. Trade deficits do not necessarily cause slower economic growth or lead to any economy- wide loss of jobs.

As seen in the 1980s and as was evident in the 1990s, the U.S. unemployment has fallen to record lows and the economy's growth rate has accelerated to record highs even as the trade deficit has risen. That deficit, therefore, does not necessarily come at the expense of current domestic economic activity. Of course, borrowing carries a cost as the lender demands that interest be paid on the funds borrowed and the principal one day be repaid. This "debt service cost" is a burden the borrower must carry tomorrow for living beyond his means today. An evaluation of the desirability or undesirability of a trade deficit will hinge on the current benefits gained from that added spending relative to the future debt service burden that is incurred. Also, reliance on foreign sources of finance often raises concern that trade deficits carry an elevated risk of instability and disruption to the economy. Finally, trade deficits have differential effects on different sectors of the economy, often placing large burdens on exporting and import-competing sectors.

Intertemporal Trade

Gains from trade can arise from *intertemporal* exchanges. These are exchanges of *current* goods and services for claims on *future* goods and services, that is, an exchange of goods and services for an asset (i.e., cash in a bank account, stock, or bond). When the United States (or any trading nation) borrows from abroad to import materials for a current investment project, it is undertaking intertemporal trade. In such a transaction, the borrowing nation gains because it can support a higher rate of investment in capital goods than what current domestic saving alone could finance. The lending nation gains an asset yielding a higher rate of return than is available in the home economy. Because of the difference in their preferences for spending over time, the international asset market allows both parties to the transaction to raise their economic well-being. The borrower's economic well-being is raised by being able to spend more in the current period than current income allows. The lender's economic well-being is raised by being able to spend more in some future period. A country that is a net borrower will also run a trade deficit, while the country that is a net lender will run a trade surplus. This type of international asset transaction allows a more global utilization of the world's saving, a more efficient allocation of investment spending across nations, and a preferred distribution of spending over time.

Since the early 1980s, the United States has incurred trade deficits of moderate to large size, using international borrowing to push spending beyond current production, pursuing desired consumption and productive investment now rather than later. Similarly, nations like Japan have been able to run trade surpluses, using international lending opportunities to earn higher returns on their excess national savings and expanding the prospects for spending in the future. Such net flows have not grown as fast as gross flows of capital so that external sources of finance still claim only a small share of the total funding of domestic investment in most industrial countries. For the United States in 2005, for example, the trade deficit was equal to 6.4% of GDP and about 38% of domestic investment spending. The trend, nevertheless, has clearly been toward larger external imbalances (surpluses and deficits).

An aspect of the current pattern of international capital flows of some concern is that the inflows to the United States are largely outflows of capital from the developing economies. This is not a pattern that makes economic sense over the longterm. The United States has a large stock of high quality capital to equip its workers with and a slow growing but rapidly ageing population. The developing world, in contrast, tends to have a low ratio of capital to labor and have young, rapidly growing populations. Economic reasoning leads to the expectation that investment opportunities are likely to be greater in the capital poor developing economies and the need for saving to support future retirees greater in the United States, and that the United States should be running trade surpluses and be a net lender to the developing economies, not vice versa.[16]

Debt Service Burden

With each successive trade deficit the stock of foreign obligations grows. The current size of this stock is formally measured by the net international investment position (NIIP). In 1981, the United States was a *net creditor* with a net accumulation of assets in the rest of the world of $374 billion. But a steady and substantial stream of net foreign borrowing has swung the NIIP to a *net debtor* position of about $2.5 trillion in 2006, up from about $2.2 trillion in 2005. Again, favorable asset valuation effects cause the net creditor position to increase by less than the size of the 2006 current account deficit. The cumulative increase in U.S. net foreign debt since 1981 is more than $3 trillion.[17]

The current annual debt service cost of America's net foreign debt can be roughly judged from the size of the investment income component of the current account balance (see **Table 1**). That series is a measure of the nation's net payments and receipts on past investment and debt. If positive, the United States earned more than it paid; if negative, the United States paid more than it earned. Over time trend movement in this measure will be reflective of changes in the stock of net indebtedness. As seen in **Table 1**, U.S. international investment income in 2006 was a surplus of \$36.6 billion, up from a surplus of \$11.3 billion in 2005, but below the recent high of \$46.3 billion in 2003.

As discussed earlier, until 2006, the investment income balance has shown a surplus in the \$20 billion — \$30 billion range for the past 30 years. In recent years, the surplus of investment income has persisted despite the United States having a large *negative* international investment position (i.e., a large external debt). This continuing surplus meant that, so far, there has been no true debt service burden to the U.S. economy from its external debt. This has happened because there has been no net outflow of investment income, meanings there was no net diversion of U.S. real output to the rest of the world to service the external debt. In part, this lack of burden has been the result of the favorable effects of the recently strong dollar on the value of external assets and of recent low interest rates on the magnitude of external payments. However, the dollar is now on a downward path and interest rates have risen. Over the long run, if the trade deficit remains on its current upward trajectory, the volume of debt obligations will continue to grow, and as a result it is credible to expect U.S. international debt payments to also grow. It is possible that U.S. foreign debt service payments will reach or exceed \$100 billion before the current account deficit is erased and net foreign borrowing stops.

A \$100 billion transfer of real income to the rest of the world would be significant, but it would not be an overwhelming outflow for the world's largest economy. In 2006, the United States has a GDP valued at more than \$12 trillion, and by decades end, it will likely exceed \$13 trillion. For an economy of this size, a \$100 billion foreign debt service burden amounts to 0.8% of GDP. Clearly, insolvency is not lurking just over the horizon, particularly since the economy in the future will be larger and more capable of meeting debt service payments.

Nevertheless, a debt service payment of this size would be significant, particularly if viewed in the context of the economy's average annual growth rate of real GDP. For a mature industrial economy like the United States, the long-term growth rate of real output can optimistically be expected to average as much as 3.0 % per annum. Thus, a yearly debt service burden of about 1.0% of GDP would mean that the rate of growth of output that is effectively available to the domestic economy is reduced to 2.0%. That would be a significant erosion of the rate of improvement in the U.S. living standard. At a 3.0% annual growth rate, national income doubles about every 24 years, whereas at a 2.0% annual rate, doubling occurs every 35 years. Put another way, if the per capita GDP in 2002 of $36,600 grows on average at 3.0% for 24 years, GDP per capita would equal about $75,000, whereas growing at 2.0% for that same period would bring per capita GDP to only $59,000 or about 21% less.

The degree of burden actually incurred, however, will depend in part on how the nation uses what it borrows. If foreign borrowing has financed an increase in domestic consumption (public or private), there will not be any boost to future productive capacity. Therefore, to meet debt service expense, future consumption must be reduced below what it otherwise would have been. Such a reduction represents the burden of foreign borrowing. This is not necessarily bad; it all depends on how current versus future consumption is valued. If, on the other hand, foreign saving is used to increase domestic investment the burden could be avoided or at least reduced. Investment spending increases the nation's capital stock and expands the economy's capacity to produce goods and services. The value of this added output may be sufficient to both pay foreign creditors and also augment domestic spending. In this case, because future consumption need not fall below what it otherwise would have been, there would be no true economic burden.

It is difficult to assess to what extent U.S. debt service cost will be attenuated by the shift in the 1990s to the pattern of supporting rising domestic investment using foreign borrowing from the pattern of the 1980s of support, more or less exclusively, added domestic consumption with foreign borrowing. (Keep in mind, however, that the accelerated rate of investment makes only a small net contribution to the size of the nation's huge capital stock. Thus its growth-accelerating effect is commensurately modest. In the calculations of debt burden done just above a relatively high rate of long-term growth was assumed. Therefore the possible boost from earlier elevated rates of investment has probably been accounted for.)

Instability

Trade deficits often raise concern about the potential instability of external sources of finance. What if foreign investors begin to pull their funds out of the United States, disrupting domestic capital markets and the wider economy? There are good reasons to doubt that a sharp turnaround in foreign capital flows is likely. Recent experience of other countries with the panic of foreign investors has shown that such behavior most often results from the growing likelihood that they would not be repaid, that debt service payments were doubtful. Very often because many economies, particularly emerging economies, are not able to borrow in their own currency, a weakening of the home currency can lead to sharp increases in the cost of servicing such external debt. This ability to pay problem would also be exacerbated by weak economic growth or the rapid consumption of the nation's foreign exchange reserves in the defense of an overvalued currency. These are not risk factors that have much relevance to the circumstances of the United States, which has strong growth, does not fix its exchange rate, and borrows in its own currency.

In addition, a large proportion of investments made in the United States have been long-term in nature and not particularly prone to quick changes in commitment. It is very likely that many foreign investors generally see the U.S. economy as a bastion of long-run economic strength and will continue to invest for long-term gain. It is true that a sizeable share of the stock of U.S. foreign debt is in short term assets that can move quickly. That these types of assets will change direction as relative yields rise abroad is quite likely and does raise the risk of instability somewhat. But given the absence of the risk factors noted just above, it is far more likely that such capital outflows will be part of an orderly adjustment process and not lead to undue economic instability. The impact of any exodus of foreign capital, absent any compensating increase in domestic saving, would tend to raise interest rates and dampen credit sensitive activities. It is very likely that a falling dollar and a shrinking U.S. trade deficit would be more disruptive to the more export dependent and exchange rate sensitive economies of Europe and Japan.

The United States underwent a very orderly correction from a large trade deficit in the 1985-1990 period. However, the current task is likely to be more difficult and carry a higher risk of a disorderly adjustment for four reasons. One, oil prices were falling sharply in the late 1980s, but now oil prices are rising sharply. This will add to the inflation impact of a falling exchange rate and hamper the Federal Reserve's ability to counter the interest rate spike. Two, in the 1986-1990 episode, other economies central banks, particularly

Japan's, were willing to buy a large volume of dollar assets, providing a stabilizing counter force on the falling dollar and the rising yen. Given the already huge stocks of dollar assets being held abroad this action seems improbable today. Three, in the 1986-1990 period, Europe, the strongest market for U.S. exports, was booming. Today economic growth in Europe is slower. Four, holders of the U.S. external debt are accepting yields that seem too low given the likelihood that to keep the volume of external debt in realistic bounds the dollar must continue to fall, perhaps even faster than has occurred so far. And five, the size of the imbalance is now more than twice as large.

For the United States, the pain of such an adjustment would be somewhat muted by the large size of the overall U.S. capital market relative to the scale of the foreign capital flows. In recent years, the total funds raised in U.S. credit markets have been around $2,200 billion. Therefore, net borrowing from the rest of the world at around $600 billion to $800 billion per year represents 25% to 30% of the nations annual flow of credit. This is a magnitude of significance, but if withdrawn gradually it is not necessarily overwhelming for the United States.

Effects on Total Output and Employment

Standard economic analysis indicates that a trade deficit does not cause a net loss of output or jobs in the overall economy. Trade deficits will, however, likely change the composition of output and employment. This compositional effect occurs because the forces generating the trade deficit will tend to increase the dollar's exchange rate, raising the incentive to substitute some types of foreign output for similar types of domestic output. But this dampening effect on some domestic industries will tend to be offset by the positive effects of the trade deficits associated capital inflow on other parts of the economy. With a trade deficit some import sensitive industries (i.e., textiles) will have their output and employment decline, but some credit sensitive industries (i.e., housing) will have their output and employment increase. Recently, some domestic manufacturing industries have been harmed by the trade deficit, but there has also been a great surge in home building stimulated by lower interest rates afforded by the trade deficits attendant inflow of foreign capital.

Also, the Federal Reserve, using monetary policy, can set the overall level of spending in the economy to a level consistent with full employment.[18]

Although deviations from full employment can occur, a well-run monetary policy will minimize the incidence and duration of such episodes and help keep the total level of employment high in most years with or without outsourcing, trade deficits, or trade in general.

Trade deficits are most often a means of augmenting the level of goods and services available to domestic purchasers, in effect, allowing the nation to spend beyond current domestic output by means of importing foreign output. Both domestic and foreign output are used to meet current domestic demand. With strong demand in an economy operating near or at its productive capacity, and unable to generate a near-term expansion of that productive capacity sufficient to meet that demand, it is possible for domestic industries to be working at full capacity, even as there are also large inflows of similar or related foreign products.

Another reason why more imports do not lead to a reduction of domestic output and employment is because a very large share of U.S. trade is *intraindustry* trade in intermediate products — trade within the same industry due to an internationally fragmented production process — a final product will often be composed of several components, some of domestic origin and some of foreign origin.[19] With this structure of production, an increase in the demand for the final product will increase both domestic output and imported foreign output of necessary components, regardless the level of capacity utilization. Finally, there may simply be no domestic counterpart for some goods because product differentiation has led to specialization across countries in the production of particular goods. (The economic gain from such specialization arises from economies of scale, not comparative advantage and is common among high income economies with very similar resource endowments).

For these reasons, to a substantial degree the size of the trade deficit during an economic expansion, as during the 1980s and 1990s, cannot be taken as a one-for-one measure of reduced domestic output and the loss of the associated jobs. Since the end of the recession in 2001, the trade deficit has increased about $400 billion, whereas the unemployment rate fell from 6% in 2003 to 4.6% in 2006 and total civilian employment climbed from a low of 136 million workers in 2002 to 144 million workers in 2006.[20]

Effects on Particular Sectors

Although large trade deficits do not necessarily reduce the total level of economic activity, they can alter the composition of domestic output. Evidence shows that over the past 20 years, persistent trade deficits may have caused a reduction in the size of the domestic manufacturing sector.[21] The trade deficit exerts some downward pressure on the size of the domestic manufacturing sector because the trade inflow cannot easily augment the full spectrum of goods and services that comprise the nation's increase in domestic demand. About 70% of domestic spending is on services, but because trade is a relatively poor vehicle for acquiring services, only about 15% of U.S. imports are services. Therefore the trade deficit, largely a net inflow of manufactured goods, may not meet the augmented domestic demand for goods and services. In this circumstance, relative prices can be expected to change so as to reallocate some resources out of the domestic manufacturing sector and into the production of services to help meet the added domestic demand for services. This, in turn, should induce a greater reliance on the net inflow of foreign manufactured goods to help meet the added domestic demand for manufactures. The outcome will be greater real output by the domestic service sector and smaller real output by the domestic manufacturing sector.[22]

Recent surges of the trade deficit have clearly had a sharp negative impact on particular sectors. On the export side, agriculture and commercial aircraft experienced dampened export sales, mainly due to general weakness in other economies, particularly in Asia. On the import side, the steel industry and the textile and apparel industries came under considerable pressure from low price competition from countries affected by economic crises. The trade deficit is certainly a factor in the fall of employment in the U.S. manufacturing sector from 17 million in 2000 to 14 million in 2006. (However, of greater importance in the reduction of jobs in manufacturing is the rapid increase in worker productivity.) Adjustment to such trade effects can be economically painful for workers in these harmed sectors. Many economists argue that it is usually more beneficial to the overall economy to encourage adjustment than it is to protect sectors from the disruptive effects of trade. There are government programs that provide some amount of *trade adjustment assistance*, but there are important questions about the adequacy of these programs.

Looking to the future, trade deficit induced erosion of the U.S. manufacturing sector may also undercut the country's ability to make future debt service payments to foreign creditors. Manufacturing is a major part of the exporting sector and it is that sector which will be the means for paying debt service. A healthy manufacturing sector is likely to make that task easier.

POLICY RESPONSES TO TRADE DEFICITS

So long as domestic saving in the United States falls short of domestic investment and an inflow of foreign saving is available to fill all or part of the gap, the United States will run a trade deficit. This suggests that the use of trade policy tools to alter the flow of exports or imports, while imposing efficiency costs on the domestic economy, would not *over time* change the domestic investment-saving imbalance, and therefore would not change the overall size of the trade deficit.[23] On the other hand, macroeconomic policy tools have the potential to alter the saving- investment balance and the trade balance, but the realistic scope for their use is limited.

Trade Policy Responses

Trade policy involves actions to directly stimulate or retard the flows of imports and exports such as the erection or removal of tariffs and subsidies. Such actions will have significant impacts on the level of trade and economic efficiency (positive or negative) but will not change the balance of trade. In each instance action aimed at altering one side of the trade equation tends to induce effects via the exchange rate that will cause the other side of the equation to change in the same direction and by an equal amount. For example, using a tariff or quota as a barrier to stem the flow of imports into the United States would also reduce the demand for foreign exchange needed by the United States to purchase imports, appreciate the dollar's exchange rate, and induce an equivalent curtailment of export sales. With this policy, the level of trade has been reduced along with the economic *gains from trade* and general economic well-being, but the trade deficit would be unchanged. Alternatively, getting the trading partners to remove trade barriers would stimulate export sales, but would increase the demand for dollars by foreigners, appreciate the dollar exchange rate and induce an equivalent increase of imports. In this case, the level of trade is increased along with the gains from trade and economic well-being, but the trade deficit would be unchanged. Finally, an export subsidy would also stimulate export sales but an exchange rate induced rise of import sales would also leave the trade balance unchanged. (In the case of the subsidy, economic theory holds that a higher level of trade does not lead to an increase in economic welfare as the gains from trade are more than offset by the economic inefficiency of distorting the allocation of resources towards the export sector.)

Macroeconomic Policy Responses

To reduce and eliminate the U.S. trade deficit, there must be a rebalancing of global spending. The United States must reduce domestic spending and the economies with trade surpluses must increase domestic spending. In the framework of the saving-investment relationship, this rebalancing means that the United States faces three options. One, the rate of domestic investment falls. Two, the level of domestic saving rises (due to reduced consumption spending). Or three, some combination of one and two occurs. Macroeconomic policy, the use of monetary and fiscal policy tools, can in theory effect changes in these saving and spending flows. In all cases the dollar will have to fall to induce changes in spending at home and abroad. The inducement is caused by the depreciating dollar increasing the relative price of foreign goods in the U.S. market and decreasing the relative price of U.S. goods in foreign markets.

Monetary policy, by raising domestic interest rates and braking economic activity, can lower the rate of domestic investment and likely narrow the trade deficit. (At the extreme, a recession would likely dramatically reduce the trade deficit as it did in 2001.) Because of its negative effects on economic growth, decreasing the rate of domestic investment is not generally considered the most desirable economic course to follow, however.

The second course to a smaller trade deficit, raising the domestic saving rate, while having considerable economic merit, is a very problematic goal for macroeconomic policy. As explained above, fiscal decisions on taxing and spending influence the deficit or surplus position of the federal budget and the rate of public saving. As seen in the late 1990s, a rise in the U.S. overall saving rate as a consequence of a rising public saving rate stemmed from the sharp swing of the federal budget from a deficit of $290 billion in 1992 to a surplus of $236 billion in 2000. Since 2002, budget deficits have fallen and the government saving rate has increased accordingly. This change has restrained the growth of the trade deficit, but to eliminate the trade deficit by this means the government would likely have to run a sizable and sustained budget surplus. Given the political nature of budget deliberations, it seems problematic whether the federal budget can be an easily exploitable policy tool for eliminating the trade deficit.

Also, keep in mind, that there is less than a one-for-one change in the total saving rate from a given reduction of the budget deficit. The lower interest rates that come from the smaller budget deficit will also tend to stimulate some amount of domestic spending and reduce national saving accordingly. The ultimate effect on the overall saving rate is likely to be $0.50 to $0.80 for each dollar reduction in the budget deficit. This also means that a dollar of budget deficit reduction results in less than a dollar of trade deficit reduction, other factors constant. Therefore, if prospective budget deficits will be in the range of about $300 billion to $500 billion, an elimination of the trade deficit achieved through an increase of government saving would require running large budget surpluses.

Can macroeconomic policy lift the low private saving rate? Proposals have been made to use the tax code to raise incentives for saving by households. Careful analysis reveals that such proposals most often have uncertain effects on the saving-investment balance, as they tend to raise both saving and investment.[24] Other proposals, such as individual retirement accounts, may just redistribute saving, raising the household rate (a little), but lowering the public rate by an offsetting amount.

The Effect of Economic Policy Abroad

Foreign economic policy can help or hinder efforts by the United States to decrease the size of its trade deficit. As discussed above, the U.S. trade deficit is a two-way affair, reflecting the behavior of borrower and lender alike. The need to borrow must be met by a willingness to lend. On the other side of the U.S. inclination to spend beyond current domestic output is a symmetrical inclination of foreign nations to spend well short of domestic output and export the difference. It seems that American spending is as important to these economies as foreign borrowing is to the United States.

The most orderly adjustment to a smaller U.S. trade deficit is likely to occur through mutual policy actions — as the United States brings domestic spending *down* closer to domestic output and its major trading partners bring domestic spending *up* closer to their domestic output. In so doing, the U.S. efforts to become less dependent on imports is complemented by foreign efforts to become less dependent on exports to the United States. As already noted above, this change would require a substantial appreciation of foreign currencies relative to the dollar.

The less willing foreign economies are to change this current pattern of spending, the more protracted and difficult shrinking the U.S. current account deficit could be. If foreign economic policies work to counter U.S. policies attempting to raise domestic saving by reducing their domestic saving, then the dollar depreciation needed to induce a sizable reduction of the U.S. trade deficit would be larger than if foreign policies were more supportive of the change in spending patterns.

Without such mutually supporting policies, the dollar might have to fall 40% to 50% to achieve any sizable reduction of the U.S. trade deficit. A depreciation of that magnitude is risky for two reasons. One, some would argue that the greater the size of the currency's fall, the greater the chance that it will fall too far, too fast, sending a jolt to world financial markets that could possibly precipitate a world recession. Two, the dollar may not fall evenly against other currencies. From 2002 through 2004, the dollar fell by more than 30% against the euro but only about 15% against the Japanese yen. This has occurred because Japan has more actively tried to limit the strengthening of the yen relative to the dollar, accumulating a large stock of dollar assets. If such behavior becomes widespread, then the burden of adjustment of trade flows would fall heavily on the euro area and raise the risk of major economic collapse there.

Because of their size and degree of economic interaction with the United States, Japan and the euro zone (particularly Germany) would likely have to play a key role in assuring the world economy has an orderly adjustment to a weaker dollar and a much smaller American trade deficit. Yet neither has had a recent history of economic strength and there are reasons to doubt their willingness to undertake the actions that would better insure an orderly adjustment to a smaller U.S. trade deficit. Japan has struggled with poor economic performance for more than a decade and despite much better performance recently it is unclear that it is willing to overcome its fears of deflation and move strongly toward a stronger yen and reduced dependence on exports to support economic activity there. In Europe, structural rigidities continue to slow economic growth and a distinct bias towards tight macroeconomic polices further inhibits economic activity. In addition, there is an evident tendency of the euro zone to also use exports to support economic activity and therefore an inclination to avoid significant strengthening of the euro.

Of course, this adjustment process would also be assisted by the appreciation of other currencies, particularly in other Asian economies that have "pegged" their currency to the dollar. Much attention has been focused on China and its pegged currency, but the case for a stronger yuan is more tentative. Unlike Japan and the euro zone economies, China does not have a convertible currency or a well-developed and stable financial system. As a result, it probably has limited ability to successfully contend with currency instability. Nevertheless, many economists would argue that there is a need for China to allow its currency to appreciate and for that economy to channel more of its large saving pool into domestic investment. An appreciation of the yuan without changes in the saving-investment asymmetries between the United States and China would not lead to any significant changes in each trade imbalance. At present, it can be argued, China, by accumulating short-term reserves to maintain an undervalued exchange rate, is running a "neo-mercantilist" policy that allows it to run a large trade surplus to generate demand for its products and also have a large net inflow of long-term capital to help propel its economic development. For an economy of China's, this is not likely to be a sustainable process from the viewpoint of its trading partners. If it needs the inflow of long-term capital, then it should allow the real transfer of those resources by running a trade deficit or be prepared to use more of its own saving to support domestic investment rather than transfer those saving to the rest of the world.

In general, policies that improve the investment climate in many developing countries such as improved macroeconomic stability, increased financial transparency, and better bank regulation will tend to redirect international lending toward them and away from the United States. Nevertheless, it would seem quite problematic whether other countries will follow polices that would greatly increase the prospect for an orderly or quick shrinking of the U.S. current account deficit.

CONCLUSION

A trade deficit is not necessarily bad. It is most useful to see it as a vehicle to achieve an economic end, conferring some benefit at some cost. Whether the trade deficit is good or bad will hinge on a weighing of these benefits and costs. The overriding benefit is the ability to borrow internationally so as to push current spending beyond current production. Trade deficits in the 1990s have been a means to help finance an elevated level of domestic investment. Investment augments the nation's future productive possibilities and is a boon to long-term economic welfare. In contrast, the large trade deficits of the 2000s have been used to finance greater public and private consumption. In this situation, the benefit of an increase in current consumption must be weighed against the cost of a reduction of future consumption.

The cost of the trade deficit is the debt service that must be paid on the associated borrowing from the rest of the world. The U.S. debt service has grown steadily and will soon reach a size that could impose a significant decrement to the rate of growth of its living standard. It is a burden that is still well within the U.S. means to pay, but some might argue it is a burden that needs to be curtailed.

Certainly true that standard trade policy tools such as tariffs, quotas, and subsidies will not significantly change saving or investment behavior and, therefore, will not reduce the trade deficit. But in most cases will create distortions that reduce national economic welfare. Macroeconomic policy can affect the saving-investment balance and can change the trade deficit, but how to do so by raising domestic saving rather than reducing domestic investment remains unclear. The government budget deficit and government saving have improved in recent years, but a much more sizable increase would be needed to eliminate the trade deficit by this means alone. Over the long-term, many economists see the budget balance moving in the opposite direction under the pressures of rising entitlement spending. However, the prospect of more vigorous economic growth in the euro area and Japan could cause greater opportunities for investment in those economies, slowing their saving outflow to the United States, and working to shrink the U.S. trade deficit. Generating a sustained increase in the U.S. economy's rate of saving by reversing the steadily sagging rate of household saving would reduce the trade deficit, but how to raise that rate is uncertain.

It is possible that the trade deficit could correct itself without any inducement by economic policy. There are good reasons to expect that economic forces will work to sate the demand for foreign borrowing as well as reduce the supply of foreign funds being offered. A significant acceleration of the rate of growth abroad relative to that of the United States (raising domestic investment relative to domestic saving abroad) would likely initiate such a process. A change in relative growth rates would most likely alter rates of return between the United States and the rest of the world, redirect a larger share of international investment flows towards destinations other than the United States, and shrink the U.S. trade deficit.

This correction does not necessarily have to lead to an elimination of the trade deficit. It might only fall enough to assure a more sustainable rate of accumulation of foreign debt that stabilizes the ratio of external debt to GDP. Nevertheless, a smaller trade deficit, lacking an increase in the rate of U.S.

domestic saving, will mean that the reduced saving inflow from abroad will have shrunk without any offsetting increase in domestic saving. This will increase U.S. interest rates and force a reduction of domestic investment to the level of the smaller flow of saving available to finance it.

End Notes

[1] The balance on current account is the nation's most comprehensive measure of international transactions, reflecting exports and imports of goods and services, investment income (earnings and payments), and unilateral transfers.

[2] Complete current account data on trade performance in 2006 will not be available until March 2007.

[3] Trade balance data for the full year 2006 are not yet available, but through three quarters the trade deficit on current account has been running at an annual rate of near $860 billion.

[4] The level and composition of the United States' accumulated net indebtedness to foreigners is found in the annual tally of the nation's *net international investment position* (NIIP) by the U.S. Department of Commerce and published in the June *Survey of Current Business*. In 2005, the NIIP was a deficit of $2.7 trillion. The capital inflow manifests in foreign holdings of several different types of assets including bank accounts, stocks, bonds, and real property. For more detail on cross-border capital flows, see CRS Report RL3 2462, *Foreign Investment in U.S. Securities*, by James Jackson.

[5] It is useful to remember that "income"/"spending" are the flip side of "production"/ "output." Any given value of production generates an equal value of income. Thus the income the economy earns can support spending sufficient to purchase the economy's current output. With international trade, however, it is possible for there to be a divergence of spending and production through the borrowing and lending of current income and output between nations.

[6] See CRS Report RL32462, *Foreign Investment in U.S. Securities*, by James Jackson.

[7] Saving in a macroeconomic framework is the portion of current income that is left after households, businesses, and government pay for their current consumption. A household that diverts some amount of current income to a bank, mutual fund, or government bond is saving. Similarly the tax revenue that the government has left after paying for its spending is (public) saving.

[8] See CRS Report RS20224, *The Collapse of Household Saving: Why Has it Happened and What Are its Implications?*, by Brian Cashell and Gail Makinen.

[9] For a fuller discussion of this analytical framework, see N. Gregory Mankiw, *Principles of Economics* (Fort Worth, TX: The Dryden Press, 1997), p. 659; and also, Congressional Budget Office, *Causes and Consequences of the Trade Deficit: An Overview*, CBO Memorandum, March 2000.

[10] See forecasts by Global Insight, *The U.S. Economy*, June 2006.

[11] See Catherine L. Mann, *Is the Trade Deficit Sustainable* (Washington, DC: Institute for International Economics, 1999), p. 156.

[12] On the subject of sustainability of the trade deficit see CRS Report RL33 186, *Is the U.S. Current Account Deficit Sustainable*? by Marc Labonte.

[13] See U.S. Treasury Department, *Treasury Bulletin*, April 2002.

[14] *The Economist*, September 18, 2003.

[15] See Global Insight, *U.S. Economic Outlook*, June 2007; and OECD, *Economic Outlook*, June 2007.

[16] See Ben S. Bernanke, "The Global Saving Glut and the U.S. Current Account Deficit," speech delivered March 10, 2005, The Federal Reserve Board.

[17] See U.S. Department of Commerce, Bureau of Economic Analysis, *2005 Year-end Net International Investment Position*, June 30, 2006. The term "net debtor" is somewhat inaccurate in that only a fraction is a true debt obligation, such as a bond, where there is a fixed term and contractual obligation to pay a fixed amount to the holder. Holdings of equities carry the expectation of earnings , but there is no obligation to pay if no earnings are made.

[18] Economies always have some amount of unemployment. Each economy will tend to have a natural rate of unemployment around which the actual unemployment rate fluctuates. This natural rate will also represent the rate at which the economy is effectively at full employment because a lower rate of unemployment would not be sustainable due to the inducement of higher a rate of inflation. The natural rate is not zero because at any point in time there will be some people who are changing jobs and other people who normal market forces have temporarily displaced. More fluid the economy's labor markets the lower its natural rate of unemployment is likely to be. For most of the last 30 years the United States economy's natural rate was judged to be in the 5.5% to 6.0% range. Since the mid-1990s, the natural rate has likely fallen to the 4.5% to 5.0% range. Most often an appropriate level of aggregate spending is that consistent with employment at the natural rate. There is no theory or evidence to indicate full employment is influenced by the trade deficit.

[19] The significance of intraindustry trade varies by industry. For industries that make sophisticated manufactured goods it tends to be very high with over 90% of trade of this form. In labor intensive industries, that manufacture less sophisticated products, very little trade is intraindustry. Intraindustry trade is to a great degree a manifestation of a wide spread move towards more fragmented production processes, or what is called *vertical specialization*. It is estimated that about one-third of the growth of world trade since 1970 is the result of this phenomenon and can be expected to be even higher for the trade of an advanced industrial economy such as the United States. For further examination of the nature and significance of intraindustry trade, see Paul Krugman and Maurice Obstfeld, *International Economics: Theory and Policy* (Reading, MA: Addison Wesely, 1997), pp. 139-142. For further examination of the *vertical specialization* phenomenon, see David Hummels, Dana Rapoport, and Kei-Mu Yi, "The Nature and Growth of Vertical Specialization," *Journal of International Economics*, vol. 54 (June 2001), pp. 75-96.

[20] See the *Economic Report of the President*, February 2006, Appendix B: Statistical Tables.

[21] See CRS Report RL32350, *Deindustrialization of the U.S. Economy: The Roles of Trade, Productivity, and Recession*, by Craig K. Elwell; CRS Report RL32 179, *Manufacturing Output, Employment, and Productivity*, by Stephen Cooney; and Robert Rowthorn and Ramana Ramaswamy, "Deindustrialization: Causes and Implications," *Staff Studies for the World Economic Outlook*, IMF, 1997.

[22] This argument is not likely undermined by the development of U.S. trade surpluses in services in this period as *tradable* services are a small sub-set of the full spectrum of, largely non-tradable, services in domestic demand.

[23] Similarly, the removal of U.S. trade barriers, while conferring efficiency gains, would not change the domestic investment-saving imbalance, and therefore would not widen the trade deficit.

[24] See CRS Report RL321 19, *Can Public Policy Raise the Saving Rate?* by Brian Cashell.

In: United States Trade Deficit Issues
Editor: Carl T. Yankovich
ISBN: 978-1-60692-090-9

Chapter 3

IS THE UNITED STATES TRADE DEFICIT CAUSED BY A GLOBAL SAVING GLUT?*

Marc Labonte
Specialist in Macroeconomics
Government and Finance Division

SUMMARY

The U.S. trade deficit is equal to net foreign capital inflows. Because U.S. investment rates exceed U.S. saving rates, the gap must be financed by foreign borrowing. Net capital inflows have grown over recent years to a record 6.6% of gross domestic product (GDP) in 2006. Economists have long argued that the low U.S. saving rate, which is much lower than most foreign countries, is the underlying cause of the trade deficit and that policies aimed at reducing the trade deficit should focus on boosting national saving. The most straightforward policy would be to reduce the budget deficit, which directly increases national saving.

In an often-cited speech in early 2005, Ben Bernanke, now the chairman of the Federal Reserve, argued that the underlying cause of the trade deficit was not insufficient domestic saving, but rather a "global saving glut." He argued that there was too much saving worldwide and not enough investment

* This is an edited, reformatted and augmented version of a CRS Report for Congress publication dated June 2007.

demand, and that the United States was the natural destination for this excess saving. As a result of the global saving glut, the trade deficit increased, interest rates remained low, demand for capital and residential investment rose, and the incentive to save decreased in the United States. He argued that because the trade deficit was not "made in the U.S.A.," policy steps to reduce the budget deficit or raise private saving were unlikely to significantly reduce the trade deficit until the global saving glut ended.

The conventional view and the global saving glut view are not necessarily mutually exclusive. To an extent, the difference between the two is tautological — the conventional view stresses that U.S. saving is too low relative to foreign saving, and the global saving glut view stresses that foreign saving is too high relative to U.S. saving. It is important to acknowledge foreign causes for international capital movements, but in doing so, changes in domestic conditions should not be neglected. Although neither view leads to any hard conclusions about whether the trade deficit is good or bad, the global saving glut implies that reducing it is largely out of American hands.

Contrary to the global saving glut hypothesis, data show that world saving is close to its lowest level in decades. However, low interest rates (although not unusually low by historical standards) suggest that worldwide investment demand is probably low as well. Data also show that the rise in saving in the developing world (notably among oil producers and East Asian countries) over the past few years has gone hand-in-hand with the significant accumulation of official foreign exchange reserves. At the same time, there has been a decrease in government saving in the United States since the 1990s. In recent years, a large fraction of U.S. net capital inflows have been the result of foreign reserve accumulation by other countries rather than coming from private sources, which suggests that global imbalances are not primarily the result of decisions by private investors and that (because of the fall in U.S. government saving) the trade deficit to a great extent may indeed have been "made in the U.S.A."

This report will be updated as events warrant.

INTRODUCTION

Members of Congress from both parties have expressed concern about the size of the U.S. current account deficit, popularly known as the trade deficit.[1] The current account deficit rose from 1.3% of gross domestic product (GDP) in 1997 to a record- high 6.6% of GDP in 2006. By definition, the current account deficit equals the foreign capital flowing into the country on net. In other words, American purchases of imports can exceed foreign purchases of U.S. exports only if the United States borrows from abroad. Congress is concerned that a trade deficit of this size may not be sustainable and could disrupt the smooth functioning of the U.S. economy.

Conventional economic analysis suggests that the cause of the current account deficit is insufficient national saving.[2] Because the U.S. saving rate is too low to finance national demand for physical capital investment, the United States must borrow from abroad to bridge the gap. The conventional policy prescription for reducing the current account deficit has been to boost the national saving rate by reducing the budget deficit and encouraging higher rates of private saving.

In March 2005, Ben Bernanke — then a Governor of the Federal Reserve (Fed) system and now Fed Chairman — made an often-cited speech arguing that the conventional view was wrong. Instead, he "locat(ed) the principal causes of the U.S. current account deficit outside the country's borders," in the "global saving glut."[3] The global saving glut view implies that conventional policy prescriptions may have little success in reducing the current account deficit.

Whether the source of the growing trade deficit is domestic or international, it could nevertheless be a cause for concern. The counterpart to a larger U.S. trade deficit is larger trade surpluses among certain trading partners. In the April 2007 *World Economic Outlook*, the International Monetary Fund (IMF) notes that "[p]articular concerns (for the outlook) include ... the low probability but high cost risk of a disorderly unwinding of large global imbalances."[4]

This report compares and analyzes the conventional view with the global saving glut view, and discusses the implications of each for the U.S. economy.

THE CONVENTIONAL VIEW

The conventional view among economists attributes the cause of the U.S. current account deficit to the country's low national saving rate. As seen in **Table 1**, the United States has a lower national saving rate than any of the regional groupings in the world. The United States' saving rate is less than half the rate of some regions and less than one-third the rate of China. Moreover, the United States has a negative public saving rate that reduces the overall national saving rate.[5] The federal budget deficit peaked at 3.5% of GDP in 2004, and equaled 1.9% of GDP in 2006.

Table 1. World Saving, Investment, and Current Account Balance as a Percentage of GDP, 2006

	Saving	Investment	Current Account Balance
United States	13.7	20.0	-6.5
Japan	28.0	24.1	3.9
Euro Area	21.3	21.3	-0.3
China	58.6	50.2	8.3
Other East Asia	29.0	23.4	5.7
Other Emerging Markets	21.0	22.5	-1.5
Oil Producers	33.2	21.4	11.8

Source: CRS calculations based on data from IMF, *World Economic Outlook*, April 2007; IMF, World Economic Outlook database.

Although U.S. investment rates are lower than the rates of other regions, the disparity is smaller than for saving rates. As seen in **Table 1**, the United States was the only economy whose investment rate significantly exceeded its national saving rate in 2006; as a result, large foreign capital inflows (which come to the country in the form of a current account deficit) are needed to bridge the gap. Although other countries have a current account deficit, none of the regions in **Table 1** has an aggregate current account deficit except the United States.

Economic theory predicts that capital will flow to the country where it can earn the highest real rate of return. Although some economists are concerned by the scale of U.S. borrowing, most believe that international capital flows are generally mutually beneficial: they allow the borrowing country access to more capital than domestic saving would allow, and they allow the lending country to earn a higher rate of return than could be earned at home. If rates of return (adjusted for risk)[6] were higher in the United States than abroad, then capital would flow into the United States and a current account deficit would result. Rates of return might be higher in the United States than abroad for several reasons.

First, the United States has enjoyed an increase in productivity growth since the mid-1990s that has not been experienced widely abroad. As a result, U.S. economic growth has tended to consistently outpace growth in most other industrial countries in the past 10 years. At least in the short run, this productivity boom might be expected to raise U.S. rates of return above foreign rates.

Second, interest rates are determined by the intersection of the supply of national saving and the demand for investment spending. Because saving rates are so much lower in the United States than abroad, one would expect higher interest rates in the United States.

Third, demand for U.S. investment spending is being crowded out by budget deficits that are competing for the same pool of private saving, which increases interest rates.[7] Because the budget deficit pushes up interest rates (which attract foreign capital inflows), the budget deficit and trade deficit are often referred to as "twin deficits."[8]

Fourth, economic theory suggests that additional investment is subject to diminishing returns. For example, adding a second machine at a factory would be expected to yield less additional output than the first machine for a given labor force. Many countries have higher investment rates than the United States; therefore, rates of return may be lower abroad because of diminishing returns. (This assumption would be less applicable to developing countries because their capital stocks are so much smaller than those of industrial countries.) For example, despite persistently low economic growth and low rates of return during the past decade, Japan's investment rate was still roughly 4 percentage points of GDP higher than America's in 2006. With investment rates so high, perhaps it is of little surprise that the Japanese would prefer to invest their remaining saving in foreign assets.

THE GLOBAL SAVING GLUT VIEW

Although Bernanke does not deny that the low U.S. saving rate and large budget deficit contribute to the current account deficit, his emphasis lies elsewhere. He argues that the current account deficit is not primarily "made in the U.S.A." — the result of domestic conditions or policies — but, rather, the result of what he calls a global saving glut. As **Table 1** illustrates, the counterpart to large U.S. trade deficits is large foreign trade surpluses, particularly in East Asia and among oil producers, a situation that is often to referred to as "global imbalances." Bernanke argues that world saving is so abundant because foreign saving rates in the industrialized world are high and investment demand is low as a result of its rapidly aging populations. However, to explain the change in current account balances in the past few years, the relevant measure is the change in global saving. The increase in global saving, he argues, is the result of the developing world's shift from a net borrower to a net lender. This has occurred, he believes, for several reasons.

First, the series of financial crises in the developing world in the late 1990s (e.g., Mexico, Southeast Asia, Turkey, and Argentina) reduced the developing world's ability to borrow. As a result, capital that was previously flowing in the developing world needed a new destination. These crises also motivated developing nations to improve their fiscal position through less borrowing, lower budget deficits, and higher foreign exchange reserves. An accumulation of foreign exchange reserves by the central bank is a form of capital outflows (lending abroad) and corresponds to an increase in the current account surplus. Accumulating foreign reserves represents a form of national saving that is undertaken by the central bank rather than private citizens. Bernanke likens foreign reserve accumulation to a country building a "war chest" to make it less vulnerable to future financial crises.[9]

Finally, the rise in oil prices has caused a sudden increase in income and saving (because the increase in income has not immediately been spent) for many developing countries that are oil producers.[10] Between 2002 and 2005, the IMF estimates that revenue that oil producers earned from oil exports increased by $437 billion, and only about half of the increase was offset by higher imports, whereas the other half was saved.[11] Some of that additional saving has been invested in U.S. assets.

Bernanke does not dispute that the U.S. national saving rate has fallen in recent years and contributed to the rising current account deficit. Instead, he argues that the global saving glut has, in large part, caused the decline in U.S. saving. According to Bernanke, the rise in foreign capital inflows pushed up U.S. equity and other asset prices in the late 1990s, making Americans wealthier. Similarly, after the stock market crash, foreign capital inflows resulted in lower interest rates which, in turn, boosted U.S. housing prices.[12] He argues that, in both cases, Americans responded to increased wealth by saving less and consuming more.

Why did this global saving glut come to the United States, causing the current account deficit? In Bernanke's view, conditions in the United States were ideal to attract the foreign capital.[13] In the 1990s, the high-tech boom led to productivity gains and profit growth that, sustainable or not, made the United States highly attractive to foreign investors. Furthermore, the United States has deep, diverse, and well-governed capital markets that made it a more attractive investment destination than other countries.[14] The United

States has often been viewed as a "safe haven" for capital in times of international market unrest. Finally, Bernanke points to the dollar's unique role as the international reserve currency. In particular, many Asian countries sought to limit their currency's movements against the dollar in recent years by accumulating dollar-denominated foreign exchange reserves.[15]

Although the United States was the primary recipient of the world's global saving glut, in Bernanke's view, it was not the only one. He believes the global saving glut is also responsible for the deterioration in the current account balances and rise in asset prices and household wealth of France, Italy, Spain, Australia, and the United Kingdom. Two notable exceptions to this trend are Japan and Germany, which still have large current account surpluses and little asset price appreciation, in spite of both running large budget deficits. Likewise, U.S. budget surpluses in the late 1990s did not prevent the current account deficit from rising.

Differing perspectives on the cause of the current account deficit have different implications for policy options to reduce it. In the global saving glut view, the U.S. current account deficit is due to global forces largely beyond our control. For this reason, Bernanke argues that eliminating the budget deficit, although desirable in itself, would probably have only a modest effect on the current account deficit. He points to research that finds a $1 decline in the budget deficit would reduce the current account deficit by less than $0.20.[16] Likewise, he argues that policy measures to induce higher household saving, although desirable, would most likely be ineffective as long as interest rates are low and housing prices are high. He argues that the global saving glut is unlikely to diminish until capital begins flowing on net into — rather than out of — the developing world.

ANALYSIS

The debate between the conventional view and the global saving glut view cannot be settled by looking at absolute levels of saving worldwide. There is no such thing as too much or too little saving in an absolute sense. As **Table 1** indicates, regions of the world are capable of widely disparate saving and investment rates. High saving/investment rates are found in both economically dynamic (China) and stagnant (Japan) countries. Rather, the debate centers on relative saving rates.

Fundamentally, the conventional view and global saving view can be thought of as two different ways to say the same thing. To paraphrase, the conventional view can be stated as "the trade deficit is caused by the United States saving too little compared to the rest of the world," whereas the global saving glut view can be stated as "the trade deficit is caused by the rest of the world saving too much compared to the United States." What is indisputable, even tautological, is the observation that saving rates are lower in the United States than abroad and that current account imbalances allows more convergence in countries' investment rates than their disparate saving rates. Economists call these *positive* statements, or statements of fact, as opposed to *normative* statements, or statements of judgment. Although the conventional view and global saving glut view are based on the same positive statements, they lead — at least implicitly — to different normative views. The conventional view implies that the United States should save more to bring its saving rates into line with the rest of the world; the global saving glut view implies that the rest of the world should save less (consume more) and become more similar to the United States.

Despite being based on the same positive statement, the conventional and global saving glut views differ because economists have only *ex post* data on the economy: one can observe (after the fact) that, for some reason, U.S. investment rates significantly exceeded domestic saving rates and that the difference was bridged by the large current account deficit. However, theory and analysis are needed to describe the underlying factors leading to those results. In the conventional view, the saving and investment rates are likely to be thought of as determined by domestic factors, and the foreign capital flows (current account deficit) are likely to be thought of as the residual variable that equilibrates the other two. In the global saving glut view, the foreign capital inflows are the predetermined variable and the domestic saving and investment rates must adjust to accommodate them.

Although the world saving rate has been rising since 2002, it was still below its historical average as a share of GDP in 2006, as shown in **Figure 1**.[17] As the IMF has argued, these data contradict the underlying premise of the global saving glut view, unless the saving glut is taken to mean a dearth of global investment opportunities (worldwide, saving and investment must be equal).[18] If so, then global imbalances may subside when investment demand in the rest of the world increases. The figure also shows that the decline in saving by industrial countries has been sharper than the decline in world saving, whereas saving by developing countries has been rising since the 1980s. Corporate saving has recently risen in industrial countries, but not enough to offset the decline in household and government saving.

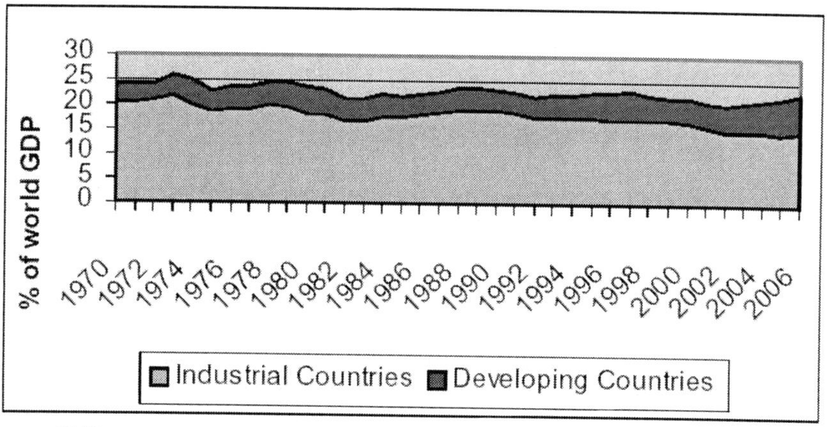

Source: IMF.

Figure 1. World Saving as a Share of World GDP, 1970-2006

Real (inflation-adjusted) interest rates are another piece of evidence that might help determine what is driving saving and investment patterns. (Nominal interest rates are lower than in recent decades because of the decline in inflation; however, this information is not useful by itself because saving and investment behavior is influenced by real, not nominal, interest rates.[19]) The conventional view would predict that the foreign capital inflows would be attracted to the United States by high and rising interest rates caused by the falling supply of national saving (due to a rising budget deficit or lower private saving) and the rising demand for investment spending. In contrast, the global saving glut view would predict that the abundance of saving (or dearth of investment demand) abroad would cause low and falling interest rates worldwide.

As seen in **Figure 2**, real interest rates, as measured by the 10-year U.S. Treasury bond yield, have been low and falling compared with recent years.[20] Long-term interest rates have also been unusually low relative to short-term rates since the Fed tightened monetary policy. Despite an uptick in 2006, interest rates remained below rates in the 1980s and 1990s. The same broad pattern has been seen in longterm government bond yields for the other major industrial economies. This pattern would support the global saving glut view — although global saving is currently at low levels, perhaps global investment demand is even lower. However, in the 1960s and 1970s, real interest rates were lower than present. That pattern would also hold true if the chart included rates from earlier years; suggesting that in the long-term, current interest rates are not unusually low and therefore do not provide clear evidence of a saving glut.[21] Arguably, however, international capital flows have only been an important determinant of interest rates more recently, so the older data are not a relevant comparison.

Worldwide, current account balances sum to zero; thus, a rise in one country's trade balance must be offset by a fall in another's. **Table 2** offers a more sophisticated picture of what is driving global capital flows by breaking down regional changes in saving, investment, and current account patterns since 1997. Over that period, there was a large move to current account surpluses in the developing world (mainly as a result of developing world financial crises and the higher oil price), and a large increase in the U.S. current account deficit. This movement is the opposite of what simple economic theory would predict — that capital should flow into capital-poor developing countries and out of the industrial world. Indeed, when large current account deficits have emerged in the past, they have usually been in developing countries. The increase in Japan's current account surplus is also notable. Although the increase in Japan's current account surplus was smaller as a share of its GDP than in developing countries, the increase was significant in dollar terms because its GDP is much larger. In other regions, the changes in the current account were more modest.

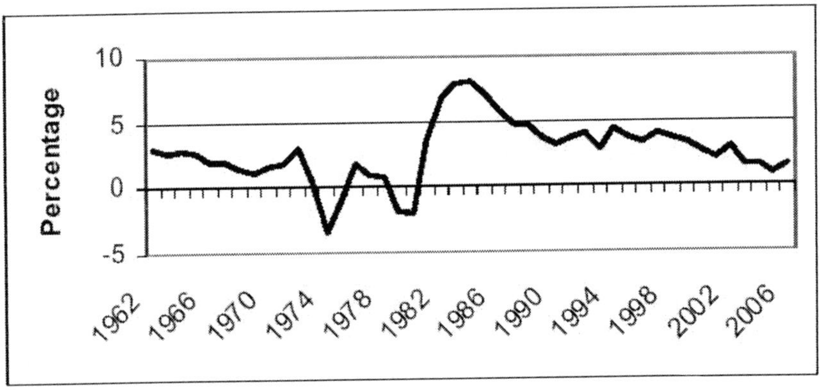

Source: CRS calculations based on data from Federal Reserve and Bureau of Labor Statistics

Note: Real interest rates = (interest rates) — (change in the consumer price index)

Figure 2. Real 10-Year Treasury Yields, 1962-2006

Table 2. Change in Saving, Investment, and Current Account Balance as a Percentage of GDP, 1997-2006

	Saving	Investment	Current Account Balance
United States	-3.9	+0.2	-4.8
Japan	-2.7	-4.3	+1.6
Euro Area	-0.3	+1.1	-1.7
China	+16.6	+12.0	+4.5
Other East Asia	-2.9	-11.0	+8.2
Other Emerging Markets	+2.4	+0.6	+1.7
Oil Producers	+6.7	-4.0	+10.7

Source: CRS calculations based on data from IMF, *World Economic Outlook*, April 2007; IMF, World Economic Outlook database.

Another major change during this period was the large decline in investment as a share of GDP in Japan, the Other East Asia region, and the Oil Producing region, which led to increases in the current account surplus in all three regions. Investment fell in Japan because of the persistent economic slowdown. It fell in East Asia — by more than 10 percentage points of GDP — because of the Asian financial crisis of the late 1990s. For the world as a whole, only China saw a large increase in investment spending, so world investment rates fell. These data support the saving glut hypothesis only if the glut is defined in terms of weak investment demand.

As can be seen in the table, a case for a global glut (due to excess saving) can be made only for China, Other Emerging Markets, and the Oil Producing Region, which all have seen significant increases in their saving rate since 1997. (In China's case, the large increase in the saving rate was accompanied by a large increase in the investment rate, so the increase in its current account surplus was smaller.) However, those saving increases were offset by saving declines in the other regions of the world, so that world saving fell. The decline in saving was particularly pronounced in the United States (which supports the view that the current account deficit was "made in the U.S.A.," and not the result of greater foreign demand for U.S. assets) and Japan.

In many regions, the change in the saving rate over this period was driven more by changes in public saving (the government budget balance) than private saving. This observation casts doubt on the global saving glut argument that the imbalances are being driven by market forces seeking out the highest rate of return. If foreign governments had not begun saving more, and the U.S. government saving less,[22] then global current account imbalances might have been much smaller. This evidence is consistent with the conventional view and its "twin deficits" prediction, and inconsistent with the global saving glut view that the fall in U.S. saving is primarily the rational response of private individuals to higher house values. Because the budget deficit was "made in the U.S.A.," it is difficult to argue that the current account deficit was not.

Role of Foreign Reserves

In determining why international capital flows have changed, an important consideration is the form they have taken. Official foreign exchange reserves in developing countries more than doubled in dollar terms from 2003 to 2006, and more than tripled from 2001 to 2006, rising to $3 trillion in 2006.[23] In many East Asian countries, although overall saving has fallen, there have been large increases in foreign exchange reserves, as shown in **Figure 3**.[24] When a country accumulates foreign reserves, its trade surplus increases (or trade deficit decreases) and its currency appreciates less than it would otherwise. Many Asian countries, including China and Japan, have not seen their currencies significantly appreciate against the dollar in recent years.[25] These countries presumably were attempting to maintain the attractiveness of their exports, but may also have been attempting to strengthen their fiscal position to stave off future financial crises (à la Bernanke's war chest analogy). The accumulation of foreign reserves in oil-exporting countries stems from their higher oil revenues in recent years, which has not been completely offset by higher imports. Furthermore, not all state-controlled capital flows in oil-exporting countries are recorded as foreign reserves.[26] The *Economist* recently estimated that $2.5 trillion may be held in various countries' sovereign-wealth funds.[27]

A large share of U.S. net capital inflows have come from official rather than private sources in recent years. Reserve accumulation by foreign governments accounted for 67% of U.S. net capital inflows in 2004 and 42% in 2006. If domestic interest rates are being held down by official foreign capital inflows, foreign central banks are preventing the market from sending a signal to Americans to save more or invest less.[28] The effect on the U.S. economy is the same whether capital inflows come from private or official sources; however, the motivation is quite different, and the global saving glut view is meant to explain the motivation. If Asian governments are motivated to accumulate foreign reserves primarily to boost the competitiveness of their export industries, then this casts doubt on the inevitability of the U.S. current account deficit stressed in the global saving glut view. Had foreign governments not intervened in foreign exchange markets, private foreigners might have raised domestic investment rates or lowered their national saving rates, thereby preventing any foreign saving glut from emerging.[29] The fact that a large share of foreign capital inflows have taken the form of official purchases of U.S. government bonds, as opposed to private investors buying private U.S. assets, suggests that recent capital flows have not been primarily motivated by rate of return considerations.

Future Prospects

Many observers are concerned whether the presence of global imbalances (large U.S. trade deficits and foreign trade surpluses) is sustainable.[30] Although current account imbalances are larger than in the past, international capital markets are deeper, barriers to international capital movements are low, and capital is more mobile. On the other hand, larger and more mobile capital flows create the potential for more significant economic disruption if they were to reverse.

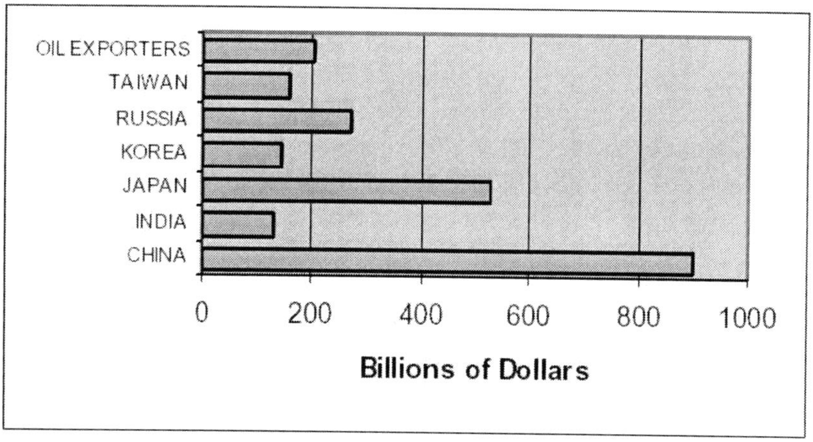

Source: Economist Intelligence Unit.

Figure 3. Cumulative Increase in Foreign Exchange Reserves in Selected Countries, 2000-2006

Economic theory cannot predict how much a country should borrow abroad (at low levels), but if borrowing were becoming burdensome, one would expect net investment income payments abroad to be large. Despite being the world's largest debtor country, the United States earns more abroad on its foreign assets than it pays out to foreign lenders. (Although its liabilities exceed its assets, the United States is earning more on its assets than it is paying on its liabilities.) As long as this is the case, it is difficult to see why the current account deficit is not sustainable — although it is implausible that the United States could borrow *limitlessly* without foreign debt payments becoming unsustainably large. Bernanke points out that one potentially troubling feature of the current situation is that so much investment has been residential, which is unlikely to increase the nation's productive capacity and reduce the burden of paying back foreign debt in the future.

So far, global imbalances have not disrupted economic activity and have arguably been mutually beneficial, since they have allowed low saving economies like the United States to increase their investment rates and high saving economies like Japan to earn a higher rate of return. Thus, the mere existence of current account imbalances cannot be seen as problematic per se. If one were to argue that the current account deficit were harmful to the United States, it would have to be on the grounds of its future, rather than current, economic effects. The most widely cited worst-case scenario is if foreigners became unwilling to lend further to the United States, causing the current account deficit and the dollar to suddenly plummet. This event would presumably cause unrest in financial markets, leading to broader economic disruption. The gap between domestic saving and investment would suddenly need to be bridged through higher domestic saving and lower domestic investment, which would require a sharp rise in interest rates to occur.

If, on the other hand, the current account deficit and dollar were to decline slowly, there would be little reason to expect it to cause economic disruption because the decline in investment spending would be offset by higher production in export- and import-competing industries. Domestic investment would have to fall and domestic saving would have to rise to restore equilibrium to financial markets. Higher interest rates would be the channel through which these changes would occur, and how much interest rates rose would depend on how sensitive saving and investment are to interest rate changes. This would be true in both the conventional view and the global saving glut view.

The worst-case scenario is presumably based on an assumption that recent lending to the United States has been irrationally high. If financial market participants act rationally, there is little reason to think that foreigners would be lending the United States too much right now and suddenly stop lending money in the future. A related concern is that large capital inflows have stoked asset bubbles in U.S. stock or housing markets, which could also be ruled out if market are rational. Nevertheless, if bubbles were present, it could make the effects of a potential reversal in capital inflows more damaging to the overall economy. Both the conventional and global saving glut views are based on an assumption of market rationality and, therefore, cannot directly address this concern. Nonetheless, the saving glut view may be more reassuring than the conventional view. The saving glut view stresses that foreign capital is flowing into the United States because it has nowhere else to go, and assumes that domestic saving would rise relatively quickly to take its place were interest rates to begin to rise. Some economists have argued that global imbalances will persist because the countries (particularly in East Asia) lending to the United States are just as dependent as the United States on maintaining them in order to sustain domestic economic growth.[31] By contrast, the conventional view stresses that the United States has put itself in a position — through its low household and government saving rates — where it is reliant on foreign capital inflows, and would presumably find it painful to replace that foreign capital were it to dry up.

How long global imbalances persist depend on a number of factors that could be either temporary or permanent. Differences in the business cycle at home and abroad are one temporary factor. The United States is further into the current economic expansion than some other industrial countries, which likely means that consumption and investment demand are stronger in the United States than abroad at the moment. (The U.S. economy may be slowing in 2007, bringing its business cycle more closely in line with foreign economies.) Some of the factors identified as causing the glut — including the decline in investment rates in East Asian economies outside of China, the desire by East Asian central banks to increase their foreign exchange reserves, and the desire by other developing countries to reduce their foreign borrowing — could be temporary or permanent. Government intervention to reduce exchange rate appreciation in East Asia has also had an effect on current account balances worldwide. In the long run, real exchange rates cannot be permanently depressed (because of price adjustment), but adjustment could take several years, and trade flows do not respond to exchange rate changes immediately. The disparity in saving rates between Asia and the United States is also likely to be a longer lasting, if not permanent, factor.[32]

Simulation Results

Of course, a dollar collapse is only one possible (and unlikely) outcome for the current account's future movement. The IMF recently estimated what would happen to the U.S. current account deficit under a variety of different scenarios based on historical data.[33] According to their estimates:

If the U.S. saving rate rose by one percentage point of GDP, the current account deficit would fall by 0.5 percentage points in three years (this estimate is much higher than the one cited by Bernanke).

If the Federal Reserve raised short-term interest rates by two percentage points over three years, the U.S. current account deficit would decline by only 0.1 percentage points.

If GDP growth in Japan or the large continental European countries were to rise by 0.5%, the U.S. current account deficit would fall by 0.2 percentage points (and the Japanese/European current account surplus would fall by 0.3 percentage points) over three years.

If the investment rate in Indonesia, Korea, Malaysia, the Philippines, and Thailand rose by five percentage points of GDP (which would still leave them with lower investment rates than before the Asian crisis), the U.S. deficit would fall by 0.75% of GDP in three years. If the oil-producing countries raised their investment rates by five percentage points of GDP, the effect on the U.S. deficit would be similar.

Continuing trade surpluses in oil-producing countries will depend on whether high oil prices persist, and, if so, whether oil producers respond by increasing consumption. If oil producers increase their imports by $150 billion initially and $350 after five years, the U.S. current account deficit would decline by nearly 0.75% of GDP after five years. But the decline in saving by oil producers would increase world interest rates by 0.4 percentage points.[34]

These examples point to both domestic and foreign causes of the U.S. current account deficit and suggest that no single change in conditions would eliminate it.

Similarly, Economist Sebastian Edwards runs regressions based on historical data to estimate whether faster economic growth abroad would significantly reduce global imbalances. He estimates that if a country's GDP growth rises (declines) by one percentage point above (below) trend, then the current account would deteriorate (improve) by one quarter of a percentage point. Since Japan and the euro area are the economies that have been growing below trend and running trade surpluses, he looks at what would happen to global imbalances if they grew faster. For 2005, Edwards estimates that if Japan's economy grew 3.3% faster its trade surplus would fall by $27 billion, and if the euro area's economy grew 1% faster its trade surplus would fall by $13 billion. As a result, the U.S. trade deficit would fall by $23 billion — less than one-tenth the overall deficit.[35]

CONCLUSION

The difference between the conventional view and the global saving glut view is mainly one of perspective. The conventional view focuses on the low level of U.S. saving relative to the rest of the world; the global saving glut view focuses on the high level of world saving relative to the United States. The two theories are not necessarily mutually exclusive; they are different interpretations of the same set of facts.

Developing countries outside of China have seen a large increase in their current account balances in recent years due to higher saving rates and lower investment rates. (China has also seen a large increase in its current account balance because saving has risen faster than investment.) Two main forces seem to be driving the shift. First, oil producing countries have chosen to reinvest rather than consume a significant portion of their increased oil revenues. Second, many East Asian countries have responded to the financial crises of the 1990s by increasing government saving and official foreign reserve accumulation. These have been important factors, in recent years, driving international capital flows traditionally neglected by the conventional view, with its focus on domestic causes of the U.S. trade deficit. Nevertheless, the global saving glut has likewise neglected an important domestic cause of the trade deficit: the large decline in domestic saving — particularly government saving — in recent years. This decline makes the United States far from the passive actor in the movements of international capital that it appears to be in the global saving glut view.

Casting doubt on the global saving glut view are data that show that global saving is close to a four-decade low at present. The recent decline in real interest rates suggests that global investment demand may currently be low as well. However, real interest rates are not particularly low by historical standards.

The risk that the record current account deficit could lead to economic disruption for the United States is still considered small by most economists, but potentially dangerous. Raising national saving through policy changes such as reducing the budget deficit remains the best defense against this risk. At worst, those measures would prove ineffective, as the global saving glut view predicts, but would still have a salutary effect on the U.S. economy in their own right.

End Notes

[1] Technically, the current account deficit is the sum of the trade deficit, net investment income, and net unilateral transfers. However, net investment income and net unilateral transfers are typically small compared with the trade deficit, so the current account deficit and trade deficit are similar in size. For practical purposes, the terms can be used interchangeably.

[2] For more information, see CRS Report RL3 1032, *The U.S. Trade Deficit: Causes, Consequences, and Cures*, by Craig Elwell.

[3] Ben Bernanke, "The Global Saving Glut and the U.S. Current Account Deficit," the Sandridge Lecture, Virginia Association of Economics, March 10, 2005, available on the Federal Reserve Board of Governors website. These are Bernanke's personal views, and not the official views of the Federal Reserve or the Administration.

[4] International Monetary Fund, *World Economic Outlook*, April 2007, p. 1.

[5] National saving consists of household saving, business saving, and public saving. Government budget deficits reduce public saving.

[6] Although some countries (particularly developing countries) offer higher rates of return than the United States, they may still not attract significant international capital flows because their investment opportunities are too risky to appeal to investors. The United States, on the other hand, has often been viewed as a "safe haven" for investors and may be able to attract capital with lower rates of return than other countries.

[7] See CRS Report RL3 1775, *Do Budget Deficits Push Up Interest Rates and Is This The Relevant Question?*, by Marc Labonte.

[8] See CRS Report RS21409, *The Budget Deficit and the Trade Deficit: What Is Their Relationship?*, by Marc Labonte and Gail Makinen.

[9] Gruber and Kamin provide econometric evidence supporting this argument. They show that including a financial crisis variable in their regressions helps better explain the shift to current account surpluses in Asia in recent years. Their results should be viewed with caution, however, since their model predicts a large current account surplus in the United States, presumably because it does not take differences in saving rates into account. As they note, even if their model can explain why current account surpluses have increased in East Asia, it cannot explain why that capital has been overwhelmingly invested in the United States. Joseph Gruber and Steven Kamin, "Explaining the Global Pattern of Current Account Imbalances," Federal Reserve Board of Governors, *International Finance and Discussion Papers 846*, November 2005.

[10] Likewise, oil consuming countries, such as the United States, could have reacted to higher oil prices by reducing their saving rate, which would, all else equal, widen their current account deficits.

[11] International Monetary Fund, "Oil Prices and Global Imbalances," *World Economic Outlook*, April 2006, Chapter 2. According to the IMF, oil producers have mostly invested their trade surpluses in portfolio investments in recent years, unlike the 1970s when they invested their trade surpluses mostly in official reserves and bank deposits.

A study from the New York Fed estimated that oil revenues to oil exporters increased by $670 billion between 2002 and 2006, and those revenues have been split about evenly between imports and foreign investments. Matthew Higgins et al, "Recycling Petrodollars," *Current Issues in Economics and Finance*, Federal Reserve Bank of New York, vol. 12, no. 9, December 2006.

[12] Bernanke does not explain why the global saving glut did not prevent the stock market from crashing since, in his view, U.S. assets were highly desirable to foreigners.

[13] Note that Bernanke's views on trade deficits, in which capital seeks out the country with the highest rate of return, are identical to the conventional view. The difference is that the conventional view focuses on what makes U.S. rates of return higher, whereas Bernanke focuses on what makes foreign rates of return low.

[14] Similarly, Caballero describes the developing world as having a shortage of financial assets in which to invest relative to its high saving, creating a high demand for U.S. assets that pushes up their price and drives down U.S. interest rates. He believes the global saving glut will persist until developing countries strengthen their financial systems enough to become more attractive investment destinations. Richard Caballero, *On the Macroeconomics of Asset Shortages*, National Bureau of Economic Research, Working Paper no. 12753, December 2006.

[15] See CRS Report RS21951, *The U.S. Trade Deficit: Role of Foreign Governments*, by Marc Labonte and Gail Makinen.

[16] Christopher Erceg, Luca Guerrieri, and Christopher Gust, "Expansionary Fiscal Shocks and the Trade Deficit." *International Finance Discussion Paper 2005-825*, Board of Governors of the Federal Reserve System (Washington: January, 2005). This estimate is lower than typically found in other research.

[17] Even when the United States is excluded from data on saving worldwide, no evidence of a global saving glut exists: saving has stayed between 24-25% of GDP each year since 1990.

[18] International Monetary Fund, *World Economic Outlook*, September 2005, chapter 2. Unless otherwise noted, all further references to the IMF refer to this document. Other studies include Richard Cooper, *Understanding Global Imbalances*, Federal Reserve Bank of Boston, Conference Series 51, June 2006; Menzie Chinn and Hiro Ito, *Current Account Balances*, Financial Development, and Institutions," National Bureau of Economic Research, Working Paper no. 11761, November 2005.

[19] Ideally, real interest rates would be determined by *ex ante* expectations of inflation at the time saving and investment decisions were taken. Economists can reliably measure real interest rates only with *ex post* inflation data. As a result, if inflation were higher than anticipated, it may appear that real interest rates were lower than individuals believed at the time they made their saving and investment decisions. This factor may explain why real interest rates were periodically negative during the 1970s.

[20] The IMF estimates that capital inflows have lowered 10-year Treasury rates by 0.86 percentage points, as of May 2005. International Monetary Fund, "Oil Prices and Global Imbalances," *World Economic Outlook*, April 2006, Chapter 2.

[21] See Luis Catao and George Mackenzie, *Perspectives on Low Global Interest Rates,* International Monetary Fund, Working Paper 06/76, March 2006.

[22] In the United States, the decline in national saving was dominated by a decline in private saving from 1997 to 2000, and a decline in public saving from 2001 to 2004.

[23] International Monetary Fund, *World Economic Outlook*, Statistical Appendix, April 2007.

[24] A fraction of foreign reserves are held in U.S. assets. No data source by country exists to determine what share of the increase in foreign reserves were in U.S. assets. Overall, foreign official holdings of U.S. government debt roughly doubled from $1,034 billion in 2000 to $2,105 billion in 2006.

[25] See CRS Report RL32 165, *China's Currency Peg: Economic Issues and Options for U.S. Trade Policy*, by Wayne Morrison and Marc Labonte.

[26] Matthew Higgins et al., "Recycling Petrodollars," *Current Issues in Economics and Finance*, Federal Reserve Bank of New York, vol. 12, no. 9, December 2006.

[27] "The World's Most Expensive Club," *Economist*, May 26, 2007, p. 79.

[28] Dooley et al. argue that long-term interest rates are unusually low relative to short-term rates because investors believe that this pattern will continue in the future. Michael Dooley et al., *Saving Gluts and Interest Rates: The Missing Link to Europe*, National Bureau of Economic Research, Working Paper no. 11520, July 2005.

[29] For more information, see CRS Report RS2 1951, *U.S. Trade Deficit: Role of Foreign Governments*, by Marc Labonte and Gail Makinen.

[30] For a detailed analysis, see CRS Report RL33186, *Is the U.S. Current Account Deficit Sustainable?,* by Marc Labonte.

[31] Michael Dooley et al., "An Essay on the Revised Bretton Woods System," National Bureau of Economic Research, working paper 9971, September 2003.

[32] See Zanny Minton Beddoes, "The Great Thrift Shift," *The Economist*, September 24, 2005.

[33] Except where noted, estimates are from International Monetary Fund, *World Economic Outlook*, September 2005, Chapter 2.

[34] International Monetary Fund, "Oil Prices and Global Imbalances," *World Economic Outlook*, April 2006, Chapter 2.

[35] Sebastian Edwards, *On Current Account Surpluses and the Correction of Global Imbalances*, National Bureau of Economic Research, Working Paper no. 12904, February 2007. Edwards points out that faster growth would not necessarily reduce a trade surplus. For example, if the source of faster growth were higher exports, the trade surplus would likely increase.

In: United States Trade Deficit Issues
Editor: Carl T. Yankovich
ISBN: 978-1-60692-090-9

Chapter 4

FINANCING THE UNITED STATES TRADE DEFICIT*

James K. Jackson
Specialist in International Trade and Finance
Foreign Affairs, Defense, and Trade Division

SUMMARY

The U.S. merchandise trade deficit is a part of the overall U.S. balance of payments, a summary statement of all economic transactions between the residents of the United States and the rest of the world, during a given period of time. Some Members of Congress and other observers have grown concerned over the magnitude of the growing U.S. merchandise trade deficit and the associated increase in U.S. dollar-denominated assets owned by foreigners. This report provides an overview of the U.S. balance of payments, an explanation of the broader role of capital flows in the U.S. economy, an explanation of how the country finances its trade deficit or a trade surplus, and the implications for Congress and the country of the large inflows of capital from abroad. The major observations indicate that:

* This is an edited, reformatted and augmented version of a CRS Report for Congress publication dated April 2008.

Foreign private investors sharply increased their purchases of U.S. Treasury securities in 2007 as they reduced their purchases of U.S. corporate bonds. At the same time, foreign official purchases of U.S. Treasury securities plummeted in 2007 as foreign governments curtailed their purchases of such securities.

The inflow of capital from abroad supplements domestic sources of capital and likely allows the United States to maintain its current level of economic activity at interest rates that are below the level they likely would be without the capital inflows.

Foreign official and private acquisitions of dollar-denominated assets likely will generate a stream of returns to overseas investors that would have stayed in the U.S. economy and supplemented other domestic sources of capital had the assets not been acquired by foreign investors.

This report will be updated as events warrant.

BACKGROUND

By standard convention, the balance of payments accounts are based on a double-entry bookkeeping system. As a result, each transaction that is entered into the accounts as a credit must have a corresponding debit and vice versa. This means that a surplus or deficit in one part of the accounts necessarily will be offset by a deficit or surplus, respectively, in another account so that, overall, the accounts are in balance. This convention also means that a deficit in one account, such as the merchandise trade account, is not necessarily the same as a debt.[1] The trade deficit can become a debt equivalent depending on how the deficit is financed and the expectations of those who hold the offsetting dollar-denominated U.S. assets. The balance of payments accounts are divided into three main sections: the current account, which includes the exports and imports of goods and services and personal and government transfer payments; the capital account, which includes such capital transfers as international debt forgiveness; and the financial account, which includes official transactions in financial assets and private transactions in financial assets and direct investment in businesses and real estate.

When the basic structure of the balance of payments was established, merchandise trade transactions dominated the accounts. Financial transactions recorded in the capital accounts generally reflected the payments and receipts of funds that corresponded to the importing and exporting of goods and services. As a result, the capital accounts generally represented "accommodating" transactions, or financial transactions associated directly with the buying and selling of goods and services. During this early period, exchange rates between currencies were fixed, and private capital flows, such as foreign investment, were heavily regulated so that nearly all international flows of funds were associated with merchandise trade transactions and with some limited government transactions.

Since the 1970s, however, private capital flows have grown markedly as countries have liberalized their rules governing overseas investing and as nations have adopted a system of floating exchange rates, where the rates are set by market forces. Floating exchange rates have spurred demand for the dollar. The dollar also is sought for investment purposes as it has become a vehicle itself for investment and speculation. This means that the balance of payments record not only the accommodating flows of capital which correspond to imports and exports of goods and services, but also autonomous flows of capital that are induced by a broad range of economic factors that are unrelated directly to the trading of merchandise goods.

CAPITAL FLOWS AND THE DOLLAR

Liberalized capital flows and floating exchange rates have greatly expanded the amount of autonomous capital flows between countries. These capital transactions are undertaken in response to commercial incentives or political considerations that are independent of the overall balance of payments or of particular accounts. As a result of these transactions, national economies have become more closely linked, the process some refer to as "globalization." The data in **Table 1** provide selected indicators of the relative sizes of the various capital markets in various countries and regions and the relative importance of international foreign exchange markets. In 2006, these markets amounted to nearly $600 trillion, or more than 30 times the size of the U.S. economy. Worldwide, foreign exchange and interest rate derivatives, which are the most widely used hedges against movements in currencies, were valued at $395 trillion in 2007, 50% larger than the combined total of all public and private bonds, equities, and bank assets. For the United States, such derivatives total three as much as all U.S. bonds, equities, and bank assets.

Another aspect of capital mobility and capital inflows is the impact such capital flows have on the international exchange value of the dollar. Demand for U.S. assets, such as financial securities, translates into demand for the dollar, since U.S. securities are denominated in dollars. As demand for the dollar rises or falls according to overall demand for dollar-denominated assets, the value of the dollar changes. These exchange rate changes, in turn, have secondary effects on the prices of U.S. and foreign goods, which tend to alter the U.S. trade balance. At times, foreign governments have intervened in international capital markets to acquire the dollar directly or to acquire Treasury securities in order to strengthen the value of the dollar against particular currencies. In addition, various central banks moved aggressively following the Asian financial crisis in the 1990s to bolster their holdings of dollars in order to use the dollars to support their currencies should the need arise.

Furthermore, the dollar is heavily traded in financial markets around the globe and, at times, plays the role of a global currency. Disruptions in this role have important implications for the United States and for the smooth functioning of the international financial system. This prominent role means that the exchange value of the dollar often acts as a mechanism for transmitting economic and political news and events across national borders. While such a role helps facilitate a broad range of international economic and financial activities, it also means that the dollar's exchange value can vary greatly on a daily or weekly basis as it is buffeted by international events. A triennial survey of the world's leading central banks conducted by the Bank for International Settlements in April 2007 indicates that the **daily** trading of foreign currencies through traditional foreign exchange markets[2] totals more than $3.2 trillion, up sharply from the $1.9 trillion reported in the previous survey conducted in 2004. In addition to the traditional foreign exchange market, the over-the-counter (OTC)[3] foreign exchange derivatives market reported that daily turnover of interest rate and non-traditional foreign exchange derivatives contracts reached $2.1 trillion in April 2007. The combined amount of $5.3 trillion for daily foreign exchange trading in the traditional and OTC markets is more than three times the **annual** amount of U.S. exports of goods and services. The data also indicate that 86.3% of the global foreign exchange turnover is in U.S. dollars, slightly lower than the 88.7% share reported in a similar survey conducted in 2004.[4]

Table 1. Selected Indicators of the Size of the Global Capital Markets, 2006 (in billions of U.S. dollars)

	Gross Domestic Product (GDP)	Total Official Reserves	Bonds, Equities, and Bank Assets				Exchange Market Derivatives		
			Total	Stock Market Capitalization	Debt Securities	Bank Assets	Total	OTC Foreign Exchange Derivatives	OTC Interest Rate Derivatives
World	48,434.4	5,091.5	194,452.7	50,826.6	68,200.9	74,465.2	395,557.0	48,620.0	211,970.0
European Union	13,658.0	252.7	73,983.7	13,068.8	23,192.3	37,736.3	N.A.	N.A.	N.A.
Euro Area	10,586.1	157.5	54,129.5	8,419.1	18,761.1	26,719.2	145,903.0	18,280.0	81,442.0
United States	13,194.7	54.9	56,822.0	19,569.0	27,050.1	10,202.9	154,799.0	40.488.0	74,441.0
Japan	4,377.1	879.7	20,109.5	4,795.8	8,723.7	6,590.0	58,329.0	10,579.0	25,605.0
Emerging Market Countries	14,262.9	1,932.0	30,984.4	11,692.4	6,072.7	13,219.4	N.A.	N.A.	N.A.

Source: *Global Financial Stability Report*, International Monetary Fund, April 2008. Statistical Appendix, Table 3. *Quarterly Review*, Bank for International Settlements, March 2008, Tables 20b and 21b. Total derivatives does not include equity and commodity-linked derivatives.

The U.S. Balance of Payments

Table 2 presents a summary of the major accounts in the U.S. balance of payments over the last six quarters. The data indicate that in 2006 and 2007 the U.S. current account, or the balance of exports and imports of goods, services and transfers, was in deficit, or the United States imported more than it exported. According to the accounts, the United States experienced a deficit in the merchandise trade goods accounts in all four quarters in 2007 and a surplus in the services accounts. In the income accounts, which represent inflows of income on U.S. assets abroad relative to outflows of income earned on U.S. assets owned by foreigners, the net balance of the accounts was in surplus in 2006 and in all four quarters of 2007.

Table 2. U.S. International Transactions, Selected Accounts (in billions of U.S. dollars)

	2006			2007				
		III	IV	2007	I	II	III	IV
Current account								
Balance on current account	-811	-217	-188	-739	-198	-190	-177	-173
Balance on goods and services	-759	-199	-177	-709	-179	-179	-173	-178
Balance on goods	-838	-219	-200	-815	-202	-205	-201	-208
Exports	1,023	260	266	1,149	269	279	297	304
Imports	-1,861	-479	-467	-1,965	-471	-484	-498	-512
Balance on services	80	20	23	107	23	26	28	30
Exports	423	106	111	479	112	117	123	128
Imports	-343	-86	-88	-372	-89	-91	-95	-98
Balance on income	37	6	10	74	7	13	21	33
Income Receipts	650	167	173	782	176	195	206	204
Income Payments	-614	-161	-163	-708	-169	-183	-185	-171
Unilateral current transfers	-90	-24	-21	74	7	13	21	33
Capital account								
Capital account transactions	-4	-1	-1	-1	-1	-1	-1	0
Financial account								
Balance on financial account	833	255	225	657	183	156	111	230
U.S.-owned assets abroad, net	-1,055	-210	-289	-1,206	-450	-466	-174	-116
U.S. official reserve assets, net	2	1	1	-0	-0	0	-0	-0

Table 2. (Continued)

	2006			2007				
		III	IV	2007	I	II	III	IV
U.S. Government assets, net	5	2	1	-23	0	0	1	-24
U.S. private assets, net	-1,063	-212	-291	-1,183	-450	-466	-175	-93
Foreign-owned assets in the U.S.	1,860	450	516	1,864	618	623	277	347
Foreign official assets,net	440	109	85	413	152	70	39	151
U.S. Treasury Securities	189	53	47	50	38	-13	-12	37
Foreign private assets,net	1,419	341	431	1,451	466	552	238	195
U.S. Treasury Securities	-36	-13	22	166	45	2	50	70
Financial derivatives	29	15	-2		15	-1	9	0
Statistical discrepancy	-18	-37	-37	84	16	35	67	-57

Source: Bach, Christopher L., *U.S. International Transactions in 2007*. Survey of Current Business, April 2008.

The data also indicate that the U.S. financial accounts were in substantial surplus, because they represent the opposite and offsetting transactions to deficits in the current account. Indeed, the accounting of the balance of payments is such that the surplus in the financial accounts is equivalent to the deficit in the combined balance in the capital account, the statistical discrepancy, and the balance on the current account. The balance in the financial accounts represents the difference between the capital outflows associated with U.S. investments abroad, which are recorded as a negative value, and the capital inflows associated with foreign investment in the United States, which are recorded as a positive value. This investment is a combination of both private and official investments, or investments by private individuals and institutions and investments by governments and governmental institutions, respectively. Data for 2007 indicate that foreign official purchases of U.S. Treasury securities were down substantially from similar purchases in 2006 and private foreign purchases of Treasury securities in 2007 rose sharply from the negative amount recorded for 2006.

The data in **Table 2** also indicate that private capital flows account for the largest share of both U.S. capital inflows and outflows. Perhaps of more importance, however, are the data in **Table 3** which show the *net* amount of the flows in the major accounts, or the difference between the inflows and outflows. In 2007, for instance, total net capital inflows representing the net balance on the current account, the capital account, and the statistical discrepancy, were a negative $657 billion, markedly less than the record deficit of $833 set in 2006. This decrease in the overall net capital inflows occurred in part because of a slight decrease in the deficit in trade in manufactured goods and an increase in the surplus in trade in services.

Commerce Department data also indicate that foreign private purchases of Treasury securities turned negative between 1998 and 2001 as foreign private investors experienced net sales of Treasury securities, as indicated in **Figure 1**. By 2002, foreign private investors returned to acquiring Treasury securities, but the amount they acquired remained relatively level at $100 billion per year from 2002 to 2005. In contrast, foreign official net acquisitions of Treasury securities trended slightly upward between 2000 and 2002, but such net acquisitions more than doubled over the 2002 to 2004 period, rising to $261 billion in 2004. In 2005, though, official purchases of Treasury securities plummeted to less than $100 billion and were less than private purchases. In 2006, private foreign investors again reduced their net holdings of Treasury securities. This action was offset by a large increase in acquisitions of Treasury securities by foreign governments, directed at least in part to slow the decline in the international exchange value of the dollar. In 2007, however, foreign private investors accumulated more than $166 billion in Treasury securities, as foreign governments sharply reduced their net purchases of Treasury securities from$189 billion in 2006 to $50 billion in 2007.

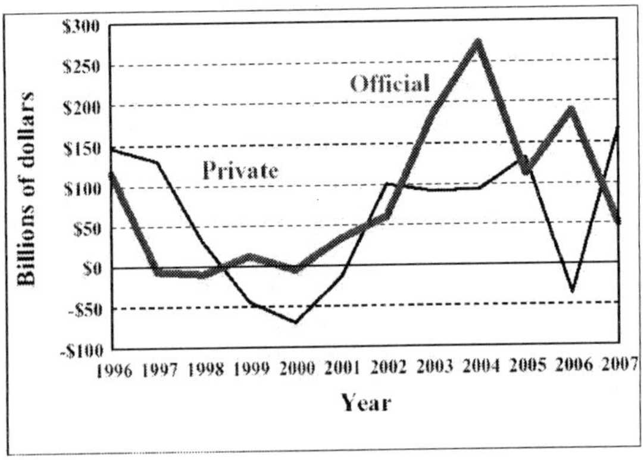

Source: Department of Commerce

Figure 1. Foreign Official and Private Purchases of U.S. Treasury Securities, 1996-2007

Table 3. Summary of the Net Balances by Major Accounts in the U.S. Balance of Payments (in billions of U.S. dollars)

	2000	2001	2002	2003	2004	2005	2006	2007
Total Net Capital Inflows	$-477	$-416	$-570	$-546	$-585	$-777	$-833	$-657
Total Net Goods	-452	-427	-483	-548	-665	-787	-838	-815
Total Net Services	74	64	61	51	48	73	80	107
Total Net Income	21	24	7	33	30	48	37	74
Total Net Transfers	-56	-47	-59	-67	-81	-89	-90	-104
Total Net Capital Account	-1	-1	-1	-3	-2	-4	-4	-2
Statistical Discrepancy	-63	-29	-95	-12	85	-18	-18	84
Total Net Financial Account	477	416	570	546	585	777	833	657
Total Net Official	42	23	111	251	399	279	448	390
Total Net Private	436	393	460	295	186	498	356	268
Direct Investment	162	25	-62	-134	-145	117	-55	-131
Portfolio Investment	268	295	402	292	374	386	267	284
Other Private (Banks)	6	74	120	137	-43	-4	145	114
Financial Derivatives	n.a.	n.a.	n.a.	n.a.	n.a.	n.a.	29	n.a.

Source: Data developed by CRS from data published by the Department of Commerce.

The deficit in the net capital inflow account was financed by an offsetting net inflow in the financial account. One striking feature of the financial flows is the recent change in the composition of the balances in the net financial account. Except for 2004, total net private inflows were greater than total net official inflows. This trend was reversed in 2004, when net official inflows were nearly double that of the net private inflows, as indicated in **Figure 2**. In 2006 and 2007, net official inflows exceeded net private inflows. In 2007, foreign private inflows of capital increased by more than 2%, but similar private outflows by U.S. citizens increased by more than 11%, so that the overall net private flows fell in 2007, or were sightly more than half of those received in 2005. The decline in net private inflows in 2007 reflects a higher level of U.S. direct investment abroad, rising to over $335 billion in 2007, from $235 billion in 2006, which is entered into the balance of payments accounts as a negative amount and lower holdings of foreign assets by U.S. banks. Data for 2007 also indicate that the United States again experienced a net positive income inflow from U.S. assets held abroad as U.S. investors received more in income on their investments held abroad than foreign investors received from their investments in the United States.

The data in **Table 4** show the total net accumulation of U.S. securities, or the amount of securities purchased less those that were sold, by foreign private and official sources from 2000-2007. The data indicate that in 2007, the net accumulation of U.S. securities fell in 2007 from the amount recorded in 2006, largely due to reduced official purchases of U.S. Treasury securities and corporate stocks. Private foreign investors in Asia and operating through financial centers in the Caribbean corporate stocks increased their net purchases of corporate stocks, while sharply smaller net accumulations of corporate bonds by European investors led to a 40% drop in the net accumulation of such securities. In addition, foreign investors, both private and official reduced their net accumulation of other U.S. government agency bonds.

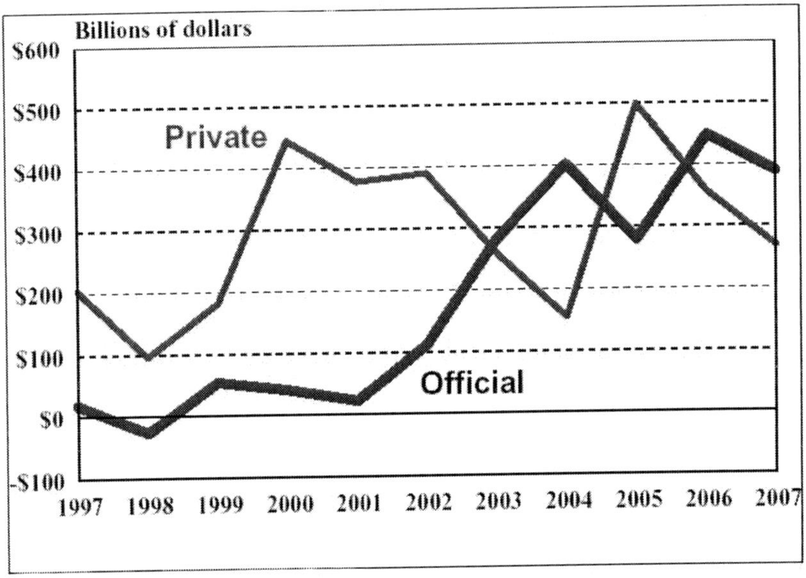

Source: Department of Commerce

Figure 2. Net Inflows of Foreign Private and Official Sources of Capital, 1997-2007

Table 4. Net Foreign Purchases of Long-Term U.S. Securities (in billions of dollars)

	2000	2001	2002	2003	2004	2005	2006	2007
Total private and official net purchases of U.S. securities	$437.3	$430.3	$428.3	$520.5	$767.8	$875.7	$982.5	$807.4
Total private purchases	394.6	370.7	361.7	311.7	455.6	598.3	542.5	528.4
Corporate stocks	192.5	119.5	56.1	34.3	59.5	88.3	142.8	183.4
Europe	181.6	86.8	31.5	22.1	35.3	44.0	94.2	91.6
United Kingdom	71.8	37.3	14.4	0.2	28.9	24.2	74.8	68.8
Canada	7.7	11.7	12.9	11.5	3.9	21.0	12.8	9.3
Caribbean financial centers	-20.7	-5.8	-17.1	-2.3	3.1	14.8	34.3	47.4
Latin America	3.5	6.8	0.8	0.5	-0.4	-0.4	1.9	1.3
Asia	20.0	20.2	23.0	2.8	5.5	8.7	-1.1	29.1
Of which: Japan	1.9	6.6	12.2	-2.3	4.9	-0.1	-0.8	-5.1
Africa	0.4	-0.4	-0.1	0.2	-0.1	0.3	0.1	-0.3
Corporate bonds	166.4	191.6	145.4	223.2	254.6	312.3	412.3	246.7
Europe	111.7	108.4	78.9	130.9	126.3	199.8	242.1	111.2
United Kingdom	95.2	84.1	55.8	89.0	69.6	144.7	192.4	121.4
Canada	3.0	3.3	-0.0	5.2	6.0	1.9	7.9	12.6
Caribbean financial centers	25.0	49.6	35.5	54.0	47.1	40.2	91.1	41.4
Latin America	4.3	5.0	4.6	6.7	20.2	7.3	9.3	4.6
Asia	21.4	24.2	22.7	24.2	51.9	54.4	53.9	71.1
Japan	15.6	6.1	10.8	10.5	33.5	25.6	12.3	38.5
Africa	0.1	0.3	0.1	0.4	0.6	0.6	0.2	-0.4
Other	0.9	0.9	3.6	1.7	2.6	8.1	7.7	6.2
U.S. Treasury bonds	-65.3	-23.2	78.4	91.0	74.1	147.9	-49.5	136.5
Europe	-54.9	-30.2	38.7	18.1	38.2	65.2	-37.8	153.4
Canada	2.1	0.2	-5.0	11.4	16.3	21.8	14.7	-2.9
Caribbean financial centers	-5.1	1.0	14.8	6.2	22.1	44.9	-10.6	3.8

Table 4. (Continued)

	2000	2001	2002	2003	2004	2005	2006	2007
Latin America	-1.2	-3.3	3.1	3.0	-3.4	10.4	5.5	24.5
Asia	-7.2	8.1	22.3	46.4	1.0	1.3	-20.3	-42.8
Africa	-0.0	0.0	1.1	-0.2	0.7	1.7	1.1	1.5
Other	1.1	1.0	3.6	6.1	-0.8	2.5	-2.1	-1.1
Federal agency bonds	101.0	82.8	81.8	-36.8	67.4	49.8	36.9	-38.2
Europe	36.8	29.6	4.7	-29.4	13.3	-11.9	11.6	53.0
United Kingdom	28.5	33.4	22.4	14.6	31.4	-1.3	13.6	81.0
Canada	7.6	-0.7	-1.9	-4.0	5.0	12.1	9.6	2.2
Caribbean financial centers	17.5	6.4	23.2	6.0	11.3	3.0	29.8	-21.9
Latin America	5.7	4.6	7.5	4.9	1.8	7.1	3.4	1.9
Asia	33.0	45.3	49.3	-11.9	36.4	40.2	-17.7	-73.7
Japan	21.3	12.6	16.8	-16.4	16.5	15.6	-5.4	-22.4
Africa	0.1	0.2	0.3	0.2	-0.1	-0.3	-0.2	-0.1
Other	0.3	-2.6	-1.2	-2.7	-0.3	-0.4	0.5	0.3
Total official purchases	42.8	59.6	66.5	208.7	312.2	277.4	440.0	279.0
U.S. Treasury bonds	-1.3	32.9	32.4	163.5	256.8	156.9	214.1	30.3
Other U.S. Government securities	40.9	20.9	30.5	39.9	41.7	100.5	191.6	182.0
Corporate bonds	2.0	3.8	5.6	5.6	11.5	19.1	28.6	51.6
Corporate stocks	1.1	2.0	-2.0	-0.3	2.2	1.0	5.8	15.1

Source: Bach, Christopher L., *U.S. International Transactions in 2007*. Survey of Current Business, April 2008.

THE U.S. NET INTERNATIONAL INVESTMENT POSITION

As indicated above, the data in **Tables 2** and **3** show that the trade deficit is accompanied by an equal capital inflow that represents an accumulation of dollar-denominated assets by foreigners. Some observers have equated the trade deficit and the associated accumulation of foreign-owned dollar-denominated assets as a debt that the U.S. economy owes to foreigners that will have to be repaid. This characterization, however, is not entirely appropriate. The debts owned by foreign investors represents claims on assets, rather than loans where payments on the principle and interest are specified according to a fixed schedule and where failure to meet the repayment schedule can result in the loans being called in and made payable in full. While foreign investors have expectations of a positive return on their dollar-denominated assets, returns, except for Treasury securities, are not guaranteed, but are subject to market forces. An important feature of claims by foreign investors on U.S. assets is that some or all of the profits or returns on the assets can be repatriated to the home country of the foreign investor, thereby reducing the returns that would otherwise remain in the U.S. economy.

According to the most commonly accepted approach to the balance of payments, macroeconomic developments in the U.S. economy are the major driving forces behind the magnitudes of capital flows, because the macroeconomic factors determine the overall demand for and supply of capital in the economy. Economists generally conclude that the rise in capital inflows can be attributed to comparatively favorable returns on investments in the United States when adjusted for risk, a surplus of saving in other areas of the world, the well-developed U.S. financial system, and the overall stability of the U.S. economy. In turn, these net capital inflows (inflows net of outflows) bridge the gap in the United States between the amount of credit demanded and the domestic supply of funds, likely keeping U.S. interest rates below the level they would have reached without the foreign capital. These capital inflows also allow the United States to spend beyond its means, including financing its trade deficit, because foreigners are willing to lend to the United States in the form of exchanging goods, represented by U.S. imports, for such U.S. assets as stocks, bonds, U.S. Treasury securities, and real estate and U.S. businesses.

While this exchange of assets is implicit in the balance of payments, the Department of Commerce explicitly accounts for this broad flow of dollar-denominated assets through the nation's net international investment position. The U.S. net international investment position represents the accumulated value of U.S.- owned assets abroad and foreign-owned assets in the United States measured on an annual basis at the end of the calendar year. Some observers refer to the net of this investment position (or the difference between the value of U.S.-owned assets abroad and the value of foreign-owned assets in the United States) as a debt, or indicate that the United States is a net debtor nation, because the value of foreign-owned assets in the United States is greater than the value of U.S.-owned assets abroad.

In fact, the nation's net international investment position is not a measure of the nation's indebtedness similar to the debt borrowed by some developing countries, but it is simply an accounting of assets. By year-end 2006, the latest year for which data are available, the overseas assets of U.S. residents totaled approximately $12 trillion, while foreigners had acquired about $14.8 trillion in assets in the United States, with direct investment measured at historical cost. As a result, the U.S. net international investment position was about a negative $2.8 trillion, with direct investment measured at historical cost, as indicated in **Table 5**.

Foreign investors who acquire U.S. assets do so at their own risk and accept the returns accordingly, unlike the debt owed by developing countries where principle and debt service payments are guaranteed in advance. While foreign investors likely expect positive returns from their dollar-denominated assets, the returns on most of the assets in the international investment position, except for bonds, are not guaranteed and foreign investors stand to gain or lose on them similar to the way U.S. domestic investors gain or lose.

As **Table 5** indicates, the investments in the international investment position include such financial assets as corporate stocks and bonds, government securities, and direct investment[5] in businesses and real estate. The value of these assets, measured on an annual basis, can change as a result of purchases and sales of new or existing assets; changes in the financial value of the assets that arise through appreciation, depreciation, or inflation; changes in the market values of stocks and bonds; or changes in the value of currencies. The Department of Commerce also uses three different methods for valuing direct investments that yield roughly comparable estimates for the net position, although the three methods do provide estimates on U.S. direct investment abroad and foreign direct investment that can be considerably different at times.[6]

Table 5. U.S. Net International Investment Position (in billions of dollars)

Type of Investment	2003	2004	2005	2006
Net international investment position of the United States:				
With direct investment at current cost	-2,140.4	-2,294.4	-2,296.3	-2,598.6
With direct investment at market value	-2,339.6	-2,396.7	-2,199.0	-2,199.4
With direct investment at historical cost	-2,232.6	-2,485.3	-2,422.2	-2,759.8
U.S.-owned assets abroad:				
With direct investment at current cost	7,643.5	9,257.1	10,386.3	12,517.4
With direct investment at market value	8,318.2	10,130.0	11,421.4	14,039.6
With direct investment at historical cost	7,380.9	8,844.7	9,986.6	12,045.8
U.S. official reserve assets	183.6	189.6	188.0	219.9
U.S. Government assets, other	84.8	83.1	77.5	72.2
U.S. private assets:				
With direct investment at current cost	7,375.1	8,984.4	10,120.7	12,225.4
With direct investment at market value	8,049.8	9,857.3	11,155.8	13,747.6
With direct investment at historical cost	7,112.6	8,572.0	9,721.0	11,753.8
Direct investment abroad:				
— At current cost	2,054.5	2,463.6	2,535.2	2,855.6
— At market value	2,729.1	3,336.4	3,570.3	4,377.8
— At historical cost	1,791.9	2,051.2	2,135.5	2,384.0
Foreign securities	2,953.8	3,553.4	4,345.9	5,432.3
Bonds	874.4	993.0	1,028.2	1,180.8
Corporate stocks	2,079.4	2,560.4	3,317.7	4,251.5
U.S. claims by US nonbanking concerns	594.0	737.6	734.0	848.5
U.S. claims reported by US banks	1,772.9	2,229.8	2,505.6	3,089.0
Foreign-owned assets in the United States:				
With direct investment at current cost	9,783.9	11,551.5	12,682.6	15,116.0
With direct investment at market value	10,657.7	12,526.6	13,620.4	16,239.0

Table 5. (Continued)

Type of Investment	2003	2004	2005	2006
With direct investment at historical cost	9,613.5	11,330.0	12,408.8	14,805.7
Foreign official assets in the United States	1,562.6	2,011.9	2,306.3	2,770.2
Foreign private assets:				
With direct investment at current cost	8,221.3	9,539.6	10,376.3	12,345.8
With direct investment at market value	9,095.2	10,514.7	11,314.1	13,468.9
With direct investment at historical cost	8,051.0	9,318.1	10,102.5	12,035.5
Direct investment in the United States:				
— At current cost	1,581.0	1,742.2	1,868.2	2,099.4
— At market value	2,454.9	2,717.4	2,806.0	3,222.5
— At historical cost	1,410.7	1,520.7	1,594.5	1,789.1
U.S. Treasury securities	527.2	561.6	643.8	594.2
U.S. other securities	3,422.9	3,995.5	4,353.0	5,228.5
— Corporate and other bonds	1,710.8	2,035.1	2,243.1	2,689.8
— Corporate stocks	1,712.1	1,960.3	2,109.9	2,538.7
U.S. currency	317.9	332.7	351.7	364.3
U.S. liabilities by U.S. nonbanking concerns	450.9	508.3	557.8	740.4
U.S. liabilities reported by U.S. banks	1,921.4	2,399.2	2,601.7	3,319.0

Source: Nguyen, Elena L., The International Investment Position of the United States at Yearend 2006, *Survey of Current Business*, July 2007. p. 17.

The foreign investment position in the United States continues to increase as foreigners acquire additional U.S. assets and as the value of existing assets appreciates. These assets are broadly divided into official and private investments reflecting transactions by governments among themselves and transactions among the public. While the foreign official share of the overall amount of capital inflows has grown sharply as indicated in **Table 3**, the overall foreign official share of foreign-owned assets in the United States has remained relatively modest.

As **Figure 3** indicates, official asset holdings were valued at about $2.8 trillion in 2006, or about 16% of the total foreign investment position, a share that has remained relatively stable over the 13-year period of 1993 to 2006. Official assets include such monetary reserve assets as gold, the reserve position with the International Monetary Fund (IMF), and holdings of foreign currency. An important component of foreign official holdings in the United States is the acquisitions of U.S. Treasury securities by foreign governments. At times, such acquisitions are used by foreign governments, either through coordinated actions or by themselves, to affect the foreign exchange price of the dollar. Foreign currency holdings account for a relatively small share of the total foreign investment position.[7]

Private asset holdings are comprised primarily of direct investment in businesses and real estate, purchases of publicly traded government securities, and corporate stocks and bonds. As indicated in **Figure 4**, the composition of U.S. assets abroad and foreign-owned assets in the United States differ in a number of ways. The strength and uniqueness of the U.S. Treasury securities markets make these assets sought after by both official and private foreign investors, whereas U.S. investors hold few foreign government securities. As a result, foreign official assets in the United States far outweigh U.S. official assets abroad. Both foreign private and official investors have been drawn at times to U.S. government securities as a safe haven investment during troubled or unsettled economic conditions.

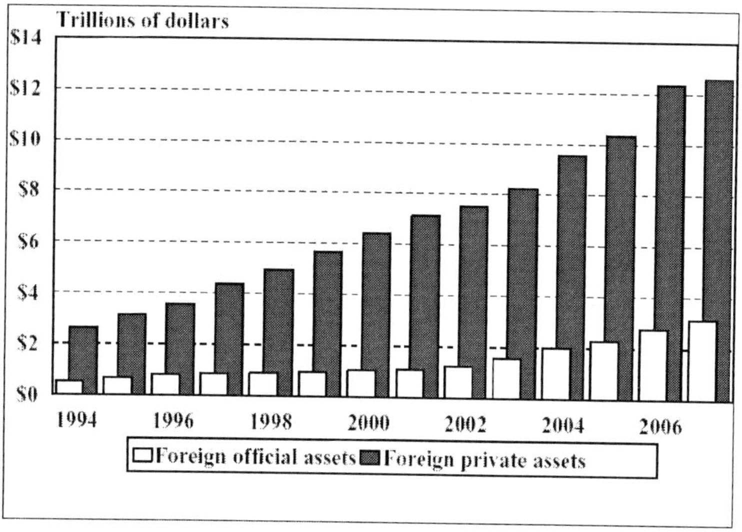

Source: Department of Commerce

Figure 3. Foreign Official and Private Investment Positions in the United States, 1994-2007

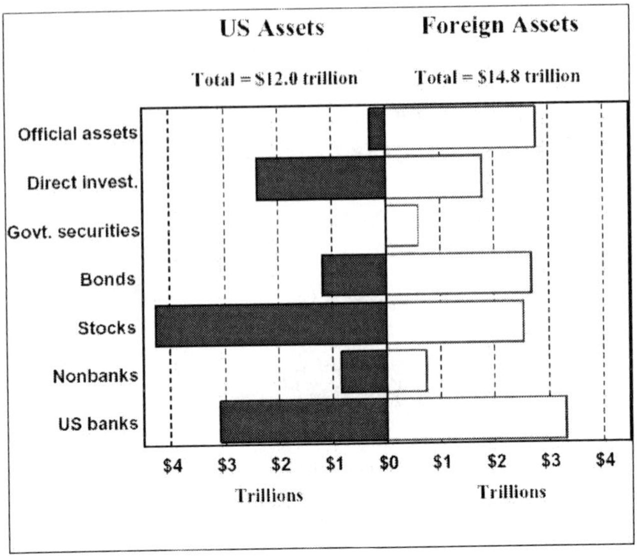

Source: Department of Commerce

Figure 4. U.S. and Foreign Investment Position, by Major Component, 2006

IMPLICATIONS

The persistent U.S. trade deficit raises concerns in Congress and elsewhere because of the potential risks such deficits may pose for the long term rate of growth for the economy. In particular, some observers are concerned that foreigners will become saturated with dollar-denominated assets and will become unwilling to accommodate the trade deficit by holding more dollar-denominated assets. The shift in 2004 in the balance of payments toward a larger share of assets being acquired by official sources generated speculation that foreign private investors had indeed reached the point where they were no longer willing to add more dollar-denominated assets to their portfolios. This shift was reversed in 2005, however, as foreign private investments rebounded.

Another concern is with the outflow of profits that arise from the dollar-denominated assets owned by foreign investors. This outflow arises from the profits or interest generated by the assets and represent a clear outflow of capital from the economy that otherwise would not arise if the assets were owned by U.S. investors. These capital outflows represent the most tangible cost to the economy of the present mix of economic policies in which foreign capital inflows are needed to fill the gap between the demand for capital in the economy and the domestic supply of capital.

Indeed, as the data presented indicate, it is important to consider the underlying cause of the trade deficit. According to the most commonly accepted economic approach, in a world with floating exchange rates and the free flow of large amounts dollars in the world economy and international access to dollar-denominated assets, macroeconomic developments, particularly the demand for and supply of credit in the economy, are the driving forces behind the movements in the dollar's international exchange rate and, therefore, the price of exports and imports in the economy. As a result, according to this approach, the trade deficit is a reflection of macroeconomic conditions within the domestic economy and an attempt to address the issue of the trade deficit without addressing the underlying macroeconomic factors in the economy likely would prove to be of limited effectiveness.

In addition, the nation's net international investment position indicates that the largest share of U.S. assets owned by foreigners is held by private investors who acquired the assets for any number of reasons. As a result, the United States is not in debt to foreign investors or to foreign governments similar to some developing countries that run into balance of payments problems, because the United States has not borrowed to finance its trade deficit. Instead the United States has traded assets with foreign investors who are prepared to gain or lose on their investments in the same way private U.S. investors can gain or lose. It is certainly possible that foreign investors, whether they are private or official, could eventually decide to limit their continued acquisition of dollar-denominated assets or even reduce the size of their holdings, but there is no firm evidence that such presently is the case.

End Notes

1 For additional information about the causes of the U.S. trade deficit, see CRS Report RL31032, *The U.S. Trade Deficit: Causes, Consequences, and Cures*, by Craig Elwell.

2 Traditional foreign exchange markets are organized exchanges which trade primarily in foreign exchange futures and options contracts where the terms and condition of the contracts are standardized.

3 The over-the-counter foreign exchange derivatives market is an informal market consisting of dealers who custom-tailor agreements to meet the specific needs regarding maturity, payments intervals or other terms that allow the contracts to meet specific requirements for risk.

[4] *Triennial Central Bank Survey: Foreign Exchange and Derivatives Market Activity in 2007.* Bank for International Settlement, September 2007. pp. 1-2. A copy of the report is available at: [http://www.bis.org/publ/rpfx07.pdf]

[5] The United States defines foreign direct investment as the ownership or control, directly or indirectly, by one foreign person (individual, branch, partnership, association, government, etc.) of 10% or more of the voting securities of an incorporated U.S. business enterprise or an equivalent interest in an unincorporated U.S. business enterprise. 15 CFR § 806.15 (a) (1). Similarly, the United States defines direct investment abroad as the ownership or control, directly or indirectly, by one person (individual, branch, partnership, association, government, etc.) of 10% or more of the voting securities of an incorporated business enterprise or an equivalent interest in an unincorporated business enterprise. 15 CFR § 806.15 (a)(1).

[6] For additional information, see CRS Report RL32964, *The United States as a Net Debtor Nation: Overview of the Net International Investment Position*, by James K. Jackson.

[7] For additional information, see CRS Report RL32462, *Foreign Investment in U.S. Securities*, by James K. Jackson.

In: United States Trade Deficit Issues
Editors: Carl T. Yankovich
ISBN: 978-1-60692-090-9

Chapter 5

UNITED STATES TRADE DEFICIT AND THE IMPACT OF RISING OIL PRICES*

James K. Jackson
Specialist in International Trade and Finance Foreign Affairs, Defense, and Trade Division

SUMMARY

Petroleum prices have risen sharply since early 2005. At the same time the average monthly volume of imports of energy-related petroleum products has fallen slightly. The combination of sharply rising prices and a slightly lower level of imports of energy-related petroleum products translates into an escalating cost for those imports. This rising cost added an estimated $70 billion to the nation's trade deficit in 2005 and $50 billion in 2006. Imported energy prices moderated in early 2007, before rising again through the summer and more sharply in the fall, following a pattern of rising energy import prices in the spring and summer. This report provides an estimate of the initial impact of the rising oil prices on the nation's merchandise trade deficit. This report will be updated as warranted by events.

* This is an edited, reformatted and augmented version of a CRS Report for Congress publication dated January 2008.

BACKGROUND

According to data published by the Census Bureau of the Department of Commerce,[1] the prices of petroleum products over the past year have fluctuated sharply, at times rising considerably faster than the change in demand for those products. As a result, the price increases of imported energy-related petroleum products worsened the U.S. trade deficit in 2005 and 2006, and will do so again in 2007, although modestly. Energy-related petroleum products is a term used by the Census Bureau that includes crude oil, petroleum preparations, and liquefied propane and butane gas. Crude oil comprises the largest share by far within this broad category of energy-related imports. The increase in the trade deficit is expected to have a slightly negative impact on U.S. gross domestic product (GDP) and could place further downward pressure on the dollar against a broad range of other currencies. To the extent that the additions to the merchandise trade deficit are returned to the U.S. economy as payment for additional U.S. exports or to acquire such assets as securities or U.S. businesses, some of the negative effects could be mitigated.

Table 1 presents summary data from the Census Bureau for the change in the volume, or quantity, of energy-related petroleum imports and the change in the price, or the value, of those imports for 2006 and for 2007. The data indicate that the United States imported 4.9 billion barrels of total energy-related petroleum products in 2006, valued at $291 billion. From January-November 2007, the quantity of energy-related petroleum imports fell by 1.7% compared with the comparable period in 2006, while crude oil imports fell by 1.5% from the same period in 2006, reflecting a milder-than-normal winter in 2007. During the same eleven-month period, the average value of energy-related petroleum products imports rose by 6.1%, while the average value of crude oil imports rose by 5.7%. At these rates, the value of U.S. energy imports for 2007 would be slightly higher than those for 2006. As **Figure 1** shows, imports of energy-related petroleum products can vary sharply on a monthly basis, but averaged about 407 barrels a month in 2006 and about 402 barrels a month in the January-November period of 2007.

Table 1. Summary Data of U.S. Imports of Energy-Related Petroleum Products, Including Oil (not Seasonally Adjusted)

	January through November					
	2006		2007			
	Quantity (thousands of barrels)	Value (thousands of dollars)	Quantity (thousands of barrels)	Percent change 2006 to 2007	Value (thousands of dollars)	Percent change 2006 to 2007
Total energy-related Petroleum Products	4,499,138	$269,983,312	4,422,080	-1.7%	$286,483,138	6.1%
Crude oil	3,440,583	$200,818,503	3,390,083	-1.5%	$212,321,512	5.7%
	January through December					
	2006		2007			
	(Actual values)		(Estimated values)			
	Quantity (thousands of barrels)	Value (thousands of dollars)	Quantity (thousands of barrels)	Percent change 2006 to 2007	Value (thousands of dollars)	Percent change 2006 to 2007
Total energy-related Petroleum Products	4,880,734	$290,923,833	4,797,140	-1.7%	$308,703,423	6.1%
Crude oil	3,734,229	$216,627,331	3,679,419	-1.5%	$229,035,880	5.7%

Source: Census Bureau, Department of Commerce. Report FT900, *U.S. International Trade in Goods and Services,* January 11, 2007. Table 17.

Note: Estimates for January through December of 2007 were developed by CRS from data through eleven months of 2007 and data through 2006 published by the Census Bureau using a straight line extrapolation.

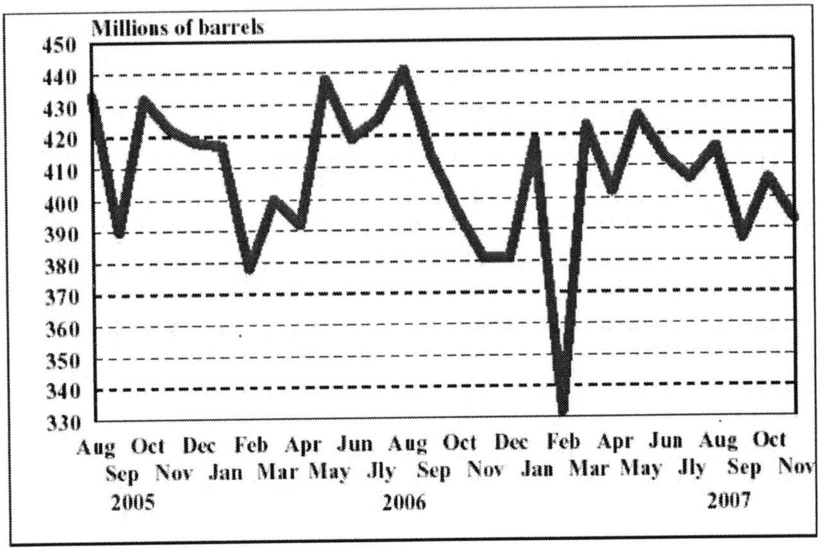

Source: Department of Commerce

Figure 1. Quantity of U.S. Imports of Energy-Related Petroleum Products

In value terms, energy-related imports rose from about $243 billion in 2005 to $291 billion in 2006, or an increase of 19.6% to account for about 16% of the value of total U.S. merchandise imports. An estimate for 2007, based on data for eleven months of 2007, indicates that there was a slower start to the seasonal rise in energy prices, compared with the sharp rise experienced in the spring of 2005 and 2006. Price data for the April-November period of 2007, however, show a sharp run-up in the price of imported energy in those months, which has continued into December 2007, compared with price data for 2006. In 2006, oil import prices peaked in August. As **Figure 2** shows, the cost of U.S. imports of energy-related petroleum products has risen from about $15 billion per month in early 2005 to more than $30 billion a month in August 2006, before falling back to $20 billion a month in December 2006 and $31 billion in November 2007. The average price of imported oil in November 2007 was up 52% from the average price in November 2006, reflecting the continued run-up in imported oil prices in 2007, as indicated in **Table 2**.

As a result of the overall rise in the value of energy-related imports in 2006, the trade deficit of such imports rose to $270 billion to account for 32% of the total $836 billion U.S. trade deficit, up from one-fifth of the total trade deficit in less than two years. In the January-November 2007 period, the trade deficit in energy-related imports amounted to $261 billion, or 35% of the total U.S. trade deficit of $744 billion. The oil-related deficit in November, however, accounted for 41% of the U.S. trade deficit for that month, the highest share recorded since 1998.

Recent data indicate that the drop in imported energy prices to about $54 per barrel toward the end of 2006 from the high of an average of $66 per barrel reached in August 2006 helped reduce the overall cost of energy imports so that the trade deficit in 2006 rose by about $50 billion, an amount equivalent to an increase of about 7% of the merchandise trade deficit due to higher oil prices. As long as the quantity of energy imports for the rest of 2007 remains below the quantity experienced in 2006, the total price of U.S. energy imports likely will be about $20 billion above that for 2006, as a result of the rise in the prices of imported energy in the October-December period of 2007. In terms of the U.S. economy, the estimated rise in the trade deficit from the increase in oil prices in 2005 is equivalent to about one-half of a percentage point of U.S. nominal GDP. In testimony before Congress, Federal Reserve Board Chairman Ben Bernanke indicated that the rise in oil prices, along with other commodity prices, likely would increase the overall rate of inflation in the economy, an important consideration in policy-making by the Federal Reserve.[2]

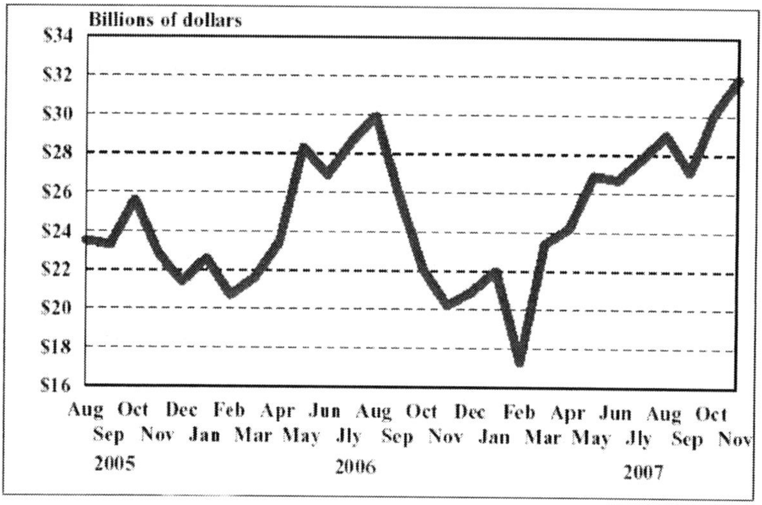

Source: Department of Commerce

Figure 2. Value of U.S. Imports of Energy-Related Petroleum Products

Table 2. U.S. Imports of Energy-Related Petroleum Products, Including Crude Oil (not seasonally adjusted

Period	Total energy-related petroleum products[a]		Crude oil			
	Quantity (thousands of barrels)	Value (thousands of dollars)	Quantity (thousands of barrels)	Thousands of barrels per day average)	Value (thousands Of ollars)	Unit price (dollars)
2006						
Jan. - Dec.	4,880,734	$290,923,833	3,734,229	10,231	$216,627,331	$58.01
Jan. - Nov.	4,499,138	269,983,312	3,440,583	10,301	200,818,503	58.37
August	440,997	29,872,301	336,528	10,856	22,255,220	66.13
September	413,902	25,786,512	316,381	10,546	19,740,688	62.40
October	395,656	22,055,963	308,602	9.955	17,119,687	55.47
November	380,813	20,208,933	299,010	9,967	15,615,178	52.22
December	381,597	20,940,521	293,645	9,472	15,808,828	53.84
2007						
Jan. - Nov.	4,422,080	286,483,138	3,390,083	10,150	212,321,512	62.63
January	418,158	22,010,536	320,108	10,326	16,720,818	52.23
February	331,818	17,347,440	252,869	9,031	12,822,771	50.71
March	422,671	23,366,614	324,248	10,460	17,186,586	53.00
April	402,043	24,238,490	304,775	10,159	17,456,146	57.28
May	426,026	26,934,778	320,208	10,329	19,006,138	59.36
June	413,312	26,654,260	321,260	10,709	19,580,491	60.95
July	406,427	27,769,362	310,320	10,010	20,344,172	65.56
August	416,130	28,988,603	319,197	10,297	21,733,947	68.09
September	387,135	27,146,183	297,503	9,917	20,383,148	68.51
October	405,860	30,079,622	316,184	10,199	22,919,110	72.49
November	392,500	31,947,251	303,411	10,114	24,168,187	79.65

Source: Census Bureau, Department of Commerce. Report FT900, *U.S. International Transactions in Goods and Services*. January 11, 2008. Table 17.

a. Energy-related petroleum products is a term used by the Census Bureau and includes crude oil, petroleum preparations, and liquefied propane and butane gas.

Crude oil comprises the largest share of energy-related petroleum products imports. According to Census Bureau data[3] as shown in **Table 2**, imports of crude oil fell from an average of 10.28 million barrels of crude oil imports per day in 2005 to an average of 10.23 million barrels per day in 2006, or a decrease of less than one percent. In December 2006, such imports averaged 9.5 million barrels per day, or a decrease of 6.6% from the volume of such imports recorded in December 2005. Overall, data for crude oil imports based on January through November data indicate that oil volumes had decreased by 1.5% in 2007 from the comparable period in 2006. From 2005 to 2006, the average price of crude oil increased from $46.81 per barrel to $58.00 per barrel for an increase of 24%, as shown in **Figure 3**. As a result, the value of U.S. energy-related imports rose from about $18 billion a month in March 2005 to about $30 billion a month in September 2006, before falling to $21 billion a month in December 2006, the lowest monthly total recorded since July 2005.

Data for 2007 indicate that a milder-than-normal winter reduced crude oil imports through July 2007 compared with comparable data for 2006 and average oil import prices, which had dropped nearly 4% from the average prices recorded in January 2007, started rising after March. The declines in prices and volumes of oil imports experienced in January and February, turned around in the April to September period, although import volumes continue to lag behind those recorded for the comparable period in 2006. Data for October and preliminary data for November and December 2007 presage higher energy-related imports costs in those months. Average crude oil prices in October 2007 were nearly 40% higher than in January 2007. Also, on November 8, 2007, crude oil traded for a record high of over $98 per barrel in world markets, before falling back to about $91 per barrel the following week.[4] At an average price of $80 per barrel, energy- related import prices could add as much as $100 billion to the U.S. trade deficit in 2008

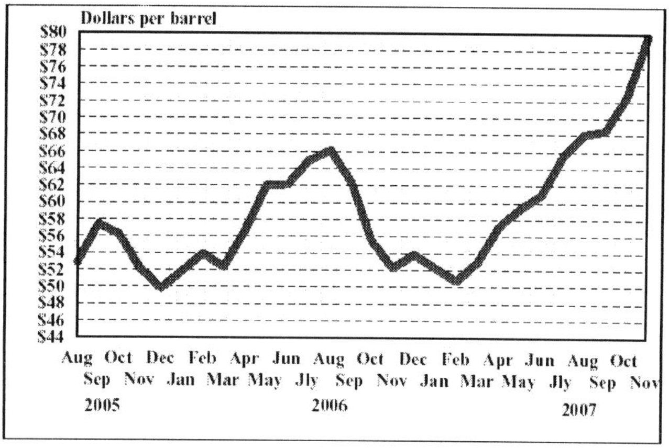

source: Department of Commerce

Figure 3. U.S. Import Price of Crude Oil

Issues for Congress

The rise in prices of energy imports experienced since early 2004 is expected to have a relatively minor impact on the rate of economic growth in 2006, but could pose a number of policy issues for Congress. The impact of the rise in energy import prices may well lessen somewhat as energy prices stabilize of fall slightly for the rest of 2006. It is likely, however, that energy prices will rise as rapidly again in 2007, especially in the late spring-early summer period of 2007. An important factor is the impact Atlantic hurricanes have on the production of crude oil in the Gulf of Mexico Most immediately, higher prices for energy imports will worsen the nation's merchandise trade deficit and have a disproportionate impact on the energy-intensive sectors of the economy and on households on fixed incomes.

Over the long run, a sustained increase in the prices of energy imports will permanently increase the nation's merchandise trade deficit, although some of this impact could be offset if some of the dollars are returned to the U.S. economy through increased purchases of U.S. goods and services or through purchases of such other assets as securities or U.S. businesses. Also, over the long-run it is possible for the economy to adjust to the higher prices of energy imports by improving its energy efficiency, finding alternative sources of energy, or searching out additional supplies of energy.

For Congress, the increase in the nation's merchandise trade deficit could add to existing pressures to examine the causes of the deficit and to address the underlying factors that are generating that deficit. In addition, the rise in prices of energy imports could add to concerns about the nation's reliance on foreign supplies for energy imports and add impetus to examining the nation's energy strategy. The increased outflow of dollars may well add to public and Congressional concerns about foreign acquisitions of U.S. firms and to concerns about the growing share of outstanding U.S. Treasury securities that are owned by foreigners. While the rise in energy prices can be expected to lead eventually to improvements in energy efficiency and to alternative sources of energy, there may well be increased pressure applied to Congress to assist in this process.

End Notes

[1] Census Bureau, Department of Commerce. Report FT900, *U.S. International Trade in Goods and Services,* January 11, 2008. Table 17. The report and supporting tables are available at [http://www.census.gov/foreign-trade/Press-Release/current_press_release/ftdpress.pdf].

[2] Bernanke, Ben, *The Economic Outlook,* Testimony Before the Joint Economic Committee, U.S. Congress, November 8, 2007.

[3] Report FT900, *U.S. International Trade in Goods and Services,* January 11, 2008. Table 17.

[4] Wong, Gillian, Oil Prices Rebound in Asian Trading, *The Washington Post.* November 14, 2007.

CHAPTER SOURCES

The following chapters have been previously published:

Chapter 1 – This is an edited, reformatted and augmented version of a Congressional Research Service publication, Report Order Code RL33577, updated January 4, 2008.

Chapter 2 - This is an edited, reformatted and augmented version of a Congressional Research Service publication, Report Order Code RL31032, updated January 25, 2008.

Chapter 3 - This is an edited, reformatted and augmented version of a Congressional Research Service publication, Report Order Code RL33140, updated June 20, 2007.

Chapter 4 - This is an edited, reformatted and augmented version of a Congressional Research Service publication, Report Order Code RL33274, updated April 22, 2008.

Chapter 5 - This is an edited, reformatted and augmented version of a Congressional Research Service publication, Report Order Code RS22204, updated January 15, 2008.

INDEX

A

B

C

D

E

F

G

H

I

J

L

M

N

O

P

Q

R

S

T

U

V

W

Y

Topics in Contemporary Mathematical Analysis and Applications

Mathematics and its Applications
Modelling, Engineering, and Social Sciences

Series Editor:
Hemen Dutta
Department of Mathematics, Gauhati University

Tensor Calculus and Applications
Simplified Tools and Techniques
Bhaben Kalita

Discrete Mathematical Structures
A Succinct Foundation
Beri Venkatachalapathy Senthil Kumar and Hemen Dutta

Methods of Mathematical Modelling
Fractional Differential Equations
Edited by Harendra Singh, Devendra Kumar, and Dumitru Baleanu

Mathematical Methods in Engineering and Applied Sciences
Edited by Hemen Dutta

Sequence Spaces
Topics in Modern Summability Theory
Mohammad Mursaleen and Feyzi Başar

Fractional Calculus in Medical and Health Science
Devendra Kumar and Jagdev Singh

Topics in Contemporary Mathematical Analysis and Applications
Hemen Dutta

Sloshing in Upright Circular Containers
Theory, Analytical Solutions, and Applications
Alexander Timokha and Ihor Raynovskyy

ISSN (online): 2689-0224
ISSN (print): 2689-0232

For more information about this series, please visit:
https://www.routledge.com/Mathematics-and-its-applications/book-series/MES

Topics in Contemporary Mathematical Analysis and Applications

Edited by

Hemen Dutta

CRC Press
Taylor & Francis Group
Boca Raton London New York

CRC Press is an imprint of the
Taylor & Francis Group, an **informa** business

First edition published 2021
by CRC Press
6000 Broken Sound Parkway NW, Suite 300, Boca Raton, FL 33487-2742

and by CRC Press
4 Park Square, Milton Park, Abingdon, Oxon OX14 4RN

ISBN: 978-0-367-53266-6 (hbk)
ISBN: 978-1-003-08119-7 (ebk)

Typeset in Times
by codeMantra

Contents

Preface

This book covers certain aspects of contemporary mathematical analysis and its applications. It focuses on enriching the understanding of several methods, problems, and applications in the area of mathematical analysis having contemporary research and study significances. Each chapter of this book aims to offer readers the understanding of discussed research problems by presenting related developments in reasonable details. This book is expected to be a valuable resource for graduate students, researchers, educators, and teachers interested in contemporary mathematical analysis. There are 12 chapters in this book, and they are organized as follows.

Chapter "Certain Banach-Space Operators Acting on Free Poisson Elements Induced by Orthogonal Projections" investigates the free (weighted-) Poisson elements in the Banach $*$-probability space generated by integer-many mutually free, semicircular elements, induced by mutually orthogonal integer-many projections in a fixed C^*-probability space. It constructs corresponding $*$-homomorphisms acting on the Banach $*$-probability space in order to study how they affect the free (weighted-) Poisson distributions and the free distributions of free (weighted-) Poisson elements. It also constructs certain Banach-space operators generated by the $*$-homomorphisms to examine how such operators deform free probability and to characterize how the free (weighted-) Poisson distributions are deformed by the action of those operators.

Chapter "Linear positive operators involving orthogonal polynomials" aims to survey extensively on the available research work regarding approximations by the linear positive operators defined by using orthogonal polynomials. In the literature, several sequences of linear positive operators involving orthogonal polynomials have been defined, and their Durrmeyer and Kantorovich-type variants have been investigated. In recent years, there has been a significant increase in activities in the approximation of continuous functions on $[0, \infty)$ by the linear positive operators based on orthogonal polynomials.

Chapter "Approximation by Kantorovich variant of λ-Schurer operators and related numerical results" aims to construct Kantorovich variant of λ-Schurer operators using certain polynomials in order to study Voronovskaja-type theorems and obtain a global approximation formula for such operators. It presents a local direct estimate of the rate of convergence by Lipschitz-type function involving two parameters. The proposed operators reduce to the classical Schurer-Kantorovich operators as well as to the classical Bernstein-Kantorovich operators and λ-Bernstein-Kantorovich operators under certain special cases. Finally, it provides tables and graphs based on numerical experiments in order to justify the efficiency of the results in comparison with other available results.

Chapter "Characterizations of rough fractional-type integral operators on variable exponent vanishing Morrey-type spaces" aims to apply relevant properties of variable exponent to study on Adams and Spanne-type estimates for a class of fractional integral operators with variable orders on variable exponent vanishing generalized Morrey spaces. Finally, it claims to introduce the variable exponent-generalized Campanato spaces and then obtain the boundedness of the commutators of these operators on such spaces.

Chapter "Compact-like operators in vector lattices normed by locally solid lattices" investigates continuous, bounded, and compact operators on locally solid Riesz spaces with respect to a concept of convergence, which was introduced and investigated on locally solid Riesz spaces. This chapter describes the generalization of several known classes of operators on Riesz spaces and Banach lattices such as norm continuous, order continuous, order bounded, bounded, and compact operators. It also presents the relations among such operators and examines the basic properties of the operators.

Chapter "On indexed product summability of an infinite series" presents the findings based on the indexed product summability of an infinite series by using Nörlund mean. In summability theory, indexed summability and indexed product summability of an infinite series have significant importance and relevance.

Chapter "On some important inequalities" aims to present some useful mathematical inequalities such as the Jensen, Hermite-Hadamard, Rogers-Hölder, and Minkowski inequalities. The aforementioned four inequalities have been presented in discrete and integral forms, and their generalizations have also been discussed. The Jensen and Hermite-Hadamard inequalities have been considered in more detail. An expansion of the initial integral form of Jensen's inequality is promoted for convex functions of several variables. The Rogers-Hölder and Minkowski inequalities have been derived from the integral form of Jensen's inequality for convex functions of several variables. The Minkowski inequality is realized independently of the Rogers-Hölder inequality.

Chapter "Refinements of Young integral inequality via fundamental inequalities and mean value theorems for derivatives" reviews several refinements of Young's integral inequality via several mean value theorems, such as Lagrange's and Taylor's mean value theorems of Lagrange's and Cauchy's type remainders, and via several fundamental inequalities, such as Čebyšev's integral inequality, Hermite-Hadamard's type integral inequalities, Hölder's integral inequality, and Jensen's discrete and integral inequalities, in terms of higher-order derivatives and their norms. It also surveys several applications of several refinements of Young's integral inequality and further refines Young's integral inequality via Pólya's type integral inequalities.

Chapter "On the coefficient estimates for new subclasses of bi-univalent functions associated with subordination and Fibonacci numbers" investigates new subclasses of the bi-univalent function class associated with subordination and Fibonacci numbers in the open unit disc. It obtains estimates on the first two Taylor-Maclaurin coefficients, derives Fekete-Szegö inequalities for functions belonging to the newly defined classes, and also discusses relevant connections to some of the earlier known results.

Chapter "Fixed point problems of multivalued mappings" aims to construct the fixed-point results of multivalued mappings subject to the satisfaction of generalized cyclic F-contractive conditions in metric spaces. It obtains the fixed points of multivalued mappings under cyclic simulation functions, and then establishes the stability of fixed-point sets of generalized cyclic F-contractive mappings and mappings under cyclic simulation function. The results have been obtained without using any form of continuity of multivalued mappings involved. Further, suitable examples have also been given to support the results.

Chapter "Significance and relevance of functional equations in various fields" aims to impart the significant role of functional equations in various fields. The study of functional equations is a growing, and an important, area in mathematics. It covers many other areas of mathematics, and recently, their role in science and engineering has found to be very attractive. It also portrays a few applications of functional equations in geometry, finance, information theory, wireless sensor networks and electric circuits with parallel resistances, physics, and electromagnetism.

Chapter "Unified type nondifferentiable second-order symmetric duality results over arbitrary cones" claims to formulate a new mixed-type second-order nondifferentiable symmetric duality in scalar-objective programming over arbitrary cones. It first discusses mixed-type primal-dual results based on available literature and constructs some numerical examples to justify the presented definitions. It derives the combined result with one model over arbitrary cones, and the duality theorems have been derived for some problems under bonvexity and pseudobonvexity with respect to η assumptions over arbitrary cones.

The editor sincerely acknowledges the cooperation and patience of contributors during the entire process of handling their works submitted for this book. Reviewers deserve deep gratitude for selflessly offering their help for successfully bringing out this book. The editor also thankfully acknowledges the support of editorial staff at Taylor & Francis. Encouragement from several colleagues and friends is the primary source of inspiration to work for such book projects, and the editor gratefully acknowledges their mental support.

Hemen Dutta
Guwahati, India
26th April, 2020

Editor

Hemen Dutta is a regular faculty member in Mathematics at Gauhati University, India. He did his Master of Science (MSc) in Mathematics, Post Graduate Diploma in Computer Application (PGDCA), Master of Philosophy (MPhil) in Mathematics, and Doctor of Philosophy (PhD) in Mathematics, respectively. His topics of primary research interest are in the area of mathematical analysis. He has contributed in authoring around 150 items so far as research papers for journals, chapters for books, and proceedings papers. He has already published 20 books as textbooks, reference books, edited books, and proceedings of conferences. He has organized many academic events for researchers and academicians, and also associated with several other such activities in different capacities. He has contributed several general and popular articles in newspaper, science magazines, science portals, popular books, etc. He has offered his service as a resource person/invited speaker in workshops, conferences, teachers' training program, faculty development programs, etc. He has also visited foreign institutions on invitation for research collaboration and delivering talks.

Contributors

Mujahid Abbas
Department of Mathematics
Government College University Lahore
Lahore, Pakistan

P. N. Agrawal
Department of Mathematics
IIT Roorkee
Roorkee, India

Şahsene Altınkaya
Department of Mathematics
Bursa Uludag University
Bursa, Turkey

Abdullah Aydın
Department of Mathematics
Muş Alparslan University
Muş, Turkey

P. Baliarsingh
Department of Mathematics
Gangadhar Meher University
Sambalpur, Odisha, India

Ruchi Chauhan
Department of Mathematics
IIT Roorkee
Roorkee, India

Ilwoo Cho
Department of Mathematics and Statistics
Saint Ambrose University
Davenport, Iowa, U.S.A.

Kamil Demirci
Department of Mathematics
Sinop University
Sinop, Turkey

Ramu Dubey
Department of Mathematics
J.C. Bose University of Science and Technology
Faridabad, India

Hemen Dutta
Department of Mathematics
Gauhati University
Guwahati, India

Shenghu Ding
School of Mathematics and Statistics
Ningxia University
Yinchuan, P. R. China

Ferit Gürbüz
Faculty of Education, Department of Mathematics Education
Hakkari University
Hakkari, Turkey

Bai-Ni Guo
School of Mathematics and Informatics
Henan Polytechnic University
Jiaozuo, China

Huili Han
School of Mathematics and Statistics
Ningxia University
Yinchuan, P. R. China

Wen-Hui Li
Department of Fundamental Courses
Zhengzhou University of Science and Technology
Zhengzhou, China

Pinhong Long
School of Mathematics and Statistics
Ningxia University
Yinchuan, P. R. China

Vishnu Narayan Mishra
Department of Mathematics
Indira Gandhi National Tribal University
Lalpur, Amarkantak, India

Talat Nazir
Department of Mathematical Sciences
University of South Africa
Johannesburg, South Africa
and
Department of Mathematics
COMSATS University Islamabad
Abbottabad, Pakistan

Faruk Özger
Department of Engineering Sciences
İzmir Kâtip Çelebi University
İzmir, Turkey

B. P. Padhy
School of Applied Sciences, Department of Mathematics
KIIT Deemed to be University
Bhubaneswar, India

Zlatko Pavić
Department of Mathematics
Mechanical Engineering Faculty in Slavonski Brod
University of Osijek
Osijek, Croatia

Feng Qi
Institute of Mathematics, Henan Polytechnic University, Jiaozuo 454010, Henan, China
College of Mathematics and Physics
Inner Mongolia University for Nationalities Tongliao, China
and
School of Mathematical Sciences
Tianjin Polytechnic University
Tianjin, China

B. V. Senthil Kumar
Department of Information Technology
Nizwa College of Technology
Nizwa, Oman

Guo-Sheng Wu
School of Computer Science
Sichuan Technology and Business University
Chengdu, China

Sevda Yıldız
Department of Mathematics
Sinop University
Sinop, Turkey

1 Certain Banach-Space Operators Acting on Free Poisson Elements Induced by Orthogonal Projections

Ilwoo Cho
Saint Ambrose University

CONTENTS

1.1 INTRODUCTION

Let (A, ψ) be a *C^*-probability space* containing mutually orthogonal $|\mathbb{Z}|$-many *projections* $\{q_j\}_{j\in\mathbb{Z}}$. Such projections q_j's induce the corresponding *free weighted-semicircular family* $\{u_j\}_{j\in\mathbb{Z}}$ in a certain *Banach $*$-probability space* $(\mathfrak{L}_Q, \tau)$, and under additional conditions, this free family $\{u_j\}_{j\in\mathbb{Z}}$ generates the *free semicircular family* $\{U_j\}_{j\in\mathbb{Z}}$ in $(\mathfrak{L}_Q, \tau)$; see [6]. This free semicircular family $\{U_j\}_{j\in\mathbb{Z}}$ generates the Banach $*$-probabilistic substructure $(\mathbb{L}_Q, \tau)$ of $(\mathfrak{L}_Q, \tau)$. The free probability on $\mathbb{L}_Q$ was studied in [7,8,10,11].

There are ways to construct semicircular elements in earlier works, e.g., see [1,2,17,18,19,20,21,29,30]. However, our construction is different from those of them. Ours is motivated by the construction of the *weighted-semicircular elements* of [5,9,11]. In [5,9,11], (weighted-)semicircular elements are naturally constructed from analyses on the *p-adic number fields* $\mathbb{Q}_p$, for primes p (and their globalization, the analysis on the *finite Adelic ring* $A_{\mathbb{Q}}$), from $|\mathbb{Z}|$-many orthogonal projections induced by $|\mathbb{Z}|$-many measurable *p-adic characteristic functions* of spheres in the p-adic number fields $\mathbb{Q}_p$ (e.g., [26] and [27]). Motivated by these, we mimic the construction of [5,9,11], in the cases where a C^*-probability space (A, ψ) has mutually orthogonal $|\mathbb{Z}|$-many projections in [6] (also, see below). For more about details and applications, see [7,8,10] and [11].

The main purposes of this paper are (i) to construct *free (weighted-)Poisson elements* of the *Banach $*$-probability space* $(\mathbb{L}_Q, \tau)$, (ii) to consider the $*$-homomorphisms $\{\beta_\pm^n\}_{n\in\mathbb{N}_0}$ acting on $\mathbb{L}_Q$ induced by certain order-preserving bijective functions $h_\pm$ on the set $\mathbb{Z}$ of all integers, (iii) to study how these $*$-homomorphisms of (ii) affect the free probability on $\mathbb{L}_Q$, (iv) to consider how the *free (weighted-)Poisson distributions*, which are the free distributions of our free (weighted-)Poisson elements of $(\mathbb{L}_Q, \tau)$, are affected by the action of $\{\beta_\pm^n\}_{n\in\mathbb{N}_0}$, based on (iii), where

$$\mathbb{N}_0 = \mathbb{N} \cup \{0\},$$

and (v) to construct a certain Banach $*$-algebra $\mathfrak{B}$ generated by $\{\beta_\pm^n\}_{n\in\mathbb{N}_0}$, and to investigate how the operators of $\mathfrak{B}$ distort the free probability on $(\mathbb{L}_Q, \tau)$.

Our main results show that (I) typical types of free (weighted-)Poisson elements generated by (weighted-)semicircular elements are characterized by the construction of $\mathbb{L}_Q$, and the universality of the semicircular law; (II) our free weighted-Poisson distributions are completely characterized by free Poisson distributions; (III) the $*$-homomorphisms of (ii) are *free-homomorphisms*, i.e., $*$-homomorphisms of (ii) preserve the free probability on $\mathbb{L}_Q$, and hence, the free (weighted-)Poisson distributions of (i) are preserved by the action of these $*$-homomorphisms on $\mathbb{L}_Q$; and (IV) the distortion of free probability on $\mathbb{L}_Q$, under the action of the Banach algebra $\mathfrak{B}$ of (v), is characterized, and it shows how our free (weighted-)Poisson distributions are deformed by the action of $\mathfrak{B}$ on $\mathbb{L}_Q$.

In earlier works, free Poisson elements have been studied. Even though free Poisson elements and free Poisson distributions are well known (e.g., see [15,16] and [17]), our free "weighted-Poisson" elements are newly introduced here. Moreover, their free distributions, the *free weighted-Poisson distributions*, are completely characterized with respect to certain free Poisson distributions. In the long run, we show that free weighted-Poisson elements are factorized by certain operators and free Poisson elements. More interestingly, distorted free (weighted-)Poisson distributions are studied under the action of $\mathfrak{B}$ on $\mathbb{L}_Q$.

1.2 PRELIMINARIES

Free probability is the noncommutative operator-algebraic version of classical *measure theory* and *statistical analysis*. The operator-algebraic *freeness* plays like the classical functional *independence* by replacing measures on sets to linear functionals on noncommutative algebras (e.g., [17,22,23,28] and [30]). It is one of the main subjects not only in pure mathematics (e.g., [3,4,20,21,24,25] and [29]), but also in related fields (e.g., [5] through [12]). In particular, here, the combinatorial free probability is used (e.g., [17,22] and [23]).

In the text, without definitions and backgrounds, *free moments* and *free cumulants* of operators will be computed for analyzing free distributions of the operators. Also, we use *free product $*$-probability spaces*, without a detailed introduction.

By the *central limit theorem(s)*, studying semicircular elements whose free distributions are *the semicircular law*, is one of the main topics in free probability theory (e.g., [1,2,18,19,20,21] and [29]). As an application, *free Poisson elements* whose free distributions are the free Poisson distributions, have been considered (e.g., [15,16] and [17]).

1.3 SOME BANACH $*$-ALGEBRAS INDUCED BY PROJECTIONS

In this section, we establish backgrounds of our proceeding works. Let (B, φ) be a topological $*$-probability space (a *C^*-probability space*, or a *W^*-probability space*, or a *Banach $*$-probability space*, etc.), where B is a topological $*$-algebra (a C^*-algebra, resp., a W^*-algebra, resp., a Banach $*$-algebra, etc.), and φ is a bounded linear functional on B.

An operator a of B is said to be a *free random variable* whenever it is regarded as an element of (B, φ). As usual in *operator theory*, a free random variable a is said to be *self-adjoint* in (B, φ) if $a^* = a$ in B, where a^* is the *adjoint of a* (e.g., [14]).

Definition 1.1. *A self-adjoint free random variable a is said to be weighted-semicircular in (B, φ) with its weight $t_0 \in \mathbb{C}^\times = \mathbb{C} \setminus \{0\}$ (or, in short, t_0-semicircular), if a satisfies the free-cumulant computations,*

$$k_n(a, ..., a) = \begin{cases} k_2(a,\, a) = t_0 & \text{if } n = 2 \\ 0 & \text{otherwise,} \end{cases} \tag{1.1}$$

for all $n \in \mathbb{N}$, where $k_\bullet(...)$ is the free cumulant on B in terms of φ under the Möbius inversion of [17,22,23].

If $t_0 = 1$ in (1.1), the 1-semicircular element a is said to be semicircular in (B, φ), i.e., a is semicircular in (B, φ) if a satisfies

$$k_n(a, ..., a) = \begin{cases} 1 & \text{if } n = 2 \\ 0 & \text{otherwise,} \end{cases} \tag{1.2}$$

for all $n \in \mathbb{N}$.

By the Möbius inversion of [17,22] and [23], one can characterize the weighted-semicircularity (1.1) as follows: A self-adjoint operator a is t_0-semicircular in (B, φ) if and only if

$$\varphi(a^n) = \omega_n \left(t_0^{\frac{n}{2}} c_{\frac{n}{2}}\right), \tag{1.3}$$

where

$$\omega_n \overset{def}{=} \begin{cases} 1 & \text{if } n \text{ is even} \\ 0 & \text{if } n \text{ is odd,} \end{cases}$$

for all $n \in \mathbb{N}$, and c_k are the k-th *Catalan numbers*,

$$c_k \overset{def}{=} \frac{1}{k+1} \begin{pmatrix} 2k \\ k \end{pmatrix} = \frac{1}{k+1} \left(\frac{(2k)!}{k!(2k-k)!}\right) = \frac{(2k)!}{k!(k+1)!},$$

for all $k \in \mathbb{N}_0$.

Similarly, a self-adjoint free random variable a is semicircular in (B, φ) if and only if a is 1-semicircular in (B, φ), and if and only if

$$\varphi(a^n) = \omega_n c_{\frac{n}{2}}, \tag{1.4}$$

by (1.2) and (1.3), for all $n \in \mathbb{N}$, where ω_n are in the sense of (1.3).

So we use the t_0-semicircularity (1.1) (or, the semicircularity (1.2)) and its characterization (1.3) (resp., (1.4)) alternatively from below.

If a is a self-adjoint free random variable in (B, φ), then the sequences consisting of

$$\text{the } \textit{free moments } (\varphi(a^n))_{n=1}^{\infty},$$

and

$$\text{the } \textit{free cumulants } (k_n(a, ..., a))_{n=1}^{\infty}$$

provide equivalent free-distributional data of a in (B, φ), characterizing the *free distribution of* a (e.g., [17,22] and [23]).

In the rest of this paper, we fix a C^*-probability space (A, ψ) and assume that there are $|\mathbb{Z}|$-many projections $\{q_j\}_{j\in\mathbb{Z}}$ in the C^*-algebra A, i.e., the operators q_j satisfy

$$q_j^* = q_j = q_j^2 \text{ in } A,$$

for all $j \in \mathbb{Z}$ (e.g., [14]). Assume further that these projections $\{q_j\}_{j\in\mathbb{Z}}$ are *mutually orthogonal* in A, in the sense that:

$$q_i q_j = \delta_{i,j} q_j \text{ in } A, \text{ for all } i, j \in \mathbb{Z}, \tag{1.5}$$

where δ is the *Kronecker delta*. Now, we fix the family

$$\mathbf{Q} = \{q_j\}_{j \in \mathbb{Z}} \tag{1.6}$$

of mutually orthogonal projections (1.5) of A.

Remark 1.1. *One can have such a C^*-algebraic structure A containing a family $\mathbf{Q}$ of (1.6), naturally or artificially. Clearly, in the settings of [5,9,12], one can naturally take such structures.*

Suppose there is a C^*-algebra A_0 containing a family $\mathbf{Q}_N = \{q_1, ..., q_N\}$ of mutually orthogonal N-many projections $q_1, ..., q_N$, for $N \in \mathbb{N}_\infty = \mathbb{N} \cup \{\infty\}$. Then, under a suitable direct product, or tensor product, or free product of copies of A_0 under product topology, one can construct a C^*-algebra A containing a family $\mathbf{Q}$ with $|\mathbb{Z}|$-many mutually orthogonal projections, containing $\mathbf{Q}_N$ under unitarily equivalence. For example, see [10].

Let Q be the C^*-subalgebra of A generated by the family $\mathbf{Q}$ of (1.6),

$$Q \overset{def}{=} C^*(\mathbf{Q}) \subseteq A. \tag{1.7}$$

Proposition 1.1. *Let Q be a C^*-subalgebra (1.7) of a fixed C^*-algebra A. Then*

$$Q \overset{*\text{-iso}}{=} \underset{j \in \mathbb{Z}}{\oplus} (\mathbb{C} \cdot q_j) \overset{*\text{-iso}}{=} \mathbb{C}^{\oplus |\mathbb{Z}|}, \text{ in } (A, \psi). \tag{1.8}$$

Proof. The proof of (1.8) is done by the orthogonality (1.5) of $\mathbf{Q}$ in A. □

Define now linear functionals ψ_j on the C^*-algebra Q of (1.7) by

$$\psi_j(q_i) = \delta_{ij}\psi(q_j), \text{for all } i \in \mathbb{Z}, \tag{1.9}$$

for all $j \in \mathbb{Z}$, where ψ is the linear functional of the fixed C^*-probability space (A, ψ). The linear functionals $\{\psi_j\}_{j \in \mathbb{Z}}$ of (1.9) are well defined on Q by (1.8).

Assumption Let (A, ψ) be a fixed C^*-probability space, and let Q be the C^*-subalgebra (1.7) of A. In the rest of this paper, we assume that

$$\psi(q_j) \in \mathbb{C}^\times, \text{ for all } j \in \mathbb{Z}.$$

□

Definition 1.2. *The C^*-probability spaces (Q, ψ_j) are called the j-th filters of Q in a given C^*-probability space (A, ψ), where Q is in the sense of (1.7) and ψ_j are the linear functionals of (1.9), for all $j \in \mathbb{Z}$.*

Now, let's define the bounded linear transformations $\mathbf{c}$ and $\mathbf{a}$ acting on the C^*-algebra Q, by linear morphisms satisfying

$$\mathbf{c}(q_j) = q_{j+1}, \text{and } \mathbf{a}(q_j) = q_{j-1}, \tag{1.10}$$

for all $j \in \mathbb{Z}$. Then, $\mathbf{c}$ and $\mathbf{a}$ are the well-defined bounded linear operators "on Q." One can understand that they are *Banach-space operators* in the *operator space* $B(Q)$, consisting of all bounded linear transformations acting on Q, by regarding Q as a *Banach space* equipped with its C^*-*norm* (e.g., [13]).

Definition 1.3. *We call these Banach-space operators* $\mathbf{c}$ *and* $\mathbf{a}$ *of (1.10) the* creation *and, respectively, the* annihilation *on* Q.

Define now a new Banach-space operator $\mathbf{l}$ on Q by

$$\mathbf{l} = \mathbf{c} + \mathbf{a} \in B(Q). \tag{1.11}$$

Definition 1.4. *The Banach-space operator* $\mathbf{l} \in B(Q)$ *of (1.11) is called the* radial operator on Q.

Note that if $\mathbf{l}$ is in the sense of (1.11), then the powers $\mathbf{l}^n$ are also contained in $B(Q)$, for all $n \in \mathbb{N}_0$, with axiomatization:

$$\mathbf{l}^0 = 1_Q, \text{ the identity operator of } B(Q).$$

Now, define a closed subspace $\mathfrak{L}$ of the operator space $B(Q)$ by

$$\mathfrak{L} \overset{def}{=} \overline{\mathbb{C}[\{\mathbf{l}\}]}^{\|.\|} = \overline{span_{\mathbb{C}}\{\mathbf{l}^n : n \in \mathbb{N}_0\}}^{\|.\|}, \tag{1.12}$$

generated by the radial operator $\mathbf{l}$, where $\|.\|$ is the operator norm on $B(Q)$, defined to be

$$\|T\| = \sup\{\|Tq\|_Q : \|q\|_Q = 1\},$$

for all $T \in B(Q)$, where $\|.\|_Q$ is the C^**-norm on* Q, and $\overline{X}^{\|.\|}$ are the *operator-norm closures* of subsets X of the *operator space* $B(Q)$ (e.g., [13]). It is not difficult to check that this subspace $\mathfrak{L}$ forms an algebra in the vector space $B(Q)$, by (1.12). So, it forms a Banach algebra in the topological vector space $B(Q)$.

On this Banach algebra $\mathfrak{L}$ of (1.12), define a unary operation $(*)$ by

$$\left(\sum_{n=0}^{\infty} t_n \mathbf{l}^n\right)^* = \sum_{n=0}^{\infty} \overline{t_n}\, \mathbf{l}^n \text{ in } \mathfrak{L}, \tag{1.13}$$

where $\overline{z}$ are the *conjugates of* $z \in \mathbb{C}$.

Then, this operation (1.13) is a well-defined *adjoint on* the Banach algebra $\mathfrak{L}$ (e.g., [6] and [12]), and hence, every element of $\mathfrak{L}$ is *adjointable* in $B(Q)$ in the sense of [13]. So the algebra $\mathfrak{L}$ forms a *Banach* $*$*-algebra* in $B(Q)$ with (1.13).

Now, let $\mathfrak{L}$ be the Banach $*$-algebra (1.12). Define the *tensor product Banach* $*$*-algebra* $\mathfrak{L}_Q$ by

$$\mathfrak{L}_Q = \mathfrak{L} \otimes_{\mathbb{C}} Q, \tag{1.14}$$

where $\otimes_{\mathbb{C}}$ is the tensor product of Banach $*$-algebras.

Definition 1.5. *We call the Banach* $*$*-algebra* $\mathfrak{L}_Q$ *of (1.14) the radial projection (Banach* $*$*-)algebra on* Q.

1.4 WEIGHTED-SEMICIRCULAR ELEMENTS INDUCED BY Q

We here construct the weighted-semicircular elements induced by the family $\mathbf{Q}$ of mutually orthogonal projections in a fixed C^*-probability space (A, ψ), inducing the radial projection algebra $\mathfrak{L}_Q$ of (1.14). Let $(Q,\ \psi_j)$ be the j-th filters of Q in $(A,\ \psi)$, where ψ_j are the linear functionals (1.9), for all $j \in \mathbb{Z}$.

Remark that if u_j are the operators of $\mathfrak{L}_Q$,

$$u_j \overset{def}{=} \mathbf{l} \otimes q_j \in \mathfrak{L}_Q, \text{ for all } j \in \mathbb{Z}, \tag{1.15}$$

then

$$u_j^n = (\mathbf{l} \otimes q_j)^n = \mathbf{l}^n \otimes q_j, \text{ for all } n \in \mathbb{N},$$

with axiomatization:

$$u_j^0 \overset{\text{axiom}}{=} \mathbf{l}^0 \otimes q_j = 1_Q \otimes q_j,$$

for all $n \in \mathbb{N}_0$, for $j \in \mathbb{Z}$. That is, the operators $\{u_j\}_{j\in\mathbb{Z}}$ of (1.15) generate $\mathfrak{L}_Q$, by (1.8) and (1.12).

One can construct a linear functional φ_j on $\mathfrak{L}_Q$ by a linear morphism satisfying that

$$\varphi_j\left(u_i^n\right) = \varphi_j\left(\mathbf{l}^n \otimes q_i\right) \overset{def}{=} \psi_j\left(\mathbf{l}^n(q_i)\right), \tag{1.16}$$

for all $n \in \mathbb{N}_0$, for all $i,\ j \in \mathbb{Z}$.

These linear functionals $\{\varphi_j\}_{j\in\mathbb{Z}}$ of (1.16) are well defined by (1.8), (1.12), and (1.14).

Definition 1.6. *We call the Banach $*$-probability spaces*

$$\left(\mathfrak{L}_Q,\ \varphi_j\right),\ for\ all\ j \in \mathbb{Z}, \tag{1.17}$$

the j-th (Banach-$*$-probability) *spaces on* Q.

Observe that if $\mathbf{c}$ and $\mathbf{a}$ are the creation, and, respectively, the annihilation, then

$$\mathbf{ca} = 1_Q = \mathbf{ac} \text{ on } Q.$$

More generally, one has

$$\mathbf{c}^n\mathbf{a}^n = (\mathbf{ca})^n = 1_Q = (\mathbf{ac})^n = \mathbf{a}^n\mathbf{c}^n,\ \forall n \in \mathbb{N},$$

and hence, (1.18)

$$\mathbf{c}^{n_1}\mathbf{a}^{n_2} = \mathbf{a}^{n_2}\mathbf{c}^{n_1},\ \forall n_1,\ n_2 \in \mathbb{N}.$$

Thus, one obtains that

$$\mathbf{l}^n = (\mathbf{c}+\mathbf{a})^n = \Sigma_{k=0}^{n}\begin{pmatrix} n \\ k \end{pmatrix}\mathbf{c}^k\mathbf{a}^{n-k}, \tag{1.19}$$

for all $n \in \mathbb{N}$, by (1.18), where

$$\begin{pmatrix} n \\ k \end{pmatrix} = \frac{n!}{k!(n-k)!},\ \forall k \leq n \in \mathbb{N}_0.$$

Note that, for any $n \in \mathbb{N}$,

$$\mathbf{l}^{2n-1} = \Sigma_{k=0}^{2n-1} \begin{pmatrix} 2n-1 \\ k \end{pmatrix} \mathbf{c}^k \mathbf{a}^{n-k}, \tag{1.20}$$

by (1.19). So formula (1.20) does not contain 1_Q-terms by (1.18).

Note also that for any $n \in \mathbb{N}$, one has

$$\mathbf{l}^{2n} = \Sigma_{k=0}^{2n} \begin{pmatrix} 2n \\ k \end{pmatrix} \mathbf{c}^k \mathbf{a}^{n-k} = \begin{pmatrix} 2n \\ n \end{pmatrix} \mathbf{c}^n \mathbf{a}^n + [\text{Rest terms}], \tag{1.21}$$

by (1.19). So $\mathbf{l}^{2n}$ contains $\begin{pmatrix} 2n \\ n \end{pmatrix}$-many 1_Q-terms by (1.18) and (1.21).

Proposition 1.2. *Let $\mathbf{l}$ be the radial operator on Q. Then for any $n \in \mathbb{N}$,*

$$\mathbf{l}^{2n-1} \text{ does not contain } 1_Q\text{-terms in } \mathfrak{L}, \tag{1.22}$$

$$\mathbf{l}^{2n} \text{ contains } \begin{pmatrix} 2n \\ n \end{pmatrix} \cdot 1_Q \text{ in } \mathfrak{L}. \tag{1.23}$$

Proof. Statements (1.22) and (1.23) are proven by (1.20), respectively, by (1.21). □

Remark that one has

$$\varphi_j \left(u_j^{2n-1} \right) = \psi_j \left(\mathbf{l}^{2n-1} (q_j) \right) = 0, \tag{1.24}$$

for all $n \in \mathbb{N}$, by (1.9) and (1.22).

Similarly, we have

$$\varphi_j \left(u_j^{2n} \right) = \psi_j \left(\mathbf{l}^{2n} (q_j) \right) = \psi_j \left(\begin{pmatrix} 2n \\ n \end{pmatrix} q_j + [\text{Rest terms}](q_j) \right)$$

by (1.21)

$$= \begin{pmatrix} 2n \\ n \end{pmatrix} \psi_j (q_j) = \begin{pmatrix} 2n \\ n \end{pmatrix} \psi (q_j),$$

by (1.9) and (1.23). That is,

$$\varphi_j \left(u_j^{2n} \right) = \begin{pmatrix} 2n \\ n \end{pmatrix} \psi (q_j), \tag{1.25}$$

for all $n \in \mathbb{N}$.

Proposition 1.3. *Fix $j \in \mathbb{Z}$, and let $u_k = \mathbf{1} \otimes q_k$ be the k-th generating operators of the j-th space $(\mathfrak{L}_Q, \varphi_j)$, for all $k \in \mathbb{Z}$. Then,*

$$\varphi_j \left(u_k^n \right) = \delta_{j,k} \omega_n \left(\left(\frac{n}{2} + 1 \right) \psi (q_j) \right) c_{\frac{n}{2}}, \tag{1.26}$$

where ω_n are in the sense of (1.3) for all $n \in \mathbb{N}$, and c_k are the k-th Catalan numbers for all $k \in \mathbb{N}_0$.

Proof. First, take the j-th generating operator u_j in $(\mathfrak{L}_Q,\ \varphi_j)$. By (1.24) and (1.25), one can get that:

$$\varphi_j\left(u_j^{2n-1}\right) = 0,$$

and

$$\varphi_j\left(u_j^{2n}\right) = \begin{pmatrix} 2n \\ n \end{pmatrix} \psi(q_j) = \left(\tfrac{n+1}{n+1}\right) \begin{pmatrix} 2n \\ n \end{pmatrix} \psi(q_j)$$

$$= ((n+1)\psi(q_j))\, c_n,$$

for all $n \in \mathbb{N}$, where c_n are the n-th Catalan numbers.

Assume now that $k \neq j$ in $\mathbb{Z}$. Then, by (1.9), (1.16), and (1.23),

$$\varphi_j\left(u_k^n\right) = 0, \text{ for all } n \in \mathbb{N}.$$

Therefore, formula (1.26) holds. □

Motivated by (1.26), we define a linear morphism,

$$E_{j,Q} : \mathfrak{L}_Q \to \mathfrak{L}_Q$$

by a bounded linear transformation satisfying

$$E_{j,Q}\left(u_i^n\right) \overset{def}{=} \begin{cases} \frac{\psi(q_j)^{n-1}}{([\frac{n}{2}]+1)}\, u_j^n & \text{if } i = j \\ 0_{\mathfrak{L}_Q}, \text{ the zero operator of } \mathfrak{L}_Q & \text{otherwise,} \end{cases} \tag{1.27}$$

for all $n \in \mathbb{N}$, $i,\ j \in \mathbb{Z}$, where $[\frac{n}{2}]$ mean the *minimal integers* greater than or equal to $\frac{n}{2}$, e.g.,

$$[\tfrac{3}{2}] = 2 = [\tfrac{4}{2}].$$

The linear transformations $E_{j,Q}$ of (1.27) are the well-defined bounded linear transformations on $\mathfrak{L}_Q$, because of the cyclicity (1.12) of the tensor factor $\mathfrak{L}$ of $\mathfrak{L}_Q$, and the structure theorem (1.8) of the other tensor factor Q of $\mathfrak{L}_Q$, for all $j \in \mathbb{Z}$.

Define now the new linear functionals τ_j on $\mathfrak{L}_Q$ by

$$\tau_j \overset{def}{=} \varphi_j \circ E_{j,Q} \text{ on } \mathfrak{L}_Q, \text{ for all } j \in \mathbb{Z}, \tag{1.28}$$

where φ_j are in the sense of (1.16), and $E_{j,Q}$ are in the sense of (1.27).

Definition 1.7. *The Banach $*$-probability spaces*

$$\mathfrak{L}_Q(j) \overset{denote}{=} (\mathfrak{L}_Q,\ \tau_j) \tag{1.29}$$

are called the j-th filtered (Banach-$*$-probability) spaces of $\mathfrak{L}_Q$, where τ_j are the linear functionals (1.28) on the radial projection algebra $\mathfrak{L}_Q$, for all $j \in \mathbb{Z}$.

On the j-th filtered space $\mathfrak{L}_Q(j)$ of (1.29), one can get that

$$\begin{aligned}\tau_j\left(u_j^n\right) &= \varphi_j\left(E_{j,Q}\left(u_j^n\right)\right)\\ &= \varphi_j\left(\frac{\psi(q_j)^{n-1}}{\left([\frac{n}{2}]+1\right)}\left(u_j^n\right)\right) = \frac{\psi(q_j)^{n-1}}{\left([\frac{n}{2}]+1\right)}\varphi_j\left(u_j^n\right)\\ &= \frac{\psi(q_j)^{n-1}}{\left([\frac{n}{2}]+1\right)}\omega_n\left(\left(\tfrac{n}{2}+1\right)\psi(q_j)\right)c_{\frac{n}{2}},\end{aligned}$$

by (1.26), i.e.,

$$\tau_j\left(u_j^n\right) = \omega_n\psi(q_j)^n c_{\frac{n}{2}}, \tag{1.30}$$

for all $n \in \mathbb{N}$, for $j \in \mathbb{Z}$, where ω_n are in the sense of (1.3).

Lemma 1.1. *Let $\mathfrak{L}_Q(j) = (\mathfrak{L}_Q, \tau_j)$ be the j-th filtered space of $\mathfrak{L}_Q$, for $j \in \mathbb{Z}$. Then*

$$\tau_j\left(u_i^n\right) = \delta_{j,i}\left(\omega_n\psi(q_j)^n c_{\frac{n}{2}}\right), \tag{1.31}$$

for all $n \in \mathbb{N}$, for all $i \in \mathbb{Z}$.

Proof. If $i = j$ in $\mathbb{Z}$, then formula (1.31) holds by (1.30), for all $n \in \mathbb{N}$. If $i \neq j$ in $\mathbb{Z}$, then, by (1.16) and (1.27),

$$\tau_j\left(u_i^n\right) = 0, \text{ for all } n \in \mathbb{N}.$$

Therefore, the free-distributional data (1.31) holds true for all $i \in \mathbb{Z}$. □

The following theorem is proven by the aforementioned free-distributional data (1.31).

Theorem 1.1. *Let $\mathfrak{L}_Q(j)$ be the j-th filtered space $(\mathfrak{L}_Q, \tau_j)$ of $\mathfrak{L}_Q$ for $j \in \mathbb{Z}$. Then, the "j-th" generating operator u_j is $\psi(q_j)^2$-semicircular in $\mathfrak{L}_Q(j)$. Meanwhile, for all $i \neq j \in \mathbb{Z}$, the i-th generating operators u_i of $\mathfrak{L}_Q$ have the zero free distribution.*

Proof. First of all, the generating operators u_i are self-adjoint in $\mathfrak{L}_Q$, for all $i \in \mathbb{Z}$, since

$$u_i^* = (\mathbf{1}\otimes q_i)^* = \mathbf{1}\otimes q_i = u_i \text{ in } \mathfrak{L}_Q,$$

for all $i \in \mathbb{Z}$, by (1.13).

Let's fix $j \in \mathbb{Z}$, and let $u_j = \mathbf{1}\otimes q_j$ be the j-th generating operator (1.15) of $\mathfrak{L}_Q(j)$. Then, by (1.31), we have that

$$\tau_j\left(u_j^n\right) = \omega_n\left(\psi(q_j)^2\right)^{\frac{n}{2}} c_{\frac{n}{2}},$$

for all $n \in \mathbb{N}$, where c_k are the k-th Catalan numbers, for all $k \in \mathbb{N}_0$. Therefore, this self-adjoint element u_j is $\psi(q_j)^2$-semicircular in $\mathfrak{L}_Q(j)$, by (1.3).

Consider now the i-th generating operators u_i of $\mathfrak{L}_Q(j)$, for any $i \neq j$ in $\mathbb{Z}$. Since u_i are self-adjoint in $\mathfrak{L}_Q$, the free distributions of u_i are completely characterized by the free-moment sequences,

$$\left(\tau_j(u_i^n)\right)_{n=1}^{\infty} = (0,\ 0,\ 0,\ ...),$$

the zero sequence, by (1.31). So the free distributions of $u_i \in \mathfrak{L}_Q(j)$ are the zero free distribution, whenever $i \neq j$ in $\mathbb{Z}$. □

The above theorem characterizes the free-probabilistic information of the generators $\{u_i\}_{i\in\mathbb{Z}}$ in the j-th filtered space $\mathfrak{L}_Q(j)$, for $j \in \mathbb{Z}$.

Note that, by the Möbius inversion of [17], if u_i are the i-th generating operators of the j-th filtered space $\mathfrak{L}_Q(j)$, then

$$k_n^j(u_i,\ ...,\ u_i) = \begin{cases} \delta_{j,i}\psi(q_j)^2 & \text{if } n = 2 \\ 0 & \text{otherwise,} \end{cases} \tag{1.32}$$

for all $n \in \mathbb{N}$, and $i \in \mathbb{Z}$, by (1.31), where $k_\bullet^j(...)$ is the free cumulant on $\mathfrak{L}_Q$ with respect to the linear functional τ_j, for $j \in \mathbb{Z}$.

1.5 SEMICIRCULAR ELEMENTS INDUCED BY Q

As in Section 1.4, let $\mathfrak{L}_Q(j)$ be the j-th filtered space (1.29) of Q for $j \in \mathbb{Z}$. Then, the j-th generating operator u_j is $\psi(q_j)^2$-semicircular in $\mathfrak{L}_Q(j)$, satisfying that

$$\tau_j\left(u_j^n\right) = \omega_n \psi(q_j)^n c_{\frac{n}{2}},$$

equivalently, (1.33)

$$k_n^j(u_j,\ ...,\ u_j) = \begin{cases} \psi(q_j)^2 & \text{if } n = 2 \\ 0 & \text{otherwise,} \end{cases}$$

for all $n \in \mathbb{N}$, by (1.31) and (1.32).

By the weighted-semicircularity (1.33), one may/can obtain the following semicircular element U_j of $\mathfrak{L}_Q(j)$ (under an additional condition),

$$U_j \overset{def}{=} \frac{1}{\psi(q_j)}\, u_j \in \mathfrak{L}_Q(j), \tag{1.34}$$

for $j \in \mathbb{Z}$. Recall that we assumed $\psi(q_k) \in \mathbb{C}^\times$, for all $k \in \mathbb{Z}$, and hence, the above operator U_j of (1.34) is well defined in $\mathfrak{L}_Q(j)$.

Theorem 1.2. *Let $U_j = \frac{1}{\psi(q_j)}\, u_j$ be a free random variable (1.34) of $\mathfrak{L}_Q(j)$, for $j \in \mathbb{Z}$, where u_j is the j-th generating operator of $\mathfrak{L}_Q$. If*

$$\psi(q_j) \in \mathbb{R}^\times = \mathbb{R} \setminus \{0\} \text{ in } \mathbb{C}^\times,$$

then U_j is semicircular in $\mathfrak{L}_Q(j)$.

Proof. Fix $j \in \mathbb{Z}$, and assume $\psi(q_j) \in \mathbb{R}^{\times}$ in $\mathbb{C}^{\times}$. Then,

$$U_j^* = \left(\frac{1}{\psi(q_j)} u_j\right)^* = U_j,$$

by the self-adjointness of u_j in $\mathfrak{L}_Q$. Observe that

$$\begin{aligned} \tau_j\left(U_j^n\right) &= \left(\frac{1}{\psi(q_j)}\right)^n \tau_j\left(u_j^n\right) \\ &= \left(\frac{1}{\psi(q_j)^n}\right)\left(\omega_n \psi(q_j)^n c_{\frac{n}{2}}\right) = \omega_n c_{\frac{n}{2}}, \end{aligned} \tag{1.35}$$

for all $n \in \mathbb{N}$. So this operator U_j is semicircular in $\mathfrak{L}_Q(j)$, whenever $\psi(q_j) \in \mathbb{R}^{\times}$, by (1.35) and (1.4). □

Assumption 1.1 (in short, **A 1.1**, from below) We further assume that

$$\psi(q_j) \in \mathbb{R}^{\times} \text{ in } \mathbb{C}, \text{ for } q_j \in \mathbf{Q},$$

for all $j \in \mathbb{Z}$. □

1.6 THE SEMICIRCULAR FILTERIZATION ($\mathbb{L}_Q$, τ)

Let (A, ψ) be a fixed C^*-probability space containing a family $\mathbf{Q} = \{q_k\}_{k \in \mathbb{Z}}$ of mutually orthogonal projections satisfying

$$\psi(q_k) \in \mathbb{R}^{\times}, \text{ for all } k \in \mathbb{Z},$$

(under **A 1.1**). For the system

$$\{\mathfrak{L}_Q(j) : j \in \mathbb{Z}\}$$

of j-th filtered spaces (1.29), define the *free product Banach $*$-probability space* $\mathfrak{L}_Q(\mathbb{Z})$ by

$$\begin{aligned} \mathfrak{L}_Q(\mathbb{Z}) &\overset{denote}{=} (\mathfrak{L}_Q(\mathbb{Z}), \tau) \\ &\overset{def}{=} \underset{j \in \mathbb{Z}}{\star} \mathfrak{L}_Q(j) = \left(\underset{j \in \mathbb{Z}}{\star} \mathfrak{L}_{Q,j}, \underset{j \in \mathbb{Z}}{\star} \tau_j\right). \end{aligned} \tag{1.36}$$

That is, our j-th filtered spaces $\mathfrak{L}_Q(j)$ form the *free blocks of* $\mathfrak{L}_Q(\mathbb{Z})$, for all $j \in \mathbb{Z}$ (e.g., [17] and [30]).

Definition 1.8. *Let $\mathfrak{L}_Q(\mathbb{Z})$ be the free product Banach $*$-probability space (1.36) of the filtered spaces $\{\mathfrak{L}_Q(j)\}_{j \in \mathbb{Z}}$. Then, it is said to be the free filterization of Q.*

Now, construct two subsets $\mathcal{X}$ and $\mathcal{S}$ of $\mathfrak{L}_Q(\mathbb{Z})$,

$$\mathcal{X} = \{u_j \in \mathfrak{L}_Q(j) : j \in \mathbb{Z}\},$$

and (1.37)

$$\mathcal{S} = \{U_j \in \mathfrak{L}_Q(j) : j \in \mathbb{Z}\},$$

where u_j are the j-th generating operators (1.15) of $\mathfrak{L}_Q(j)$, and $U_j = \frac{1}{\psi(q_j)}u_j$ are the operators (1.34) in $\mathfrak{L}_Q(j)$ (under **A 1.1**), for all $j \in \mathbb{Z}$.

Recall that a subset $\mathcal{Y}$ of an arbitrary topological $*$-probability space (B, φ) is said to be a *free family* if all elements of $\mathcal{Y}$ are mutually free from each other in (B, φ). Also, a free family $\mathcal{Y}$ is called a *free (weighted-)semicircular family* in (B, φ) if this family $\mathcal{Y}$ is not only a free family in (B, φ), but also a subset of B whose elements are (weighted-)semicircular in (B, φ). (e.g., [6] and [30]).

Theorem 1.3. *Let $\mathcal{X}$ and $\mathcal{S}$ be the subsets (1.37) of the free filterization $\mathfrak{L}_Q(\mathbb{Z})$.*
(1.38) The family $\mathcal{X}$ is a free weighted-semicircular family in $\mathfrak{L}_Q(\mathbb{Z})$.
(1.39) The family $\mathcal{S}$ is a free semicircular family in $\mathfrak{L}_Q(\mathbb{Z})$.

Proof. Let $\mathcal{X}$ be in the sense of (1.37) in $\mathfrak{L}_Q(\mathbb{Z})$. All elements u_j of $\mathcal{X}$ are taken from mutually distinct free blocks $\mathfrak{L}_Q(j)$ of $\mathfrak{L}_Q(\mathbb{Z})$, for all $j \in \mathbb{Z}$, and hence, they are free from each other in $\mathfrak{L}_Q(\mathbb{Z})$. Thus, this family $\mathcal{X}$ is a free family in $\mathfrak{L}_Q(\mathbb{Z})$. Moreover, the n-th powers u_j^n of $u_j \in \mathcal{X}$ are again contained in the free block $\mathfrak{L}_Q(j)$ as free reduced words with their lengths-1, for all $n \in \mathbb{N}$ and for $j \in \mathbb{Z}$. Thus,

$$\tau\left(u_j^n\right) = \tau_j\left(u_j^n\right) = \omega_n \psi(q_j)^n c_{\frac{n}{2}},$$

by (1.33), for all $n \in \mathbb{N}$ and for all $j \in \mathbb{Z}$. It shows every element $u_j \in \mathcal{X}$ is $\psi(q_j)^2$-semicircular in $\mathfrak{L}_Q(\mathbb{Z})$, for all $j \in \mathbb{Z}$. Therefore, the family $\mathcal{X}$ is a free weighted-semicircular family in $\mathfrak{L}_Q(\mathbb{Z})$. Equivalently, statement (1.38) holds.

Similarly, one can verify that the family $\mathcal{S}$ of (1.37) is a free semicircular family in $\mathfrak{L}_Q(\mathbb{Z})$ (under **A 1.1**). That is, statement (1.39) holds. □

By (1.31), (1.32), (1.36), (1.38), and (1.39), the only "j-th" generating operators u_j of the free blocks $\mathfrak{L}_Q(j)$ provide possible nonzero free distributions on $\mathfrak{L}_Q(\mathbb{Z})$. More precisely, all free reduced words of $\mathfrak{L}_Q(\mathbb{Z})$ in

$$\bigcup_{j \in \mathbb{Z}} \{u_i \in \mathfrak{L}_Q(j) : i \in \mathbb{Z}\},$$

are the free reduced words in $\mathcal{X}$, having their nonzero free distributions in $\mathfrak{L}_Q(\mathbb{Z})$. So we now restrict our interests to the Banach $*$-subalgebra $\mathbb{L}_Q$ of the free filterization $\mathfrak{L}_Q(\mathbb{Z})$, whose elements have possible nonzero free distributions in $\mathfrak{L}_Q(\mathbb{Z})$.

Definition 1.9. *Let $\mathfrak{L}_Q(\mathbb{Z})$ be the free filterization of Q. Define a Banach $*$-subalgebra $\mathbb{L}_Q$ of $\mathfrak{L}_Q(\mathbb{Z})$ by*

$$\mathbb{L}_Q \overset{def}{=} \overline{\mathbb{C}[\mathcal{X}]}, \tag{1.40}$$

where $\mathcal{X}$ is the free weighted-semicircular family (1.38) in $\mathfrak{L}_Q(\mathbb{Z})$, and $\overline{Y}$ are the Banach-topology closures of subsets Y of $\mathfrak{L}_Q(\mathbb{Z})$. Construct the Banach $*$-probability space,

$$\mathbb{L}_Q \overset{denote}{=} \left(\mathbb{L}_Q,\ \tau = \tau\,|_{\mathbb{L}_Q}\right), \tag{1.41}$$

as a free-probabilistic substructure of $\mathfrak{L}_Q(\mathbb{Z}) = (\mathfrak{L}_Q(\mathbb{Z}),\ \tau)$.

We call the Banach $*$-algebra $\mathbb{L}_Q$ of (1.40), or the Banach $*$-probability space $\mathbb{L}_Q$ of (1.41), the semicircular (free-sub-)filterization of $\mathfrak{L}_Q(\mathbb{Z})$.

The semicircular filterization $\mathbb{L}_Q$ satisfies the following structure theorem.

Theorem 1.4. *Let $\mathbb{L}_Q$ be the semicircular filterization (1.40) of $\mathfrak{L}_Q(\mathbb{Z})$. Then,*

$$\begin{aligned} \mathbb{L}_Q &\overset{def}{=} \overline{\mathbb{C}[\mathcal{X}]} = \overline{\mathbb{C}[\mathcal{S}]} \\ &\overset{*\text{-}iso}{=} \underset{j\in\mathbb{Z}}{\star}\, \overline{\mathbb{C}[\{u_j\}]} \overset{*\text{-}iso}{=} \overline{\mathbb{C}\left[\underset{j\in\mathbb{Z}}{\star}\{u_j\}\right]}, \end{aligned} \tag{1.42}$$

in $\mathfrak{L}_Q(\mathbb{Z})$, where "$\overset{*\text{-}iso}{=}$" means "being Banach-$*$-isomorphic," and where ($\star$) in the first $*$-isomorphic relation of (1.42) is the free-probabilistic free product of [17,30], and ($\star$) in the second $*$-isomorphic relation of (1.42) is the pure-algebraic free product inducing noncommutative free words in $\mathcal{X}$.

Proof. The free weighted-semicircular family $\mathcal{X}$ of (1.38) can be rewritten as

$$\mathcal{X} = \{\psi(q_j)U_j \in \mathfrak{L}_Q(j) : U_j \in \mathcal{S}\}$$

in the free filterization $\mathfrak{L}_Q(\mathbb{Z})$ of Q, where $\mathcal{S}$ is the free semicircular family (1.39). Therefore,

$$\overline{\mathbb{C}[\mathcal{X}]} = \overline{\mathbb{C}[\mathcal{S}]} \text{ in } \mathfrak{L}_Q(\mathbb{Z}),$$

by (1.40). It shows that the set equality (=) of (1.42) holds.

By definition (1.40) of $\mathbb{L}_Q$, it is generated by the free family $\mathcal{X}$ by (1.38), and hence, the first $*$-isomorphic relation of (1.42) holds in the free filterization $\mathfrak{L}_Q(\mathbb{Z})$ by (1.36), because

$$\overline{\mathbb{C}[\{u_j\}]} \subset \mathfrak{L}_Q(j) \text{ in } \mathfrak{L}_Q(\mathbb{Z}), \text{ for all } j \in \mathbb{Z}.$$

Since

$$\mathbb{L}_Q \overset{*\text{-iso}}{=} \underset{j\in\mathbb{Z}}{\star}\, \overline{\mathbb{C}[\{u_j\}]} \text{ in } \mathfrak{L}_Q(\mathbb{Z}),$$

every element T of $\mathbb{L}_Q$ is a limit of linear combinations of free reduced words in $\mathcal{X}$. Also, all (pure-algebraic) free words in $\mathcal{X}$ have their unique free-reduced-word forms under operator-multiplication on $\mathfrak{L}_Q(\mathbb{Z})$. Therefore, the second $*$-isomorphic relation of (1.42) holds, too. □

1.7 FREE POISSON ELEMENTS OF $\mathbb{L}_Q$

Let (A, ψ) be a fixed C^*-probability space, containing a family $\mathbf{Q} = \{q_j\}_{j \in \mathbb{Z}}$ of mutually orthogonal projections, and let $\mathbb{L}_Q$ be the semicircular filterization (1.41) of the free filterization $\mathfrak{L}_Q(\mathbb{Z})$ of the C^*-subalgebra $Q = C^*(\mathbf{Q})$ of A. Throughout this section, we also assume **A 1.1**, and hence, the family $\mathcal{S}$ of (1.37) is a well-determined free semicircular family in $\mathfrak{L}_Q(\mathbb{Z})$, generating $\mathbb{L}_Q$ by (1.39) and (1.42). From the generating free family $\mathcal{S}$ of $\mathbb{L}_Q$, we here study free Poisson elements.

1.7.1 FREE POISSON ELEMENTS

Let (B, φ) be a topological $*$-probability space. If $x \in (B, \varphi)$ is a free random variable, then the free distribution of x is characterized by the *joint free moments of* $\{x, x^*\}$,

$$\varphi\left(x^{r_1} x^{r_2} ... x^{r_n}\right),$$

or, by the *joint free cumulants of* $\{x, x^*\}$,

$$k_n^B\left(x^{r_1}, x^{r_2}, ..., x^{r_n}\right),$$

for all $(r_1, ..., r_n) \in \{1, *\}^n$, and for all $n \in \mathbb{N}$, where $k_n^B(..)$ is the free cumulant on B in terms of φ under the Möbius inversion of [17,22,23]. And they provide equivalent free-distributional data of $x \in (B, \varphi)$, representing its free distribution.

Thus, if x is a self-adjoint free random variable of (B, φ_B), satisfying $x = x^*$ in B, then the free distribution of x is characterized by the free-moment sequence

$$(\varphi(x^n))_{n=1}^{\infty} = \left(\varphi(x), \varphi(x^2), \varphi(x^3), ...\right),$$

or, by the free-cumulant sequence

$$\left(k_n^B(x, ..., x)\right)_{n=1}^{\infty} = \left(k_1^B(x) = \varphi(x), k_2^B(x, x), ...\right).$$

For example, every semicircular element $s \in (B, \varphi)$ has its free distribution, the semicircular law, characterized by the free-moment sequence

$$(0, c_1, 0, c_2, 0, c_3, ...),$$

or, by the free-cumulant sequence

$$(0, 1, 0, 0, 0, ...),$$

where c_k are the k-th Catalan numbers for all $k \in \mathbb{N}$.

Notation From below, we will write " a free random variable $x \in (B, \varphi)$ has its free distribution $(\varphi(x^n))_{n=1}^{\infty}$," and equivalently, "$x \in (B, \varphi)$ has its free distribution $\left(k_n^B(x, ..., x)\right)_{n=1}^{\infty}$," if (i) x is self-adjoint in B and (ii) the free distribution of x is characterized by

$$(\varphi(x^n))_{n=1}^{\infty}, \text{ or, } \left(k_n^B(x,...,x)\right)_{n=1}^{\infty}.$$

□

Definition 1.10. *Let $s \in (B, \varphi)$ be a semicircular element, and let a be a self-adjoint free random variable of (B, φ), having its free distribution $(\varphi(a^n))_{n=1}^{\infty}$. Assume that a and s are free in (B, φ). Then, a new free random variable*

$$W_s^a = sas \in (B, \varphi) \quad (1.43)$$

is called the free Poisson element generated by s and a.

By definition (1.43), a free Poisson element W_s^a is a free reduced word with its length-3 in (B, φ). Also, by (1.43),

$$(W_s^a)^* = (sas)^* = s^*a^*s^* = sas = W_s^a \quad (1.44)$$

in B, and hence, it is a self-adjoint free random variable of (B, φ), too.

Let $\Omega = \{e_1, ..., e_n\}$ be a finite set with its cardinality $n \in \mathbb{N}$. Then, the *lattice* $NC(\Omega)$ *of noncrossing partitions of* Ω is well defined with its partial ordering $\leq$,

$$\theta_1 \leq \theta_2 \Longleftrightarrow \forall V_1 \in \theta_1, \exists V_2 \in \theta_2, \text{ s.t., } V_1 \subseteq V_2,$$

where $\subseteq$ is the usual set inclusion, where "$V \in \theta$" means "V is a block of θ."

For example, if $\Omega_5 = \{1, 2, ..., 5\}$, and if

$$\theta_1 = \{(1, 4), (2, 3), (5)\},$$

and

$$\theta_2 = \{(1, 2, 3, 4), (5)\}$$

in $NC(\Omega_5)$, then $\theta_1 \leq \theta_2$.

Notation From below, if a given finite set Ω is a subset $\{1, 2, ..., n\}$ of $\mathbb{N}$, for some $n \in \mathbb{N}$, then we denote Ω by Ω_n. □

Under ($\leq$), the lattice $NC(\Omega)$ has its maximal element,

$$1_\Omega = \{(e_1, ..., e_n)\}, \text{ the 1-block partition,}$$

and its minimal element,

$$0_\Omega = \{(e_1), (e_2), ..., (e_n)\}, \text{ the } n\text{-block partition.}$$

Suppose

$$\Omega = \Omega^1 \sqcup \Omega^2, \text{ with } \Omega^l \subset \Omega, \forall l = 1, 2.$$

where $\sqcup$ is the disjoint union, and let $NC\left(\Omega^l\right)$ be the noncrossing partition lattices for Ω^l, for $l = 1, 2$.

Then, for $\theta_l \in NC(\Omega^l)$, for $l = 1, 2$, one can construct a noncrossing partition $\theta \in NC(\Omega)$ as the join of θ_1 and θ_2,

$$\theta = \theta_1 \vee \theta_2 \in NC(\Omega),$$

as in [17,22,23]. For example, if

$$\theta_1 = \{(2, 5), (3)\} \in NC(\{2, 3, 5\}),$$

and

$$\theta_2 = \{(4), (1, 6, 7)\} \in NC(\{1, 4, 6, 7\}),$$

then, we obtain

$$\theta_1 \vee \theta_2 = \{(1,6,7), (2, 5), (3), (4)\},$$

in $NC\left(\Omega_7\right)$.

Now, fix $n \in \mathbb{N}$, and let $NC(\Omega_{3n})$ be the noncrossing partition lattice, and let

$$\Omega_{3n}^1 = \{1, 3, 4, 6, 7, 9, 10, ..., 3n-3, 3n-2, 3n\},$$

and (1.45)

$$\Omega_{3n}^2 = \Omega_{3n} \setminus \Omega_{3n}^1 = \{2, 5, 8, 11, ..., 3n-1\},$$

satisfying

$$\Omega_{3n} = \Omega_{3n}^1 \sqcup \Omega_{3n}^2.$$

And then take $\theta_o \in NC\left(\Omega_{3n}^1\right)$,

$$\theta_o = \{(1, 3n), (3,4), (6,7), ..., (3n-3, 3n-2)\}, \tag{1.46}$$

where Ω_{3n}^1 is in the sense of (1.45).

The following lemma is already shown (e.g., in the page 207 of [17]), but we provide a sketch of the proof for our future works.

Lemma 1.2. *Let $a \in (B, \varphi)$ be a self-adjoint free random variable having its free distribution $(\varphi(a^n))_{n=1}^{\infty}$, and let $s \in (B, \varphi)$ be a semicircular element, free from a in (B, φ). If $W_s^a = sas$ is a free Poisson element (1.43), then*

$$k_n^B\left(\underbrace{W_s^a, W_s^a, ..., W_s^a}_{n\text{-times}}\right) = \varphi(a^n), \tag{1.47}$$

for all $n \in \mathbb{N}$.

Proof. By the semicircularity (1.2) of s,

$$k_n^B(s, ..., s) = \begin{cases} 1 & \text{if } n = 2 \\ 0 & \text{otherwise,} \end{cases} \tag{1.48}$$

for all $n \in \mathbb{N}$. So,

$$k_n^B(W_s^a, ..., W_s^a) = k_n^B(sas,\ sas,\ ...,\ sas)$$

$$= \sum_{\theta \in NC(\Omega_{3n}^2),\ \theta \vee \pi_0 \leq 1_{3n}} k_\theta^B(sas,\ ...,\ sas)$$

where Ω_{3n}^2 is the set (1.45), and $k_\theta^B(...)$ are the block-depending free cumulants of [27], and 1_{3n} is the maximal 1-block partition of $NC(\Omega_{3n})$, and

$$\pi_0 = \{(1, 2, 3), (4, 5, 6), ..., (3n-2, 3n-1, 3n)\}$$

(see [17,22] and [23] for details), and hence, it goes to

$$= \sum_{\theta \in NC(\Omega_{3n}^2),\ \theta_o \vee \theta \in NC(\Omega_{3n})} k_{\theta_o \vee \theta}^B(sas,\ ...,\ sas)$$

by (1.48), where Ω_{3n}^2 is in the sense of (1.45), and θ_o is the partition (1.46)

$$= \sum_{\theta \in NC(\Omega_{3n}^2)} k_{\theta_o}^B\left(\underbrace{s,\ s,\ s,\ ...,\ s}_{2n\text{-times}}\right) k_\theta^B\left(\underbrace{a,\ a,\ ...,\ a}_{n\text{-times}}\right)$$

since all "mixed" free cumulants of s and a vanish by the freeness of s and a

$$= \sum_{\theta \in NC(\Omega_{3n}^2)} \left((k_2^B(s,\ s))^n\right) k_\theta^B\left(\underbrace{a,\ a,\ ...,\ a}_{n\text{-times}}\right)$$

$$= \sum_{\theta \in NC(\Omega_{3n}^2)} k_\theta^B\left(\underbrace{a,\ a,\ ...,\ a}_{n\text{-times}}\right)$$

by (1.2)

$$= \sum_{\pi \in NC(\Omega_n)} k_\pi^B(a,\ ...,\ a)$$

since the sublattice $NC\left(\Omega_{3n}^2\right)$ of $NC(\Omega_{3n})$ is equivalent to the lattice $NC(\Omega_n)$

$$= \varphi(a^n)$$

by the Möbius inversion of [17], for all $n \in \mathbb{N}$. Therefore, the free-distributional data (1.47) is obtained. □

The free-cumulant formula (1.47) shows that a *free Poisson distribution*, and the free distribution of a free Poisson element W_s^a, is characterized by the free distribution $(\varphi(a^n))_{n=1}^{\infty}$ of a fixed self-adjoint free random variable $a \in (B, \varphi)$.

Theorem 1.5. *Let $W_s^a = sas \in (B, \varphi)$ be a free Poisson element (1.43). Then,*

$$\varphi((W_s^a)^n) = k_n^B \left(\underbrace{a, a, ..., a}_{n\text{-times}} \right), \tag{1.49}$$

for all $n \in \mathbb{N}$, where $|V|$ are the cardinalities of blocks V.

Proof. Observe that

$$\varphi((W_s^a)^n) = \sum_{\theta \in NC(\Omega_n)} k_\theta^B (W_s^a, ..., W_s^a)$$

by the Möbius inversion

$$= \sum_{\theta \in NC(\Omega_n)} \left(\prod_{V \in \theta} k_{|V|}^B \left(\underbrace{W_s^a, ..., W_s^a}_{|V|\text{-times}} \right) \right)$$

$$= \sum_{\theta \in NC(\Omega_n)} \left(\prod_{V \in \theta} \varphi\left(a^{|V|}\right) \right)$$

by (1.47)

$$= k_n^B(a, ..., a),$$

by the Möbius inversion, for all $n \in \mathbb{N}$. So formula (1.49) holds. □

1.7.2 CERTAIN FREE POISSON ELEMENTS INDUCED BY $\mathcal{S}$

Let $\mathbb{L}_Q = (\mathbb{L}_Q, \tau)$ be the semicircular filterization (1.41). In this section, we fix a semicircular element $U_j \in \mathcal{S}$ in $\mathbb{L}_Q$, for a fixed $j \in \mathbb{Z}$. By Section 1.7.1, if $T \in \mathbb{L}_Q$ is a self-adjoint operator, and if T is free from U_j in $\mathbb{L}_Q$, then one obtains the corresponding free Poisson element

$$W_j^T = U_j T U_j \text{ in } \mathbb{L}_Q,$$

satisfying that

$$k_n\left(W_j^T, ..., W_j^T\right) = \tau(T^n),$$

and (1.50)

$$\tau\left(\left(W_j^T\right)^n\right) = k_n(T, ..., T),$$

by (1.47) and (1.49), for all $n \in \mathbb{N}$, where $k_{\bullet}(...)$ is the free cumulant on $\mathbb{L}_Q$ in terms of the linear functional τ of (1.41).

Define free Poisson elements $W_j^k = W_j^{U_k}$ of (1.50) by

$$W_j^k \overset{def}{=} U_j U_k U_j \in \mathbb{L}_Q, \tag{1.51}$$

where $j \neq k$ in $\mathbb{Z}$. Then, one has that

$$k_n\left(W_j^k, ..., W_j^k\right) = \tau\left(U_k^n\right) = \omega_n c_{\frac{n}{2}},$$

and (1.52)

$$\tau\left(\left(W_j^k\right)^n\right) = k_n\left(U_k, ..., U_k\right) = \delta_{n,2}$$

by (1.50) and (1.2), for all $n \in \mathbb{N}$, where δ is the Kronecker delta.

More generally, for $k \neq j \in \mathbb{Z}$, define a free Poisson element,

$$W_j^{k,N} = U_j U_k^N U_j \in \mathbb{L}_Q, \text{ for } N \in \mathbb{N}. \tag{1.53}$$

Theorem 1.6. *Let $W_j^{k,N}$ be a free Poisson element (1.53) for $N \in \mathbb{N}$. Then,*

$$k_n\left(W_j^{k,N}, ..., W_j^{k,N}\right) = \omega_{nN} c_{\frac{nN}{2}},$$

and *(1.54)*

$$\tau\left(\left(W_j^{k,N}\right)^n\right) = \begin{cases} \sum\limits_{\pi \in NC(\Omega_n)} \left(\prod\limits_{B \in \theta} c_{\frac{N|B|}{2}}\right) & \text{if } N \text{ is even} \\ \omega_n\left(\sum\limits_{\theta \in NC_e(\Omega_n)} \left(\prod\limits_{V \in \theta} c_{\frac{N|V|}{2}}\right)\right) & \text{if } N \text{ is odd,} \end{cases}$$

for all $n \in \mathbb{N}$, where

$$NC_e(\Omega_n) = \{\pi \in NC(\Omega_n) : |V| \text{ is even}, \forall V \in \pi\}.$$

Proof. Observe first that

$$k_n\left(W_j^{k,N}, ..., W_j^{k,N}\right) = \tau\left(\left(U_k^N\right)^n\right) = \tau\left(U_k^{nN}\right) = \omega_{nN} c_{\frac{nN}{2}},$$

by (1.47), for all $n \in \mathbb{N}$. Thus, the free-cumulant formula of (1.54) holds.

Consider now that

$$\tau\left(\left(W_j^{k,N}\right)^n\right) = k_n\left(U^N, ..., U^N\right)$$

by (1.50)

$$= \sum_{\pi \in NC(\Omega_n)} \left(\prod_{V \in \pi} \left(\tau \left(U_k^{N|V|} \right) \right) \right)$$

by the Möbius inversion

$$= \sum_{\pi \in NC(\Omega_n)} \left(\prod_{V \in \pi} \left(\omega_{N|V|} c_{\frac{N|V|}{2}} \right) \right)$$

by the semicircularity (1.4) of $U_k \in \mathcal{S}$ in $\mathbb{L}_Q$

$$= \begin{cases} \sum_{\pi \in NC(\Omega_n)} \left(\prod_{B \in \theta} c_{\frac{N|B|}{2}} \right) & \text{if } N \text{ is even} \\ \omega_n \left(\sum_{\theta \in NC_e(\Omega_n)} \left(\prod_{V \in \theta} c_{\frac{N|V|}{2}} \right) \right) & \text{if } N \text{ is odd,} \end{cases}$$

because

if N is even, then lN is even for all $l \in \mathbb{N}$,

respectively,

if N is odd, then lN is even if and only if l is even in $\mathbb{N}$.

Therefore, the free-moment formula of (1.54) holds true. □

Trivially, if $N = 1$ in (1.54), then relation (1.52) is automatically obtained.

1.7.3 SOME FREE POISSON ELEMENTS INDUCED BY $\mathcal{S} \cup \mathcal{X}$

As in Section 1.7.2, let's fix a semicircular element $U_j \in \mathcal{S}$, and let $\mathcal{X}$ be the free weighted-semicircular family (1.38) in the semicircular filterization $\mathbb{L}_Q$. For any $k \neq j$ in $\mathbb{Z}$, we have the corresponding free Poisson elements

$$Y_j^{k,N} = U_j u_k^N U_j \text{ in } \mathbb{L}_Q, \tag{1.55}$$

where $u_k \in \mathcal{X}$ is a $\psi(q_j)^2$-semicircular element of $\mathbb{L}_Q$, for all $N \in \mathbb{N}$.

Since

$$u_k = \psi(q_k) U_k \in \mathcal{X}, \text{ in } \mathbb{L}_Q, \tag{1.56}$$

by (1.55)

$$Y_j^{k,N} = \psi(q_k)^N U_j U_k^N U_{p,j} = \psi(q_k)^N W_j^{k,N}, \tag{1.57}$$

in $\mathbb{L}_Q$, by (1.56), where $W_j^{k,N}$ is the free Poisson element (1.55).

Theorem 1.7. *Let $Y_j^{k,N}$ be a free Poisson element (1.55) in $\mathbb{L}_Q$, for $N \in \mathbb{N}$. Then*

$$k_n \left(Y_j^{k,N}, \ldots, Y_j^{k,N} \right) = \omega_{nN} \psi(q_k)^{nN} c_{\frac{nN}{2}},$$

and *(1.58)*

$$\tau\left(\left(Y_j^{k,N}\right)^n\right) = \begin{cases} \psi(q_k)^{nN}\left(\sum\limits_{\pi\in NC(\Omega_n)}\left(\prod\limits_{B\in\theta} c_{\frac{N|B|}{2}}\right)\right) & \text{if } N \text{ is even} \\ \omega_n\psi(q_k)^{nN}\left(\sum\limits_{\theta\in NC_e(\Omega_n)}\left(\prod\limits_{V\in\theta} c_{\frac{N|V|}{2}}\right)\right) & \text{if } N \text{ is odd,} \end{cases}$$

for all $n \in \mathbb{N}$.

Proof. Consider that

$$k_n\left(Y_j^{k,N}, \ldots, Y_j^{k,N}\right) = k_n\left(\psi(q_k)^N W_j^{k,N}, \ldots, \psi(q_k)^N W_j^{k,N}\right)$$

by (1.57)

$$= \psi(q_k)^{nN} k_n\left(W_j^{k,N}, \ldots, W_j^{k,N}\right)$$

by the bimodule-map property of free cumulants (e.g., [17,22] and [23])

$$= \psi(q_k)^{nN}\, \tau\left(U_k^{nN}\right) = \psi(q_k)^{nN}\left(\omega_{nN} c_{\frac{nN}{2}}\right)$$

$$= \omega_{nN}\psi(q_k)^{nN} c_{\frac{nN}{2}} = \tau\left(u_k^{nN}\right),$$

for all $n \in \mathbb{N}$, by (1.54).

Similarly, for any $n \in \mathbb{N}$, one obtains that

$$\tau\left(\left(Y_j^{k,N}\right)^n\right) = \tau\left(\psi(q_k)^{nN}\left(W_j^{k,N}\right)^n\right)$$

by (1.57)

$$= \psi(q_k)^{nN}\tau\left((W_j^{k,N})^n\right)$$

$$= \begin{cases} \psi(q_k)^{nN}\left(\sum\limits_{\pi\in NC(\Omega_n)}\left(\prod\limits_{B\in\theta} c_{\frac{N|B|}{2}}\right)\right) & \text{if } N \text{ is even} \\ \omega_n\psi(q_k)^{nN}\left(\sum\limits_{\theta\in NC_e(\Omega_n)}\left(\prod\limits_{V\in\theta} c_{\frac{N|V|}{2}}\right)\right) & \text{if } N \text{ is odd,} \end{cases}$$

by (1.54).

Therefore, the free-distributional data (1.58) hold in $\mathbb{L}_Q$. □

The above theorem shows that the free Poisson elements $Y_j^{k,N}$ of (1.55) induced by the free weighted-semicircular family $\mathcal{X}$ of (1.38) have their free Poisson distributions, affected by the weights of fixed weighted-semicircular elements of $\mathcal{X}$ in $\mathbb{L}_Q$.

Corollary 1.1. *Let $Y_j^{k,1} = U_j u_k U_j$ be a free Poisson element (1.55) in $\mathbb{L}_Q$. Then,*

$$k_n\left(Y_j^{k,1}, ..., Y_j^{k,1}\right) = \omega_n \psi(q_k)^n c_{\frac{n}{2}},$$

and *(1.59)*

$$\tau\left(\left(Y_j^{k,1}\right)^n\right) = \delta_{n,2}\psi(q_k)^2,$$

for all $n \in \mathbb{N}$.

Proof. The free-distributional data (1.59) is directly obtained by (1.58), by replacing N to 1. □

1.8 FREE WEIGHTED-POISSON ELEMENTS OF $\mathbb{L}_Q$

In this section, we are interested in free-Poisson-like free random variables in our semicircular filterization $\mathbb{L}_Q$.

1.8.1 FREE WEIGHTED-POISSON ELEMENTS

Let (B, φ) be an arbitrary topological $*$-probability space, and let $x \in (B, \varphi)$ be a t_0-semicircular element for some $t_0 \in \mathbb{C}^\times$, satisfying

$$\varphi(x^n) = \omega_n\, t_0^{\frac{n}{2}} c_{\frac{n}{2}},$$

and (1.60)

$$k_n^B(x, ..., x) = \delta_{n,2} t_0$$

for all $n \in \mathbb{N}$, where $k_n^B(...)$ is the free cumulant on B in terms of φ.

Definition 1.11. *Let $x \in (B, \varphi)$ be a t_0-semicircular element (1.60). Suppose $a \in (B, \varphi)$ is a self-adjoint free random variable, which is free from x in (B, φ). A free random variable*

$$T_x^a = xax \in (B, \varphi) \tag{1.61}$$

is called a free weighted-Poisson element with its weight t_0 (in short, free t_0-Poisson element) of (B, φ).

Let's consider free-distributional data of a free t_0-Poisson element T_x^a of (1.61).

Theorem 1.8. *Let $T_x^a = xax$ be a free t_0-Poisson element (1.61), where x is a fixed t_0-semicircular element (1.60) in (B, φ), and a has its free distribution $(\varphi(a^n))_{n=1}^{\infty}$. Then,*

$$k_n^B\left(\underbrace{T_x^a,\ T_x^a,\ \ldots,\ T_x^a}_{n\text{-times}}\right) = t_0^n\left(\varphi(a^n)\right), \tag{1.62}$$

for all $n \in \mathbb{N}$.

Proof. Observe that

$$k_n^B\left(T_x^a,\ \ldots,\ T_x^a\right) = k_n^B\left(xax,\ xax, \ldots,\ xax\right)$$

$$= \sum_{\theta \in NC(\Omega_{3n}),\ \theta \vee \pi_0 \leq 1_{3n}} k_\theta^B\left(xax,\ \ldots, xax\right)$$

where Ω_{3n} is in the sense of (1.45), and $k_\theta^B(\ldots)$ are the block-depending free cumulants of [17], and

$$\pi_0 = \{(1,\ 2,\ 3),\ (4,\ 5,\ 6),\ \ldots,\ (3n-2,\ 3n-1\ ,3n)\},$$

and hence, it goes to

$$= \sum_{\theta \in NC\left(\Omega_{3n}^2\right),\ \theta_o \vee \theta \in NC(\Omega_{3n})} k_{\theta_o \vee \theta}^B\left(xax,\ \ldots,\ xax\right)$$

by (1.48), where θ_o is in the sense of (1.46)

$$= \sum_{\theta \in NC\left(\Omega_{3n}^2\right)} k_{\theta_o}^B\left(\underbrace{x,\ x,\ x,\ \ldots,\ x}_{2n\text{-times}}\right) k_\theta^B\left(\underbrace{a,\ a,\ \ldots,\ a}_{n\text{-times}}\right)$$

$$= \sum_{\theta \in NC\left(\Omega_{3n}^2\right)} \left(\left(k_2^B(x,\ x)\right)^n\right) k_\theta^B\left(a,\ a,\ \ldots,\ a\right)$$

$$= t_0^n\left(\sum_{\theta \in NC\left(\Omega_{3n}^2\right)} k_\theta^B\left(a,\ a,\ \ldots,\ a\right)\right)$$

by (1.48), because x is a t_0-semicircular element satisfying (1.60)

$$= t_0^n\left(\sum_{\pi \in NC(\Omega_n)} k_\pi^B\left(a,\ \ldots,\ a\right)\right)$$

since the sublattice $NC\left(\Omega_{3n}^2\right)$ of $NC\left(\Omega_{3n}\right)$ is equivalent to the lattice $NC(\Omega_n)$

$$= t_0^n\left(\varphi(a^n)\right),$$

by the Möbius inversion, for all $n \in \mathbb{N}$. Therefore, the free-distributional data (1.62) is obtained. □

The above theorem illustrates that the free distributions of our free weighted-Poisson elements T_x^a of (1.61) are depending not only on the free distributions of a, but also on the weights of fixed weighted-semicircular elements x in (B, φ), by (1.62). By the Möbius inversion, we obtain the following equivalent result.

Theorem 1.9. *Let T_x^a be a free t_0-Poisson element (1.61) in (B, φ). Then,*

$$\varphi\left((T_x^a)^n\right) = t_0^n \left(k_n^B \left(\underbrace{a, a, \ldots\ldots, a}_{n\text{-times}} \right) \right), \tag{1.63}$$

for all $n \in \mathbb{N}$.

Proof. Let $T_x^a \in (B, \varphi)$ be a free t_0-Poisson element (1.61). Then,

$$\varphi\left((T_x^a)^n\right) = \sum_{\pi \in NC(\Omega_n)} \left(\prod_{V \in \pi} k_{|V|}^B \left(T_x^a, \ldots, T_x^a\right) \right)$$

by the Möbius inversion

$$= \sum_{\pi \in NC(\Omega_n)} \left(\prod_{V \in \pi} \left(t_0^{|V|} \varphi\left(a^{|V|}\right) \right) \right)$$

by (1.62)

$$= \sum_{\pi \in NC(\Omega_n)} \left(\prod_{V \in \pi} t_0^{|V|} \right) \left(\prod_{V \in \pi} \varphi\left(a^{|V|}\right) \right)$$

$$= \sum_{\pi \in NC(\Omega_n)} \left(t_0^{\sum_{V \in \pi} |V|} \right) \left(\prod_{V \in \pi} \varphi\left(a^{|V|}\right) \right)$$

$$= \sum_{\pi \in NC(\Omega_n)} \left(t_0^n\right) \left(\prod_{V \in \pi} \varphi\left(a^{|V|}\right) \right)$$

since $\sum_{V \in \pi} |V| = |\Omega_n| = n$, for all $\pi \in NC(\Omega_n)$

$$= \left(t_0^n\right) \left(\sum_{\pi \in NC(\Omega_n)} \left(\prod_{V \in \pi} \varphi\left(a^{|V|}\right) \right) \right),$$

for all $n \in \mathbb{N}$. Therefore, the free-momental data (1.63) is obtained by the Möbius inversion. □

The aforementioned free-distributional data (1.62) and (1.63) provide the following free-distributional information for the free weighted-Poisson elements.

Theorem 1.10. *Let T_x^a be a free t_0-Poisson element (1.61) in (B, φ), and let W_s^a be a free Poisson element (1.43) of (B, φ), where s is an arbitrary semicircular element of (B, φ), which is free from a fixed self-adjoint free random variable a of (B, φ). Then,*

$$k_n^B(T_x^a, ..., T_x^a) = t_0^n k_n^B(W_s^a, ..., W_s^a) = t_0^n \varphi(a^n),$$

and *(1.64)*

$$\varphi((T_x^a)^n) = t_0^n\ \varphi((W_s^a)^n) = t_0^n k_n\left(\underbrace{a, ..., a}_{n\text{-times}}\right),$$

for all $n \in \mathbb{N}$.

Proof. Under hypothesis, one has that

$$k_n^B(T_x^a, ..., T_x^a) = t_0^n\ \varphi(a^n) = t_0^n\ k_n^B(W_s^a, ..., W_s^a),$$

for all $n \in \mathbb{N}$, by (1.47) and (1.62).

Similarly, we have

$$\varphi((T_x^a)^n) = t_0^n\,(k_n(a, ..., a)) = t_0^n\ \varphi((W_s^a)^n),$$

for all $n \in \mathbb{N}$, by (1.49) and (1.63).

Therefore, relation (1.64) holds in (B, φ). □

The above theorem characterizes the difference between the free Poisson distributions and the free weighted-Poisson distributions by (1.64). It also shows how our weights act free-probabilistically.

1.8.2 FREE WEIGHTED-POISSON ELEMENTS INDUCED BY $\mathcal{S} \cup \mathcal{X}$

Let $\mathbb{L}_Q$ be the semicircular filterization, and let $\mathcal{S}$ be the free semicircular family (1.39) in $\mathbb{L}_Q$. Let's fix a $\psi(q_j)^2$-semicircular element $u_j \in \mathcal{X}$ in $\mathbb{L}_Q$, where $\mathcal{X}$ is the free weighted-semicircular family (1.38) of $\mathbb{L}_Q$. Then, as in (1.61), one can define the free $\psi(q_j)^2$-Poisson elements

$$T_j^{k,N} = u_j U_k^N u_j \in \mathbb{L}_Q, \tag{1.65}$$

for $U_k \in \mathcal{S}$, any $N \in \mathbb{N}$, whenever $k \neq j$ in $\mathbb{Z}$.

By (1.62), (1.63), and (1.64), we obtain the following free-distributional data of free $\psi(q_j)^2$-Poisson elements (1.65) in $\mathbb{L}_Q$.

Theorem 1.11. *Let $T_j^{k,N} = u_j U_k^N u_j$ be a free $\psi(q_j)^2$-Poisson element (1.65) in $\mathbb{L}_Q$, for $N \in \mathbb{N}$. If $W_j^{k,N} = U_j U_k^N U_j$ is a free Poisson element (1.53) in $\mathbb{L}_Q$, then*

$$k_n\left(T_j^{k,N}, ..., T_j^{k,N}\right) = \psi(q_j)^{2n} k_n\left(W_j^{l,N}, ..., W_j^{l,N}\right)$$
$$= \psi(q_j)^{2n}\left(\omega_{nN} c_{\frac{nN}{2}}\right),$$

and (1.66)

$$\tau\left(\left(T_j^{k,N}\right)^n\right) = \psi(q_j)^{2n}\tau\left(\left(W_j^{l,N}\right)^n\right)$$
$$= \begin{cases} \psi(q_j)^{2n}\left(\sum_{\pi\in NC(\Omega_n)}\left(\prod_{V\in\pi} c_{\frac{N|V|}{2}}\right)\right) & \text{if } N \text{ is even} \\ \omega_n\psi(q_j)^{2n}\left(\sum_{\theta\in NC_e(\Omega_n)}\left(\prod_{V\in\theta} c_{\frac{N|V|}{2}}\right)\right) & \text{if } N \text{ is odd,} \end{cases}$$

for all $n \in \mathbb{N}$, where $NC_e(\Omega_n)$ are the subsets (1.54) of the lattices $NC(\Omega_n)$.

Proof. The proof of (1.66) is done by (1.54) and (1.64). □

The following corollary is obtained immediately by (1.66).

Corollary 1.2. *Let $T_j^{k,1}$ be a $\psi(q_j)^2$-free Poisson element (1.65) with $N = 1$. Then*

$$k_n\left(T_j^{k,1}, ..., T_j^{k,1}\right) = \omega_n\psi(q_j)^{2n} c_{\frac{n}{2}},$$

and (1.67)

$$\tau\left(\left(T_j^{k,1}\right)^n\right) = \delta_{n,2}\psi(q_j)^2,$$

for all $n \in \mathbb{N}$.

Proof. The free-distributional data (1.67) of $T_j^{k,1}$ holds by (1.52) and (1.66). □

The above corollary shows the connections between our $\psi(q_j)^2$-semicircular laws, and the $\psi(q_j)^2$-free Poisson distributions on $\mathbb{L}_Q$, by (1.67).

1.8.3 FREE WEIGHTED-POISSON ELEMENTS INDUCED BY $\mathcal{X}$

Let $\mathbb{L}_Q$ be the semicircular Adelic filterization, and $\mathcal{X}$, the free weighted-semicircular family (1.38) of $\mathbb{L}_Q$, and let's fix $u_j \in \mathcal{X}$ in $\mathbb{L}_Q$. For any $k \neq j$ in $\mathbb{Z}$, define the corresponding free $\psi(q_j)^2$-Poisson elements

$$X_j^{k,N} = u_j u_k^N u_j \in \mathbb{L}_Q, \tag{1.68}$$

for $N \in \mathbb{N}$.

Since

$$U_j = \frac{1}{\psi(q_j)} u_j \text{ in } \mathcal{S} \Longleftrightarrow u_j = \psi(q_j)U_j \text{ in } \mathcal{X},$$

in $\mathbb{L}_Q$, for all $j \in \mathbb{Z}$, our free $\psi(q_j)^2$-Poisson elements $X_j^{k,N}$ of (1.68) are also understood as

$$\begin{aligned} X_j^{k,N} &= \psi(q_j)^2 \psi(q_k)^N U_j U_k^N U_j \\ &= \left(\psi(q_j)^2 \psi(q_k)^N\right) W_j^{k,N}, \end{aligned} \tag{1.69}$$

in $\mathbb{L}_Q$, where $W_j^{k,N}$ are the free Poisson element (1.53) of $\mathbb{L}_Q$, for all $N \in \mathbb{N}$.

Theorem 1.12. *Let $X_j^{k,N} = u_j u_k^N u_j$ be a free $\psi(q_j)^2$-Poisson element (1.68) of $\mathbb{L}_Q$, for $N \in \mathbb{N}$. Then,*

$$\begin{aligned} k_n\left(X_j^{k,N}, \ldots, X_j^{k,N}\right) &= \beta_n k_n\left(W_j^{l,N}, \ldots, W_j^{l,N}\right) \\ &= \beta_n\left(\omega_{nN} c_{\frac{nN}{2}}\right), \end{aligned}$$

and *(1.70)*

$$\tau\left(\left(X_j^{k,N}\right)^n\right) = \beta_n \tau\left(\left(W_j^{l,N}\right)^n\right)$$

$$= \begin{cases} \beta_n\left(\sum\limits_{\pi \in NC(\Omega_n)}\left(\prod\limits_{V \in \pi} c_{\frac{N|V|}{2}}\right)\right) & \textit{if } N \textit{ is even} \\ \omega_n \beta_n\left(\sum\limits_{\theta \in NC_e(\Omega_n)}\left(\prod\limits_{V \in \theta} c_{\frac{N|V|}{2}}\right)\right) & \textit{if } N \textit{ is odd,} \end{cases}$$

with

$$\beta_n = \left(\psi(q_j)^2 \psi(q_k)^N\right)^n = \psi(q_j)^{2n} \psi(q_k)^{nN},$$

in $\mathbb{R}^{\times}$, for all $n \in \mathbb{N}$.

Proof. The proof of the free-distributional data (1.70) is done by (1.58) and (1.69). □

The above theorem shows that the free weighted-Poisson distributions induced by the free weighted-semicircular family $\mathcal{X}$ are characterized by the free Poisson distributions induced by the free semicircular family $\mathcal{S}$ in the semicircular filterization $\mathbb{L}_Q$ up to the weights $\{\psi(q_j)^2\}_{j \in \mathbb{Z}}$ from $\mathcal{X}$, where the quantities $\{\psi(q_j)\}_{j \in \mathbb{Z}}$ represent the free distributions of our mutually orthogonal projections $\{q_j\}_{j\in\mathbb{Z}}$ in the fixed C^*-probability space $(A,\ \psi)$. That is, the study of our free weighted-Poisson elements of $\mathbb{L}_Q$ is to investigate the free Poisson elements of $\mathbb{L}_Q$ up to certain scalar multiples, characterized by (1.70). Therefore, from below, we concentrate on studying the free Poisson elements of $\mathbb{L}_Q$.

1.9 SHIFTS ON $\mathbb{Z}$ AND INTEGER-SHIFTS ON $\mathbb{L}_Q$

As before, let $(A,\ \psi)$ be a fixed C^*-probability space containing a family $\mathbf{Q} = \{q_j\}_{j\in\mathbb{Z}}$ of mutually orthogonal projections q_j's having

$$\psi(q_j) \in \mathbb{R}^{\times}, \text{ for all } j \in \mathbb{Z},$$

(under **A 1.1**), and let $\mathbb{L}_Q$ be the semicircular filterization.

1.9.1 $(\pm)$-SHIFTS ON $\mathbb{Z}$

Define bijections h_+ and h_- on the set $\mathbb{Z}$ of all integers by

$$h_{\pm}(j) = j \pm 1, \tag{1.71}$$

for all $j \in \mathbb{Z}$. By definition (1.71), indeed, these functions are bijective on $\mathbb{Z}$, since $h_+^{-1} = h_-$, where f^{-1} means the inverses of bijections f.

Then, for these bijections $h_{\pm}$ of (1.71), one can construct the following bijections $h_{\pm}^{(n)}$ on $\mathbb{Z}$,

$$h_{\pm}^{(n)} = \underbrace{h_{\pm} \circ h_{\pm} \circ \cdots \circ h_{\pm}}_{n\text{-times}}, \tag{1.72}$$

for all $n \in \mathbb{N}$, with identities, $h_{\pm}^{(1)} = h_{\pm}$, where $(\circ)$ is the composition. Then,

$$h_{\pm}^{(n)}(j) = j \pm n, \text{ for all } j \in \mathbb{Z},$$

satisfying $\left(h_{+}^{(n)}\right)^{-1} = h_{-}^{(n)}$ on $\mathbb{Z}$, for all $n \in \mathbb{N}_0$, with axiomatization:

$$h_{\pm}^{(0)} = id_{\mathbb{Z}}, \text{ the identity function on } \mathbb{Z}.$$

Definition 1.12. *Let $h_{\pm}^{(n)}$ be the bijections (1.72) on $\mathbb{Z}$, for all $n \in \mathbb{N}_0$. Then, we call $h_{\pm}^{(n)}$, the n-$(\pm)$-shifts on $\mathbb{Z}$.*

1.9.2 INTEGER-SHIFTS ON $\mathbb{L}_Q$

Let $h_{\pm}^{(n)}$ be n-$(\pm)$-shifts (1.72) on $\mathbb{Z}$, for $n \in \mathbb{N}_0$. In this section, by using $h_{\pm}^{(n)}$, certain $*$-isomorphisms $\beta_{\pm}^{(n)}$ on $\mathbb{L}_Q$ are constructed, and we study how these $*$-isomorphisms act on $\mathbb{L}_Q$, for $n \in \mathbb{N}_0$.

Define "multiplicative" bounded linear transformations $\beta_{\pm}$ on $\mathbb{L}_Q$ by the morphisms satisfying that:

$$\beta_{\pm}(U_j) = U_{h_{\pm}(j)} = U_{j\pm 1}, \tag{1.73}$$

for $U_j \in \mathcal{S}$, and for all $j \in \mathbb{Z}$, where $\mathcal{S}$ is the free semicircular family (1.39).

By the structure theorem (1.42), the aforementioned multiplicative linear transformations $\beta_{\pm}$ of (1.73) are well defined on $\mathbb{L}_Q$. More precisely, one obtains the following computations.

Lemma 1.3. *Let* $Y = \prod_{l=1}^{N} U_{j_l}^{n_l}$ *be a free reduced word of* $\mathbb{L}_Q$ *with its length-N, for* $U_{j_1}, ..., U_{j_N} \in \mathcal{S}$, *and* $n_1, ..., n_N \in \mathbb{N}$, *where* $(j_1, ..., j_N)$ *is alternating in* $\mathbb{Z}^N$, *in the sense that:*

$$j_1 \neq j_2,\ j_2 \neq j_3,\ ...,\ j_{N-1} \neq j_N \text{ in } \mathbb{Z},$$

for $N \in \mathbb{N}$. *Then,* $\beta_{\pm}(Y)$ *become new free reduced words of* $\mathbb{L}_Q$ *with their lengths-N in* $\mathcal{S}$,

$$\beta_{\pm}(Y) = \prod_{l=1}^{N} U_{j_l \pm 1}^{n_l}, \text{ in } \mathbb{L}_Q. \tag{1.74}$$

Proof. Let Y be given as above in $\mathbb{L}_Q$. Then, by the multiplicativity of the linear transformations $\beta_{\pm}$ of (1.73), one has that

$$\beta_{\pm}(Y) = \prod_{l=1}^{N} \beta_{\pm}\left(U_{j_l}^{n_l}\right) = \prod_{l=1}^{N} \left(\beta_{\pm}\left(U_{j_l}\right)\right)^{n_l} = \prod_{l=1}^{N} U_{h_{\pm}(j_l)}^{n_l}.$$

Therefore, formula (1.74) holds.

Moreover, it is easily checked that if $(j_1, ..., j_N)$ is an alternating N-tuple of $\mathbb{Z}^N$, then the N-tuples

$$(j_1 \pm 1,\ j_2 \pm 1,\ ...,\ j_N \pm 1)$$

are alternating in $\mathbb{Z}^N$, too. Therefore, the images $\beta_{\pm}(Y)$ form new free reduced words of $\mathbb{L}_Q$ with their lengths-N in $\mathcal{S}$. □

As one can see in (1.74), the morphisms $\beta_{\pm}$ of (1.73) preserve the freeness on $\mathbb{L}_Q$, by (1.42).

Lemma 1.4. *The morphisms* $\beta_{\pm}$ *of (1.73) are* $*$*-isomorphisms on* $\mathbb{L}_Q$.

Proof. By (1.40), (1.41), and (1.42), all elements of the semicircular filterization $\mathbb{L}_Q$ are the limits of linear combinations of free reduced words in the free semicircular family $\mathcal{S}$ of (1.39). So, let's focus on the free reduced words of $\mathbb{L}_Q$ in $\mathcal{S}$.

Let $(j_1, ..., j_N)$ be an alternating N-tuple of $\mathbb{Z}^N$ for $N \in \mathbb{N}$, and

$$Y = \prod_{l=1}^{N} U_{j_l}^{n_l}, \text{ for } n_1, ..., n_N \in \mathbb{N}.$$

Then, by (1.74),

$$\beta_{\pm}(Y) = \prod_{l=1}^{N} U_{h_{\pm}(j_l)}^{n_l}, \tag{1.75}$$

where $h_{\pm}$ are the ($\pm$)-shifts (1.71) on $\mathbb{Z}$.

By the bijectivity of $h_{\pm}$, relation (1.75) implies the bijectivity of $\beta_{\pm}$ on $\mathbb{L}_Q$. That is, these multiplicative linear transformations $\beta_{\pm}$ of (1.73) are generator-preserving (bijective), and bounded on $\mathbb{L}_Q$.

Consider now that if Y is as above, then

$$\beta_{\pm}(Y^*) = \beta_{\pm}\left(\prod_{l=1}^{N} U_{j_{N-l+1}}^{n_{N-l+1}}\right) = \prod_{l=1}^{N} U_{h_{\pm}(j_{N-l+1})}^{n_{N-l+1}}$$

by (1.74)

$$= \left(\prod_{l=1}^{N} U_{h_{\pm}(j_l)}^{n_l}\right)^* = \left(\beta_{\pm}(Y)\right)^*. \tag{1.76}$$

So

$$\beta_{\pm}(S^*) = \left(\beta_{\pm}(S)\right)^*, \text{ for all } S \in \mathbb{L}_Q,$$

by (1.76). Therefore, the bounded, bijective, multiplicative linear transformations $\beta_{\pm}$ are adjoint-preserving on $\mathbb{L}_Q$, by (1.77). That is, they are $*$-isomorphisms on $\mathbb{L}_Q$. □

The above lemma shows that the ($\pm$)-shifts $h_{\pm}$ on $\mathbb{Z}$ induce the corresponding $*$-isomorphisms $\beta_{\pm}$ on $\mathbb{L}_Q$.

Let $\beta_{\pm}$ be the $*$-isomorphisms (1.73). Then, one can construct $*$-isomorphisms,

$$\beta_{\pm}^n = \underbrace{\beta_{\pm}\beta_{\pm}\cdot\cdots\cdot\beta_{\pm}}_{n\text{-times}} \text{ on } \mathbb{L}_Q, \tag{1.77}$$

for all $n \in \mathbb{N}_0$, with identity: $\beta_{\pm}^0 = 1_{\mathbb{L}_Q}$, the identity map on $\mathbb{L}_Q$.

Since $\beta_{\pm}$ and $1_{\mathbb{L}_Q}$ are $*$-isomorphisms, the morphisms $\beta_{\pm}^n$ of (1.77) are well-defined $*$-isomorphisms on $\mathbb{L}_Q$, too, for all $n \in \mathbb{N}_0$.

Definition 1.13. *The $*$-isomorphisms $\beta_{\pm}^n$ of (1.77) are called the n-($\pm$)-(integer-)shifts on $\mathbb{L}_Q$, for all $n \in \mathbb{N}_0$.*

These $*$-isomorphisms $\{\beta_{\pm}^n\}_{n\in\mathbb{N}_0}$ satisfy the following identity relation on $\mathbb{L}_Q$.

Proposition 1.4. *Let $\beta_{\pm}^n$ be the n-($\pm$)-integer-shifts (1.77) on $\mathbb{L}_Q$. Then,*

$$(\beta_+\beta_-)^n = \beta_+^n\beta_-^n = 1_{\mathbb{L}_Q} = \beta_-^n\beta_+^n = (\beta_-\beta_+)^n \text{ on } \mathbb{L}_Q, \tag{1.78}$$

for all $n \in \mathbb{N}_0$. Moreover,

$$\beta_+^{n_1}\beta_-^{n_2} = \beta_-^{n_2}\beta_+^{n_1} = \begin{cases} 1_{\mathbb{L}_Q} & \text{if } n_1 = n_2 \\ \beta_+^{n_1-n_2} & \text{if } n_1 > n_2 \\ \beta_-^{n_2-n_1} & \text{if } n_1 < n_2, \end{cases} \tag{1.79}$$

on $\mathbb{L}_Q$, for all $n_1, n_2 \in \mathbb{N}_0$.

Proof. As we discussed above, it suffices to consider the cases where we have the free reduced words

$$Y = \prod_{l=1}^{N} U_{j_l}^{n_l} \text{ of } \mathbb{L}_Q, \text{ for } n_1, ..., n_N \in \mathbb{N},$$

for $N \in \mathbb{N}$, by (1.74) and (1.42). Observe that

$$\beta_+\beta_-(Y) = \beta_+\left(\prod_{l=1}^{N} U_{j_l-1}^{n_l}\right) = \prod_{l=1}^{N} U_{(j_l-1)+1}^{n_l}$$
$$= Y = \prod_{l=1}^{N} U_{(j_l+1)-1}^{n_l}$$
$$= \beta_-\left(\prod_{l=1}^{N} U_{j_l+1}^{n_l}\right) = \beta_-\beta_+(Y).$$

Therefore,

$$\beta_+\beta_- = 1_{\mathbb{L}_Q} = \beta_-\beta_+ \text{ on } \mathbb{L}_Q. \tag{1.80}$$

By (1.80), one can get that

$$\beta_+^n\beta_-^n = (\beta_+\beta_-)^n = 1_{\mathbb{L}_Q} = (\beta_-\beta_+)^n = \beta_-^n\beta_+^n,$$

on $\mathbb{L}_Q$, for all $n \in \mathbb{N}_0$. Therefore, formula (1.78) holds.

By (1.78), one has that if $n_1 > n_2$ in $\mathbb{N}_0$, then

$$\beta_+^{n_1}\beta_-^{n_2} = \beta_+^{n_1-n_2}\beta_+^{n_2}\beta_-^{n_2} = \beta_+^{n_1-n_2} \text{ on } \mathbb{L}_Q,$$

and similarly, if $n_1 < n_2$ in $\mathbb{N}_0$, then

$$\beta_+^{n_1}\beta_-^{n_2} = \beta_+^{n_1}\beta_-^{n_1}\beta_-^{n_2-n_1} = \beta_-^{n_2-n_1}.$$

Therefore, formula (1.79) holds. □

The above relations (1.78) and (1.79) can be re-expressed simply by

$$\beta_{e_1}^{n_1}\beta_{e_2}^{n_2} = \beta_{e_2}^{n_2}\beta_{e_1}^{n_1} = \beta_{sgn(e_1n_1+e_2n_2)}^{|e_1n_1+e_2n_2|} \text{ on } \mathbb{L}_Q, \tag{1.81}$$

for all $e_1, e_2 \in \{\pm\}$, and $n_1, n_2 \in \mathbb{N}_0$, where $sgn(\cdot)$ is the sign-map on $\mathbb{Z}$,

$$sgn(j) = \begin{cases} + & \text{if } j \geq 0 \\ - & \text{if } j < 0 \end{cases}$$

for all $j \in \mathbb{Z}$, and where $|.|$ is the absolute value on $\mathbb{Z}$.

Now, consider the system $\mathfrak{B}$ of all n-($\pm$)-shifts $\beta_\pm^n$ on $\mathbb{L}_Q$, i.e.,

$$\mathfrak{B} = \{\beta_\pm^n\}_{n \in \mathbb{N}_0}. \tag{1.82}$$

Let $Aut(\mathbb{L}_Q)$ be the *automorphism group*

$$Aut(\mathbb{L}_Q) = \left(\left\{\alpha : \mathbb{L}_Q \to \mathbb{L}_Q \;\middle|\; \begin{array}{c}\alpha \text{ is a} \\ *\text{-isomorphism} \\ \text{on } \mathbb{L}_Q\end{array}\right\}, \cdot\right) \tag{1.83}$$

where the operation $(\cdot)$ is the product of $*$-isomorphisms.

By definition (1.82), the system $\mathfrak{B}$ is contained in the automorphism group $Aut(\mathbb{L}_Q)$ of (1.83). Note that the operation $(\cdot)$ is closed on $\mathfrak{B}$, in the sense that:

$$\left(\beta_{e_1}^{n_1}, \beta_{e_2}^{n_2}\right) \in \mathfrak{B} \times \mathfrak{B} \longmapsto \beta_{e_1}^{n_1} \beta_{e_2}^{n_2} \in \mathfrak{B}, \tag{1.84}$$

for all $e_1, e_2 \in \{\pm\}$, and $n_1, n_2 \in \mathbb{N}_0$, by (1.81).

Clearly, by (1.84), one can get that

$$\left(\beta_e^{n_1} \beta_e^{n_2}\right) \beta_e^{n_3} = \beta_e^{n_1+n_2+n_3} = \beta_e^{n_1}\left(\beta_e^{n_2} \beta_e^{n_3}\right), \tag{1.85}$$

for all $e \in \{\pm\}$, and $n_1, n_2, n_3 \in \mathbb{N}_0$.

Observe now that

$$\left(\beta_{e_1}^{n_1} \beta_{e_2}^{n_2}\right) \beta_{e_3}^{n_3} = \beta_{sgn(e_1 n_1 e_2 n_2)}^{|e_1 n_1 e_2 n_2|} \beta_{e_3}^{n_3} = \beta_{sgn(e_1 n_1 e_2 n_2 e_3 n_3)}^{|e_1 n_1 e_2 n_2 e_3 n_3|},$$

and (1.86)

$$\beta_{e_1}^{n_1}\left(\beta_{e_2}^{n_2} \beta_{e_3}^{n_3}\right) = \beta_{e_1}^{n_1} \beta_{sgn(e_2 n_2 e_3 n_3))}^{|e_2 n_2 e_3 n_3|} = \beta_{sgn(e_1 n_1 e_2 n_2 e_3 n_3))}^{|e_1 n_1 e_2 n_2 e_3 n_3)|}.$$

Thus, by (1.85) and (1.86),

$$\left(\beta_{e_1}^{n_1} \beta_{e_2}^{n_2}\right) \beta_{e_3}^{n_3} = \beta_{e_1}^{n_1}\left(\beta_{e_2}^{n_2} \beta_{e_3}^{n_3}\right) \text{ on } \mathbb{L}_Q, \tag{1.87}$$

for all $e_1, e_2, e_3 \in \{\pm\}$, and $n_1, n_2, n_3 \in \mathbb{N}_0$.

Theorem 1.13. *If $\mathfrak{B}$ is the set (1.82), then $\mathfrak{B}$ is an abelian subgroup of $Aut(\mathbb{L}_Q)$.*

Proof. By (1.81), the operation $(\cdot)$ is closed on $\mathfrak{B}$. So the algebraic pair $\mathfrak{B} = (\mathfrak{B}, \cdot)$ is a well-defined algebraic substructure of $Aut(\mathbb{L}_Q)$. By (1.87), this operation $(\cdot)$ is associative on $\mathfrak{B}$, and hence, the pair forms a semigroup. Since

$$\beta_+^0 = 1_{\mathbb{L}_Q} = \beta_-^0 \in \mathfrak{B},$$

and since

$$\beta_e^n \cdot 1_{\mathbb{L}_Q} = \beta_e^n = 1_{\mathbb{L}_Q} \cdot \beta_e^n \text{ on } \mathbb{L}_Q,$$

for all $e \in \{\pm\}$, and $n \in \mathbb{N}_0$, the semigroup $\mathfrak{B}$ contains its $(\cdot)$-identity $1_{\mathbb{L}_Q}$, and hence, it forms a monoid.

By (1.78), all elements $\beta_\pm^n \in \mathfrak{B}$ have their unique $(\cdot)$-inverses $\beta_\mp^n \in \mathfrak{B}$, for all $n \in \mathbb{N}_0$. So this monoid $\mathfrak{B}$ is a group.

The commutativity on $\mathfrak{B}$ is clear by (1.79). Therefore, the system $\mathfrak{B}$ is an abelian subgroup of the automorphism group $Aut(\mathbb{L}_Q)$. □

The above theorem characterizes the system $\mathfrak{B}$ of (1.82) as an abelian subgroup of $Aut(\mathbb{L}_Q)$. As a group, $\mathfrak{B}$ satisfies the following group-property.

Theorem 1.14. *Let $\mathfrak{B}$ be the abelian group (1.82). Then,*

$$\mathfrak{B} \overset{Group}{=} (\mathbb{Z}, +), \tag{1.88}$$

where "$\overset{Group}{=}$" means "being group-isomorphic to."

Proof. Define now a function $\Phi : \mathbb{Z} \to \mathfrak{B}$ by

$$\Phi : j \in \mathbb{Z} \longmapsto \beta_{sgn(j)}^{|j|} \in \mathfrak{B}, \tag{1.89}$$

with identity: $\Phi(0) = 1_{\mathbb{L}_Q}$ in $\mathfrak{B}$. By (1.79), this map Φ is a well-defined bijection from $\mathbb{Z}$ onto $\mathfrak{B}$. Observe that

$$\begin{aligned}\Phi(j_1 + j_2) = \beta_{sgn(j_1+j_2)}^{|j_1+j_2|} &= \beta_{sgn(j_1)}^{|j_1|}\beta_{sgn(j_2)}^{|j_2|} \\ &= \Phi(j_1)\Phi(j_2),\end{aligned} \tag{1.90}$$

in $\mathfrak{B}$, by (1.81), for all $j_1, j_2 \in \mathbb{Z}$.

So the bijection Φ of (1.89) is a group-homomorphism by (1.90). Therefore, the group-isomorphic relation (1.88) holds true. □

The above theorem characterizes the group-structure of the subgroup $\mathfrak{B} = \{\beta_{\pm}^{n}\}_{n\in\mathbb{N}_0}$ in $Aut(\mathbb{L}_Q)$. That is, $\mathfrak{B}$ is an infinite abelian cyclic group $\langle\beta_+\rangle = \langle\beta_-\rangle$.

Definition 1.14. *Let $\mathfrak{B}$ be the abelian group (1.82). We call $\mathfrak{B}$ the integer-shift (sub)group (of the automorphism group $Aut(\mathbb{L}_Q)$ acting) on $\mathbb{L}_Q$.*

1.9.3 FREE PROBABILITY ON $\mathbb{L}_Q$ UNDER THE GROUP-ACTION OF $\mathfrak{B}$

Let $\mathfrak{B}$ be the integer-shift group (1.84) acting on the semicircular filterization $\mathbb{L}_Q$, which is an infinite abelian cyclic subgroup of the automorphism group $Aut(\mathbb{L}_Q)$, by (1.88). In this section, we consider how our $*$-isomorphisms $\beta_{\pm}^{n} \in \mathfrak{B}$ affect the free probability on $\mathbb{L}_Q$. Throughout this section, let's fix $n_0 \in \mathbb{N}_0$ and $\beta_{\pm}^{n_0} \in \mathfrak{B}$.

Lemma 1.5. *Let $u_j \in \mathcal{X}$ be the $\psi(q_j)^2$-semicircular element, and $U_j \in \mathcal{S}$, a semicircular element of $\mathbb{L}_Q$. Then,*

$$\tau\left(\left(\beta_{\pm}^{n_0}(u_j)\right)^n\right) = \omega_n \psi(q_j)^n c_{\frac{n}{2}} = \tau\left(u_j^n\right),$$

and *(1.91)*

$$\tau\left(\left(\beta_{\pm}^{n_0}(U_j)\right)^n\right) = \omega_n c_{\frac{n}{2}} = \tau\left(U_j^n\right),$$

for all $n \in \mathbb{N}$.

Proof. Observe that, for any $n \in \mathbb{N}$, one has that

$$\tau\left(\left(\beta_{\pm}^{n_0}(u_j)\right)^n\right) = \tau\left(\left(\psi(q_j)\beta_{\pm}^{n_0}(U_j)\right)^n\right)$$

since $\beta_{\pm}^{n_0}$ are linear on $\mathbb{L}_Q$ and $u_j = \psi(q_j)U_j$ in $\mathbb{L}_Q$

$$= \psi(q_j)^n\, \tau\left(U_{j\pm n_0}^n\right) = \psi(q_j)^n\left(\omega_n c_{\frac{n}{2}}\right) \tag{1.92}$$

by the semicircularity (1.39) of $U_{j \pm n_0} \in \mathcal{S}$

$$= \omega_n \left(\psi(q_j)^2\right)^{\frac{n}{2}} c_{\frac{n}{2}} = \tau\left(u_j^n\right), \tag{1.93}$$

by (1.38). Therefore, the first free-distributional data of (1.91) hold by (1.93).

As one can see in (1.92), we have that

$$\tau\left(\left(\beta_{\pm}^{n_0}(U_j)\right)^n\right) = \omega_n c_{\frac{n}{2}} = \tau\left(U_j^n\right), \text{ for all } n \in \mathbb{N},$$

by (1.39), for all $j \in \mathbb{Z}$. So the second free-distributional data of (1.91) hold. □

The above lemma shows how the original free-distributional data on $\mathbb{L}_Q$ is affected by the group-action of $\mathfrak{B}$. That is, the action preserves the free distributions of generating operators of $\mathbb{L}_Q$.

Definition 1.15. *Let (B_1, φ_1) and (B_2, φ_2) be arbitrary topological $*$-probability spaces. We say that they are free-($*$-)isomorphic if (i) B_1 and B_2 are $*$-isomorphic via a $*$-isomorphism $\Omega : B_1 \to B_2$, and (ii)*

$$\varphi_2(\Omega(a)) = \varphi_1(a), \forall a \in (B_1, \varphi_1).$$

In such a case, we call the $*$-isomorphism Ω a free-isomorphism.

By (1.91), one obtains the following theorem.

Theorem 1.15. *All integer-shifts of $\mathfrak{B}$ are free-isomorphisms on $\mathbb{L}_Q$.*

Proof. Let $\beta_e^n \in \mathfrak{B}$, for $e \in \{\pm\}$ and $n \in \mathbb{N}_0$. Since $\mathfrak{B}$ is a subgroup of $Aut(\mathbb{L}_Q)$, a group-element $\beta_e^n \in \mathfrak{B}$ is a $*$-isomorphisms on $\mathbb{L}_Q$. Moreover, by (1.42) and (1.91),

$$\tau\left(\beta_e^n(T)\right) = \tau(T), \text{ for all } T \in \mathbb{L}_Q.$$

Therefore, the $*$-isomorphism $\beta_e^n \in \mathfrak{B}$ is a free-isomorphism. Since β_e^n is arbitrary in $\mathfrak{B}$, all integer-shifts of $\mathfrak{B}$ are free-isomorphisms on $\mathbb{L}_Q$. □

The above theorem illustrates that the free probability on the semicircular filterization $\mathbb{L}_Q$ is preserved by the action of the integer-shift group $\mathfrak{B}$.

1.10 BANACH-SPACE OPERATORS ON $\mathbb{L}_Q$ GENERATED BY $\mathfrak{B}$

Throughout this section, let $\mathbb{L}_Q$ be the semicircular filterization, and let $\mathfrak{B}$ be the integer-shift group acting on $\mathbb{L}_Q$. In this section, we consider certain Banach-space operators acting "on $\mathbb{L}_Q$," generated by $\mathfrak{B}$, by regarding $\mathbb{L}_Q$ as a Banach space (e.g., [13]).

Let $B(\mathbb{L}_Q)$ be the operator space consisting of all Banach-space operators on the Banach space $\mathbb{L}_Q$ equipped with its operator norm,

$$\|T\| = \sup\left\{ \|Tv\|_{\mathbb{L}_Q} \,\middle|\, \begin{array}{c} v \in \mathbb{L}_Q, \text{ and} \\ \|v\|_{\mathbb{L}_Q} = 1 \end{array} \right\}, \tag{1.94}$$

for all $T \in B(\mathbb{L}_Q)$, where $\|.\|_{\mathbb{L}_Q}$ is the norm on the Banach $*$-algebra $\mathbb{L}_Q$ (e.g., [13] and [14]).

Define now a (closed) subspace $\mathfrak{A}$ of the vector space $B(\mathbb{L}_Q)$ by

$$\mathfrak{A} \overset{def}{=} \overline{span_{\mathbb{C}}(\mathfrak{B})} = \overline{\mathbb{C}[\mathfrak{B}]}^{\|.\|}, \tag{1.95}$$

where $\mathfrak{B}$ is the integer-shift group, and $\overline{Y}^{\|.\|}$ are the operator-norm topology closures of the subsets Y of $B(\mathbb{L}_Q)$, where $\|.\|$ is in the sense of (1.94). Note that since $\mathfrak{B}$ is a group, the set equality of (1.95) holds. That is, $\mathfrak{A}$ is not only a closed subspace, but also an algebra of $B(\mathbb{L}_Q)$.

On this Banach algebra $\mathfrak{A}$, define a unary operation $(*)$ by

$$\left(\sum_{(e,n)\in\{\pm\}\times\mathbb{N}_0} t_{(e,n)} \beta_e^n \right)^* \overset{def}{=} \sum_{(e,n)\in\{\pm\}\times\mathbb{N}_0} \overline{t_{(e,n)}}\, \beta_{-e}^n, \tag{1.96}$$

on $\mathfrak{A}$, for all $t_{(e,n)} \in \mathbb{C}$ with their conjugates $\overline{t_{(e,n)}} \in \mathbb{C}$.

Proposition 1.5. *The subspace $\mathfrak{A}$ of (1.95) forms a Banach $*$-algebra in $B(\mathbb{L}_Q)$.*

Proof. First of all, for any $\beta_e^n \in \mathfrak{B} \subset \mathfrak{A}$, there always exists $(\beta_e^n)^* = \beta_{-e}^n \in \mathfrak{B} \subset \mathfrak{A}$, for all $e \in \{\pm\}$ and $n \in \mathbb{N}_0$. So for any $A \in \mathfrak{A}$, there exists a unique A^* in $\mathfrak{A}$. So the operation $(*)$ of (1.96) is closed on $\mathfrak{A}$. Observe that

$$((\beta_e^n)^*)^* = (\beta_{-e}^n)^* = \beta_{-(-e)}^n = \beta_e^n \text{ in } \mathfrak{A},$$

by (1.96), for all $e \in \{\pm\}$, and $n \in \mathbb{N}_0$. So if $A \in \mathfrak{A}$, then

$$A^{**} = A, \text{ in } \mathfrak{A}. \tag{1.97}$$

By the very definition (1.96), one immediately obtain that

$$(zA)^* = \overline{z}\, A^*, \forall z \in \mathbb{C}, \text{ and } A \in \mathfrak{A}. \tag{1.98}$$

Now, observe that

$$\left(\beta_{e_1}^{n_1} + \beta_{e_2}^{n_2}\right)^* = \beta_{-e_1}^{n_1} + \beta_{-e_2}^{n_2} = \left(\beta_{e_1}^{n_1}\right)^* + \left(\beta_{e_2}^{n_2}\right)^*,$$

in $\mathfrak{A}$, by (1.96), for all $e_1, e_2 \in \{\pm\}$, and $n_1, n_2 \in \mathbb{N}_0$. Thus, if $A_1, A_2 \in \mathfrak{A}$,

$$(A_1 + A_2)^* = A_1^* + A_2^* \text{ in } \mathfrak{A}, \tag{1.99}$$

by (1.98). Also, one can get that

$$\left(\beta_{e_1}^{n_1} \beta_{e_2}^{n_2}\right)^* = (\beta_e^n)^* = \beta_{-e}^n,$$

and

$$\left(\beta_{e_2}^{n_2}\right)^* \left(\beta_{e_1}^{n_1}\right)^* = \beta_{-e_2}^{n_2} \beta_{-e_1}^{n_1} = \beta_{-e_1}^{n_1} \beta_{-e_2}^{n_2} = \beta_{-e}^n,$$

where $e = sgn(e_1n_1 + e_2n_2) \in \{\pm\}$, and $n = |e_1n_1 + e_2n_2| \in \mathbb{N}_0$.

And hence,

$$\left(\beta_{e_1}^{n_1}\beta_{e_2}^{n_2}\right)^* = \left(\beta_{e_2}^{n_2}\right)^*\left(\beta_{e_1}^{n_1}\right)^*,$$

in $\mathfrak{A}$, for all $e_1, e_2 \in \{\pm\}$, and $n_1, n_2 \in \mathbb{N}_0$. So

$$(A_1A_2)^* = A_2^*A_1^* \text{ in } \mathfrak{A}, \tag{1.100}$$

for all $A_1, A_2 \in \mathfrak{A}$.

Therefore, the operation $(*)$ of (1.96) is a well-defined adjoint on $\mathfrak{A}$, by (1.97), (1.98), (1.99), and (1.100). So the Banach algebra $\mathfrak{A}$ forms a Banach $*$-algebra. □

The above proposition shows that every element of $\mathfrak{A}$ is an adjointable Banach-space operator on $\mathbb{L}_Q$ in the sense of [13].

Definition 1.16. *Let $\mathfrak{A}$ be the Banach $*$-algebra (1.95) embedded in the operator space $B(\mathbb{L}_Q)$. Then, we call $\mathfrak{A}$ the integer-shift operator algebra (on $\mathbb{L}_Q$). All elements of $\mathfrak{A}$ are said to be integer-shift operators on $\mathbb{L}_Q$.*

1.10.1 DEFORMED FREE PROBABILITY OF $\mathbb{L}_Q$ BY $\mathfrak{A}$

Let $\mathbb{L}_Q$ be the semicircular filterization, and $\mathfrak{B}$, the integer-shift group acting on $\mathbb{L}_Q$, and let $\mathfrak{A}$ be the integer-shift-operator algebra (1.95) generated by $\mathfrak{B}$ in the operator space $B(\mathbb{L}_Q)$. In this section, we act operators of $\mathfrak{A}$ on $\mathbb{L}_Q$ and study how the original free-distributional data on $\mathbb{L}_Q$ are deformed by the action. By (1.40) and (1.42), we focus on how our (weighted-)semicircularity induced by $(\mathcal{X}\cup)S$ is affected by the action of $\mathfrak{A}$ on $\mathbb{L}_Q$.

Since we already considered how the integer-shift group $\mathfrak{B}$, the generator set of $\mathfrak{A}$, affects the free probability on $\mathbb{L}_Q$ in Section 1.9, we here are interested in the distorted (weighted-)semicircular law(s) by the action of nongenerator operators A of $\mathfrak{A}$, formed by

$$A = \sum_{(e,n)\in\mathbb{N}_0^{\pm}} t_{(e,n)}\beta_e^n \in \mathfrak{A}. \tag{1.101}$$

Note again that if $A \in \mathfrak{B} \subset \mathfrak{A}$, then such an integer-shift operator A is an integer-shift, which is free-isomorphism on $\mathbb{L}_Q$, and hence, it preserves the free probability on $\mathbb{L}_Q$. However, if $A \in \mathfrak{A} \setminus \mathfrak{B}$, then we cannot guarantee that A preserves the free-distributional data on $\mathbb{L}_Q$.

Notation From below, for convenience, we let

$$\mathbb{N}_0^{\pm} \overset{denote}{=} \{\pm\} \times \mathbb{N}_0.$$

□

Lemma 1.6. *Let $A = t\beta_e^k \in \mathfrak{A}$, for $t \in \mathbb{C}^{\times}$, and $(e,k) \in \mathbb{N}_0^{\pm}$, and let $u_j \in \mathcal{X}$ be a $\psi(q_j)^2$-semicircular element in $\mathbb{L}_Q$, for $j \in \mathbb{Z}$. Then,*

$$\tau((A(u_j))^n) = \omega_n\,(t\psi(q_j))^n\, c_{\frac{n}{2}},$$

and (1.102)

$$\tau\left((A(u_j)^*)^n\right) = \omega_n \left(\bar{t}\psi(q_j)\right)^n c_{\frac{n}{2}},$$

for all $n \in \mathbb{N}$.

Proof. Let $A = t\beta_e^k \in \mathfrak{A}$, for $(e, k) \in \mathbb{N}_0^{\pm}$, and let $t \in \mathbb{C}^{\times}$. Then,

$$\begin{aligned}\tau\left(A(u_j)^n\right) &= \tau\left(\left(t\beta_e^k(u_j)\right)^n\right) = \tau\left(\left(t\psi(q_j)U_{jek}\right)^n\right) \\ &= t^n\psi(q_j)^n\tau\left(U_{jek}^n\right) = \omega_n t^n\psi(q_j)^n c_{\frac{n}{2}},\end{aligned}$$

and

$$\begin{aligned}\tau\left((A(u_j)^*)^n\right) &= \tau\left(\left(\left(t\beta_e^k(u_j)\right)^*\right)^n\right) \\ &= \omega_n\bar{t}^n\psi(q_j)^n c_{\frac{n}{2}},\end{aligned}$$

for all $n \in \mathbb{N}$, and $j \in \mathbb{Z}$, implying the formulas of (1.104). □

By (1.102), we obtain the following result.

Theorem 1.16. *Let* $A = t\beta_e^n \in \mathfrak{A}$, *for* $t \in \mathbb{C}^{\times}$, *and* $(e, n) \in \mathbb{N}_0^{\pm}$. *Then,*

if $t \in \mathbb{R}^{\times}$, *then* $t\beta_e^n(u_j) \in \mathbb{L}_Q$ *are* $(t\psi(q_j))^2$*-semicircular,* (1.103)

in $\mathbb{L}_Q$, *for all* $(e, n) \in \mathbb{N}_0^{\pm}$ *and for all* $j \in \mathbb{Z}$.

Proof. Let $t \in \mathbb{R}^{\times}$ in $\mathbb{C}$, and let $A = t\beta_e^n$, for $(e, n) \in \mathbb{N}_0^{\pm}$, then, for any $j \in \mathbb{Z}$, one has that

$$\tau\left((A(u_j))^k\right) = \omega_k\left(t\psi(q_j)\right)^k c_{\frac{k}{2}} = \tau\left((A(u_j)^*)^k\right),$$

for all $k \in \mathbb{N}$, by (1.102).

Indeed, since $t \in \mathbb{R}^{\times}$, we have

$$(A(u_j))^* = \left(t\psi(q_j)U_{jek}\right)^* = t\psi(q_j)U_{jek} = A(u_j),$$

in $\mathbb{L}_Q$ (under **A 1.1**); equivalently, $A(u_j)$ is self-adjoint in $\mathbb{L}_Q$, for all $j \in \mathbb{Z}$.

Therefore, $t\beta_e^n(u_j)$ is $(t\psi(q_j))^2$-semicircular in $\mathbb{L}_Q$, for all $j \in \mathbb{Z}$, whenever $t \in \mathbb{R}^{\times}$, for all $(e,n) \in \mathbb{N}_0^{\pm}$. □

The above theorem shows that the integer-shift operators $t\beta_e^n \in \mathfrak{A}$ distort the original $\psi(q_j)^2$-semicircular laws to the $(t\psi(q_j))^2$-semicircular laws on $\mathbb{L}_Q$, for all $(e, n) \in \mathbb{N}_0^{\pm}$, and $j \in \mathbb{Z}$, whenever $t \in \mathbb{R}^{\times} \setminus \{1\}$, by (1.103).

Corollary 1.3. *Let* $A = t\beta_e^n \in \mathfrak{A}$, *for* $t \in \mathbb{R}^{\times}$, *and* $(e, n) \in \mathbb{N}_0^{\pm}$, *and let* $U_j \in \mathcal{S}$ *be a semicircular element in* $\mathbb{L}_Q$, *for* $j \in \mathbb{Z}$. *Then,*

if $t \in \mathbb{R}^{\times}$, *then* $t\beta_e^n(U_j)$ *is* t^2*-semicircular in* $\mathbb{L}_Q$, (1.104)

for all $(e, n) \in \mathbb{N}_0^{\pm}$ *and for all* $j \in \mathbb{Z}$.

Proof. Statement (1.104) is shown by the proof of (1.103). □

Now, let $A \in \mathfrak{A}$ be in the sense of (1.101), and assume further that A has more than one summand. Then, for any $u_j \in \mathcal{X}$ and $U_j \in \mathcal{S}$, one can have that

$$A\left(U_j^n\right) = \sum_{(e,k)\in\mathbb{N}_0} t_{(e,k)} U_{jek}^n \text{ in } \mathbb{L}_Q,$$

and hence, (1.105)

$$A\left(u_j^n\right) = \psi(q_j)^n \left(\sum_{(e,k)\in\mathbb{N}_0^{\pm}} t_{(e,k)} U_{jek}^n \right) \text{ in } \mathbb{L}_Q,$$

for all $n \in \mathbb{N}$.

Theorem 1.17. *Let $A \in \mathfrak{A}$ be an integer-shift operator (1.101), and $u_j \in \mathcal{X}$, $U_j \in \mathcal{S}$ in $\mathbb{L}_Q$. Then,*

$$\begin{aligned}\tau\left(A\left(u_j^n\right)\right) &= \left(\omega_n \psi(q_j)^n c_{\frac{n}{2}}\right) \left(\sum_{(e,k)\in\mathbb{N}_0^{\pm}} t_{(e,k)} \right) \\ &= \tau\left(u_j^n\right) \left(\sum_{(e,k)\in\mathbb{N}_0^{\pm}} t_{(e,k)} \right),\end{aligned}$$

and (1.106)

$$\begin{aligned}\tau\left(A\left(U_j^n\right)\right) &= \left(\omega_n c_{\frac{n}{2}}\right) \left(\sum_{(e,k)\in\mathbb{N}_0^{\pm}} t_{(e,k)} \right) \\ &= \tau\left(U_j^n\right) \left(\sum_{(e,k)\in\mathbb{N}_0^{\pm}} t_{(e,k)} \right),\end{aligned}$$

for all $n \in \mathbb{N}$.

Proof. Remark that if $A \in \mathfrak{A}$ is in the sense of (1.101), then

$$\begin{aligned}A\left(u_j^n\right) &= \sum_{(e,k)\in\mathbb{N}_0^{\pm}} t_{(e,k)} \beta_e^k\left(u_j^n\right) \\ &= \sum_{(e,k)\in\mathbb{N}_0^{\pm}} t_{(e,k)} \left(\psi(q_j)^n U_{jek}^n\right),\end{aligned}$$

by (1.105). So

$$\tau\left(A\left(u_j^n\right)\right) = \psi(q_j)^n \left(\sum_{(e,k)\in\mathbb{N}_0^{\pm}} t_{(e,k)} \tau\left(U_{jek}^n\right) \right)$$

$$= \psi(q_j)^n \left(\sum_{(e,k)\in\mathbb{N}_0^{\pm}} t_{(e,k)} \left(\omega_n c_{\frac{n}{2}}\right)\right) \tag{1.107}$$

$$= \left(\omega_n \psi(q_j)^n c_{\frac{n}{2}}\right) \left(\sum_{(e,k)\in\mathbb{N}_0^{\pm}} t_{(e,k)} \right)$$

$$= \left(\tau\left(u_j^n\right)\right) \left(\sum_{(e,k)\in\mathbb{N}_0^{\pm}} t_{(e,k)} \right), \tag{1.108}$$

for all $n \in \mathbb{N}$.

By (1.107), one obtains that

$$\tau\left(A\left(U_j^n\right)\right) = \left(\omega_n c_{\frac{n}{2}}\right) \left(\sum_{(e,k)\in\mathbb{N}_0^{\pm}} t_{(e,k)} \right)$$

$$= \tau\left(U_j^n\right) \left(\sum_{(e,k)\in\mathbb{N}_0^{\pm}} t_{(e,k)} \right),$$

for all $n \in \mathbb{N}$.

Therefore, by (1.107) and (1.109), the free-distributional data (1.106) hold. □

In the formulas of (1.106), the quantity

$$t_A \overset{def}{=} \sum_{(e,k)\in\mathbb{N}_0^{\pm}} t_{(e,k)} \in \mathbb{C} \tag{1.109}$$

is the sum of all coefficients $\{t_{(e,k)}\}_{(e,k)\in\mathbb{N}_0^{\pm}}$ of the operator $A \in \mathfrak{A}$. So

$$\tau\left(A(U_j^n)\right) = t_A \left(\omega_n c_{\frac{n}{2}}\right), \forall n \in \mathbb{N}, \tag{1.110}$$

for all $j \in \mathbb{Z}$, by (1.106) and (1.109). And, similar to (1.110),

$$\tau\left(A(u_j^n)\right) = \left(t_A \psi(q_j)^n\right) \left(\omega_n c_{\frac{n}{2}}\right), \forall n \in \mathbb{N}, \tag{1.111}$$

for all $j \in \mathbb{Z}$, where t_A is in the sense of (1.109).

Formulas (1.110) and (1.111) show how the integer-shift-operator algebra $\mathfrak{A}$ deforms the (weighted-)semicircular law(s) on $\mathbb{L}_Q$.

1.10.2 DEFORMED SEMICIRCULAR LAWS ON $\mathbb{L}_Q$ BY $\mathfrak{A}$

We, here, concentrate on the distortions of the semicircular law on $\mathbb{L}_Q$ by acting the integer-shift-operator algebra $\mathfrak{A}$. Now, observe that if A is an integer-shift operator,

$$A = \sum_{(e,k)\in\mathbb{N}_0^{\pm}} t_{(e,k)} \beta_e^k \in \mathfrak{A}, \tag{1.112}$$

then

$$A^2 = \sum_{((e_1,k_1),(e_2,k_2)) \in \mathbb{N}_0^{\pm} \times \mathbb{N}_0^{\pm}} t_{(e_1,k_1)} t_{(e_2,k_2)} \beta_{e_1}^{k_1} \beta_{e_2}^{k_2}$$

$$= \sum_{((e_1,k_1),(e_2,k_2)) \in \mathbb{N}_0^{\pm} \times \mathbb{N}_0^{\pm}} t_{(e_1,k_1)} t_{(e_2,k_2)} \beta_{sgn(e_1k_1+e_2k_2)}^{|e_1k_1+e_2k_2|},$$

and hence,

$$A^2 = \sum_{(e,k) \in \mathbb{N}_0^{\pm}} \left(\sum_{((e_1,k_1),(e_2,k_2)) \in [e,k]_2} t_{(e_1,k_1)} t_{(e_2,k_2)} \right) \beta_e^k,$$

where (1.113)

$$[e,k]_2 = \left\{ ((e_1,k_1),(e_2,k_2)) \,\middle|\, \begin{array}{c} (e_1,k_1),\ (e_2,k_2) \in \mathbb{N}_0^{\pm}, \\ e = sgn(e_1k_1 + e_2k_2), \\ \text{and } k = |e_1k_1 + e_2k_2| \end{array} \right\},$$

for all $(e, k) \in \mathbb{N}_0^{\pm}$, because the integer-shift group $\mathfrak{B}$, the generator set of $\mathfrak{A}$, is abelian.

Lemma 1.7. *Let $A \in \mathfrak{A}$ be an integer-shift operator (1.112). Then,*

$$A^n = \sum_{(e,k) \in \mathbb{N}_0^{\pm}} \left(\sum_{((e_l,k_l))_{l=1}^n \in [e,k]_n} \left(\prod_{l=1}^{n} t_{(e_l,k_l)} \right) \right) \beta_e^k \in \mathfrak{A},$$

with *(1.114)*

$$[e,k]_n = \left\{ ((e_l,k_l))_{l=1}^n \,\middle|\, \begin{array}{c} (e_l,k_l) \in \mathbb{N}_0^{\pm},\ \forall l = 1, \ldots, n, \\ e = sgn\,(\sum_{l=1}^n e_l k_l) \in \{\pm\}, \\ and\ k = |\sum_{l=1}^n e_l k_l| \in \mathbb{N}_0 \end{array} \right\},$$

for all $n \in \mathbb{N}$.

Proof. The operator equality (1.114) is obtained by the induction on (1.113). □

Notation Let A^n be as in (1.114) for an integer-shift operator $A \in \mathfrak{A}$ of (1.112), for $n \in \mathbb{N}$. Then, we denote the quantities

$$\sum_{((e_l,k_l))_{l=1}^n \in [e,k]_n} \left(\prod_{l=1}^{n} t_{(e_l,k_l)} \right) \overset{denote}{=} t_{[e,k]_n}, \tag{1.115}$$

for all $(e, k) \in \mathbb{N}_0^{\pm}$, where $[e, k]_n$ are in the sense of (1.114). □

By notation (1.115), one can re-express (1.115) by

$$A^n = \sum_{(e,k) \in \mathbb{N}_0^{\pm}} t_{[e,k]_n} \beta_e^k \text{ in } \mathfrak{A},$$

for all $n \in \mathbb{N}$.

Theorem 1.18. *Let $U_j \in \mathcal{S}$ in $\mathbb{L}_Q$, and let $A \in \mathfrak{A}$ be an integer-shift operator (1.112). Then,*

$$\tau\left(A^{n_1}\left(U_j^{n_2}\right)\right) = \left(\omega_{n_2} c_{\frac{n_2}{2}}\right)\left(\sum_{(e,k)\in\mathbb{N}_0^{\pm}} t_{[e,k]_{n_1}}\right) \tag{1.116}$$

where $[e,\, k]_{n_1}$ are in the sense of (1.115), for all $(e,\, k) \in \mathbb{N}_0^{\pm}$, and $n_1, n_2 \in \mathbb{N}$.

Proof. Now, let $n_1, n_2 \in \mathbb{N}$, and $j \in \mathbb{Z}$. Then,

$$\tau\left(A^{n_1}\left(U_j^{n_2}\right)\right) = \tau\left(\sum_{(e,k)\in\mathbb{N}_0^{\pm}} t_{[e,k]_{n_1}} \beta_e^k\left(U_j^{n_2}\right)\right)$$

by (1.115)

$$= \sum_{(e,k)\in\mathbb{N}_0^{\pm}} t_{[e,k]_{n_1}}\, \tau\left(U_{jek}^{n_2}\right)$$

where $[e,k]_{n_1}$ are in the sense of (1.115) for all $(e,k) \in \mathbb{N}_0^{\pm}$

$$= \sum_{(e,k)\in\mathbb{N}_0^{\pm}} t_{[e,k]_{n_1}} \left(\omega_{n_2} c_{\frac{n_2}{2}}\right)$$

by the semicircularity of $U_{jek} \in \mathcal{S}$ in $\mathbb{L}_Q$, for all $j \in \mathbb{Z}$, and $(e,\, k) \in \mathbb{N}_0^{\pm}$

$$= \left(\omega_{n_2} c_{\frac{n_2}{2}}\right)\left(\sum_{(e,k)\in\mathbb{N}_0^{\pm}} t_{[e,k]_{n_1}}\right).$$

Therefore, formula (1.116) holds. □

Similar to (1.116), we also have the following free-distributional data on $\mathbb{L}_Q$.

Theorem 1.19. *Let $u_j \in \mathcal{X}$ in $\mathbb{L}_Q$, and let A be an integer-shift operator (1.112) in $\mathfrak{A}$. Then,*

$$\tau\left(A^{n_1}(u_j^{n_2})\right) = \left(\omega_{n_2} \psi(q_j)^{n_2} c_{\frac{n_2}{2}}\right)\left(\sum_{(e,k)\in\mathbb{N}_0^{\pm}} t_{[e,k]_{n_1}}\right), \tag{1.117}$$

for all $n_1, n_2 \in \mathbb{N}$.

Proof. The proof of (1.117) is similarly done by (1.114) and (1.116). □

The above two theorems generalize the distorted free-distributional data (1.106) of the semicircular law on $\mathbb{L}_Q$. Similar to the notation t_A of (1.109), one can define the following quantities.

Notation Let's denote the quantity

$$\sum_{(e,k)\in\mathbb{N}_0^{\pm}} t_{[e,k]_n} \overset{denote}{=} t_A^{(n)} \text{ in } \mathbb{C}, \tag{1.118}$$

where $\{t_{[e,k]_n}\}_{(e,k)\in\mathbb{N}_0^{\pm}}$ are the coefficients (1.115) of $A^n \in \mathfrak{A}$ of the integer-shift operator A of (1.112). Remark that, by (1.118),

$$t_A \text{ of } (1.109) = t_A^{(1)} \text{ of } (1.118).$$

□

By using the above new notation (1.118), formulas (1.116) and (1.117) can be re-expressed simply by

$$\tau\left(A^{n_1}\left(U_j^{n_2}\right)\right) = t_A^{(n_1)}\left(\omega_{n_2} c_{\frac{n_2}{2}}\right) = t_A^{(n_1)}\tau\left(U_j^{n_2}\right),$$

and (1.119)

$$\tau\left(A^{n_1}\left(u_j^{n_2}\right)\right) = t_A^{(n_1)}\left(\omega_{n_2}\psi(q_j)^{n_2} c_{\frac{n_2}{2}}\right) = t_A^{(n_1)}\tau\left(u_j^{n_2}\right),$$

for all $n_1, n_1 \in \mathbb{N}$, and for all $j \in \mathbb{Z}$.

1.11 DEFORMED FREE POISSON DISTRIBUTIONS ON $\mathbb{L}_Q$ BY $\mathfrak{A}$

In this section, as an application of Section 1.10, we study the deformed free (weighted-)Poisson distributions on $\mathbb{L}_Q$ under the action of the integer-shift-operator algebra $\mathfrak{A}$.

Throughout this section, we fix a free Poisson element

$$W_j^{m,N} = U_j U_m^N U_j \in \mathbb{L}_Q, \tag{1.120}$$

for $U_j, U_m \in \mathcal{S}$, and a free $\psi(q_j)^2$-Poisson element

$$Y_j^{m,N} = u_j U_m^N u_j \in \mathbb{L}_Q, \tag{1.121}$$

for $u_j \in \mathcal{X}$, where $j \neq m$ in $\mathbb{Z}$, for $N \in \mathbb{N}$.

By (1.54) and (1.66), we have the following free Poisson distribution of $W_j^{m,N}$ and the free $\psi(q_j)^2$-Poisson distribution of $Y_j^{m,N}$:

$$\tau\left(\left(W_j^{m,N}\right)^n\right) = \begin{cases} \sum\limits_{\pi\in NC(\Omega_n)}\left(\prod\limits_{V\in\pi} c_{\frac{N|V|}{2}}\right) & \text{if } N \text{ is even} \\ \omega_n \sum\limits_{\pi\in NC_e(\Omega_n)}\left(\prod\limits_{V\in\pi} c_{\frac{N|V|}{2}}\right) & \text{if } N \text{ is odd,} \end{cases} \tag{1.122}$$

and

$$\tau\left(\left(Y_j^{m,N}\right)^n\right) = \psi(q_j)^{2n}\,\tau\left(\left(W_j^{m,N}\right)^n\right), \tag{1.123}$$

for all $n \in \mathbb{N}$.

Corollary 1.4. *Let $W_j^{m,N}$ be the free Poisson element (1.120) of $\mathbb{L}_Q$. If $A \in \mathfrak{A}$, an integer-shift operator (1.112), then*

$$\tau\left(A^{n_1}\left(\left(W_j^{m,N}\right)^{n_2}\right)\right) = \begin{cases} t_A^{(n_1)}\left(\sum_{\pi \in NC(\Omega_{n_2})}\left(\prod_{V\in\pi} c_{\frac{n_2|V|}{2}}\right)\right) & \text{if } N \text{ is even} \\ \omega_n t_A^{(n_1)}\left(\sum_{\pi \in NC_e(\Omega_{n_2})}\left(\prod_{V\in\pi} c_{\frac{n_2|V|}{2}}\right)\right) & \text{if } N \text{ is odd,} \end{cases} \tag{1.124}$$

with

$$t_A^{(n_1)} = \sum_{(e,k)\in\mathbb{N}_0^{\pm}}\left(\sum_{((e_l,k_l))_{l=1}^{n}\in[e,k]_{n_1}}\left(\prod_{l=1}^{n} t_{(e_l,k_l)}\right)\right), \tag{1.125}$$

for all $n_1, n_2 \in \mathbb{N}$, where

$$[e,k]_{n_1} = \left\{ ((e_l,k_l))_{l=1}^{n_1} \;\middle|\; \begin{array}{c} (e_l,k_l)\in\mathbb{N}_0^{\pm},\ \forall l=1,\dots,n_1, \\ e = sgn\left(\sum_{l=1}^{n} e_l n_l\right)\in\{\pm\}, \\ \text{and } k = \left|\sum_{l=1}^{n} e_l n_l\right|\in\mathbb{N}_0 \end{array}\right\}.$$

Proof. Fix $n_1, n_2 \in \mathbb{N}$, and let

$$T_{n_1,n_2} = A^{n_1}\left(\left(W_j^{m,N}\right)^{n_2}\right)\in\mathbb{L}_Q.$$

Then

$$\begin{aligned} T_{n_1,n_2} &= A^{n_1}\left((U_j U_m^N U_j)^{n_2}\right) \\ &= \sum_{(e,k)\in\mathbb{N}_0^{\pm}} t_{[e,k]_{n_1}}\beta_e^k\left((U_j U_m^N U_j)^{n_2}\right) \end{aligned}$$

with

$$t_{[e,k]_{n_1}} = \sum_{((e_l,k_l))_{l=1}^{n_1}\in[e,k]_{n_1}}\left(\prod_{l=1}^{n_1} t_{(e_l,k_l)}\right)$$

by (1.115), where

$$[e,\,k]_{n_1} = \left\{ ((e_l,k_l))_{l=1}^{n_1} \;\middle|\; \begin{array}{c} (e_l,k_l)\in\mathbb{N}_0^{\pm},\ \forall l=1,\dots,n_1, \\ e = sgn\left(\sum_{l=1}^{n} e_l n_l\right)\in\{\pm\}, \\ \text{and } k = \left|\sum_{l=1}^{n} e_l n_l\right|\in\mathbb{N}_0 \end{array}\right\},$$

by (1.114), for all $(e,\,k)\in\mathbb{N}_0^{\pm}$, and hence, it goes to

$$= \sum_{(e,k)\in\mathbb{N}_0^{\pm}} t_{[e,k]_{n_1}}\left(U_{jek}U_{mek}^N U_{jek}\right)^{n_2}, \tag{1.126}$$

in $\mathbb{L}_Q$.

Note that in (1.126), the summands $U_{jek}U_{mek}^{N}U_{jek}$ are the free Poisson elements of $\mathbb{L}_Q$, because the freeness of semicircular elements U_{jek} and U_{mek} is preserved from the freeness of U_j and U_m in $\mathbb{L}_Q$ (by the action of the integer-shift group $\mathfrak{B}$), for all $j \neq m \in \mathbb{Z}$. Thus,

$$\tau(T_{n_1,n_2}) = \sum_{(e,k)\in\mathbb{N}_0^{\pm}} t_{[e,k]_{n_1}} \, \tau\left(\left(U_{jek}U_{mek}^{N}U_{jek}\right)^{n_2}\right)$$

$$= \sum_{(e,k)\in\mathbb{N}_0^{\pm}} t_{[e,k]_{n_1}} \, \tau\left(\left(U_{jek}U_{mek}^{N}U_{jek}\right)^{n_2}\right)$$

$$= \sum_{(e,k)\in\mathbb{N}_0^{\pm}} t_{[e,k]_{n_1}} \, \tau\left(\left(U_jU_m^{N}U_j\right)^{n_2}\right)$$

by Theorem 1.15

$$= \tau\left(\left(U_jU_m^{N}U_j\right)^{n_2}\right)\left(\sum_{(e,k)\in\mathbb{N}_0^{\pm}} t_{[e,k]_{n_1}}\right)$$

$$= t_A^{(n_1)} \, \tau\left(\left(W_j^{m,N}\right)^{n_2}\right), \tag{1.127}$$

where $t_A^{(n_1)}$ is in the sense of (1.125). Therefore, by (1.54) and (1.127), the free-distributional data (1.124) hold true. □

The aforementioned free-distributional data (1.124) shows how our integer-shift operators $A \in \mathfrak{A}$ of (1.112) distort the free Poisson distribution of $W_j^{m,N}$ on $\mathbb{L}_Q$. As a special case of (1.124), one obtains the following fact.

Corollary 1.5. *Let $W_j^{m,1}$ be the free Poisson element (1.120) of $\mathbb{L}_Q$. If $A \in \mathfrak{A}$, an integer-shift operator (1.112), then*

$$\tau\left(A^{n_1}\left(\left(W_j^{m,1}\right)^{n_2}\right)\right) = \delta_{n_2,2}\, t_A^{(n_1)}$$

with

$$t_A^{(n_1)} = \sum_{(e,k)\in\mathbb{N}_0^{\pm}} \left(\sum_{((e_l,k_l))_{l=1}^{n}\in[e,k]_{n_1}} \left(\prod_{l=1}^{n} t_{(e_l,k_l)}\right)\right),$$

for all $n_1, n_2 \in \mathbb{N}$. □

Also, we obtain the following corollary.

Corollary 1.6. *Let $Y_j^{m,N}$ be the free $\psi(q_j)^2$-Poisson element (1.121) of $\mathbb{L}_Q$, and let $A \in \mathfrak{A}$ be an integer-shift operator (1.112). Then,*

$$\tau\left(A^{n_1}\left(Y_j^{m,N}\right)^{n_2}\right) = \begin{cases} t_A^{(n_1)}\psi(q_j)^{2n_2}\left(\sum\limits_{\pi\in NC(\Omega_n)}\left(\prod\limits_{V\in\pi} c_{\frac{N|V|}{2}}\right)\right) & \text{if } N \text{ is even} \\ \omega_n t_A^{(n_1)}\psi(q_j)^{2n_2}\left(\sum\limits_{\pi\in NC_e(\Omega_n)}\left(\prod\limits_{V\in\pi} c_{\frac{N|V|}{2}}\right)\right) & \text{if } N \text{ is odd,} \end{cases} \tag{1.128}$$

for all $n_1, n_2 \in \mathbb{N}$, where $t_A^{(n_1)}$ are in the sense of (1.125).

Proof. The free-distributional data (1.128) is proven by (1.66), (1.126), and (1.127). □

The free-distributional data (1.128) illustrates how the integer-shift operator $A \in \mathfrak{A}$ distorts the free $\psi(q_j)^2$-Poisson distribution of $Y_j^{m,N}$ on $\mathbb{L}_Q$, in general. As a special case of (1.128), one has the following corollary.

Corollary 1.7. *Let $Y_j^{m,1}$ be the free $\psi(q_j)^2$-Poisson element (1.121) of $\mathbb{L}_Q$, and let $A \in \mathfrak{A}$ be an integer-shift operator (1.112). Then,*

$$\tau\left(A^{n_1}\left(Y_j^{m,1}\right)^{n_2}\right) = \delta_{n_2,2}\left(t_A^{(n_1)}\psi(q_j)^4\right),$$

for all $n_1, n_2 \in \mathbb{N}$, where $t_A^{(n_1)}$ are in the sense of (1.125). □

REFERENCES

[1] M. Ahsanullah, Some Inferences on Semicircular Distribution, *J. Stat. Theo. Appl.*, 15, no. 3, (2016) 207–213.

[2] H. Bercovici, and D. Voiculescu, Superconvergence to the Central Limit and Failure of the Cramer Theorem for Free Random Variables, *Probab. Theo. Related Fields,* 103, no. 2, (1995) 215–222.

[3] M. Bozejko, W. Ejsmont, and T. Hasebe, Noncommutative Probability of Type *D*, *Internat. J. Math.*, 28, no. 2, (2017) 1750010, 30.

[4] M. Bozheuiko, E. V. Litvinov, and I. V. Rodionova, An Extended Anyon Fock Space and Non-commutative Meixner-Type Orthogonal Polynomials in the Infinite-Dimensional Case, *Uspekhi Math. Nauk.*, 70, no. 5, (2015) 75–120.

[5] I. Cho, Semicircular Families in Free Product Banach $*$-Algebras Induced by p-Adic Number Fields over Primes p, *Compl. Anal. Oper. Theo.*, 11, no. 3, (2017) 507–565.

[6] I. Cho, Semicircular-Like Laws and the Semicircular Law Induced by Orthogonal Projections, *Compl. Anal. Oper. Theo.*, 12, no.1, DOI:10.1007/s11785-018-0781-x, (2018).

[7] I. Cho, Banach-Space Operators Acting on Semicircular Elements Induced by Orthogonal Projections, *Compl. Anal. Oper. Theo.*, 13, Issue 8, (2019) 4065–4115.

[8] I. Cho, Acting Semicircular Elements Induced by Orthogonal Projections on von Neumann Algebras, *Mathematics,* 5, 74, DOI:10.3390/math5040074, (2017).

[9] I. Cho, Semicircular-Like and Semicircular Laws on Banach $*$-Probability Spaces Induced by Dynamical Systems of the Finite Adele Ring, Adv. Oper. Theo., Special Issue: Trends in Operators on Banach Spaces (dedicated to Prof. S. Banach), *Adv. Oper. Theo.,* 4, no. 1, (2019) 24–70.
[10] I. Cho, and P. E. T. Jorgensen, *Semicircular Elements Induced by Projections on Separable Hilbert Spaces,* Monograph Ser., Operator Theory: Advances & Applications, Published by Birkhauser, Basel, (2019) To Appear.
[11] I. Cho, and P. E. T. Jorgensen, Banach $*$-Algebras Generated by Semicircular Elements Induced by Certain Orthogonal Projections, Opuscula Math., 38, no. 4, (2018) 501–535.
[12] I. Cho, and P. E. T. Jorgensen, Semicircular Elements Induced by p-Adic Number Fields, *Opuscula Math.,* 35, no. 5, (2017) 665–703.
[13] A. Connes, *Noncommutative Geometry,* ISBN: 0-12-185860-X, (1994) Academic Press (San Diego, CA).
[14] P. R. Halmos, *Hilbert Space Problem Books,* Grad. Texts in Math., 19, ISBN: 978-0387906850, (1982) Published by Springer.
[15] I. Kaygorodov, and I. Shestakov, Free Generic Poisson Fields and Algebras, *Comm. Alg.,* 46, issue 4, DOI:10.1080/00927872.2017.1358269, (2018).
[16] L. Makar-Limanov, and I. Shestakov, Polynomials and Poisson Dependence in Free Poisson Algebras and Free Poisson Fields, *J. Alg.,* vol. 349, issue 1, (2012) 372–379.
[17] A. Nica, and R. Speicher, *Lectures on the Combinatorics of Free Probability* (1-st Ed.), London Math. Soc. Lecture Note Ser., 335, ISBN-13:978-0521858526, (2006) Cambridge Univ. Press.
[18] I. Nourdin, G. Peccati, and R. Speicher, Multi-Dimensional Semicircular Limits on the Free Wigner Chaos, *Progr. Probab.,* 67, (2013) 211–221.
[19] V. Pata, The Central Limit Theorem for Free Additive Convolution, *J. Funct. Anal.,* 140, no. 2, (1996) 359–380.
[20] F. Radulescu, Random Matrices, Amalgamated Free Products and Subfactors of the C^*-Algebra of a Free Group of Nonsingular Index, *Invent. Math.,* 115, (1994) 347–389.
[21] F. Radulescu, Free Group Factors and Hecke Operators, notes taken by N. Ozawa, Proceed. 24-th Conference in Oper. Theo., Theta Advanced Series in Math., (2014) Theta Foundation.
[22] R. Speicher, Combinatorial Theory of the Free Product with Amalgamation and Operator-Valued Free Probability Theory, *Amer. Math. Soc. Mem.,* vol 132, no. 627, (1998).
[23] R. Speicher A Conceptual Proof of a Basic Result in the Combinatorial Approach to Freeness, Infinit. Dimention. *Anal. Quant. Prob. & Related Topics,* 3, (2000) 213–222.
[24] R. Speicher, and T. Kemp, Strong Haagerup Inequalities for Free R-Diagonal Elements, *J. Funct. Anal.,* 251, Issue 1, (2007) 141–173.
[25] R. Speicher, and U. Haagerup, Brown's Spectrial Distribution Measure for R-Diagonal Elements in Finite Von Neumann Algebras, *J. Funct. Anal.,* 176, Issue 2, (2000) 331–367.
[26] V. S. Vladimirov, p-Adic Quantum Mechanics, *Comm. Math. Phy.,* 123, no. 4, (1989) 659–676.
[27] V. S. Vladimirov, I. V. Volovich, and E. I. Zelenov, *p-Adic Analysis and Mathematical Physics,* Ser. Soviet & East European Math., vol 1, ISBN: 978-981-02-0880-6, (1994) World Scientific.

[28] D. Voiculescu, Aspects of Free Analysis, *Jpn. J. Math.,* 3, no. 2, (2008) 163–183.
[29] D. Voiculescu, Free Probability and the Von Neumann Algebras of Free Groups, *Rep. Math. Phy.,* 55, no. 1, (2005) 127–133.
[30] D. Voiculescu, K. Dykemma, and A. Nica, Free Random Variables, CRM Monograph Series, vol 1., ISBN-13: 978-0821811405, (1992) Published by Amer. Math. Soc.

2 Linear Positive Operators Involving Orthogonal Polynomials

P. N. Agrawal and Ruchi Chauhan
IIT Roorkee

CONTENTS

2.1 OPERATORS BASED ON ORTHOGONAL POLYNOMIALS

In recent years, there has been a significant increase in activities in approximation of continuous functions on the semi-real axis by the linear positive operators based on orthogonal polynomials. Jakimovski and Leviatan [21] initiated the study in this direction by defining the generalization of Szász operators based on Appell polynomials. Ismail [19] generalized the Szász operators by means of Sheffer polynomials.

Varma and Tasdelen [42] proposed Szász-type operators involving Charlier polynomials. Kajla and Agrawal [24] introduced the Szász-Durrmeyer-type operators involving Charlier polynomials. Varma et al. [41] proposed Szász-type operators based on Brenke-type polynomials. Sucu et al. [37] defined Szász-type operators involving Boas-Buck polynomials that include Brenke-type polynomials, Sheffer polynomials, and Appell polynomials. In the literature, several sequences of linear positive operators have been defined, involving orthogonal polynomials, and their Durrmeyer and Kantorovich-type variants have been investigated. Our aim in this chapter is to make a survey of the research work available on approximation by the linear positive operators defined by using orthogonal polynomials.

Throughout this chapter, we shall use the following notations and definitions.

2.1.1 NOTATIONS

$\mathbb{R}^+$	$(0,\infty)$,
$C[0,\infty)$	the space of all continuous functions on $[0,\infty)$,
$C_B[0,\infty)$	the space of all continuous and bounded functions on $[0,\infty)$,
E_1	$\left\{f:[0,\infty)\to\mathbb{R}: x\in[0,\infty), \lim_{x\to\infty}\frac{f(x)}{1+x^2} \text{ exists}\right\}$,
$\tilde{C}[0,\infty)$	the space of all uniformly continuous functions on $[0,\infty)$,
$\tilde{C}^r[0,\infty)$	the space of r-times differentiable functions such that $f^{(r)}$ is uniformly continuous on $[0,\infty)$,
$\tilde{C}_B[0,\infty)$	the space of all real-valued bounded and uniformly continuous functions f on $[0,\infty)$, endowed with the norm $\parallel f \parallel = \sup_{x\in[0,\infty)} \lvert f(x)\rvert$,
$C_\gamma[0,\infty)$	$\{f\in C[0,\infty): \lvert f(x)\rvert \le M_f(1+x^\gamma), \gamma>0\}$,
$B_2[0,\infty)$	the space of all real-valued functions on $[0,\infty)$ satisfying the condition $\lvert f(x)\rvert \le M_f(1+x^2)$, where M_f is a positive constant depending only on f and $1+x^2$ is a weight function,
$C_2[0,\infty)$	the space of all continuous functions in $B_2[0,\infty)$ with the norm $\lVert f\rVert_2 := \sup_{x\in[0,\infty)} \frac{\lvert f(x)\rvert}{1+x^2}$
$C_2^*[0,\infty)$	$\left\{f\in C_2[0,\infty): \lim_{x\to\infty}\frac{\lvert f(x)\rvert}{1+x^2} \text{ is finite}\right\}$,
E_2	$\{f:[0,\infty)\to\mathbb{R}: \lvert f(x)\rvert \le Me^{Ax}, \text{ for some } A, M\in\mathbb{R}^+\}$,
E_3	$\{f:[0,\infty)\to\mathbb{R}: \lvert f(x)\rvert = \lvert\int_0^x f(s)ds\rvert \le Ke^{Bx}, \text{ for some } B, K\in\mathbb{R}^+\}$.

2.1.2 DEFINITIONS

Let $f\in\tilde{C}[0,\infty)$ and $\delta>0$. The modulus of continuity $\omega(f;\delta)$ of the function f is defined by

$$\omega(f;\delta) = \sup_{0<|h|<\delta}\ \sup_{x,x+h\in[0,\infty)} |f(x+h)-f(x)|. \tag{2.1}$$

Lipschitz-type maximal function of order r introduced is defined by Lenze [29] as

$$\widetilde{\omega}_r(f,x) = \sup_{t\neq x,\ t\in[0,\infty)} \frac{|f(t)-f(x)|}{|t-x|^r},\quad x\in[0,\infty) \text{ and } r\in(0,1]. \tag{2.2}$$

In what follows, let $\tilde{C}_B[0,\infty)$ be the space of all real-valued bounded and uniformly continuous functions f on $[0,\infty)$, endowed with the norm $||f||_{\tilde{C}_B[0,\infty)} = \sup_{x\in[0,\infty)} |f(x)|$.

Further, let us define the following Peetre's K-functional:

$$K_2(f,\delta) = \inf_{g\in W^2}\{||f-g||+\delta||g''||\},\ \delta>0,$$

where $W^2 = \{g \in \tilde{C_B}[0,\infty) : g', g'' \in \tilde{C_B}[0,\infty)\}$ and the norm

$$\| f \|_{W^2}=\| f \|_{\tilde{C_B}[0,\infty)} + \| f' \|_{\tilde{C_B}[0,\infty)} + \| f'' \|_{\tilde{C_B}[0,\infty)} .$$

By ([9], p. 177, Theorem 2.4), there exists an absolute constant $M > 0$ such that

$$K_2(f,\delta) \leq M\left\{\omega_2(f,\sqrt{\delta})+\min(1,\delta)\ \| f \|_{\tilde{C_B}[0,\infty)}\right\}, \tag{2.3}$$

where the second-order modulus of smoothness is defined as

$$\omega_2(f,\sqrt{\delta}) = \sup_{0<|h|\leq\sqrt{\delta}}\ \sup_{x\in[0,\infty)} |f(x+2h)-2f(x+h)+f(x)|.$$

The modulus $\omega_{\phi^\tau}(f,t), 0 \leq \tau \leq 1$, is given by

$$\omega_{\phi^\tau}(f,t) = \sup_{0\leq h\leq t}\ \sup_{x\pm\frac{h\phi^\tau(x)}{2}\in[0,\infty)} \left| f\left(x+\frac{h\phi^\tau(x)}{2}\right) - f\left(x-\frac{h\phi^\tau(x)}{2}\right)\right|. \tag{2.4}$$

Now for $0 < r \leq 1$, the Lipschitz-type space [26] is defined as:

$$Lip^*_M(r) := \left\{f \in C[0,\infty) : |f(t)-f(x)| \leq M_f\frac{|t-x|^r}{(t+x)^{\frac{r}{2}}}; t\in(0,\infty), x>0\right\}, \tag{2.5}$$

for some $M_f > 0$.

For $f \in C_2[0,\infty)$, Ispir and Atakut [20] introduced the weighted modulus of continuity as follows:

$$\Omega(f;\delta) = \sup_{0\leq|h|<\delta, x\in[0,\infty)} \frac{f(x+h)-f(x)|}{(1+x^2)(1+h^2)}. \tag{2.6}$$

If $f \in C_2^*[0,\infty)$, then $\lim_{\delta\to 0}\Omega(f;\delta) = 0$.

2.1.3 APPELL POLYNOMIALS

Appell [4] introduced a sequence of polynomials $P_n(x)$ of degree n which satisfies the differential equation

$$DP_n(x) = nP_{n-1}(x),\ D \equiv \frac{d}{dx},$$

known as Appell polynomials. In [35], Sheffer extended the class of Appell polynomials and called these polynomials as zero-type polynomials. The very well-known Szász operator is defined in the following.

For $f \in C[0,\infty)$ and $n \in \mathbb{N}$, we have

$$S_n(f;x) = e^{-nx} \sum_{k=0}^{\infty} \frac{(nx)^k}{k!} f\left(\frac{k}{n}\right) \quad x \geq 0, \tag{2.7}$$

whenever the series on the right side converges. Using Appell polynomials, Jakimovski and Leviatan [21] introduced a generalization of the Szász operators as

$$P_n(f;x) = \frac{e^{-nx}}{g(1)} \sum_{k=0}^{\infty} p_k(nx) f\left(\frac{k}{n}\right), \tag{2.8}$$

where

$$g(u)e^{ux} = \sum_{k=0}^{\infty} p_k(x)u^k \tag{2.9}$$

is the generating function for the Appell polynomials $p_k(x) \geq 0$, with $g(u) = \sum_{n=0}^{\infty} a_n u^n$, $|u| < r$, $r > 1$, and $g(1) \neq 0$, and established several approximation properties of these operators.

Later, Ismail [19] gave another generalization of Szász operators by means of Sheffer polynomials. Let $A(z) = \sum_{k=0}^{\infty} a_k z^k$, $(a_0 \neq 0)$, and $H(z) = \sum_{k=1}^{\infty} h_k z^k$ $(h_k \neq 0$ $\forall k$ be the analytic functions in the disk $|z| \leq R$ $(R > 1)$, where a_k and h_k are real. The Sheffer polynomials $p_k(x)$ have the generating functions of the form $A(t)e^{xH(t)} = \sum_{k=0}^{\infty} p_k(x)t^k$, $|t| < R$. By assuming $p_k(x) \geq 0$, $\forall x \in [0,\infty)$, $A(1) \neq 0$, and $H'(1) = 1$, Ismail introduced and studied the convergence properties of the positive linear operators defined by

$$T_n(f;x) = \frac{e^{-nx}}{A(1)} \sum_{k=0}^{\infty} p_k(nx) f\left(\frac{k}{n}\right).$$

In [8], Ciupa considered the following operators of general form

$$D_n(f;x) = \frac{e^{-nx}}{g(1)} \sum_{k=0}^{\infty} p_k(nx) A_{k,n}(f), \; x \geq 0,$$

where $p_k(x)$ are the Appell polynomials defined by the relation

$$g(u)e^{ux} = \sum_{k=0}^{\infty} p_k(u)u^k, \; g(1) \neq 0.$$

The main result of this paper is that the rth derivative of $D_n(f;x)$ is given by

$$(D_n(f))^{(r)}(x) = \frac{n^r}{g(1)} \sum_{k=0}^{\infty} e^{-nx} p_k(nx) \sum_{i=0}^{r} (-1)^i \binom{r}{i} A_{k+r-i,n}(f).$$

Choosing different expressions for $A_{k,n}(f)$, the known formulas for the cases such as the Jakimovski-Leviatan operators, Favard-Szász operators, the Durrmeyer variant of

Jakimovski-Leviatan operators, and the Durrmeyer variant of Favard-Szász operators may be obtained.

Brenke-type polynomials [7] have the generating functions of the type

$$A(t)B(xt) = \sum_{k=0}^{\infty} p_k(x)t^k, \tag{2.10}$$

where $A(t)$ and $B(t)$ are the analytic functions given by

$$A(t) = \sum_{i=0}^{\infty} a_i t^i,\ a_0 \neq 0 \tag{2.11}$$

$$B(t) = \sum_{j=0}^{\infty} b_j t^j,\ b_j \neq 0,\ \forall\ j \tag{2.12}$$

and $p_k(x) = \sum_{i=0}^{k} a_{k-i} b_i x^i$, $k = 0,1,2...$, which includes Appell polynomials for $B(t) = e^t$, as a particular case. Assuming that $A(1) \neq 0$, $\dfrac{a_{k-i}b_i}{A(1)} \geq 0$, $0 \leq i \leq k$, $k = 0,1,2...$, $B : [0,\infty) \to (0,\infty)$ and (2.10)–(2.12) converge for $|t| < R$ $(R > 1)$, Verma et al. [40] proposed the following operators:

$$L_n(f;x) = \frac{1}{A(1)B(nx)} \sum_{k=0}^{\infty} p_k(nx) f\left(\frac{k}{n}\right),\ x \in [0,\infty) \tag{2.13}$$

and studied some results concerning the rate of convergence of these operators. In particular, if $B(t) = e^t$ and $A(t) = g(t)$, then the operators given by (2.13) reduce to the operators defined by (2.8).

2.1.4 BOAS-BUCK-TYPE POLYNOMIALS

For $f \in C[0,\infty)$, Sucu et. al [37] considered the Szász operators based on Boas-Buck-type polynomials as follows:

$$B_n(f;x) = \frac{1}{A(1)G(nxH(1))} \sum_{k=0}^{\infty} p_k(nx) f\left(\frac{k}{n}\right),\ x \geq 0,\ n \in \mathbb{N},$$

where the generating function of the Boas-Buck-type polynomials is given by

$$A(u)G(xH(u)) = \sum_{k=0}^{\infty} p_k(x)u^k,$$

and $A(u)$, $G(u)$, and $H(u)$ are the analytic functions described by $A(u) = \sum_{k=0}^{\infty} a_k u^k$, $(a_0 \neq 0$, $G(u) = \sum_{k=0}^{\infty} g_k u^k$, $(g_k \neq 0, \forall k)$, and $H(u) = \sum_{k=1}^{\infty} h_k u^k$, $(h_1 \neq 0$, and studied some approximation properties of these operators. As a particular case, Boas-Buck polynomials include Sheffer polynomials and Appell polynomials.

Yilik et al. [44] estimated the approximation degree of the operators B_n for bounded variation functions using some results of the probability theory. The authors also investigated the Voronovskaja and Grüss-Voronovskaja-type theorems in the quantitative form.

2.1.5 CHARLIER POLYNOMIALS

In 1950, Szász [38] introduced the following linear positive operators:

$$S_n(f;x) = e^{-nx} \sum_{k=0}^{\infty} \frac{(nx)^k}{k!} f\left(\frac{k}{n}\right), \tag{2.14}$$

where $x \in [0,\infty)$ and $f(x)$ is a continuous function on $[0,\infty)$ whenever the above sum converges uniformly. These polynomials [18] have the generating functions of the form

$$e^t \left(1 - \frac{t}{a}\right)^u = \sum_{k=0}^{\infty} C_k^{(a)}(u) \frac{t^k}{k!}, \ |t| < a, \tag{2.15}$$

where $C_k^{(a)}(u) = \sum_{r=0}^{k} \binom{k}{r} (-u)_r \left(\frac{1}{a}\right)^r$ and $(m)_0 = 1, (m)_j = m(m+1)\cdots(m+j-1)$ for $j \geq 1$. For $C_A[0,\infty)$, Varma and Taşdelen [42] defined the following Szász-type operators involving Charlier polynomials

$$\mathcal{L}_n(f;x,a) = e^{-1}\left(1 - \frac{1}{a}\right)^{(a-1)nx} \sum_{k=0}^{\infty} \frac{C_k^{(a)}(-(a-1)nx)}{k!} f\left(\frac{k}{n}\right), \tag{2.16}$$

where $a > 1$ and $x \in [0,\infty)$, and studied the degree of approximation of these operators.

2.1.6 APPROXIMATION BY APPELL POLYNOMIALS

For $f \in C_B[0,\infty)$, Karaisa [26] introduced a Durrmeyer-type modification based on Appell polynomials as follows:

$$\begin{aligned} L_n(f;x) = {} & \frac{e^{-nx}}{g(1)} \sum_{k=1}^{\infty} \frac{p_k(nx)}{B(n+1,k)} \int_0^{\infty} b_{n,k}(t) f(t)\,dt \\ & + \frac{e^{-nx}}{g(1)} a_0 f(0), \ x \geq 0, \end{aligned} \tag{2.17}$$

where $B(k+1,n)$ is the beta function, $b_{n,k}(t) = \frac{t^{k-1}}{(1+t)^{n+k+1}}$, and studied the local approximation properties and the convergence in a weighted space of functions. A Voronovskaja-type theorem for these operators was also proved. Gupta and Agrawal [14] established the rate of convergence for a Lipschitz-type space and obtained the degree of approximation in terms of Lipschitz-type maximal function for the Durrmeyer-type modification of Jakimovski-Leviatan operators based on Appell polynomials.

2.1.7 APPROXIMATION BY OPERATORS INCLUDING GENERALIZED APPELL POLYNOMIALS

For $f \in C[0,\infty)$, Icoz et al. [17] considered the linear operators

$$M_n(f;x) := \frac{1}{A(g(1))B(nxg(1))} \sum_{k=0}^{\infty} p_k(nx) f\left(\frac{k}{n}\right), \tag{2.18}$$

where $p_k(x)$ are the generalized Appell polynomials [4] having the generating functions of the following form:

$$A(g(t))B(xg(t)) = \sum_{k=0}^{\infty} p_k(x)t^k \tag{2.19}$$

and A, B, and g are the analytic functions such that

$$A(t) = \sum_{k=0}^{\infty} a_k t^k \ (a_0 \neq 0), \quad B(t) = \sum_{k=0}^{\infty} b_k t^k \ (b_k \neq 0), \quad g(t) = \sum_{k=1}^{\infty} g_k t^k \ (g_1 \neq 0). \tag{2.20}$$

Assuming that the generalized Appell polynomials (2.19) satisfy

1. $A(g(1)) \neq 0,\ g'(1) = 1,\ p_k(x) \geq 0\ k = 0,1,2,\ldots,$
2. $B : \mathbb{R} \to (0,\infty),$
3. (2.19) and the power series (2.20) converges for $|t| < R\ (R > 1)$,

it turns out that the linear operators M_n defined by (2.18) are positive.

Remark 2.1. *Let $g(t) = t$, the operators* (2.18) *reduce to the operators L_n involving Brenke-type polynomials.*

Remark 2.2. *Let $g(t) = t$ and $B(t) = e^t$, one can get the operators* (2.8). *In addition, if we choose $A(t) = 1$, we meet the well-known Szász operators* (2.7).

Icoz et al. [17] proved the qualitative and quantitative approximation theorems. Icoz et al. [17] obtained the qualitative convergence result by means of M_n operators with the help of universal Korovkin-type property with respect to positive linear operators. Next, they stated the quantitative results for estimating the error of approximation using the classical approach, the second modulus of continuity, and Peetre's K-functional in the continuous functions space and the Lipschitz class.

Neer et al. [32] defined Baskakov-Durrmeyer-type operators based on the generalized Appell polynomials and established some results in weighted approximation besides the quantitative Voronovskaja and Grüss-Voronovskaja-type theorems. The approximation for functions having derivatives of bounded variation was also studied.

2.1.8 SZÁSZ-TYPE OPERATORS INVOLVING MULTIPLE APPELL POLYNOMIALS

First, let us recall the definition of multiple Appell polynomials [28]. A set of polynomials $\{p_{k_1,k_2}(x)\}_{k_1,k_2=0}^{\infty}$ with degree (k_1+k_2) for $k_1,k_2 \geq 0$, is called multiple polynomial system (multiple PS), and a multiple PS is called multiple Appell if it is generated by the relation

$$A(t_1,t_2)e^{x(t_1+t_2)} = \sum_{k_1=0}^{\infty}\sum_{k_2=0}^{\infty} \frac{p_{k_1,k_2}(x)}{k_1!k_2!} t_1^{k_1} t_2^{k_2}, \tag{2.21}$$

where $A(t_1,t_2)$ is given by

$$A(t_1,t_2) = \sum_{k_1=0}^{\infty}\sum_{k_2=0}^{\infty} \frac{a_{k_1,k_2}}{k_1!k_2!} t_1^{k_1} t_2^{k_2}, \tag{2.22}$$

with $A(0,0) = a_{0,0} \neq 0$.

Theorem 2.1. *For multiple PS,* $\{p_{k_1,k_2}(x)\}_{k_1,k_2=0}^{\infty}$, *the following statements are equivalent:*

a. $\{p_{k_1,k_2}(x)\}_{k_1,k_2=0}^{\infty}$ *is a set of multiple Appell polynomials.*
b. *There exists a sequence* $\{a_{k_1,k_2}\}_{k_1,k_2=0}^{\infty}$ *with* $a_{0,0} \neq 0$ *such that*

$$p_{k_1,k_2}(x) = \sum_{r_1=0}^{\infty}\sum_{r_2=0}^{\infty} \binom{k_1}{r_1}\binom{k_2}{r_2} a_{k_1-r_1,k_2-r_2} x^{r_1+r_2}.$$

c. *For every* $k_1+k_2 \geq 1$, *we have*

$$p'_{k_1,k_2}(x) = k_1 p_{k_1-1,k_2}(x) + k_2 p_{k_1,k_2-1}(x).$$

Utilizing these polynomials, for any $f \in C[0,\infty)$, Varma [40] defined a sequence of linear positive operators as

$$K_n(f;x) = \frac{e^{-nx}}{A(1,1)} \sum_{k_1=0}^{\infty}\sum_{k_2=0}^{\infty} \frac{p_{k_1,k_2}\left(\frac{nx}{2}\right)}{k_1!k_2!} f\left(\frac{k_1+k_2}{n}\right), \tag{2.23}$$

provided $A(1,1) \neq 0$, $\frac{a_{k_1,k_2}}{A(1,1)} \geq 0$ for $k_1,k_2 \in \mathbb{N}$, and series (2.21) and (2.22) converge for $|t_1| < R_1$, $|t_2| < R_2$ $(R_1,R_2 > 1)$, respectively.

Remark 2.3. *Let us note the following special cases:*

1. *For* $t_2 = 0$, *the generating functions given by* (2.21) *reduce to the generating functions for the Appell polynomials given by* (2.9).
2. *For* $t_2 = 0$ *and* $A(t_1,0) = 1$, *from the generating function given by* (2.21), *we easily find* $p_k(x) = x^k$. *From this fact, one can obtain Szász operators* (2.7).

We use the following notation for the partial derivatives:

$$\frac{\partial A}{\partial t_i} = A_{t_i} \textit{ and } A_{t_i t_j} = \frac{\partial^2 A}{\partial t_i \partial t_j} \quad i,j = 1,2,3,4.$$

From definition (2.23) and relation (2.21), we obtain the following auxiliary result

Lemma 2.1. *[40] The operator (2.23) satisfies the following inequalities:*

1. $K_n(1;x) = 1;$
2. $K_n(s;x) = x + \frac{A_{t_1}(1,1)+A_{t_2}(1,1)}{nA(1,1)};$
3. $K_n(s^2;x) = x^2 + \frac{x}{n}\left(1 + \frac{2(A_{t_1}(1,1)+A_{t_2}(1,1))}{A(1,1)}\right)$
   $+\frac{1}{n^2A(1,1)}\{A_{t_1}(1,1)+A_{t_2}(1,1)+A_{t_1t_1}(1,1)+2A_{t_1t_2}(1,1)+A_{t_2t_2}(1,1)\},$

where $x \geq 0$. The following theorem shows that the operator defined by (2.23) is an approximation process for continuous functions contained in E.

Theorem 2.2. *[40] Let $f \in C[0,\infty) \cap E_1$. Then,*

$$\lim_{n\to\infty} K_n(f;x) = f(x),$$

the convergence being uniform in each compact subset of $[0,\infty)$.

Theorem 2.3. *[40] Let $f \in \tilde{C}[0,\infty) \cap E_1$, we have the following inequality for the operator* (2.23)

$$|K_n(f;x) - f(x)|$$

$$\leq \left\{1 + \sqrt{x + \frac{1}{nA(1,1)}\{A_{t_1}(1,1)+A_{t_2}(1,1)+A_{t_1t_1}(1,1)+2A_{t_1t_2}(1,1)+A_{t_2t_2}(1,1)\}}\right\}$$

$$\times\, \omega\left(f;\frac{1}{\sqrt{n}}\right).$$

The following theorem shows that the operators (2.23) possess the simultaneous approximation.

Theorem 2.4. *[40] For $f \in \tilde{C}^r[0,\infty) \cap E_1$, the following inequality holds:*

$$|K_n^{(r)}(f;x) - f^{(r)}(x)|$$

$$\leq \left\{1 + \sqrt{x + \frac{1}{nA(1,1)}\{A_{t_1}(1,1)+A_{t_2}(1,1)+A_{t_1t_1}(1,1)+2A_{t_1t_2}(1,1)+A_{t_2t_2}(1,1)\}}\right\}$$

$$\times\, \omega\left(f^{(r)};\frac{1}{\sqrt{n}}+\frac{r}{n}\right) + \omega\left(f^{(r)};\frac{r}{n}\right).$$

2.1.9 KANTOROVICH-TYPE GENERALIZATION OF K_n OPERATORS

Also, Varma [40] gave a Kantorovich-type generalization of the operators K_n (2.23) with the same restrictions

$$K_n^*(f;x) = \frac{ne^{-nx}}{A(1,1)} \sum_{k_1=0}^{\infty}\sum_{k_2=0}^{\infty} \frac{p_{k_1,k_2}\left(\frac{nx}{2}\right)}{k_1!k_2!} \int_{\frac{k_1+k_2}{n}}^{\frac{k_1+k_2+1}{n}} f(s)ds. \tag{2.24}$$

In order to study the approximation properties of the operators K_n^*, the first author gave a lemma for the moments of these operators:

Lemma 2.2. *[40] The operators (2.24) satisfy the following equalities:*

1. $K_n^*(1;x) = 1;$
2. $K_n^*(s;x) = x + \frac{A_{t_1}(1,1)+A_{t_2}(1,1)}{nA(1,1)} + \frac{1}{2n};$
3. $K_n^*(s^2;x) = x^2 + \frac{2x}{n}\left(1 + \frac{(A_{t_1}(1,1)+A_{t_2}(1,1))}{A(1,1)}\right)$
   $+\frac{1}{n^2A(1,1)}\{2(A_{t_1}(1,1)+A_{t_2}(1,1)+A_{t_1t_2}(1,1))A_{t_1t_1}(1,1)+A_{t_2t_2}(1,1)\}+\frac{1}{3n^2};$
4. $K_n^*(s^3;x) = \frac{1}{4n^3A(1,1)}\Bigg[\Bigg(36A_{t_1}(1,1)+36A_{t_2}(1,1)+14A(1,1)+12A_{t_2t_2}(1,1)+$
   $12A_{t_1t_1}(1,1)+24A_{t_1t_2}(1,1)\Bigg)nx+\Bigg(48A_{t_1}(1,1)+48A_{t_2}(1,1)+72A(1,1)\Bigg)\frac{n^2x^2}{4}$
   $+32A(1,1)\frac{n^3x^3}{8}+\Bigg(14A_{t_1}(1,1)+14A_{t_2}(1,1)+18A_{t_2t_2}(1,1)+18A_{t_1t_1}(1,1)+$
   $36A_{t_1t_2}(1,1)+4A_{t_2t_2}(1,1)+4A_{t_1t_1t_1}(1,1)+12A_{t_1t_2t_2}(1,1)+12A_{t_1t_1t_2}(1,1)\Bigg)\Bigg];$
5. $K_n^*(s^4;x) = \frac{1}{n^4A(1,1)}\Bigg[\frac{nx}{2}\Bigg(12A(1,1)+60A_{t_1}(1,1)+60A_{t_2}(1,1)+48A_{t_1t_1}(1,1)+$
   $48A_{t_2t_2}(1,1)+8A_{t_1t_1t_1}(1,1)+8A_{t_2t_2t_2}(1,1)+96A_{t_1t_2}(1,1)+12A_{t_1t_1t_2}(1,1)+$
   $12A_{t_1t_2t_2}(1,1)\Bigg)+\frac{n^2x^2}{4}\Bigg(54A(1,1)+78A_{t_2}(1,1)+78A_{t_2}(1,1)+18A_{t_1t_1}(1,1)+$
   $18A_{t_2t_2}(1,1)+24A_{t_1t_2}(1,1)\Bigg)+\frac{n^3x^3}{8}\Bigg(64A(1,1)+32A_{t_1}(1,1)+32A_{t_2}(1,1)\Bigg)+$
   $n^4x^4A(1,1)+4A_{t_1}(1,1)+4A_{t_2}(1,1)+13A_{t_1t_1}(1,1)+13A_{t_2t_2}(1,1)+$
   $9A_{t_1t_1t_1}(1,1)+9A_{t_2t_2t_2}(1,1)+6A_{t_1t_1t_2t_2}(1,1)+6A_{t_1t_1t_2}(1,1)+6A_{t_1t_2t_2}+16A_{t_1t_1}+$
   $6A_{t_1t_2t_2}+\frac{1}{5}\Bigg].$

In the following, the authors show that the uniform convergence of $K_n^*(f)$ to f is established.

Theorem 2.5. *[40] Let $f \in C[0,\infty) \cap E_1$. Then,*

$$\lim_{n\to\infty} K_n^*(f;x) = f(x),$$

the convergence being uniform in each compact subset of $[0,\infty)$.

In the next theorem, the authors obtained the order of approximation $K_n^*(f)$ to f.

Theorem 2.6. *[40] Let $f \in \tilde{C}[0,\infty) \cap E_1$, we have the following inequality for the operator* (2.24)

$$|K_n^*(f;x) - f(x)|$$

$$\leq \left\{1 + \sqrt{x + \frac{1}{nA(1,1)}\{2(A_{t_1}(1,1) + A_{t_2}(1,1) + A_{t_1t_2}(1,1)) + A_{t_1t_1}(1,1) + A_{t_2t_2}(1,1)\} + \frac{1}{3n}}\right\}$$
$$\times \omega\left(f; \frac{1}{\sqrt{n}}\right).$$

Lemma 2.3. *[15] For all $x \geq 0$ and $n > 2$, we have*

$$K_n^*(|s-x|;x) \leq \sqrt{\gamma_n(x)},$$

where $\gamma_n(x) = K_n^*((s-x)^2;x)$.

Theorem 2.7. *[15] Let $0 < r \leq 1$ and $f \in Lip_M^*(r)$. Then for all $x > 0$ and $n > 2$, we have*

$$|K_n^*(f;x) - f(x)| \leq M\left(\frac{\gamma_n(x)}{x}\right)^{\frac{r}{2}},$$

where $\gamma_n(x)$ is defined as in Lemma 2.3.

In order to study the estimate of the error in terms of the second-order modulus of continuity via Peetre's K-functional, we define an auxiliary operator

$$K_n^{**}(f;x) = K_n^*(f;x) + f(x) - f\left(x + \frac{A_{t_1}(1,1) + A_{t_2}(1,1)}{nA(1,1)} + \frac{1}{2n}\right), \tag{2.25}$$

Applying Lemma 2.2, we have $K_n^{**}(1;x) = 1$ and $K_n^{**}(t;x) = x$.

Theorem 2.8. *[15] Let $f \in \tilde{C}_B[0,\infty)$. Then for all $x \geq 0$, the following inequality holds:*

$$|K_n^*(f;x) - f(x)| \leq C\omega_2(f, \sqrt{\psi_n(x)}) + \omega\left(f; \frac{2(A_{t_1}(1,1) + A_{t_2}(1,1)) + A(1,1)}{2A(1,1)n}\right),$$

where $\psi_n(x) = \left(\gamma_n(x) + \left(\frac{2(A_{t_1}(1,1)+A_{t_2}(1,1))+A(1,1)}{2A(1,1)n}\right)^2\right)$.

In order to obtain the next result, the authors adopt an approach of Steklov mean. For $f \in \tilde{C}_B[0,\infty)$, the Steklov mean is defined as

$$f_h(x) = \frac{4}{h^2}\int_0^{\frac{h}{2}}\int_0^{\frac{h}{2}} [2f(x+\xi+\eta) - f(x+2(\xi+\eta))]d\xi d\eta. \tag{2.26}$$

The Steklov mean verifies the following inequalities:

1. $\|f_h - f\| \leq \omega_2(f,h)$;
2. $f_h', f_h'' \in \tilde{C}_B[0,\infty)$ and $\|f_h'\| \leq \frac{5}{n}\omega(f,h), \|f_h''\| \leq \frac{9}{h^2}\omega_2(f,h)$.

Theorem 2.9. *[15] Let $f \in \tilde{C}_B[0,\infty)$. Then, for every $x \geq 0$, the following inequality holds:*

$$|K_n^*(f;x) - f(x)| \leq 5\omega(f, \sqrt{\gamma_n(x)}) + \frac{13}{2}\omega_2(f, \sqrt{\gamma_n(x)}).$$

Theorem 2.10. *[15] For any $f \in C_B^1[0,\infty)$ and $x \in [0,\infty)$, we have*

$$|K_n^*(f,x) - f(x)| \leq |f'(x)| \left| \frac{2(A_{t_1}(1,1) + A_{t_2}(1,1)) + A(1,1)}{2A(1,1)n} \right| + 2\omega(f', \delta)\sqrt{\gamma_n(x)}.$$

Theorem 2.11. *[15] Let $f \in \tilde{C}_B[0,\infty)$, then for every $x \in (0,\infty)$, we have*

$$|K_n^*(f;x) - f(x)| \leq C\omega_\tau\left(f; \sqrt{\frac{\mu}{n}}\right).$$

where $\mu \geq \max\left\{1, \left(\frac{2A_{t_1}(1,1)+2A_{t_2}(1,1)+2A_{t_1t_2}(1,1)A_{t_1t_1}(1,1)+A_{t_2t_2}(1,1)}{A(1,1)} + \frac{1}{3}\right)\right\}$ is any real constant.

In the next result, the authors establish a quantitative Voronovskaja-type theorem by means of the weighted modulus of continuity defined in (2.6).

Theorem 2.12. *Let $f \in C_2^*[0,\infty)$ such that $f'' \in C_2^*[0,\infty)$. Then, the inequality*

$$\left| n(K_n^*(f;x) - f(x)) - f'(x)\left(\frac{A_{t_2}(1,1) + A_{t_1}(1,1)}{A(1,1)} + \frac{1}{2}\right) - \frac{xf''(x)}{2} \right.$$
$$\left. - \frac{f''(x)}{2n}\left(\frac{2A_{t_1}(1,1) + 2A_{t_2}(1,1) + 2A_{t_1t_2t_2}(1,1) + A_{t_1t_2}(1,1) + A_{t_1t_1t_2t_2}(1,1)}{A(1,1)} + \frac{1}{3}\right)\right|$$
$$= O(1)\Omega(f''; 1/\sqrt{n}), \quad as \ n \to \infty$$

holds true.

Now the Grüss-Voronovskaja-type theorem for the operators K_n^*, we state.

Theorem 2.13. *Let $f', g', f'', g'' \in C_2^*[0,\infty)$, then for every $x \in [0,\infty)$*

$$\lim_{n\to\infty} n(K_n^*(fg)(x) - K_n^*(f;x)K_n^*(g;x)) = xf'(x)g'(x).$$

Ansari et al. [3] introduced Jakimovski-Leviatan-Durrmeyer-type operators involving multiple Appell polynomials, and investigated Korovkin-type theorem and the order of convergence by means of the modulus of continuity. Some results in the weighted approximation were also discussed in this paper.

2.1.10 KANTOROVICH VARIANT OF SZÁSZ OPERATORS BASED ON BRENKE-TYPE POLYNOMIALS

For $f \in C[0,\infty)$, Varma et al. [41] defined another generalization of the Szász operators by using Brenke-type polynomials, which are as follows:

$$L_n(f;x) = \frac{1}{A(1)B(nx)} \sum_{k=0}^{\infty} p_k(nx) f\left(\frac{k}{n}\right), \tag{2.27}$$

where $x \geq 0$ and $n \in \mathbb{N}$. Taşdelen et al. [39] introduced the Kantorovich modification of the operators (2.27), which is as follows:

$$K_n(f;x) = \frac{n}{A(1)B(nx)} \sum_{k=0}^{\infty} p_k(nx) \int_{k/n}^{(k+1)/n} f(t)\,dt, \tag{2.28}$$

where $n \in \mathbb{N}$, $x \geq 0$, and $f \in C[0,\infty)$. If we take $B(t) = e^t$ and $A(t) = 1$, then it reduces to the Szász Mirakyan-Kantorovich operators defined by

$$K_n(f;x) = ne^{-nx} \sum_{k=0}^{\infty} \frac{(nx)^k}{k!} \int_{k/n}^{(k+1)/n} f(t)\,dt. \tag{2.29}$$

Mursaleen and Ansari [30] introduced a Chlodowsky-type generalization of Szász operators defined by means of the Brenke-type polynomials, proved basic convergence theorem, and also established the order of approximation with the aid of the second-order modulus of continuity and the Peetre's K-functional.

Öksüzer et al. [33] estimated the rate of convergence of the operators (2.28) for the functions of bounded variations using the techniques of probability theory. The authors rewrite the operator (2.28) as:

$$K_n(f;x) = \int_0^{\infty} f(t) M_n(x,t)dt, \tag{2.30}$$

where

$$M_n(x,t) = \frac{n}{A(1)B(nx)} \sum_{k=0}^{\infty} p_k(nx) \chi_{n,k}(t)$$

$\chi_{n,k}(t)$ is the characteristic function of the interval $[k/n,(k+1)/n]$ with respect to $I = [0,\infty)$.

Lemma 2.4. *[39] For the operator K_n, there hold the equalities*

1. $K_n(1;x) = 1$;
2. $K_n(t;x) = \dfrac{B'(nx)}{B(nx)} + \dfrac{aA'(1)+A(1)}{2nA(1)}$;
3. $K_n(t^2;x) = \dfrac{B''(nx)}{B(nx)}x^2 + \dfrac{2B'(nx)[A'(1)+A(1)]}{nA(1)B(nx)}x$
$+\dfrac{1}{n^2A(1)}\left\{A''(1)+2A'(1)+\dfrac{A(1)}{3}\right\}$;
4. $K_n((t-x)^2;x) = \left\{\dfrac{B''(nx)-2B'(nx)+B(nx)}{B(nx)}\right\}x^2 +$
$\left\{\dfrac{2A'(1)[B'(nx)-B(nx)]+A(1)[2B'(nx)-B(nx)]}{}\right\}x$
$+\dfrac{1}{n^2A(1)}\left\{A''(1)+2A'(1)+\dfrac{A(1)}{3}\right\}.$

Theorem 2.14. *[39] Let*

$$\lim_{y\to\infty}\frac{B'(y)}{B(y)}=1,\quad \lim_{y\to\infty}\frac{B''(y)}{B(y)}=1.$$

If $f\in C[0,\infty)\cap E_1$, then

$$\lim_{n\to\infty}K_n(f;x)=f(x),$$

and the operators K_n converge uniformly in each compact subset of $[0,\infty)$.

Next theorem gives the rate of convergence for the operator K_n.

Theorem 2.15. *[39] Let $f\in\tilde{C}[0,\infty)\cap E$, the operators K_n satisfy the following inequality:*

$$|K_n(f;x)-f(x)|\leq 2\omega\left(f;\sqrt{\delta_n(x)}\right),$$

where $\delta_n(x)=K_n\left((t-x)^2;x\right)$.

Theorem 2.16. *[39] Let $f\in C_B^2[0,\infty)$. There holds the inequality*

$$|K_n(f;x)-f(x)|\leq\zeta||f||_{C_B^2},$$

where

$$\zeta=\zeta_n(x)=\left\{\frac{B''(nx)-2B'(nx)+B(nx)}{2B(nx)}\right\}+\left\{\frac{2A'(1)\left(B'(nx)-B(nx)\right)}{2nA(1)B(nx)}\right.$$
$$\left.+\frac{A(1)\left(2(n+1)B'(nx)-(2n+1)B(nx)\right)}{2nA(1)B(nx)}\right\}x+\frac{2A'(1)+A(1)}{2nA(1)}$$
$$+\frac{1}{2n^2A(1)}\left\{A''(1)+2A(1)+\frac{A(1)}{3}\right\}.$$

Theorem 2.17. *[39] Let $f\in\tilde{C}_B[0,\infty)$. There holds*

$$|K_n(f;x)-f(x)|\leq 2\,M\left\{\omega_2(f;\sqrt{\delta})+\min(1,\delta)||f||_{C_B}\right\},$$

where

$$\delta=\delta_n(x)=\frac{1}{2}\zeta_n(x),$$

and $M>0$ is a constant, which is independent of f and δ.

Atakut and Buyukyazici [6] considered a generalization of the Kantorovich-Szász-type operators involving Brenke-type polynomials as follows:

$$L_n^{\alpha_n,\beta_n}(f;x)=\frac{\beta_n}{A(1)B(\alpha_nx)}\sum_{k=0}^{\infty}p_k(\alpha_nx)\int_{\frac{k}{\beta_n}}^{\frac{k+1}{\beta_n}}f(t)dt, \tag{2.31}$$

where α_n and β_n are strictly increasing sequence of positive numbers such that $\lim_{n\to\infty}\frac{1}{\beta_n}=0, \frac{\alpha_n}{\beta_n}=1+O\left(\frac{1}{\beta_n}\right)$, as $n\to\infty$ and $p_k(x), k=1,1,2...$ are Brenke-type polynomials.

Assuming that $\lim_{x\to\infty}\frac{B^{(k)}(x)}{B(x)}=1$ as $k=1,2,3,4$, Atakut and Buyukyazici obtained the order of convergence of the operators given by (2.31). Subsequently, Garg et al. [12] investigated the degree of approximation of these operators by means of Peetre's K-functional and the Ditizian-Totik modulus of smoothness. The rate of approximation of functions having derivatives equivalent with a function of bounded variation was also obtained.

2.1.11 OPERATORS DEFINED BY MEANS OF BOAS-BUCK-TYPE POLYNOMIALS

Sidharth et al. [36] introduced the Szász-Durrmeyer-type polynomials based on Boas-Buck-type polynomials and established a direct approximation theorem with the aid of unified Ditzian-Totik modulus of smoothness. The approximation of functions whose derivative are locally of bounded variation are also discussed. For a function $f\in C_\gamma[0,\infty)$, Sidharth et al. [36] defined the Szász-Durrmeyer-type operators based on Boas-Buck-type polynomials as follows:

$$\begin{aligned} M_n(f;x) &= \frac{1}{A(1)G(nxH(1))}\sum_{k=1}^{\infty}\frac{p_k(nx)}{B(k,n+1)}\int_0^\infty \frac{t^{k-1}}{(1+t)^{n+k+1}}f(t)dt \\ &+\frac{a_0b_0}{A(1)G(nxH(1))}f(0), \end{aligned} \tag{2.32}$$

where $B(k,n+1)$ is the beta function and $x\geq 0,\ n\in\mathbb{N}$.

Lemma 2.5. *[36] For the operator M_n, the following equalities hold:*

1. $M_n(1;x)=1$;

2. $M_n(t;x)=\frac{1}{n}\left(\frac{G'(nxH(1))}{G(nxH(1))}nx+\frac{A'(1)}{A(1)}\right)$;

3. $M_n(t^2;x)=\frac{1}{n(n-1)}\left[\frac{G''(nxH(1))}{G(nxH(1))}n^2x^2+\left(2\frac{A'(1)}{A(1)}+H''(1)+2\right)\right.$
$\left.\times\frac{G'(nxH(1))}{G(nxH(1))}nx+2\frac{A'(1)}{A(1)}+\frac{A''(1)}{A(1)}\right]$;

4. $M_n(t^3;x)=\frac{1}{n(n-1)(n-2)}\left[\frac{G'''(nxH(1))}{G(nxH(1))}n^3x^3+\left(3\frac{A'(1)}{A(1)}+6+3H''(1)\right)\right.$
$\times\frac{G''(nxH(1))}{G(nxH(1))}n^2x^2+\left(12\frac{A'(1)}{A(1)}+H''(1)+3\frac{A'(1)}{A(1)}H''(1)+H'''(1)+4\right)$
$\left.\times\frac{G'(nxH(1))}{G(nxH(1))}nx+7\frac{A''(1)}{A(1)}+6\frac{A'(1)}{A(1)}\right]$;

5. $$M_n(t^4;x) = \frac{1}{n(n-1)(n-2)(n-3)}\left[\frac{G^{iv}(nxH(1))}{G(nxH(1))}n^4x^4 + \left(4\frac{A'(1)}{A(1)} + 6H''(1)\right.\right.$$
$$\left. + 12\right)\frac{G'''(nxH(1))}{G(nxH(1))}n^3x^3 + \left(6\frac{A''(1)}{A(1)} + 12\frac{A'(1)}{A(1)}H''(1) + 21\frac{A'(1)}{A(1)} + 3\frac{H''(1)}{A(1)}\right.$$
$$\left. + 4H'''(1) + 18H''(1) + 3(H''(1))^2 + 21\right)\frac{G''(nxH(1))}{G(nxH(1))}n^2x^2 + \left(4\frac{A''(1)}{A(1)}\right.$$
$$+ 6\frac{A''(1)}{A(1)}H''(1) + 36\frac{A''(1)}{A(1)}H''(1) + 42\frac{A'(1)}{A(1)} + 4\frac{A'(1)}{A(1)}H'''(1) + 36\frac{A''(1)}{A(1)}$$
$$\left. + H^{iv}(1) + 12H'''(1) + 36H''(1) + 24\right)\frac{G'(nxH(1))}{G(nxH(1))}nx + \frac{A^{iv}(1)}{A(1)} + 48\frac{A''(1)}{A(1)}$$
$$\left. + 13\frac{A'(1)}{A(1)} + 11\right].$$

Lemma 2.6. *[36] For the operator (2.32), the following results hold:*

1. $$M_n((t-x);x) = \left(\frac{G'(nxH(1))}{G(nxH(1))} - 1\right)x + \frac{A'(1)}{nA(1)};$$

2. $$M_n((t-x)^2;x) = \left(\frac{n}{n-1}\frac{G''(nxH(1))}{G(nxH(1))} - 2\frac{G'(nxH(1))}{G(nxH(1))} + 1\right)x^2$$
$$+ \left(\frac{1}{n-1}\left(2\frac{A'(1)}{A(1)} + H''(1) + 2\right)\frac{G'(nxH(1))}{G(nxH(1))} - \frac{2}{n}\frac{A'(1)}{A(1)}\right)x$$
$$+ \frac{1}{n(n-1)}\left(2\frac{A'(1)}{A(1)} + \frac{A''(1)}{A(1)}\right);$$

3. $$M_n((t-x)^4;x) = \left\{\frac{n^3}{(n-1)(n-2)(n-3)}\frac{G^{iv}(nxH(1))}{G(nxH(1))}\right.$$
$$\left. - \frac{4n^2}{(n-1)(n-2)}\frac{G'''(nxH(1))}{G(nxH(1))} + \frac{6n}{(n-1)}\frac{G''(nxH(1))}{G(nxH(1))} - 4\frac{G'(nxH(1))}{G(nxH(1))} + 1\right\}x^4$$
$$+ \left\{\frac{n^2}{(n-1)(n-2)(n-3)}\frac{G'''(nxH(1))}{G(nxH(1))}\left(4\frac{A'(1)}{A(1)} + 6H''(1) + 12\right)\right.$$
$$- \frac{4n}{(n-1)(n-2)}\frac{G''(nxH(1))}{G(nxH(1))}\left(3\frac{A'(1)}{A(1)} + 3H''(1) + 6\right) + \frac{6}{(n-1)}\frac{G'(nxH(1))}{G(nxH(1))}$$
$$\left.\times\left(2\frac{A'(1)}{A(1)} + H''(1) + 2\right) - \frac{4}{n}\frac{A'(1)}{A(1)}\right\}x^3 + \left\{\frac{n}{(n-1)(n-2)(n-3)}\frac{G''(nxH(1))}{G(nxH(1))}\right.$$
$$\times\left(6\frac{A''(1)}{A(1)} + 12\frac{A'(1)}{A(1)}H''(1) + 21\frac{A'(1)}{A(1)} + 3\frac{H''(1)}{A(1)} + 4H'''(1) + 18H''(1)\right.$$
$$\left. + 3(H''(1))^2 + 21\right) - \frac{4}{(n-1)(n-2)}\frac{G'(nxH(1))}{G(nxH(1))}\left(12\frac{A'(1)}{A(1)} + H''(1) + 3\frac{A'(1)}{A(1)}H''\right.$$
$$\left.\left.(1) + H''(1) + 4\right)\right\}x^2 + \left\{\frac{1}{(n-1)(n-2)(n-3)}\frac{G'(nxH(1))}{G(nxH(1))}\left(4\frac{A''(1)}{A(1)}\right.\right.$$
$$+ 6\frac{A''(1)}{A(1)}H''(1) + 36\frac{A''(1)}{A(1)}H''(1) + 42\frac{A'(1)}{A(1)} + 4\frac{A'(1)}{A(1)}H'''(1) + 36\frac{A''(1)}{A(1)}$$

$$+H^{iv}(1)+12H'''(1)+36H''(1)+24\Big)-\frac{4}{n(n-1)(n-2)}\left(7\frac{A''(1)}{A(1)}+6\frac{A'(1)}{A(1)}\right)\Big\}x$$
$$+\frac{1}{(n-1)(n-2)(n-3)}\left(\frac{A^{iv}(1)}{A(1)}+48\frac{A''(1)}{A(1)}+13\frac{A'(1)}{A(1)}+11\right).$$

Lemma 2.7. *[36] For the operator (2.32), the equalities hold:*

1. $\lim_{n\to\infty} nM_n((t-x);x) = l_1(x)x+\frac{A'(1)}{A(1)}$;
2. $\lim\limits_{n\to\infty} nM_n((t-x)^2;x) = l_2(x)x^2+x(H''(1)+2) = \eta(x), (say)$;
3. $\lim\limits_{n\to\infty} n^2M_n((t-x)^4;x) = l_4(x)x^4+l_3(x)x^3+\Big(6\frac{A''(1)}{A(1)}-27\frac{A'(1)}{A(1)}+\frac{H''(1)}{A(1)}+ 14H''(1)+3(H''(1))^2+5\Big) = \nu(x), (say)$.

The following theorem shows that the operators defined by (2.32) are an approximation process for $f\in C_\gamma[0,\infty)$, using the Bohman-Korovkin theorem.

Theorem 2.18. *[36] Let $f\in C_\gamma[0,\infty)$. Then,*

$$\lim_{n\to\infty} M_n(f;x) = f(x),$$

holds uniformly in $x\in[0,a]$, $a>0$.

Proof. From Lemma 2.5, it follows that

$$\lim_{n\to\infty} M_n(t^i;x) = x^i,\ i=0,1,2$$

uniformly in $x\in[0,a]$. Hence by Bohman-Korovkin theorem, the required result is immediate. □

Theorem 2.19. *[36] Let $f\in C_\gamma[0,\infty)$, admitting a derivative of second order at a point $x\in[0,\infty)$, then there holds*

$$\lim_{n\to\infty} n(M_n(f;x)-f(x)) = \left\{l_1(x)x+\frac{A'(1)}{A(1)}\right\}f'(x)+\Big\{l_2(x)x^2 \tag{2.33}$$
$$+x(H''(1)+2)\Big\}\frac{f''(x)}{2}. \tag{2.34}$$

If f'' is continuous on $[0,\infty)$, then the limit in (2.33) holds uniformly in $x\in[0,a]\subset[0,\infty), a>0$.

In 2018, Mursaleen et al. [31] considered a Chlodowsky variant of generalized Szász-type operators involving Boas-Buck-type polynomials and studied some approximation properties of these operators in a weighted space of continuous functions on $[0,\infty)$.

2.1.12 OPERATORS DEFINED BY MEANS OF CHARLIER POLYNOMIALS

In 1950, Szász [38] introduced the following linear positive operators

$$S_n(f;x) = e^{-nx} \sum_{k=0}^{\infty} \frac{(nx)^k}{k!} f\left(\frac{k}{n}\right), \tag{2.35}$$

where $x \in [0,\infty)$ and $f(x)$ is a continuous function on $[0,\infty)$ whenever the above sum converges uniformly. These polynomials [18] have the generating functions of the form

$$e^t\left(1-\frac{t}{a}\right)^u = \sum_{k=0}^{\infty} C_k^{(a)}(u)\frac{t^k}{k!}, \ |t| < a, \tag{2.36}$$

where $C_k^{(a)}(u) = \sum_{r=0}^{k} \binom{k}{r}(-u)_r\left(\frac{1}{a}\right)^r$ and $(m)_0 = 1, (m)_j = m(m+1)\cdots(m+j-1)$ for $j \geq 1$. For $f \in C[0,\infty) \cap E_2$, Varma and Taşdelen [42] defined the following Szász-type operators involving Charlier polynomials

$$\mathcal{L}_n(f;x,a) = e^{-1}\left(1-\frac{1}{a}\right)^{(a-1)nx} \sum_{k=0}^{\infty} \frac{C_k^{(a)}(-(a-1)nx)}{k!} f\left(\frac{k}{n}\right), \tag{2.37}$$

where $a > 1$ and $x \in [0,\infty)$. For the special case, $a \to \infty$ and $x - \frac{1}{n}$ instead of x, these operators reduce to the operators (2.35).

Lemma 2.8. *[42] The operators (2.37) satisfy the following equalities:*

1. $L_n(1;x,a) = 1$;
2. $L_n(t;x,a) = x + \frac{1}{n}$;
3. $L_n(t^2;x,a) = x^2 + \frac{x}{n}\left(3 + \frac{1}{a-1}\right) + \frac{2}{n^2}$

where $x \geq 0$.

Theorem 2.20. *[42] Let* $f \in C[0,\infty) \cap E_2$, *then*

$$\lim_{n\to\infty} L_n(f;x,a) = f(x),$$

the sequence of operators given by (2.37) *converges uniformly in each compact subset of* $[0,\infty)$.

Theorem 2.21. *[42] Let* $f \in \tilde{C}[0,\infty) \cap E_2$. *For the operators* L_n *given by* (2.37), *there holds the inequality:*

$$|L_n(f;x,a) - f(x)| \leq \left\{1 + \sqrt{x\left(1+\frac{1}{a-1}\right) + \frac{2}{n}}\right\} \omega\left(f;\frac{1}{\sqrt{n}}\right).$$

Also, Varma and Taşdelen [42] considered Kantorovich-type generalization of the operators $L_n(f;x,a)$ for a function

$$f \in \bar{C}[0,\infty) := \left\{ f \in C[0,\infty) : |F(x)| = \left| \int_0^x f(s)ds \right| \leq Ke^{Bx}, B \in \mathbb{R} \text{ and } K \in \mathbb{R}^+ \right\}$$

as follows :

$$L^*_{n,a}(f;x) = ne^{-1}\left(1-\frac{1}{a}\right)^{(a-1)nx} \sum_{k=0}^{\infty} \frac{C_k^{(a)}(-(a-1)nx)}{k!} \int_{\frac{k}{n}}^{\frac{k+1}{n}} f(t)dt, \quad (2.38)$$

where $a > 1$ and $x \geq 0$, and studied the uniform convergence of $L^*_{n,a}(f;x)$ to f on each compact subset of $[0,\infty)$ and the degree of approximation in terms of the classical modulus of continuity.

Lemma 2.9. *[42] The operators given by* (2.38) *satisfy the following equalities:*

1. $L_n^*(1;x,a) = 1;$
2. $L_n^*(t;x,a) = x + \frac{3}{2n};$
3. $L_n^*(t^2;x,a) = x^2 + \frac{x}{n}\left(4 + \frac{1}{a-1}\right) + \frac{10}{3n^2}.$

Theorem 2.22. *[42] Let $f \in C[0,\infty) \cap E_3$, then*

$$\lim_{n\to\infty} L_n^*(f;x,a) = f(x),$$

holds uniformly in each compact subset of $[0,\infty)$.

Theorem 2.23. *[42] Let $f \in \tilde{C}[0,\infty) \cap E_3$. For the operators L_n*, there holds the following inequality:*

$$|L_n^*(f;x,a) - f(x)| \leq \left\{ 1 + \sqrt{x + \left(1 + \frac{1}{a-1}\right) + \frac{10}{3n}} \right\} \omega\left(f; \frac{1}{\sqrt{n}}\right).$$

Further, for the operator L_n (2.37), Kajla and Agrawal [23] proved some approximation theorems. Let $e_i(x) = x^i, i = 0,1,2,\cdots$

Lemma 2.10. *[23] For the operators $\mathcal{L}_n(e_s(t);x,a)$, $s = 3,4$, we have*

1. $\mathcal{L}_n(e_3(t);x,a) = x^3 + \frac{x^2}{n}\left(6 + \frac{3}{a-1}\right) + \frac{2x}{n^2}\left(\frac{1}{(a-1)^2} + \frac{3}{a-1} + 5\right) + \frac{5}{n^3};$
2. $\mathcal{L}_n(e_4(t);x,a) = x^4 + \frac{x^3}{n}\left(10 + \frac{6}{a-1}\right) + \frac{x^2}{n^2}\left(31 + \frac{30}{a-1} + \frac{11}{(a-1)^2}\right)$
$+ \frac{x}{n^3}\left(67 + \frac{31}{a-1} + \frac{20}{(a-1)^2} + \frac{6}{(a-1)^3}\right) + \frac{15}{n^4}.$

Let $e_i^x(t) = (t-x)^i, i = 0,1,2\cdots$

Lemma 2.11. *[23] For the operators $\mathcal{L}_n(f;x,a)$, we have*

1. $\mathcal{L}_n(e_1^x(t);x,a) = \frac{1}{n}$;
2. $\mathcal{L}_n(e_2^x(t);x,a) = \frac{ax}{n(a-1)} + \frac{2}{n^2}$;
3. $\mathcal{L}_n(e_4^x(t);x,a) = \frac{x}{n^3}\left(17 + \frac{49}{(a-1)} - \frac{20}{(a-1)^2} + \frac{6}{(a-1)^3}\right)$ $+ \frac{x^2}{n^2}\left(19 - \frac{46}{(a-1)} + \frac{3}{(a-1)^2}\right) + \frac{15}{n^4}$.

Proof. Using ([42], p. 119, Lemma 1) and Lemma 2.10, the proof of this lemma easily follows. Hence, the details are omitted. □

To study the rate of convergence of functions having a derivative of bounded variation, let us rewrite the operators (2.37) as

$$\mathcal{L}_n(f;x,a) = \int_0^\infty f(w)\frac{\partial}{\partial w}\{\mathcal{K}_n(x,w,a)\}\,dw, \tag{2.39}$$

where

$$\mathcal{K}_n(x,w,a) = \begin{cases} \sum\limits_{k\le nw} e^{-1}\left(1-\frac{1}{a}\right)^{(a-1)nx}\frac{C_k^{(a)}(-(a-1)nx)}{k!}, & \text{if } 0 < w < \infty, \\ 0, & \text{if } w = 0. \end{cases}$$

From Lemma 2.11, for $x \in (0,\infty)$ and sufficiently large n, we have

$$\mathcal{L}_n(|e_1^x(t)|;x,a) \le \left(\mathcal{L}_n((t-x)^2;x,a)\right)^{1/2} \le \sqrt{\frac{\lambda(a)x}{n}}, \tag{2.40}$$

where $\lambda(a)$ is some positive constant depending on a.
Also the authors get, for $r \ge 2$ and fixed $x \in [0,\infty)$,

$$\mathcal{L}_n(e_{2r}^x(t);x,a) = O(n^{-r});\ n \to \infty. \tag{2.41}$$

Lemma 2.12. *[23] For all $x \in (0,\infty)$ and sufficiently large n, we have*

1. $\vartheta_{n,a}(x,t) = \int_0^t \frac{\partial}{\partial w}\{\mathcal{K}_n(x,w,a)\}\,dw \le \frac{1}{(x-t)^2}\frac{\lambda(a)x}{n}$, $0 \le t < x$;
2. $1 - \vartheta_{n,a}(x,z) = \int_z^\infty \frac{\partial}{\partial w}\{\mathcal{K}_n(x,w,a)\}\,dw \le \frac{1}{(z-x)^2}\frac{\lambda(a)x}{n}$, $x < z < \infty$,

where $\lambda(a)$ is a constant as described in (2.40).

Proof. First, we prove (i).

$$\vartheta_{n,a}(x,t) = \int_0^t \frac{\partial}{\partial w}\{\mathcal{K}_n(x,w,a)\}\,dw \le \int_0^t \left(\frac{x-w}{x-t}\right)^2 \frac{\partial}{\partial w}\{\mathcal{K}_n(x,w,a)\}\,dw$$

$$\leq \frac{1}{(x-t)^2}\mathcal{L}_n((w-x)^2;x,a)$$
$$\leq \frac{1}{(x-t)^2}\frac{\lambda(a)x}{n}.$$

The proof of (ii) is similar, and hence, it is omitted. □

Theorem 2.24. *[23] Let $f \in Lip_M^*(r)$ and $r \in (0,1]$. Then, for all $x \in (0,\infty)$, we have*

$$\mid \mathcal{L}_n(f;x,a) - f(x) \mid \leq M\left(\frac{\zeta_{n,a}(x)}{a_1x^2+a_2x}\right)^{\frac{r}{2}},$$

where $\zeta_{n,a}(x) = \mathcal{L}_n((t-x)^2;x,a)$.

Proof. Applying the Hölder's inequality with $p = \frac{2}{r}$ and $q = \frac{2}{2-r}$, we find that

$$\mid \mathcal{L}_n(f;x,a) - f(x) \mid \leq \left\{ e^{-1}\left(1-\frac{1}{a}\right)^{(a-1)nx} \sum_{k=0}^{\infty} \frac{C_k^{(a)}(-(a-1)nx)}{k!} \left| f\left(\frac{k}{n}\right) - f(x)\right|^{\frac{2}{r}} \right\}^{r/2}$$
$$\leq M\left\{ e^{-1}\left(1-\frac{1}{a}\right)^{(a-1)nx} \sum_{k=0}^{\infty} \frac{C_k^{(a)}(-(a-1)nx)}{k!} \frac{\left(\frac{k}{n}-x\right)^2}{\left(\frac{k}{n}+a_1x^2+a_2x\right)} \right\}^{r/2}.$$

Since $f \in Lip_M^*(r)$ and $\frac{1}{\sqrt{\frac{k}{n}+a_1x^2+a_2x}} < \frac{1}{\sqrt{a_1x^2+a_2x}}, \forall x \in (0,\infty)$, we have

$$\mid \mathcal{L}_n(f;x,a) - f(x) \mid \leq \frac{M}{(a_1x^2+a_2x)^{\frac{r}{2}}} \left\{ e^{-1}\left(1-\frac{1}{a}\right)^{(a-1)nx} \right.$$
$$\left. \times \sum_{k=0}^{\infty} \frac{C_k^{(a)}(-(a-1)nx)}{k!} \left(\frac{k}{n}-x\right)^2 \right\}^{r/2}$$
$$= \frac{M}{(a_1x^2+a_2x)^{\frac{r}{2}}} (\mathcal{L}_n|t-x|;x,a)^r$$
$$\leq M\left(\frac{\zeta_{n,a}(x)}{a_1x^2+a_2x}\right)^{\frac{r}{2}}.$$

This completes the proof of the theorem. □

Theorem 2.25. *[23] Let $f \in \tilde{C}_B[0,\infty)$ and $0 < r \leq 1$. Then, for all $x \in [0,\infty)$, we have*

$$|\mathcal{L}_n(f;x,a) - f(x)| \leq \widetilde{\omega}_r(f,x)(\zeta_{n,a}(x))^{\frac{r}{2}}.$$

Proof. From equation (2.2), we have

$$|\mathcal{L}_n(f;x,a) - f(x)| \leq \widetilde{\omega}_r(f,x)\mathcal{L}_n(|t-x|^r;x,a).$$

Applying the Hölder's inequality with $p = \frac{2}{r}$ and $q = \frac{2}{2-r}$, we get

$$|\mathcal{L}_n(f;x,a) - f(x)| \leq \widetilde{\omega}_r(f,x)(\mathcal{L}_n((t-x)^2;x,a))^{\frac{r}{2}} \leq \widetilde{\omega}_r(f,x)(\zeta_{n,a}(x))^{\frac{r}{2}}.$$

Thus, the proof is completed. □

Theorem 2.26. *[23] Let $f \in C_2^*[0,\infty)$. Then, we have*

$$\lim_{n\to\infty} \|\mathcal{L}_n(f;\cdot,a) - f\|_2 = 0. \tag{2.42}$$

Proof. From [10], we know that it is sufficient to verify the following three equations

$$\lim_{n\to\infty} \|\mathcal{L}_n(e_m;\cdot,a) - e_m\|_2 = 0,\ m = 0,1,2. \tag{2.43}$$

Since $\mathcal{L}_n(1;x,a) = 1$, the condition in (2.43) holds true for $m = 0$.

By ([42], Lemma 1), we have

$$\|\mathcal{L}_n(e_1;\cdot,a) - e_1\|_2 = \sup_{x\geq 0} \frac{1}{1+x^2}\left|x + \frac{1}{n} - x\right| \leq \frac{1}{n}.$$

Thus, $\lim_{n\to\infty} \|\mathcal{L}_n(t;\cdot,a) - e_1\|_2 = 0$. Similarly, we get

$$\begin{aligned}\|\mathcal{L}_n(e_2;\cdot,a) - e_2\|_2 &= \sup_{x\geq 0} \frac{1}{1+x^2}\left|x^2 + \frac{x}{n}\left(3 + \frac{1}{a-1}\right) + \frac{2}{n^2} - x^2\right| \\ &\leq \frac{1}{n}\left(3 + \frac{1}{(a-1)}\right) + \frac{2}{n^2},\end{aligned}$$

which implies that $\lim_{n\to\infty} \|\mathcal{L}_n(e_2;\cdot,a) - e_2\|_2 = 0$. This completes the proof. □

Next, the authors [23] gave a theorem to approximate all functions in $C_2[0,\infty)$. This type of result is discussed in [11] for locally integrable functions.

Theorem 2.27. *[23] For each $f \in C_2[0,\infty)$ and $\beta > 0$, we have*

$$\lim_{n\to\infty} \sup_{x\in[0,\infty)} \frac{|\mathcal{L}_n(f;x,a) - f(x)|}{(1+x^2)^{1+\beta}} = 0.$$

Proof. For any fixed $x_0 > 0$,

$$\begin{aligned}\sup_{x\in[0,\infty)} \frac{|\mathcal{L}_n(f;x,a) - f(x)|}{(1+x^2)^{1+\beta}} &\leq \sup_{x\leq x_0} \frac{|\mathcal{L}_n(f;x,a) - f(x)|}{(1+x^2)^{1+\beta}} + \sup_{x\geq x_0} \frac{|\mathcal{L}_n(f;x,a) - f(x)|}{(1+x^2)^{1+\beta}} \\ &\leq \| \mathcal{L}_n(f) - f \|_{C[0,x_0]} + \| f \|_2 \sup_{x\geq x_0} \frac{|\mathcal{L}_n(1+t^2;x,a)|}{(1+x^2)^{1+\beta}}\end{aligned}$$

$$+\sup_{x\geq x_0}\frac{|f(x)|}{(1+x^2)^{1+\beta}},$$
$$=: I_1+I_2+I_3,\ \text{say.} \tag{2.44}$$

Since $|f(x)| \leq ||f||_2(1+x^2)$, we have

$$I_3=\sup_{x\geq x_0}\frac{|f(x)|}{(1+x^2)^{1+\beta}}\leq \sup_{x\geq x_0}\frac{||f||_2}{(1+x^2)^{\beta}}\leq \frac{||f||_2}{(1+x_0^2)^{\beta}}.$$

Let $\varepsilon>0$ be arbitrary.

$$\frac{M_f}{(1+x_0^2)^{\gamma}}<\frac{\varepsilon}{3}, \tag{2.45}$$

In view of ([42], Theorem 1), there exists $n_1\in\mathbb{N}$ such that

$$\| f \|_2\frac{|\mathcal{L}_n(1+t^2;x,a)|}{(1+x^2)^{1+\beta}}<\frac{1}{(1+x^2)^{1+\beta}}\| f \|_2\left((1+x^2)+\frac{\varepsilon}{3||f||_2}\right),\forall n\geq n_1$$
$$<\frac{||f||_2}{(1+x^2)^{\beta}}+\frac{\varepsilon}{3},\forall n\geq n_1. \tag{2.46}$$

Hence, $||f||_2\sup\limits_{x\geq x_0}\dfrac{|\mathcal{L}_n(1+t^2;x,a)|}{(1+x^2)^{1+\beta}}<\dfrac{||f||_2}{(1+x_0^2)^{\beta}}+\dfrac{\varepsilon}{3},\ \forall n\geq n_1.$

Thus, $I_2+I_3<\dfrac{2||f||_{\varphi}}{(1+x_0^2)^{\beta}}+\dfrac{\varepsilon}{3},\ \forall n\geq n_1.$

Now, let us choose x_0 to be so large that $\dfrac{||f||_{\varphi}}{(1+x^2)^{\beta}}<\dfrac{\varepsilon}{6}.$

Then,

$$I_2+I_3<\frac{2\varepsilon}{3},\ \forall n\geq n_1. \tag{2.47}$$

By Theorem (2.28), there exists $n_2\in\mathbb{N}$ such that

$$I_1=\| \mathcal{L}_n(f)-f \|_{C[0,x_0]}<\frac{\varepsilon}{3},\ \forall n\geq n_2. \tag{2.48}$$

Let $n_0=\max(n_1,n_2)$. Then, combining (2.44)–(2.48)

$$\sup_{x\in[0,\infty)}\frac{|\mathcal{L}_n(f;x,a)-f(x)|}{(1+x^2)^{1+\beta}}<\varepsilon,\ \forall n\geq n_0.$$

This completes the proof. □

Theorem 2.28. *[23] Let $f\in C_2[0,\infty)$. Then, we have*

$$||\mathcal{L}_n(f;\cdot,a)-f||_{C[0,b]}\leq 4M_f(1+b^2)\zeta_{n,a}(b)+2\omega_{b+1}(f,\sqrt{\zeta_{n,a}(b)}),$$

where $\zeta_{n,a}(b)=\dfrac{ab}{n(a-1)}+\dfrac{2}{n^2}.$

Proof. From [16], for $x \in [0,b]$ and $t \geq 0$, we have

$$|f(t)-f(x)| \leq 4M_f(1+x^2)(t-x)^2 + \left(1+\frac{|t-x|}{\delta}\right)\omega_{b+1}(f,\delta), \delta > 0.$$

Hence applying Cauchy-Schwarz inequality, we get

$$\begin{aligned} |\mathcal{L}_n(f;x,a)-f(x)| &\leq 4M_f(1+x^2)\mathcal{L}_n((t-x)^2;x,a) \\ &\quad + \omega_{b+1}(f,\delta)\left(1+\frac{1}{\delta}\mathcal{L}_n(|t-x|;x,a)\right) \\ &\leq 4M_f(1+x^2)\zeta_{n,a}(x) + \omega_{b+1}(f,\delta)\left(1+\frac{1}{\delta}\sqrt{\zeta_{n,a}(x)}\right) \\ &\leq 4M_f(1+b^2)\zeta_{n,a}(b) + \omega_{b+1}(f,\delta)\left(1+\frac{1}{\delta}\sqrt{\zeta_{n,a}(b)}\right). \end{aligned}$$

Choosing $\delta = \sqrt{\zeta_{n,a}(b)}$, we get the desired result. □

Further, Kajla and Agrawal [25] considered Kantorovich-type generalization of the operators $L_n(f;x,a)$ for a function $f \in \tilde{C}[0,\infty) := \{f \in C[0,\infty) : |F(x)| = |\int_0^x f(s)ds| \leq Ke^{Bx}, B \in \mathbb{R} \text{ and } K \in \mathbb{R}^+\}$, and established some more approximation properties of the operators $L^*_{n,a}$ such as weighted approximation, A-statistical convergence, and approximation of functions with a derivative of bounded variation. They also presented some moment estimates and a result needed to study approximation of functions with derivatives of bounded variation. They discussed the main results of this paper wherein we establish approximation in a Lipschitz-type space, weighted approximation theorems, and A-statistical convergence properties for the operators $L^*_{n,a}$. Lastly, they obtained the rate of convergence for functions having a derivative of bounded variation on every finite subinterval of $[0,\infty)$, for these operators.

In 2016, Agrawal and Ispir [2] introduced a new bivariate operator associated with a combination of Chlodowsky and generalized Szász-Charlier-type operators as follows:

$$T_{n,m}(f;x,y,a) = \sum_{k=0}^{n}\sum_{j=0}^{\infty} p_{n,k}\left(\frac{x}{\alpha_n}\right) s_{m,j}(\beta_{my},a) f\left(\frac{k\alpha_n}{n}, \frac{j}{\gamma_m}\right).$$

for all $n,m \in \mathbb{N}$, $f \in C(A_{\alpha_n})$ with $A_{\alpha_n} = \{(x,y) : 0 \leq x \leq \alpha_n,\ 0 \leq y \leq \infty\}$ and $C(A_{\alpha_n}) = \{f : A_{\alpha_n} \to \mathbb{R} \text{ is continuous}\}$. Here, α_n is an unbounded sequence of positive numbers such that $\lim_{n\to\infty}\left(\frac{\alpha_n}{n}\right) = 0$, and also γ_m and β_m denote the unbounded sequences of positive numbers such that $\frac{\beta_m}{\gamma_m} = 1 + O\left(\frac{1}{\gamma_m}\right)$. Also, the basic elements are $p_{n,k}\left(\frac{x}{\alpha_n}\right) = \binom{n}{k}\left(\frac{x}{\alpha_n}\right)\left(1-\frac{x}{\alpha_n}\right)^{n-k}$ and $s_{m,j}(\beta_m y,a) = e^{-1}\left(1-\frac{1}{a}\right)^{(a-1)\beta_m y}\frac{C_j^{(a)}(-(a-1)\beta_m y)}{j!}$, where $C_j^{(a)}(u)$ is Charlier polynomial and $a > 1$. For the special case, $a \to \infty$ and $y - \left(\frac{x}{m}\right)$ instead of y, the operators $T_{n,m}$ reduce to the operators studied by Gazanfer and Buyukyazici [13]. They give the degree of approximation for these bivariate operators by means of the complete and partial modulus of continuity, and also by using weighted modulus of continuity. Furthermore, they construct a GBS (generalized Boolean sum) operator of bivariate Chlodowsky-Szász-Charlier type and estimate the order of approximation in terms of mixed modulus of continuity.

Motivated by the above development, Wafi et al. [43] defined a new sequence of Kantorovich-Szász-type operators which preserves constant and quadratic test functions, i.e., $e_0(x)$ and $e_2(x)$, where $e_i(x) = x^i$, i = 0,2

$$K^*_{n,a}(f;r^*_{n,a}(x)) = ne^{-1}\left(1-\frac{1}{a}\right)^{(a-1)nr^*_{n,a}(x)} \sum_{k=0}^{\infty} \frac{C_k^{(a)}(-(a-1)nr^*_{n,a}(x))}{k!} \int_{\frac{k}{n}}^{\frac{k+1}{n}} f(t)dt \tag{2.49}$$

where $r^*_{n,a}(x) = \frac{\left(-4+\frac{1}{a-1}\right)+\sqrt{\left(4+\frac{1}{a-1}\right)^2+4\left(n^2x^2-\frac{10}{3}\right)}}{2n}$ and $r^*_{n,a}(x) \geq 0$ for $x \in \left[\frac{\sqrt{\frac{10}{3}}}{n}, \infty\right)$.

For a fixed $x \in \left[\frac{\sqrt{\frac{10}{3}}}{n}, \infty\right)$, $r^*_{n,a}(x) \to x$, as $n \to \infty$, and the operators (2.49) reduce to operators (2.38). Wafi et al. [43] discussed the rate of convergence by determining better error estimates. Further, the authors investigated the order of approximation by means of local approximation results with the help of Ditzian-Totik modulus of smoothness, second-order modulus of continuity, Peetre's K-functional, and Lipschitz class.

2.1.13 OPERATORS DEFINED BY USING Q-CALCULUS

First, we shall give some definitions.

Following [5,22], for any fixed real number $q > 0$, satisfying the condition $0 < q < 1$, the q-integer $[k]_q$, for $k \in \mathbb{N}$, and q-factorial $[k]_q!$ are defined as

$$[k]_q = \begin{cases} \dfrac{(1-q^k)}{(1-q)}, & \text{if } q \neq 1 \\ k, & \text{if } q = 1, \end{cases}$$

and

$$[k]_q! = \begin{cases} [k]_q[k-1]_q \dots 1, & \text{if } k \geq 1 \\ 1, & \text{if } k = 0, \end{cases}$$

respectively. For any integers n, k satisfying $0 \leq k \leq n$, the q-binomial coefficient is given by

$$\binom{n}{k}_q = \frac{[n]_q!}{[n-k]_q![k]_q!}.$$

The q-analogue of $(1-x)^n$ is given by

$$(1-x)_q^n = \begin{cases} \prod_{j=0}^{n-1}(1-q^j x), & n=1,2,... \\ 1, & n=0. \end{cases}$$

The q-integration in the interval [0,a] is defined by

$$\int_0^a f(t)d_qt = a(1-q)\sum_{n=0}^{\infty} f(aq^n)q^n \quad 0<q<1,$$

provided the series converges.
Karaisa [27] introduced a Stancu-type generalization of the q-Favard-Szász operator as follows:

$$T_{n,t}^{\alpha,\beta}(f;q,x) = \frac{E_q^{-[n]_qt}}{A(1)}\sum_{k=0}^{\infty}\frac{P_k(q;[n]_qt)}{[k]_q!}f\left(x+\frac{[k]_q+\alpha}{[n]_q+\beta}\right),$$

where $P_k(q;.)\geq 0$ for each k is a q-Appell generated by

$$B(u)e^{[n]_qtu} = \sum_{k=0}^{\infty}\frac{P_k(q;[n]_qt)u^k}{[k]_q!}$$

and $B(u)$ is defined by

$$B(u) = \sum_{k=0}^{\infty} a_k u^k,$$

and studied Korovkin-type statistical approximation properties and rate of convergence using modulus of continuity. He also obtained some local approximation results for these operators.
For $f\in C_\gamma[0,\infty)$, Agrawal and Gupta [1] defined the q-analogue of the operators (2.17) defined in [26] as follows:

$$\mathcal{L}_n(f;q,x) = \frac{E^{-[n]_qx}}{g(1)}\sum_{k=0}^{\infty}\frac{P_k(q;[n]_qx)}{[k]_q!B_q(n+1,k)}q^{\frac{k(k-1)}{2}} \int_0^{\infty}\frac{t^{k-1}}{(1+t)_q^{n+k+1}}f(q^kt)d_qt,$$

and obtained the rate of convergence in terms of the weighted modulus of continuity and a Lipschitz-type maximal function for these operators.

ACKNOWLEDGMENT

Many thanks to our TEX-pert for developing this class file.

REFERENCES

[1] P. N. Agrawal and P. Gupta, Durrmeyer variant of q-Favard-Szász operators based on Appell polynomials. *Creat. Math. Inform.* **26**(1) (2017) 9–7.

[2] P. N. Agrawal, and N. Ispir, Degree of approximation for bivariate Chlodowsky-Szász-Charlier type operators. *Results Math.,* **69**(3–4) (2016) 369–385.

[3] K. J. Ansari, M. Mursaleen and S. Rahman, Approximation by Jakimovski-Leviatan operators of Durrmeyer type involving multiple Appell polynomials. *RACSAM* **113** (2019) 1007–1024.

[4] P. E. Appell, Sur une classe de polynomes. *Annales scientifique de l'E.N.S.* **2**(9) (1880) 119–144.

[5] A. Aral, V. Gupta and R. P. Agarwal, *Application of q-Calculus in Operator Theory.* Springer, New York (2013).

[6] Ç. Atakut and I. Büyükyazici, Approximation by Kantorovich-Szász type operators based on Brenke type polynomials. *Numer. Funct. Anal. Optim.* **37(12)** (2016), 1488–1502.

[7] T. S. Chihara, *An Introduction to Orthogonal Polynomials*, Gordon and Breach, NewYork, 1978.

[8] A. Ciupa, Positive linear operators obtained by means of Appell polynomials. in *Approximation and optimization,* Vol. II (Cluj-Napoca, 1996), 63–68, Transilvania, Cluj.

[9] R. A. Devore and G. G. Lorentz, *Constructive Approximation.* Springer, Berlin (1993).

[10] A. D. Gadjiev., On P. P. Korovkin type theorems. *Math. Zametki* **20**(5) (1976) 781–786.

[11] A. D. Gadjiev, R. O. Efendiyev and E. Ibikli, On Korovkin type theorems in space of locally integrable functions. *Czechoslovak Math. J.* **53(128)**(1) (2003) 45–53.

[12] T. Garg, P. N. Agrawal and S. Araci, Rate of convergence by Kantorovich-Szász type operators based on Brenke type polynomials. *J. Inequal. Appl.* 2017 **(156)**.

[13] A. F. Gazanfer and I. Büyükyazici, Approximation by certain linear positive operators of two variables. *Abstr. Appl. Anal.* 2014, Art. ID 782080 (2014).

[14] P. Gupta and P. N. Agrawal, Jakimovski-Leviatan operators of Durrmeyer type involving Appell polynomials. *Turk. J. Math.* **42** (2018) 1457–1470.

[15] P. Gupta and P. N. Agrawal, Quantitative Voronovskaja and Grüss Voronovskaja-type theorems for operators of Kantorovich type involving multiple Appell polynomials. *Iran. J. Sci. Technol. Trans. Sci.* **43** (2019) 1679–1687.

[16] E. Ibikli and E. A. Gadjiev, The order of approximation of some unbounded function by the sequences of positive linear operators. *Turk. J. Math.* **19**(3) (1995) 331–337.

[17] G. İçöz, S. Varma and S. Sucu, Approximation by operators including generalized Appell polynomials, *Filomat* **30** (2) (2016) 429–440.

[18] M. E. H. Ismail, *Classical and Quantum Orthogonal Polynomials in One Variable.* Cambridge University Press, Cambridge (2005).

[19] M. E. H. Ismail, On a generalization of Szász operators. *Mathematica (Cluj),* **39** (1974) 259–267.

[20] N. Ispir and Ç. Atakut, Approximation by modified Szász-Mirakjan operators on weighted space. *Proc. Indian Acad. Sci. Math. Sci.* **112**(4) (2002) 571–578.

[21] A. Jakimovski and D. Leviatan, Generalized Szász operators for the approximation in the infinite interval. *Mathematica (Cluj),* **34** (1969) 97–103.

[22] V. Kac and P. Cheung, *Quantum Calculus.* Universitext, Springer, New York (2002).

[23] A. Kajla and P. N. Agrawal, Approximation properties of Szász type operators based on Charlier polynomials. *Turk. J. Math.* **39** (2015) 990–1003.

[24] A. Kajla and P. N. Agrawal, Szász-Durrmeyer type operators based on Charlier polynomials. *Appl. Math. Comput.* **268** (2015) 1001–1014.

[25] A. Kajla and P. N. Agrawal, Szász-Kantorovich type operators based on Charlier polynomials. *Kyungpook Math. J.* **56**(3) (2016) 877–897.

[26] A. Karaisa, Approximation by Durrmeyer type Jakimovski-Leviatan operators. *Math. Meth. Appl. Sci.* **39**(9) (2016) 2401–2410.

[27] A. Karaisa, D. Turgut and Y. Asar, Stancu type generalization of q-Favard-Szász operators. *Appl. Math. Comput.* **264** (2015) 249–257.

[28] D. Lee, On multiple Appell polynomials. *Proc. Amer. Math. Soc.* **139**(6) (2011), 2133–2141.

[29] B. Lenze, On Lipschitz type maximal functions and their smoothness spaces. *Nederl. Akad. Indag. Math.* **50** (1) (1988) 53–63.

[30] M. Mursaleen and K. J. Ansari, On Chlodowsky variant of Szász operators by Brenke type polynomials. *Appl. Math. Comput.* **271** (2015) 991–1003.

[31] M. Mursaleen, A. H. Al-Abied and A. M. Acu, Approximation by Chlodowsky type of Szász operators based on Boas-Buck type polynomials. *Turk. J. Math.* **42** (2018) 2243–2259.

[32] T. Neer, A. M. Acu and P. N. Agrawal, Baskakov-Durrmeyer type operators involving generalized Appell polynomials. *Math. Meth. Appl. Sci.* 2019: 1–13, http://doi.org/10.1002/mma.6089.

[33] Ö. Öksüzer, H. Karsli and F. Taşdelen, Approximation by Kantorovich variant of Szász operators based on Brenke type polynomials. Mediterr. *J. Math.* **13** (2016) 3327–3340.

[34] M. A. Özarslan and O. Duman, Local approximation behaviour of modified SMK operators. *Miskolc Math. Notes.* **11**(1) (2010) 87–99.

[35] I. M. Sheffer, Some properties of polynomial sets of type zero. *Duke Math. J.* **5** (1939) 590–622.

[36] M. Sidharth, P. N. Agrawal and S. Araci, Szász-Durrmeyer operators involving Boas-Buck polynomials of blending type. *J. Inequal. Appl.* 2017, **127**.

[37] S. Sucu, G. İçöz and S. Varma, *On some extension of Szász operators including Boas-Buck type polynomials*, Absr. Appl. Anal. volume 2012. Hindawi Publishing Corporation, (2012).

[38] O. Szász, Generalization of S. Bernstein's polynomials to the infinite interval. *J. Res. Nat. Bur. Standards* **45** (1950) 239–245.

[39] F. Taşdelen, R. Aktaş, and A. Altin, A Kantorovich type of Szász operators including Brenke type polynomials , *Abs. Appl. Anal.* Artical Number 867203 (2012) DOI: 10.1155/2012/867203.

[40] S. Varma, On a generalization of Szász operators by multiple Appell polynomials. Studia Universitatis Babes-Bolyai, *Mathematica* **58**(3) (2013) 361–369.

[41] S. Varma, S. Sucu and G. Icoz, Generalization of Szász operators involving Brenke type polynomials, *Comput. Math. Appl.* **64**(2) (2012) 121–127.

[42] S. Varma and F. Taşdelen, Szász type operators involving Charlier polynomials. *Math. Comput. Modelling,* **56** (2012) 118–122.

[43] A. Wafi, N. Rao and Deepmala, On Kantorovich form of generalized Szász type operators using Charlier polynomials. *Korean J. Math.* **25**(1) (2017) 99–116.

[44] Ö Ö Yilik, T. Garg and P. N. Agrawal, Convergence rate of Szász operators involving Boas-Buck type polynomials. *Proc. Natl. Acad. Sci., India, Sect. A Phys. Sci.,* DOI 10.1007/s40010-020-00663-3.

3 Approximation by Kantorovich Variant of $\lambda-$Schurer Operators and Related Numerical Results

Faruk Özger
İzmir Katip Çelebi University

Kamil Demirci and Sevda Yıldız
Sinop University

CONTENTS

3.1 INTRODUCTION

Functions have been widely approximated by positive linear operators over the past decades. Sergei Natanovich Bernstein first used the known polynomials in the approximation theory to prove Weierstrass' well-known theorem [6]. Bernstein polynomials of order n are given by

$$B_n(h;z) = \sum_{i=0}^{n} \binom{n}{i} z^i \,(1-z)^{n-i} h\left(\frac{i}{n}\right) \quad (z \in [0,1]), \tag{3.1}$$

for any continuous function $h(z)$ defined on $C[0,1]$, the space of all real-valued continuous functions on $[0,1]$ endowed with the norm $\|h\|_{C[0,1]} = \sup_{z\in[0,1]} |h(z)|$. The Bernstein basis polynomials play an important role in approximations of functions, computer-aided geometric design, differential equations, numerical analysis, and constructing Bézier curves [12,13,15,21,22].

A shape parameter $\lambda \in [-1,1]$ was used to construct new Bernstein bases by Ye et al. in [30] since shape parameter λ provides more modeling flexibility. Shape parameter λ was also used by Cai et al. [7] to construct λ-Bernstein operators:

$$B_{n,\lambda}(h;z) = \sum_{i=0}^{n} \tilde{b}_{n,i}(\lambda;z)\, h\left(\frac{i}{n}\right). \tag{3.2}$$

Considering two nonnegative parameters α and β, which satisfy $0 \leq \alpha \leq \beta$, the λ-Stancu operators $S_n^{\alpha,\beta}(h;z;\lambda) : C[0,1] \longrightarrow C[0,1]$ were defined by Srivastava et al. [23] as

$$S_n^{\alpha,\beta}(h;z;\lambda) = \sum_{i=0}^{n} h\left(\frac{i+\alpha}{n+\beta}\right) \tilde{b}_{n,i}(\lambda;z),$$

for any $n \in \mathbb{N}$. Many approximation properties of the bivariate variant of these operators were also investigated. The direct approximation theorem with the help of second-order modulus of smoothness was established, and the rate of convergence was calculated via Lipschitz-type function. Srivastava et al. also constructed the bivariate case of Stancu-type λ-Bernstein operators and studied their approximation behaviors.

Kantorovich modified the well-known Bernstein polynomials (3.1) to approximate the Lebesgue integrable functions on the interval $[0,1]$ in [14]. Acu et al. [3] introduced the following integral modification of Bernstein operators:

$$K_{n,\lambda}(h;z) = (n+1)\sum_{i=0}^{n} \tilde{b}_{n,i}(\lambda;z) \int_{\frac{i}{n+1}}^{\frac{i+1}{n+1}} h(t)dt. \tag{3.3}$$

They generalized both Bernstein (3.1) and λ-Bernstein (3.2) operators and obtained some asymptotic type results. Also, Cai proposed λ-Kantorovich operators (3.3) and the following Bézier variant of Kantorovich-type λ-Bernstein operators [8]:

$$L_{n,\lambda,\beta}(h;z) = (n+1)\sum_{i=0}^{n} Q_{n,i}^{(\beta)}(\lambda;z) \int_{\frac{i}{n+1}}^{\frac{i+1}{n+1}} h(t)dt,$$

where

$$Q_{n,i}^{(\beta)}(\lambda;z) = \left[J_{n,i}^{(\beta)}(\lambda;z)\right]^{\beta} - \left[J_{n,i+1}^{(\beta)}(\lambda;z)\right]^{\beta} \quad \text{and} \quad J_{n,i}^{(\beta)}(\lambda;z) = \sum_{j=i}^{n} \tilde{b}_{n,j}(\lambda;z).$$

Note that Bézier variants of Kantorovich-type λ-Bernstein operators reduce to the λ-Kantorovich operators (3.3) when $\beta = 0$.

Approximation properties of λ-Kantorovich operators with shifted knots were introduced by Rahman et al. [24] as

$$K_{n,\lambda}^{(\alpha,\beta)}(h;z) = \left(\frac{n+\beta}{n}\right)^{n} (n+\beta+1)\sum_{i=0}^{n} \hat{b}_{n,i}^{(\alpha,\beta)}(\lambda;z) \int_{\frac{i+\alpha}{n+\beta+1}}^{\frac{i+\alpha+1}{n+\beta+1}} h(t)dt.$$

A family of GBS operators of bivariate tensor product of λ-Kantorovich type was constructed in [9]. An estimate for the rate of convergence of such operators was given for B-continuous and B-differentiable functions. Also, a Voronovskaja-type asymptotic formula was established for the bivariate case. Many researchers established some Kantorovich-type operators by modifying Bernstein-type operators to have better error estimation [16,24,26].

More recently, statistical approximation properties of univariate and bivariate λ-Kantorovich operators were considered by Özger in [28]. The rate of weighted A-statistical convergence was estimated. A Voronovskaja-type approximation theorem by a family of linear operators was proved using the notion of weighted A-statistical convergence. Some estimates for differences of λ-Bernstein and λ-Durrmeyer, and λ-Bernstein and λ-Kantorovich operators were given. Finally, a Voronovskaja-type approximation theorem by weighted A-statistical convergence was established for the bivariate case of operators.

Acu et al. extended λ-Bernstein operators to introduce a new type genuine Bernstein-Durrmeyer operators in [4]:

$$U^{\rho}_{n,\lambda}(h;z)=\sum_{i=1}^{n-1}\int_0^1\left[\frac{t^{i\rho-1}(1-t)^{(n-i)\rho-1}}{B(i\rho,(n-i)\rho)}h(t)dt\right]\tilde{b}_{n,i}(\lambda;z)$$
$$+\ h(0)\tilde{b}_{n,0}(\lambda;z)+h(1)\tilde{b}_{n,n}(\lambda;z).$$

Here, $B(a,b)$ is Euler's beta function and $\tilde{b}_{n,i}(\lambda;z)$ is the new Bernstein base, which was introduced by Ye et al. in [30].

In [29], Qi et al. constructed λ-Szász-Mirakian operators

$$M_{n,\lambda}(h;z)=\sum_{i=0}^{n}\tilde{m}_{n,i}(\lambda;z)\,h\left(\frac{i}{n}\right),\quad z\in[0,\infty),$$

where

$$\tilde{m}_{n,0}(\lambda;z)=m_{n,0}(z)-\frac{\lambda}{n+\alpha+1}m_{n+1,1}(z),$$
$$\tilde{m}_{n,i}(\lambda;z)=m_{n,i}(z)+\frac{\lambda}{n^2-1}\left[(n-2i+1)m_{n+1,i}(z)-(n-2i-1)m_{n+1,i+1}(z)\right],$$
$$\tilde{m}_{n,n}(\lambda;z)=m_{n,n}(z)-\frac{\lambda}{n+1}m_{n+1,n}(z),$$

and

$$m_{n,,i}(z)=e^{-nz}\frac{(nz)^i}{i!}.$$

The Schurer polynomials $s_{n,i}(z)$ were introduced by Frans Schurer in [20] as

$$s_{n,i}(z)=\binom{n+\alpha}{i}z^i\,(1-z)^{n+\alpha-i}\qquad(i=0,1,\ldots,n+\alpha),\tag{3.4}$$

where α is a nonnegative integer. The operators generated by these polynomials are called Schurer operators, which were introduced to extend the domain of function from $C[0,1]$ to $C[0,1+\alpha]$. Some relevant works about the Schurer polynomials and Schurer operators may be found in [5,17–19].

The bases in [30] were modified by adding parameter α to introduce the following new bases in [27]:

$$\begin{aligned}
\tilde{s}_{n,0}(\lambda;z) &= s_{n,0}(z) - \frac{\lambda}{n+\alpha+1} s_{n+1,1}(z), \\
\tilde{s}_{n,i}(\lambda;z) &= s_{n,i}(z) + \frac{\lambda}{(n+\alpha)^2-1}\left[(n+\alpha-2i+1)s_{n+1,i}(z)\right. \\
&\quad \left. -(n+\alpha-2i-1)s_{n+1,i+1}(z)\right] \; (i=1,2\ldots,n+\alpha-1), \\
\tilde{s}_{n,n+\alpha}(\lambda;z) &= s_{n,n+\alpha}(z) - \frac{\lambda}{n+\alpha+1} s_{n+1,n+\alpha}(z), \qquad (3.5)
\end{aligned}$$

where shape parameter $\lambda \in [-1,1]$. In the same work, the λ-Schurer operators were introduced, and some approximation and statistical approximation properties were studied. Also, an estimate for the rate of weighted A-statistical convergence was obtained. Moreover, two Voronovskaja-type theorems, including a Voronovskaja-type approximation theorem using weighted A-statistical convergence, were proved.

The rest of this chapter is organized as follows. In Section 3.2, we construct the λ-Schurer-Kantorovich operators, and find moments and central moments. Section 3.3 investigates the approximation behavior of defined λ-Schurer-Kantorovich operators (3.6) and obtains a global and a local direct estimate for the rate of convergence. Section 3.4 establishes three Voronovskaja-type theorems, including a quantitative type. Section 3.5 analyzes the approximation behavior of the defined operators by supporting theoretical results with numerical experiments and graphs. Finally, Section 3.6 summarizes our work and gives some suggestions for readers to carry out further after reading the work.

3.2 AUXILIARY RESULTS

Considering a given nonnegative integer α, we now introduce λ-Schurer-Kantorovich operators $K_{n,\alpha}^{\lambda} : C[0,1+\alpha] \longrightarrow C[0,1]$ for any $n \in \mathbb{N}$ as

$$K_{n,\alpha}^{\lambda}(h;z) = (n+\alpha+1)\sum_{i=0}^{n+\alpha} \tilde{s}_{n,i}(\lambda;z) \int_{\frac{i}{n+\alpha+1}}^{\frac{i+1}{n+\alpha+1}} h(t)dt, \qquad (3.6)$$

where new Schurer polynomials $\tilde{s}_{n,i}(\lambda;z)$ are given in (3.5).

Based on the above definition, we reveal the special cases of our new Schurer operators.

Remark 3.1. *We have the following results:*

a. *The λ-Schurer-Kantorovich operators (3.6) are reduced to the classical Schurer-Kantorovich operators if $\lambda = 0$.*

b. *The λ-Schurer-Kantorovich operators (3.6) are reduced to the classical Bernstein-Kantorovich operators if $\alpha = \lambda = 0$.*

c. *The λ-Schurer-Kantorovich operators (3.6) are reduced to the λ-Bernstein-Kantorovich operators if $\alpha = 0$.*

Now, we find moments and central moments of λ-Schurer-Kantorovich operators (3.6). First, we recall the following lemma.

Lemma 3.1. *[27] We have the following results for λ-Schurer operators:*

$$S^{\lambda}_{n,\alpha}(1;z) = 1,$$

$$S^{\lambda}_{n,\alpha}(t;z) = \frac{n+\alpha}{n}z + \frac{1-2z+z^{n+\alpha+1}-(1-z)^{n+\alpha+1}}{n(n+\alpha-1)}\lambda,$$

$$S^{\lambda}_{n,\alpha}(t^2;z) = \frac{(n+\alpha)^2}{n^2}z^2 + \frac{n+\alpha}{n^2}(z-z^2) + \frac{2(n+\alpha)z-1-4(n+\alpha)z^2+(2(n+\alpha)+1)z^{n+\alpha+1}+(1-z)^{n+\alpha+1}}{n^2(n+\alpha-1)}\lambda.$$

Lemma 3.2. *Let $\lambda \in [-1,1]$ and α be a nonnegative integer, then the moments of λ-Schurer-Kantorovich operators are as follows:*

$$K^{\lambda}_{n,\alpha}(1;z) = 1,$$

$$K^{\lambda}_{n,\alpha}(t;z) = \frac{1+2(n+\alpha)z}{2(n+\alpha+1)} + \frac{1-2z+z^{n+\alpha+1}-(1-z)^{n+\alpha+1}}{(n+\alpha)^2-1}\lambda,$$

$$K^{\lambda}_{n,\alpha}(t^2;z) = \frac{(n+\alpha)^2}{(n+\alpha+1)^2}z^2 + \frac{n+\alpha}{(n+\alpha+1)^2}z(2-z) + \frac{1+6z\lambda}{3(n+\alpha+1)^2} + \frac{2z^{n+\alpha+1}}{(n+\alpha)^2-1}\lambda - \frac{4(n+\alpha)z^2}{(n+\alpha+1)((n+\alpha)^2-1)}\lambda.$$

Proof. Proof of the first part of the lemma is provided by the partition of unity property of Schurer and Kantorovich operators. Bearing in mind the definition of operators (3.6) and Lemma 3.1, we have

$$\begin{aligned}
K^{\lambda}_{n,\alpha}(t;z) &= (n+\alpha+1)\sum_{i=0}^{n+\alpha}\tilde{s}_{n,i}(\lambda;z)\int_{\frac{i}{n+\alpha+1}}^{\frac{i+1}{n+\alpha+1}} t\,dt \\
&= \sum_{i=0}^{n+\alpha}\tilde{s}_{n,i}(\lambda;z)\frac{2i+1}{2(n+\alpha+1)} \\
&= \frac{n}{n+\alpha+1}S^{\lambda}_{n,\alpha}(t;z) + \frac{1}{2(n+\alpha+1)}S^{\lambda}_{n,\alpha}(1;z) \\
&= \frac{1+2(n+\alpha)z}{2(n+\alpha+1)} + \frac{1-2z+z^{n+\alpha+1}-(1-z)^{n+\alpha+1}}{(n+\alpha)^2-1}\lambda,
\end{aligned}$$

which completes the proof of the second part. Now, we prove the third part:

$$
\begin{aligned}
K_{n,\alpha}^{\lambda}(t^2;z) &= (n+\alpha+1)\sum_{i=0}^{n+\alpha}\tilde{s}_{n,i}(\lambda;z)\int_{\frac{i}{n+\alpha+1}}^{\frac{i+1}{n+\alpha+1}} t^2\,dt \\
&= \sum_{i=0}^{n+\alpha}\tilde{s}_{n,i}(\lambda;z)\,\frac{3i^2+3i+1}{3(n+\alpha+1)^2} \\
&= \frac{n^2}{(n+\alpha+1)^2}S_{n,\alpha}^{\lambda}(t^2;z)+\frac{n}{(n+\alpha+1)^2}S_{n,\alpha}^{\lambda}(t;z)+\frac{1}{3(n+\alpha+1)^2}S_{n,\alpha}^{\lambda}(1;z) \\
&= \frac{(n+\alpha)^2}{(n+\alpha+1)^2}z^2+\frac{n+\alpha}{(n+\alpha+1)^2}z(2-z)+\frac{1+6z\lambda}{3(n+\alpha+1)^2} \\
&\quad +\frac{2z^{n+\alpha+1}}{(n+\alpha)^2-1}\lambda-\frac{4(n+\alpha)z^2}{(n+\alpha+1)((n+\alpha)^2-1)}\lambda.
\end{aligned}
$$

Thus, Lemma 3.2 is proved. □

Corollary 3.1. *Let $z\in[0,1]$, α be a nonnegative integer, $\lambda\in[-1,1]$, and $\psi_z=t-z$, then we have the following central moments:*

$$
\begin{aligned}
K_{n,\alpha}^{\lambda}(\psi_z;z) &= \frac{1-2z}{2(n+\alpha+1)}+\frac{1-2z+z^{n+\alpha+1}-(1-z)^{n+\alpha+1}}{(n+\alpha)^2-1}\lambda, \\
K_{n,\alpha}^{\lambda}(\psi_z^2;z) &= \frac{z-z^2}{n+\alpha+1}+\frac{1+6z\lambda}{3(n+\alpha+1)^2} \\
&\quad -\frac{z(1-2z)+z^{n+\alpha+1}(z-1)-z(1-z)^{n+\alpha+1}}{(n+\alpha)^2-1}2\lambda \\
&\quad -\frac{4(n+\alpha)z^2}{(n+\alpha+1)((n+\alpha)^2-1)}\lambda.
\end{aligned}
$$

Corollary 3.2. *The following relations hold for operators $K_{n,\alpha}^{\lambda}(\psi_z;z)$ and $K_{n,\alpha}^{\lambda}(\psi_z^2;z)$:*

$$
\begin{aligned}
\lim_{n\to\infty} n\,K_{n,\alpha}^{\lambda}(\psi_z;z) &= \frac{1-2z}{2}, \\
\lim_{n\to\infty} n\,K_{n,\alpha}^{\lambda}(\psi_z^2;z) &= z-z^2.
\end{aligned}
$$

3.3 APPROXIMATION BEHAVIOR OF λ-SCHURER-KANTOROVICH OPERATORS

The following theorem gives the uniform convergence property of λ-Schurer-Kantorovich operators (3.6) by the well-known Bohman-Korovkin-Popoviciu theorem:

Theorem 3.1. *Let $h\in C[0,1+\alpha]$, then*

$$\lim_{n\to\infty} K_{n,\alpha}^{\lambda}(h;z)=h(z)$$

uniformly on $[0,1]$.

Proof. As stated in the Bohman-Korovkin-Popoviciu theorem, it is sufficient to show that

$$\lim_{n\to\infty} K_{n,\alpha}^{\lambda}(t^i;z) = z^i, \quad i = 0,1,2$$

uniformly on $[0,1]$. Using Lemma 3.2, we can easily get these three conditions. Hence, we have the result. □

We need the following notions and notation to achieve a local direct estimate for the rate of convergence of λ-Schurer-Kantorovich operators (3.6) and obtain a global approximation formula.

Definition 3.1. *Global approximation formulas via Ditzian-Totik uniform modulus of smoothness of first and second orders are defined by*

$$\omega_{\xi}(h,\delta) := \sup_{0<|\rho|\leq\delta} \; \sup_{z,z+\rho\xi(z)\in[0,1]} \{|h(z+\rho\xi(z)) - h(z)|\};$$

$$\omega_2^{\beta}(h,\delta) := \sup_{0<|\rho|\leq\delta} \; \sup_{z,z\pm\rho\beta(z)\in[0,1]} \{|h(z+\rho\beta(z)) - 2h(z) + h(z-\rho\beta(z))|\},$$

respectively, where β is an admissible step-weight function on $[a,b]$, i.e., $\beta(z) = [(z-a)(b-z)]^{1/2}$ if $z \in [a,b]$, [11]. We denote absolutely continuous functions by AC, and so K-functional is

$$K_{2,\beta(z)}(h,\delta) = \inf_{g\in W^2(\beta)} \{||h-g||_{C[0,1+\alpha]} + \delta||\beta^2 g''||_{C[0,1+\alpha]} : g \in C^2[0,1+\alpha]\},$$

where $\delta > 0$, $W^2(\beta) = \{g \in C[0,1+\alpha] : g' \in AC[0,1+\alpha],\ \beta^2 g'' \in C[0,1+\alpha]\}$ and $C^2[0,1+\alpha] = \{g \in C[0,1+\alpha] : g', g'' \in C[0,1+\alpha]\}$.

Remark 3.2. *[10] There is an absolute constant $\Omega > 0$, such that*

$$\Omega^{-1}\omega_2^{\beta}(h,\sqrt{\delta}) \leq K_{2,\beta(z)}(h,\delta) \leq \Omega\omega_2^{\beta}(h,\sqrt{\delta}). \tag{3.7}$$

First, we obtain the global approximation formula in terms of Ditzian-Totik uniform modulus of smoothness of first and second orders.

Theorem 3.2. *Let $\beta(z)$ $(\beta \neq 0)$ be an admissible step-weight function of modulus of smoothness in Definition 3.1 such that β^2 is concave and let $\psi_z = t - z$, $h \in C[0,1+\alpha]$, $z \in [0,1]$, and $\lambda \in [-1,1]$. Then for $\Omega > 0$, λ-Schurer-Kantorovich operators (3.6) verify*

$$|K_{n,\alpha}^{\lambda}(h;z) - h(z)| \leq \Omega\ \omega_2^{\beta}\left(h, \frac{[\chi_{n,\alpha,\lambda}(z) + \bar{\chi}_{n,\alpha,\lambda}^2(z)]^{1/2}}{2[(z-a)(b-z)]^{1/2}}\right) + \omega_{\xi}\left(h, \frac{\bar{\chi}_{n,\alpha,\lambda}(z)}{\xi(z)}\right),$$

where $\bar{\chi}_{n,\alpha,\lambda}(z) = K_{n,\alpha}^{\lambda}(\psi_z;z)$ and $\chi_{n,\alpha,\lambda}(z) = K_{n,\alpha}^{\lambda}(\psi_z^2;z)$ are given in Corollary 3.1.

Proof. We define the following operators:

$$\breve{K}_{n,\alpha}^{\lambda}(h;z) = K_{n,\alpha}^{\lambda}(h;z) + h(z) - h\Big(\frac{1+2(n+\alpha)z}{2(n+\alpha+1)} + \frac{1-2z+z^{n+\alpha+1}-(1-z)^{n+\alpha+1}}{(n+\alpha)^2-1}\lambda\Big) \tag{3.8}$$

where $h \in C[0,1+\alpha]$, $z \in [0,1]$, and $\lambda \in [-1,1]$. We have the following relations

$$\breve{K}_{n,\alpha}^{\lambda}(1;z) = 1 \text{ and } \breve{K}_{n,\alpha}^{\lambda}(t;z) = x$$

by Lemma 3.2. These relations imply $\breve{K}_{n,\alpha}^{\lambda}(\psi_z;z) = 0$.

Let $u = \rho z + (1-\rho)t$, $\rho \in [0,1]$. Since β^2 is concave on $[0,1]$, it follows that $\beta^2(u) \geq \rho\beta^2(z) + (1-\rho)\beta^2(t)$ and

$$\frac{|t-u|}{\beta^2(u)} \leq \frac{\rho|z-t|}{\rho\beta^2(z)+(1-\rho)\beta^2(t)} \leq \frac{|\psi_z|}{\beta^2(z)}. \tag{3.9}$$

Hence, the following inequalities hold:

$$\begin{aligned} |\breve{K}_{n,\alpha}^{\lambda}(h;z) - h(z)| &\leq |\breve{K}_{n,\alpha}^{\lambda}(h-g;z)| + |\breve{K}_{n,\alpha}^{\lambda}(g;z) - g(z)| + |h(z) - g(z)| \\ &\leq 4\|h-g\|_{C[0,1+\alpha]} + |\breve{K}_{n,\alpha}^{\lambda}(g;z) - g(z)|. \end{aligned} \tag{3.10}$$

Applying Taylor's formula, we obtain

$$\begin{aligned} &|\breve{K}_{n,\alpha}^{\lambda}(g;z) - g(z)| \\ &\leq K_{n,\alpha}^{\lambda}\left(\left|\int_z^t |t-u|\ |g''(u)|du\right|;z\right) + \left|\int_z^{z+\bar{\chi}_{n,\alpha,\lambda}(z)} |z+\bar{\chi}_{n,\alpha,\lambda}(z)-u|\ |g''(u)|\ du\right| \\ &\leq \|\beta^2 g''\|_{C[0,1+\alpha]} K_{n,\alpha}^{\lambda}\left(\left|\int_z^t \frac{|t-u|}{\beta^2(u)}du\right|;z\right) + \|\beta^2 g''\|_{C[0,1+\alpha]} \\ &\times \left|\int_z^{z+\bar{\chi}_{n,\alpha,\lambda}(z)} \frac{|z+\bar{\chi}_{n,\alpha,\lambda}(z)-u|}{\beta^2(u)}du\right| \\ &\leq \beta^{-2}(z)\|\beta^2 g''\|_{C[0,1+\alpha]} K_{n,\alpha}^{\lambda}(\psi_z^2;z) + \beta^{-2}(z)\|\beta^2 g''\|_{C[0,1+\alpha]} \bar{\chi}_{n,\alpha,\lambda}^2(z). \end{aligned} \tag{3.11}$$

By definition of K-functional with relation (3.7) and inequalities (3.10)–(3.11), we have

$$\begin{aligned} |\breve{K}_{n,\alpha}^{\lambda}(h;z) - h(z)| &\leq 4\|h-g\|_{C[0,1+\alpha]} + \beta^{-2}(z)\|\beta^2 g''\|_{C[0,1+\alpha]}\left(\chi_{n,\alpha,\lambda}(z) + \bar{\chi}_{n,\alpha,\lambda}^2(z)\right) \\ &\leq \Omega\ \omega_2^{\beta}\left(h, \frac{[\chi_{n,\alpha,\lambda}(z) + \bar{\chi}_{n,\alpha,\lambda}^2(z)]^{1/2}}{2\beta(z)}\right). \end{aligned}$$

Also, by the help of uniform modulus of smoothness of first order in Definition 3.1, we have

$$|h(z+\bar{\chi}_{n,\alpha,\lambda}(z)) - h(z)| = \left|h\left(z + \xi(z)\frac{\bar{\chi}_{n,\alpha,\lambda}(z)}{\xi(z)}\right) - h(z)\right| \leq \omega_{\xi}\left(h, \frac{\bar{\chi}_{n,\alpha,\lambda}(z)}{\xi(z)}\right).$$

Therefore, the following inequalities, which complete the proof, hold:

$$|K_{n,\alpha}^{\lambda}(h;z)-h(z)| \leq |\breve{K}_{n,\alpha}^{\lambda}(h;z)-h(z)| + \left|h(z+\bar{\chi}_{n,\alpha,\lambda}(z))-h(z)\right|$$
$$\leq \Omega\, \omega_2^{\beta}\left(h, \frac{[\chi_{n,\alpha,\lambda}(z)+\bar{\chi}_{n,\alpha,\lambda}^2(z)]^{1/2}}{2[(z-a)(b-z)]^{1/2}}\right) + \omega_{\xi}\left(h, \frac{\bar{\chi}_{n,\alpha,\lambda}(z)}{\xi(z)}\right).$$

□

Theorem 3.3. *Let $h,h' \in C[0,1+\alpha]$ and $z \in [0,1]$, then the following inequality is satisfied:*

$$|K_{n,\alpha}^{\lambda}(h;z)-h(z)| \leq |\bar{\chi}_{n,\alpha,\lambda}(z)|\;|h'(z)| + 2\sqrt{\chi_{n,\alpha,\lambda}(z)}w(h', \sqrt{\chi_{n,\alpha,\lambda}(z)}\,),$$

where $\chi_{n,\alpha,\lambda}(z)$ and $\bar{\chi}_{n,\alpha,\lambda}(z)$ are given in Theorem 3.2.

Proof. We have the following relation

$$h(t)-h(z) = \psi_z h'(z) + \int_z^t (h'(u)-h'(z))du \tag{3.12}$$

for any $t,z \in [0,1]$. Applying operators $K_{n,\alpha}^{\lambda}(h;z)$ to both sides of (3.12), we have

$$K_{n,\alpha}^{\lambda}(h(t)-h(z);z) = h'(z)K_{n,\alpha}^{\lambda}(\psi_z;z) + K_{n,\alpha}^{\lambda}\left(\int_z^t (h'(u)-h'(z))du;z\right).$$

The following inequality holds for any $\delta > 0$, $u \in [0,1]$, and $h \in C[0,1+\alpha]$:

$$|h(u)-h(z)| \leq w(h,\delta)\left(\frac{|u-z|}{\delta}+1\right),$$

With above inequality, we get

$$\left|\int_z^t (h'(u)-h'(z))du\right| \leq w(h',\delta)\left(\frac{\psi_z^2}{\delta}+|\psi_z|\right).$$

Hence, we have

$$|K_{n,\alpha}^{\lambda}(h;z)-h(z)| \leq |h'(z)|\;|K_{n,\alpha}^{\lambda}(\psi_z;z)| + w(h',\delta)\left\{\frac{1}{\delta}K_{n,\alpha}^{\lambda}(\psi_z^2;z) + K_{n,\alpha}^{\lambda}(\psi_z;z)\right\}.$$

Applying Cauchy-Schwarz inequality on the right-hand side of above inequality, we have

$$|K_{n,\alpha}^{\lambda}(h;z)-h(z)| \leq h'(z)|\bar{\chi}_{n,\alpha,\lambda}(z)| + w(h',\delta)\left\{\frac{1}{\delta}\sqrt{K_{n,\alpha}^{\lambda}(\psi_z^2;z)}+1\right\}\sqrt{K_{n,\alpha}^{\lambda}(|\psi_z|;z)}.$$

□

In the following theorem, we obtain a local direct estimate of the rate of convergence via Lipschitz-type function involving two parameters for the operators $K^{\lambda}_{n,\alpha}$. Before proceeding further, let us recall that

$$Lip_M^{(k_1,k_2)}(\eta) := \left\{h \in C[0,1] : |h(t)-h(z)| \leq M\frac{|\psi_z|^{\eta}}{(k_1z^2+k_2z+t)^{\frac{\eta}{2}}};\ z \in (0,1], t \in [0,1]\right\}$$

for $k_1 \geq 0, k_2 > 0$, where $\eta \in (0,1]$ and M is a positive constant (see [25]).

Theorem 3.4. *Let $\lambda \in [-1,1]$, $z \in (0,1]$, and $\eta \in (0,1]$ $h \in Lip_M^{(k_1,k_2)}(\eta)$, then*

$$|K^{\lambda}_{n,\alpha}(h;z)-h(z)| \leq M\sqrt{\frac{\chi^{\eta}_{n,\alpha,\lambda}(z)}{(k_1z^2+k_2z)^{\eta}}},$$

where $\chi_{n,\alpha,\lambda}(z)$ is defined in Theorem 3.2.

Proof. Let $h \in Lip_M^{(k_1,k_2)}(\eta)$ and $\eta \in (0,1]$. First, we show that the statement holds for $\eta = 1$. Since we can express λ-Schurer-Kantorovich operators as

$$K^{\lambda}_{n,\alpha}(h;z) = (n+\alpha+1)\sum_{i=0}^{n+\alpha}\tilde{s}_{n,i}(\lambda;z)\int_0^1 h\left(\frac{i+t}{n+\alpha+1}\right)dt,$$

we have

$$\begin{aligned}
|K^{\lambda}_{n,\alpha}(h;z)-h(z)| &\leq |K^{\lambda}_{n,\alpha}(|h(t)-h(z)|;z)| + h(z)\,|K^{\lambda}_{n,\alpha}(1;z)-1| \\
&\leq \sum_{i=0}^{n+\alpha}\left|h\left(\frac{i+t}{n+\alpha+1}\right)-h(z)\right|\tilde{s}_{n,i}(\lambda;z) \\
&\leq M\sum_{i=0}^{n+\alpha}\frac{\left|\frac{i+t}{n+\alpha+1}-z\right|}{(k_1z^2+k_2z+t)^{\frac{1}{2}}}\tilde{s}_{n,i}(\lambda;z)
\end{aligned}$$

for $h \in Lip_M^{(k_1,k_2)}(1)$. By using

$$(k_1z^2+k_2z+t)^{-1/2} \leq (k_1z^2+k_2z)^{-1/2} \quad (k_1 \geq 0, k_2 > 0)$$

and applying Cauchy-Schwarz inequality, we obtain

$$\begin{aligned}
|K^{\lambda}_{n,\alpha}(h;z)-h(z)| &\leq M(k_1z^2+k_2z)^{-1/2}\sum_{i=0}^{n+\alpha}\left|\frac{i+t}{n+\alpha+1}-z\right|\tilde{s}_{n,i}(\lambda;z) \\
&= M(k_1z^2+k_2z)^{-1/2}|K^{\lambda}_{n,\alpha}(\psi_z;z)| \\
&\leq M|\chi_{n,\alpha,\lambda}(z)|^{1/2}(k_1z^2+k_2z)^{-1/2}.
\end{aligned}$$

Hence, the statement is true for $\eta = 1$. By the monotonicity of $K_{n,\alpha}^{\lambda}(h;z)$ and applying Hölder's inequality two times with $a = 2/\eta$ and $b = 2/(2-\eta)$, we can see that the statement is true for $\eta \in (0,1]$, as follows:

$$\begin{aligned}
\left|K_{n,\alpha}^{\lambda}(h;z)-h(z)\right| &\le \sum_{i=0}^{n+\alpha}\left|h\left(\frac{i+t}{n+\alpha+1}\right)-h(z)\right|\tilde{s}_{n,i}(\lambda;z)\\
&\le \left(\sum_{i=0}^{n+\alpha}\left|h\left(\frac{i+t}{n+\alpha+1}\right)-h(z)\right|^{\frac{2}{\eta}}\tilde{s}_{n,i}(\lambda;z)\right)^{\frac{\eta}{2}}\left(\sum_{i=0}^{n+\alpha}\tilde{s}_{n,i}(\lambda;z)\right)^{\frac{2-\eta}{2}}\\
&\le M\left(\sum_{i=0}^{n+\alpha}\frac{\left(\frac{i+t}{n+\alpha+1}-z\right)^2\tilde{s}_{n,i}(\lambda;z)}{\frac{i+t}{n+\alpha+1}+k_1z^2+k_2z}\right)^{\frac{\eta}{2}}\\
&\le M(k_1z^2+k_2z)^{-\eta/2}\left\{\sum_{i=0}^{n+\alpha}\left(\frac{i+t}{n+\alpha+1}-z\right)^2\tilde{s}_{n,i}(\lambda;z)\right\}^{\frac{\eta}{2}}\\
&\le M(k_1z^2+k_2z+t)^{-\eta/2}\left[K_{n,\alpha}^{\lambda}(\psi_z^2;z)\right]^{\frac{\eta}{2}}\\
&= M\sqrt{\frac{\chi_{n,\alpha,\lambda}^{\eta}(z)}{(k_1z^2+k_2z)^{\eta}}}.
\end{aligned}$$

□

3.4 VORONOVSKAJA-TYPE APPROXIMATION THEOREMS

In this section, we establish a quantitative Voronovskaja-type and a Grüss-Voronovskaja type theorem for $K_{n,\alpha}^{\lambda}(h;z)$ using modulus of smoothness, which is given in Definition 3.1. This modulus is defined as

$$\omega_{\beta}(h,\delta) := \sup_{0<|\rho|\le\delta}\left\{\left|h\left(z+\frac{\rho\beta(z)}{2}\right)-h\left(z-\frac{\rho\beta(z)}{2}\right)\right|, z\pm\frac{\rho\beta(z)}{2}\in[0,1]\right\}.$$

Here, $\beta(z) = (z-z^2)^{1/2}$ and $h \in C[0,1+\alpha]$, and the related Peetre's K-functional is known as

$$K_{\beta}(h,\delta) = \inf_{g\in W_{\beta}[0,1+\alpha]}\{||h-g||+\delta||\beta g'|| : g\in C^1[0,1+\alpha], \delta>0\},$$

where $W_{\beta}[0,1+\alpha] = \{g : g \in AC_{loc}[0,1+\alpha], \ ||\beta g'|| < \infty\}$ and $AC_{loc}[0,1+\alpha]$ is the class of absolutely continuous functions defined on $[a,b] \subset [0,1+\alpha]$. There is a constant $\Omega > 0$ so that

$$K_{\beta}(h,\delta) \le \Omega\ \omega_{\beta}(h,\delta).$$

Theorem 3.5. *Let $h \in C^2[0,1+\alpha]$, then we have*

$$\left|K_{n,\alpha}^{\lambda}(h;z)-h(z)-\bar{\chi}_{n,\alpha,\lambda}(z)h'(z)-\frac{\chi_{n,\alpha,\lambda}(z)}{2}h''(z)\right| \le \frac{\Omega}{n}\beta^2(z)\omega_{\beta}\left(h'',\frac{1}{\sqrt{n}}\right)$$

for every $z \in [0,1]$ and sufficiently large n, where Ω is a positive constant, and $\chi_{n,\alpha,\lambda}(z)$ and $\bar{\chi}_{n,\alpha,\lambda}(z)$ are defined in Theorem 3.2.

Proof. Consider the following equality:

$$h(t) - h(z) - \psi_z h'(z) = \int_z^t (t-u)h''(u)du$$

for $h \in C[0,1+\alpha]$. It means we have

$$h(t) - h(z) - \psi_z h'(z) - \frac{\psi_z^2}{2} h''(z) = \int_z^t (t-u)[h''(u) - h''(z)]du. \tag{3.13}$$

Applying $K_{n,\alpha}^{\lambda}(h;z)$ to both sides of (3.13), we obtain

$$\left| K_{n,\alpha}^{\lambda}(h;z) - h(z) - K_{n,\alpha}^{\lambda}(\psi_z;z)h'(z) - \frac{K_{n,\alpha}^{\lambda}(\psi_z^2;z)}{2} h''(z) \right|$$
$$\leq K_{n,\alpha}^{\lambda}\left(\left| \int_z^t |t-u| \, |h''(u) - h''(z)| \, du \right| ; z \right). \tag{3.14}$$

The expression in the right-hand side of (3.14) can be estimated as

$$\left| \int_z^t |t-u| \, |h''(u) - h''(z)| \, du \right| \leq 2\|h'' - g\| \psi_z^2 + 2\|\beta g'\| \beta^{-1}(z) |\psi_z|^3, \tag{3.15}$$

where $g \in W_\beta[0,1+\alpha]$. There exists $\Omega > 0$ such that

$$K_{n,\alpha}^{\lambda}(\psi_z^2;z) \leq \frac{\Omega}{2n}\beta^2(z) \quad \text{and} \quad K_{n,\alpha}^{\lambda}(\psi_z^4;z) \leq \frac{\Omega}{2n^2}\beta^4(z) \tag{3.16}$$

for sufficiently large n. Using Cauchy-Schwarz inequality, we have

$$\left| K_{n,\alpha}^{\lambda}(h;z) - h(z) - K_{n,\alpha}^{\lambda}(\psi_z;z)h'(z) - \frac{K_{n,\alpha}^{\lambda}(\psi_z^2;z)}{2} h''(z) \right|$$
$$\leq 2\|h'' - g\| K_{n,\alpha}^{\lambda}(\psi_z^2;z) + 2\|\beta g'\| \beta^{-1}(z) K_{n,\alpha}^{\lambda}(|\psi_z|^3;z)$$
$$\leq \frac{\Omega}{n}(z - z^2)\|h'' - g\| + 2\|\beta g'\| \beta^{-1}(z) \{K_{n,\alpha}^{\lambda}(\psi_z^2;z)\}^{1/2} \{K_{n,\alpha}^{\lambda}(\psi_z^4;z)\}^{1/2}$$
$$\leq \frac{\Omega}{n}\beta^2(z) \left\{ \|h'' - g\| + n^{-1/2}\|\beta g'\| \right\}$$

by (3.14)–(3.16). Taking infimum on the right-hand side over all $g \in W_\beta[0,1+\alpha]$, we deduce

$$\left| K_{n,\alpha}^{\lambda}(h;z) - h(z) - \bar{\chi}_{n,\alpha,\lambda}(z)h'(z) - \frac{\chi_{n,\alpha,\lambda}(z)}{2} h''(z) \right| \leq \frac{\Omega}{n}\beta^2(z)\omega_\beta\left(h'', \frac{1}{\sqrt{n}} \right).$$

The result follows immediately by applying Corollaries 3.1 and 3.2. □

As an immediate consequence of Theorem 3.5, we have the following result.

Corollary 3.3. *Let $h \in C^2[0,1+\alpha]$, then*

$$\lim_{n\to\infty} n\left[K_{n,\alpha}^{\lambda}(h;z) - h(z) - \bar{\chi}_{n,\alpha,\lambda}(z)h'(z) - \frac{\chi_{n,\alpha,\lambda}(z)}{2}h''(z)\right] = 0,$$

where $\chi_{n,\alpha,\lambda}(z)$ and $\bar{\chi}_{n,\alpha,\lambda}(z)$ are defined in Theorem 3.2.

A Grüss inequality for the positive linear operators was first given by Acu et al. in [2] by using the least concave majorant of the modulus of continuity. Then, Acar et al. [1] obtained a Grüss-type approximation theorem and a Grüss-Voronovskaja-type theorem for a class of sequences of linear positive operators. Now, we will obtain a Grüss-Voronovskaja-type theorem for λ-Schurer-Kantorovich operators $K_{n,\alpha}^{\lambda}$:

Theorem 3.6. *Let $h,k \in C^2[0,1+\alpha]$. Then, for each $z \in [0,1]$,*

$$\lim_{n\to\infty} n\left\{K_{n,\alpha}^{\lambda}((hk);z) - K_{n,\alpha}^{\lambda}(h;z)K_{n,\alpha}^{\lambda}(k;z)\right\} = h'(z)k'(z)\left(z-z^2\right).$$

Proof. It can be easily seen that the following equality holds:

$$\begin{aligned}
&K_{n,\alpha}^{\lambda}((hk);z) - K_{n,\alpha}^{\lambda}(h;z)K_{n,\alpha}^{\lambda}(k;z)\\
&= K_{n,\alpha}^{\lambda}((hk);z) - h(z)k(z) - (hk)'(z)\overline{\chi}_{n,\alpha,\lambda}(z) - (hk)''(z)\frac{\chi_{n,\alpha,\lambda}(z)}{2}\\
&\quad - k(z)\left\{K_{n,\alpha}^{\lambda}(h;z) - h(z) - h'(z)\overline{\chi}_{n,\alpha,\lambda}(z) - h''(z)\frac{\chi_{n,\alpha,\lambda}(z)}{2}\right\}\\
&\quad - K_{n,\alpha}^{\lambda}(h;z)\left\{K_{n,\alpha}^{\lambda}(k;z) - k(z) - k'(z)\overline{\chi}_{n,\alpha,\lambda}(z) - k''(z)\frac{\chi_{n,\alpha,\lambda}(z)}{2}\right\}\\
&\quad + \frac{\chi_{n,\alpha,\lambda}(z)}{2}\left\{h(z)k''(z) + 2h'(z)k'(z) - k''(z)K_{n,\alpha}^{\lambda}(h;z)\right\}\\
&\quad + \overline{\chi}_{n,\alpha,\lambda}(z)\left\{h(z)k'(z) - k'(z)K_{n,\alpha}^{\lambda}(h;z)\right\}.
\end{aligned}$$

Hence, by using Theorem 3.1 and Corollary 3.3, we have

$$\begin{aligned}
&\lim_{n\to\infty} n\left\{K_{n,\alpha}^{\lambda}((hk);z) - K_{n,\alpha}^{\lambda}(h;z)K_{n,\alpha}^{\lambda}(k;z)\right\}\\
&= \lim_{n\to\infty} nk''(z)\left\{h(z) - K_{n,\alpha}^{\lambda}(h;z)\right\}\frac{\chi_{n,\alpha,\lambda}(z)}{2} + \lim_{n\to\infty} 2nh'(z)k'(z)\frac{\chi_{n,\alpha,\lambda}(z)}{2}\\
&\quad + \lim_{n\to\infty} nk'(z)\left\{h(z) - K_{n,\alpha}^{\lambda}(h;z)\right\}\overline{\chi}_{n,\alpha,\lambda}(z)\\
&= h'(z)k'(z)\left(z-z^2\right).
\end{aligned}$$

□

Finally, we obtain the following theorem by Taylor's expansion theorem and Lemma 3.2, and Corollaries 3.1 and 3.2:

Theorem 3.7. *Let $h \in C^2[0,1+\alpha]$, then for each $z \in [0,1]$*

$$\lim_{n\to\infty} n\{K_{n,\alpha}^{\lambda}(h;z)-h(z)\} = (1-2z)\,\frac{h'(z)}{2} + (z-z^2)\,\frac{h''(z)}{2}$$

uniformly on $[0,1]$.

Proof. We first write the following equality by Taylor's expansion theorem of function $h(z)$ in $C[0,1]$:

$$h(t) = h(z) + \psi_z h'(z) + \frac{1}{2}\psi_z^2 h''(z) + \psi_z^2\, r_z(t), \tag{3.17}$$

where $r_z(t)$ is Peano form of the remainder, $r_z \in C[0,1]$ and $r_z(t) \to 0$ as $t \to z$. Applying the operators $K_{n,\alpha}^{\lambda}(\cdot;z)$ to identity (3.17), we have

$$K_{n,\alpha}^{\lambda}(h;z) - h(z) = h'(z)K_{n,\alpha}^{\lambda}(\psi_z;z) + \frac{h''(z)}{2}K_{n,\alpha}^{\lambda}(\psi_z^2;z) + K_{n,\alpha}^{\lambda}(\psi_z^2 r_z(t);z).$$

Using Cauchy-Schwarz inequality, we have

$$K_{n,\alpha}^{\lambda}(\psi_z^2 r_z(t);z) \le \sqrt{K_{n,\alpha}^{\lambda}(\psi_z^4;z)}\sqrt{K_{n,\alpha}^{\lambda}(r_z^2(t);z)}. \tag{3.18}$$

We observe that $\lim_n K_{n,\alpha}^{\lambda}(r_z^2(t);z) = 0$ and hence

$$\lim_{n\to\infty} n\{K_{n,\alpha}^{\lambda}(\psi_z^2 r_z(t);z)\} = 0.$$

Thus,

$$\lim_{n\to\infty} n\{K_{n,\alpha}^{\lambda}(h;z)-h(z)\} = \lim_{n\to\infty} n\Big\{K_{n,\alpha}^{\lambda}(\psi_z;z)h'(z) + \frac{h''(z)}{2}K_{n,\alpha}^{\lambda}(\psi_z^2;z) + K_{n,\alpha}^{\lambda}(\psi_z^2 r_z(t);z)\Big\}.$$

□

3.5 GRAPHICAL AND NUMERICAL RESULTS

The aim of this section is to support the results given in the previous sections by graphs and numerical examples. We first study on the behavior of polynomials $\tilde{s}_{n,i}(\lambda;z)$ for different values of shape parameter λ. In Figure 3.1, we demonstrate the classical Bernstein polynomials and λ-Schurer polynomials $\tilde{s}_{n,i}(\lambda;z)$ to see the difference.

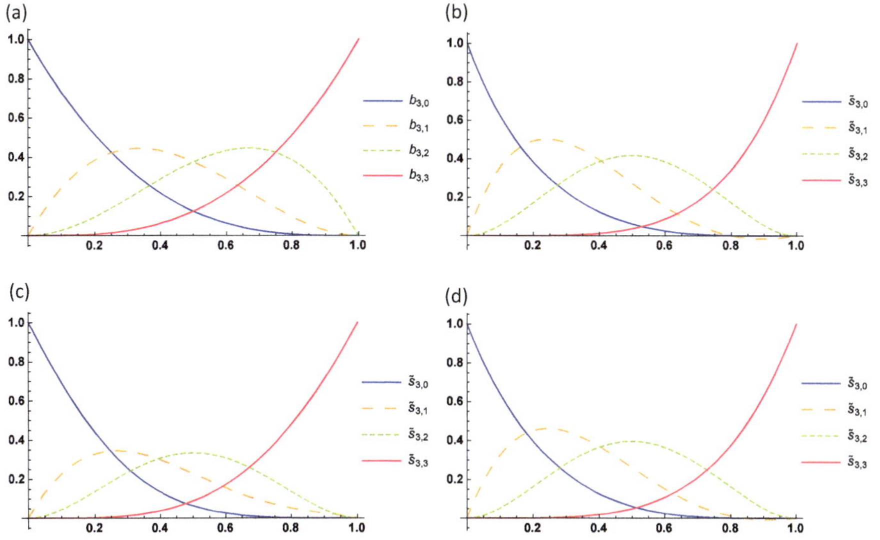

Figure 3.1 Behavior of polynomials $b_{n,i}(z)$ and $\tilde{s}_{n,i}(\lambda;z)$ for $n=3$ and $i=0,1,\ldots,3$. (a) $b_{3,i}(z)$ for $i=0,1,\ldots,3$, (b) $\tilde{s}_{3,i}(\lambda;z)$ with $\lambda=1$ and $\alpha=1$, (c) $\tilde{s}_{3,i}(\lambda;z)$ with $\lambda=-1$ and $\alpha=1$, and (d) $\tilde{s}_{3,i}(\lambda;z)$ with $\lambda=0.5$ and $\alpha=1$.

Example 3.1. *Let $\alpha=2$, $\lambda=0.5$, $h(z)=\cos(\pi z)$, and $E^{\lambda}_{n,\alpha}(h;z)=\left|h(z)-K^{\lambda}_{n,\alpha}(h;z)\right|$ be the error function of λ-Schurer-Kantorovich operators. The graphs of operators $K^{\lambda}_{n,\alpha}$ for $n=20$, $n=50$, $n=100$ and the graph of the function h are illustrated in Figure 3.2a. The error functions $E^{\lambda}_{n,\alpha}$ are given in Figure 3.2b. Hence, we show the convergence and error of approximation of λ-Schurer-Kantorovich operators to the function h. Also, we see the error estimation from Table 3.1.*

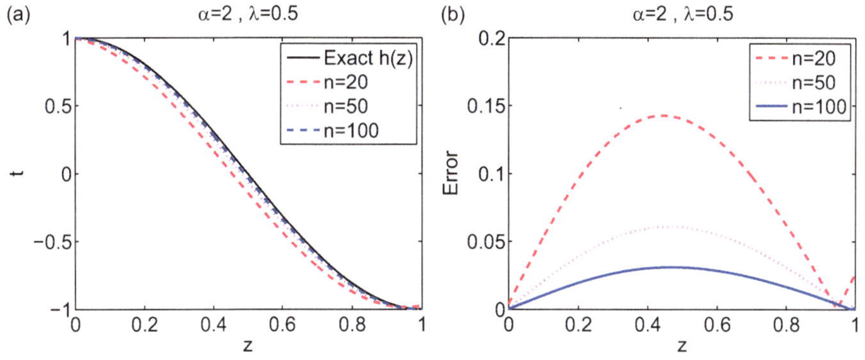

Figure 3.2 Convergence of our operators to $h(z)=\cos(\pi z)$. (a) Approximation process and (b) error of approximation.

Table 3.1
The Errors of the Approximation

n	α	λ	**Error**
20	2	0.5	1.42e−01
50	2	0.5	6.05e−02
100	2	0.5	3.09e−02

Example 3.2. *Let* $n = 10$, $h(z) = \left(z-\frac{1}{2}\right)\left(z-\frac{3}{8}\right)\left(z-\frac{1}{4}\right)$. *In Figure 3.3a, we see the graphs of* λ*-Schurer-Kantorovich operators* $K^1_{n,2}$, λ*-Kantorovich operators* $K^1_{n,0}$ *that are given by Acu et al.[3], and* $K^0_{10,0}$ *that are the classical Kantorovich operators and the graph of function h. The error functions* $E^{\lambda}_{n,\alpha}$ *are given in Figure 3.3b. Also, we see the error estimation from Table 3.2. Hence, we show that the error for* λ*-Schurer-Kantorovich operators* $K^1_{n,2}$ *is smaller than the ones for* $K^1_{n,0}$ *and* $K^0_{10,0}$.

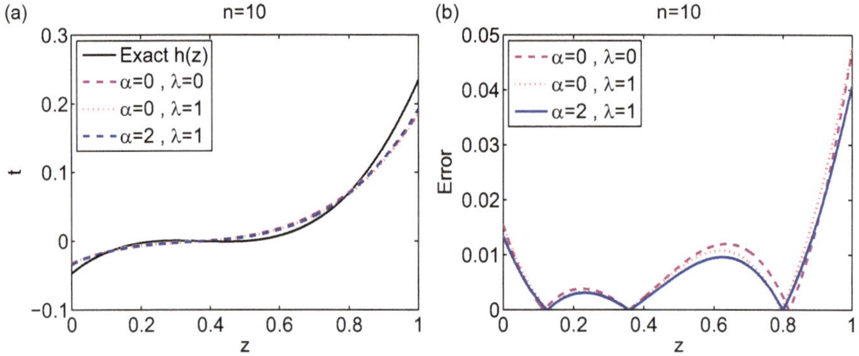

Figure 3.3 Convergence of our operators to $h(z) = \left(z-\frac{1}{2}\right)\left(z-\frac{3}{8}\right)\left(z-\frac{1}{4}\right)$. (a) Approximation process and (b) error of approximation.

Table 3.2
Comparison of Operators via Errors

n	α	λ	**Error**
10	0	0	4.76e−02
10	0	1	4.76e−02
10	2	1	4.09e−02

When we compare the numerical results of this section and the results in [3,7,8,27], we see that our operators have less error of approximation.

3.6 CONCLUSION

One of the main contributions of our work is to approximate the Lebesgue integrable functions on the interval $[0,1]$ more precisely. This is achieved by considering new Schurer polynomials defined in [27] instead of the polynomials defined in [7].

We provide a comprehensive literature review about λ-Bernstein-type operators, Bernstein operators, Schurer operators, and Schurer and Bernstein polynomials. We obtain some Voronovskaja-type theorems, including a Grüss-Voronovskaja and a quantitative Voronovskaja-type theorem for λ-Schurer-Kantorovich operators. We explore the convergence of our operators, and we see that our new operators have several advantages. As it is theoretically and numerically shown, the new operators defined in this chapter generalize the results in [3,5–9,17,20,27]. We investigate some approximation properties and show the relevance of the results by examples, and hence, we get better error estimation for our newly defined operators.

This study may be extended by considering q and (p,q) analogues of λ-Schurer, λ-Schurer-Kantorovich, λ-Schurer-Stancu, and λ-Schurer-Durrmeyer operators after introducing λ-Schurer-Durrmeyer and λ-Schurer-Stancu operators. All these operators may be considered for the functions of two variables, too.

REFERENCES

[1] Acar T, Aral A, Rasa I. The new forms of Voronovskaja's theorem in weighted spaces. *Positivity* 2016; 20(1):25–40.

[2] Acu A M, Gonska H, Rasa I. Grüss-type and Ostrowski-type inequalities in approximation theory. *Ukr. Math. J.* 2011; 63(6):843–864.

[3] Acu AM, Manav N, Sofonea S. Approximation properties of λ-Kantorovich operators. *J Inequal Appl.* 2018; 2018:202.

[4] Acu A M, Acar T, Radu V A. Approximation by modified $U^{\rho}_{n,\lambda}$ operators. *RACSAM* 2019; 113:2715–2729.

[5] Bărbosu D, Bărbosu M. Some properties of the fundamental polynomials of Bernstein-Schurer. Bul Ştiinţ Univ Baia Mare Ser B, *Mat-Inf.* 2002; 18(2):133–136.

[6] Bernstein SN. Démonstration du théorème de Weierstrass fondée sur le calcul des probabilités. *Communications of the Kharkov Mathematical Society* 1912; 13(2):1–2.

[7] Cai QB, Lian B-Y, Zhou G. Approximation properties of λ-Bernstein operators. *J Ineq and App* 2018; 2018:61.

[8] Cai QB. The Bézier variant of Kantorovich type λ-Bernstein operators. *J Inequal Appl.* 2018; 2018:90.

[9] Cai QB, Zhou G. Blending type approximation by GBS operators of bivariate tensor product of λ-Bernstein-Kantorovich type. *J Inequal Appl.* 2018; 2018:268.

[10] DeVore RA, Lorentz GG. *Constructive Approximation.* Berlin: Springer; 1993.

[11] Ditzian Z, Totik V. *Moduli of Smoothness.* New York: Springer; 1987.

[12] Farouki RT. The Bernstein polynomials basis: a centennial retrospective. *Comput Aided Geom Des.* 2012; 29:379–419.

[13] Goldman R. *Pyramid algorithms, a dynamic programming approach to curves and surfaces for geometric modeling*. The Morgan Kaufmann Series in Computer Graphics and Geometric Modeling San Francisco: Elsevier Science; 2002.

[14] Kantorovich LV. Sur certains developements suivant les polynmes de la forme de S. Bernstein I, II. *Dokl Akad Nauk SSSR* 1930; (563)568:595–600.

[15] Lorentz GG. *Bernstein polynomials*. Chelsea Pub. Comp: New York, 1986.

[16] Mohiuddine SA, F. Özger. Approximation of functions by Stancu variant of Bernstein-Kantorovich operators based on shape parameter α, *Rev. R. Acad. Cienc. Exactas Fís. Nat. Ser. A Math. RACSAM* 2020; 114:70.

[17] Muraru C. On the monotonicity of Schurer type polynomials. *Carpathian J Math*. 2005; 21(1–2):89–94.

[18] Mursaleen M, Ahasan M, Ansari KJ. Bivariate BernsteinSchurerStancu type GBS operators in (p,q)-analogue. *Adv Differ Equ*. 2020; 76(2020).

[19] Mursaleen M, Al-Abeid AH, Ansari KJ. On approximation properties of Baskakov-Schurer-Szász-Stancu operators based on q-integers, *Filomat* 2018; 32(41):359-1378.

[20] Schurer F. Linear positive operators in approximation theory. Math Inst Techn Univ Delft Report 1962.

[21] Simsek Y. Construction a new generating function of Bernstein type polynomials. *Appl Math Comput*. 2011; 218:1072–1076.

[22] Simsek Y. Analysis of the Bernstein basis functions: an approach to combinatorial sums involving binomial coefficients and Catalan numbers. *Math Method Appl Sci*. 2015; 38:3007–3021.

[23] Srivastava HM, Özger F, Mohiuddine SA. Construction of Stancu-type Bernstein operators based on Bézier bases with shape parameter λ. *Symmetry* 2019; 11(3):316. DOI:10.3390/symxx010005.

[24] Rahman S, Mursaleen M, Acu AM. Approximation properties of λ-Bernstein Kantorovich operators with shifted knots. *Math Meth Appl Sci*. 2019; 42(11):042–4053.

[25] Özarslan MA, Aktuğlu H. Local approximation for certain King type operators. *Filomat* 2013; 27(1):173–181.

[26] Özarslan MA, Duman O. Smoothness properties of modified Bernstein-Kantorovich operators. *Numer Func Anal Opt*. 2016; 37(1):92–105.

[27] Özger F. On new Bézier bases with Schurer polynomials and corresponding results in approximation theory. *Commun Fac Sci Univ Ank Ser A1 Math Stat*. 2019; 69(1): 376–393.

[28] Özger F. Weighted statistical approximation properties of univariate and bivariate λ-Kantorovich operators. *Filomat* 2019; 33(11):3473–3486.

[29] Qi Q, Guo D, Yang G. Approximation Properties of λ-Szász-Mirakian Operators. *International Journal of Engineering Research and Technology*. 2019; 12(5):662–669.

[30] Ye Z, Long X, Zeng X-M. Adjustment algorithms for Bézier curve and surface. *International Conference on Computer Science and Education* 2010; 1712–1716. DOI: 10.1109/ICCSE.2010.5593563.

4 Characterizations of Rough Fractional-Type Integral Operators on Variable Exponent Vanishing Morrey-Type Spaces

Ferit Gürbüz
Hakkari University

Shenghu Ding, Huili Han, and Pinhong Long
Ningxia University

CONTENTS

4.1 INTRODUCTION

In this work, we mainly focus on some operators and commutators on the variable exponent-generalized Morrey-type space. Precisely, our aim is to characterize the boundedness for the maximal operator, fractional integral operator, and fractional maximal operator with rough kernel as well as the corresponding commutators on the variable exponent vanishing generalized Morrey spaces.

We first list a series of (somewhat standard) notation needed for later sections.

1. Let $x=(x_1,x_2,\ldots,x_n)$, $\xi=(\xi_1,\xi_2,\ldots,\xi_n)\ldots$. etc. be the points of the real n-dimensional space $\mathbb{R}^n$. Let $x.\xi=\sum_{i=1}^{n}x_i\xi_i$ stand for the usual dot product in $\mathbb{R}^n$ and $|x|=\left(\sum_{i=1}^{n}x_i^2\right)^{\frac{1}{2}}$ for the Euclidean norm of x.
2. By x', we always mean the unit vector corresponding to x, i.e., $x'=\frac{x}{|x|}$ for any $x\neq 0$.
3. $S^{n-1}=\{x\in\mathbb{R}^n:|x|=1\}$ represents the unit sphere in Euclidean n-dimensional space $\mathbb{R}^n$ $(n\geq 2)$, and dx' is its surface measure.
4. $B(x,r)=\{y\in\mathbb{R}^n:|x-y|<r\}$ denotes x-centered Euclidean ball with radius r, $B^C(x,r)$ denotes its complement, and $|B(x,r)|$ is the Lebesgue measure of the ball $B(x,r)$, $|B(x,r)|=v_nr^n$, where $v_n=|B(0,1)|=\frac{2\pi^{\frac{n}{2}}}{n\Gamma\left(\frac{n}{2}\right)}$ and $\tilde{B}(x,r)=B(x,r)\cap E$, where $E\subset\mathbb{R}^n$ is an open set. Finally, we use the notation

$$f_{B(x,r)}=\frac{1}{|B(x,r)|}\int\limits_{\tilde{B}(x,r)}f(y)\,dy.$$

5. C stands for a positive constant that can change its value in each statement without explicit mention.
6. The exponents $p'(\cdot)$ and $s'(\cdot)$ always denote the conjugate index of any exponent $1<p(x)<\infty$ and $1<s(x)<\infty$, i.e., $\frac{1}{p'(x)}:=1-\frac{1}{p(x)}$ and $\frac{1}{s'(x)}:=1-\frac{1}{s(x)}$.
7. In the sequel, for any exponent $1<p(x)<\infty$ and bounded sets $E\subset\mathbb{R}^n$, if we use

$$|p(x)-p(y)|\leq\frac{-C}{\log(|x-y|)}\qquad |x-y|\leq\frac{1}{2},\qquad x,y\in E,\qquad (4.1)$$

where $C=C(p)>0$ does not depend on x, y, then we call that $p(\cdot)$ satisfies the local log-Hölder continuity condition or Dini-Lipschitz condition. The important role of the local log-Hölder continuity of $p(x)$ is well known in variable analysis. On the other hand, the condition

$$|p(x)-p(y)|\leq\frac{C}{\log(e+|x|)}\qquad |y|\geq|x|,\qquad x,y\in E,$$

introduced by Cruz-Uribe et al. in [4] is known as the log-Hölder decay condition used for unbounded sets E. It is equivalent to the condition that there exists a number $p_\infty\in[1,\infty)$ such that

$$\left|\frac{1}{p_\infty}-\frac{1}{p(x)}\right|\leq\frac{C_\infty}{\log(e+|x|)}\qquad \text{for all } x\in E,\qquad (4.2)$$

where $p_\infty=\lim_{|x|\to\infty}p(x)$.

If $p(\cdot)$ satisfies both (4.1) and (4.2), then we say that it is log-Hölder continuous.

8. Let $F, G \geq 0$. Here and henceforth, the symbol $F \approx G$ means that $F \lesssim G$ and $G \lesssim F$ happen simultaneously, while $F \lesssim G$ and $G \lesssim F$ mean that there exists a constant $C > 0$ such that $F \leq CG$.
9. Let $\Omega \in L_s(S^{n-1})$ with $1 < s \leq \infty$ be the homogeneous function of degree 0 on $\mathbb{R}^n$ and satisfy the integral zero property over the unit sphere S^{n-1}. Moreover, note that $\|\Omega\|_{L_s(S^{n-1})} := \left(\int\limits_{S^{n-1}} |\Omega(z')|^s d\sigma(z') \right)^{\frac{1}{s}}$ and

$$\begin{aligned}\|\Omega(z-y)\|_{L_s(\tilde{B}(x,r))} &= \left(\int\limits_{\tilde{B}(x,r)} |\Omega((z-y))|^s dz \right)^{\frac{1}{s}} \\ &\lesssim \left(\int\limits_{\tilde{B}(x,r)} \Omega(\sigma)^s \int\limits_0^r \rho^{n-1} d\rho d\sigma \right)^{\frac{1}{s}} \\ &\lesssim \|\Omega\|_{L_s(S^{n-1})} r^{\frac{n}{s}},\end{aligned} \tag{4.3}$$

for $z \in B(x,r)$.
10. Suppose that $0 < \alpha(x) < n, x \in E \subset \mathbb{R}^n$. Then, the rough Riesz-type potential operator with variable order $I_{\Omega,\alpha(\cdot)}$ and the corresponding rough fractional maximal operator with variable order $M_{\Omega,\alpha(\cdot)}$ are defined, respectively, by

$$I_{\Omega,\alpha(\cdot)} f(x) = \int\limits_E \frac{\Omega(x-y)}{|x-y|^{n-\alpha(x)}} f(y) dy$$

and

$$M_{\Omega,\alpha(\cdot)} f(x) = \sup_{r>0} |B(x,r)|^{\frac{\alpha(x)}{n}-1} \int\limits_{\tilde{B}(x,r)} |\Omega(x-y)| |f(y)| dy,$$

where $E \subset \mathbb{R}^n$ is an open set. On the other hand, if $\alpha(\cdot) = 0$, then the rough Calderón-Zygmund-type singular integral operator T_Ω in the sense of principal value Cauchy integral is defined by

$$T_\Omega f(x) = p.v. \int\limits_E \frac{\Omega(x-y)}{|x-y|^n} f(y) dy,$$

and especially in the limiting case $\alpha(\cdot) = 0$, the rough fractional maximal operator with variable order $M_{\Omega,\alpha}$ reduces to the rough Hardy-Littlewood maximal operator M_Ω, and M_Ω is also defined by

$$M_\Omega f(x) = \sup_{r>0} \frac{1}{|B(x,r)|} \int\limits_{\tilde{B}(x,r)} |\Omega(y)| |f(x-y)| dy,$$

where $E \subset \mathbb{R}^n$ is an open set. In fact, we can easily see that when $\Omega \equiv 1$, $M_{1,\alpha(\cdot)} \equiv M_{\alpha(\cdot)}$ and $I_{1,\alpha(\cdot)} \equiv I_{\alpha(\cdot)}$ are the fractional maximal operator with variable order and the Riesz-type potential operator with variable order, and similarly, M and T are the Hardy-Littlewood maximal operator and the standard Calderón-Zygmund-type singular integral operator, respectively.

11. The boundedness properties of commutator operators is also an important aspect of harmonic analysis as these are useful in the study of characterization of function spaces and regularity theory of partial differential equations. The commutators of the operators T_Ω, M_Ω with rough kernel Ω with locally integrable function b are given by

$$\begin{aligned}[b,T_\Omega] f(x) &= b(x) T_\Omega f(x) - T_\Omega (bf)(x) \\ &= p.v. \int_E \frac{\Omega(x-y)}{|x-y|^n} (b(x) - b(y)) f(y) dy\end{aligned}$$

and

$$\begin{aligned}[b,M_\Omega] f(x) &= b(x) M_\Omega f(x) - M_\Omega (bf)(x) \\ &= \sup_{r>0} \frac{1}{|B(x,r)|} \int_{\tilde{B}(x,r)} |\Omega(x-y)| (b(x) - |b(y)|) |f(y)| dy,\end{aligned}$$

similarly, define the rough commutators $[b, I_{\Omega,\alpha(\cdot)}]$, $[b, M_{\Omega,\alpha(\cdot)}]$ generated by the function b and the operators $I_{\Omega,\alpha(\cdot)}$ and $M_{\Omega,\alpha(\cdot)}$ with rough kernel Ω and variable order $\alpha(\cdot)(0 \leq \alpha(\cdot) < n)$ by

$$\begin{aligned}[b, I_{\Omega,\alpha(\cdot)}] f(x) &= b(x) I_{\Omega,\alpha(\cdot)} f(x) - I_{\Omega,\alpha(\cdot)} (bf)(x) \\ &= \int_E \frac{\Omega(x-y)}{|x-y|^{n-\alpha(x)}} (b(x) - b(y)) f(y) dy\end{aligned}$$

and

$$\begin{aligned}[b, M_{\Omega,\alpha(\cdot)}] f(x) &= b(x) M_{\Omega,\alpha(\cdot)} f(x) - M_{\Omega,\alpha(\cdot)} (bf)(x) \\ &= \sup_{r>0} |B(x,r)|^{\frac{\alpha(x)}{n}-1} \int_{\tilde{B}(x,r)} |\Omega(x-y)| (b(x) - |b(y)|) |f(y)| dy.\end{aligned}$$

Later, Morrey spaces can complement the boundedness properties of operators that Lebesgue spaces can not handle. Morrey spaces that we have been handling are called classical Morrey spaces (see [16]). But classical Morrey spaces are not totally enough to describe the boundedness properties. To this end, we need to generalize parameters p and q, among others p, but this issue will exceed the scope of this chapter, so we pass this part. Though we do not consider the direct applications of

Morrey spaces to PDEs, Morrey spaces can be applied to PDEs. Applications to the second-order elliptic partial differential equations can be found in [9] and [21].

Recently, while we try out to resolve somewhat modern problems emerging inherently such that nonlinear elasticity theory, fluid mechanics, etc., it is well-known that classical function spaces are not anymore suitable spaces. It thus becomes essential to introduce and analyze the diverse function spaces from diverse viewpoints. One of such spaces is the variable exponent Lebesgue space $L^{p(\cdot)}$. This space is a generalization of the classical $L^p(\mathbb{R}^n)$ space, in which the constant exponent p is replaced by an exponent function $p(\cdot):\mathbb{R}^n \to (0,\infty)$, and it consists of all functions f such that $\int_{\mathbb{R}^n} |f(x)|^{p(x)}\,dx < \infty$. This theory got a boost in 1931 when Orlicz published his seminal paper [17]. The next major step in the investigation of variable exponent spaces was the comprehensive paper by Kováčik and Rákosník in the early 1990s [14]. Since then, the theory of variable exponent spaces was applied to many fields: Refer to [3,23] for the image processing, [2] for thermorheological fluids, [19] for electrorheological fluids, and [11] for the differential equations with nonstandard growth. For the nonweighted and weighted variable exponent settings, refer to [5–8]. On the other hand, Kováčik and Rákosník [14] established many of the basic properties of Lebesgue and Sobolev spaces. Moreover, since these authors clarified fundamental properties of the variable exponent Lebesgue and Sobolev spaces, there are many spaces studied, such as variable exponent Morrey, generalized Morrey, vanishing generalized Morrey, and Herz-Morrey spaces (see [1,10,12,13,15,20,22,24]). In the last decade, when the parameters that define the operator have changed from point to point, there has been a strong interest in fractional-type operators and the "variable setting" function spaces. The field called variable exponent analysis has become a fairly branched area with many interesting results obtained in the last decade, such as harmonic analysis, approximation theory, operator theory, and pseudo-differential operators. But the results in this paper lie in these spaces known as variable exponent Morrey-type spaces on the rough fractional-type operators with variable order of harmonic analysis, which has been extensively developed for the last ten years and continues to attract attention of researchers from various fields of mathematics. Many of problems about such spaces have been solved both in the classical setting and in the Euclidean setting, including fractional upper and lower dimensions. For example, in 2008, variable exponent Morrey spaces $L^{p(\cdot),\lambda(\cdot)}$ were introduced to study the boundedness of M and $I_{\alpha(\cdot)}$ in the Euclidean setting by Almeida et al. [1]. In 2010, variable exponent-generalized Morrey spaces $L^{p(\cdot),w(\cdot)}(E)$ were introduced to consider the boundedness of $M, I_{\alpha(\cdot)}, T$ for bounded sets $E \subset \mathbb{R}^n$ on $L^{p(\cdot),w(\cdot)}(E)$ in [10]. In 2016, variable exponent vanishing generalized Morrey spaces $VL_{\Pi}^{p(\cdot),w(\cdot)}(E)$ were introduced to characterize the boundedness of $M, I_{\alpha(\cdot)}, T$ for bounded or unbounded sets E on $VL_{\Pi}^{p(\cdot),w(\cdot)}(E)$ in [15]. These results inspire us to ask whether the above operators ($I_{\Omega,\alpha(\cdot)}$, $M_{\Omega,\alpha(\cdot)}$, T_{Ω}, and M_{Ω}) have the similar mapping properties on variable exponent $VL_{\Pi}^{p(\cdot),w(\cdot)}(E)$, which includes variable exponent $L^{p(\cdot),\lambda(\cdot)}$ and $L^{p(\cdot)}$ spaces. Our first results (see Theorem 4.3, Theorem 4.5, and Theorem 4.6 below) will give some affirmative answers to these questions. Another purpose of this chapter is to prove the boundedness of above operators ($[b, I_{\Omega,\alpha(\cdot)}]$, $[b, M_{\Omega,\alpha(\cdot)}]$, $[b, T_\Omega]$, and $[b, M_\Omega]$) on $VL_{\Pi}^{p(\cdot),w(\cdot)}(E)$ spaces (see Theorem 4.7 below).

4.2 PRELIMINARIES AND MAIN RESULTS

In this section, we first recall the definitions and some properties of basic spaces that we need and then give the main results.

4.2.1 VARIABLE EXPONENT LEBESGUE SPACES $L^{p(\cdot)}$

Unfortunately, the variable exponent Lebesgue spaces $L^{p(\cdot)}$ and the classical cases have some undesired properties. For example, the variable $L^{p(\cdot)}$ spaces are not translation invariant. As a consequence, the variable exponent Lebesgue spaces are not rearrangement-invariant Banach spaces, and so neither good-λ techniques nor rearrangement inequalities may be applied for a generalization of some standard results in classical Lebesgue spaces to the case of $L^{p(\cdot)}$.

Now, we begin with a brief and necessarily incomplete review of the variable exponent Lebesgue spaces $L^{p(\cdot)}$.

Definition 4.1. *[18] Given an open set $E \subset \mathbb{R}^n$ and a measurable function $p(\cdot): E \to [1,\infty)$. We assume that $1 \le p_-(E) \le p_+(E) < \infty$, where $p_-(E) = \operatorname{essinf}_{x\in E} p(x)$ and $p_+(E) = \operatorname{esssup}_{x\in E} p(x)$. The variable exponent Lebesgue space $L^{p(\cdot)}(E)$ is the collection of all measurable functions f such that, for some $\lambda > 0$, $\rho(f/\lambda) < \infty$, where the modular is defined by*

$$\rho(f) = \rho_{p(\cdot)}(f) = \int_E |f(x)|^{p(x)}\,dx.$$

Then, the spaces $L^{p(\cdot)}(E)$ and $L^{p(\cdot)}_{loc}(E)$ are defined by

$$L^{p(\cdot)}(E) = \{f \text{ is measurable} : \rho_{p(\cdot)}(\lambda^{-1}f) < \infty \text{ for some } \lambda > 0\}$$

and

$$L^{p(\cdot)}_{loc}(E) = \left\{f \text{ is measurable} : f \in L^{p(\cdot)}(K) \text{ for all compact } K \subset E\right\}.$$

Moreover, we define $\|\cdot\|_{L^{p(\cdot)}(E)}$, which is called the variable Lebesgue norm or the Luxemburg norm as follows:

$$\|f\|_{L^{p(\cdot)}(E)} = \inf\left(\{\lambda \in (0,\infty) : \rho_{p(\cdot)}(\lambda^{-1}f) \le 1\} \cup \{\infty\}\right) \qquad f \in L^{p(\cdot)}(E). \tag{4.4}$$

Since $p_-(E) \ge 1$, $\|\cdot\|_{L^{p(\cdot)}(E)}$ is a norm and $\left(L^{p(\cdot)}(E), \|\cdot\|_{L^{p(\cdot)}(E)}\right)$ is a Banach space. However, if $p_-(E) < 1$, then $\|\cdot\|_{L^{p(\cdot)}(E)}$ is a quasinorm and $\left(L^{p(\cdot)}(E), \|\cdot\|_{L^{p(\cdot)}(E)}\right)$ is a quasi-Banach space. The variable exponent norm has the following property

$$\left\|f^\lambda\right\|_{L^{p(\cdot)}(E)} = \|f\|^\lambda_{L^{\lambda p(\cdot)}(E)},$$

for $\lambda \geq \frac{1}{p_-}$. Moreover, these spaces are referred to as the variable L^p spaces since they generalize the standard L^p spaces: If $p(x) = p$ is constant, then $L^{p(\cdot)}(E)$ is isometrically isomorphic to $L^p(E)$. As a result, using notations above ($p_-(E)$ and $p_+(E)$), we define a class of variable exponent as follows:

$$\Phi(E) = \{p(\cdot) : E \to [1,\infty),\ p_-(E) \geq 1,\ p_+(E) < \infty\}.$$

Now, we define two sets of exponents $p(x)$ with $1 \leq p_-(E) \leq p_+(E) < \infty$. These will be denoted as follows:

$$\mathcal{P}^{\log}(E) = \left\{ \begin{array}{c} p(\cdot) : p_-(E) \geq 1,\ p_+(E) < \infty \text{ and } p(\cdot) \text{ satisfy both conditions (4.1) and (4.2)} \\ \text{(the latter required if } E \text{ is unbounded)} \end{array} \right\}$$

and

$$\mathcal{B}(E) = \left\{ p(\cdot) : p(\cdot) \in \mathcal{P}^{\log}(E),\ M \text{ is bounded on } L^{p(\cdot)}(E) \right\},$$

where M is the Hardy-Littlewood maximal operator. We recall that the generalized Hölder inequality on Lebesgue spaces with the variable exponent

$$\left| \int_E f(x)\, g(x)\, dx \right| \leq \int_E |f(x)\, g(x)|\, dx \leq C_p \|f\|_{L^{p(\cdot)}(E)} \|g\|_{L^{p'(\cdot)}(E)} \quad C_p = 1 + \frac{1}{p_-} - \frac{1}{p_+},$$

is known to hold for $p(\cdot) \in \Phi(E)$, $f \in L^{p(\cdot)}(E)$, and $g \in L^{p'(\cdot)}(E)$ (see Theorem 2.1 in [14]). Now, we recall some recent results for the rough Riesz-type potential operator with the variable order $I_{\Omega,\alpha(\cdot)}$ and the corresponding rough fractional maximal operator with variable order $M_{\Omega,\alpha(\cdot)}$ on the variable exponent Lebesgue space $L^{p(\cdot)}(E)$. The order $\alpha(x)$ of the potential is not assumed to be continuous. We assume that it is a measurable function on E satisfying the following assumptions:

$$\left. \begin{array}{l} \alpha_0 = \operatorname*{ess\,inf}_{x \in E} \alpha(x) > 0 \\ \operatorname*{ess\,sup}_{x \in E} \alpha(x)\, p(x) < n \end{array} \right\}. \tag{4.5}$$

First, the norm in the space $L^{p(\cdot)}(E)$ seems to be complicated in a sense, to be calculated or estimated. So the following basic estimation of the boundedness of an operator B:

$$\|Bf\|_{L^{p(\cdot)}(E)} \lesssim \|f\|_{L^{p(\cdot)}(E)} \tag{4.6}$$

is not easy. However, in the case of linear operators, the above inequality between the norm and the modular and the homogeneity property

$$\|B\|_{X \to X} = \sup_{f \in X} \frac{\|Bf\|_X}{\|f\|_X} = \sup_{\|f\|_X = 1} \|Bf\|_X$$

allow us to replace checking of (4.6) by a work with a modular:

$$\int_E |Bf(x)|^{p(x)}\, dx, \text{ for all } f \text{ with } \|f\|_{L^{p(\cdot)}(E)} \leq 1,$$

which is certainly easier. In that respect, the boundedness of the rough Riesz-type potential operator from the space $L^{p(\cdot)}(\mathbb{R}^n)$ with the variable exponent $p(x)$ into the space $L^{q(\cdot)}(\mathbb{R}^n)$ with the limiting Sobolev exponent

$$\frac{1}{q(x)} = \frac{1}{p(x)} - \frac{\alpha(x)}{n} \tag{4.7}$$

was an open problem for a long time. It was solved in the case of bounded domains. First, in [18], in the case of bounded domains E, there has the following conditional result.

Theorem 4.1. *[18] Let E be a bounded open set, $\Omega \in L_s(S^{n-1})$ with $1 < s \leq \infty$, $p(x) \in \mathcal{P}^{\log}(E)$, $\alpha(x)$ satisfying assumptions (4.5) and $(p')_+ \leq s$. Define $q(x)$ by (4.7). Then, the rough Riesz-type potential operator $I_{\Omega,\alpha(\cdot)}$ is $\left(L^{p(\cdot)}(E) \to L^{q(\cdot)}(E)\right)$-bounded, i.e., the Sobolev-type theorem*

$$\left\|I_{\Omega,\alpha(\cdot)}f\right\|_{L^{q(\cdot)}(E)} \lesssim \|f\|_{L^{p(\cdot)}(E)} \tag{4.8}$$

is valid.

Corollary 4.1. *Let E be a bounded open set, $\Omega \in L_s(S^{n-1})$ with $1 < s \leq \infty$ being a homogeneous function of degree 0 on $\mathbb{R}^n$, $\frac{p}{s'} \in \mathcal{B}(E)$, and $(p')_+ \leq s$. Under the conditions of Theorem 4.1 (taking $\alpha(\cdot) = 0$ there), the operator T_Ω is $\left(L^{p(\cdot)}(E) \to L^{p(\cdot)}(E)\right)$-bounded, i.e.,*

$$\|T_\Omega f\|_{L^{p(\cdot)}(E)} \lesssim \|f\|_{L^{p(\cdot)}(E)} \tag{4.9}$$

is valid.

On the other hand, the pointwise inequalities on variable exponent Lebesgue spaces are very useful. Indeed, we have

$$|f(x)| \leq |h(x)| \text{ implies that } \|f\|_{L^{p(\cdot)}(E)} \lesssim \|h\|_{L^{p(\cdot)}(E)}.$$

Thus, if one operator is pointwise dominated by another one:

$$|Bf(x)| \leq |Df(x)|,$$

and we know that the operator D is bounded, then the boundedness of the operator B immediately follows. For example, by Theorem 4.1, we get the following:

Theorem 4.2. *Under the conditions of Theorem 4.1, the operator $M_{\Omega,\alpha(\cdot)}$ is $\left(L^{p(\cdot)}(E) \to L^{q(\cdot)}(E)\right)$-bounded, i.e., the Sobolev-type theorem*

$$\left\|M_{\Omega,\alpha(\cdot)}f\right\|_{L^{q(\cdot)}(E)} \lesssim \|f\|_{L^{p(\cdot)}(E)} \tag{4.10}$$

is valid.

Corollary 4.2. *Let E be a bounded open set, $\Omega \in L_s(S^{n-1})$ with $1 < s \leq \infty$ being a homogeneous function of degree 0 on $\mathbb{R}^n$, $\frac{p}{s'} \in \mathcal{B}(E)$, and $(p')_+ \leq s$. Under the conditions of Theorem 4.2 (taking $\alpha(\cdot) = 0$ there), the operator M_Ω is $\left(L^{p(\cdot)}(E) \to L^{p(\cdot)}(E)\right)$-bounded, i.e.,*

$$\|M_\Omega f\|_{L^{p(\cdot)}(E)} \lesssim \|f\|_{L^{p(\cdot)}(E)} \tag{4.11}$$

is valid.

We are now in a place of proving (4.10) in Theorem 4.2.

Remark 4.1. *The conclusion of (4.10) is a direct consequence of the following Lemma 4.1 and (4.8). In order to do this, we need to define an operator by*

$$\widetilde{T}_{|\Omega|,\alpha(\cdot)}(|f|)(x) = \int_E \frac{|\Omega(x-y)|}{|x-y|^{n-\alpha(x)}} |f(y)|\, dy \qquad 0 < \alpha(x) < n,$$

where $\Omega \in L_s(S^{n-1})\,(s > 1)$ is homogeneous of degree zero on $\mathbb{R}^n$.

Using the idea of proving Corollary 3.1. in [22], we can obtain the following pointwise relation.

Lemma 4.1. *Let $0 < \alpha(x) < n$ and $\Omega \in L_s(S^{n-1})\,(s > 1)$. Then, we have*

$$M_{\Omega,\alpha(\cdot)}(f)(x) \leq C\widetilde{T}_{|\Omega|,\alpha(\cdot)}(|f|)(x) \qquad \text{for } x \in \mathbb{R}^n, \tag{4.12}$$

where C does not depend on f and x.

Proof. To prove (4.12), we observe that for any $x \in \mathbb{R}^n$, there exists an $r = r_x$ such that

$$M_{\Omega,\alpha(\cdot)}(f)(x) \leq \frac{2}{|B(x,r_x)|^{n-\alpha(x)}} \int_{B(x,r_x)} |\Omega(x-y)|\,|f(y)|\,dy,$$

and by the inequality above, we get

$$\begin{aligned} \widetilde{T}_{|\Omega|,\alpha(\cdot)}(|f|)(x) &\geq \int_{B(x,r_x)} \frac{|\Omega(x-y)|}{|x-y|^{n-\alpha(x)}} |f(y)|\, dy \\ &\geq \frac{C}{|B(x,r_x)|^{n-\alpha(x)}} \int_{B(x,r_x)} |\Omega(x-y)|\,|f(y)|\, dy. \end{aligned}$$

□

From the process proving (4.8) in [18], it is easy to see that the conclusions of (4.8) also hold for $\widetilde{T}_{|\Omega|,\alpha(\cdot)}$. Combining this with (4.12), we can immediately obtain (4.10), which completes the proof of Theorem 4.2.

Remark 4.2. *Taking $\alpha(\cdot) = 0$ in Lemma 4.1 and the inequality*

$$M_\Omega(f)(x) \le C\widetilde{T}_{|\Omega|}(|f|)(x) \qquad \text{for } x \in \mathbb{R}^n,$$

which follows from the definitions of the operators.

The above theorems (Theorem 4.1 and Theorem 4.2) allow us to use the known results for the boundedness of the operators $M_{\Omega,\alpha(\cdot)}$ and $I_{\Omega,\alpha(\cdot)}$ that are transferred to the various function spaces. The following fact is known (see Lemma 3.1. in [15]).

Lemma 4.2. *[15] Let E be a bounded open set, $p(x) \in \mathcal{P}^{\log}(E)$ and $\alpha(x)$ satisfying assumptions (4.5). Then,*

$$\left\| |x-\cdot|^{\alpha(x)-n} \chi_{\tilde{B}(x,r)} \right\|_{L^{p(\cdot)}(E)} \lesssim r^{\alpha(x)-\frac{n}{p(x)}}.$$

We will also make use of the estimate provided by the following fact (see [15]).

$$\left\| \chi_{\tilde{B}(x,r)} \right\|_{L^{p(\cdot)}(E)} \lesssim r^{\psi_p(x,r)}, \qquad x \in E,\ p(x) \in \mathcal{P}^{\log}(E), \tag{4.13}$$

where

$$\psi_p(x,r) = \begin{cases} \frac{n}{p(x)}, & r \le 1 \\ \frac{n}{p(\infty)}, & r > 1. \end{cases}$$

4.2.2 VARIABLE EXPONENT MORREY SPACES $L^{p(\cdot),\lambda(\cdot)}$

Here, we recall the variable exponent Morrey spaces and the integral inequalities.

Definition 4.2. *[1] Let E be a bounded open set and $\lambda(x)$ be a measurable function on E with values in $[0,n]$. Then, the variable exponent Morrey space $L^{p(\cdot),\lambda(\cdot)} \equiv L^{p(\cdot),\lambda(\cdot)}(E)$ is defined by*

$$L^{p(\cdot),\lambda(\cdot)} \equiv L^{p(\cdot),\lambda(\cdot)}(E) = \left\{ \begin{array}{c} f \in L^{p(\cdot)}_{loc}(E): \\ \|f\|_{L^{p(\cdot),\lambda(\cdot)}} = \sup\limits_{x\in E, r>0} r^{-\frac{\lambda(x)}{p(x)}} \left\| f\chi_{\tilde{B}(x,r)} \right\|_{L^{p(\cdot)}(E)} < \infty \end{array} \right\}.$$

Note that $L^{p(\cdot),0}(E) = L^{p(\cdot)}(E)$ and $L^{p(\cdot),n}(E) = L^\infty(E)$. If $\lambda_- > n$, then $L^{p(\cdot),\lambda(\cdot)}(E) = \{0\}$.

Lemma 4.3. *Let E be a bounded open set, $\Omega \in L_s(S^{n-1})$ with $1 < s < \infty$, $p(x), q(x) \in \mathcal{P}^{\log}(E)$, $\alpha(x)$ satisfying the following assumptions:*

$$\left.\begin{array}{c} \alpha_0 = \operatorname*{essinf}\limits_{x\in E} \alpha(x) > 0 \\ \operatorname*{esssup}\limits_{x\in E} [\lambda(x) + \alpha(x)p(x)] < n \end{array}\right\} \tag{4.14}$$

and $(p')_+ \leq s$. *Define* $q(x)$ *by* $\frac{1}{q(\cdot)} = \frac{1}{p(\cdot)} - \frac{\alpha(\cdot)}{n-\lambda(\cdot)}$. *Then, the rough Riesz-type potential operator* $I_{\Omega,\alpha(\cdot)}$ *is* $\left(L^{p(\cdot),\lambda(\cdot)}(E) \to L^{q(\cdot),\lambda(\cdot)}(E)\right)$*-bounded. Moreover,*

$$\left\|I_{\Omega,\alpha(\cdot)}f\right\|_{L^{q(\cdot),\lambda(\cdot)}(E)} \lesssim \|f\|_{L^{p(\cdot),\lambda(\cdot)}(E)}.$$

Proof. By the embedding property in Lemma 7 in [1], we only need to prove that the operator $I_{\Omega,\alpha(\cdot)}$ is bounded in $L^{p(\cdot),\lambda(\cdot)}(E)$.

Hedberg's trick:

$$\begin{aligned} I_{\Omega,\alpha(\cdot)}f(x) &= \int\limits_{B(x,2r)} \frac{\Omega(x-y)}{|x-y|^{n-\alpha(x)}} f(y)dy + \int\limits_{B^C(x,2r)} \frac{\Omega(x-y)}{|x-y|^{n-\alpha(x)}} f(y)dy \\ &= \mathcal{F}(x,r) + \mathcal{G}(x,r). \end{aligned} \tag{4.15}$$

We may assume that $\|f\|_{L^{p(\cdot),\lambda(\cdot)}(E)} \leq 1$. For $\mathcal{F}(x,r)$, we first have to prove the following:

$$\mathcal{F}(x,r) := \left| \int\limits_{|x-y|<r} \frac{\Omega(x-y)}{|x-y|^{n-\alpha(x)}} f(y)dy \right| \lesssim \frac{2^n r^{\alpha(x)}}{2^{\alpha(x)}-1} M_\Omega f(x). \tag{4.16}$$

Indeed, for $f(x) \geq 0$, we have

$$\begin{aligned} \mathcal{F}(x,r) &= \sum_{j=0}^{\infty} \int\limits_{2^{-j-1}r \leq |x-y| < 2^{-j}r} \frac{\Omega(x-y)}{|x-y|^{n-\alpha(x)}} f(y)dy \\ &\leq \sum_{j=0}^{\infty} \frac{1}{(2^{-j-1}r)^{n-\alpha(x)}} \int\limits_{|x-y|<2^{-j}r} \Omega(x-y)f(y)dy \\ &\leq 2^{n-\alpha(x)} M_\Omega f(x) \sum_{j=0}^{\infty} \frac{|B(x,2^{-j}r)|}{(2^{-j}r)^{n-\alpha(x)}}. \end{aligned}$$

Hence, by $|B(x,2^{-j}r)| \lesssim (2^{-j}r)^n$, we obtain

$$\mathcal{F}(x,r) \lesssim 2^{n-\alpha(x)} r^{\alpha(x)} M_\Omega f(x) \sum_{j=0}^{\infty} \left(2^{-j\alpha(x)}\right),$$

which gives estimate (4.16). Then by (4.16):

$$|\mathcal{F}(x,r)| \lesssim r^{\alpha(x)} M_\Omega f(x).$$

For $\mathcal{G}(x,r)$, from Lemma 4.2 and the procedure of Theorem 3 in [1], we may show that

$$|\mathcal{G}(x,r)| \lesssim r^{\alpha(x)-\frac{n-\lambda(x)}{p(x)}}.$$

Then, from (4.15), we get

$$I_{\Omega,\alpha(\cdot)}f(x) \lesssim \left[r^{\alpha(x)}M_{\Omega}f(x) + r^{\alpha(x)-\frac{n-\lambda(x)}{p(x)}}\right]. \tag{4.17}$$

As usual in Hedberg approach, we choose

$$r = [M_{\Omega}f(x)]^{-\frac{p(x)}{n-\lambda(x)}}.$$

Substituting this into (4.17), we get

$$\left|I_{\Omega,\alpha(\cdot)}f(x)\right| \lesssim (M_{\Omega}f(x))^{\frac{p(x)}{q(x)}},$$

here, we need (4.3). Therefore, by Theorem 5.1 in [18], we know that

$$\int_{\tilde{B}(x,r)} \left|I_{\Omega,\alpha(\cdot)}f(y)\right|^{q(y)} dy \lesssim \int_{\tilde{B}(x,r)} |M_{\Omega}f(y)|^{p(y)} dy \lesssim r^{\lambda(x)},$$

which completes the proof of Lemma 4.3. □

Theorem 4.3. *Let E be a bounded open set, $\Omega \in L_s(S^{n-1})$ with $1 < s < \infty$, $p(x), q(x) \in \mathcal{P}^{\log}(E)$, $\alpha(x)$ satisfying (4.14) and $(p')_+ \leq s$. Define $q(x)$, $\mu(x)$ by $\frac{1}{q(\cdot)} = \frac{1}{p(\cdot)} - \frac{\alpha(\cdot)}{n}$, $\frac{n-\mu(\cdot)}{q(\cdot)} = \frac{n-\lambda(\cdot)}{p(\cdot)} - \alpha(\cdot)$, respectively. Then, the rough Riesz-type potential operator $I_{\Omega,\alpha(\cdot)}$ is $\left(L^{p(\cdot),\lambda(\cdot)}(E) \to L^{q(\cdot),\mu(\cdot)}(E)\right)$-bounded. Moreover,*

$$\left\|I_{\Omega,\alpha(\cdot)}f\right\|_{L^{q(\cdot),\mu(\cdot)}(E)} \lesssim \|f\|_{L^{p(\cdot),\lambda(\cdot)}(E)}, \tag{4.18}$$

where

$$1 \leq q(\cdot) \leq \frac{p(\cdot)(n-\lambda(\cdot))}{n-\lambda(\cdot)-\alpha(\cdot)p(\cdot)}.$$

Proof. Since

$$\frac{p(\cdot)(n-\lambda(\cdot))}{n-\lambda(\cdot)-\alpha(\cdot)p(\cdot)} < \frac{np(\cdot)}{n-\alpha(\cdot)p(\cdot)},$$

from Lemma 4.3 and Theorem 4.1, we obtain

$$\begin{aligned}\left\|I_{\Omega,\alpha(\cdot)}f\right\|_{L^{q(\cdot),\mu(\cdot)}(E)} &= \sup_{x\in E, r>0} r^{-\frac{\mu(x)}{q(x)}} \left\|I_{\Omega,\alpha(\cdot)}f\chi_{\tilde{B}(x,r)}\right\|_{L^{q(\cdot)}(E)} \\ &\lesssim \sup_{x\in E, r>0} r^{-\frac{\lambda(x)}{p(x)}} \left\|f\chi_{\tilde{B}(x,r)}\right\|_{L^{p(\cdot)}(E)} \\ &= \|f\|_{L^{p(\cdot),\lambda(\cdot)}(E)}.\end{aligned}$$

Clearly, Theorem 4.3 holds. □

Theorem 4.4. *Under the conditions of Theorem 4.3,*

$$\left\|M_{\Omega,\alpha(\cdot)}f\right\|_{L^{q(\cdot),\mu(\cdot)}(E)} \lesssim \|f\|_{L^{p(\cdot),\lambda(\cdot)}(E)}. \tag{4.19}$$

Proof. Similar to the proof of Theorem 4.2, conclusion (4.19) is a direct consequence of (4.12) and (4.18). Indeed, from the process proving (4.18) in Theorem 4.3, it is easy to see that conclusion (4.18) also holds for $\widetilde{T}_{|\Omega|,\alpha(\cdot)}$. Combining this with (4.12), we can immediately obtain (4.19), which completes the proof. □

4.2.3 VARIABLE EXPONENT VANISHING GENERALIZED MORREY SPACES

Having set down the boundedness properties of the rough operators on variable exponent Morrey spaces, in this section, we are now interested in the boundedness properties of the rough operators on variable exponent vanishing generalized Morrey spaces. For this, we first consider the generalized Morrey spaces $L^{p(\cdot),w(\cdot)}(E)$ with a variable exponent $p(x)$ and a general function $w(x,r):\Pi\times(0,diam(E))\to\mathbb{R}_+$, $\Pi\subset E\subset\mathbb{R}^n$, defining the Morrey-type norm on sets $E\subset\mathbb{R}^n$ which may be both bounded and unbounded; see the definition of the spaces $L^{p(\cdot),w(\cdot)}(E)$ in (4.21).

Everywhere in the sequel, the functions $w(x,r)$, $w_1(x,r)$, $w_2(x,r)$ used in the body of this paper are nonnegative measurable functions on $E\times(0,\infty)$, where $E\subset\mathbb{R}^n$ is an open set. We recall the definition of variable exponent-generalized Morrey space in the following.

Definition 4.3. *[10] Let $1\le p(x)\le p_+<\infty$, $\Pi\subset E\subset\mathbb{R}^n$, $x\in\Pi$, $w(x,r):\Pi\times(0,diam(E))\to\mathbb{R}_+$, where*

$$\inf_{x\in\Pi} w(x,r)>0 \qquad r>0. \tag{4.20}$$

Then, the variable exponent-generalized Morrey space $L_{\Pi}^{p(\cdot),w(\cdot)}\equiv L_{\Pi}^{p(\cdot),w(\cdot)}(E)$ is defined by

$$L_{\Pi}^{p(\cdot),w(\cdot)}\equiv L_{\Pi}^{p(\cdot),w(\cdot)}(E)=\left\{\begin{array}{c} f\in L_{loc}^{p(\cdot)}(E): \\ \|f\|_{L_{\Pi}^{p(\cdot),w(\cdot)}}=\sup\limits_{x\in\Pi,r>0} w(x,r)^{-\frac{1}{p(x)}}\|f\|_{L^{p(\cdot)}(\tilde{B}(x,r))}<\infty \end{array}\right\}, \tag{4.21}$$

and one can also see that for bounded exponents p, there holds the following equivalence:

$$f\in L_{\Pi}^{p(\cdot),w(\cdot)} \text{ if and only if } \sup_{x\in\Pi,r>0}\int_{\tilde{B}(x,r)}\left|\frac{f(y)}{w(x,r)}\right|^{p(y)}dy<\infty.$$

On the other hand, the above definition recovers the definition of $L^{p(\cdot),\lambda(\cdot)}(E)$ if we choose $w(x,r)=r^{\frac{\lambda(x)}{p(x)}}$ and $\Pi=E$, i.e.,

$$L^{p(\cdot),\lambda(\cdot)}(E)=L_{\Pi}^{p(\cdot),w(\cdot)}(E)\Big|_{w(x,r)=r^{\frac{\lambda(x)}{p(x)}}}.$$

Also, when $\Pi = \{x_0\}$ and $\Pi = E$, $L_{\Pi}^{p(\cdot),w(\cdot)}$ turns into the local generalized Morrey space $L_{\{x_0\}}^{p(\cdot),w(\cdot)}(E)$ and the global generalized Morrey space $L_{E}^{p(\cdot),w(\cdot)}(E)$, respectively. Moreover, we point out that $w(x,r)$ is a measurable nonnegative function and no monotonicity-type condition is imposed on these spaces. Note that by the above definition of the norm in $L^{p(\cdot)}(E)$ (see 4.4), we can also write that

$$\|f\|_{L_{\Pi}^{p(\cdot),w(\cdot)}} = \sup_{x\in\Pi, r>0} \inf \left\{ \lambda = \lambda(x,r) : \int_{\tilde{B}(x,r)} \left| \frac{f(y)}{\lambda w(x,r)} \right|^{p(y)} dy \le 1 \right\}.$$

Then, recall that the concept of the variable exponent vanishing generalized Morrey space $VL_{\Pi}^{p(\cdot),w(\cdot)}(E)$ has been introduced in [15] in the following form.

Definition 4.4. *[15] Let $1 \le p(x) \le p_+ < \infty$, $\Pi \subset E \subset \mathbb{R}^n$, $x \in \Pi$, $w(x,r)\colon \Pi \times (0, diam(E)) \to \mathbb{R}_+$. Then, the variable exponent vanishing generalized Morrey space $VL_{\Pi}^{p(\cdot),w(\cdot)} \equiv VL_{\Pi}^{p(\cdot),w(\cdot)}(E)$ is defined by*

$$\left\{ f \in L_{\Pi}^{p(\cdot),w(\cdot)}(E) : \lim_{r\to 0} \sup_{x\in\Pi} \mathfrak{M}_{p(\cdot),w(\cdot)}(f;x,r) = 0 \right\},$$

where

$$\mathfrak{M}_{p(\cdot),w(\cdot)}(f;x,r) := \frac{r^{-\frac{n}{p(x)}} \|f\|_{L^{p(\cdot)}(\tilde{B}(x,r))}}{w(x,r)^{\frac{1}{p(x)}}}.$$

Naturally, it is suitable to impose on $w(x,t)$ with the following conditions:

$$\lim_{t\to 0} \sup_{x\in\Pi} \frac{t^{-\psi_p(x,t)}}{w(x,t)^{\frac{1}{p(x)}}} = 0 \tag{4.22}$$

and

$$\inf_{t>1} \sup_{x\in\Pi} w(x,t) > 0. \tag{4.23}$$

From (4.22) and (4.23), we easily know that the bounded functions with compact support belong to $VL_{\Pi}^{p(\cdot),w(\cdot)}(E)$, which make the spaces $VL_{\Pi}^{p(\cdot),w(\cdot)}(E)$ nontrivial.

The spaces $VL_{\Pi}^{p(\cdot),w(\cdot)}(E)$ are the Banach spaces with respect to the norm

$$\|f\|_{VL_{\Pi}^{p(\cdot),w(\cdot)}} \equiv \|f\|_{L_{\Pi}^{p(\cdot),w(\cdot)}} = \sup_{x\in\Pi, r>0} \mathfrak{M}_{p(\cdot),w(\cdot)}(f;x,r).$$

The spaces $VL_{\Pi}^{p(\cdot),w(\cdot)}(E)$ are also the closed subspaces of the Banach spaces $L_{\Pi}^{p(\cdot),w(\cdot)}(E)$, which may be shown by standard means.

Furthermore, we have the following embeddings:

$$VL_{\Pi}^{p(\cdot),w(\cdot)} \subset L_{\Pi}^{p(\cdot),w(\cdot)}, \qquad \|f\|_{L_{\Pi}^{p(\cdot),w(\cdot)}} \le \|f\|_{VL_{\Pi}^{p(\cdot),w(\cdot)}}.$$

In 2016, for bounded or unbounded sets E, Long and Han [15] considered the Spanne-type boundedness of operators $M_{\alpha(\cdot)}$ and $I_{\alpha(\cdot)}$ on $VL_{\Pi}^{p(\cdot),w(\cdot)}(E)$.

Now, in this section, we extend Theorem 4.3. in [15] to rough kernel versions. In other words, Theorem 4.3. in [15] allows us to use the known results for the boundedness of the operators $I_{\alpha(\cdot)}$ and $M_{\alpha(\cdot)}$ in generalized variable exponent Morrey spaces to transfer them to the operators $I_{\Omega,\alpha(\cdot)}$ and $M_{\Omega,\alpha(\cdot)}$. We give two versions of such an extension, the one being a generalization of Spanne's result for rough potential operators with variable order and the other extending the corresponding Adams' result, respectively.

In this context, we will give some answers to the above explanations in the following.

Theorem 4.5. ***(Spanne-type result with variable*** $\alpha(x)$***)*** *(our main result) Let E be a bounded open set, $\Omega \in L_s(S^{n-1})$, $1 < s \le \infty$, $\Omega(\mu x) = \Omega(x)$ for any $\mu > 0$, $x \in \mathbb{R}^n \setminus \{0\}$, $p(x) \in \mathcal{P}^{\log}(E)$, $\alpha(x)$ satisfying assumption (4.5). Define $q(x)$ by (4.7). Suppose that $q(\cdot)$ and $\alpha(\cdot)$ satisfy (4.1). For $\frac{s}{s-1} < p^- \le p(\cdot) < \frac{n}{\alpha(\cdot)}$, the following pointwise estimate*

$$\left\| I_{\Omega,\alpha(\cdot)} f \right\|_{L^{q(\cdot)}\left(\tilde{B}(x,r)\right)} \lesssim r^{\frac{n}{q(x)}} \int_r^{diam(E)} \|f\|_{L^{p(\cdot)}\left(\tilde{B}(x,t)\right)} \frac{dt}{t^{\frac{n}{q(x)}+1}} \tag{4.24}$$

holds for any ball $\tilde{B}(x,r)$ and for all $f \in L_{loc}^{p(\cdot)}(E)$.

If the functions $w_1(x,r)$ and $w_2(x,r)$ satisfy (4.20) as well as the following Zygmund condition

$$\int_r^{diam(E)} \frac{w_1^{\frac{1}{p(x)}}(x,t)}{t^{1-\alpha(x)}} dt \lesssim w_2^{\frac{1}{q(x)}}(x,r), \qquad r \in (0, diam(E)] \tag{4.25}$$

and additionally these functions satisfy the conditions (4.22)-(4.23),

$$c_\delta := \int_\delta^{diam(E)} \sup_{x\in\Pi} \frac{w_1^{\frac{1}{p(x)}}(x,t)}{t^{1-\alpha(x)}} dt < \infty, \qquad \delta > 0 \tag{4.26}$$

then the operators $I_{\Omega,\alpha(\cdot)}$ and $M_{\Omega,\alpha(\cdot)}$ are $\left(VL_{\Pi}^{p(\cdot),w_1(\cdot)}(E) \to VL_{\Pi}^{q(\cdot),w_2(\cdot)}(E)\right)$-bounded. Moreover,

$$\left\| I_{\Omega,\alpha(\cdot)} f \right\|_{VL_{\Pi}^{q(\cdot),w_2(\cdot)}(E)} \lesssim \|f\|_{VL_{\Pi}^{p(\cdot),w_1(\cdot)}(E)}, \tag{4.27}$$

$$\left\| M_{\Omega,\alpha(\cdot)} f \right\|_{VL_{\Pi}^{q(\cdot),w_2(\cdot)}(E)} \lesssim \|f\|_{VL_{\Pi}^{p(\cdot),w_1(\cdot)}(E)}.$$

Proof. Since inequality (4.24) is the key of the proof of (4.27), we first prove (4.24).

For any $x \in E$, we write as

$$f(y) = f_1(y) + f_2(y), \tag{4.28}$$

where $f_1(y) = f(y)\chi_{\tilde{B}(x,2r)}(y)$, $r > 0$ such that

$$I_{\Omega,\alpha(\cdot)}f(y) = I_{\Omega,\alpha(\cdot)}f_1(y) + I_{\Omega,\alpha(\cdot)}f_2(y).$$

By using triangle inequality, we get

$$\left\|I_{\Omega,\alpha(\cdot)}f\right\|_{L^{q(\cdot)}(\tilde{B}(x,r))} \leq \left\|I_{\Omega,\alpha(\cdot)}f_1\right\|_{L^{q(\cdot)}(\tilde{B}(x,r))} + \left\|I_{\Omega,\alpha(\cdot)}f_2\right\|_{L^{q(\cdot)}(\tilde{B}(x,r))}.$$

Now, let us estimate $\left\|I_{\Omega,\alpha(\cdot)}f_1\right\|_{L^{q(\cdot)}(\tilde{B}(x,r))}$ and $\left\|I_{\Omega,\alpha(\cdot)}f_2\right\|_{L^{q(\cdot)}(\tilde{B}(x,r))}$, respectively.

By Hardy-Littlewood-Sobolev-type inequality and Theorem 4.1, we obtain that

$$\begin{aligned}\left\|I_{\Omega,\alpha(\cdot)}f_1\right\|_{L^{q(\cdot)}(\tilde{B}(x,r))} &\leq \left\|I_{\Omega,\alpha(\cdot)}f_1\right\|_{L^{q(\cdot)}(E)} \lesssim \|f_1\|_{L^{p(\cdot)}(E)} = \|f\|_{L^{p(\cdot)}(\tilde{B}(x,2r))} \\ &\approx r^{\frac{n}{q(x)}} \|f\|_{L^{p(\cdot)}(\tilde{B}(x,2r))} \int_{2r}^{diam(E)} \frac{dt}{t^{\frac{n}{q(x)}+1}} \\ &\leq r^{\frac{n}{q(x)}} \int_{r}^{diam(E)} \|f\|_{L^{p(\cdot)}(\tilde{B}(x,t))} \frac{dt}{t^{\frac{n}{q(x)}+1}},\end{aligned}$$

where in the last inequality, we have used the following fact:

$$\|f\|_{L^{p(\cdot)}(\tilde{B}(x,2r))} \leq \|f\|_{L^{p(\cdot)}(\tilde{B}(x,t))}, \text{ for } t > 2r.$$

Now, let us estimate the second part $(= \left\|I_{\Omega,\alpha(\cdot)}f_2\right\|_{L^{q(\cdot)}(\tilde{B}(x,r))})$.

If $|x-z| \leq r$ and $|z-y| \geq r$, then $|x-y| \leq |x-z| + |y-z| \leq 2|y-z|$. By the generalized Minkowski's inequality, we get

$$\begin{aligned}\left\|I_{\Omega,\alpha(\cdot)}f_2\right\|_{L^{q(\cdot)}(\tilde{B}(x,r))} &= \left\| \int_{E\backslash\tilde{B}(x,2r)} \frac{\Omega(z-y)}{|z-y|^{n-\alpha(x)}} f(y)dy \right\|_{L^{q(\cdot)}(\tilde{B}(x,r))} \\ &\lesssim \int_{E\backslash\tilde{B}(x,2r)} \frac{|\Omega(z-y)|\,|f(y)|}{|x-y|^{n-\alpha(x)}} dy \left\|\chi_{\tilde{B}(x,r)}\right\|_{L^{q(\cdot)}(E)}.\end{aligned}$$

Put $\gamma > \frac{n}{q(\cdot)}$. Provided that $1 < s' < p^- \leq p^+ < \infty$, $\sup\limits_{x\in E}(\alpha(x)+\gamma-n) < \infty$, and $\inf\limits_{x\in E}\left(n+(\alpha(x)+\gamma-n)\left(\frac{p(\cdot)}{s'}\right)'\right) < \infty$, by generalized Hölder's inequality for $L^{p(\cdot)}(E)$,Fubini's theorem, and Lemma 4.2 and (4.3), we obtain

$$\int\limits_{E\setminus\tilde{B}(x,2r)} \frac{|\Omega(z-y)|\,|f(y)|}{|x-y|^{n-\alpha(x)}}dy$$

$$\lesssim \int\limits_{E\setminus\tilde{B}(x,2r)} \frac{|\Omega(z-y)|\,|f(y)|}{|x-y|^{n-\alpha(x)-\gamma}}dy \int\limits_{|x-y|}^{diam(E)} \frac{dt}{t^{\gamma+1}}$$

$$= \int\limits_{2r}^{diam(E)} \frac{dt}{t^{\gamma+1}} \int\limits_{\{y\in E:2r\leq|x-y|\leq t\}} \frac{|\Omega(z-y)|\,|f(y)|}{|x-y|^{n-\alpha(x)-\gamma}}dy$$

$$\lesssim \int\limits_{2r}^{diam(E)} \|f\|_{L^{p(\cdot)}(\tilde{B}(x,t))} \left\| |x-\cdot|^{\alpha(x)+\gamma-n} \right\|_{L^{v(\cdot)}(\tilde{B}(x,t))} \|\Omega(z-y)\|_{L_s(\tilde{B}(x,t))} \frac{dt}{t^{\gamma+1}}$$

$$\lesssim \int\limits_{r}^{diam(E)} \|f\|_{L^{p(\cdot)}(\tilde{B}(x,t))} \frac{dt}{t^{\frac{n}{q(x)}+1}} \tag{4.29}$$

for $\frac{1}{p(\cdot)}+\frac{1}{s}+\frac{1}{v(\cdot)}=1$. Thus, by (4.13), we get

$$\left\|I_{\Omega,\alpha(\cdot)}f_2\right\|_{L^{q(\cdot)}(\tilde{B}(x,r))} \lesssim r^{\frac{n}{q(x)}} \int\limits_{r}^{diam(E)} \|f\|_{L^{p(\cdot)}(\tilde{B}(x,t))} \frac{dt}{t^{\frac{n}{q(x)}+1}}.$$

Combining all the estimates for $\left\|I_{\Omega,\alpha(\cdot)}f_1\right\|_{L^{q(\cdot)}(\tilde{B}(x,r))}$ and $\left\|I_{\Omega,\alpha(\cdot)}f_2\right\|_{L^{q(\cdot)}(\tilde{B}(x,r))}$, we get (4.24).

At last, by Definition 4.4, (4.24), and (4.25), we get

$$\begin{aligned}
\left\|I_{\Omega,\alpha(\cdot)}f\right\|_{VL_{\Pi}^{q(\cdot),w_2(\cdot)}(E)} &= \sup_{x\in\Pi,r>0} \frac{r^{-\frac{n}{q(x)}}\left\|I_{\Omega,\alpha(\cdot)}f\right\|_{L^{q(\cdot)}(\tilde{B}(x,r))}}{w_2(x,r)^{\frac{1}{q(x)}}} \\
&\lesssim \sup_{x\in\Pi,r>0} \frac{1}{w_2(x,r)^{\frac{1}{q(x)}}} \int\limits_{r}^{diam(E)} \|f\|_{L^{p(\cdot)}(\tilde{B}(x,t))} \frac{dt}{t^{\frac{n}{q(x)}+1}} \\
&\lesssim \|f\|_{VL_{\Pi}^{p(\cdot),w_1(\cdot)}(E)} \sup_{x\in\Pi,r>0} \frac{1}{w_2(x,r)^{\frac{1}{q(x)}}} \int\limits_{r}^{diam(E)} \frac{w_1^{\frac{1}{p(x)}}(x,t)}{t^{1-\alpha(x)}}dt \\
&\lesssim \|f\|_{VL_{\Pi}^{p(\cdot),w_1(\cdot)}(E)}
\end{aligned}$$

and

$$\limsup_{r\to 0}\sup_{x\in\Pi} \frac{r^{-\frac{n}{q(x)}}\left\|I_{\Omega,\alpha(\cdot)}f\right\|_{L^{q(\cdot)}(\tilde{B}(x,r))}}{w_2(x,t)^{\frac{1}{q(x)}}} \lesssim \limsup_{r\to 0}\sup_{x\in\Pi} \frac{r^{-\frac{n}{p(x)}}\|f\|_{L^{p(\cdot)}(\tilde{B}(x,r))}}{w_1(x,t)^{\frac{1}{p(x)}}} = 0.$$

Thus, (4.27) holds. On the other hand, since $M_{\Omega,\alpha(\cdot)}(f) \lesssim I_{|\Omega|,\alpha(\cdot)}(|f|)$ (see Lemma 4.1), we can also use the same method for $M_{\Omega,\alpha(\cdot)}$, so we omit the details. As a result, we complete the proof of Theorem 4.5. □

Definition 4.5. *[13] **(Rough** (p,q)**-admissible** $T_{\Omega,\alpha(\cdot)}$**-potential type operator with variable order)** Let $1 \le p_-(E) \le p(\cdot) \le p_+(E) < \infty$. A rough sublinear operator with variable order $T_{\Omega,\alpha(\cdot)}$, i.e., $\left|T_{\Omega,\alpha(\cdot)}(f+g)\right| \le \left|T_{\Omega,\alpha(\cdot)}(f)\right| + \left|T_{\Omega,\alpha(\cdot)}(g)\right|$ and for $\forall\lambda \in \mathbb{C}$ $\left|T_{\Omega,\alpha(\cdot)}(\lambda f)\right| = |\lambda|\left|T_{\Omega,\alpha(\cdot)}(f)\right|$, will be called rough (p,q)-admissible $T_{\Omega,\alpha(\cdot)}$-potential type operator with variable order if*

· $T_{\Omega,\alpha(\cdot)}$ fulfills the following size condition:

$$\chi_{B(z,r)}(x)\left|T_{\Omega,\alpha(\cdot)}\left(f\chi_{E\setminus B(z,2r)}\right)(x)\right| \le C\chi_{B(z,r)}(x)\int\limits_{E\setminus B(z,2r)}\frac{|\Omega(x-y)|}{|x-y|^{n-\alpha(\cdot)}}|f(y)|\,dy, \tag{4.30}$$

· $T_{\Omega,\alpha(\cdot)}$ is $\left(L^{p(\cdot)}(E) \to L^{q(\cdot)}(E)\right)$-bounded.

Remark 4.3. *Note that rough (p,q)-admissible potential type operators were introduced to study their boundedness on Morrey spaces with variable exponents in [13]. The operators $M_{\Omega,\alpha(\cdot)}$ and $I_{\Omega,\alpha(\cdot)}$ are also rough (p,q)-admissible potential type operators. Moreover, these operators satisfy (4.30).*

Corollary 4.3. *Obviously, under the conditions of Theorem 4.5, if the rough (p,q)-admissible $T_{\Omega,\alpha(\cdot)}$-potential type operator is $\left(L^{p(\cdot)}(E) \to L^{q(\cdot)}(E)\right)$-bounded and satisfies (4.30), the result in Theorem 4.5 still holds.*

For $\alpha(x) = 0$ in Theorem 4.5, we get the following new result.

Corollary 4.4. *Let E, Ω, $p(x)$ be the same as in Theorem 4.5. Then, for $\frac{s}{s-1} < p^- \le p(\cdot) \le p^+ < \infty$, the following pointwise estimate*

$$\|T_\Omega f\|_{L^{p(\cdot)}(\tilde{B}(x,r))} \lesssim r^{\frac{n}{p(x)}}\int\limits_r^{diam(E)} t^{-\frac{n}{p(x)}-1}\|f\|_{L^{p(\cdot)}(\tilde{B}(x,t))}\,dt$$

holds for any ball $\tilde{B}(x,r)$ and for all $f \in L^{p(\cdot)}_{loc}(E)$.

If the function $w(x,r)$ satisfies (4.20) as well as the following Zygmund condition

$$\int\limits_r^{diam(E)}\frac{w^{\frac{1}{p(x)}}(x,t)}{t}dt \lesssim w^{\frac{1}{p(x)}}(x,r), \qquad r \in (0, diam(E)]$$

and additionally this function satisfies conditions (4.22) and (4.23),

$$c_\delta := \int\limits_\delta^{diam(E)}\sup_{x\in\Pi}\frac{w^{\frac{1}{p(x)}}(x,t)}{t}dt < \infty, \qquad \delta > 0$$

then the operators T_Ω *and* M_Ω *are bounded on* $VL_\Pi^{p(\cdot),w(\cdot)}(E)$. *Moreover,*

$$\|T_\Omega f\|_{VL_\Pi^{p(\cdot),w(\cdot)}(E)} \lesssim \|f\|_{VL_\Pi^{p(\cdot),w(\cdot)}(E)},$$
$$\|M_\Omega f\|_{VL_\Pi^{p(\cdot),w(\cdot)}(E)} \lesssim \|f\|_{VL_\Pi^{p(\cdot),w(\cdot)}(E)}. \tag{4.31}$$

Theorem 4.6. ***(Adams-type result with variable*** $\alpha(x)$***)*** *(our main result) Let* E, Ω, $p(x)$, $q(x)$, $\alpha(x)$ *be the same as in Theorem 4.5. Then, for* $\frac{s}{s-1} < p^- \le p(\cdot) < \frac{n}{\alpha(\cdot)}$, *the following pointwise estimate*

$$\left|I_{\Omega,\alpha(\cdot)}f(x)\right| \lesssim r^{\alpha(x)} M_\Omega f(x) + \int_r^{diam(E)} t^{\alpha(x)-\frac{n}{p(x)}-1} \|f\|_{L_p(\tilde{B}(x,t))}\,dt \tag{4.32}$$

holds for any ball $\tilde{B}(x,r)$ *and for all* $f \in L_{loc}^{p(\cdot)}(E)$.

The function $w(x,t)$ *satisfies (4.20), (4.22)-(4.23) as well as the following conditions:*

$$\int_r^{diam(E)} \frac{w^{\frac{1}{p(x)}}(x,t)}{t}\,dt \lesssim w^{\frac{1}{p(x)}}(x,r),$$
$$\int_r^{diam(E)} \frac{w^{\frac{1}{p(x)}}(x,t)}{t^{1-\alpha(x)}}\,dt \lesssim r^{-\frac{\alpha(x)p(x)}{q(x)-p(x)}}, \tag{4.33}$$

where $p(x) < q(x)$. *Then, the operators* $I_{\Omega,\alpha(\cdot)}$ *and* $M_{\Omega,\alpha(\cdot)}$ *are* $\left(VL_\Pi^{p(\cdot),w^{\frac{1}{p(\cdot)}}}(E) \to VL_\Pi^{q(\cdot),w^{\frac{1}{q(\cdot)}}}(E)\right)$*-bounded. Moreover,*

$$\left\|I_{\Omega,\alpha(\cdot)}f\right\|_{VL_\Pi^{q(\cdot),w^{\frac{1}{q(\cdot)}}}(E)} \lesssim \|f\|_{VL_\Pi^{p(\cdot),w^{\frac{1}{p(\cdot)}}}(E)},$$
$$\left\|M_{\Omega,\alpha(\cdot)}f\right\|_{VL_\Pi^{q(\cdot),w^{\frac{1}{q(\cdot)}}}(E)} \lesssim \|f\|_{VL_\Pi^{p(\cdot),w^{\frac{1}{p(\cdot)}}}(E)}.$$

Proof. As in the proof of Theorem 4.5, we represent the function f in the form (4.28) and have

$$I_{\Omega,\alpha(\cdot)}f(x) = I_{\Omega,\alpha(\cdot)}f_1(x) + I_{\Omega,\alpha(\cdot)}f_2(x).$$

For $I_{\Omega,\alpha(\cdot)}f_1(x)$, similar to the proof of (4.17), we obtain the following pointwise estimate:

$$\left|I_{\Omega,\alpha(\cdot)}f_1(x)\right| \lesssim t^{\alpha(x)} M_\Omega f(x). \tag{4.34}$$

For $I_{\Omega,\alpha(\cdot)}f_2(x)$, similar to the proof of (4.29), applying Fubini's theorem, Hölder's inequality, and (4.3), we get

$$\left|I_{\Omega,\alpha(\cdot)}f_2(x)\right| \lesssim \int_r^{diam(E)} t^{\alpha(x)-\frac{n}{p(x)}-1} \|f\|_{L_p(\tilde{B}(x,t))}\,dt \tag{4.35}$$

and by (4.34) and (4.35) complete the proof of (4.32).

Since $M_{\Omega,\alpha(\cdot)}(f) \lesssim I_{|\Omega|,\alpha(\cdot)}(|f|)$ (see Lemma 4.1), it suffices to treat only the case of the operator $I_{\Omega,\alpha(\cdot)}$. In this sense, by (4.32) and (4.33), we obtain

$$\left|I_{\Omega,\alpha(\cdot)}f(x)\right| \lesssim r^{\alpha(x)} M_{\Omega}f(x) + r^{-\frac{\alpha(x)p(x)}{q(x)-p(x)}} \|f\|_{VL_{\Pi}^{p(\cdot),w(\cdot)}(E)}.$$

Then, choosing $r = \left(\frac{\|f\|_{VL_{\Pi}^{p(\cdot),w(\cdot)}(E)}}{M_{\Omega}f(x)}\right)^{\frac{q(x)-p(x)}{\alpha(x)p(x)}}$ for every $x \in E$ supposing that f is not equal 0, thus we have

$$\left|I_{\Omega,\alpha(\cdot)}f(x)\right| \lesssim (M_{\Omega}f(x))^{\frac{p(x)}{q(x)}} \|f\|_{VL_{\Pi}^{p(\cdot),w(\cdot)}(E)}^{1-\frac{p(x)}{q(x)}}. \tag{4.36}$$

Finally, by Definition 4.4, (4.36), and (4.31), we get

$$\begin{aligned}
\left\|I_{\Omega,\alpha(\cdot)}f\right\|_{VL_{\Pi}^{q(\cdot),w^{\frac{1}{q(\cdot)}}}(E)} &= \sup_{x\in\Pi, r>0} \frac{r^{-\frac{n}{q(x)}} \left\|I_{\Omega,\alpha(\cdot)}f\right\|_{L^{p(\cdot)}(\tilde{B}(x,r))}}{w(x,r)^{\frac{1}{q(x)}}} \\
&\lesssim \|f\|_{VL_{\Pi}^{p(\cdot),w(\cdot)}(E)}^{1-\frac{p(x)}{q(x)}} \sup_{x\in\Pi, r>0} \frac{r^{-\frac{n}{q(x)}}}{w(x,r)^{\frac{1}{q(x)}}} \|M_{\Omega}f\|_{L^{p(\cdot)}(\tilde{B}(x,r))}^{\frac{p(x)}{q(x)}} \\
&\lesssim \|f\|_{VL_{\Pi}^{p(\cdot),w(\cdot)}(E)}^{1-\frac{p(x)}{q(x)}} \left(\sup_{x\in\Pi, r>0} \frac{r^{-\frac{n}{p(x)}}}{w(x,r)^{\frac{1}{p(x)}}} \|M_{\Omega}f\|_{L^{p(\cdot)}(\tilde{B}(x,r))}\right)^{\frac{p(x)}{q(x)}} \\
&\lesssim \|f\|_{VL_{\Pi}^{p(\cdot),w(\cdot)}(E)}^{1-\frac{p(x)}{q(x)}} \|M_{\Omega}f\|_{VL_{\Pi}^{p(\cdot),w^{\frac{1}{p(\cdot)}}}(E)}^{\frac{p(x)}{q(x)}} \\
&\lesssim \|f\|_{VL_{\Pi}^{p(\cdot),w^{\frac{1}{p(\cdot)}}}(E)}
\end{aligned}$$

if $p(x) < q(x)$ and

$$\limsup_{r\to 0} \sup_{x\in\Pi} \frac{r^{-\frac{n}{q(x)}} \left\|I_{\Omega,\alpha(\cdot)}f\right\|_{L^{q(\cdot)}(\tilde{B}(x,r))}}{w_2(x,t)^{\frac{1}{q(x)}}} \lesssim \limsup_{r\to 0} \sup_{x\in\Pi} \frac{r^{-\frac{n}{p(x)}} \|f\|_{L^{p(\cdot)}(\tilde{B}(x,r))}}{w_1(x,t)^{\frac{1}{p(x)}}} = 0,$$

which completes the proof of Theorem 4.6. □

Corollary 4.5. *Obviously, under the conditions of Theorem 4.6, if the rough (p,q)-admissible $T_{\Omega,\alpha(\cdot)}$-potential type operator is $\left(L^{p(\cdot)}(E) \to L^{q(\cdot)}(E)\right)$-bounded and satisfies (4.30), the result in Theorem 4.6 still holds.*

Remark 4.4. *Let E be a bounded open set and $\lambda(x)$ be a measurable function on E with values in $[0,n]$. Then, the variable exponent vanishing Morrey space*

$VL_{\Pi}^{p(\cdot),\lambda(\cdot)} \equiv VL_{\Pi}^{p(\cdot),\lambda(\cdot)}(E)$ *is defined by*

$$VL_{\Pi}^{p(\cdot),\lambda(\cdot)} \equiv VL_{\Pi}^{p(\cdot),\lambda(\cdot)}(E) = \left\{ \begin{array}{c} f \in L^{p(\cdot),\lambda(\cdot)}(E) : \\ \|f\|_{VL_{\Pi}^{p(\cdot),\lambda(\cdot)}} = \lim\limits_{r\to 0} \sup\limits_{\substack{x\in E \\ 0<t<r}} t^{-\frac{\lambda(x)}{p(x)}} \left\| f\chi_{\tilde{B}(x,t)} \right\|_{L^{p(\cdot)}(E)} = 0 \end{array} \right\}.$$

Corollary 4.6. *Let E, Ω, $p(x)$, $\alpha(x)$ be the same as in Theorem 4.5. Define $q(x)$ by $\frac{1}{q(x)} = \frac{1}{p(x)} - \frac{\alpha(x)}{n-\lambda(x)}$. Let also the following conditions hold:*

$$\lambda(x) \geq 0, \qquad \operatorname*{esssup}_{x\in E} [\lambda(x) + \alpha(x) p(x)] < n.$$

Then for $(p_-)' \leq s$, the operators $I_{\Omega,\alpha(\cdot)}$ and $M_{\Omega,\alpha(\cdot)}$ are $\left(VL_{\Pi}^{p(\cdot),\lambda(\cdot)}(E) \to VL_{\Pi}^{q(\cdot),\lambda(\cdot)}(E)\right)$-bounded. Moreover,

$$\left\| I_{\Omega,\alpha(\cdot)} f \right\|_{VL_{\Pi}^{q(\cdot),\lambda(\cdot)}(E)} \lesssim \|f\|_{VL_{\Pi}^{p(\cdot),\lambda(\cdot)}(E)},$$

$$\left\| M_{\Omega,\alpha(\cdot)} f \right\|_{VL_{\Pi}^{q(\cdot),\lambda(\cdot)}(E)} \lesssim \|f\|_{VL_{\Pi}^{p(\cdot),\lambda(\cdot)}(E)}.$$

In the case of $\lambda(x) \equiv 0$, for the spaces $L^{p(\cdot)}(E)$, from Corollary 4.6, we get the following.

Corollary 4.7. *Let E, Ω, $p(x)$, $q(x)$, $\alpha(x)$ be the same as in Theorem 4.5. Then, the operators $I_{\Omega,\alpha(\cdot)}$ and $M_{\Omega,\alpha(\cdot)}$ are $\left(L^{p(\cdot)}(E) \to L^{q(\cdot)}(E)\right)$-bounded. Moreover,*

$$\left\| I_{\Omega,\alpha(\cdot)} f \right\|_{L^{q(\cdot)}(E)} \lesssim \|f\|_{L^{p(\cdot)}(E)},$$

$$\left\| M_{\Omega,\alpha(\cdot)} f \right\|_{L^{q(\cdot)}(E)} \lesssim \|f\|_{L^{p(\cdot)}(E)}.$$

4.2.4 VARIABLE EXPONENT-GENERALIZED CAMPANATO SPACES $C_{\Pi}^{Q(\cdot),\gamma(\cdot)}$

In this section, we first introduce the variable exponent-generalized Campanato spaces and then obtain the boundedness of the commutators of the operators $I_{\Omega,\alpha(\cdot)}$, $M_{\Omega,\alpha(\cdot)}$, T_Ω, and M_Ω on the spaces $VL_{\Pi}^{p(\cdot),w(\cdot)}(E)$.

Definition 4.6. *Let $1 \leq q(\cdot) \leq q^+ < \infty$ and $0 \leq \gamma(\cdot) < \frac{1}{n}$. Define the generalized Campanato space $C_{\Pi}^{q(\cdot),\gamma(\cdot)}$ with variable exponents $q(\cdot)$, $\gamma(\cdot)$ as follows:*

$$C_{\Pi}^{q(\cdot),\gamma(\cdot)}(E) = \left\{ f \in L_{loc}^{q(\cdot)}\left(\tilde{B}(x,r)\right) : \|f\|_{C_{\Pi}^{q(\cdot),\gamma(\cdot)}(E)} < \infty \right\},$$

where

$$\|f\|_{C_{\Pi}^{q(\cdot),\gamma(\cdot)}(E)} = \sup_{x\in\Pi, r>0} |B(x,r)|^{-\frac{1}{q(x)}-\gamma(x)} \left\| f - f_{B(x,r)} \right\|_{L^{q(\cdot)}\left(\tilde{B}(x,r)\right)}$$

such that

$$\left\| f - f_{B(x,r)} \right\|_{L^{q(\cdot)}(\tilde{B}(x,r))} \lesssim r^{\frac{n}{q(x)}+n\gamma(x)} \left\| f \right\|_{C_{\Pi}^{q(\cdot),\gamma(\cdot)}(E)}. \tag{4.37}$$

When $\Pi = \{x_0\}$ *and* $\Pi = E$, $C_{\Pi}^{q(\cdot),\gamma(\cdot)}(E)$ *turns into the local generalized Campanato space* $C_{\{x_0\}}^{q(\cdot),\gamma(\cdot)}(E)$ *and the global generalized Campanato space* $C_{E}^{q(\cdot),\gamma(\cdot)}(E)$, *respectively. If* $q(\cdot)$, $\gamma(\cdot)$ *are the constant functions and* $\Pi = E$, *then the variable exponent-generalized Campanato space* $C_{\Pi}^{q(\cdot),\gamma(\cdot)}(E)$ *is exactly the usual Campanato space* $C^{q,\gamma}(E)$. *If* $\gamma(\cdot) \equiv 0$ *and* $q(\cdot) \equiv q$, *the generalized Campanato space* $C_{\Pi}^{q(\cdot),\gamma(\cdot)}(E)$ *is just the central* $BMO(E)$ *(the local version of* $BMO(E)$*).*

Theorem 4.7. *Let* E, Ω, $p(x)$, $q(x)$, $\alpha(x)$ *be the same as in Theorem 4.5. Let also* $\frac{1}{p(\cdot)} = \frac{1}{p_1(\cdot)} + \frac{1}{p_2(\cdot)}$, $\frac{1}{q_1(\cdot)} = \frac{1}{p_1(\cdot)} - \frac{\alpha(\cdot)}{n}$ *and* $b \in C_{\Pi}^{p_2(\cdot),\gamma(\cdot)}(E)$. *Suppose that* $p_1(\cdot)$, $p_2(\cdot)$, $q(\cdot)$, $q_1(\cdot)$, *and* $\alpha(\cdot)$ *satisfy (4.1). Then, for* $\frac{s}{s-1} < p^- \le p(\cdot) < \frac{n}{\alpha(\cdot)}$, *the following pointwise estimate*

$$\left\| \left[b, I_{\Omega,\alpha(\cdot)}\right] f \right\|_{L_q(\tilde{B}(x,r))} \lesssim \|b\|_{C_{\Pi}^{p_2(\cdot),\gamma(\cdot)}} r^{\frac{n}{q(x)}} \int_{2r}^{diam(E)} \left(1+\ln\frac{t}{r}\right) t^{n\gamma(x)-\frac{n}{q_1(x)}-1} \|f\|_{L^{p_1(\cdot)}(\tilde{B}(x,t))}\, dt \tag{4.38}$$

holds for any ball $\tilde{B}(x,r)$ *and for all* $f \in L_{loc}^{p_1(\cdot)}(E)$.

If the functions $w_1(x,r)$ *and* $w_2(x,r)$ *satisfy (4.20) as well as the following Zygmund condition*

$$\int_{r}^{diam(E)} \left(1+\ln\frac{t}{r}\right) \frac{w_1^{\frac{1}{p_1(x)}}(x,t)}{t^{1-(\alpha(x)+n\gamma(x))}} dt \lesssim w_2^{\frac{1}{q(x)}}(x,r), \qquad r \in (0, diam(E)] \tag{4.39}$$

and additionally these functions satisfy conditions (4.22) and (4.23),

$$d_\delta := \int_{\delta}^{diam(E)} \sup_{x\in\Pi} \left(1+\ln\frac{t}{r}\right) \frac{w_1^{\frac{1}{p_1(x)}}(x,t)}{t^{1-(\alpha(x)+n\gamma(x))}} dt < \infty, \qquad \delta > 0,$$

then the operators $\left[b, I_{\Omega,\alpha(\cdot)}\right]$ *and* $\left[b, M_{\Omega,\alpha(\cdot)}\right]$ *are* $\left(VL_{\Pi}^{p_1(\cdot),w_1(\cdot)}(E) \to VL_{\Pi}^{q(\cdot),w_2(\cdot)}(E)\right)$*-bounded. Moreover,*

$$\left\| \left[b, I_{\Omega,\alpha(\cdot)}\right] f \right\|_{VL_{\Pi}^{q(\cdot),w_2(\cdot)}(E)} \lesssim \|b\|_{C_{\Pi}^{p_2(\cdot),\gamma(\cdot)}} \|f\|_{VL_{\Pi}^{p_1(\cdot),w_1(\cdot)}(E)},$$

$$\left\| \left[b, M_{\Omega,\alpha(\cdot)}\right] f \right\|_{VL_{\Pi}^{q(\cdot),w_2(\cdot)}(E)} \lesssim \|b\|_{C_{\Pi}^{p_2(\cdot),\gamma(\cdot)}} \|f\|_{VL_{\Pi}^{p_1(\cdot),w_1(\cdot)}(E)}.$$

Proof. Since $\left[b, M_{\Omega,\alpha(\cdot)}\right](f) \lesssim \left[b, I_{|\Omega|,\alpha(\cdot)}\right](|f|)$, it suffices to treat only the case of the operator $\left[b, I_{\Omega,\alpha(\cdot)}\right]$. As in the proof of Theorem 4.5, we represent the function f in the form (4.28) and have

$$\left[b, I_{\Omega,\alpha(\cdot)}\right] f(x) = \left(b(x) - b_{B(x,r)}\right) I_{\Omega,\alpha(\cdot)} f_1(x) - I_{\Omega,\alpha(\cdot)}\left(\left(b(\cdot) - b_{B(x,r)}\right) f_1\right)(x)$$

$$
\begin{aligned}
&+\left(b(x)-b_{B(x,r)}\right)I_{\Omega,\alpha(\cdot)}f_2(x)-I_{\Omega,\alpha(\cdot)}\left(\left(b(\cdot)-b_{B(x,r)}\right)f_2\right)(x)\\
&\equiv F_1+F_2+F_3+F_4.
\end{aligned}
$$

Hence, we get

$$
\begin{aligned}
\left\|\left[b,I_{\Omega,\alpha(\cdot)}\right]f\right\|_{L^{q(\cdot)}(\tilde{B}(x,r))} \leq{}& \|F_1\|_{L^{q(\cdot)}\left(\tilde{B}(x,r)\right)}+\|F_2\|_{L^{q(\cdot)}\left(\tilde{B}(x,r)\right)}+\|F_3\|_{L^{q(\cdot)}\left(\tilde{B}(x,r)\right)}\\
&+\|F_4\|_{L^{q(\cdot)}\left(\tilde{B}(x,r)\right)}. \qquad (4.40)
\end{aligned}
$$

First, we use the Hölder's inequality such that $\frac{1}{q(\cdot)}=\frac{1}{p_2(\cdot)}+\frac{1}{q_1(\cdot)}$, the boundedness of $I_{\Omega,\alpha(\cdot)}$ from $L^{p(\cdot)}$ into $L^{q(\cdot)}$ (see Theorem 4.1) and (4.37) to estimate $\|F_1\|_{L^{q(\cdot)}\left(\tilde{B}(x,r)\right)}$, and we obtain

$$
\begin{aligned}
\|F_1\|_{L^{q(\cdot)}\left(\tilde{B}(x,r)\right)} &= \left\|\left(b(\cdot)-b_B\right)I_{\Omega,\alpha(\cdot)}f_1(\cdot)\right\|_{L^{q(\cdot)}\left(\tilde{B}(x,r)\right)}\\
&\lesssim \left\|\left(b(\cdot)-b_B\right)\right\|_{L^{p_2(\cdot)}\left(\tilde{B}(x,r)\right)}\left\|I_{\Omega,\alpha(\cdot)}f_1(\cdot)\right\|_{L^{q_1(\cdot)}\left(\tilde{B}(x,r)\right)}\\
&\lesssim r^{\frac{n}{p_2(x)}+n\gamma(x)}\|b\|_{C_\Pi^{p_2(\cdot),\gamma(\cdot)}}\|f_1\|_{L^{p_1(\cdot)}\left(\tilde{B}(x,r)\right)}\\
&= \|b\|_{C_\Pi^{p_2(\cdot),\gamma(\cdot)}} r^{\frac{n}{p_2(x)}+\frac{n}{q_1(x)}+n\gamma(x)}\|f\|_{L^{p_1(\cdot)}\left(\tilde{B}(x,2r)\right)}\int_{2r}^{diam(E)} t^{-1-\frac{n}{q_1(x)}}dt\\
&\lesssim \|b\|_{C_\Pi^{p_2(\cdot),\gamma(\cdot)}} r^{\frac{n}{q(x)}}\int_{2r}^{diam(E)}\left(1+\ln\frac{t}{r}\right)\|f\|_{L^{p_1(\cdot)}\left(\tilde{B}(x,t)\right)}t^{n\gamma(x)-\frac{n}{q_1(x)}-1}dt.
\end{aligned}
$$

Second, for $\|F_2\|_{L^{q(\cdot)}\left(\tilde{B}(x,r)\right)}$, applying the boundedness of $I_{\Omega,\alpha(\cdot)}$ from $L^{p(\cdot)}$ into $L^{q(\cdot)}$ (see Theorem 4.1), generalized Hölder's inequality such that $\frac{1}{p(\cdot)}=\frac{1}{p_1(\cdot)}+\frac{1}{p_2(\cdot)}$, $\frac{1}{q(\cdot)}=\frac{1}{p_2(\cdot)}+\frac{1}{q_1(\cdot)}$ and (4.37), we know that

$$
\begin{aligned}
\|F_2\|_{L^{q(\cdot)}\left(\tilde{B}(x,r)\right)} &= \left\|I_{\Omega,\alpha(\cdot)}\left(b(\cdot)-b_{B(x,r)}\right)f_1\right\|_{L^{q(\cdot)}\left(\tilde{B}(x,r)\right)}\\
&\lesssim \left\|\left(b(\cdot)-b_B\right)f_1\right\|_{L^{p(\cdot)}\left(\tilde{B}(x,r)\right)}\\
&\lesssim \left\|\left(b(\cdot)-b_B\right)\right\|_{L^{p_2(\cdot)}\left(\tilde{B}(x,r)\right)}\|f_1\|_{L^{p_1(\cdot)}\left(\tilde{B}(x,r)\right)}\\
&\lesssim \|f\|_{C_\Pi^{p_2(\cdot),\gamma(\cdot)}} r^{\frac{n}{p_2(x)}+\frac{n}{q_1(x)}+n\gamma(x)}\|f\|_{L^{p_1(\cdot)}\left(\tilde{B}(x,2r)\right)}\int_{2r}^{diam(E)} t^{-1-\frac{n}{q_1(x)}}dt\\
&\lesssim \|b\|_{C_\Pi^{p_2(\cdot),\gamma(\cdot)}} r^{\frac{n}{q(x)}}\int_{2r}^{diam(E)}\left(1+\ln\frac{t}{r}\right)\|f\|_{L^{p_1(\cdot)}\left(\tilde{B}(x,t)\right)}t^{n\gamma(x)-\frac{n}{q_1(x)}-1}dt.
\end{aligned}
$$

Third, for $\|F_3\|_{L^{q(\cdot)}(\tilde{B}(x,r))}$, similar to the proof of (4.29), when $\frac{s}{s-1} \le p_1(\cdot)$, by Fubini's theorem, generalized Hölder's inequality, and (4.3), we have

$$\begin{aligned} \left|I_{\Omega,\alpha(\cdot)} f_2(x)\right| &\lesssim \int\limits_{E \setminus \tilde{B}(x,2r)} \frac{|\Omega(z-y)|\,|f(y)|}{|x-y|^{n-\alpha(x)}} dy \\ &\lesssim \int\limits_{2r}^{diam(E)} \|f\|_{L^{p_1(\cdot)}(\tilde{B}(x,t))} t^{-1-\frac{n}{q_1(x)}} dt. \end{aligned} \tag{4.41}$$

Thus, by generalized Hölder's inequality such that $\frac{1}{q(\cdot)} = \frac{1}{p_2(\cdot)} + \frac{1}{q_1(\cdot)}$, (4.37), and (4.41), we obtain

$$\begin{aligned} \|F_3\|_{L^{q(\cdot)}(\tilde{B}(x,r))} &= \left\| \left(b(\cdot) - b_{B(x,r)}\right) I_{\Omega,\alpha(\cdot)} f_2(\cdot) \right\|_{L^{q(\cdot)}(\tilde{B}(x,r))} \\ &\lesssim \left\| \left(b(\cdot) - b_{B(x,r)}\right) \right\|_{L^{p_2(\cdot)}(\tilde{B}(x,r))} \left\| I_{\Omega,\alpha(\cdot)} f_2(\cdot) \right\|_{L^{q_1(\cdot)}(\tilde{B}(x,r))} \\ &\lesssim r^{\frac{n}{p_2(x)} + n\gamma(x)} \|b\|_{C_{\Pi}^{p_2(\cdot),\gamma(\cdot)}} r^{\frac{n}{q_1(x)}} \int\limits_{2r}^{diam(E)} \|f\|_{L^{p_1(\cdot)}(\tilde{B}(x,t))} t^{-1-\frac{n}{q_1(x)}} dt \\ &\lesssim \|b\|_{C_{\Pi}^{p_2(\cdot),\gamma(\cdot)}} r^{\frac{n}{q(x)}} \int\limits_{2r}^{diam(E)} \left(1 + \ln \frac{t}{r}\right) \|f\|_{L^{p_1(\cdot)}(\tilde{B}(x,t))} t^{n\gamma(x) - \frac{n}{q_1(x)} - 1} dt. \end{aligned}$$

Finally, we consider the term $\|F_4\|_{L^{q(\cdot)}(\tilde{B}(x,r))} = \left\| I_{\Omega,\alpha(\cdot)} \left(\left(b(\cdot) - b_{B(x,r)}\right) f_2 \right)(\cdot) \right\|_{L^{q(\cdot)}(\tilde{B}(x,r))}$. For $z \in B(x,r)$, when $\frac{s}{s-1} \le p(\cdot)$, by the Fubini's theorem, applying the generalized Hölder's inequality, and from (4.3) and (4.37), we have

$$\begin{aligned} &\left| I_{\Omega,\alpha(\cdot)} \left(\left(b(\cdot) - b_{B(x,r)}\right) f_2 \right)(z) \right| \\ &\lesssim \int\limits_{2r}^{diam(E)} \left| b(y) - b_{B(x,r)} \right| \left| \Omega(z-y) \right| \frac{|f(y)|}{|x-y|^{n-\alpha(x)}} dy \\ &\approx \int\limits_{2r}^{diam(E)} \int\limits_{2r<|x-y|<t} \left| b(y) - b_{B(x,r)} \right| \left| \Omega(z-y) \right| |f(y)| \, dy \frac{dt}{t^{n-\alpha(x)+1}} \\ &\lesssim \int\limits_{2r}^{diam(E)} \int\limits_{B(x,t)} \left| b(y) - b_{B(x,t)} \right| \left| \Omega(z-y) \right| |f(y)| \, dy \frac{dt}{t^{n-\alpha(x)+1}} \\ &+ \int\limits_{2r}^{diam(E)} \int\limits_{B(x,t)} \left| b_{B(x,r)} - b_{B(x,t)} \right| \left| \Omega(z-y) \right| |f(y)| \, dy \frac{dt}{t^{n-\alpha(x)+1}} \\ &\lesssim \int\limits_{2r}^{diam(E)} \left\| \left(b(\cdot) - b_{B(x,r)}\right) \right\|_{L^{p_2(\cdot)}(\tilde{B}(x,t))} \|f\|_{L^{p_1(\cdot)}(\tilde{B}(x,t))} \|\Omega(z-\cdot)\|_{L_s(\tilde{B}(x,t))} \\ &t^{-\frac{n}{q(x)} - \frac{n}{s} - 1} dt \\ &+ \int\limits_{2r}^{diam(E)} \left\| \left(b_{B(x,r)} - b_{B(x,t)}\right) \right\|_{L^{p_2(\cdot)}(\tilde{B}(x,t))} \|f\|_{L^{p_1(\cdot)}(\tilde{B}(x,t))} \|\Omega(z-\cdot)\|_{L_s(\tilde{B}(x,t))} \\ &t^{-\frac{n}{q(x)} - \frac{n}{s} - 1} dt \end{aligned}$$

$$\lesssim \int_{2r}^{diam(E)} \left\|\left(b(\cdot)-b_{B(x,r)}\right)\right\|_{L^{p_2(\cdot)}(\tilde{B}(x,t))} \|f\|_{L^{p_1(\cdot)}(\tilde{B}(x,t))} t^{-\frac{n}{q(x)}-1} dt$$
$$+\|b\|_{C_{\Pi}^{p_2(\cdot),\gamma(\cdot)}} \int_{2r}^{diam(E)} \left(1+\ln \tfrac{t}{r}\right) \|f\|_{L^{p_1(\cdot)}(\tilde{B}(x,t))} t^{n\gamma(x)-\frac{n}{q_1(x)}-1} dt$$

$$\lesssim \|b\|_{C_{\Pi}^{p_2(\cdot),\gamma(\cdot)}} \int_{2r}^{diam(E)} \left(1+\ln \frac{t}{r}\right) \|f\|_{L^{p_1(\cdot)}(\tilde{B}(x,t))} t^{n\gamma(x)-\frac{n}{q_1(x)}-1} dt. \tag{4.42}$$

Then, by (4.42), we have

$$\|F_4\|_{L^{q(\cdot)}(\tilde{B}(x,r))} = \left\|I_{\Omega,\alpha(\cdot)}\left(\left(b(\cdot)-b_{B(x,r)}\right) f_2\right)(x)\right\|_{L^{q(\cdot)}(\tilde{B}(x,r))}$$
$$\lesssim \|b\|_{C_{\Pi}^{p_2(\cdot),\gamma(\cdot)}} r^{\frac{n}{q(x)}} \int_{2r}^{diam(E)} \left(1+\ln \frac{t}{r}\right) \|f\|_{L^{p_1(\cdot)}(\tilde{B}(x,t))} t^{n\gamma(x)-\frac{n}{q_1(x)}-1} dt.$$

Combining all the estimates of $\|F_1\|_{L^{q(\cdot)}(\tilde{B}(x,r))}$, $\|F_2\|_{L^{q(\cdot)}(\tilde{B}(x,r))}$, $\|F_3\|_{L^{q(\cdot)}(\tilde{B}(x,r))}$, $\|F_4\|_{L^{q(\cdot)}(\tilde{B}(x,r))}$, we get (4.38).

At last, by Definition 4.4, (4.38), and (4.39), we get

$$\left\|\left[b,I_{\Omega,\alpha(\cdot)}\right] f\right\|_{VL_{\Pi}^{q(\cdot),w_2(\cdot)}(E)} = \sup_{x\in\Pi,r>0} \frac{r^{-\frac{n}{q(x)}} \left\|\left[b,I_{\Omega,\alpha(\cdot)}\right] f\right\|_{L^{q(\cdot)}(\tilde{B}(x,r))}}{w_2(x,r)^{\frac{1}{q(x)}}}$$
$$\lesssim \|b\|_{C_{\Pi}^{p_2(\cdot),\gamma(\cdot)}} \sup_{x\in\Pi,r>0} \frac{1}{w_2(x,r)^{\frac{1}{q(x)}}} \int_{2r}^{diam(E)} \left(1+\ln \frac{t}{r}\right) t^{n\gamma(x)-\frac{n}{q_1(x)}-1}$$
$$\times \|f\|_{L^{p_1(\cdot)}(\tilde{B}(x,t))} dt$$
$$\lesssim \|b\|_{C_{\Pi}^{p_2(\cdot),\gamma(\cdot)}} \|f\|_{VL_{\Pi}^{p_1(\cdot),w_1(\cdot)}(E)} \sup_{x\in\Pi,r>0} \frac{1}{w_2(x,r)^{\frac{1}{q(x)}}} \int_{r}^{diam(E)} \left(1+\ln \frac{t}{r}\right)$$
$$\times t^{\alpha(x)+n\gamma(x)} w_1^{\frac{1}{p_1(x)}}(x,t) \frac{dt}{t}$$
$$\lesssim \|b\|_{C_{\Pi}^{p_2(\cdot),\gamma(\cdot)}} \|f\|_{VL_{\Pi}^{p(\cdot),w_1(\cdot)}(E)}$$

and

$$\limsup_{r\to 0} \sup_{x\in\Pi} \frac{r^{-\frac{n}{q(x)}} \left\|\left[b,I_{\Omega,\alpha(\cdot)}\right] f\right\|_{L^{q(\cdot)}(\tilde{B}(x,r))}}{w_2(x,t)^{\frac{1}{q(x)}}} \lesssim \limsup_{r\to 0} \sup_{x\in\Pi} \frac{r^{-\frac{n}{p(x)}} \|f\|_{L^{p(\cdot)}(\tilde{B}(x,r))}}{w_1(x,t)^{\frac{1}{p(x)}}} = 0,$$

which completes the proof of Theorem 4.7. □

Corollary 4.8. *Let E, Ω, $p(x)$, $q(x)$, $\alpha(x)$ be the same as in Theorem 4.5. Suppose that $q(\cdot)$ and $\alpha(\cdot)$ satisfy (4.1). Then, for $\frac{s}{s-1} < p^- \le p(\cdot) < \frac{n}{\alpha(\cdot)}$ and $b \in BMO(E)$, the following pointwise estimate*

$$\| [b, I_{\Omega,\alpha(\cdot)}] f\|_{L^{q(\cdot)}(\tilde{B}(x,r))} \lesssim \|b\|_{BMO} r^{\frac{n}{q(x)}} \int_{2r}^{diam(E)} \left(1+\ln\frac{t}{r}\right) t^{-\frac{n}{q(x)}-1} \|f\|_{L^{p(\cdot)}(\tilde{B}(x,t))} dt$$

holds for any ball $\tilde{B}(x,r)$ and for all $f \in L^{p(\cdot)}_{loc}(E)$.

If the functions $w_1(x,r)$ and $w_2(x,r)$ satisfy (4.20) as well as the following Zygmund condition

$$\int_r^{diam(E)} \left(1+\ln\frac{t}{r}\right) \frac{w_1^{\frac{1}{p(x)}}(x,t)}{t^{1-\alpha(x)}} dt \lesssim w_2^{\frac{1}{q(x)}}(x,r), \qquad r \in (0, diam(E)]$$

and additionally these functions satisfy conditions (4.22) and (4.23),

$$d_\delta := \int_\delta^{diam(E)} \sup_{x\in\Pi} \left(1+\ln\frac{t}{r}\right) \frac{w_1^{\frac{1}{p(x)}}(x,t)}{t^{1-\alpha(x)}} dt < \infty, \qquad \delta > 0,$$

then the operators $[b, I_{\Omega,\alpha(\cdot)}]$ and $[b, M_{\Omega,\alpha(\cdot)}]$ are $\left(VL_\Pi^{p(\cdot),w_1(\cdot)}(E) \to VL_\Pi^{q(\cdot),w_2(\cdot)}(E)\right)$-bounded. Moreover,

$$\left\| [b, I_{\Omega,\alpha(\cdot)}] f\right\|_{VL_\Pi^{q(\cdot),w_2(\cdot)}(E)} \lesssim \|b\|_{BMO} \|f\|_{VL_\Pi^{p_1(\cdot),w_1(\cdot)}(E)},$$

$$\left\| [b, M_{\Omega,\alpha(\cdot)}] f\right\|_{VL_\Pi^{q(\cdot),w_2(\cdot)}(E)} \lesssim \|b\|_{BMO} \|f\|_{VL_\Pi^{p_1(\cdot),w_1(\cdot)}(E)}.$$

For $\alpha(x) = 0$ in Theorem 4.7, we get the following new result.

Corollary 4.9. *Let E, Ω, $p(x)$ be the same as in Theorem 4.5. Let also $\frac{1}{p(\cdot)} = \frac{1}{p_1(\cdot)} + \frac{1}{p_2(\cdot)}$ and $b \in C_\Pi^{p_2(\cdot),\gamma(\cdot)}(E)$. Suppose that $p_1(\cdot)$ and $p_2(\cdot)$ satisfy (4.1). Then, for $\frac{s}{s-1} < p^- \le p(\cdot) \le p^+ < \infty$, the following pointwise estimate*

$$\| [b, T_\Omega] f\|_{L^{p(\cdot)}(\tilde{B}(x,r))} \lesssim \|b\|_{C_\Pi^{p_2(\cdot),\gamma(\cdot)}} r^{\frac{n}{p(x)}} \int_{2r}^{diam(E)} \left(1+\ln\frac{t}{r}\right) t^{n\gamma(x)-\frac{n}{p_1(x)}-1} \|f\|_{L^{p_1(\cdot)}(\tilde{B}(x,t))} dt$$

holds for any ball $\tilde{B}(x,r)$ and for all $f \in L^{p_1(\cdot)}_{loc}(E)$.

If the function $w(x,r)$ satisfies (4.20) as well as the following Zygmund condition

$$\int_r^{diam(E)} \left(1+\ln\frac{t}{r}\right) \frac{w^{\frac{1}{p_1(x)}}(x,t)}{t^{1-n\gamma(x)}} dt \lesssim w^{\frac{1}{p(x)}}(x,r), \qquad r \in (0, diam(E)]$$

and additionally this function satisfies conditions (4.22) and (4.23),

$$d_\delta := \int_\delta^{diam(E)} \sup_{x\in\Pi} \left(1+\ln\frac{t}{r}\right) \frac{w^{\frac{1}{p_1(x)}}(x,t)}{t^{1-n\gamma(x)}} dt < \infty, \qquad \delta > 0,$$

then the operators $[b,T_\Omega]$ *and* $[b,M_\Omega]$ *are* $\left(VL_\Pi^{p_1(\cdot),w(\cdot)}(E) \to VL_\Pi^{p(\cdot),w(\cdot)}(E)\right)$*-bounded. Moreover,*

$$\|[b,T_\Omega]f\|_{VL_\Pi^{p(\cdot),w(\cdot)}(E)} \lesssim \|b\|_{C_\Pi^{p_2(\cdot),\gamma(\cdot)}} \|f\|_{VL_\Pi^{p_1(\cdot),w(\cdot)}(E)},$$

$$\|[b,M_\Omega]f\|_{VL_\Pi^{p(\cdot),w(\cdot)}(E)} \lesssim \|b\|_{C_\Pi^{p_2(\cdot),\gamma(\cdot)}} \|f\|_{VL_\Pi^{p_1(\cdot),w(\cdot)}(E)}.$$

From Corollary 4.9, we get the following.

Corollary 4.10. *Let* E, Ω, $p(x)$ *be the same as in Theorem 4.5. Then, for* $\frac{s}{s-1} < p^- \le p(\cdot) \le p^+ < \infty$ *and* $b \in BMO(E)$, *the following pointwise estimate*

$$\|[b,T_\Omega]f\|_{L^{p(\cdot)}(\tilde{B}(x,r))} \lesssim \|b\|_{BMO} r^{\frac{n}{p(x)}} \int_{2r}^{diam(E)} \left(1+\ln\frac{t}{r}\right) t^{\frac{n}{p(x)}-1} \|f\|_{L^{p(\cdot)}(\tilde{B}(x,t))} dt$$

holds for any ball $\tilde{B}(x,r)$ *and for all* $f \in L_{loc}^{p(\cdot)}(E)$.

If the function $w(x,r)$ *satisfies (4.20) as well as the following Zygmund condition*

$$\int_r^{diam(E)} \left(1+\ln\frac{t}{r}\right) \frac{w^{\frac{1}{p(x)}}(x,t)}{t} dt \lesssim w^{\frac{1}{p(x)}}(x,r), \qquad r \in (0, diam(E)]$$

and additionally this function satisfies conditions (4.22) and (4.23),

$$d_\delta := \int_\delta^{diam(E)} \sup_{x\in\Pi} \left(1+\ln\frac{t}{r}\right) \frac{w^{\frac{1}{p(x)}}(x,t)}{t} dt < \infty, \qquad \delta > 0,$$

then the operators $[b,T_\Omega]$ *and* $[b,M_\Omega]$ *are bounded on* $VL_\Pi^{p(\cdot),w(\cdot)}(E)$. *Moreover,*

$$\|[b,T_\Omega]f\|_{VL_\Pi^{p(\cdot),w(\cdot)}(E)} \lesssim \|b\|_{BMO} \|f\|_{VL_\Pi^{p(\cdot),w(\cdot)}(E)},$$

$$\|[b,M_\Omega]f\|_{VL_\Pi^{p(\cdot),w(\cdot)}(E)} \lesssim \|b\|_{BMO} \|f\|_{VL_\Pi^{p(\cdot),w(\cdot)}(E)}.$$

4.3 CONCLUSION

It is well known that, for the purpose of researching non-smoothness partial differential equation, mathematicians pay more attention to the singular integrals with rough kernel. Moreover, the fractional-type operators and their weighted boundedness theory play important roles in harmonic analysis and other fields, and the multilinear operators arise in numerous situations involving product-like operations. Moreover, the multilinear operators are natural generalizations of linear case. In recent years, these topics gain the attention from a vast number of researchers in different function spaces. Especially, more and more researches focus on function spaces based on variable exponent Morrey spaces to fill in some gaps in the theory of Morrey-type spaces. Moreover, these spaces are useful in harmonic analysis and PDEs. But this topic exceeds the scope of this paper. Thus, we omit the details here. In this paper, we have shown that various classical operators (such as rough maximal, potential, and singular integral operators) and their commutators are bounded in different proper closed subspaces of variable exponent-generalized Morrey spaces. On the other hand, all these subspaces together provide an explicit description of the closure of nice functions in variable exponent Morrey norm in terms of vanishing properties of Morrey functions. Therefore, our results give a contribution for the development of harmonic analysis on variable exponent-generalized Morrey spaces.

As is well known, variable exponent Morrey-type spaces attract a lot of attention from the applications side. By this reason, we are convinced that the results exhibited in this paper can also be useful for regularity results in the theory of certain partial differential equations.

Finally, the results presented here are sure to be new and potentially useful. Since the research subject here and its related ones are so popular, the content of this paper may attract interested readers who have been interested in this and related research subjects. Therefore, the results in this paper are worthwhile to record.

FUNDING

This work is funded by Hakkari University Scientific Research Project (Grant No. FM18BAP1) under the research project "Some estimates for rough Riesz-type potential operator with variable order and rough fractional maximal operator with variable order both on generalized variable exponent Morrey spaces and on vanishing generalized variable exponent Morrey spaces," Institution of Higher Education Scientific Research Project in Ningxia (Grant No. NGY2017011) and Natural Science Foundation of China (Grant Nos. 11461053 and 11762016).

REFERENCES

[1] A. Almeida, J.J. Hasanov and S.G. Samko, Maximal and potential operators in variable exponent Morrey spaces, *Georgian Math. J.*, 2008, 15(2): 195–208.

[2] S.N. Antontsev and J.F. Rodrigues, On stationary thermorheological viscous flows, *Ann. Univ. Ferrara, Sez. VII, Sci. Mat.*, 2006, 52(1): 19–36.

[3] Y. Chen, S.E. Levine and M. Rao, Variable exponent, linear growth functionals in image restoration, *SIAM J. Appl. Math.*, 2006, 66(4): 1383–1406.

[4] D. Cruz-Uribe, A. Fiorenza, C.J. Neugebauer, The maximal function on variable L_p spaces, *Ann. Acad. Sci Fenn. Math.*, 2003, 28(1): 223–238.

[5] L. Diening, P. Harjulehto, P. Hästö and M. Růžička, *Lebesgue and Sobolev Space with Variable Exponents,* Springer Lecture Notes, Vol. 2017, Berlin: Springer-Verlag, 2011.

[6] L. Diening, P. Hästö and A. Nekvinda, Open problems in variable exponent Lebesgue and Sobolev spaces, in Proceedings of the Function Spaces, Differential Operators and Nonlinear Analysis (FSDONA'04), pp. 38–58, Milovy, Czech, 2004.

[7] L. Diening and M. Rüžička, Calderón-Zygmund operators on generalized Lebesgue Spaces $L^{p(x)}(\Omega)$ and problems related to fluid dynamics, *J. Reine Angew. Math.*, 2003, 563: 197–220.

[8] X.L. Fan and D. Zhao, On the spaces $L^{p(x)}(\Omega)$ and $W^{m,p(x)}(\Omega)$, *J. Math. Anal. Appl.*, 2001, 263(2): 424–446.

[9] M. Giaquinta, *Multiple integrals in the calculus of variations and non-linear elliptic systems.* Princeton, New Jersey: Princeton Univ. Press, 1983.

[10] V.S. Guliyev, J.J. Hasanov and S.G. Samko, Boundedness of the maximal, potential and singular integral operators in generalized variable exponent Morrey spaces, *Math. Scand.*, 2010, 107(2): 285–304.

[11] P. Harjulehto, P. Hästö, Út V. Lê and M. Nuortio, Overview of differential equations with nonstandard growth, *Nonlinear. Anal.*, 2010, 72(12): 4551–4574.

[12] K. Ho, The fractional integral operators on Morrey spaces with variable exponent on unbounded domains, *Math. Inequal. Appl.*, 2013, 16(2): 363–373.

[13] K. Ho, Fractional integral operators with homogeneous kernels on Morrey spaces with variable exponents, *J. Math. Soc. Japan*, 2017, 69(3): 1059–1077.

[14] O. Kováčik and J. Rákosník, On spaces $L^{p(x)}$ and $W^{k,p(x)}$, *Czechoslovak Math. J.*, 1991, 41(11): 592–618.

[15] P. Long and H. Han, Characterizations of some operators on the vanishing generalized Morrey spaces with variable exponent, *J. Math. Anal. Appl.*, 2016, 437(1): 419–430.

[16] C.B. Morrey, On the solutions of quasi-linear elliptic partial differential equations, *Trans. Amer. Math. Soc.,* 1938, 43: 126–166.

[17] W. Orlicz, Über konjugierte Exponentenfolgen, *Studia Math.*, 1931, 3: 200–211.

[18] H. Rafeiro and S.G. Samko, On maximal and potential operators with rough kernels in variable exponent spaces, *Rend. Lincei Mat. Appl.*, 2016,27(3): 309–325.

[19] M. Ružička, *Electrorheological fluids: modeling and mathematical theory,* Berlin: Springer, 2013.

[20] Y. Sawano, K. Ho, D.C. Yang and S. Yang, Hardy spaces for ball quasi-Banach function spaces, *Dissertationes Math.*, 2017, 525: 102 pp.

[21] M.E. Taylor, *Tools for PDE: Pseudodifferential Operators, Paradifferential Operators, and Layer Potentials,* Volume 81 of Math. Surveys and Monogr. AMS, Providence, R.I., 2000.

[22] J. Wu, Boundedness for Riesz-type potential operators on Herz-Morrey spaces with variable exponent, *Math. Inequal. Appl.*, 2015, 18(2): 471–484.

[23] T. Wunderli, On time flows of minimizers of general convex functionals of linear growth with variable exponent in BV space and stability of pseudosolutions, *J. Math. Anal. Appl.*, 2010, 364(2): 591–598.

[24] L.J. Wang and Sh. P. Tao, Boundedness of Littlewood-Paley operators and their commutators on Herz-Morrey spaces with variable exponent, *J. Inequal. Appl.*, 2014, 2014: 227.

5 Compact-Like Operators in Vector Lattices Normed by Locally Solid Lattices

Abdullah Aydın
Muş Alparslan University

CONTENTS

5.1 INTRODUCTION

Lattice-valued norms on vector lattices play an important and effective role in the functional analysis. It is well known that order convergence in vector lattice is not topological unless dimension is finite. However, thanks to the order convergence, some properties like order continuous in vector lattice can be defined. We refer the reader for an exposition on basic notions and properties of vector lattice (or, Riesz space) to [1–3,13,16,25–27,31,32] and on the theory of lattice-normed vector lattices to [9–11,16,23,24] and to locally solid vector lattices [2–6,20,32]. In this chapter, we introduce and study continuous and bounded operators with respect to the p_τ-convergence, which was introduced and investigated by Aydın in [5], and we also introduce the compact operators in vector lattice normed by locally solid lattices.

The concept of the unbounded convergence is crucial for the concept of p_τ-convergence. The *uo-convergence* was introduced in [28] under the name *individual convergence* and the name "unbounded order convergence" was first proposed by DeMarr in [14]. The relation between weak and *uo*-convergence in Banach lattices was studied by Wickstead in [30], and Kaplan established two characterizations of *uo*-convergence on Dedekind complete Riesz spaces with the weak unit in [22], and the *un-convergence* was introduced in [29] under the name *d-convergence*. We refer the reader for an exposition on *uo*-convergence to [15,17–19], on *un*-convergence to

[15,21,29], on the unbounded p-convergence to [10–12], and on the p_τ-convergence to [5,6]. For applications of uo-convergence, we refer to [4,7,8,18,19].

The structure of this chapter is as follows. In Section 5.2, we give some basic notions and properties of vector lattices, lattice-normed spaces, locally solid Riesz spaces, unbounded convergence, and unbounded p_τ-convergence.

In Section 5.3, we introduce the definitions of the p_τ-continuous and the p_τ-bounded operators between lattice-normed locally solid vector lattices. We show that p-boundedness coincides with p_τ-boundedness, and also, we prove that a dominated operator is p_τ-bounded; see Propositions 5.1 and 5.2, respectively. Also, we get a relation between the order continuity and p_τ-continuity; see Proposition 5.3. We show that a sequentially p_τ-continuous operator is norm continuous; see Proposition 5.4.

In Section 5.4, we introduce the notions of up_τ-continuous and sequentially up_τ-continuous operator between lattice-normed locally solid vector lattices. We prove that a dominated surjective lattice homomorphism operator is sequentially up_τ-continuous; see Theorem 5.1. We give some kind of up_τ-continuous operator; see Propositions 5.6 and 5.7.

In the last section, we introduce the notions of sequentially p_τ-compact and p_τ-compact operators, and we give some basic properties of them. We show that a sequence of order-bounded sequentially p_τ-compact operators is sequentially p_τ-compact (see Theorem 5.2). Also, it holds for the equicontinuously and uniformly convergence (see Theorem 5.3). We prove that a sequentially p_τ-compact operator is compact (see Proposition 5.9). Also, a GAM-compact operator is sequentially p_τ-compact (see Proposition 5.12).

5.2 PRELIMINARIES

First of all, let us recall some notations and terminologies used in this paper. In this chapter, all vector spaces are supposed to be real. Let E be a vector space. Then, E is called *ordered vector space* if it has an order relation "$\leq$" (i.e, it is reflexive, antisymmetric, and transitive) that is compatible with the algebraic structure of E, it means that $y \leq x$ implies $y+z \leq x+z$ for all $z \in E$ and $\lambda y \leq \lambda x$ for each positive scalar $\lambda \geq 0$.

An ordered vector E is said to be *vector lattice* (or, *Riesz space*) if, for each pair of vectors $x, y \in E$, the supremum $x \vee y = \sup\{x,y\}$ and the infimum $x \wedge y = \inf\{x,y\}$ both exist in E. Then, $x^+ := x \vee 0$, $x^- := (-x) \vee 0$, and $|x| := x \vee (-x)$ are called the *positive* part, the *negative* part, and the *absolute value* of $x \in E$, respectively. Also, two vectors x and y in a vector lattice are said to be *disjoint* whenever $|x| \wedge |y| = 0$. A vector lattice is called *order complete* if every nonempty bounded above subset has a supremum (or, equivalently, whenever every nonempty bounded below subset has an infimum).

A partially ordered set I is called *directed* if, for each $a_1, a_2 \in I$, there is another $a \in I$ such that $a \geq a_1$ and $a \geq a_2$ (or, $a \leq a_1$ and $a \leq a_2$). A function from a directed set I into a set E is called a *net* in E. A vector lattice is order complete if $0 \leq x_\alpha \uparrow \leq x$ implies the existence of sup x_α. A net $(x_\alpha)_{\alpha \in A}$ in a vector lattice X is called *order convergent* (or shortly, *o-convergent*) to $x \in X$ if there exists another net $(y_\beta)_{\beta \in B}$

satisfying $y_\beta \downarrow 0$, and for any $\beta \in B$, there exists $\alpha_\beta \in A$ such that $|x_\alpha - x| \leq y_\beta$ for all $\alpha \geq \alpha_\beta$. In this case, we write $x_\alpha \xrightarrow{o} x$; for more details, see, for example, [3,31,32]. In a vector lattice X, a net (x_α) is *unbounded order convergent* to $x \in X$ if $|x_\alpha - x| \wedge u \xrightarrow{o} 0$ for every $u \in X_+$; see, for example, [15,17–19,28].

Recall that every linear topology τ on a vector space E has a base $\mathcal{N}$ for the zero neighborhoods satisfying the following four properties: For each $V \in \mathcal{N}$, we have $\lambda V \subseteq V$ for all scalar $|\lambda| \leq 1$; for any $V_1, V_2 \in \mathcal{N}$, there is another $V \in \mathcal{N}$ such that $V \subseteq V_1 \cap V_2$; for each $V \in \mathcal{N}$, there exists another $U \in \mathcal{N}$ with $U + U \subseteq V$; and for any scalar λ and each $V \in \mathcal{N}$, the set λV is also in $\mathcal{N}$; for much more detail, see [2,3].

A subset A of a vector lattice is called *solid* whenever $|x| \leq |y|$ and $y \in A$ imply $x \in A$. A solid vector subspace is referred to as an *order ideal*. An order closed ideal is referred to as a *band*. A sublattice Y of a vector lattice is majorizing E if, for every $x \in E$, there exists $y \in Y$ with $x \leq y$; see, for example, [1–3,32]. Let E be a vector lattice and τ be a linear topology on E that has a base at zero consisting of solid sets. Then, the pair (E, τ) is said to be a *locally solid vector lattice* (or, *locally solid Riesz space*).

It should be noted that all topologies considered throughout this chapter are assumed to be Hausdorff. It follows from [2, Thm. 2.28.] that a linear topology τ on a vector lattice E is a locally solid if it is generated by a family of Riesz pseudonorms $\{\rho_j\}_{j \in J}$. Moreover, if a family of Riesz pseudonorms generates a locally solid topology τ on a vector lattice E, then $x_\alpha \xrightarrow{\tau} x$ if $\rho_j(x_\alpha - x) \to 0$ in $\mathbb{R}$ for each $j \in J$. Since E is Hausdorff, the family $\{\rho_j\}_{j \in J}$ of Riesz pseudonorms is separating; i.e., if $\rho_j(x) = 0$ for all $j \in J$, then $x = 0$. A locally solid vector lattice is said to have *Lebesgue property* if $x_\alpha \xrightarrow{o} 0$ in E implies $x_\alpha \xrightarrow{\tau} 0$. In this chapter, unless otherwise, the pair (E, τ) refers to as a locally solid vector lattice, and the topologies in locally solid vector lattices are generated by a family of Riesz pseudonorms $\{\rho_j\}_{j \in J}$.

Let X be a vector space, E be a vector lattice, and $p : X \to E_+$ be a vector norm (i.e., $p(x) = 0 \Leftrightarrow x = 0$, $p(\lambda x) = |\lambda| p(x)$ for all $\lambda \in \mathbb{R}$, $x \in X$, and $p(x+y) \leq p(x) + p(y)$ for all $x, y \in X$), then the triple (X, p, E) is called a *lattice-normed space*, abbreviated as *LNS*. The lattice norm p in an LNS (X, p, E) is said to be *decomposable* if, for all $x \in X$ and $e_1, e_2 \in E_+$, it follows from $p(x) = e_1 + e_2$ that there exists $x_1, x_2 \in X$ such that $x = x_1 + x_2$ and $p(x_k) = e_k$ for $k = 1, 2$. We refer the reader for more information on *LNS*s to [13,23,24] and [10–12]. A linear operator T between two *LNS*s (X, p, E) and (Y, m, F) is said to be *dominated* if there is a positive operator $S : E \to F$ satisfying $m(Tx) \leq S(p(x))$ for all $x \in X$. In an *LNS* (X, p, E), a subset A of X is called *p-bounded* if there exists $e \in E$ such that $p(a) \leq e$ for all $a \in A$; see [11, Def. 2.].

If X is a vector lattice and the vector norm p is monotone (i.e., $|x| \leq |y| \Rightarrow p(x) \leq p(y)$), then the triple (X, p, E) is called a *lattice-normed vector lattice*, abbreviated as *LNVL*; see [10–12]. Let (X, p, E) be an LNVL with (E, τ), which is a locally solid vector lattice, then (X, p, E_τ) is said to be a *lattice-normed locally solid Riesz space* (or *lattice-normed locally solid vector lattice*), abbreviated as *LSNVL* in [5]. Throughout this chapter, we use X instead of (X, p, E_τ) and Y instead of $(Y, m, F_{\hat{\tau}})$.

Note also that $L(X,Y)$ denotes the space of all linear operators between vector spaces X and Y. If X is a normed space, then X^* denotes the topological dual of X and B_X denotes the closed unit ball of X.

We abbreviate the convergence $p(x_\alpha - x) \xrightarrow{\tau} 0$ as $x_\alpha \xrightarrow{p_\tau} x$, and say in this case that (x_α) p_τ-converges to x. A net $(x_\alpha)_{\alpha\in A}$ in an $LSNVL$ (X,p,E_τ) is said to be p_τ-*Cauchy* if the net $(x_\alpha - x_{\alpha'})_{(\alpha,\alpha')\in A\times A}$ p_τ-converges to 0. An $LSNVL$ (X,p,E_τ) is called (*sequentially*) p_τ-*complete* if every p_τ-Cauchy (sequence) net in X is p_τ-convergent. In an $LSNVL$ (X,p,E_τ), a subset A of X is called p_τ-*bounded* if $p(A)$ is τ-bounded in E. An $LSNVL$ (X,p,E_τ) is called op_τ-*continuous* if $x_\alpha \xrightarrow{o} 0$ implies that $p(x_\alpha) \xrightarrow{\tau} 0$. A net (x_α) in an $LSNVL$ (X,p,E_τ) is said to be *unbounded* p_τ-*convergent* to $x \in X$ (shortly, (x_α) up_τ-converges to x or $x_\alpha \xrightarrow{up_\tau} x$) if $p(|x_\alpha - x| \wedge u) \xrightarrow{\tau} 0$ for all $u \in X_+$; see for much more information [5].

Let (X,p,E) be an LNS and $(E,\|\cdot\|_E)$ be a normed vector lattice. The *mixed-norm* on X is defined by $p\text{-}\|x\|_E = \|p(x)\|_E$ for all $x \in X$. In this case, the normed space $(X, p\text{-}\|\cdot\|_E)$ is called a *mixed-normed space*; see [23, 7.1.1, p. 292].

Lastly, it should be noticed that the theory of lattice-normed spaces is well developed in the case of decomposable lattice norms. In this chapter, we usually do not assume lattice norms to be decomposable. On the other hand, throughout this chapter, all vector lattices are assumed to be Archimedean, and also, we frequently use the following lemmas and so we shall keep in mind them; see [5, Lem. 1.1.] and [11, Lem. 1.], respectively.

Lemma 5.1. *If* $(x_\alpha)_{\alpha\in A}$ *and* $(y_\alpha)_{\alpha\in A}$ *be two nets in a locally solid vector lattice* (E,τ) *such that* $|x_\alpha| \leq |y_\alpha|$ *for all* $\alpha \in A$ *and* $y_\alpha \xrightarrow{\tau} 0$, *then* $x_\alpha \xrightarrow{\tau} 0$.

Lemma 5.2. *Let* (X,p,E) *be an LNS such that* $(E,\|\cdot\|_E)$ *is a Banach space. If* (X,p,E) *is sequentially p-complete, then* $(X,p\text{-}\|\cdot\|_E)$ *is the Banach space.*

5.3 p_τ-CONTINUOUS AND p_τ-BOUNDED OPERATORS

In this section, we define the notions of p_τ-continuous and p_τ-bounded operators between LSNVLs. Recall that an operator T between two LNVLs X and Y is called *p-continuous* if $x_\alpha \xrightarrow{p} 0$ in X implies $Tx_\alpha \xrightarrow{p} 0$ in Y, and if the condition holds only for sequences, then T is called *sequentially p-continuous*. Moreover, T is also called *p-bounded* if it maps p-bounded sets in X to p-bounded sets in Y; see [11]. Motivated by these definitions, we give the following notions.

Definition 5.1. *Let X and Y be two LSNVLs and* $T \in L(X,Y)$. *Then, T is called*

1. p_τ-*continuous if* $x_\alpha \xrightarrow{p_\tau} 0$ *in X implies* $Tx_\alpha \xrightarrow{p_\tau} 0$ *in Y, and if the condition holds only for sequences, then T is called sequentially* p_τ-*continuous,*
2. p_τ-*bounded if it maps* p_τ-*bounded sets to* p_τ-*bounded sets.*

Remark 5.1.

i. *Let T be an operator between LSNVLs (X,p,E_τ) and $(Y,m,F_{\acute{\tau}})$ with (E,τ) and $(F,\acute{\tau})$ having order-bounded neighborhoods of zero. Then, by applying [2, Thm. 2.19(i)] and [20, Thm. 2.2.], one can see that T is p-bounded if it is p_τ-bounded. Moreover, $T:(E,|\cdot|,E_\tau)\to(F,|\cdot|,F_{\acute{\tau}})$ is p_τ-bounded if $T:X\to Y$ is order-bounded.*

ii. *Let X be a vector lattice and $(Y,\|\cdot\|_Y)$ be a normed space. Then, $T\in L(X,Y)$ is called order-to-norm continuous if $x_\alpha\xrightarrow{o}0$ in X implies $Tx_\alpha\xrightarrow{\|\cdot\|_Y}0$; see [27, Sec. 4., p. 468]. For a locally solid lattice (X,τ) with the Lebesgue property, the p_τ-continuity of $T:(X,|\cdot|,X_\tau)\to(Y,\|\cdot\|_Y,\mathbb{R})$ implies order-to-norm continuity of it.*

iii. *Let X be a vector lattice and $(Y,m,F_{\acute{\tau}})$ be an LSNVL, and $T:X\to Y$ be a strictly positive operator. Define $p:X\to F_+$, by $p(x)=(m\circ T)(|x|)$. Then, $(X,p,F_{\acute{\tau}})$ is an LSNVL, and also, the map $T:(X,p,F_{\acute{\tau}})\to(Y,m,F_{\acute{\tau}})$ is p_τ-continuous.*

In the following work, we show that the collection of all p_τ-continuous operators between *LSNVLs* is the vector space.

Lemma 5.3. *Let (X,p,E_τ) and $(Y,m,F_{\acute{\tau}})$ be two LSNVLs.*

i. *If $T,S:(X,p,E_\tau)\to(Y,m,F_{\acute{\tau}})$ are p_τ-continuous operators, then $\lambda S+\mu T$ is p_τ-continuous for any real numbers λ and μ. In particular, if $H=T-S$, then H is p_τ-continuous.*

ii. *If $-T_1\le T\le T_2$ with T_1 and T_2 positive and p_τ-continuous operators, then T is p_τ-continuous.*

Proof. (i) We show $x_\alpha\xrightarrow{p_\tau}0$ in X implies $m(Sx_\alpha+Tx_\alpha)\xrightarrow{\acute{\tau}}0$ in F. To do this, we consider the following inequality:

$$m(Sx_\alpha+Tx_\alpha)\le m(Sx_\alpha)+m(Tx_\alpha)\xrightarrow{\acute{\tau}}0.$$

So $S+T$ is also p_τ-continuous. Now, for arbitrary real numbers λ and μ, we have

$$\begin{aligned}m(\lambda Sx_\alpha+\mu Tx_\alpha)&\le|\lambda|m(Sx_\alpha)+|\mu|m(Tx_\alpha)\\&\le(|\lambda|+|\mu|)\big(m(Sx_\alpha)+m(Tx_\alpha)\big)\xrightarrow{\acute{\tau}}0.\end{aligned}$$

Therefore, $\lambda S+\mu T$ is p_τ-continuous.

(ii) If $-T_1\le T\le T_2$ with T_1 *and* T_2 positive and p_τ-continuous, then we have

$$0\le T+T_1\le T_2+T_1$$

where $T+T_1$ is positive and p_τ-continuous. Thus, it follows from (i) that $T=(T+T_1)-T_1$ is p_τ-continuous. □

By the following result, we prove that there is a relation between p- and p_τ-bounded notions.

Proposition 5.1. *Let T be an operator between LSNVLs (X,p,E_τ) and $(Y,m,F_{\acute{\tau}})$ with (E,τ) and $(F,\acute{\tau})$ having order-bounded neighborhoods of zero. Then, T is p-bounded if it is p_τ-bounded.*

Proof. We show only one direction. Assume T is p-bounded. Suppose A is p_τ-bounded subset in X, and so $p(A)$ is τ-bounded in E. Thus, $p(A)$ is also order-bounded in E; see [20, Thm. 2.2.]. Since T is p-bounded, $T(A)$ is p-bounded in Y, and so $m\big(T(A)\big)$ is order-bounded in F. Therefore, $m\big(T(A)\big)$ is $\acute{\tau}$-bounded in F; see [2, Thm. 2.19(i)]. Hence, $T(A)$ is p_τ-bounded in Y. □

Proposition 5.2. *Any dominated operator T from an LSNVL (X,p,E_τ) with (E,τ) having order-bounded τ-neighborhood of zero to an LSNVL $(Y,m,F_{\acute{\tau}})$ is p_τ-bounded.*

Proof. Consider a p_τ-bounded subset A in X. That is, $p(A)$ is τ-bounded in E. So $p(A)$ is order-bounded in E; see [20, Thm. 2.2.]. Let S be the dominant of T. Since S is a positive operator, $S\big(p(A)\big)$ is order-bounded in F. Also, we know that $m\big(T(a)\big) \leq S\big(p(a)\big)$ for all $a \in A$, and so $m\big(T(A)\big)$ is order-bounded in F. Hence, by applying [2, Thm. 2.19(i)], $m\big(T(A)\big)$ is $\acute{\tau}$-bounded in F. Therefore, T is p_τ-bounded. □

The converse of Proposition 5.2 is not true in general. For instance, consider ℓ_∞ with the norm topology and $\mathbb{R}$ with the usual topology, and the identity operator $I : (\ell_\infty, |\cdot|, \ell_\infty) \to (\ell_\infty, \|\cdot\|, \mathbb{R})$. It is p_τ-bounded. Indeed, for any p_τ-bounded set A in ℓ_∞, $|A|$ is τ-bounded in ℓ_∞. Thus, $\big\||A|\big\| = \|A\|$ is bounded in $\mathbb{R}$. But it is not dominated; see [13, Rem., p. 388]. □

The next proposition gives a relation between the p_τ- and order continuity.

Proposition 5.3. *Let $(Y,m,F_{\acute{\tau}})$ be arbitrary and (X,p,E_τ) be op_τ-continuous LSNVLs and $T : (X,p,E_\tau) \to (Y,m,F_{\acute{\tau}})$ be a (sequentially) p_τ-continuous positive operator. Then, $T : X \to Y$ is (σ-) order continuous operator.*

Proof. Assume $x_\alpha \downarrow 0$ in X. Since X is op_τ-continuous, we have $p(x_\alpha) \xrightarrow{\tau} 0$, and so $x_\alpha \xrightarrow{p_\tau} 0$ in X. By the p_τ-continuity of T, $m(Tx_\alpha) \xrightarrow{\acute{\tau}} 0$ in F. It can be seen that $Tx_\alpha \downarrow$ because T is positive. Then, applying [5, Prop. 2.4.], we get $Tx_\alpha \downarrow 0$. Thus, T is order continuous. □

Corollary 5.1. *Let (X,p,E) be an op_τ-continuous LSNVL and $(Y,m,F_{\acute{\tau}})$ be an LSNVL with Y being order complete. If $T : (X,p,E) \to (Y,m,F)$ is p_τ-continuous and $T \in L^\sim(X,Y)$, then $T : X \to Y$ is order continuous.*

Proof. Since Y is order-complete and T is order-bounded, by Riesz-Kantorovich formula, we have $T = T^+ - T^-$. Now, Proposition 5.3 implies that T^+ and T^- are both order continuous, and so T is order continuous. □

In the following result, which is p_τ-version of [11, Prop. 3.], we give norm continuity of sequentially p_τ-continuous operator on the mixed-norms.

Proposition 5.4. *Let (X,p,E_τ) and $(Y,m,F_{\acute{\tau}})$ be two LSNVLs with $(E,\|\cdot\|_E)$ and $(F,\|\cdot\|_F)$ being normed vector lattices, and where τ and $\acute{\tau}$ are generated by the norms. If $T:(X,p,E_\tau)\to(Y,m,F_{\acute{\tau}})$ is sequentially p_τ-continuous, then $T:(X,p\text{-}\|\cdot\|_E)\to(Y,m\text{-}\|\cdot\|_F)$ is norm continuous.*

Proof. $(\Rightarrow)$ Assume $T:(X,|\cdot|,X)\to(X,\|\cdot\|_X,\mathbb{R})$ to be sequentially p_τ-continuous, and a sequence $x_n\xrightarrow{\|\cdot\|}0$ in X. Thus, $x_n\xrightarrow{\tau}0$ in X, and since T is sequentially p_τ-continuous, $Tx_n\xrightarrow{\|\cdot\|}0$.

$(\Leftarrow)$ Assume that T is norm continuous, and let $x_n\xrightarrow{p_\tau}0$ in $(X,|\cdot|,X)$. Then, $|x_n|\xrightarrow{\tau}0$ or $x_n\xrightarrow{\|\cdot\|}0$ in X. Hence, $Tx_n\xrightarrow{\|\cdot\|}0$. Therefore, $T:(X,|\cdot|,X)\to(X,\|\cdot\|_X,\mathbb{R})$ is sequentially p-continuous. □ □

Remark 5.2. *By applying [2, Thm. 2.19(i)] and [11, Prop. 4.], one can see that every p_τ-continuous operator is p_τ-bounded. But a p_τ-continuous operator $T:(X,p,E_\tau)\to(Y,m,F_{\acute{\tau}})$ need not to be order-bounded from X to Y. Indeed, consider the classical "Fourier coefficients" operator $T:L_1[0,1]\to c_0$ defined by the formula*

$$T(f)=\left(\int_0^1 f(x)sinx\,dx,\int_0^1 f(x)sin2x\,dx,...\right).$$

Then, $T:L_1[0,1]\to c_0$ is norm-bounded, but it is not order-bounded; see [2, Exer. 10., p. 289]. So $T:(L_1[0,1],\|\cdot\|_{L_1},\mathbb{R})\to(c_0,\|\cdot\|_\infty,\mathbb{R})$ is p_τ-continuous and is not order-bounded.

Using [20, Thm. 2.2.] in Remark 5.2, it can be seen that p_τ-continuity implies order boundedness if $(F,\acute{\tau})$ has order-bounded $\acute{\tau}$-neighborhood of zero. Recall that an operator $T\in L(X,Y)$, where X and Y are the normed spaces, is called *Dunford-Pettis* if $x_n\xrightarrow{w}0$ in X implies $Tx_n\xrightarrow{\|\cdot\|}0$ in Y. We show the following result, which is p_τ-version of [11, Prop. 5.], so we omit its proof.

Proposition 5.5. *Let $(X,\|\cdot\|_X)$ be a normed vector lattice and $(Y,\|\cdot\|_Y)$ be a normed space. Put $E:=\mathbb{R}^{X^*}$ and define $p:X\to E_+$, by $p(x)[f]=|f|(|x|)$ for $f\in X^*$. It is easy to see that (X,p,E_τ), where τ is the topology generated by the norm $\|\cdot\|_{X^*}$, is an LSNVL. Then, the followings hold:*

i. *If $T\in L(X,Y)$ is a Dunford-Pettis operator then $T:(X,p,E_\tau)\to(Y,\|\cdot\|_Y,\mathbb{R})$ is sequentially p_τ-continuous,*
ii. *The converse holds if the lattice operations of X are weakly sequentially continuous.*

5.4 up_τ-CONTINUOUS OPERATORS

Recall that a net (x_α) in an *LSNVL* (X,p,E_τ) is said to be *unbounded* p_τ*-convergent* to x if $p(|x_\alpha - x| \wedge u) \xrightarrow{\tau} 0$ for all $u \in X_+$; see [5]. Motivated by *up*-continuous operators in [11] and *un*-continuous functionals in [21, p. 16], and by using the up_τ-convergence, we introduce the following notion.

Definition 5.2. *An operator T between two LSNVLs X and Y is called* up_τ*-continuous if it maps the* up_τ*-convergent net to* up_τ*-convergent nets. If it holds only for sequence, then T is called sequentially* up_τ*-continuous.*

It is clear that if T is (sequentially) p_τ-continuous operator, then T is (sequentially) up_τ-continuous. For an *LSNVL* (X,p,E_τ), a sublattice Y of X is called up_τ*-regular* if, for any net (y_α) in Y, the convergence $y_\alpha \xrightarrow{\mathrm{up}_\tau} 0$ in Y implies $y_\alpha \xrightarrow{\mathrm{up}_\tau} 0$ in X. The following is a more general extension of [21, Prop. 9.4.].

Theorem 5.1. *Let* (X,p,E_τ) *and* $(Y,m,F_{\acute{\tau}})$ *be LSNVLs with* $(E,\|\cdot\|_E)$ *being a Banach lattice and* $(F,\|\cdot\|_F)$ *being a normed vector lattice, and also* τ *and* $\acute{\tau}$ *are being generated by the norms. Then, the followings hold:*

i. *A dominated surjective lattice homomorphism operator* $T \in L(X,Y)$ *is sequentially* up_τ*-continuous;*
ii. *If* $T \in L(X,Y)$ *is a dominated lattice homomorphism operator and* $T(X)$ *is* up_τ*-regular in Y, then it is sequentially* up_τ*-continuous;*
iii. *If* $T \in L(X,Y)$ *is a dominated lattice homomorphism operator and* $I_{T(X)}$ *(the ideal generated by* $T(X)$*) is* up_τ*-regular in Y, then it is sequentially* up_τ*-continuous.*

Proof. (i) Let's fix a sequence $x_n \xrightarrow{\mathrm{up}_\tau} 0$ in X and $u \in Y_+$. Since T is a surjective lattice homomorphism, we have some $v \in X_+$ such that $Tv = u$. So we have $p(|x_n| \wedge v) \xrightarrow{\tau} 0$ in E. Since T is dominated, there is a positive operator $S : E \to F$ such that

$$m\big(T(|x_n| \wedge v)\big) \leq S\big(p(|x_n| \wedge v)\big).$$

Taking into account that T is a lattice homomorphism and $Tv = u$, we get $m\big(|Tx_n| \wedge u\big) \leq S\big(p(|x_n| \wedge v)\big)$. By using [2, Thm. 4.3.], we know that every positive operator from a Banach lattice to the normed vector lattice is continuous, and so S is continuous. Hence, we get $S\big(p(|x_n| \wedge v)\big) \xrightarrow{\acute{\tau}} 0$ in F. That is, $m\big(|Tx_n| \wedge u\big) \xrightarrow{\acute{\tau}} 0$, and we get the desired result.

(ii) Since T is a lattice homomorphism, $T(X)$ is a vector sublattice of Y. So $\big(T(X),m,F_{\acute{\tau}}\big)$ is an *LSNVL*. Thus, by (i), we have $T : (X,p,E_\tau) \to \big(T(X),m,F_{\acute{\tau}}\big)$ is sequentially up_τ-continuous.

Next, we show that $T : (X,p,E_\tau) \to (Y,m,F_{\acute{\tau}})$ is sequentially up_τ-continuous. Consider an up_τ-convergent to zero sequence (x_n) in X. That is, $Tx_n \xrightarrow{\mathrm{up}_\tau} 0$ in $T(X)$.

Since $T(X)$ is up_τ-regular in Y, $T(x_n)\xrightarrow{\mathrm{up}_\tau}0$ in Y. Therefore, T is sequentially up_τ-continuous.

(iii) Let $(x_n)\xrightarrow{\mathrm{up}_\tau}0$ sequence in X. Thus, $p(|x_n|\wedge u)\xrightarrow{\tau}0$ in E for all $u\in X_+$. Fix $0\leq w\in I_{T(X)}$. Then, there is $x\in X_+$ such that $0\leq w\leq Tx$. For a dominant S, we have $m\big(T(|x_n|\wedge x)\big)\leq S\big(p(|x_n|\wedge x)\big)$, and so, by taking lattice homomorphism of T, we have

$$m\big((|Tx_n|\wedge Tx)\big)\leq S\big(p(|x_n|\wedge x)\big).$$

It follows from $0\leq w\leq Tx$ that $m\big((|Tx_n|\wedge w)\big)\leq S\big(p(|Tx_n|\wedge x)\big)$. Now, the argument given in the proof of (i) can be repeated here as well. Thus, we see that $T:(X,p,E_\tau)\to\big(I_{T(X)},m,F_{\acute{\tau}}\big)$ is sequentially up_τ-continuous. Since $I_{T(X)}$ is up_τ-regular in Y, it can be easily seen by (ii) that $T:X\to Y$ is sequentially up_τ-continuous. □

It should be mentioned, by using Theorem 5.1, that an operator, surjective lattice homomorphism with order continuous dominant, is up_τ-continuous.

Proposition 5.6. *Let (X,p,E_τ) and $(Y,m,F_{\acute{\tau}})$ be two LSNVLs with Y being order-complete vector lattice. For a positive up_τ-continuous operator $T:(X,p,E_\tau)\to(Y,m,F_{\acute{\tau}})$, consider the operator $S:(X_+,p,E_\tau)\to(Y_+,m,F_{\acute{\tau}})$ defined by $S(x)=\sup\{T(x_\alpha\wedge x):x_\alpha\in X_+,x_\alpha\xrightarrow{\mathrm{up}_\tau}0\}$ for each $x\in X_+$. Then, we have the followings:*

i. S is the up_τ-continuous operator;
ii. The Kantorovich extension of S is the up_τ-continuous operator.

Proof. (i) Suppose $X_+\ni y_\beta\xrightarrow{\mathrm{up}_\tau}0$. Then, $Ty_\beta\xrightarrow{\mathrm{up}_\tau}0$ in Y, and so $m\big(Ty_\beta\wedge w\big)\xrightarrow{\acute{\tau}}0$ in F for all $w\in Y_+$. For any net $x_\alpha\in X_+$ and fixed $w\in Y_+$, we have

$$T(x_\alpha\wedge y_\beta)\wedge w\leq T(y_\beta)\wedge w\xrightarrow{\acute{\tau}}0.$$

Therefore, we get the desired result.

(ii) We show first that S has the Kantorovich extension. To show this, let's see additivity of it. By using [3, Lem. 1.4.], for any up_τ-null net (x_α) in X_+, we have

$$T\big((x+y)\wedge x_\alpha\big)\leq T(x\wedge x_\alpha)+T(y\wedge x_\alpha)\leq S(x)+S(y).$$

So by taking supremum, we get $S(x+y)\leq S(x)+S(y)$. On the other hand, for any two up_τ-null nets (x_α) and (y_β) in X_+, using the formula in the proof of [3, Thm. 1.28.], we get

$$T(x\wedge x_\alpha)+T(y\wedge y_\beta)=T(x\wedge x_\alpha+y\wedge y_\beta)\leq T\big((x+y)\wedge(x_\alpha+y_\beta)\big)\leq S(x+y).$$

So $S(x)+S(y)\leq S(x+y)$. By [3, Thm. 1.10.], S extends to a positive operator, denoted by $\hat{S}:(X,p,E_\tau)\to(Y,m,F_{\acute{\tau}})$. That is, $\hat{S}x=S(x^+)-S(x^-)$ for all $x\in X$. Now, we show up_τ-continuity of $\hat{S}$. Fix a net $w_\beta\xrightarrow{\mathrm{up}_\tau}0$ in X. Then, $w_\beta^+\xrightarrow{\mathrm{up}_\tau}0$ and $w_\beta^-\xrightarrow{\mathrm{up}_\tau}0$ in X, and so $S(w_\beta^+)\xrightarrow{\mathrm{up}_\tau}0$ and $S(w_\beta^-)\xrightarrow{\mathrm{up}_\tau}0$ in Y. Hence, $\hat{S}w_\beta=S(w_\beta^+)-S(w_\beta^-)\xrightarrow{\mathrm{up}_\tau}0$ in Y. □

We complete this section with the following technical work.

Proposition 5.7. *Consider a positive up_τ-continuous operator T between LSNVLs X and Y, and an ideal A in X. Then, an operator $S:(X,p,E_\tau)\to(Y,m,F_{\hat{\tau}})$ defined by $S(x)=\sup_{a\in A}T(|x|\wedge a)$ for each $x\in X$ is up_τ-continuous operator.*

Proof. Let $x_\alpha \xrightarrow{\mathrm{up}_\tau} 0$ be a net in X. Then, $|x_\alpha| \xrightarrow{\mathrm{up}_\tau} 0$, and so $T(|x_\alpha|) \xrightarrow{\mathrm{up}_\tau} 0$ in Y. Thus, for each $u\in Y_+$, we have

$$|S(x_\alpha)|\wedge u=\left|\sup_{a\in A}T(|x_\alpha|\wedge a)\right|\wedge u\le |T(|x_\alpha|)|\wedge u\le T(|x_\alpha|)\wedge u\xrightarrow{\mathrm{up}_\tau}0.$$

Therefore, $S(x_\alpha)\xrightarrow{\mathrm{up}_\tau}0$ in Y. □

5.5 THE COMPACT-LIKE OPERATORS

In this section, we define the notions of p_τ-compact and sequentially p_τ-compact operators in *LSNVLs* and study their properties. A linear operator T between normed spaces is called compact if $T(B_X)$ is relatively compact, or equivalently, T is compact if, for any norm-bounded sequence (x_n), there is a subsequence (x_{n_k}) such that the sequence (Tx_{n_k}) is convergent. Similarly, we introduce the following notions.

Definition 5.3. *Let X and Y be two LSNVLs and $T\in L(X,Y)$. Then, T is called p_τ-compact if, for any p_τ-bounded net (x_α) in X, there is a subnet (x_{α_β}) such that $Tx_{\alpha_\beta}\xrightarrow{\mathrm{p}_\tau}y$ in Y for some $y\in Y$. If it holds only for sequence, then T is called sequentially p_τ-compact.*

Example 5.1.

i. *Let $(X,\|\cdot\|_X)$ and $(Y,\|\cdot\|_Y)$ be the normed spaces. Then, $T:(X,\|\cdot\|_X,\mathbb{R})\to(Y,\|\cdot\|_Y,\mathbb{R})$ is (sequentially) p_τ-compact if $T:X\to Y$ is compact.*
ii. *Let X be a vector lattice and Y be a normed space. An operator $T\in L(X,Y)$ is said to be AM-compact if $T[-x,x]$ is relatively compact for every $x\in X_+$; see [26, Def. 3.7.1.]. Let (X,τ) be a locally solid vector lattice with order-bounded τ-neighborhood and $(Y,\|\cdot\|_Y)$ be a normed vector lattice. Then, $T\in L(X,Y)$ is the AM-compact operator if $T:(X,|\cdot|,X_\tau)\to(Y,\|\cdot\|_Y,\mathbb{R})$ is p_τ-compact; apply [20, Thm. 2.2.] and [2, Thm. 2.19(i)].*
iii. *Consider a topology τ in ℓ_2 with the norm $\|\cdot\|_2$, and so $(\ell_2,|\cdot|,\ell_{2\tau})$ and $(\ell_2,\|\cdot\|_2,\mathbb{R})$ are two LSNVLs. Thus, a linear operator $T_n:(\ell_2,|\cdot|,\ell_{2\tau})\to(\ell_2,\|\cdot\|_2,\mathbb{R})$ defined by $T_nx=(x_1,x_2,\cdots,x_n,0,0\cdots)$ for all $x\in\ell_2$ is p_τ-compact. Indeed, let (x_n) be a p_τ-bounded, or $|(x_n)|$ is $\|\cdot\|_2$-bounded sequence in ℓ_2. Hence, (Tx_n) is $\|\cdot\|_2$-bounded in ℓ_2. Since every bounded sequence in $\mathbb{R}^n$ has a convergent subsequence, it follows that T_n is p_τ-compact.*

Lemma 5.4. *If S and T are (sequentially) p_τ-compact operators between LSNVLs, then $T+S$ and λT, for any real number λ, are also (sequentially) p_τ-compact operators.*

Proof. We show that only $T+S$ is p_τ-compact, and the other cases are analogous. Let (x_α) be a p_τ-bounded net in X. Since T is p_τ-compact, there is a subnet (x_{α_β}) such that $m(Tx_{\alpha_\beta}-y)\xrightarrow{\acute{\tau}}0$ in F for some $y\in Y$. On the other hand, (x_{α_β}) is also p_τ-bounded in X and S is p_τ-compact, and then there is a subnet $(x_{\alpha_{\beta_\gamma}})$ such that $m(Sx_{\alpha_{\beta_\gamma}}-z)\xrightarrow{\acute{\tau}}0$ in F for some $z\in Y$. Also, we have $m(Tx_{\alpha_{\beta_\gamma}}-y)\xrightarrow{\acute{\tau}}0$ in F. Thus, $m[(S+T)(x_{\alpha_{\beta_\gamma}})-y-z)]\xrightarrow{\acute{\tau}}0$. Hence, $S+T$ is p_τ-compact. □

Proposition 5.8. *Let (X,p,E_τ) be an LSNVL and $R,T,S\in L(X)$.*

i. If T is a (sequentially) p_τ-compact and S is a (sequentially) p_τ-continuous operator, then $S\circ T$ is (sequentially) p_τ-compact.
ii. If T is a (sequentially) p_τ-compact and R is a p_τ-bounded operator, then $T\circ R$ is (sequentially) p_τ-compact.

Proof. We give the only p_τ-compactness, and the sequential case is analogous.

i. Consider a p_τ-bounded net (x_α) in X. Since T is p_τ-compact, there are a subnet (x_{α_β}) and $x\in X$ such that $Tx_{\alpha_\beta}\xrightarrow{p_\tau}x$. By p_τ-continuity of S, we have $S(Tx_{\alpha_\beta})\xrightarrow{p_\tau}Sx$ in E. Therefore, $S\circ T$ is p_τ-compact.
ii. Suppose (x_α) is a p_τ-bounded net in X. Since R is p_τ-bounded, (Rx_α) is p_τ-bounded. Then, by p_τ-compact of T, there are a subnet (x_{α_β}) and $y\in X$ such that $T(Rx_{\alpha_\beta})\xrightarrow{p_\tau}y$. Therefore, $T\circ R$ is p_τ-compact.

□

Remark 5.3.

i. Let X be an LSNVL and $(Y,\acute{\tau})$ be a locally solid vector lattice with Y being compact. Then, each operator $T:(X,p,E_\tau)\to(Y,|\cdot|,Y_{\acute{\tau}})$ is (sequentially) p_τ-compact.
ii. Let X be an LSNVL and $(Y,\|\cdot\|_Y)$ be a finite dimensional normed space, and $\acute{\tau}$ be the topology generated by this norm. If $T:(X,p,E_\tau)\to(Y,|\cdot|,Y_{\acute{\tau}})$ is p_τ-bounded operator, then it is sequentially p_τ-compact.
iii. Let (X,τ) be a locally solid vector lattice with an order-bounded τ-neighborhood of zero and $(Y,m,F_{\acute{\tau}})$ be an op_τ-continuous LSNVL with Y being an atomic KB-space. If $T:X\to Y$ is an order-bounded operator, then $T:(X,|\cdot|,X_\tau)\to(Y,m,F_{\acute{\tau}})$ is p_τ-compact; see [20, Thm. 2.2.] and [11, Rem. 6.].

Remark 5.4. *Let (T_m) be a sequence of sequentially p_τ-compact operators from X to Y. For a given p_τ-bounded sequence (x_n) in X, by a standard diagonal argument, there exists a subsequence (x_{n_k}) such that, for any $m\in\mathbb{N}$, $T_m x_{n_k}\xrightarrow{p_\tau}y_m$ for some $y_m\in Y$.*

Theorem 5.2. *Let (T_m) be a sequence of order-bounded sequentially p_τ-compact operators from (X,p,E_τ) to a sequentially p_τ-complete op_τ-continuous $(Y,q,F_{\acute{t}})$ with Y being order complete. If $T_m \xrightarrow{o} T$ in $L_b(X,Y)$, then T is sequentially p_τ-compact.*

Proof. Let (x_n) be a p_τ-bounded sequence in X. By Remark 5.4, there exists a subsequence (x_{n_k}) such that, for any $m \in \mathbb{N}$, $T_m x_{n_k} \xrightarrow{p_\tau} y_m$ for some $y_m \in Y$. We show that (y_m) is a p_τ-Cauchy sequence. Consider the following formula

$$q(y_m - y_j) \leq q(y_m - T_m x_{n_k}) + q(T_m x_{n_k} - T_j x_{n_k}) + q(T_j x_{n_k} - y_j). \tag{5.1}$$

The first and the third terms in the last inequality both $\acute{t}$-converge to zero as $m \to \infty$ and $j \to \infty$, respectively. Since $T_m \xrightarrow{o} T$, we have $T_m x_{n_k} \xrightarrow{o} T x_{n_k}$ for all x_{n_k}; see [31, Thm. VIII.2.3.]. Then, for a fixed index k, we have

$$|T_m x_{n_k} - T_j x_{n_k}| \leq |T_m x_{n_k} - T x_{n_k}| + |T x_{n_k} - T_j x_{n_k}| \xrightarrow{o} 0$$

as $m, j \to \infty$, and so $(T_m - T_j)x_{n_k} \xrightarrow{o} 0$ in Y. Hence, by op_τ-continuity of $(Y,q,F_{\acute{t}})$, we get $q(T_m x_{n_k} - T_j x_{n_k}) \xrightarrow{\acute{t}} 0$ in F. By formula (1), (y_m) is p_τ-Cauchy. Since Y is sequentially p_τ-complete, there is $y \in Y$ such that $q(y_m - y) \xrightarrow{\acute{t}} 0$ in F as $m \to \infty$. So, for arbitrary m, if we take $\acute{t}$-limit with k in the following formula

$$q(T x_{n_k} - y) \leq q(T x_{n_k} - T_m x_{n_k}) + q(T_m x_{n_k} - y_m) + q(y_m - y),$$

we get $\acute{t} - \lim q(T x_{n_k} - y) \leq q(T x_{n_k} - T_m x_{n_k}) + q(y_m - y)$ because of $q(T_m x_{n_k} - y_m) \xrightarrow{\acute{t}} 0$. Since m is arbitrary, $\acute{t} - \lim q(T x_{n_k} - y) \xrightarrow{\acute{t}} 0$. Thus, T is sequentially p_τ-compact. □

Similar to Theorem 5.2, we give the following theorem by using equicontinuously and uniformly convergence.

Theorem 5.3. *Let (T_m) be a sequence of sequentially p_τ-compact operators from $(X,|\cdot|,X_\tau)$ to a sequentially p_τ-complete LSNVL $(Y,|\cdot|,Y_\tau)$. Then, the followings hold:*

i. If (T_m) converges equicontinuously to an operator $T : (X,|\cdot|,X_\tau) \to (Y,|\cdot|,Y_{\acute{t}})$, then T is sequentially p_τ-compact,

ii. If (T_m) uniformly converges on zero neighborhoods to an operator $T : (X,|\cdot|,X_\tau) \to (Y,|\cdot|,Y_{\acute{t}})$, then T is sequentially p_τ-compact.

Let (X,E) be a decomposable *LNS* and (Y,F) be an *LNS* with F being order complete. Then, each dominated operator $T : X \to Y$ has the exact dominant $|T| : E \to F$; see [23, 4.1.2., p. 142]. For a sequence (T_n) in the set of dominated operators $M(X,Y)$, we call $T_n \to T$ in $M(X,Y)$ whenever $|T_n - T|(e) \xrightarrow{\acute{t}} 0$ in F for each $e \in E$.

Theorem 5.4. *Let (X,p,E_τ) be a decomposable and $(Y,q,F_{\acute{t}})$ be a sequentially p_τ-complete LSNVLs with F being order complete. If (T_m) is a sequence of sequentially p_τ-compact operators and $T_m \to T$ in $M(X,Y)$ then T is sequentially p_τ-compact.*

Proof. Let (x_n) be a p_τ-bounded sequence in X. By Remark 5.4, there exists a subsequence (x_{n_k}) and a sequence (y_m) in Y such that, for any $m \in \mathbb{N}$, $T_m x_{n_k} \xrightarrow{p_\tau} y_m$. We show that (y_m) is p_τ-Cauchy sequence in Y. Consider formula (1) of Theorem 5.2. Similarly, the first and the third terms in the last inequality of (1) both $\acute{\tau}$-converge to zero as $m \to \infty$ and $j \to \infty$, respectively. Since $T_m \in M(X,Y)$ for all $m \in \mathbb{N}$,

$$q(T_m x_{n_k} - T_j x_{n_k}) \leq |T_m - T_j|(p(x_{n_k})) \leq |T_m - T|(p(x_{n_k})) + |T - T_j|(p(x_{n_k})) \xrightarrow{\acute{\tau}} 0$$

as $m, j \to \infty$. Thus, $q(y_m - y_j) \xrightarrow{\acute{\tau}} 0$ in F as $m, j \to \infty$. Therefore, (y_m) is p_τ-Cauchy. Since Y is sequentially p_τ-complete, there is $y \in Y$ such that $q(y_m - y) \xrightarrow{\acute{\tau}} 0$ in F as $m \to \infty$. By the following formula

$$\begin{aligned} q(Tx_{n_k} - y) &\leq q(Tx_{n_k} - T_m x_{n_k}) + q(T_m x_{n_k} - y_m) + q(y_m - y) \\ &\leq |T_m - T|(p(x_{n_k})) + q(T_m x_{n_k} - y_m) + q(y_m - y) \end{aligned}$$

and by repeating the same of last part of Theorem 5.2, we get $q(Tx_{n_k} - y) \xrightarrow{\acute{\tau}} 0$. Therefore, T is sequentially p_τ-compact. □

Proposition 5.9. *Let (X, p, E_τ) be an LSNVL, where $(E, \|\cdot\|_E)$ is an AM-space with a strong unit, and $(Y, m, F_{\acute{\tau}})$ be an LSNVL, where $(F, \|\cdot\|_F)$ is the normed vector lattice and $\acute{\tau}$ is generated by the norm $\|\cdot\|_F$. If $T : (X, p, E_\tau) \to (Y, m, F_{\acute{\tau}})$ is sequentially p_τ-compact, then $T : (X, p\text{-}\|\cdot\|_E) \to (Y, m\text{-}\|\cdot\|_F)$ is compact.*

Proof. Let (x_n) be a normed bounded sequence in $(X, p\text{-}\|\cdot\|_E)$. That is, $p\text{-}\|x_n\|_E = \|p(x_n)\|_E < \infty$ for all $n \in N$. Since $(E, \|\cdot\|_E)$ is an AM-space with a strong unit, $p(x_n)$ is order-bounded in E. Thus, $p(x_n)$ is τ-bounded in E; see [2, Thm. 2.19(i)]. So (x_n) is a p_τ-bounded sequence in (X, p, E_τ). Since T is sequentially p_τ-compact, there are a subsequence x_{n_k} and $y \in Y$ such that $m(Tx_{n_k} - y) \xrightarrow{\acute{\tau}} 0$ in F. Then, $\|m(Tx_{n_k} - y)\|_F \to 0$ or $m\text{-}\|Tx_{n_k} - y\|_F \to 0$ in F. Thus, the operator $T : (X, p\text{-}\|\cdot\|_E) \to (Y, m\text{-}\|\cdot\|_F)$ is compact. □

It is known that a finite rank operator is compact. Similarly, we give the following result.

Proposition 5.10. *Let (X, p, E_τ) and $(Y, m, F_{\acute{\tau}})$ be LSNVLs with $(F, \acute{\tau})$ having the Lebesgue property. Consider an operator $T : (X, p, E_\tau) \to (Y, m, F_{\acute{\tau}})$ defined by $Tx = f(x)y_0$, where $y_0 \in Y$ and f is a linear functional on X. If $f : (X, p, E_\tau) \to (\mathbb{R}, |\cdot|, \mathbb{R})$ is p_τ-bounded, then T is (sequentially) p_τ-compact.*

Proof. Suppose (x_α) is a p_τ-bounded net in X. Since f is p_τ-bounded, $f(x_\alpha)$ is bounded in $\mathbb{R}$. Then, there is a subnet (x_{α_β}) such that $f(x_{\alpha_\beta}) \to \lambda$ for some $\lambda \in \mathbb{R}$. For $y_0 \in Y$, we have the following formula:

$$m(Tx_{\alpha_\beta}-\lambda y_0)=m(f(x_{\alpha_\beta})y_0-\lambda y_0)=m((f(x_{\alpha_\beta})-\lambda)y_0)=|f(x_{\alpha_\beta})-\lambda|m(y_0)\xrightarrow{o}0.$$

By the Lebesgue property of F, we get $m(Tx_{\alpha_\beta}-\lambda y)\xrightarrow{\tau}0$ in E. Thus, T is p_τ-compact. □

Proposition 5.11. *Let (X,p,E_τ) be an LSNVL with (E,τ) having an order-bounded τ-neighborhood and $(Y,m,F_{\acute{t}})$ be an LSNVL, where $(Y,\|\cdot\|_Y)$ is an order continuous atomic KB-space and $\acute{t}$ is generated by $\|\cdot\|_Y$. If $T:(X,p,E_\tau)\to(Y,|\cdot|,Y_{\acute{t}})$ is p-bounded or dominated operator, then it is p_τ-compact.*

Recall that a linear operator T from an LNS (X,E) to a Banach space $(Y,\|\cdot\|_Y)$ is called the *generalized AM-compact* or *GAM-compact* if, for any p-bounded set A in X, $T(A)$ is relatively compact in $(Y,\|\cdot\|_Y)$.

Proposition 5.12. *Let (X,p,E_τ) be an LSNVL with (E,τ) having an order-bounded τ-neighborhood and $(Y,m,F_{\acute{t}})$ be an op_τ-continuous LSNVL with a Banach lattice $(Y,\|\cdot\|_Y)$. If $T:(X,p,E_\tau)\to(Y,\|\cdot\|_Y)$ is GAM-compact, then $T:(X,p,E_\tau)\to(Y,m,F_{\acute{t}})$ is sequentially p_τ-compact.*

Proof. Let (x_n) be a p_τ-bounded sequence in X. By [20, Thm. 2.2.], (x_n) is p-bounded in (X,p,E_τ). Since T is GAM-compact, there are a subsequence (x_{n_k}) and some $y\in Y$ such that $\|Tx_{n_k}-y\|_Y\to 0$. Since $(Y,\|\cdot\|_Y)$ is Banach lattice then, by [31, Thm. VII.2.1.], there is a further subsequence $(x_{n_{k_j}})$ such that $Tx_{n_{k_j}}\xrightarrow{o}y$ in Y. Then, by op_τ-continuity of $(Y,m,F_{\acute{t}})$, we get $Tx_{n_{k_j}}\xrightarrow{p_\tau}y$ in Y. Hence, T is sequentially p_τ-compact. □

Proposition 5.13. *Let $(X,\|\cdot\|_X)$ be a normed lattice and $(Y,\|\cdot\|_Y)$ be a Banach lattice. If $T:(X,\|\cdot\|_X,\mathbb{R})\to(Y,|\cdot|,Y_{\acute{t}})$ is sequentially p_τ-compact and p-bounded, and $f:Y\to\mathbb{R}$ is σ-order continuous, then $(f\circ T):X\to\mathbb{R}$ is compact.*

Proof. Assume (x_n) be a norm-bounded sequence in X. Since T is sequentially p_τ-compact, there are a subsequence (x_{n_k}) and $y\in Y$ such that $Tx_{n_k}\xrightarrow{p_\tau}y$ or $|Tx_{n_k}-y|\xrightarrow{\acute{t}}0$ or $Tx_{n_k}\xrightarrow{\|\cdot\|_Y}y$ in Y. Since $(Y,\|\cdot\|_Y)$ be a Banach lattice, there is a further subsequence $(x_{n_{k_j}})$ such that $Tx_{n_{k_j}}\xrightarrow{o}y$ in Y; see [31, Thm. VII.2.1.]. By σ-order continuity of f, we have $(f\circ T)x_{n_{k_j}}\to f(y)$ in $\mathbb{R}$. □

We now turn our attention to the up_τ-compact operators.

Definition 5.4. *Let X and Y be two LSNVLs and $T\in L(X,Y)$. Then, T is called up_τ-compact if, for any p_τ-bounded net (x_α) in X, there is a subnet (x_{α_β}) such that $Tx_{\alpha_\beta}\xrightarrow{up_\tau}y$ in Y for some $y\in Y$. If the condition holds only for sequences, then T is called sequentially-up_τ-compact.*

It is clear that a p_τ-compact operator is up_τ-compact, and similar to Lemma 5.4, linear properties hold for up_τ-compact operators. Moreover, an operator $T\in L(X,Y)$

is (sequentially) un-compact if $T:(X,\|\cdot\|_X,\mathbb{R})\to(Y,\|\cdot\|_Y,\mathbb{R})$ is (sequentially) up_τ-compact; see [21, Sec. 9., p. 28]. Similar to Proposition 5.8, we give the following results.

Proposition 5.14. *Let (X,p,E_τ) be an LSNVL and $R,T,S,H\in L(X)$.*

i. *If T is an (sequentially) up_τ-compact and S is a (sequentially) p_τ-continuous, then $S\circ T$ is (sequentially) up_τ-compact.*
ii. *If T is an (sequentially) up_τ-compact and R is a p_τ-bounded, then $T\circ R$ is (sequentially) up_τ-compact.*

Now, we investigate a relation between sequentially up_τ-compact operators and dominated lattice homomorphisms. The following is a more general extension of [21, Prop. 9.4.] and [11, Thm. 8.], and its proof is similar to Theorem 5.1.

Theorem 5.5. *Let (X,p,E_τ), $(Y,m,F_{\acute{\tau}})$, and $(Z,q,G_{\hat{\tau}})$ be LSNVLs with $(F,\|\cdot\|_F)$ being Banach lattice and $(G,\|\cdot\|_G)$ normed lattice, and $\acute{\tau}$ and $\hat{\tau}$ are being generated by the norms. Then, the followings hold:*

i. *If $T\in L(X,Y)$ is a sequentially up_τ-compact operator and $S\in L(Y,Z)$ is a dominated surjective lattice hòmomorphism, then $S\circ T$ is sequentially up_τ-compact;*
ii. *If $T\in L(X,Y)$ is a sequentially up_τ-compact, $S\in L(Y,Z)$ is a dominated lattice homomorphism, and $S(Y)$ is up_τ-regular in Z, then $S\circ T$ is sequentially up_τ-compact;*
iii. *If $T\in L(X,Y)$ is a sequentially up_τ-compact, $S\in L(Y,Z)$ is a dominated lattice homomorphism operator, and $I_{S(Y)}$ (the ideal generated by $S(Y)$) is up_τ-regular in Z, then $S\circ T$ is sequentially up_τ-compact.*

Proposition 5.15. *Let (X,p,E_τ) be an LSNVL and $(Y,m,F_{\acute{\tau}})$ be an up_τ-complete LSNVL, and S, $T:(X,p,E_\tau)\to(Y,m,F_{\acute{\tau}})$ be operators with $0\le S\le T$. If T is a lattice homomorphism and (sequentially) up_τ-compact, then S is (sequentially) up_τ-compact.*

Proof. We will prove the sequential case; the other case is similar. Let (x_n) be a p_τ-bounded sequence in X. So there are a subsequence (x_{n_k}) and some $y\in Y$ such that $Tx_{n_k}\xrightarrow{up_\tau}y$ in Y. In particular, it is up_τ-Cauchy. Fix $u\in Y_+$, and note that

$$|Sx_{n_k}-Sx_{n_j}|\wedge u\le(S|x_{n_k}-x_{n_j}|)\wedge u\le(T|x_{n_k}-x_{n_j}|)\wedge u=|Tx_{n_k}-Tx_{n_j}|\wedge u\xrightarrow{\acute{\tau}}0$$

as $k,j\to\infty$. Thus, we get (Sx_{n_k}), which is a up_τ-Cauchy sequence in Y. Therefore, it follows from up_τ-complete of Y. □

Lemma 5.5. *Let (X,p,E_τ) and $(Y,m,F_{\acute{\tau}})$ be two LSNVLs with Y being order-complete vector lattice. If $T:(X,p,E_\tau)\to(Y,m,F_{\acute{\tau}})$ is a positive up_τ-compact operator, then the operator $S:(X_+,p,E_\tau)\to(Y_+,m,F_{\acute{\tau}})$ defined by $S(x)=\sup\{T(u\wedge x):u\in X_+\}$ for each $x\in X_+$ is also up_τ-compact operator.*

Proof. Suppose (y_β) is a p_τ-bounded net in X_+. Then, there is a subnet (y_{β_γ}) such that $Ty_{\beta_\gamma} \xrightarrow{\mathrm{up}_\tau} y$ for some $y \in Y$, and so $m(|Ty_{\beta_\gamma} - y| \wedge w) \xrightarrow{\hat{\tau}} 0$ in F for all $w \in Y_+$. For $u \in X_+$ and fixed $w \in Y_+$, we have $0 \leq T(u \wedge y_{\beta_\gamma}) \leq T(y_{\beta_\gamma})$, and so $|T(u \wedge y_{\beta_\gamma}) - y| \wedge w \leq |T(y_{\beta_\gamma}) - y| \wedge w$. By taking supremum over $u \in X_+$, we get $|Sy_{\beta_\gamma} - y| \wedge w \leq |T(y_{\beta_\gamma}) - y| \wedge w \xrightarrow{\hat{\tau}} 0$, and so we get the desired result. □

Remark 5.5. *The sum of two p_τ-bounded subsets is also p_τ-bounded since the sum of two solid subsets is solid. Moreover, for a p_τ-bounded net (x_α) in an LSNVL (X, p, E_τ), the nets (x_α^+) and (x_α^-) are p_τ-bounded.*

The following theorem is up_τ-compact version of Proposition 5.6, so we omit its proof.

Theorem 5.6. *Let (X, p, E_τ) and $(Y, m, F_{\hat{\tau}})$ be two LSNVLs with Y being order-complete vector lattice. If $T : (X, p, E_\tau) \to (Y, m, F_{\hat{\tau}})$ is a positive up_τ-compact operator, then the Kantorovich extension of $S : (X_+, p, E_\tau) \to (Y_+, m, F_{\hat{\tau}})$ defined by $S(x) = \sup\{T(x_\alpha \wedge x) : x_\alpha \in X_+$ is p_τ-bounded$\}$ for each $x \in X_+$ is also up_τ-compact.*

BIBLIOGRAPHY

[1] Y.A. Abramovich and C.D. Aliprantis, *An invitation to operator theory*, Graduate Studies in Mathematics, Vol. 50, American Mathematical Society, Rhoda Island, (2002).

[2] C.D. Aliprantis and O. Burkinshaw, *Locally solid Riesz spaces with applications to economics*, Pure and Applied Mathematics, Vol. 105, American Mathematical Society, Indianapolish, (2003).

[3] C.D. Aliprantis and O. Burkinshaw, *Positive operators*, Springer, Vol. 119, Dordrecht, (2006).

[4] A. Aydın, Topological algebras of bounded operators with locally solid Riesz spaces, *Journal of Science and Technology of Erzincan University,* Vol. 11, 543–549, (2018).

[5] A. Aydın, Unbounded p_τ-convergence in vector lattices normed by locally solid lattices, Academic studies in mathematic and natural sciences, IVPE, Cetinje-Montenegro, 118–134, (2019).

[6] A. Aydın, *Convergence via filter in locally solid Riesz spaces, International Journal of Science and Research,* Vol. 8, 351–353, (2019).

[7] A. Aydın, Multiplicative order convergence in f-algebras, *Hacettepe Journal of Mathematics and Statistics,* Vol. 49, 998–1005, (2020).

[8] A. Aydın, Multiplicative norm convergence in Banach lattice f-algebras, *Hacettepe Journal of Mathematics and Statistics,* in press, (2020).

[9] A. Aydın and M. Çınar, Multiplicative norm compact operators on Banach lattice f-algebras, *International Journal on Mathematics, Engineering and Natural Science,* Vol. 9, 8–13, (2019).

[10] A. Aydın, E.Y. Emel'yanov, N.E. Özcan and M.A.A. Marabeh, Compact-like operators in lattice-normed spaces, *Indagationes Mathematicae,* Vol. 2, 633–656, (2018).

[11] A. Aydın, E.Y. Emel'yanov, N.E. Özcan and M.A.A. Marabeh, Unbounded p-convergence in lattice-normed vector lattices, *Siberian Advances in Mathematics,* Vol. 29, 164–182, (2019).

[12] A. Aydın, S.G. Gorokhova and H. Gül, Nonstandard hulls of lattice-normed ordered vector spaces, *Turkish Journal of Mathematics,* Vol. 42, 155–163, (2018).

[13] A.V. Bukhvalov, A.E. Gutman, V.B. Korotkov, A.G. Kusraev, S.S. Kutateladze and B.M. Makarov, *Vector lattices and integral operators*, Mathematics and its Applications, Vol. 358, Kluwer Academic Publishers Group, Dordrecht, (1996).

[14] R. DeMarr, Partially ordered linear spaces and locally convex linear topological spaces, *Illinois Journal of Mathematics,* Vol. 8, 601–606, (1964).

[15] Y. Deng, M. O'Brien and V.G. Troitsky, Unbounded norm convergence in Banach lattices, *Positivity,* Vol. 21, 963–974, (2017).

[16] E.Y. Emel'yanov, Infinitesimal analysis and vector lattices, *Siberian Advances in Mathematics,* Vol. 6, 19–70, (1996).

[17] N. Gao, Unbounded order convergence in dual spaces, *Journal of Mathematical Analysis and Applications,* Vol. 419, 347–354, (2014).

[18] N. Gao and F. Xanthos, Unbounded order convergence and application to martingales without probability, *Journal of Mathematical Analysis and Applications,* Vol. 415, 931–947, (2014).

[19] N. Gao, V.G. Troitsky and F. Xanthos, *Uo*-convergence and its applications to Cesáro means in Banach lattices, *Israel Journal of Mathematics,* Vol. 220, 649–689, (2017).

[20] L. Hong, On order bounded subsets of locally solid Riesz spaces, *Quaestiones Mathematicae,* Vol. 39, 381–389, (2016).

[21] M. Kandić, M.A.A. Marabeh and V.G. Troitsky, *Unbounded norm topology in Banach lattices, Mathematical Analysis and Applications,* Vol. 451, 259–279, (2017).

[22] S. Kaplan, On unbounded order convergence, *Real Analysis Exchange,* Vol. 23, 175–184, (1998).

[23] A.G. Kusraev, *Dominated operators*, Mathematics and its Applications, (2000).

[24] A.G. Kusraev and S.S. Kutateladze, *Boolean valued analysis*, Mathematics and its Applications, (1999).

[25] W.A.J. Luxemburg and A.C. Zaanen, *Riesz spaces I,* North-Holland, Amsterdam, (1971).

[26] P. Meyer-Nieberg, *Banach lattices*, Universitext, Springer-Verlag, Berlin, (1991).

[27] O.V. Maslyuchenko, V.V. Mykhaylyuk and M.M. Popov, A lattice approach to narrow operators, *Positivity,* Vol. 13, 459–495, (2009).

[28] H. Nakano, Ergodic theorems in semi-ordered linear spaces, *Annals of Mathematics,* Vol. 49, 538–556, (1948).

[29] V.G. Troitsky, Measures of non-compactness of operators on Banach lattices, *Positivity,* Vol. 8, 165–178, (2004).

[30] A.W. Wickstead, Weak and unbounded order convergence in Banach lattices, *Journal of the Australian Mathematical Society,* Vol. 24, 312–319, (1977).

[31] B.Z. Vulikh, *Introduction to the theory of partially ordered spaces*, Wolters-Noordhoff Scientific Publications, Ltd., Groningen, (1967).

[32] A.C. Zaanen, *Riesz spaces II,* North-Holland Mathematical Library, Vol. 30, North-Holland Publishing Co., Amsterdam, (1983).

6 On Indexed Product Summability of an Infinite Series

B. P. Padhy
KIIT Deemed to be University

P. Baliarsingh
Gangadhar Meher University

CONTENTS

6.1 INTRODUCTION

6.1.1 HISTORICAL BACKGROUND

Initially, in 1952, Szasz [10] published some results on products of summability methods. Subsequently, Rajgopal [7] in 1954, Parameswaran [6] in 1957, Ramanujan [8] in 1958, etc. published some more results on the products of summability methods. Later on, Das [2] in 1969 proved some related results on the absolute product summability. In 2008, Sulaiman [9] provided a result on the indexed product summability of an infinite series. The result found by Sulaiman was then extended by Paikray et al. [5] in 2010. Also, we can see some more developments on this idea in Ref. [1,3,4] in the recent past.

6.1.2 NOTATIONS AND DEFINITIONS

Let $\sum a_n$ be an infinite series with the sequence of partial sums $\{s_n\}$. Let $\{p_n\}$ be a sequence of positive real constants such that

$$P_n = p_0 + p_1 + \cdots + p_n \to \infty \; as \; n \to \infty \,(P_{-i} = p_{-1} = 0)\,. \tag{6.1}$$

The sequence-to-sequence transformation

$$t_n = \frac{1}{P_n} \sum_{v=0}^{n} p_v \, s_v \tag{6.2}$$

defines $(R,\ p_n)$ transform of $\{s_n\}$ generated by $\{p_n\}$.

The series $\sum a_n$ is said to be summable $|R, p_n|_k$, $k \geq 1$, if

$$\sum_{n=1}^{\infty} n^{k-1} \left|t_n - t_{n-1}\right|^k < \infty. \tag{6.3}$$

Similarly, the sequence-to-sequence transformation

$$T_n = \frac{1}{P_n} \sum_{v=0}^{n} p_{n-v} \, s_v$$

defines the (N, p_n) transform of $\{s_n\}$ generated by $\{p_n\}$.

Let $\{\tau_n\}$ be the sequence of (N, q_n) transform of the (N, p_n) transform of $\{s_n\}$, generated by the sequences $\{q_n\}$ and $\{p_n\}$, respectively. Then, the series $\sum a_n$ is said to be summable $|(N, q_n)\ (N, p_n)|_k$, $k \geq 1$, if

$$\sum_{n=1}^{\infty} n^{k-1} \left|\tau_n - \tau_{n-1}\right|^k < \infty, \tag{6.4}$$

and the series $\sum a_n$ is said to be summable $|(N, q_n)(N, p_n), \delta|_k, k \geq 1, 1 \geq \delta k \geq 0$, if

$$\sum_{n=1}^{\infty} n^{(\delta k + k - 1)} \left|\tau_n - \tau_{n-1}\right|^k < \infty. \tag{6.5}$$

Similarly, if $\{\alpha_n\}$ is any sequence of positive numbers, then the series $\sum a_n$ is said to be summable $|(N, q_n)\ (N, p_n)\,, \alpha_n|_k$, $k \geq 1$, if

$$\sum_{n=1}^{\infty} \alpha_n^{k-1} \left|\tau_n - \tau_{n-1}\right|^k < \infty, \tag{6.6}$$

and the series $\sum a_n$ is said to be summable $|(N, q_n)(N, p_n), \alpha_n; \delta|_k, k \geq 1, 1 \geq k\delta \geq 0$, if

$$\sum_{n=1}^{\infty} \alpha_n^{\delta k + k - 1} \left|\tau_n - \tau_{n-1}\right|^k < \infty. \tag{6.7}$$

Let f be a function of α_n, if

$$\sum_{n=1}^{\infty} \{f(\alpha_n)\}^k (\alpha_n)^{k-1} \left|\tau_n - \tau_{n-1}\right|^k < \infty, \tag{6.8}$$

then the series $\sum a_n$ is said to be $|(N, q_n)\ (N, p_n)\,, \alpha_n; f|_k, k \geq 1$ summable.

Clearly for $f(\alpha_n) = \alpha_n^{\delta}, \delta \geq 0$, $|(N, q_n)\ (N, p_n)\,, \alpha_n; f|_k = |(N, q_n)\ (N, p_n)\,, \alpha_n; \delta|_k$., and for $\delta = 0$, $|(N, q_n)\ (N, p_n)\,, \alpha_n; f|_k = |(N, q_n)\ (N, p_n)\,, \alpha_n|_k$.

We assume throughout this chapter that $Q_n = q_0 + \cdots + q_n \to \infty$ as $n \to \infty$ and $P_n = p_0 + \cdots + p_n \to \infty$ as $n \to \infty$

6.2 KNOWN RESULTS

In 2008, Sulaiman [9] has proved the following theorem.

Theorem 6.1. *Let $k \geq 1$ and (λ_m) be a sequence of constants. Let us define*

$$f_v = \sum_{r=v}^{n} \frac{q_r}{P_r}, \; F_v = \sum_{r=v}^{n} p_r \, f_r \tag{6.9}$$

Let $p_n \, Q_n = O(P_n)$ such that

$$\sum_{n=v+1}^{\infty} \frac{n^{k-1} q_n^k}{Q_n^k Q_{n-1}} = O\left(\frac{(v q_v^{k-1})}{Q_v^k}\right). \tag{6.10}$$

Then, the sufficient conditions for the implication that $\sum a_n$ is summable $|R, r_n|_k \Rightarrow \sum a_n \, \lambda_n$ is summable $|(R, q_n) \, (R, p_n)|_k$ are

$$|\lambda_v| \; F_v = O(Q_v), \tag{6.11}$$

$$|\lambda_v| = O(Q_v), \tag{6.12}$$

$$p_v \, R_v \; |\lambda_v| = O(Q_v), \tag{6.13}$$

$$p_v \, q_v \, R_v \; |\lambda_v| = O(Q_v \, Q_{v-1} r_v), \tag{6.14}$$

$$p_n \, q_n \, R_n \; |\lambda_n| = O(P_n \, Q_n \, r_n), \tag{6.15}$$

$$R_{v-1} \, |\Delta \lambda_v| \; F_{v+1} = O(Q_v \, r_v), \tag{6.16}$$

and

$$R_{v-1} \, |\Delta \lambda_v| = O(Q_v \, r_v). \tag{6.17}$$

Subsequently, Paikray et al. [5] generalized the above theorem by replacing the (R, p_n) summability by A-summability and stated the results as follows.

Theorem 6.2. *Let $k \geq 1, \{\lambda_n\}$ be a sequence of constants. Let us define*

$$f_v = \sum_{r=v}^{n} q_r \, a_{rv}, \quad F_v = \sum_{r=v}^{n} f_r. \tag{6.18}$$

Then, the sufficient conditions for the implication that $\sum a_n$ is summable $|R, r_n|_k \Rightarrow \sum a_n \, \lambda_n$ is summable $|(R, q_n) \, (A)|_k$ are

$$\sum_{n=v+1}^{m+1} \frac{n^{k-1} q_n^k}{Q_n^k Q_{n-1}} = O\left(\frac{1}{\lambda_v^k}\right), \tag{6.19}$$

$$\left(\sum_{r=v}^{n} q_r^{\frac{k}{k-1}}\right) = O(q_v), \tag{6.20}$$

$$\left(\sum_{r=v}^{n} a_{r,v}^{k}\right) = O\left(v^{k-1}\right), \tag{6.21}$$

$$R_v = O(r_v), \tag{6.22}$$

$$\frac{q_n}{Q_n} = O(1), \tag{6.23}$$

$$\frac{q_n \lambda_n a_{n,n}}{Q_{n-1}} = O(1), \tag{6.24}$$

$$\frac{(\Delta\lambda_v)^k}{q_v^{k-1}} = O\left(v^{k-1}\right), \tag{6.25}$$

$$\frac{\Delta\lambda_v}{\lambda_v} = O(1), \tag{6.26}$$

and

$$\frac{\lambda_v^k}{q_v^{k-1}} = O\left(v^{k-1}\right). \tag{6.27}$$

In this chapter, we established the following theorems on the product summability of the infinite series $\sum a_n \lambda_n$.

6.3 MAIN RESULTS

Theorem 6.3. *For the sequences of real constants* $\{p_n\}$ *and* $\{q_n\}$*, define*

$$f_v = \sum_{i=v}^{n} \frac{q_{n-i} p_{i-v}}{P_i} \text{ and } F_v = \sum_{i=v}^{n} f_i. \tag{6.28}$$

Let

$$Q_n = O(q_n P_n) \tag{6.29}$$

and

$$\sum_{n=v+1}^{m+1} \frac{n^{\delta k+k-1} q_n^k}{Q_n^k Q_{n-1}} = O\left(\frac{(v q_v)^{k-1}}{Q_v^k}\right) \text{ as } m \to \infty. \tag{6.30}$$

Then for any sequences $\{r_n\}$ *and* $\{\lambda_n\}$*, the sufficient conditions for the implication that* $\sum a_n$ *is summable* $|R, r_n|_k \Rightarrow \sum a_n \lambda_n$ *is summable* $|(N,q_n)\,(N,p_n);\delta|_k$, $k \geq 1$, $1 \geq k\delta \geq 0$, *are*

$$|\lambda_n|\ F_v = O(Q_v), \tag{6.31}$$

$$|\lambda_n| = O(Q_n), \tag{6.32}$$

$$R_v\, F_v\, |\lambda_v| = O(Q_v\, r_v), \tag{6.33}$$

$$q_n\, R_n\, F_n\, |\lambda_n| = O(Q_n\, Q_{n-1} r_n), \tag{6.34}$$

$$R_{v-1} F_{v+1}\, |\Delta\lambda_v| = O(Q_v\, r_v), \tag{6.35}$$

$$R_{v-1}\, |\Delta\lambda_v| = O(Q_v\, r_v), \tag{6.36}$$

$$q_n\, R_n\, |\lambda_n| = O(Q_n\, Q_{n-1} r_n), \tag{6.37}$$

where $R_n = r_1 + r_2 + \ldots\ldots + r_n$.

Theorem 6.4. *For the sequences of real constants $\{p_n\}$ and $\{q_n\}$ and the sequence of positive numbers $\{\alpha_n\}$, define*

$$f_v = \sum_{i=v}^{n} \frac{q_{n-i} p_{i-v}}{P_i} \text{ and } F_v = \sum_{i=v}^{n} f_i. \tag{6.38}$$

Let

$$Q_n = O(q_n P_n) \tag{6.39}$$

and

$$\sum_{n=v+1}^{m+1} \frac{\alpha_n^{k-1} q_n^k}{Q_n^k Q_{n-1}} = O\left(\frac{(vq_v)^{k-1}}{Q_v^k}\right) \text{ as } m \to \infty. \tag{6.40}$$

Then, for any sequences $\{r_n\}$ and $\{\lambda_n\}$, the sufficient conditions for the implication that $\sum a_n$ is summable $|R, r_n|_k \Rightarrow \sum a_n \lambda_n$ is summable $|(N,q_n)(N,p_n),\alpha_n|_k$, $k \geq 1$, are

$$|\lambda_v| \, F_v = O(Q_v), \tag{6.41}$$

$$|\lambda_n| = O(Q_n), \tag{6.42}$$

$$R_v F_v \, |\lambda_v| = O(Q_v \, r_v), \tag{6.43}$$

$$q_n R_n F_n \, |\lambda_n| = O(Q_n \, Q_{n-1} r_n), \tag{6.44}$$

$$R_{v-1} F_{v+1} \, |\Delta\lambda_v| = O(Q_v \, r_v), \tag{6.45}$$

$$R_{v-1} \, |\Delta\lambda_v| = O(Q_v \, r_v), \tag{6.46}$$

$$q_n R_n \, |\lambda_n| = O(Q_n \, Q_{n-1} r_n), \tag{6.47}$$

$$\sum_{n=1}^{\infty} n^{k-1} |t_n|^k = O(1), \tag{6.48}$$

and

$$\sum_{n=2}^{\infty} \alpha_n^{k-1} |t_n|^k = O(1), \tag{6.49}$$

where $R_n = r_1 + r_2 + \ldots\ldots + r_n$ $t_n = \Delta t_n'$ and t_n' is the n-th (R, r_n) transform of $\sum a_n$.

Theorem 6.5. *For the sequences of real constants $\{p_n\}$ and $\{q_n\}$ and the sequence of positive numbers $\{\alpha_n\}$, define*

$$f_v = \sum_{i=v}^{n} \frac{q_{n-i} p_{i-v}}{P_i} \text{ and } F_v = \sum_{i=v}^{n} f_i \tag{6.50}$$

Let

$$Q_n = O(q_n P_n) \tag{6.51}$$

and

$$\sum_{n=v+1}^{m+1} \frac{\alpha_n^{\delta k+k-1} q_n^k}{Q_n^k Q_{n-1}} = O\left(\frac{(vq_v)^{k-1}}{Q_v^k}\right) \text{ as } m \to \infty. \tag{6.52}$$

Then for any sequences $\{r_n\}$ and $\{\lambda_n\}$, the sufficient conditions for the implication $\sum a_n$ is summable $|R,\, r_n|_k \Rightarrow \sum a_n \lambda_n$ is summable $|(N,q_n)(N,p_n),\alpha_n;\delta|_k\,, k \geq 1, 1 \geq k\delta \geq 0$, are

$$|\lambda_n|\;F_v = O\left(Q_v\right), \tag{6.53}$$

$$|\lambda_n| = O\left(Q_n\right), \tag{6.54}$$

$$R_v\;F_v\;|\lambda_v| = O\left(Q_v\;r_v\right), \tag{6.55}$$

$$q_n\;R_n\;F_n\;|\lambda_n|\;\alpha_n^{\delta} = O\left(Q_n\;Q_{n-1} r_n\right), \tag{6.56}$$

$$R_{v-1} F_{v+1}\,|\Delta\lambda_v| = O\left(Q_v\;r_v\right), \tag{6.57}$$

$$R_{v-1}\,|\Delta\lambda_v| = O\left(Q_v\;r_v\right), \tag{6.58}$$

$$q_n\;R_n\;|\lambda_n|\;\alpha_n^{\delta} = O\left(Q_n\;Q_{n-1} r_n\right), \tag{6.59}$$

$$\sum_{n=1}^{\infty} n^{k-1}\,|t_n|^k = O(1), \tag{6.60}$$

and

$$\sum_{n=2}^{\infty} \alpha_n^{k-1}\,|t_n|^k = O(1), \tag{6.61}$$

where $R_n = r_1 + r_2 + \dots\dots + r_n$.

Theorem 6.6. *For the sequences of real constants $\{p_n\}$ and $\{q_n\}$ and the sequence of positive numbers $\{\alpha_n\}$, we define*

$$f_v = \sum_{i=v}^{n} \frac{q_{n-i} p_{i-v}}{P_i} \text{ and } F_v = \sum_{i=v}^{n} f_i. \tag{6.62}$$

Let

$$Q_n = O\left(q_n P_n\right) \tag{6.63}$$

and

$$\sum_{n=v+1}^{m+1} \frac{\{f(\alpha_n)\}^k (\alpha_n)^{k-1} q_n^k}{Q_n^k Q_{n-1}} = O\left(\frac{(v q_v)^{k-1}}{Q_v^k}\right) \text{ as } m \to \infty. \tag{6.64}$$

Then for any sequences $\{r_n\}$ and $\{\lambda_n\}$, the sufficient conditions for the implication $\sum a_n$ is summable $|R,\, r_n|_k \Rightarrow \sum a_n \lambda_n$ is $|(N,q_n)\;(N,p_n)\,,\alpha_n;f|_k\,, k \geq 1$ is summable, are

$$|\lambda_n|\;F_v = O\left(Q_v\right), \tag{6.65}$$

$$|\lambda_n| = O\left(Q_n\right), \tag{6.66}$$

$$R_v\;F_v\;|\lambda_v| = O\left(Q_v\;r_v\right), \tag{6.67}$$

$$q_n\;R_n\;F_n\;|\lambda_n| = O\left(Q_n\;Q_{n-1} r_n\right), \tag{6.68}$$

$$R_{v-1} F_{v+1}\,|\Delta\lambda_v| = O\left(Q_v\;r_v\right), \tag{6.69}$$

$$R_{v-1}\,|\Delta\lambda_v| = O\left(Q_v\;r_v\right), \tag{6.70}$$

$$q_n\, R_n\, |\lambda_n| = O\left(Q_n\, Q_{n-1} r_n\right), \tag{6.71}$$

$$\sum_{n=1}^{\infty} n^{k-1}\, |t_n|^k = O(1), \tag{6.72}$$

and

$$\sum_{n=2}^{\infty} \{f(\alpha_n)\}^k (\alpha_n)^{k-1}\, |t_n|^k = O(1), \tag{6.73}$$

where $R_n = r_1 + r_2 + \ldots\ldots + r_n$.

6.4 PROOF OF MAIN RESULTS

In this section, we provide the detailed proof of all theorems as stated above.

Proof of Theorem 6.3. Let $\{t'_n\}$ be the $(R,\, r_n)$ transform of the series $\sum a_n$. Then,

$$t'_n = \frac{1}{R} \sum_{v=0}^{n} r_v s_v\,.$$

Then

$$t_n = t'_n - t'_{n-1} = \frac{r_n}{R_n R_{n-1}} \sum_{v=1}^{n} R_{v-1} a_v.$$

Let $\{s_n\}$ be the sequence of partial sums of the series $\sum a_n\, \lambda_n$ and $\{\tau_n\}$ the sequence of $(N, q_n)\ (N, p_n)$ transform of the series $\sum a_n\, \lambda_n$. Then,

$$\begin{aligned}
\tau_n &= \frac{1}{Q_n} \sum_{r=0}^{n} q_{n-r} \frac{1}{P_r} \sum_{v=0}^{r} p_{r=v}\, s_v, \\
&\frac{1}{Q_n} \sum_{v=0}^{n} s_v \sum_{r=v}^{n} \frac{q_{n-v} p_{r-v}}{P_r}, \\
&= \frac{1}{Q_n} \sum_{v=0}^{n} f_v\, s_v.
\end{aligned} \tag{6.74}$$

Hence,

$$\begin{aligned}
T_n &= \tau_n - \tau_{n-1} \\
&= \frac{1}{Q_n} \sum_{v=0}^{n} f_v\, s_v - \frac{1}{Q_{n-1}} \sum_{v=0}^{n-1} f_v\, s_v \\
&= -\frac{q_n}{Q_n Q_{n-1}} \sum_{v=0}^{n} f_v\, s_v + \frac{f_n s_n}{Q_{n-1}} \\
&= -\frac{q_n}{Q_n Q_{n-1}} \sum_{r=0}^{n} f_r \sum_{v=0}^{r} a_v\, \lambda_v + \frac{f_n}{Q_{n-1}} \sum_{v=0}^{n} a_v\, \lambda_v \\
&= -\frac{q_n}{Q_n Q_{n-1}} \sum_{r=0}^{n} a_v\, \lambda_v \sum_{v=0}^{r} f_r + \frac{f_n}{Q_{n-1}} \sum_{v=0}^{n} a_v\, \lambda_v
\end{aligned} \tag{6.75}$$

$$
\begin{aligned}
&= -\frac{q_n}{Q_nQ_{n-1}} \sum_{v=1}^{n} R_{v-1}a_v \left(\frac{\lambda_v}{R_{v-1}} \sum_{r=v}^{n} f_r \right) + \frac{q_0p_0}{P_nQ_{n-1}} \sum_{v=1}^{n} R_{v-1}a_v \left(\frac{\lambda_v}{R_{v-1}} \right) \\
&= -\frac{q_n}{Q_nQ_{n-1}} \left[\sum_{v=1}^{n-1} \left(\sum_{r=1}^{v} R_{r-1}a_r \right) \Delta \left(\frac{\lambda_v}{R_{v-1}} \sum_{r=v}^{n} f_r \right) + \left(\sum_{v=1}^{n} R_{v-1}a_v \right) \frac{\lambda_n}{R_{n-1}} f_n \right] \\
&\quad + \frac{p_0q_0}{P_nQ_{n-1}} \left[\sum_{v=1}^{n-1} \left(\sum_{r=1}^{v} R_{r-1}a_v \right) \Delta \left(\frac{\lambda_v}{R_{v+1}} \right) + \left(\sum_{v=1}^{n} R_{v-1}a_v \right) \frac{\lambda_n}{R_{n-1}} \right] \\
&= -\frac{q_n}{Q_nQ_{n-1}} \left[\sum_{v=1}^{n-1} \left[\lambda_v F_v t_v + \frac{R_{v-1}}{r_v} f_v\, \lambda_v\, t_v + \frac{R_{v-1}}{r_v} (\Delta\lambda_v)\, F_{v+1} t_v \right] + \frac{R_n}{r_n} \lambda_n\, F_n\, t_n \right] \\
&\quad + \frac{p_0q_0}{P_nQ_{n-1}} \left[\sum_{v=1}^{n-1} \left(\lambda_v\, t_v + \frac{R_{v-1}}{r_v} (\Delta\lambda_v) t_v \right) + \frac{R_n}{r_n} \lambda_n\, t_n \right] \\
&= \sum_{i=1}^{7} T_{n,i}, \quad \text{say.} \qquad (6.76)
\end{aligned}
$$

In order to prove the theorem, using Minkowski's inequality, it is sufficient to show that

$$
\sum_{n=1}^{\infty} n^{\delta k+k-1} |T_{n,i}|^k < \infty, \quad \text{for } i = 1,2,3,4,5,6,7.
$$

Now, on applying Holder's inequality, we have

$$
\begin{aligned}
\sum_{n=2}^{m+1} n^{\delta k+k-1} |T_{n,1}|^k &= \sum_{n=2}^{m+1} n^{\delta k+k-1} \left| \frac{q_n}{Q_nQ_{n-1}} \sum_{v=1}^{n-1} \lambda_v\, F_v\, t_v \right|^k \\
&\leq \sum_{n=2}^{m+1} n^{\delta k+k-1} \frac{q_n^k}{Q_n^k Q_{n-1}} \sum_{v=1}^{n-1} \frac{|\lambda_v|^k F_v^k |t_v|^k}{q_v^{k-1}} \left(\frac{1}{Q_{n-1}} \sum_{v=1}^{n-1} q_v \right)^{k-1} \\
&= O(1) \sum_{v=1}^{m} \frac{1}{q_v^{k-1}} |\lambda_v|^k\, F_v^k\, |t_v|^k \sum_{n=v+1}^{m+1} \frac{n^{\delta k+k-1} q_n^k}{Q_n^k Q_{n-1}} \\
&= O(1) \sum_{v-1}^{m} \frac{1}{q_v^{k-1}} |\lambda_v|^k\, F_v^k\, |t_v|^k \frac{(vq_v)^{k-1}}{Q_v^k}, \text{ using (6.30)} \\
&= O(1) \sum_{v=1}^{m} v^{k-1} |t_v|^k \left(\frac{|\lambda_v| F_v}{Q_v} \right)^k \\
&= O(1) \sum_{v=1}^{m} v^{k-1} |t_v|^k, \quad \text{using (6.31)} \\
&= O(1), \ on\ m \to \infty.
\end{aligned}
$$

Next,

$$
\sum_{n=2}^{m+1} n^{\delta k+k-1} |T_{n2}|^k = \sum_{n=2}^{m+1} n^{k-1} \left| \frac{q_n}{Q_nQ_{n-1}} \sum_{v=1}^{n-1} \frac{R_{v-1}}{r_v} f_v\, \lambda_v\, t_v \right|^k
$$

$$\leq \sum_{n=2}^{m+1} n^{\delta k+k-1} \frac{q_n^k}{Q_n^k Q_{n-1}} \sum_{v=1}^{n-1} \frac{R_v^k F_v^k |\lambda_v|^k}{q_v^{k-1} r_v^k} \left(\frac{1}{Q_{n-1}} \sum_{v=1}^{n-1} q_v \right)^{k-1}$$

$$= O(1) \sum_{v=1}^{m} \frac{R_v^k F_v^k |\lambda_v|^k |t_v|^k}{q_v^{k-1} r_v^k} \sum_{n=v+1}^{m+1} \frac{n^{\delta k+k-1} q_n^k}{Q_n^k Q_{n-1}}$$

$$= O(1) \sum_{v=1}^{m} v^{k-1} |t_v|^k \left(\frac{R_v F_v |\lambda_v|}{r_v Q_v} \right)^k$$

$$= O(1) \sum_{v=1}^{m} v^{k-1} |t_v|^k \text{ , using (6.33)}$$

$$= O(1), \textit{ as } m \to \infty.$$

$$\sum_{n=2}^{m+1} n^{\delta k+k-1} |T_{n,3}|^k = \sum_{n=2}^{m+1} n^{\delta k+k-1} \left| \frac{q_n}{Q_n Q_{n-1}} \sum_{v=1}^{n-1} \frac{R_{v-1}}{r_v} (\Delta \lambda_v) F_{v+1} t_v \right|^k$$

$$\leq \sum_{n=2}^{m+1} n^{\delta k+k-1} \frac{q_n^k}{Q_n^k Q_{n-1}} \sum_{v=1}^{n-1} \frac{R_{v-1}^k}{r_v^k q_v^{k-1}} |\Delta \lambda_v|^k \; F_{v+1}^k \; |t_v|^k \left(\frac{1}{Q_{n-1}} \sum_{v=1}^{n-1} q_v \right)^{k-1}$$

$$= O(1) \sum_{v=1}^{m} \frac{R_{v-1}^k |\Delta \lambda_r|^k}{r_v^k q_v^{k-1}} F_{v+1}^k \; |t_v|^k \sum_{n=v+1}^{m+1} \frac{n^{\delta k+k-1} q_n^k}{Q_n^k Q_{n-1}}, \text{ by (6.30)}$$

$$= O(1) \sum_{v=1}^{m} v^{k-1} |t_v|^k \left(\frac{R_{v-1} F_{v+1} |\Delta \lambda_v|}{r_v Q_v} \right)^k$$

$$= O(1) \sum_{v=1}^{m} v^{k-1} |t_v|^k \text{ , using (6.35)}$$

$$= O(1), \textit{ as } m \to \infty.$$

$$\sum_{n=2}^{m+1} n^{\delta k+k-1} |T_{n,4}|^k = \sum_{n=2}^{m+1} n^{\delta k+k-1} \left| \frac{q_n}{Q_n Q_{n-1}} \frac{R_n \lambda_n f_n t_n}{r_n} \right|^k$$

$$\leq \sum_{n=2}^{m+1} n^{k-1} |t_n|^k \left(\frac{q_n R_n F_n |\lambda_n|}{Q_n Q_{n-1} r_n} \right)^k$$

$$= O(1) \sum_{n=2}^{m+1} n^{k-1} |t_n|^k, \text{ using (6.34)}$$

$$= O(1), \textit{ as } m \to \infty.$$

$$\sum_{n=2}^{m+1} n^{\delta k+k-1} |T_{n,5}|^k = \sum_{n=2}^{m+1} n^{\delta k+k-1} \left| \frac{p_0 q_0}{P_n Q_{n-1}} \sum_{v=1}^{n-1} \lambda_v t_v \right|^k$$

$$\leq O(1) \sum_{n=2}^{m+1} n^{\delta k+k-1} \frac{1}{P_n^k Q_{n-1}} \sum_{v=1}^{n-1} \frac{|\lambda_v|^k}{q_v^{k-1}} |t_v|^k \left(\frac{1}{Q_{n-1}} \sum_{v=1}^{n-1} q_v \right)^{k-1}$$

$$
\begin{aligned}
&= O(1)\sum_{v=1}^{m}\frac{|\lambda_v|^k|t_v|^k}{q_v^{k-1}}\sum_{n=v+1}^{m+1} n^{\delta k+k-1}\cdot\frac{1}{P_n^k Q_{n-1}}\\
&= O(1)\sum_{v=1}^{m}\frac{|\lambda_v|^k|t_v|^k}{q_v^{k-1}}\sum_{n=v+1}^{m+1}\frac{n^{k-1}q_n^k}{Q_n^k Q_{n-1}},\ \text{using (6.29)}\\
&= O(1)\sum_{v=1}^{m} v^k\,|t_v|^k\left(\frac{|\lambda_n|^k}{Q_v}\right)^k\\
&= O(1)\sum_{v=1}^{m} v^k\,|t_v|^k,\ \text{using (6.34)}\\
&= O(1),\ as\ m\to\infty.
\end{aligned}
$$

$$
\begin{aligned}
\sum_{n=2}^{m+1} n^{\delta k+k-1}\left|T_{n,6}\right|^k &= \sum_{n=2}^{m+1} n^{\delta k+k-1}\left|\frac{p_0q_0}{P_nQ_{n-1}}\sum_{v=1}^{n-1}\frac{R_{v-1}}{r_v}(\Delta\lambda_v)\,t_v\right|^k\\
&\le O(1)\sum_{n=2}^{m+1} n^{\delta k+k-1}\cdot\frac{1}{P_n^kQ_{n-1}}\sum_{v=1}^{n-1}\frac{R_{v-1}^k}{r_v^kq_v^{k-1}}|\Delta\lambda_v|^k\,|t_v|^k\left(\frac{1}{Q_{n-1}}\sum_{v=1}^{n-1}q_v\right)^{n-1}\\
&= O(1)\sum_{v=1}^{m}\frac{R_{v-1}^k|\Delta\lambda_v|^k|t_v|^k}{r_v^kq_v^{k-1}}\sum_{n=v+1}^{m+1} n^{\delta k+k-1}\cdot\frac{1}{P_n^kQ_{n-1}}\\
&= O(1)\sum_{v=1}^{m} v^{k-1}|t_v|^k\left(\frac{R_{v-1}|\Delta\lambda_v|}{r_vQ_v}\right)^k\\
&= O(1)\sum_{v=1}^{m} v^{k-1}|t_v|^k,\ \text{using (6.36)}\\
&= O(1),\ as\ m\to\infty.
\end{aligned}
$$

Finally,

$$
\begin{aligned}
\sum_{n=2}^{m+1} n^{\delta k+k-1}|T_{n,7}|^k &= \sum_{n=2}^{m+1} n^{\delta k+k-1}\left|\frac{p_0q_0}{P_nQ_{n-1}}\frac{R_n\lambda_nt_n}{r_n}\right|^k\\
&= O(1)\sum_{n=2}^{m+1} n^{k-1}|t_n|^k\left(\frac{R_n|\lambda_n|}{P_nQ_{n-1}r_n}\right)^k\\
&= O(1)\sum_{n=2}^{m+1} n^{k-1}|t_n|^k\left(\frac{q_nR_n|\lambda_n|}{Q_nQ_{n-1}r_n}\right)^k\\
&= O(1)\sum_{n=2}^{m+1} n^{k-1}|t_n|^k,\ \text{using (6.37)}\\
&= O(1),\ as\ m\to\infty.
\end{aligned}
$$

This completes the Proof of Theorem 6.3.

Proof of Theorem 6.4. In order to prove this theorem, using (6.76) and Minkowski's inequality, it is sufficient to show that

$$\sum_{n=1}^{\infty} \alpha_n^{k-1} |T_{n,i}|^k < \infty, \text{ for } i = 1,2,3,4,5,6,7.$$

Now, on applying Holder's inequality, we have

$$\begin{aligned}
\sum_{n=2}^{m+1} \alpha_n^{k-1} |T_{n,1}|^k &= \sum_{n=2}^{m+1} \alpha_n^{k-1} \left| \frac{q_n}{Q_n Q_{n-1}} \sum_{v=1}^{n-1} \lambda_v F_v t_v \right|^k \\
&\le \sum_{n=2}^{m+1} \alpha_n^{k-1} \frac{q_n^k}{Q_n^k Q_{n-1}} \sum_{v=1}^{n-1} \frac{|\lambda_v|^k F_v^k |t_v|^k}{q_v^{k-1}} \left(\frac{1}{Q_{n-1}} \sum_{v=1}^{n-1} q_v \right)^{k-1} \\
&= O(1) \sum_{v=1}^{m} \frac{1}{q_v^{k-1}} |\lambda_v|^k F_v^k |t_v|^k \sum_{n=v+1}^{m+1} \frac{\alpha_n^{k-1} q_n^k}{Q_n^k Q_{n-1}} \\
&= O(1) \sum_{v=1}^{m} \frac{1}{q_v^{k-1}} |\lambda_v|^k F_v^k |t_v|^k \frac{(v q_v)^{k-1}}{Q_v^k}, \text{ using (6.40)} \\
&= O(1) \sum_{v=1}^{m} v^{k-1} |t_v|^k \left(\frac{|\lambda_v| F_v}{Q_v} \right)^k \\
&= O(1) \sum_{v=1}^{m} v^{k-1} |t_v|^k, \text{ using (6.41)} \\
&= O(1), \textit{ as } m \to \infty.
\end{aligned}$$

Next,

$$\begin{aligned}
\sum_{n=2}^{m+1} \alpha_n^{k-1} |T_{n2}|^k &= \sum_{n=2}^{m+1} \alpha_n^{k-1} \left| \frac{q_n}{Q_n Q_{n-1}} \sum_{v=1}^{n-1} \frac{R_{v-1}}{r_v} f_v \lambda_v t_v \right|^k \\
&\le \sum_{n=2}^{m+1} \alpha_n^{k-1} \frac{q_n^k}{Q_n^k Q_{n-1}} \sum_{v=1}^{n-1} \frac{R_v^k F_v^k |\lambda_v|^k}{q_v^{k-1} r_v^k} \left(\frac{1}{Q_{n-1}} \sum_{v=1}^{n-1} q_v \right)^{k-1} \\
&= O(1) \sum_{v=1}^{m} \frac{R_v^k F_v^k |\lambda_v|^k |t_v|^k}{q_v^{k-1} r_v^k} \sum_{n=v+1}^{m+1} \frac{\alpha_n^{k-1} q_n^k}{Q_n^k Q_{n-1}} \\
&= O(1) \sum_{v=1}^{m} v^{k-1} |t_v|^k \left(\frac{R_v F_v |\lambda_v|}{r_v Q_v} \right)^k \\
&= O(1) \sum_{v=1}^{m} v^{k-1} |t_v|^k, \text{ using (6.43)} \\
&= O(1), \textit{ as } m \to \infty.
\end{aligned}$$

Further,

$$\begin{aligned}
\sum_{n=2}^{m+1} \alpha_n^{k-1} |T_{n,3}|^k &= \sum_{n=2}^{m+1} \alpha_n^{k-1} \left| \frac{q_n}{Q_n Q_{n-1}} \sum_{v=1}^{n-1} \frac{R_{v-1}}{r_v} (\Delta\lambda_v) F_{v+1} t_v \right|^k \\
&\leq \sum_{n=2}^{m+1} \alpha_n^{k-1} \frac{q_n^k}{Q_n^k Q_{n-1}} \sum_{v=1}^{n-1} \frac{R_{v-1}^k}{r_v^k q_v^{k-1}} |\Delta\lambda_v|^k \; F_{v+1}^k \; |t_v|^k \left(\frac{1}{Q_{n-1}} \sum_{v=1}^{n-1} q_v \right)^{k-1} \\
&= O(1) \sum_{v=1}^{m} \frac{R_{v-1}^k |\Delta\lambda_r|^k}{r_v^k q_v^{k-1}} F_{v+1}^k \; |t_v|^k \sum_{n=v+1}^{m+1} \frac{\alpha_n^{k-1} q_n^k}{Q_n^k Q_{n-1}} \\
&= O(1) \sum_{v=1}^{m} v^{k-1} |t_v|^k \left(\frac{R_{v-1} F_{v+1} |\Delta\lambda_v|}{r_v Q_v} \right)^k, \text{ by (6.40)} \\
&= O(1) \sum_{v=1}^{m} v^{k-1} |t_v|^k, \text{ using (6.45)} \\
&= O(1), \; as \; m \to \infty.
\end{aligned}$$

Again,

$$\begin{aligned}
\sum_{n=2}^{m+1} \alpha_n^{k-1} |T_{n,4}|^k &= \sum_{n=2}^{m+1} \alpha_n^{k-1} \left| \frac{q_n}{Q_n Q_{n-1}} \frac{R_n \lambda_n f_n t_n}{r_n} \right|^k \\
&\leq \sum_{n=2}^{m+1} \alpha_n^{k-1} |t_n|^k \left(\frac{q_n R_n F_n |\lambda_n|}{Q_n Q_{n-1} r_n} \right)^k \\
&= O(1) \sum_{n=2}^{m+1} \alpha_n^{k-1} |t_n|^k, \text{ using (6.44)} \\
&= O(1), \; as \; m \to \infty.
\end{aligned}$$

Next,

$$\begin{aligned}
\sum_{n=2}^{m+1} \alpha_n^{k-1} |T_{n,5}|^k &= \sum_{n=2}^{m+1} \alpha_n^{k-1} \left| \frac{p_0 q_0}{P_n Q_{n-1}} \sum_{v=1}^{n-1} \lambda_v \, t_v \right|^k \\
&\leq O(1) \sum_{n=2}^{m+1} \alpha_n^{k-1} \frac{1}{P_n^k Q_{n-1}} \sum_{v=1}^{n-1} \frac{|\lambda_v|^k}{q_v^{k-1}} |t_v|^k \left(\frac{1}{Q_{n-1}} \sum_{v=1}^{n-1} q_v \right)^{k-1} \\
&= O(1) \sum_{v=1}^{m} \frac{|\lambda_v|^k |t_v|^k}{q_v^{k-1}} \sum_{n=v+1}^{m+1} \alpha_n^{k-1} \cdot \frac{1}{P_n^k Q_{n-1}} \\
&= O(1) \sum_{v=1}^{m} \frac{|\lambda_v|^k |t_v|^k}{q_v^{k-1}} \sum_{n=v+1}^{m+1} \frac{\alpha_n^{k-1} q_n^k}{Q_n^k Q_{n-1}}, \text{ using (6.39)} \\
&= O(1) \sum_{v=1}^{m} v^k \; |t_v|^k \left(\frac{|\lambda_n|^k}{Q_v} \right)^k
\end{aligned}$$

$$= O(1)\sum_{v=1}^{m} v^k \left|t_v\right|^k, \text{ using } (6.44)$$
$$= O(1),\ as\ m \to \infty.$$

Again,

$$\sum_{n=2}^{m+1} \alpha_n^{k-1}\left|T_{n,6}\right|^k = \sum_{n=2}^{m+1} \alpha_n^{k-1}\left|\frac{p_0 q_0}{P_n Q_{n-1}}\sum_{v=1}^{n-1}\frac{R_{v-1}}{r_v}(\Delta\lambda_v)\, t_v\right|^k$$
$$\leq O(1)\sum_{n=2}^{m+1}\alpha_n^{k-1}\frac{1}{P_n^k Q_{n-1}}\sum_{v=1}^{n-1}\frac{R_{v-1}^k}{r_v^k q_v^{k-1}}\left|\Delta\lambda_v\right|^k\left|t_v\right|^k\left(\frac{1}{Q_{n-1}}\sum_{v=1}^{n-1} q_v\right)^{n-1}$$
$$= O(1)\sum_{v=1}^{m}\frac{R_{v-1}^k\left|\Delta\lambda_v\right|^k\left|t_v\right|^k}{r_v^k q_v^{k-1}}\sum_{n=v+1}^{m+1}\alpha_n^{k-1}\frac{1}{P_n^k Q_{n-1}}$$
$$= O(1)\sum_{v=1}^{m} v^{k-1}\left|t_v\right|^k\left(\frac{R_{v-1}\left|\Delta\lambda_v\right|}{r_v Q_v}\right)^k$$
$$= O(1)\sum_{v=1}^{m} v^{k-1}\left|t_v\right|^k, \text{ using } (6.46)$$
$$= O(1),\ as\ m \to \infty.$$

Finally,

$$\sum_{n=2}^{m+1}\alpha_n^{k-1}\left|T_{n,7}\right|^k = \sum_{n=2}^{m+1}\alpha_n^{k-1}\left|\frac{p_0 q_0}{P_n Q_{n-1}}\frac{R_n\lambda_n t_n}{r_n}\right|^k$$
$$= O(1)\sum_{n=2}^{m+1}\alpha_n^{k-1}\left|t_n\right|^k\left(\frac{R_n\left|\lambda_n\right|}{P_n Q_{n-1} r_n}\right)^k$$
$$= O(1)\sum_{n=2}^{m+1}\alpha_n^{k-1}\left|t_n\right|^k\left(\frac{q_n R_n\left|\lambda_n\right|}{Q_n Q_{n-1} r_n}\right)^k$$
$$= O(1)\sum_{n=2}^{m+1}\alpha_n^{k-1}\left|t_n\right|^k, \text{ using } (6.47)$$
$$= O(1),\ as\ m \to \infty.$$

This completes the Proof of Theorem 6.4.

Proof of Theorem 6.5. In order to prove this theorem, using (6.76) and Minkowski's inequality, it is sufficient to show that

$$\sum_{n=1}^{\infty}\alpha_n^{\delta k+k-1}\left|T_{n,i}\right|^k < \infty, \text{for } i = 1,2,3,4,5,6,7.$$

On applying Holder's inequality, we have

$$\begin{aligned}
\sum_{n=2}^{m+1} \alpha_n^{\delta k+k-1} |T_{n,1}|^k &= \sum_{n=2}^{m+1} \alpha_n^{\delta k+k-1} \left| \frac{q_n}{Q_n Q_{n-1}} \sum_{v=1}^{n-1} \lambda_v F_v t_v \right|^k \\
&\leq \sum_{n=2}^{m+1} \alpha_n^{\delta k+k-1} \frac{q_n^k}{Q_n^k Q_{n-1}} \sum_{v=1}^{n-1} \frac{|\lambda_v|^k F_v^k |t_v|^k}{q_v^{k-1}} \left(\frac{1}{Q_{n-1}} \sum_{v=1}^{n-1} q_v \right)^{k-1} \\
&= O(1) \sum_{v=1}^{m} \frac{1}{q_v^{k-1}} |\lambda_v|^k F_v^k |t_v|^k \sum_{n=v+1}^{m+1} \frac{\alpha_n^{\delta k+k-1} q_n^k}{Q_n^k Q_{n-1}} \\
&= O(1) \sum_{v-1}^{m} \frac{1}{q_v^{k-1}} |\lambda_v|^k F_v^k |t_v|^k \frac{(vq_v)^{k-1}}{Q_v^k}, \text{ using } (6.51) \\
&= O(1) \sum_{v=1}^{m} v^{k-1} |t_v|^k \left(\frac{|\lambda_v| F_v}{Q_v} \right)^k \\
&= O(1) \sum_{v=1}^{m} v^{k-1} |t_v|^k, \text{ using } (6.53) \\
&= O(1),\ as\, m \to \infty.
\end{aligned}$$

Next,

$$\begin{aligned}
\sum_{n=2}^{m+1} \alpha_n^{\delta k+k-1} |T_{n,2}|^k &= \sum_{n=2}^{m+1} \alpha_n^{\delta k+k-1} \left| \frac{q_n}{Q_n Q_{n-1}} \sum_{v=1}^{n-1} \frac{R_{v-1}}{r_v} f_v \lambda_v t_v \right|^k \\
&\leq \sum_{n=2}^{m+1} \alpha_n^{\delta k+k-1} \frac{q_n^k}{Q_n^k Q_{n-1}} \sum_{v=1}^{n-1} \frac{R_v^k F_v^k |\lambda_v|^k}{q_v^{k-1} r_v^k} \left(\frac{1}{Q_{n-1}} \sum_{v=1}^{n-1} q_v \right)^{k-1} \\
&= O(1) \sum_{v=1}^{m} \frac{R_v^k F_v^k |\lambda_v|^k |t_v|^k}{q_v^{k-1} r_v^k} \sum_{n=v+1}^{m+1} \frac{\alpha_n^{\delta k+k-1} q_n^k}{Q_n^k Q_{n-1}} \\
&= O(1) \sum_{v=1}^{m} v^{k-1} |t_v|^k \left(\frac{R_v F_v |\lambda_v|}{r_v Q_v} \right)^k \\
&= O(1) \sum_{v=1}^{m} v^{k-1} |t_v|^k, \text{ using } (6.55) \\
&= O(1),\ as\, m \to \infty.
\end{aligned}$$

Further,

$$\begin{aligned}
\sum_{n=2}^{m+1} \alpha_n{}^{\delta k+k-1} |T_{n,3}|^k &= \sum_{n=2}^{m+1} \alpha_n^{\delta k+k-1} \left| \frac{q_n}{Q_n Q_{n-1}} \sum_{v=1}^{n-1} \frac{R_{v-1}}{r_v} (\Delta \lambda_v) F_{v+1} t_v \right|^k \\
&\leq \sum_{n=2}^{m+1} \alpha_n^{\delta k+k-1} \frac{q_n^k}{Q_n^k Q_{n-1}} \sum_{v=1}^{n-1} \frac{R_{v-1}^k}{r_v^k q_v^{k-1}} |\Delta \lambda_v|^k F_{v+1}^k |t_v|^k \left(\frac{1}{Q_{n-1}} \sum_{v=1}^{n-1} q_v \right)^{k-1}
\end{aligned}$$

$$
\begin{aligned}
&= O(1)\sum_{v=1}^{m}\frac{R_{v-1}^{k}\left|\Delta\lambda_{r}\right|^{k}}{r_{v}^{k}q_{v}^{k-1}}F_{v+1}^{k}\left|t_{v}\right|^{k}\sum_{n=v+1}^{m+1}\frac{\alpha_{n}^{\delta k+k-1}q_{n}^{k}}{Q_{n}^{k}Q_{n-1}}, \text{ by (6.52)}\\
&= O(1)\sum_{v=1}^{m}v^{k-1}\left|t_{v}\right|^{k}\left(\frac{R_{v-1}F_{v+1}\left|\Delta\lambda_{v}\right|}{r_{v}Q_{v}}\right)^{k}\\
&= O(1)\sum_{v=1}^{m}v^{k-1}\left|t_{v}\right|^{k}, \text{ using (6.56)}\\
&= O(1),\ as\ m\to\infty.
\end{aligned}
$$

Again,

$$
\begin{aligned}
\sum_{n=2}^{m+1}\alpha_{n}^{\delta k+k-1}\left|T_{n,4}\right|^{k} &= \sum_{n=2}^{m+1}\alpha_{n}^{\delta k+k-1}\left|\frac{q_{n}}{Q_{n}Q_{n-1}}\frac{R_{n}\lambda_{n}f_{n}t_{n}}{r_{n}}\right|^{k}\\
&\leq \sum_{n=2}^{m+1}\alpha_{n}^{\delta k+k-1}\left|t_{n}\right|^{k}\left(\frac{q_{n}R_{n}F_{n}\left|\lambda_{n}\right|}{Q_{n}Q_{n-1}r_{n}}\right)^{k}\\
&= \sum_{n=2}^{m+1}\alpha_{n}^{k-1}\left|t_{n}\right|^{k}\left(\frac{q_{n}R_{n}F_{n}\left|\lambda_{n}\right|\alpha_{n}^{\delta}}{Q_{n}Q_{n-1}r_{n}}\right)^{k}\\
&= O(1)\sum_{n=2}^{m+1}\alpha_{n}^{k-1}\left|t_{n}\right|^{k}, \text{ using (6.56)}\\
&= O(1),\ as\ m\to\infty.
\end{aligned}
$$

Next,

$$
\begin{aligned}
\sum_{n=2}^{m+1}\alpha_{n}^{\delta k+k-1}\left|T_{n,5}\right|^{k} &= \sum_{n=2}^{m+1}\alpha_{n}^{\delta k+k-1}\left|\frac{p_{0}q_{0}}{P_{n}Q_{n-1}}\sum_{v=1}^{n-1}\lambda_{v}\,t_{v}\right|^{k}\\
&\leq O(1)\sum_{n=2}^{m+1}\alpha_{n}^{\delta k+k-1}\frac{1}{P_{n}^{k}Q_{n-1}}\sum_{v=1}^{n-1}\frac{\left|\lambda_{v}\right|^{k}}{q_{v}^{k-1}}\left|t_{v}\right|^{k}\left(\frac{1}{Q_{n-1}}\sum_{v=1}^{n-1}q_{v}\right)^{k-1}\\
&= O(1)\sum_{v=1}^{m}\frac{\left|\lambda_{v}\right|^{k}\left|t_{v}\right|^{k}}{q_{v}^{k-1}}\sum_{n=v+1}^{m+1}\alpha_{n}^{\delta k+k-1}\frac{1}{P_{n}^{k}Q_{n-1}}\\
&= O(1)\sum_{v=1}^{m}\frac{\left|\lambda_{v}\right|^{k}\left|t_{v}\right|^{k}}{q_{v}^{k-1}}\sum_{n=v+1}^{m+1}\frac{\alpha_{n}^{\delta k+k-1}q_{n}^{k}}{Q_{n}^{k}Q_{n-1}}, \text{ using (6.51)}\\
&= O(1)\sum_{v=1}^{m}v^{k}\left|t_{v}\right|^{k}\left(\frac{\left|\lambda_{n}\right|^{k}}{Q_{v}}\right)^{k}\\
&= O(1)\sum_{v=1}^{m}v^{k}\left|t_{v}\right|^{k}, \text{ using (6.55)}\\
&= O(1),\ \ as\ m\to\infty.
\end{aligned}
$$

Again,

$$\begin{aligned}
\sum_{n=2}^{m+1} \alpha_n{}^{\delta k+k-1} \left|T_{n,6}\right|^k &= \sum_{n=2}^{m+1} \alpha_n^{\delta k+k-1} \left| \frac{p_0 q_0}{P_n Q_{n-1}} \sum_{v=1}^{n-1} \frac{R_{v-1}}{r_v} (\Delta\lambda_v)\, t_v \right|^k \\
&\leq O(1) \sum_{n=2}^{m+1} \alpha_n^{\delta k+k-1} \frac{1}{P_n^k Q_{n-1}} \sum_{v=1}^{n-1} \frac{R_{v-1}^k}{r_v^k q_v^{k-1}} \left|\Delta\lambda_v\right|^k \left|t_v\right|^k \left(\frac{1}{Q_{n-1}} \sum_{v=1}^{n-1} q_v \right)^{n-1} \\
&= O(1) \sum_{v=1}^{m} \frac{R_{v-1}^k \left|\Delta\lambda_v\right|^k \left|t_v\right|^k}{r_v^k q_v^{k-1}} \sum_{n=v+1}^{m+1} \alpha_n^{\delta k+k-1} \frac{1}{P_n^k Q_{n-1}} \\
&= O(1) \sum_{v=1}^{m} v^{k-1} \left|t_v\right|^k \left(\frac{R_{v-1} \left|\Delta\lambda_v\right|}{r_v Q_v} \right)^k \\
&= O(1) \sum_{v=1}^{m} v^{k-1} \left|t_v\right|^k, \text{ using } (6.58) \\
&= O(1), \; as\; m \to \infty.
\end{aligned}$$

Finally,

$$\begin{aligned}
\sum_{n=2}^{m+1} \alpha_n^{\delta k+k-1} \left|T_{n,7}\right|^k &= \sum_{n=2}^{m+1} \alpha_n^{\delta k+k-1} \left| \frac{p_0 q_0}{P_n Q_{n-1}} \frac{R_n \lambda_n t_n}{r_n} \right|^k \\
&= O(1) \sum_{n=2}^{m+1} \alpha_n^{\delta k+k-1} \left|t_n\right|^k \left(\frac{R_n \left|\lambda_n\right|}{P_n Q_{n-1} r_n} \right)^k \\
&= O(1) \sum_{n=2}^{m+1} \alpha_n^{\delta k+k-1} \left|t_n\right|^k \left(\frac{q_n R_n \left|\lambda_n\right|}{Q_n Q_{n-1} r_n} \right)^k \\
&= O(1) \sum_{n=2}^{m+1} \alpha_n^{k-1} \left|t_n\right|^k \left(\frac{q_n R_n \left|\lambda_n\right| \alpha_n^{\delta}}{Q_n Q_{n-1} r_n} \right)^k \\
&= O(1) \sum_{n=2}^{m+1} \alpha_n^{k-1} \left|t_n\right|^k, \text{ using } (6.59) \\
&= O(1), \;\; as\; m \to \infty.
\end{aligned}$$

This completes the Proof of the Theorem 6.5.

Proof of Theorem 6.6. In order to prove this theorem, using (6.76) and Minkowski's inequality, it is sufficient to show that

$$\sum_{n=1}^{\infty} \{f(\alpha_n)\}^k (\alpha_n)^{k-1} \left|T_{n,i}\right|^k < \infty, \text{ for } i = 1,2,3,4,5,6,7.$$

Now, on applying Holder's inequality, we have

$$\begin{aligned}
&\sum_{n=2}^{m+1} \{f(\alpha_n)\}^k (\alpha_n)^{k-1} |T_{n,1}|^k \\
&= \sum_{n=2}^{m+1} \{f(\alpha_n)\}^k (\alpha_n)^{k-1} \left| \frac{q_n}{Q_n Q_{n-1}} \sum_{v=1}^{n-1} \lambda_v F_v t_v \right|^k \\
&\leq \sum_{n=2}^{m+1} \{f(\alpha_n)\}^k (\alpha_n)^{k-1} \frac{q_n^k}{Q_n^k Q_{n-1}} \sum_{v=1}^{n-1} \frac{|\lambda_v|^k F_v^k |t_v|^k}{q_v^{k-1}} \left(\frac{1}{Q_{n-1}} \sum_{v=1}^{n-1} q_v \right)^{k-1} \\
&= O(1) \sum_{v=1}^{m} \frac{1}{q_v^{k-1}} |\lambda_v|^k F_v^k |t_v|^k \sum_{n=v+1}^{m+1} \frac{\{f(\alpha_n)\}^k (\alpha_n)^{k-1} q_n^k}{Q_n^k Q_{n-1}} \\
&= O(1) \sum_{v-1}^{m} \frac{1}{q_v^{k-1}} |\lambda_v|^k F_v^k |t_v|^k \frac{(v q_v)^{k-1}}{Q_v^k}, \text{ using } (6.64) \\
&= O(1) \sum_{v=1}^{m} v^{k-1} |t_v|^k \left(\frac{|\lambda_v| F_v}{Q_v} \right)^k \\
&= O(1) \sum_{v=1}^{m} v^{k-1} |t_v|^k, \text{ using } (6.65) \\
&= O(1), \textit{ as } m \to \infty.
\end{aligned}$$

Next,

$$\begin{aligned}
&\sum_{n=2}^{m+1} \{f(\alpha_n)\}^k (\alpha_n)^{k-1} |T_{n,2}|^k \\
&= \sum_{n=2}^{m+1} \{f(\alpha_n)\}^k (\alpha_n)^{k-1} \left| \frac{q_n}{Q_n Q_{n-1}} \sum_{v=1}^{n-1} \frac{R_{v-1}}{r_v} f_v \lambda_v t_v \right|^k \\
&\leq \sum_{n=2}^{m+1} \{f(\alpha_n)\}^k (\alpha_n)^{k-1} \frac{q_n^k}{Q_n^k Q_{n-1}} \sum_{v=1}^{n-1} \frac{R_v^k F_v^k |\lambda_v|^k}{q_v^{k-1} r_v^k} \left(\frac{1}{Q_{n-1}} \sum_{v=1}^{n-1} q_v \right)^{k-1} \\
&= O(1) \sum_{v=1}^{m} \frac{R_v^k F_v^k |\lambda_v|^k |t_v|^k}{q_v^{k-1} r_v^k} \sum_{n=v+1}^{m+1} \frac{\{f(\alpha_n)\}^k (\alpha_n)^{k-1} q_n^k}{Q_n^k Q_{n-1}} \\
&= O(1) \sum_{v=1}^{m} v^{k-1} |t_v|^k \left(\frac{R_v F_v |\lambda_v|}{r_v Q_v} \right)^k \\
&= O(1) \sum_{v=1}^{m} v^{k-1} |t_v|^k, \text{ using } (6.67) \\
&= O(1), \textit{ as } m \to \infty.
\end{aligned}$$

Further,

$$\begin{aligned}
&\sum_{n=2}^{m+1}\{f(\alpha_n)\}^k(\alpha_n)^{k-1}\left|T_{n,3}\right|^k \\
&\quad=\sum_{n=2}^{m+1}\{f(\alpha_n)\}^k(\alpha_n)^{k-1}\left|\frac{q_n}{Q_nQ_{n-1}}\sum_{v=1}^{n-1}\frac{R_{v-1}}{r_v}(\Delta\lambda_v)F_{v+1}t_v\right|^k \\
&\quad\leq\sum_{n=2}^{m+1}\{f(\alpha_n)\}^k(\alpha_n)^{k-1}\frac{q_n^k}{Q_n^kQ_{n-1}}\sum_{v=1}^{n-1}\frac{R_{v-1}^k}{r_v^kq_v^{k-1}}\left|\Delta\lambda_v\right|^k F_{v+1}^k\left|t_v\right|^k\left(\frac{1}{Q_{n-1}}\sum_{v=1}^{n-1}q_v\right)^{k-1} \\
&\quad=O(1)\sum_{v=1}^{m}\frac{R_{v-1}^k\left|\Delta\lambda_r\right|^k}{r_v^kq_v^{k-1}}F_{v+1}^k\left|t_v\right|^k\sum_{n=v+1}^{m+1}\frac{\{f(\alpha_n)\}^k(\alpha_n)^{k-1}q_n^k}{Q_n^kQ_{n-1}},\ \text{by (6.64)} \\
&\quad=O(1)\sum_{v=1}^{m}v^{k-1}\left|t_v\right|^k\left(\frac{R_{v-1}F_{v+1}\left|\Delta\lambda_v\right|}{r_vQ_v}\right)^k \\
&\quad=O(1)\sum_{v=1}^{m}v^{k-1}\left|t_v\right|^k,\ \text{using (6.69)} \\
&\quad=O(1),\ \text{as } m\to\infty.
\end{aligned}$$

Again,

$$\begin{aligned}
&\sum_{n=2}^{m+1}\{f(\alpha_n)\}^k(\alpha_n)^{k-1}\left|T_{n,4}\right|^k \\
&\quad=\sum_{n=2}^{m+1}\{f(\alpha_n)\}^k(\alpha_n)^{k-1}\left|\frac{q_n}{Q_nQ_{n-1}}\frac{R_n\lambda_nf_nt_n}{r_n}\right|^k \\
&\quad\leq\sum_{n=2}^{m+1}\{f(\alpha_n)\}^k(\alpha_n)^{k-1}\left|t_n\right|^k\left(\frac{q_nR_nF_n\left|\lambda_n\right|}{Q_nQ_{n-1}r_n}\right)^k \\
&\quad=\sum_{n=2}^{m+1}\{f(\alpha_n)\}^k(\alpha_n)^{k-1}\left|t_n\right|^k\left(\frac{q_nR_nF_n\left|\lambda_n\right|}{Q_nQ_{n-1}r_n}\right)^k \\
&\quad=O(1)\sum_{n=2}^{m+1}\{f(\alpha_n)\}^k(\alpha_n)^{k-1}\left|t_n\right|^k,\ \text{using (6.68)} \\
&\quad=O(1),\ \text{as } m\to\infty.
\end{aligned}$$

Next,

$$\begin{aligned}
&\sum_{n=2}^{m+1}\{f(\alpha_n)\}^k(\alpha_n)^{k-1}\left|T_{n,5}\right|^k \\
&\quad=\sum_{n=2}^{m+1}\{f(\alpha_n)\}^k(\alpha_n)^{k-1}\left|\frac{p_0q_0}{P_nQ_{n-1}}\sum_{v=1}^{n-1}\lambda_v t_v\right|^k
\end{aligned}$$

$$\leq O(1)\sum_{n=2}^{m+1}\{f(\alpha_n)\}^k(\alpha_n)^{k-1}\frac{1}{P_n^kQ_{n-1}}\sum_{v=1}^{n-1}\frac{|\lambda_v|^k}{q_v^{k-1}}|t_v|^k\left(\frac{1}{Q_{n-1}}\sum_{v=1}^{n-1}q_v\right)^{k-1}$$

$$=O(1)\sum_{v=1}^{m}\frac{|\lambda_v|^k|t_v|^k}{q_v^{k-1}}\sum_{n=v+1}^{m+1}\frac{\{f(\alpha_n)\}^k(\alpha_n)^{k-1}}{P_n^kQ_{n-1}}$$

$$=O(1)\sum_{v=1}^{m}\frac{|\lambda_v|^k|t_v|^k}{q_v^{k-1}}\sum_{n=v+1}^{m+1}\frac{\{f(\alpha_n)\}^k(\alpha_n)^{k-1}q_n^k}{Q_n^kQ_{n-1}},\ \text{using (6.63)}$$

$$=O(1)\sum_{v=1}^{m}v^k\ |t_v|^k\left(\frac{|\lambda_n|^k}{Q_v}\right)^k$$

$$=O(1)\sum_{v=1}^{m}v^k\ |t_v|^k,\ \text{using (6.68)}$$

$$=O(1),\ as\ m\to\infty.$$

Again,

$$\sum_{n=2}^{m+1}\{f(\alpha_n)\}^k(\alpha_n)^{k-1}\left|T_{n,6}\right|^k$$

$$=\sum_{n=2}^{m+1}\{f(\alpha_n)\}^k(\alpha_n)^{k-1}\left|\frac{p_0q_0}{P_nQ_{n-1}}\sum_{v=1}^{n-1}\frac{R_{v-1}}{r_v}(\Delta\lambda_v)\ t_v\right|^k$$

$$\leq O(1)\sum_{n=2}^{m+1}\{f(\alpha_n)\}^k(\alpha_n)^{k-1}\frac{1}{P_n^kQ_{n-1}}\sum_{v=1}^{n-1}\frac{R_{v-1}^k}{r_v^kq_v^{k-1}}|\Delta\lambda_v|^k\ |t_v|^k\left(\frac{1}{Q_{n-1}}\sum_{v=1}^{n-1}q_v\right)^{n-1}$$

$$=O(1)\sum_{v=1}^{m}\frac{R_{v-1}^k|\Delta\lambda_v|^k|t_v|^k}{r_v^kq_v^{k-1}}\sum_{n=v+1}^{m+1}\frac{\{f(\alpha_n)\}^k(\alpha_n)^{k-1}}{P_n^kQ_{n-1}}$$

$$=O(1)\sum_{v=1}^{m}v^{k-1}|t_v|^k\left(\frac{R_{v-1}|\Delta\lambda_v|}{r_vQ_v}\right)^k$$

$$=O(1)\sum_{v=1}^{m}v^{k-1}|t_v|^k,\ \text{using (6.70)}$$

$$=O(1),\ as\ m\to\infty.$$

Finally,

$$\sum_{n=2}^{m+1}\{f(\alpha_n)\}^k(\alpha_n)^{k-1}|T_{n,7}|^k$$

$$=\sum_{n=2}^{m+1}\{f(\alpha_n)\}^k(\alpha_n)^{k-1}\left|\frac{p_0q_0}{P_nQ_{n-1}}\frac{R_n\lambda_nt_n}{r_n}\right|^k$$

$$=O(1)\sum_{n=2}^{m+1}\{f(\alpha_n)\}^k(\alpha_n)^{k-1}|t_n|^k\left(\frac{R_n|\lambda_n|}{P_nQ_{n-1}r_n}\right)^k$$

$$= O(1)\sum_{n=2}^{m+1}\{f(\alpha_n)\}^k(\alpha_n)^{k-1}|t_n|^k\left(\frac{q_nR_n|\lambda_n|}{Q_nQ_{n-1}r_n}\right)^k$$
$$= O(1)\sum_{n=2}^{m+1}\{f(\alpha_n)\}^k(\alpha_n)^{k-1}|t_n|^k\left(\frac{q_nR_n|\lambda_n|}{Q_nQ_{n-1}r_n}\right)^k$$
$$= O(1)\sum_{n=2}^{m+1}\{f(\alpha_n)\}^k(\alpha_n)^{k-1}|t_n|^k, \text{ using } (6.71)$$
$$= O(1),\ as\ m \to \infty.$$

This completes the Proof of the Theorem 6.6.

6.5 CONCLUSION

From the above results and discussions, we are in a conclusion that our results are more generalized and in particular, these generalize the results of Sulaiman [9], Paikray et al. [5], and Das [2]. We have also observed that the sufficient conditions for $\sum a_n\lambda_n$ using the absolute indexed product summability $|(N,q_n)(N,p_n),\alpha_n;\delta|_k$ with $k \geq 1, 1 \geq k\delta \geq 0$ and $|(N,q_n)\ (N,p_n),\ \alpha_n;f|_k,\ k \geq 1$ generalize the sufficient conditions for $\sum a_n\lambda_n$ using the absolute indexed product summability $|(N,q_n)\ (N,p_n),\ \alpha_n|_k,\ k \geq 1$. Similarly, the sufficient conditions for $\sum a_n\lambda_n$ using the absolute indexed product summabilities $|(N,q_n)\ (N,p_n);\delta|_k$, $k \geq 1, 1 \geq k\delta \geq 0$, and $|(N,q_n)\ (N,p_n),\alpha_n|_k,\ k \geq 1$ generalize the sufficient conditions for $\sum a_n\lambda_n$ using the absolute indexed product summability $|(N,q_n)(N,p_n)|_k$.

As a future scope of this work, one may approach in the similar way to find the sufficient conditions for

- $\sum a_n\lambda_n$ is summable $|(N,q_n)(N,p_n),\alpha_n,\delta,\mu|_k$ if $\sum a_n$ is $|R,r_n|_k$-summable, where μ is a real number.
- $\sum a_n\lambda_n$ is summable $|(R,q_n)(R,p_n),\delta|_k, |(R,q_n)(R,p_n),\alpha_n|_k, |(R,q_n)(R,p_n),\alpha_n;\delta|_k$ and $|(R,q_n)(R,p_n),\alpha_n,f|_k$ if $\sum a_n$ is $|R,r_n|_k$-summable.
- $\sum a_n\lambda_n$ is summable $|(R,q_n)(C,1),\delta|_k, |(C,1)(R,p_n),\delta|_k, |(R,q_n)(C,1),\alpha_n|_k, |(C,1)(R,p_n),\alpha_n|_k, |(C,1)(R,p_n),\alpha_n;\delta|_k, |(R,q_n)(C,1),\alpha_n;\delta|_k$ if $\sum a_n$ is $|C,1|_k$-summable.

REFERENCES

[1] Aasma, A., Dutta, H. and Natarajan, P. N., *An Introductory Course in Summability Theory,* First Edition, John Wiley & Sons, Inc., USA, (2017).

[2] Das, G., Tauberian theorems for absolute Norlund summability, *Proceedings of the London Mathematical Society,* Vol. 19(2), (1969), 357–384.

[3] Dutta, H. and Rhoades, B.E. (Eds.), *Current Topics in Summability Theory and Applications,* First Edition, Springer, Singapore, (2016).

[4] Padhy, B.P., Misra, U.K. and Misra, M., *Summability Methods and its Applications,* Lap Lambart Academic Publications, Germany, (2012).

[5] Paikray, S.K., Misra, U.K. and Sahoo, N.C., Product Summability of an Infinite Series, *International Journal of Computer and Mathematical Sciences,* Vol-1(7), (2010), 853–863.

[6] Parameswaran, M.R., Some product theorems in summability, *Mathematische Zeitscher,* Vol. 68, (1957), 19–26.

[7] Rajgopal, C.T., Theorems on product of two summability methods, The *Journal of Indian Mathematical Society,* Vol. 18(1), (1954) .

[8] Ramanujan, M.S., On products of summability methods, *Mathematische Zeitscher,* Vol. 69(1), (1958), 423–428.

[9] Sulaiman, W.T., A Note on product summability of an infinite series, *International Journal of Mathematical Sciences,* Hindawi publishing corporation, (2008), Article ID 372604.

[10] Szasz, O., On products of summability methods, *Proceedings of American Mathematical Society,* Vol. 3(2), (1952).

7 On Some Important Inequalities

Zlatko Pavić
University of Osijek

CONTENTS

7.1 CONCEPTS OF AFFINITY AND CONVEXITY

7.1.1 AFFINE AND CONVEX SETS AND FUNCTIONS

Throughout this chapter, we will use a vector space $\mathbb{X}$ over the field of real numbers $\mathbb{R}$. We think about a binomial linear combination of points $x_1, x_2 \in \mathbb{X}$ and coefficients $\lambda_1, \lambda_2 \in \mathbb{R}$ as the sum

$$\lambda_1 x_1 + \lambda_2 x_2. \tag{7.1}$$

We briefly say that the above sum is a linear combination of points x_1 and x_2.

A linear combination in formula (7.1) is said to be affine if $\lambda_1 + \lambda_2 = 1$. A set $A \subseteq \mathbb{X}$ is said to be affine if it contains each affine combination of each pair of its points. A function $h : A \to \mathbb{R}$ is said to be affine if the equality

$$h(\lambda_1 x_1 + \lambda_2 x_2) = \lambda_1 h(x_1) + \lambda_2 h(x_2) \tag{7.2}$$

holds for each affine combination $\lambda_1 x_1 + \lambda_2 x_2$ of each pair of points $x_1, x_2 \in A$.

A linear combination in formula (7.1) is said to be convex if $\lambda_1 + \lambda_2 = 1$ and $\lambda_1, \lambda_2 \geq 0$. Really, we have that $\lambda_1, \lambda_2 \in [0,1]$. A set $C \subseteq \mathbb{X}$ is said to be convex if it contains each convex combination of each pair of its points. A function $f : C \to \mathbb{R}$ is said to be convex if the inequality

$$f(\lambda_1 x_1 + \lambda_2 x_2) \leq \lambda_1 f(x_1) + \lambda_2 f(x_2) \tag{7.3}$$

holds for each convex combination $\lambda_1 x_1 + \lambda_2 x_2$ of each pair of points $x_1, x_2 \in C$. In relation to this, a function f is said to be concave if $-f$ is convex.

A convex combination is affine. An affine set is convex. The empty set and singleton are affine and convex.

Let $S \subseteq \mathbb{X}$ be a set. The affine (convex) hull aff$S$ (conv$S$) of the set S is defined as the set containing each binomial affine (convex) combination of each pair of points from S. The set aff$S$ (conv$S$) is the smallest affine (convex) set containing S.

Let $n \geq 2$ be an integer. By using the method of mathematical induction, it can be demonstrated that the set affinity (convexity), function affinity (convexity), and affine (convex) hull apply to n-member affine (convex) combinations.

Comprehensive presentation of convex sets, convex functions, and their inequalities can be found in books [12,18].

7.1.2 EFFECT OF AFFINE AND CONVEX COMBINATIONS IN $\mathbb{R}^n$

Let a and b be the distinct points in the line $\mathbb{R}$. Then, each point $x \in \mathbb{R}$ can be represented by the affine combination of points a and b as

$$x = \alpha(x)a + \beta(x)b, \tag{7.4}$$

where

$$\alpha(x) = \frac{x-b}{a-b} = \frac{\begin{vmatrix} x & 1 \\ b & 1 \end{vmatrix}}{\begin{vmatrix} a & 1 \\ b & 1 \end{vmatrix}}, \quad \beta(x) = \frac{a-x}{a-b} = \frac{\begin{vmatrix} a & 1 \\ x & 1 \end{vmatrix}}{\begin{vmatrix} a & 1 \\ b & 1 \end{vmatrix}}. \tag{7.5}$$

The convex combinations in formula (7.4) accentuating points x with $\alpha(x) \geq 0$ and $\beta(x) \geq 0$ delineate the closed interval with endpoints a and b as the set

$$\Delta_{ab} = \text{conv}\{a,b\} = \{\overline{\alpha}a + \overline{\beta}b : \overline{\alpha}, \overline{\beta} \geq 0, \ \overline{\alpha} + \overline{\beta} = 1\}. \tag{7.6}$$

Let $a = (a_1, a_2)$, $b = (b_1, b_2)$, and $c = (c_1, c_2)$ be the noncollinear points in the plane $\mathbb{R}^2$. Then, each point $x = (x_1, x_2) \in \mathbb{R}^2$ can be represented by the affine combination of points a, b, and c as

$$x = \alpha(x)a + \beta(x)b + \gamma(x)c, \tag{7.7}$$

where

$$\alpha(x)=\frac{\begin{vmatrix} x_1 & x_2 & 1\\ b_1 & b_2 & 1\\ c_1 & c_2 & 1\end{vmatrix}}{\begin{vmatrix} a_1 & a_2 & 1\\ b_1 & b_2 & 1\\ c_1 & c_2 & 1\end{vmatrix}},\ \beta(x)=\frac{\begin{vmatrix} a_1 & a_2 & 1\\ x_1 & x_2 & 1\\ c_2 & c_2 & 1\end{vmatrix}}{\begin{vmatrix} a_1 & a_2 & 1\\ b_1 & b_2 & 1\\ c_1 & c_2 & 1\end{vmatrix}},\ \gamma(x)=\frac{\begin{vmatrix} a_1 & a_2 & 1\\ b_1 & b_2 & 1\\ x_1 & x_2 & 1\end{vmatrix}}{\begin{vmatrix} a_1 & a_2 & 1\\ b_1 & b_2 & 1\\ c_1 & c_2 & 1\end{vmatrix}}. \tag{7.8}$$

The convex combinations in formula (7.7) emphasizing points x with $\alpha(x)\geq 0$, $\beta(x)\geq 0$, and $\gamma(x)\geq 0$ designate the triangle with vertices a, b, and c as the set

$$\Delta_{abc}=\operatorname{conv}\{a,b,c\}=\left\{\overline{\alpha}a+\overline{\beta}b+\overline{\gamma}c : \overline{\alpha},\overline{\beta},\overline{\gamma}\geq 0,\ \overline{\alpha}+\overline{\beta}+\overline{\gamma}=1\right\}. \tag{7.9}$$

Let $a_0=(a_{01},\dots,a_{0n}),\dots,a_n=(a_{n1},\dots,a_{nn})$ be the points in the space $\mathbb{R}^n$ such that differences $a_1-a_0,\dots,a_n-a_0$ are linearly independent. Then, each point $x=(x_1,\dots,x_n)\in\mathbb{R}^n$ can be represented by the affine combination of points a_i as

$$x=\sum_{i=0}^{n}\alpha_i(x)a_i, \tag{7.10}$$

where

$$\alpha_i(x)=\begin{vmatrix} a_{01} & \dots & a_{0n} & 1\\ \vdots & \ddots & \vdots & \vdots\\ x_1 & \dots & x_n & 1\\ \vdots & \ddots & \vdots & \vdots\\ a_{n1} & \dots & a_{nn} & 1\end{vmatrix}\cdot\begin{vmatrix} a_{01} & \dots & a_{0n} & 1\\ \vdots & \ddots & \vdots & \vdots\\ a_{i1} & \dots & a_{in} & 1\\ \vdots & \ddots & \vdots & \vdots\\ a_{n1} & \dots & a_{nn} & 1\end{vmatrix}^{-1}. \tag{7.11}$$

Since the differences $a_1-a_0,\dots,a_n-a_0$ are linearly independent, the affine combination in formula (7.10) is unique for each $x\in\mathbb{R}^n$. The affine hull of the set of simplex vertices covers the space $\mathbb{R}^n$, i.e., $\mathbb{A}_{a_0\dots a_n}=\operatorname{aff}\{a_0,\dots,a_n\}=\mathbb{R}^n$.

The convex combinations in formula (7.10) highlighting points x with all $\alpha_i(x)\geq 0$ appoint the n-simplex with vertices a_i as the set

$$\Delta_{a_0\dots a_n}=\operatorname{conv}\{a_0,\dots,a_n\}=\left\{\textstyle\sum_{i=0}^{n}\overline{\alpha}_i a_i : \overline{\alpha}_i\geq 0,\ \sum_{i=0}^{n}\overline{\alpha}_i=1\right\}. \tag{7.12}$$

7.1.3 COEFFICIENTS OF AFFINE AND CONVEX COMBINATIONS

Let $a_0,\dots,a_n\in\mathbb{R}^n$ be the points such that $a_1-a_0,\dots,a_n-a_0$ are linearly independent. The existence and uniqueness of the representation of point $x\in\mathbb{R}^n$ by the affine combination of points $a_0,\dots,a_n$ can be demonstrated in two simple steps. We first represent the difference $x-a_0$ by the unique linear combination

$$x-a_0=\sum_{i=1}^{n}\lambda_i(a_i-a_0),$$

and then express the point x, which yields the affine combination

$$x = \sum_{i=1}^{n} \lambda_i a_i + \left(1 - \sum_{i=1}^{n} \lambda_i\right) a_0.$$

We want to verify the coefficients in formula (7.11). According to the above consideration, we can suppose that

$$x = \sum_{j=0}^{n} \alpha_j(x) a_j = \left(\sum_{j=0}^{n} \alpha_j(x) a_{j1}, \ldots, \sum_{j=0}^{n} \alpha_j(x) a_{jn}\right) \tag{7.13}$$

with $\sum_{j=0}^{n} \alpha_j(x) = 1$. We still need the determinants

$$A_i(x) = \begin{vmatrix} a_{01} & \cdots & a_{0n} & 1 \\ \vdots & \ddots & \vdots & \vdots \\ x_1 & \cdots & x_n & 1 \\ \vdots & \ddots & \vdots & \vdots \\ a_{n1} & \cdots & a_{nn} & 1 \end{vmatrix}, \ A = \begin{vmatrix} a_{01} & \cdots & a_{0n} & 1 \\ \vdots & \ddots & \vdots & \vdots \\ a_{i1} & \cdots & a_{in} & 1 \\ \vdots & \ddots & \vdots & \vdots \\ a_{n1} & \cdots & a_{nn} & 1 \end{vmatrix}. \tag{7.14}$$

By exposing the ith row of $A_i(x)$ with coordinates of x in formula (7.13), and $\sum_{j=0}^{n} \alpha_j(x)$ instead of 1, we induce

$$A_i(x) = \begin{vmatrix} a_{01} & \cdots & a_{0n} & 1 \\ \vdots & \ddots & \vdots & \vdots \\ \sum_{j=0}^{n} \alpha_j(x) a_{j1} & \cdots & \sum_{j=0}^{n} \alpha_j(x) a_{jn} & \sum_{j=0}^{n} \alpha_j(x) \\ \vdots & \ddots & \vdots & \vdots \\ a_{n1} & \cdots & a_{nn} & 1 \end{vmatrix}.$$

After decomposition into $n+1$ summands by the ith row, it follows that

$$A_i(x) = \sum_{j=0}^{n} \alpha_j(x) \begin{vmatrix} a_{01} & \cdots & a_{0n} & 1 \\ \vdots & \ddots & \vdots & \vdots \\ a_{j1} & \cdots & a_{jn} & 1 \\ \vdots & \ddots & \vdots & \vdots \\ a_{n1} & \cdots & a_{nn} & 1 \end{vmatrix} = \alpha_i(x) \begin{vmatrix} a_{01} & \cdots & a_{0n} & 1 \\ \vdots & \ddots & \vdots & \vdots \\ a_{i1} & \cdots & a_{in} & 1 \\ \vdots & \ddots & \vdots & \vdots \\ a_{n1} & \cdots & a_{nn} & 1 \end{vmatrix} = \alpha_i(x) A,$$

and thus, we get the expression $\alpha_i(x) = A_i(x)/A$ corresponding to formula (7.11).

The coefficients $\alpha_i(x)$ have a geometric meaning. To present it as simple as possible, we consider the simplex $\Delta_{a_0 \ldots a_{i-1} x a_{i+1} \ldots a_n}$ as a fictive n-simplex. If x belongs to the facet $\Delta_{a_0 \ldots a_{i-1} a_{i+1} \ldots a_n}$, we assume that $\Delta_{a_0 \ldots a_{i-1} x a_{i+1} \ldots a_n} = \Delta_{a_0 \ldots a_{i-1} a_{i+1} \ldots a_n}$. In this case, the coefficient $\alpha_i(x)$ and the n-volume of the facet are equal to zero. As for the coefficients' geometric meaning, since

$$A_i(x) = \pm n! \mathrm{vol}_n(\Delta_{a_0 \ldots a_{i-1} x a_{i+1} \ldots a_n}), \ A = \pm n! \mathrm{vol}_n(\Delta_{a_0 \ldots a_n}), \tag{7.15}$$

it follows that

$$\alpha_i(x) = \pm \frac{\mathrm{vol}_n(\Delta_{a_0 \ldots a_{i-1} x a_{i+1} \ldots a_n})}{\mathrm{vol}_n(\Delta_{a_0 \ldots a_n})}. \tag{7.16}$$

The sign in formula (7.16) depends on the orientation in the space $\mathbb{R}^n$, which refers to the ordered $(n+1)$-tuples

$$(a_0,\ldots,a_{i-1},x,a_{i+1},\ldots,a_n) \text{ and } (a_0,\ldots,a_n).$$

The plus sign is related to the same orientation, and the minus sign to the opposite. If we consider only the points x belonging to the n-simplex $\Delta_{a_0 \ldots a_n}$, then the above ordered $(n+1)$-tuples have the same orientation and the coefficients $\alpha_i(x)$ are nonnegative. In that case, the plus sign obviously stands in formula (7.16).

The coefficients $\alpha_i(x)$ in formula (7.11) indicate functions $\alpha_i : \mathbb{R}^n \to \mathbb{R}$. After expanding the numerator determinant $A_i(x)$ using the ith row containing coordinates of x, and rearranging, we reach the concise representation

$$\alpha_i(x_1,\ldots,x_n) = \alpha_{i0} + \sum_{j=1}^{n} \alpha_{ij} x_j, \tag{7.17}$$

where α_{i0} and α_{ij} are the constants as the ratios of determinants without coordinates of x. Following the above formula, it is easy to show that functions α_i are affine.

Let us look at the representation of an affine function $h : \mathbb{R}^n \to \mathbb{R}$. By combining the affinity of h with representations in formulas (7.10) and (7.17), we get

$$\begin{aligned} h(x_1,\ldots,x_n) &= \sum_{i=0}^{n} \alpha_i(x_1,\ldots,x_n) h(a_i) \\ &= \sum_{i=0}^{n} \Big(\alpha_{i0} + \sum_{j=1}^{n} \alpha_{ij} x_j\Big) h(a_i) \\ &= \kappa_0 + \kappa_1 x_1 + \cdots + \kappa_n x_n, \end{aligned} \tag{7.18}$$

where $\kappa_0,\ldots,\kappa_n$ are the constants. The above representation is usually called the standard form of h. It is not difficult to prove the uniqueness of this form.

7.1.4 SUPPORT AND SECANT HYPERPLANES

Let $C \subseteq \mathbb{R}^n$ be a convex set with the nonempty interior, let c be an interior point of C, and let $f : C \to \mathbb{R}$ be a convex function. Then, the function f admits an affine function $h_1 : \mathbb{R}^n \to \mathbb{R}$, which meets the equality $h_1(c) = f(c)$, and for all $x \in C$ satisfies the inequality

$$h_1(x) \le f(x). \tag{7.19}$$

In the space $\mathbb{R}^{n+1}$, we can imagine that the graph of h_1 supports the graph of f at the point $F = (c, f(c))$. Accordingly, h_1 is called the support hyperplane of f at c. The support hyperplane of f at c is not necessarily unique. Formula (7.19) can be called the support hyperplane inequality. The existence of support hyperplanes arises from the separating and supporting hyperplane theorems.

Let $\Delta_{a_0 \dots a_n} \subset \mathbb{R}^n$ be an n-simplex, and let $f : \Delta_{a_0 \dots a_n} \to \mathbb{R}$ be a convex function. Then, the function f goes with the affine function $h_2 : \mathbb{R}^n \to \mathbb{R}$ determined by the equalities $f(a_0) = h_2(a_0), \dots, f(a_n) = h_2(a_n)$. It follows that the function h_2 for all $x \in \Delta_{a_0 \dots a_n}$ satisfies the inequality:

$$f(x) \leq h_2(x). \tag{7.20}$$

We can visualize that the graph of h_2 is a roof of the graph of f fixed at the points $F_0 = (a_0, f(a_0)), \dots, F_n = (a_n, f(a_n))$. Suitably, h_2 is called the secant hyperplane of f at vertices, and formula (7.20) can be called the secant hyperplane inequality. If we include c as an interior point of $\Delta_{a_0 \dots a_n}$ and h_1 as a support hyperplane of f at c, then for all $x \in \Delta_{a_0 \dots a_n}$, we have the support-secant hyperplane inequality:

$$h_1(x) \leq f(x) \leq h_2(x). \tag{7.21}$$

The equation of the secant hyperplane can be easily determined. By applying the affinity of h_2 to the affine combination in formula (7.10), and using the coincidences with f, we get the secant hyperplane equation:

$$h_2(x) = \sum_{i=0}^{n} \alpha_i(x) f(a_i). \tag{7.22}$$

If $n = 1$ ($n = 2$), we use terms "support" and "secant lines" (planes).

7.2 THE JENSEN INEQUALITY

The Jensen inequality is the most important. With more or less effort, almost all important and influential inequalities can be derived from Jensen's.

7.2.1 DISCRETE AND INTEGRAL FORMS OF THE JENSEN INEQUALITY

Let $\mathbb{X}$ be a real vector space, and let $\sum_{i=1}^{n} \lambda_i x_i$ be a linear combination of points $x_i \in \mathbb{X}$ such that $\lambda = \sum_{i=1}^{n} \lambda_i \neq 0$. The center of the given combination is defined as the point $\overline{x} \in \mathbb{X}$ satisfying the discrete equation

$$\sum_{i=1}^{n} \lambda_i (x_i - \overline{x}) = 0. \tag{7.23}$$

It follows that

$$\overline{x} = \sum_{i=1}^{n} \frac{\lambda_i}{\lambda} x_i. \tag{7.24}$$

So the center $\overline{x}$ is the affine combination of points x_i and coefficients $\kappa_i = \lambda_i / \lambda$. Accordingly, if the given combination is affine, then the combination center coincides with the combination itself, respectively, $\overline{x} = \sum_{i=1}^{n} \lambda_i x_i$. This is especially true for convex combinations.

Discrete form of Jensen's inequality includes a real vector space, convex combination with its center, and convex function. Regarding the strict form, we present the following theorem.

Theorem 7.1. *Let $\mathbb{X}$ be a real vector space, let $\sum_{i=1}^{n} \lambda_i x_i$ be a convex combination of points $x_i \in \mathbb{X}$, let $C \subseteq \mathbb{X}$ be a convex set containing $\{x_1, \ldots, x_n\}$, and let $f : C \to \mathbb{R}$ be a convex function.*

Then, we have the discrete inequality

$$f\left(\sum_{i=1}^{n} \lambda_i x_i\right) \leq \sum_{i=1}^{n} \lambda_i f(x_i). \tag{7.25}$$

Proof. If $n = 1$, the trivial inequality $f(x_1) \leq f(x_1)$ represents formula (7.25) regardless of the convexity of f. If $n \geq 2$, the method of mathematical induction enables us to perform formula (7.25) as follows.

The case $n = 2$ is regarded as the induction base, wherein the convexity of f provides formula (7.25).

The case $n > 2$ is considered as the induction step, wherein $\lambda_1 < 1$ is assumed without a reduction of generality. The induction base and premise are included through the next procedure. The right side of the representation

$$\sum_{i=1}^{n} \lambda_i x_i = \lambda_1 x_1 + (1 - \lambda_1) \sum_{i=2}^{n} \frac{\lambda_i}{1 - \lambda_1} x_i$$

can be regarded as a binomial convex combination. The induction base can be applied to the right side, and so gain the inequality

$$f\left(\sum_{i=1}^{n} \lambda_i x_i\right) \leq \lambda_1 f(x_1) + (1 - \lambda_1) f\left(\sum_{i=2}^{n} \frac{\lambda_i}{1 - \lambda_1} x_i\right).$$

The induction premise can be applied to the $(n-1)$-member convex combination under the function f, and so obtain the inequality

$$f\left(\sum_{i=2}^{n} \frac{\lambda_i}{1 - \lambda_1} x_i\right) \leq \sum_{i=2}^{n} \frac{\lambda_i}{1 - \lambda_1} f(x_i).$$

The coupling of the above two inequalities gives formula (7.25). □

Let X be a set with a nonnegative measure μ such that $\mu(X) > 0$, and let $g : X \to \mathbb{R}$ be a μ-integrable function. The μ-integral arithmetic mean of the function g is defined as the number $\overline{g} \in \mathbb{R}$, which satisfies the integral equation

$$\int_X (g(x) - \overline{g})\, d\mu(x) = 0. \tag{7.26}$$

A simple calculation gives

$$\overline{g} = \frac{\int_X g(x)\, d\mu(x)}{\mu(X)}. \tag{7.27}$$

If we include an affine function $h : \mathbb{R} \to \mathbb{R}$, then we have the integral equality

$$h\left(\frac{\int_X g(x)\, d\mu(x)}{\mu(X)}\right) = \frac{\int_X h(g(x))\, d\mu(x)}{\mu(X)}. \tag{7.28}$$

This is easy to prove if we use the standard representation $h(x) = \kappa_0 + \kappa_1 x$. The question is what changes in formula (7.28) if we replace the affine function h with a convex function f. This leads to Jensen's inequality.

Integral form of Jensen's inequality includes a measurable set X, integrable function $g : X \to \mathbb{R}$ with its integral arithmetic mean $\overline{g}$, and convex function f such that the composition $f(g) : X \to \mathbb{R}$ is integrable. The next appropriate lemma and theorem provide the strict form.

Lemma 7.1. *Let X be a set with a nonnegative measure μ such that $\mu(X) > 0$, and let $g : X \to \mathbb{R}$ be a μ-integrable function.*

Then, the μ-integral arithmetic mean of g is in the convex hull of the image of g.

Proof. Let $\overline{g}$ be the μ-integral arithmetic mean of g, and let $I \subseteq \mathbb{R}$ be an interval containing the image of g. Relying on proof by contradiction, we will suppose that $\overline{g}$ does not belong to I. Then, either $g(x) - \overline{g} > 0$ or $g(x) - \overline{g} < 0$ for all $x \in X$. Consequently, it implies either $\int_X (g(x) - \overline{g}) d\mu(x) > 0$ or $\int_X (g(x) - \overline{g}) d\mu(x) < 0$. Thus, $\overline{g}$ does not represent the μ-integral arithmetic mean of g.

The conclusion is that $\overline{g}$ belongs to each interval containing the image of g. This must be true even for the smallest one, the convex hull of the image of g. □

Theorem 7.2. *Let X be a set with a nonnegative measure μ such that $\mu(X) > 0$, let $g : X \to \mathbb{R}$ be a μ-integrable function, let $I \subseteq \mathbb{R}$ be an interval containing the image of g, and let $f : I \to \mathbb{R}$ be a convex function such that $f(g)$ is μ-integrable.*

Then, we have the integral inequality

$$f\left(\frac{\int_X g(x) d\mu(x)}{\mu(X)}\right) \le \frac{\int_X f(g(x)) d\mu(x)}{\mu(X)}. \tag{7.29}$$

Proof. The mean $\overline{g} = \int_X g(x) d\mu(x) / \mu(X)$ belongs to the interval I by Lemma 7.1. Thus, $\overline{g}$ is either an interior or boundary point of I.

If $\overline{g}$ is an interior point of I, then f as a convex function admits a support line h at $\overline{g}$. Thus, $h(\overline{g}) = f(\overline{g})$, and for all $x \in X$, we have the inequality

$$h(g(x)) \le f(g(x)). \tag{7.30}$$

By using the coincidence $f(\overline{g}) = h(\overline{g})$, affinity equality in formula (7.28), and support line inequality in formula (7.30), we obtain the multiple relation

$$\begin{aligned} f\left(\frac{\int_X g(x) d\mu(x)}{\mu(X)}\right) &= h\left(\frac{\int_X g(x) d\mu(x)}{\mu(X)}\right) \\ &= \frac{\int_X h(g(x)) d\mu(x)}{\mu(X)} \\ &\le \frac{\int_X f(g(x)) d\mu(x)}{\mu(X)}, \end{aligned}$$

covering the inequality in formula (7.29).

If $\overline{g}$ is a boundary point of I, then either $g(x)-\overline{g}\geq 0$ or $g(x)-\overline{g}\leq 0$ for all $x\in X$. Integral equality in formula (7.26) implies $g(x)-\overline{g}=0$, and so $g(x)=\overline{g}$ for μ-almost all $x\in X$. The trivial inequality $f(\overline{g})\leq f(\overline{g})$ represents formula (7.29). □

Versions of the discrete and integrals forms of the inequalities in formulas (7.25) and (7.29) were proven by Jensen, the discrete version in [6], and integral version in [7]. In the period 1905–1906, Jensen also defined a convex function.

7.2.2 GENERALIZATIONS OF THE JENSEN INEQUALITY

For the sake of formulae conciseness, we will sometimes omit the variable x in integral expressions. This is the case in Theorem 7.3.

Let $g_1,\ldots,g_n : X\to\mathbb{R}$ be μ-integrable functions. The μ-integral arithmetic mean of the mapping $g=(g_1,\ldots,g_n):X\to\mathbb{R}^n$ can be defined as the point $\overline{g}=(\overline{g}_1,\ldots,\overline{g}_n)\in\mathbb{R}^n$ whose coordinates satisfy the integral equations

$$\int_X (g_1(x)-\overline{g}_1)\,d\mu(x)=0,\ldots,\int_X (g_n(x)-\overline{g}_n)\,d\mu(x)=0. \tag{7.31}$$

Then, it follows that

$$\overline{g}=\left(\frac{\int_X g_1(x)\,d\mu(x)}{\mu(X)},\ldots,\frac{\int_X g_n(x)\,d\mu(x)}{\mu(X)}\right). \tag{7.32}$$

If we include an affine function $h:\mathbb{R}^n\to\mathbb{R}$, then we have the integral equality

$$h\left(\frac{\int_X g_1(x)d\mu(x)}{\mu(X)},\ldots,\frac{\int_X g_n(x)d\mu(x)}{\mu(X)}\right)=\frac{\int_X h(g_1(x),\ldots,g_n(x))\,d\mu(x)}{\mu(X)} \tag{7.33}$$

due to the representation $h(t_1,\ldots,t_n)=\kappa_0+\kappa_1 t_1+\cdots+\kappa_n t_n$.

Lemma 7.2. *Let X be a set with a nonnegative measure μ such that $\mu(X)>0$, let $g_1,\ldots,g_n : X\to\mathbb{R}$ be μ-integrable functions, and let $g=(g_1,\ldots,g_n):X\to\mathbb{R}^n$ be the corresponding $\mathbb{R}^n$-valued mapping.*

Then, the μ-integral arithmetic mean of the mapping g is in the Cartesian product of the convex hulls of the images of $g_1,\ldots,g_n$.

Proof. Let $I_1,\ldots,I_n$ be the convex hulls of images of $g_1,\ldots,g_n$, respectively. Since each $\overline{g}_i\in I_i$ by Lemma 7.1, it follows that $\overline{g}=(\overline{g}_1,\ldots,\overline{g}_n)\in I_1\times\cdots\times I_n$. □

Integral forms of Jensen's inequality for convex functions of several variables are certainly very important. We present the following expansion of Theorem 7.2.

Theorem 7.3. *Let X be a set with a nonnegative measure μ such that $\mu(X)>0$, let $g_1,\ldots,g_n : X\to\mathbb{R}$ be μ-integrable functions, let $I_1,\ldots,I_n\subseteq\mathbb{R}$ be intervals containing the images of $g_1,\ldots,g_n$, respectively, and let $f:I_1\times\cdots\times I_n\to\mathbb{R}$ be a convex function such that $f(g_1,\ldots,g_n)$ is μ-integrable.*

Then, we have the integral inequality

$$f\left(\frac{\int_X g_1\,d\mu}{\mu(X)},\ldots,\frac{\int_X g_n\,d\mu}{\mu(X)}\right)\leq\frac{\int_X f(g_1,\ldots,g_n)\,d\mu}{\mu(X)}. \tag{7.34}$$

Proof. If $n=1$, Theorem 7.3 is reduced to Theorem 7.2. Therefore, we will assume that $n \geq 2$ and consider three positions of the mean $\overline{g}=(\overline{g}_1,\dots,\overline{g}_n)$ located in the cuboid $I=I_1\times\cdots\times I_n$. The first position refers to the interior of I, and the other two positions refer to the boundary (relative interior and vertices) of I.

If $\overline{g}$ is an interior point of I (i.e., if $\overline{g}_1,\dots,\overline{g}_n$ are the interior points of $I_1,\dots,I_n$, respectively), then f as a convex function admits a support hyperplane h at $\overline{g}$. The support hyperplane inequality applied to the points $g(x)=(g_1(x),\dots,g_n(x))$ holds for all $x\in X$ in the form

$$h\big(g_1(x),\dots,g_n(x)\big) \leq f\big(g_1(x),\dots,g_n(x)\big). \tag{7.35}$$

By relying on the coincidence $f(\overline{g})=h(\overline{g})$, affinity equality in formula (7.33), and support hyperplane inequality in formula (7.35), we generate the connections

$$\begin{aligned} f\left(\frac{\int_X g_1\,d\mu}{\mu(X)},\dots,\frac{\int_X g_n\,d\mu}{\mu(X)}\right) &= h\left(\frac{\int_X g_1\,d\mu}{\mu(X)},\dots,\frac{\int_X g_n\,d\mu}{\mu(X)}\right)\\ &= \frac{\int_X h(g_1,\dots,g_n)\,d\mu}{\mu(X)}\\ &\leq \frac{\int_X f(g_1,\dots,g_n)\,d\mu}{\mu(X)}, \end{aligned} \tag{7.36}$$

including the inequality in formula (7.34).

If $\overline{g}$ is a boundary point of I so that $\overline{g}_1,\dots,\overline{g}_k$ are the interior points of $I_1,\dots,I_k$, respectively, and that $\overline{g}_{k+1},\dots,\overline{g}_n$ are the boundary points of $I_{k+1},\dots,I_n$, respectively, where $1\leq k\leq n-1$, then $\overline{g}$ is an interior point of the k-cuboid

$$J=I_1\times\cdots\times I_k\times\{\overline{g}_{k+1}\}\times\cdots\times\{\overline{g}_n\}$$

contained in the affine plane $\mathbb{A}=\mathbb{R}^k\times\{\overline{g}_{k+1}\}\times\cdots\times\{\overline{g}_n\}$ of dimension k. Therefore, we will use the restriction $f_J=f/J$. The convex function $f_J: J\to\mathbb{R}$ admits a support hyperplane $\tilde{h}_J:\mathbb{A}\to\mathbb{R}$ at $\overline{g}$ as an interior point of J. The support hyperplane inequality holds for all $x\in X$ in the form

$$\tilde{h}_J\big(g_1(x),\dots,g_k(x),\overline{g}_{k+1},\dots,\overline{g}_n\big) \leq f_J\big(g_1(x),\dots,g_k(x),\overline{g}_{k+1},\dots,\overline{g}_n\big).$$

Let $\tilde{h}:\mathbb{R}^n\to\mathbb{R}$ be any affine extension of $\tilde{h}_J$. By utilizing the connections $\tilde{h}/J=\tilde{h}_J$, $\tilde{h}_J(\overline{g})=f_J(\overline{g})$, and $f_J=f/J$, we get

$$\tilde{h}(\overline{g})=\tilde{h}_J(\overline{g})=f_J(\overline{g})=f(\overline{g}).$$

The numbers $\overline{g}_{k+1},\dots,\overline{g}_n$ are the boundary points of the intervals $I_{k+1},\dots,I_n$, respectively, which guarantees that μ-almost all $x\in X$ satisfy the equalities

$$g_{k+1}(x)=\overline{g}_{k+1},\dots,g_n(x)=\overline{g}_n.$$

All considered indicates that μ-almost all $x\in X$ satisfy the multiple relation

$$\begin{aligned}\tilde{h}(g_1(x),\dots,g_n(x)) &= \tilde{h}(g_1(x),\dots,g_k(x),\overline{g}_{k+1},\dots,\overline{g}_n)\\ &= \tilde{h}_J(g_1(x),\dots,g_k(x),\overline{g}_{k+1},\dots,\overline{g}_n)\\ &\leq f_J(g_1(x),\dots,g_k(x),\overline{g}_{k+1},\dots,\overline{g}_n)\\ &= f(g_1(x),\dots,g_k(x),\overline{g}_{k+1},\dots,\overline{g}_n)\\ &= f(g_1(x),\dots,g_n(x)),\end{aligned}$$

and so the support hyperplane inequality

$$\tilde{h}(g_1(x),\dots,g_n(x)) \leq f(g_1(x),\dots,g_n(x)).$$

The coincidence $\tilde{h}(\overline{g}) = f(\overline{g})$ and the above μ-almost everywhere inequality encourage us to put $\tilde{h}$ instead of h into formula (7.36), and thus reach formula (7.34). Similar arguments apply to any k-cuboid of I.

If $\overline{g}$ is a vertex of I (i.e., if $\overline{g}_1,\dots,\overline{g}_n$ are the boundary points of $I_1,\dots,I_n$, respectively), then $g_1(x) = \overline{g}_1,\dots,g_n(x) = \overline{g}_n$ for μ-almost all $x \in X$. The trivial inequality $f(\overline{g}_1,\dots,\overline{g}_n) \leq f(\overline{g}_1,\dots,\overline{g}_n)$ represents formula (7.34). □

Some extensions and generalizations of different variants of Jensen's inequality can be found in papers [13,16,17].

7.3 THE HERMITE-HADAMARD INEQUALITY

The Hermite-Hadamard inequality is the double inequality with harmonic form consisting of the integral member between two discrete members.

7.3.1 THE CLASSIC FORM OF THE HERMITE-HADAMARD INEQUALITY

In this subsection, we use the Riemann integral and a bounded closed interval $[a,b]$ in the line $\mathbb{R}$ with $a < b$.

By using the expression for the integral arithmetic mean

$$\overline{g} = \frac{\int_a^b g(x)\,dx}{b-a}$$

of an integrable function $g : [a,b] \to \mathbb{R}$ with $g(x) = x$, we get the barycenter

$$\overline{c} = \frac{\int_a^b x\,dx}{b-a} = \frac{a+b}{2} \tag{7.37}$$

of the interval $[a,b]$, also called the midpoint.

The classic form of the Hermite-Hadamard inequality is as follows.

Theorem 7.4. *Let $[a,b]$ be a bounded closed interval in the line $\mathbb{R}$, and let $f : [a,b] \to \mathbb{R}$ be a convex function.*

Then, we have the double inequality

$$f\left(\frac{a+b}{2}\right) \leq \frac{\int_a^b f(x)\,dx}{b-a} \leq \frac{f(a)+f(b)}{2}. \tag{7.38}$$

First Proof. By applying the convexity of f to the right side of the convex combinations equality

$$\frac{a+b}{2}=\frac{1}{2}\big((1-t)a+tb\big)+\frac{1}{2}\big((1-t)b+ta\big),$$

as well as to convex combinations $(1-t)a+tb$ and $(1-t)b+ta$, we obtain the multiple relation

$$\begin{aligned} f\left(\frac{a+b}{2}\right) &\le \frac{1}{2}f\big((1-t)a+tb\big)+\frac{1}{2}f\big((1-t)b+ta\big) \\ &\le \frac{1}{2}\big((1-t)f(a)+tf(b)\big)+\frac{1}{2}\big((1-t)f(b)+tf(a)\big) \\ &= \frac{f(a)+f(b)}{2}. \end{aligned}$$

Now we single out the double inequality

$$f\left(\frac{a+b}{2}\right)\le \frac{1}{2}f\big((1-t)a+tb\big)+\frac{1}{2}f\big((1-t)b+ta\big)\le \frac{f(a)+f(b)}{2},$$

and then integrating over the unit interval $[0,1]$, and using equalities

$$\int_0^1 f\big((1-t)a+tb\big)\,dt=\int_0^1 f\big((1-t)b+ta\big)\,dt=\frac{\int_a^b f(x)\,dx}{b-a},$$

we achieve the inequality in formula (7.38). □

Second Proof. Let h_1 be a support line of f at the midpoint $\overline{c}=(a+b)/2$, and let h_2 be the secant line of f. By integrating the support-secant line inequality

$$h_1(x)\le f(x)\le h_2(x)$$

over the interval $[a,b]$, dividing with $b-a$, and applying the affinity of h_1 and h_2 through formula (7.28) with $g(x)=x$, we get

$$h_1\left(\frac{\int_a^b x\,dx}{b-a}\right)\le \frac{\int_a^b f(x)\,dx}{b-a}\le h_2\left(\frac{\int_a^b x\,dx}{b-a}\right).$$

By using the barycenter representation in formula (7.37), we obtain

$$h_1\left(\frac{a+b}{2}\right)\le \frac{\int_a^b f(x)\,dx}{b-a}\le h_2\left(\frac{a+b}{2}\right).$$

By utilizing relations

$$h_1\left(\frac{a+b}{2}\right)=f\left(\frac{a+b}{2}\right)\ \text{and}\ h_2\left(\frac{a+b}{2}\right)=\frac{h_2(a)+h_2(b)}{2}=\frac{f(a)+f(b)}{2},$$

we attain the inequality in formula (7.38). □

The inequality of the first (last) two members in formula (7.38) is usually called the left-hand (right-hand) side of the Hermite-Hadamard inequality. The double inequality in formula (7.38) was discovered by Hermite in 1883, see [4]. Ten years later, the left-hand side of this inequality was rediscovered by Hadamard, see [3]. At that time, the notion of a convex function was not yet introduced.

7.3.2 GENERALIZATIONS OF THE HERMITE-HADAMARD INEQUALITY

In the first part of this subsection, we use versions of the Riemann integral like multiple integrals in higher dimensions.

Let Δ_{abc} a triangle in the plane $\mathbb{R}^2$. By using the expression for the integral arithmetic mean

$$\overline{g} = \left(\frac{\iint_{\Delta_{abc}} g_1(x,y)\,dxdy}{\mathrm{ar}(\Delta_{abc})}, \frac{\iint_{\Delta_{abc}} g_2(x,y)\,dxdy}{\mathrm{ar}(\Delta_{abc})} \right)$$

of the mapping $g = (g_1, g_2) : \Delta_{abc} \to \mathbb{R}^2$ with $g_1(x,y) = x$ and $g_2(x,y) = y$, we get the barycenter

$$\overline{d} = \left(\frac{\iint_{\Delta_{abc}} x\,dxdy}{\mathrm{ar}(\Delta_{abc})}, \frac{\iint_{\Delta_{abc}} y\,dxdy}{\mathrm{ar}(\Delta_{abc})} \right) = \frac{a+b+c}{3} \tag{7.39}$$

of the triangle Δ_{abc}.

The next is the generalization of the Hermite-Hadamard inequality to triangles.

Lemma 7.3. *Let Δ_{abc} be a triangle in the plane $\mathbb{R}^2$, and let $f : \Delta_{abc} \to \mathbb{R}$ be a convex function.*

Then, we have the double inequality

$$f\left(\frac{a+b+c}{3}\right) \leq \frac{\iint_{\Delta_{abc}} f(x,y)\,dxdy}{\mathrm{ar}(\Delta_{abc})} \leq \frac{f(a)+f(b)+f(c)}{3}. \tag{7.40}$$

First Proof. We put into practice the unit triangle in the plane $\mathbb{R}^2$ as the set

$$\Delta_2 = \{(t,s) : 0 \leq t \leq 1, 0 \leq s \leq 1-t\},$$

and thus, we have the correlation

$$\Delta_{abc} = \{(1-t-s)a + tb + sc : (t,s) \in \Delta_2\}.$$

Now, we can employ the bijection $g_{abc} : \Delta_2 \to \Delta_{abc}$ determined by

$$g_{abc}(t,s) = (1-t-s)a + tb + sc.$$

Then, the convexity of f applied to the convex combination on the right side produces the inequality

$$f(g_{abc}(t,s)) \leq (1-t-s)f(a) + tf(b) + sf(c) = g_{f(a)f(b)f(c)}(t,s).$$

If we put the vertices coordinates $a = (a_1, a_2)$, $b = (b_1, b_2)$, and $c = (c_1, c_2)$, and if we take the substitution

$$(x,y) = \left(g_{a_1b_1c_1}(t,s), g_{a_2b_2c_2}(t,s)\right) = g_{abc}(t,s),$$

then the corresponding Jacobian outputs as

$$J = \begin{vmatrix} \partial x/\partial t & \partial x/\partial s \\ \partial y/\partial t & \partial y/\partial s \end{vmatrix} = \begin{vmatrix} b_1-a_1 & c_1-a_1 \\ b_2-a_2 & c_2-a_2 \end{vmatrix} = \begin{vmatrix} a_1 & a_2 & 1 \\ b_1 & b_2 & 1 \\ c_1 & c_2 & 1 \end{vmatrix}$$

$$= \pm 2\operatorname{ar}(\Delta_{abc}) = \pm\frac{\operatorname{ar}(\Delta_{abc})}{\operatorname{ar}(\Delta_2)}$$

because $\operatorname{ar}(\Delta_2) = 1/2$. It follows that $|J| = \operatorname{ar}(\Delta_{abc})/\operatorname{ar}(\Delta_2)$, and we accomplish the integral relation

$$\frac{\iint_{\Delta_{abc}} f(x,y)\,dx\,dy}{\operatorname{ar}(\Delta_{abc})} = \frac{\iint_{\Delta_2} f(g_{abc}(t,s))\,dt\,ds}{\operatorname{ar}(\Delta_2)}. \tag{7.41}$$

By applying the convexity of f to the right side of the convex combinations equality

$$\frac{a+b+c}{3} = \frac{1}{3}g_{abc}(t,s) + \frac{1}{3}g_{bca}(t,s) + \frac{1}{3}g_{cab}(t,s),$$

as well as to the convex combinations of $g_{abc}(t,s)$, $g_{bca}(t,s)$, and $g_{cab}(t,s)$, we get the multiple relation

$$\begin{aligned} f\left(\frac{a+b+c}{3}\right) &\leq \frac{1}{3}f(g_{abc}(t,s)) + \frac{1}{3}f(g_{bca}(t,s)) + \frac{1}{3}f(g_{cab}(t,s)) \\ &\leq \frac{1}{3}g_{f(a)f(b)f(c)}(t,s) + \frac{1}{3}g_{f(b)f(c)f(a)}(t,s) + \frac{1}{3}g_{f(c)f(a)f(b)}(t,s) \\ &= \frac{f(a)+f(b)+f(c)}{3}, \end{aligned}$$

from which we extricate the double inequality

$$f\left(\frac{a+b+c}{3}\right) \leq \frac{f(g_{abc}(t,s))+f(g_{bca}(t,s))+f(g_{cab}(t,s))}{3} \leq \frac{f(a)+f(b)+f(c)}{3}.$$

By integrating over the unit triangle Δ_2, using equalities

$$\iint_{\Delta_2} f(g_{abc}(t,s))\,dt\,ds = \iint_{\Delta_2} f(g_{bca}(t,s))\,dt\,ds = \iint_{\Delta_2} f(g_{cab}(t,s))\,dt\,ds,$$

and dividing with $\operatorname{ar}(\Delta_2)$, we obtain

$$f\left(\frac{a+b+c}{3}\right) \leq \frac{\iint_{\Delta_2} f(g_{abc}(t,s))\,dt\,ds}{\operatorname{ar}(\Delta_2)} \leq \frac{f(a)+f(b)+f(c)}{3}.$$

Respecting the integral relation in formula (7.41), we have formula (7.40). □

Second Proof. Let h_1 be a support plane of f at the barycenter $\overline{d} = (a+b+c)/3$, and let h_2 be the secant plane of f. By integrating the support-secant plane inequality

$$h_1(x,y) \leq f(x,y) \leq h_2(x,y)$$

over the triangle Δ_{abc}, dividing with $\mathrm{ar}(\Delta_{abc})$, and applying the affinity of h_1 and h_2 through formula (7.33) with $g_1(x,y)=x$ and $g_2(x,y)=y$, we get

$$\begin{aligned} h_1\left(\frac{\iint_{\Delta_{abc}} x\,dxdy}{\mathrm{ar}(\Delta_{abc})}, \frac{\iint_{\Delta_{abc}} y\,dxdy}{\mathrm{ar}(\Delta_{abc})}\right) &= \frac{\iint_{\Delta_{abc}} h_1(x,y)\,dxdy}{\mathrm{ar}(\Delta_{abc})} \\ &\leq \frac{\iint_{\Delta_{abc}} f(x,y)\,dxdy}{\mathrm{ar}(\Delta_{abc})} \\ &\leq \frac{\iint_{\Delta_{abc}} h_2(x,y)\,dxdy}{\mathrm{ar}(\Delta_{abc})} \\ &= h_2\left(\frac{\iint_{\Delta_{abc}} x\,dxdy}{\mathrm{ar}(\Delta_{abc})}, \frac{\iint_{\Delta_{abc}} y\,dxdy}{\mathrm{ar}(\Delta_{abc})}\right). \end{aligned}$$

By taking the odd members, and referring to the barycenter representation in formula (7.39), we obtain

$$h_1\left(\frac{a+b+c}{3}\right) \leq \frac{\iint_{\Delta_{abc}} f(x,y)\,dxdy}{\mathrm{ar}(\Delta_{abc})} \leq h_2\left(\frac{a+b+c}{3}\right).$$

By utilizing coincidences

$$h_1\left(\frac{a+b+c}{3}\right) = f\left(\frac{a+b+c}{3}\right) \text{ and } h_2\left(\frac{a+b+c}{3}\right) = \frac{f(a)+f(b)+f(c)}{3},$$

we attain the inequality in formula (7.40). □

The barycenter of the n-simplex $\Delta_{a_0\ldots a_n}$ in the space $\mathbb{R}^n$ is the point

$$\overline{a} = \left(\frac{\int\ldots\int_{\Delta_{a_0\ldots a_n}} x_1\,dx_1\ldots dx_n}{\mathrm{vol}_n(\Delta_{a_0\ldots a_n})}, \ldots, \frac{\int\ldots\int_{\Delta_{a_0\ldots a_n}} x_n\,dx_1\ldots dx_n}{\mathrm{vol}_n(\Delta_{a_0\ldots a_n})}\right) = \frac{\sum_{i=0}^n a_i}{n+1}. \tag{7.42}$$

We can realize the Hermite-Hadamard inequality for simplices.

Theorem 7.5. *Let $\Delta_{a_0\ldots a_n}$ be an n-simplex in the space $\mathbb{R}^n$, and let $f:\Delta_{a_0\ldots a_n}\to\mathbb{R}$ be a convex function.*

Then, we have the double inequality

$$f\left(\frac{\sum_{i=0}^n a_i}{n+1}\right) \leq \frac{\int\ldots\int_{\Delta_{a_0\ldots a_n}} f(x_1,\ldots,x_n)\,dx_1\ldots dx_n}{\mathrm{vol}_n(\Delta_{a_0\ldots a_n})} \leq \frac{\sum_{i=0}^n f(a_i)}{n+1}. \tag{7.43}$$

To establish the relevant inequalities for convex functions defined on simplices, we will use the simplex representations presented in Section 7.1.

Lemma 7.4. *Let X be a set with a nonnegative measure μ such that $\mu(X)>0$, let $g: X\to\mathbb{R}$ be a bounded μ-integrable function, let $[a,b]$ be an interval containing the image of g, let $\overline{\alpha}a+\overline{\beta}b$ be the convex combination such that*

$$\frac{\int_X g(x)\,d\mu(x)}{\mu(X)} = \overline{\alpha}a+\overline{\beta}b, \tag{7.44}$$

and let $f : [a,b] \to \mathbb{R}$ be a convex function.

Then, we have the double inequality

$$f(\overline{\alpha}a+\overline{\beta}b) \leq \frac{\int_X f(g(x))\,d\mu(x)}{\mu(X)} \leq \overline{\alpha}f(a)+\overline{\beta}f(b). \tag{7.45}$$

Proof. As regards the equality in formula (7.44), we will determine the convex combination $\overline{\alpha}a+\overline{\beta}b$, which represents the μ-integral arithmetic mean

$$\overline{g} = \frac{\int_X g(x)\,d\mu(x)}{\mu(X)}.$$

By applying formula (7.4) to the point $\overline{g}$, and utilizing the affinity of functions α and β, we obtain the affine combination

$$\begin{aligned}\overline{g} &= \alpha(\overline{g})a+\beta(\overline{g})b \\ &= \frac{\int_X \alpha(g(x))\,d\mu(x)}{\mu(X)}a+\frac{\int_X \beta(g(x))\,d\mu(x)}{\mu(X)}b \\ &= \overline{\alpha}a+\overline{\beta}b\end{aligned}$$

with coefficients

$$\overline{\alpha} = \frac{\int_X \alpha(g(x))\,d\mu(x)}{\mu(X)} \text{ and } \overline{\beta} = \frac{\int_X \beta(g(x))\,d\mu(x)}{\mu(X)}. \tag{7.46}$$

These coefficients are nonnegative because $g(x) \in [a,b]$ for all $x \in X$, and so the affine combination $\overline{g} = \overline{\alpha}a+\overline{\beta}b$ is convex.

To prove the inequality in formula (7.45), we will consider two cases of the combination $\overline{g} = \overline{\alpha}a+\overline{\beta}b$, referring to the number of positive coefficients. So the cases specify the interior (a,b) and boundary $\{a,b\}$.

If $\overline{g} = \overline{\alpha}a+\overline{\beta}b$ with $\overline{\alpha},\overline{\beta} > 0$, then $\overline{g} \in (a,b)$. By including a support line h_1 of f at $\overline{g}$, and the secant line h_2 of f at a and b, we get the multiple inequality

$$\begin{aligned}f(\overline{\alpha}a+\overline{\beta}b) &= f(\overline{g}) = h_1(\overline{g}) = \frac{\int_X h_1(g(x))\,d\mu(x)}{\mu(X)} \\ &\leq \frac{\int_X f(g(x))\,d\mu(x)}{\mu(X)} \leq \frac{\int_X h_2(g(x))\,d\mu(x)}{\mu(X)} = h_2(\overline{g}) \\ &= \overline{\alpha}h_2(a)+\overline{\beta}h_2(b) = \overline{\alpha}f(a)+\overline{\beta}f(b),\end{aligned}$$

which contains formula (7.45). The composition $f(g)$ is μ-integrable because it is bounded on X, and continuous μ-almost everywhere on X.

If $\overline{g} = a$, then the equation $\overline{\alpha} = 1$ via formula (7.46) implies that $g(x) = a$ for μ-almost all $x \in X$ (the same arises from the equation $\overline{\beta} = 0$). It turns out that

$$\frac{\int_X f(g(x))\,d\mu(x)}{\mu(X)} = \frac{\int_X f(a)\,d\mu(x)}{\mu(X)} = f(a),$$

and so the trivial double inequality $f(a) \leq f(a) \leq f(a)$ represents formula (7.45). A similar reasoning applies for $\overline{g} = b$. $\square$

Lemma 7.5. *Let X be a set with a nonnegative measure μ such that $\mu(X) > 0$, let $g_1, g_2 : X \to \mathbb{R}$ be the bounded μ-integrable functions, let Δ_{abc} be a triangle containing the image of the mapping $g = (g_1, g_2) : X \to \mathbb{R}^2$, let $\overline{\alpha}a + \overline{\beta}b + \overline{\gamma}c$ be the convex combination such that*

$$\left(\frac{\int_X g_1(x)\, d\mu(x)}{\mu(X)}, \frac{\int_X g_2(x)\, d\mu(x)}{\mu(X)} \right) = \overline{\alpha}a + \overline{\beta}b + \overline{\gamma}c, \tag{7.47}$$

and let $f : \Delta_{abc} \to \mathbb{R}$ be a convex function.
Then, we have the double inequality

$$f(\overline{\alpha}a + \overline{\beta}b + \overline{\gamma}c) \le \frac{\int_X f(g_1(x), g_2(x))\, d\mu(x)}{\mu(X)} \le \overline{\alpha}f(a) + \overline{\beta}f(b) + \overline{\gamma}f(c). \tag{7.48}$$

Theorem 7.6. *Let X be a set with a nonnegative measure μ such that $\mu(X) > 0$, let $g_1, \ldots, g_n : X \to \mathbb{R}$ be the bounded μ-integrable functions, let $\Delta_{a_0 \ldots a_n}$ be an n-simplex containing the image of the mapping $g = (g_1, \ldots, g_n) : X \to \mathbb{R}^n$, let $\sum_{i=0}^n \overline{\alpha}_i a_i$ be the convex combination such that*

$$\left(\frac{\int_X g_1(x)\, d\mu(x)}{\mu(X)}, \ldots, \frac{\int_X g_n(x)\, d\mu(x)}{\mu(X)} \right) = \sum_{i=0}^{n} \overline{\alpha}_i a_i, \tag{7.49}$$

and let $f : \Delta_{a_0 \ldots a_n} \to \mathbb{R}$ be a convex function.
Then, we have the double inequality

$$f\left(\sum_{i=0}^{n} \overline{\alpha}_i a_i \right) \le \frac{\int_X f(g_1(x), \ldots, g_n(x))\, d\mu(x)}{\mu(X)} \le \sum_{i=0}^{n} \overline{\alpha}_i f(a_i). \tag{7.50}$$

Proof. The representation in formula (7.49) can be realized by applying formula (7.10) to the μ-integral arithmetic mean

$$\overline{g} = \left(\frac{\int_X g_1(x)\, d\mu(x)}{\mu(X)}, \ldots, \frac{\int_X g_n(x)\, d\mu(x)}{\mu(X)} \right),$$

and employing the affinity of functions α_i. This yields nonnegative coefficients

$$\overline{\alpha}_i = \frac{\int_X \alpha_i(g(x))\, dx}{\mu(X)}. \tag{7.51}$$

To prove the inequality in formula (7.50), we will consider three cases of the convex combination $\overline{g} = \sum_{i=0}^n \overline{\alpha}_i a_i$, referring to the number of positive coefficients. The first case connotes the interior of $\Delta_{a_0 \ldots a_n}$, and the other two cases connote the boundary (relative interior and vertices) of $\Delta_{a_0 \ldots a_n}$.

If $\overline{g} = \sum_{i=0}^n \overline{\alpha}_i a_i$ with $\overline{\alpha}_0, \ldots, \overline{\alpha}_n > 0$, then $\overline{g}$ is an interior point of $\Delta_{a_0 \ldots a_n}$, and f as a convex function admits a support hyperplane h_1 at $\overline{g}$. By including the secant hyperplane h_2 at vertices, we have the coincidences

$$h_1(\overline{g}) = f(\overline{g}),\ f(a_0) = h_2(a_0), \ldots, f(a_n) = h_2(a_n),$$

and for all $x \in X$ the support-secant hyperplane inequality

$$h_1(g(x)) \leq f(g(x)) \leq h_2(g(x)),$$

which is applied to the points $g(x) = (g_1(x), \ldots, g_n(x))$. By using the above coincidences and inequality, we can obtain the multiple relation

$$\begin{aligned} f\left(\sum_{i=0}^{n} \overline{\alpha}_i a_i\right) &= f(\overline{g}) = h_1(\overline{g}) = \frac{\int_X h_1(g(x))\, d\mu(x)}{\mu(X)} \\ &\leq \frac{\int_X f(g(x))\, d\mu(x)}{\mu(X)} \leq \frac{\int_X h_2(g(x))\, d\mu(x)}{\mu(X)} = h_2(\overline{g}) \qquad (7.52) \\ &= \sum_{i=0}^{n} \overline{\alpha}_i h_2(a_i) = \sum_{i=0}^{n} \overline{\alpha}_i f(a_i), \end{aligned}$$

covering the inequality in formula (7.50).

If $\overline{g} = \sum_{i=0}^{k} \overline{\alpha}_i a_i$ with $\overline{\alpha}_0, \ldots, \overline{\alpha}_k > 0$, where $1 \leq k \leq n-1$, then $\overline{g}$ is an interior point of the k-face

$$S = \Delta_{a_0 \ldots a_k}$$

contained in the affine plane $\mathbb{A} = \operatorname{aff}(S)$ of dimension k, and we rely on the restriction $f_S = f/S$. The convex function $f_S : S \to \mathbb{R}$ admits a support hyperplane $\tilde{h}_S : \mathbb{A} \to \mathbb{R}$ at $\overline{g}$, which provides the equality $\tilde{h}_S(\overline{g}) = f_S(\overline{g})$, and for all $s = (s_1, \ldots, s_n) \in S$, the support hyperplane inequality

$$\tilde{h}_S(s) \leq f_S(s). \qquad (7.53)$$

Let $\tilde{h}_1 : \mathbb{R}^n \to \mathbb{R}$ be any affine extension of $\tilde{h}_S$. Now, we have the coincidences

$$\tilde{h}_1(\overline{g}) = \tilde{h}_S(\overline{g}) = f_S(\overline{g}) = f(\overline{g}).$$

The system of equations $\overline{\alpha}_{k+1} = 0, \ldots, \overline{\alpha}_n = 0$ via formula (7.51) implies that

$$g(x) \in \Delta_{a_0 \ldots a_k a_{k+2} \ldots a_n} \cap \ldots \cap \Delta_{a_0 \ldots a_{n-1}} = \Delta_{a_0 \ldots a_k} = S$$

for μ-almost all $x \in X$. Therefore, the support hyperplane inequality in formula (7.53) applies to μ-almost all $x \in X$ in the form

$$\tilde{h}_S(g(x)) \leq f_S(g(x)).$$

Now, we include the secant hyperplane h_2 of f at vertices. Then, μ-almost all $x \in X$ satisfy the multiple relation

$$\begin{aligned} \tilde{h}_1(g(x)) = \tilde{h}_S(g(x)) &\leq f_S(g(x)) \\ = f(g(x)) &\leq h_2(g(x)), \end{aligned}$$

and consequently, the support-secant hyperplane inequality

$$\tilde{h}_1(g(x)) \leq f(g(x)) \leq h_2(g(x)).$$

The coincidence $\tilde{h}_1(\overline{g}) = f(\overline{g})$ and the above μ-almost everywhere inequality enable us to put $\tilde{h}_1$ instead of h_1 into formula (7.52), and thus reach formula (7.50). The same applies to other k-faces.

If $\overline{g} = a_0$, then the equation $\overline{\alpha}_0 = 1$ via formula (7.51) implies that $g(x) = a_0$ for μ-almost all $x \in X$. It further produces the trivial inequality $f(a_0) \leq f(a_0) \leq f(a_0)$, representing formula (7.50). The same applies to other vertices. □

The inequality in formula (7.50) is reduced to the Hermite-Hadamard inequality in formula (7.43) if we take $X = \Delta_{a_0 \ldots a_n}$ and $g_1(x) = x_1, \ldots, g_n(x) = x_n$. In this reduction, we have the correlations $\overline{\alpha}_0 = \ldots = \overline{\alpha}_n = 1/(n+1)$, $d\mu(x) = d_1 \ldots dx_n$, and $\mu(X) = \mathrm{vol}_n(\Delta_{a_0 \ldots a_n})$.

Formula (7.12) can be considered as the simplex definition in any real vector space of sufficiently large dimension. We will include this feature in the statement of the discrete version of the Hermite-Hadamard inequality.

Theorem 7.7. *Let $\mathbb{X}$ be a real vector space of dimension of at least n, let $\Delta_{a_0 \ldots a_n}$ be an n-simplex in $\mathbb{X}$, let $\sum_{j=1}^{m} \lambda_j x_j$ be a convex combination of points $x_j \in \Delta_{a_0 \ldots a_n}$, let $\sum_{i=0}^{n} \overline{\alpha}_i a_i$ be the convex combination of vertices a_i such that*

$$\sum_{j=1}^{m} \lambda_j x_j = \sum_{i=0}^{n} \overline{\alpha}_i a_i, \tag{7.54}$$

and let $f : \Delta_{a_0 \ldots a_n} \to \mathbb{R}$ be a convex function.

Then, we have the double discrete inequality

$$f\left(\sum_{i=0}^{n} \overline{\alpha}_i a_i\right) \leq \sum_{j=1}^{m} \lambda_j f(x_j) \leq \sum_{i=0}^{n} \overline{\alpha}_i f(a_i). \tag{7.55}$$

Proof. By using the simplex definition in formula (7.12), we can represent the points x_j as the convex combinations

$$x_j = \sum_{i=0}^{n} \overline{\alpha}_{ij} a_i. \tag{7.56}$$

Then, using the assumption in formula (7.54), we obtain

$$\sum_{i=0}^{n} \overline{\alpha}_i a_i = \sum_{j=1}^{m} \lambda_j x_j = \sum_{j=1}^{m} \lambda_j \left(\sum_{i=0}^{n} \overline{\alpha}_{ij} a_i\right) = \sum_{i=0}^{n} \left(\sum_{j=1}^{m} \lambda_j \overline{\alpha}_{ij}\right) a_i,$$

and since the convex combination of simplex vertices is unique, it follows that

$$\sum_{j=1}^{m} \lambda_j \overline{\alpha}_{ij} = \overline{\alpha}_i.$$

By applying Jensen's inequality to the convex combination $\sum_{j=1}^{m} \lambda_j x_j$ and subsequently through formula (7.56), and utilizing the above correlation coefficients, we produce the multiple relation

$$f\left(\sum_{i=0}^{n}\overline{\alpha}_i a_i\right)=f\left(\sum_{j=1}^{m}\lambda_j x_j\right)\leq\sum_{j=1}^{m}\lambda_j f(x_j)\leq\sum_{j=1}^{m}\lambda_j\sum_{i=0}^{n}\overline{\alpha}_{ij}f(a_i)$$
$$=\sum_{i=0}^{n}\left(\sum_{j=1}^{m}\lambda_j\overline{\alpha}_{ij}\right)f(a_i)=\sum_{i=0}^{n}\overline{\alpha}_i f(a_i),$$

including the double inequality in formula (7.55). □

Another Proof of the Case $\mathbb{X}=\mathbb{R}^n$. We will adapt Theorem 7.6 to the given discrete case. Let $x_j=(x_{j1},\dots,x_{jn})$ be the coordinate representations for $j=1,\dots,m$. Let $X=\{x_1,\dots,x_m\}$ be an m-member set with the probability measure μ given by $\mu(\{x_j\})=\lambda_j$, and let g_i be the functions determined by $g_i(x_j)=x_{ji}$. Then, we have

$$\begin{aligned}\overline{g} &= \left(\frac{\int_X g_1(x)\,d\mu(x)}{\mu(X)},\dots,\frac{\int_X g_n(x)\,d\mu(x)}{\mu(X)}\right)\\ &= \left(\sum_{j=1}^{m}g_1(x_j)\mu(\{x_j\}),\dots,\sum_{j=1}^{m}g_n(x_j)\mu(\{x_j\})\right)\\ &= \left(\sum_{j=1}^{m}\lambda_j x_{j1},\dots,\sum_{j=1}^{m}\lambda_j x_{jn}\right)=\sum_{j=1}^{m}\lambda_j x_j\end{aligned}$$

and

$$\begin{aligned}\overline{f(g)} &= \frac{\int_X f(g_1(x),\dots,g_n(x))\,d\mu(x)}{\mu(X)}\\ &= \sum_{j=1}^{m}f(g_1(x_j),\dots,g_n(x_j))\,\mu(\{x_j\})\\ &= \sum_{j=1}^{m}\lambda_j f(x_{j1},\dots,x_{jn})=\sum_{j=1}^{m}\lambda_j f(x_j).\end{aligned}$$

Thus, equality in formula (7.49) turns into equality in formula (7.54), and inequality in formula (7.50) turns into inequality in formula (7.55). □

The inequality in formula (7.55) discusses the nature of the behavior of convex functions. It shows that the convex function values taken in the form of convex combinations grow from the center, across the middle, to the vertices as ends.

Simple proof and refinement of the Hermite-Hadamard inequality was demonstrated in [2]. The Hermite-Hadamard inequality for the simplex, its refinements, and generalizations were considered in papers [1,10,11,14,15].

7.4 THE ROGERS-HÖLDER INEQUALITY

The Rogers-Hölder inequality occupies an important place in mathematical analysis, especially in the study and development of L^p spaces. Although it comes down to nonnegative real-valued functions, complex-valued functions are used due to their wider applications. This is usually done because of L^p spaces.

7.4.1 INTEGRAL AND DISCRETE FORMS OF THE ROGERS-HÖLDER INEQUALITY

Let X be a set with a nonnegative measure μ such that $\mu(X) > 0$. Let $p > 0$ be a real number, and let $L^p_\mu(X) = L^p(\mu)$ be the space of all μ-measurable functions $f : X \to \mathbb{C}$ such that f^p is μ-integrable (Lebesgue integrable with respect to the measure μ). Each function $f \in L^p(\mu)$ has the fictive p-norm

$$\|f\|_p = \left(\int_X |f(x)|^p \, d\mu(x)\right)^{1/p}. \tag{7.57}$$

If $p \geq 1$, the above definition gives the (proper) p-norm, the inequality $|f(x)| \leq |f(x)|^p$ holds for every $x \in X$, and therefore, $L^p_\mu(X) \subseteq L^1_\mu(X)$. The fundamental space $L^1_\mu(X)$ contains all complex functions on X that are μ-integrable.

Initial forms of the Rogers-Hölder inequality use a pair of positive real numbers p and q such that $p+q = pq$. It is equivalent to conditions $1/p+1/q = 1$ and $p,q > 1$. The numbers p and q are called the conjugate exponents.

All that is needed is prepared for Rogers-Hölder inequalities. The first one that follows is the integral form of the Rogers-Hölder inequality. The integral inequality in formula (7.34) adjusted to concave functions will serve as a basis of the proof.

Theorem 7.8. *Let X be a set with a nonnegative measure μ such that $\mu(X) > 0$, let $p,q > 1$ be the real numbers such that $1/p+1/q = 1$, let $f : X \to \mathbb{C}$ be a function in $L^p_\mu(X)$, and let $g : X \to \mathbb{C}$ be a function in $L^q_\mu(X)$.*

Then, we have the integral inequality

$$\int_X |f(x)g(x)| \, d\mu(x) \leq \left(\int_X |f(x)|^p \, d\mu(x)\right)^{1/p} \left(\int_X |g(x)|^q \, d\mu(x)\right)^{1/q}. \tag{7.58}$$

Proof. Since $p,q > 1$, the functions f and g are in $L^1_\mu(X)$, and therefore, their product fg is also in $L^1_\mu(X)$.

Let $I_1 \subseteq \mathbb{R}$ be an interval containing the image of $|f|^p$, let $I_2 \subseteq \mathbb{R}$ be an interval containing the image of $|g|^q$, and let $\phi : I_1 \times I_2 \to \mathbb{R}$ be a concave function. The generalized integral inequality in formula (7.34) for integer $n = 2$ adjusted to functions $g_1 = |f|^p$, $g_2 = |g|^q$ and $f = -\phi$ takes the form

$$\frac{\int_X \phi\left(|f(x)|^p, |g(x)|^q\right) d\mu(x)}{\mu(X)} \leq \phi\left(\frac{\int_X |f(x)|^p \, d\mu(x)}{\mu(X)}, \frac{\int_X |g(x)|^q \, d\mu(x)}{\mu(X)}\right).$$

If we implement the concave function $\phi : [0,\infty) \times [0,\infty) \to \mathbb{R}$ defined by

$$\phi(x,y) = x^{1/p} y^{1/q},$$

then we obtain

$$\frac{\int_X |f(x)g(x)| \, d\mu(x)}{\mu(X)} \leq \left(\frac{\int_X |f(x)|^p \, d\mu(x)}{\mu(X)}\right)^{1/p} \left(\frac{\int_X |g(x)|^q \, d\mu(x)}{\mu(X)}\right)^{1/q}.$$

After multiplying by $\mu(X)$, we achieve the inequality in formula (7.58). □

The integral inequality in formula (7.58) can be presented as the norm inequality

$$\|fg\|_1 \leq \|f\|_p \, \|g\|_q. \tag{7.59}$$

The integral form of the Rogers-Hölder inequality can be transformed into discrete form by taking advantage of the counting measure.

Theorem 7.9. *Let $x_i, y_i \in \mathbb{C}$ be the complex numbers for $i = 1, \ldots, n$, and let $p, q > 1$ be the real numbers such that $1/p + 1/q = 1$.*

Then, we have the discrete inequality

$$\sum_{i=1}^{n} |x_i y_i| \leq \left(\sum_{i=1}^{n} |x_i|^p \right)^{1/p} \left(\sum_{i=1}^{n} |y_i|^q \right)^{1/q}. \tag{7.60}$$

Proof. Let $X = \{x_1, \ldots, x_n\}$ be an n-member set with the counting measure μ as $\mu(\{x_i\}) = 1$, let f be the function as $f(x_i) = x_i$, and let g be the function as $g(x_i) = y_i$. Then, the transformation of the left side in formula (7.58) shows

$$\int_X |f(x)g(x)| \, d\mu(x) = \sum_{i=1}^{n} |f(x_i)g(x_i)| \, \mu(\{x_i\}) = \sum_{i=1}^{n} |x_i y_i|,$$

pointing the left side in formula (7.60). The same applies to the right side. □

By promoting n-tuples

$$x = (x_1, \ldots, x_n) \ \text{ and } \ y = (y_1, \ldots, y_n),$$

the product

$$x \cdot y = (x_1 y_1, \ldots, x_n y_n),$$

and norms

$$\|x\|_p = \left(\sum_{i=1}^{n} |x_i|^p \right)^{1/p}, \quad \|y\|_q = \left(\sum_{i=1}^{n} |y_i|^q \right)^{1/q}, \quad \|x \cdot y\|_1 = \sum_{i=1}^{n} |x_i y_i|,$$

the discrete inequality in formula (7.60) can be written as the norm inequality

$$\|x \cdot y\|_1 \leq \|x\|_p \, \|y\|_q. \tag{7.61}$$

In the books, formulas (7.58) and (7.60) were proved by relying on the discrete form of the Young inequality. It says that the inequality

$$ab \leq \frac{1}{p} a^p + \frac{1}{q} b^q \tag{7.62}$$

holds for every pair of nonnegative real numbers a and b.

Inequalities in formulas (7.58) and (7.60) are usually called the Hölder inequalities. Respecting the chronological publication order of paper [19] and paper [5], we preferred the name Rogers-Hölder. In the case $p = q = 2$, these inequalities are also called the Cauchy-Bunyakovsky-Schwarz inequalities. As regards the above special case, the inequality for sums was published by Cauchy (1821), the corresponding inequality for integrals was proved by Bunyakovsky in (1859), and the improved inequality for integrals was given by Schwarz (1888).

7.4.2 GENERALIZATIONS OF THE ROGERS-HÖLDER INEQUALITY

The main tool in the generalization of Rogers-Hölder inequalities are positive real numbers $p_1,\dots,p_m,p$ such that $\sum_{j=1}^m 1/p_j = 1/p$. The consequent relation

$$\frac{p}{p_1}+\cdots+\frac{p}{p_m}=1$$

is effective, implying that $p/p_j < 1$ and thus $p < p_j$ for $j=1,\dots,m$. Note that numbers p_j may be less than or equal to 1.

The generalized integral form of the Rogers-Hölder inequality is as follows.

Corollary 7.1. *Let X be a set with a nonnegative measure μ such that $\mu(X)>0$, let $p_1,\dots,p_m,p>0$ be the real numbers such that $\sum_{j=1}^m 1/p_j = 1/p$, and let $f_j : X\to\mathbb{C}$ be the functions in $L_\mu^{p_j}(X)$ for $j=1,\dots,m$.*

Then, we have the integral inequality

$$\left(\int_X |f_1\dots f_m|^p\,d\mu\right)^{1/p} \le \left(\int_X |f_1|^{p_1}\,d\mu\right)^{1/p_1}\cdots\left(\int_X |f_m|^{p_m}\,d\mu\right)^{1/p_m}. \tag{7.63}$$

Proof. Since $p<p_1,\dots,p<p_m$, it follows that

$$|f_1\dots f_m|^p \le |f_1|^{p_1}\dots|f_m|^{p_m},$$

and so the product $f_1\dots f_m$ is in $L_\mu^p(X)$.

Let $I_j\subseteq\mathbb{R}$ be an interval containing the image of $|f_j|^{p_j}$ for $j=1,\dots,m$, and let $\phi : I_1\times\cdots\times I_m\to\mathbb{R}$ be a concave function. The generalized integral inequality in formula (7.34) for integer $n=m$ with functions $g_1=|f_1|^{p_1},\dots,g_m=|f_m|^{p_m}$ and $f=-\phi$ comes out as

$$\frac{\int_X \phi\left(|f_1|^{p_1},\dots,|f_m|^{p_m}\right)d\mu}{\mu(X)} \le \phi\left(\frac{\int_X |f_1|^{p_1}\,d\mu}{\mu(X)},\dots,\frac{\int_X |f_m|^{p_m}\,d\mu}{\mu(X)}\right).$$

If we include the concave function $\phi : [0,\infty)\times\cdots\times[0,\infty)\to\mathbb{R}$ determined by

$$\phi(x_1,\dots,x_m)=x_1^{p/p_1}\dots x_m^{p/p_m},$$

then we realize

$$\frac{\int_X |f_1\dots f_m|^p\,d\mu}{\mu(X)} \le \left(\frac{\int_X |f_1|^{p_1}\,d\mu}{\mu(X)}\right)^{p/p_1}\cdots\left(\frac{\int_X |f_m|^{p_m}\,d\mu}{\mu(X)}\right)^{p/p_m}.$$

The multiplication by $\mu(X)$ and raising to the power $1/p$ gives formula (7.63). □

The integral inequality in formula (7.63) can be expressed as the fictive norm inequality

$$\|f_1\dots f_m\|_p \le \|f_1\|_{p_1}\cdots\|f_m\|_{p_m}. \tag{7.64}$$

If $m=2$ and $p=1$, formula (7.63) is reduced to formula (7.58), and formula (7.64) is reduced to formula (7.59).

The following is the generalized discrete form of the Rogers-Hölder inequality.

Corollary 7.2. *Let $x_{ij} \in \mathbb{C}$ be the complex numbers for $i = 1, \ldots, n$ and $j = 1, \ldots, m$, and let $p_1, \ldots, p_m, p > 0$ be the real numbers such that $\sum_{j=1}^{m} 1/p_j = 1/p$.*

Then, we have the discrete inequality

$$\left(\sum_{i=1}^{n} |x_{i1} \ldots x_{im}|^p\right)^{1/p} \leq \left(\sum_{i=1}^{n} |x_{i1}|^{p_1}\right)^{1/p_1} \cdots \left(\sum_{i=1}^{n} |x_{im}|^{p_m}\right)^{1/p_m}. \tag{7.65}$$

Proof. Let $X = \{x_1, \ldots, x_n\}$ be an n-member set with the counting measure μ given by $\mu(\{x_i\}) = 1$, and let f_j be the functions determined by $f_j(x_i) = x_{ij}$. Then, the transformation of pth power of the left side in formula (7.63) produces

$$\int_X |f_1(x) \ldots f_m(x)|^p d\mu(x) = \sum_{i=1}^{n} |f_1(x_i) \ldots f_m(x_i)|^p \mu(\{x_i\}) = \sum_{i=1}^{n} |x_{i1} \ldots x_{im}|^p$$

as pth power of the left side in formula (7.65). The similar applies to the right side. □

By exploiting n-tuples

$$x_1 = (x_{11}, \ldots, x_{n1}), \; \ldots, \; x_m = (x_{1m}, \ldots, x_{nm}),$$

the product

$$x_1 \cdot \ldots \cdot x_m = (x_{11} \ldots x_{1m}, \ldots, x_{n1} \ldots x_{nm}),$$

and using the corresponding fictive norms, the discrete inequality in formula (7.65) can be presented as the fictive norm inequality

$$\|x_1 \cdot \ldots \cdot x_m\|_p \leq \|x_1\|_{p_1} \cdots \|x_m\|_{p_m}. \tag{7.66}$$

Formulas (7.63) and (7.65) can be proved by applying the method of mathematical induction to integer m, wherein the case $m = 2$ serves as the induction base. These formulae can also be obtained by relying on the generalized discrete form of the Young inequality. It can be demonstrated that the inequality

$$a_1 \ldots a_m \leq \frac{p}{p_1} a_1^{p_1/p} + \ldots + \frac{p}{p_m} a_m^{p_m/p} \tag{7.67}$$

holds for every m-tuple of nonnegative real numbers $a_1, \ldots, a_m$.

More details and better insight into Young's original inequalities can be found in the proceedings [20].

7.5 THE MINKOWSKI INEQUALITY

The Minkowski inequality is the key inequality of functional analysis. It has the greatest influence in the normed vector spaces.

7.5.1 INTEGRAL AND DISCRETE FORMS OF THE MINKOWSKI INEQUALITY

Minkowski inequalities demonstrate that p-norms satisfy the triangle inequality. These inequalities are fundamental in the field of functional analysis.

Let $x, y \in \mathbb{C}$ be a pair of complex numbers. The prominent triangle inequality for absolute value as

$$|x+y| \leq |x| + |y| \tag{7.68}$$

can be obtained by applying Jensen's inequality in formula (7.25) to the convex combination $x/2 + y/2$, and convex function $\varphi : \mathbb{C} \to \mathbb{R}$ given by $\varphi(z) = 2|z|$.

The following is the integral form of the Minkowski inequality. The integral inequality in formula (7.34) will be the mainstay of the proof.

Theorem 7.10. *Let X be a set with a nonnegative measure μ such that $\mu(X) > 0$, let $p \geq 1$ be a real number, and let $f, g : X \to \mathbb{C}$ be the functions in $L^p_\mu(X)$.*

Then, we have the integral inequality

$$\left(\int_X |f(x)+g(x)|^p \, d\mu(x)\right)^{1/p} \leq \left(\int_X |f(x)|^p \, d\mu(x)\right)^{1/p} + \left(\int_X |g(x)|^p \, d\mu(x)\right)^{1/p}. \tag{7.69}$$

Proof. A slightly modified formula (7.69) with the integrand $\left(|f(x)| + |g(x)|\right)^p$ on the left side will be discussed first. The sum $|f| + |g|$ is in $L^p_\mu(X)$ because

$$\left(|f(x)| + |g(x)|\right)^p \leq 2^{p-1}\left(|f(x)|^p + |g(x)|^p\right)$$

for every $x \in X$. The above inequality can be obtained by applying Jensen's inequality in formula (7.25) to the convex combination $|f(x)|/2 + |g(x)|/2$, and convex function $\varphi : [0, \infty) \to \mathbb{R}$ given by $\varphi(t) = 2^p t^p$.

Let $I_1 \subseteq \mathbb{R}$ be an interval containing the image of $|f|^p$, let $I_2 \subseteq \mathbb{R}$ be an interval containing the image of $|g|^p$, and let $\phi : I_1 \times I_2 \to \mathbb{R}$ be a concave function. The generalized integral inequality in formula (7.34) for integer $n = 2$ with functions $g_1 = |f|^p$, $g_2 = |g|^p$, and $f = -\phi$ arises in the form

$$\frac{\int_X \phi\left(|f(x)|^p, |g(x)|^p\right) d\mu(x)}{\mu(X)} \leq \phi\left(\frac{\int_X |f(x)|^p \, d\mu(x)}{\mu(X)}, \frac{\int_X |g(x)|^p \, d\mu(x)}{\mu(X)}\right).$$

If we utilize the concave function $\phi : [0, \infty) \times [0, \infty) \to \mathbb{R}$ defined by

$$\phi(x, y) = \left(x^{1/p} + y^{1/p}\right)^p,$$

then we gain

$$\frac{\int_X \left(|f(x)| + |g(x)|\right)^p d\mu(x)}{\mu(X)} \leq \left[\left(\frac{\int_X |f(x)|^p \, d\mu(x)}{\mu(X)}\right)^{1/p} + \left(\frac{\int_X |g(x)|^p \, d\mu(x)}{\mu(X)}\right)^{1/p}\right]^p.$$

After multiplying by $\mu(X)$, and raising to the power $1/p$, we have

$$\left(\int_X \left(|f(x)| + |g(x)|\right)^p d\mu(x)\right)^{1/p} \leq \left(\int_X |f(x)|^p \, d\mu(x)\right)^{1/p} + \left(\int_X |g(x)|^p \, d\mu(x)\right)^{1/p}.$$

This inequality can be extended to the left by using the integrand $|f(x)+g(x)|^p$ because $|f(x)+g(x)|^p \leq \big(|f(x)|+|g(x)|\big)^p$ for every $x \in X$. □

The collection $L^p_\mu(X)$ with $p \geq 1$ becomes the normed vector space if the integral inequality in formula (7.69) is expressed as the norm inequality

$$\|f+g\|_p \leq \|f\|_p + \|g\|_p. \tag{7.70}$$

The discrete form of the Minkowski inequality is as follows.

Theorem 7.11. *Let $x_i, y_i \in \mathbb{C}$ be the complex numbers for $i = 1,\ldots,n$, and let $p \geq 1$ be a real number.*
Then, we have the discrete inequality

$$\left(\sum_{i=1}^{n} |x_i+y_i|^p\right)^{1/p} \leq \left(\sum_{i=1}^{n} |x_i|^p\right)^{1/p} + \left(\sum_{i=1}^{n} |y_i|^p\right)^{1/p}. \tag{7.71}$$

Proof. The integral inequality in formula (7.69) is transformed into discrete inequality in formula (7.71) by exploring the counting measure as in Theorem 7.9. □

By using n-tuples $x = (x_1,\ldots,x_n)$ and $y = (y_1,\ldots,y_n)$, and required p-norms, the discrete inequality in formula (7.71) can be presented as the norm inequality

$$\|x+y\|_p \leq \|x\|_p + \|y\|_p. \tag{7.72}$$

In the books, formulas (7.69) and (7.71) were proved by relying on the triangle inequality and corresponding Rogers-Hölder inequalities.

7.5.2 GENERALIZATIONS OF THE MINKOWSKI INEQUALITY

To generalize the integral form of the Minkowski inequality, we need a real number $p \geq 1$, and complex functions in the space $L^p_\mu(X)$. It is as follows.

Corollary 7.3. *Let X be a set with a nonnegative measure μ such that $\mu(X) > 0$, let $p \geq 1$ be a real number, and let $f_1,\ldots,f_m : X \to \mathbb{C}$ be the functions in $L^p_\mu(X)$.*
Then, we have the integral inequality

$$\left(\int_X |f_1+\cdots+f_m|^p \, d\mu\right)^{1/p} \leq \left(\int_X |f_1|^p \, d\mu\right)^{1/p} + \cdots + \left(\int_X |f_m|^p \, d\mu\right)^{1/p}. \tag{7.73}$$

Proof. The modified formula (7.73) having the integrand $\big(|f_1|+\cdots+|f_m|\big)^p$ on the left side will be considered first. The sum $|f_1|+\cdots+|f_m|$ is in $L^p_\mu(X)$ because

$$\big(|f_1(x)|+\cdots+|f_m(x)|\big)^p \leq m^{p-1}\big(|f_1(x)|^p+\cdots+|f_m(x)|^p\big)$$

for every $x \in X$. The above inequality can be obtained by applying the discrete form of Jensen's inequality to the convex combination $|f_1(x)|/m+\cdots+|f_m(x)|/m$, and convex function $\varphi : [0,\infty) \to \mathbb{R}$ given by $\varphi(t) = m^p t^p$.

Let $I_j \subseteq \mathbb{R}$ be an interval containing the image of $|f_j|^p$ for $j = 1, \dots, m$, and let $\phi : I_1 \times \cdots \times I_m \to \mathbb{R}$ be a concave function. The generalized integral inequality in formula (7.34) for integer $n = m$ with functions $g_1 = |f_1|^p, \dots, g_m = |f_m|^p$, and $f = -\phi$ appears as

$$\frac{\int_X \phi\left(|f_1|^p, \dots, |f_m|^p\right) d\mu}{\mu(X)} \leq \phi\left(\frac{\int_X |f_1|^p d\mu}{\mu(X)}, \dots, \frac{\int_X |f_m|^p d\mu}{\mu(X)}\right).$$

If we employ the concave function $\phi : [0,\infty) \times \cdots \times [0,\infty) \to \mathbb{R}$ defined by

$$\phi(x_1, \dots, x_m) = \left(x_1^{1/p} + \cdots + x_m^{1/p}\right)^p,$$

then we obtain

$$\frac{\int_X \left(|f_1| + \cdots + |f_m|\right)^p d\mu}{\mu(X)} \leq \left(\frac{\int_X |f_1|^p d\mu}{\mu(X)}\right)^p + \cdots + \left[\left(\frac{\int_X |f_m|^p d\mu}{\mu(X)}\right)^p\right]^p.$$

After multiplying by $\mu(X)$, and raising to the power $1/p$, we attain

$$\left(\int_X \left(|f_1| + \cdots + |f_m|\right)^p d\mu\right)^{1/p} \leq \left(\int_X |f_1|^p d\mu\right)^{1/p} + \cdots + \left(\int_X |f_m|^p d\mu\right)^{1/p}.$$

This inequality can be extended to the left by using the integrand $|f_1 + \cdots + f_m|^p$ because $|f_1(x) + \cdots + f_m(x)|^p \leq \left(|f_1(x)| + \cdots + |f_m(x)|\right)^p$ for every $x \in X$. □

The integral inequality in formula (7.73) can be represented as the norm inequality

$$\|f_1 + \cdots + f_m\|_p \leq \|f_1\|_p + \cdots + \|f_m\|_p. \tag{7.74}$$

The following is the generalized discrete form of the Minkowski inequality.

Corollary 7.4. *Let $x_{ij} \in \mathbb{C}$ be the complex numbers for $i = 1, \dots, n$ and $j = 1, \dots, m$, and let $p \geq 1$ be a real number.*

Then, we have the discrete inequality

$$\left(\sum_{i=1}^n |x_{i1} + \cdots + x_{im}|^p\right)^{1/p} \leq \left(\sum_{i=1}^n |x_{i1}|^p\right)^{1/p} + \cdots + \left(\sum_{i=1}^n |x_{im}|^p\right)^{1/p}. \tag{7.75}$$

Proof. The integral inequality in formula (7.73) is transformed into discrete inequality in formula (7.75) by exploring the counting measure as in Corollary 7.2. □

By using n-tuples $x_j = (x_{1j}, \dots, x_{nj})$ for $j = 1, \dots, m$, and required p-norms, the discrete inequality in formula (7.75) can be presented as the norm inequality

$$\|x_1 + \cdots + x_m\|_p \leq \|x_1\|_p + \cdots + \|x_m\|_p. \tag{7.76}$$

Formulas (7.74) and (7.76) can be easily achieved by applying the method of mathematical induction to integer m, wherein the case $m = 2$ is as the induction base. In doing so, formulas (7.73) and (7.76) would also be verified as equivalents of (7.74) and (7.76), respectively.

Original details concerning Minkowski's inequalities can be seen in his book [9].

BIBLIOGRAPHY

[1] M. Bessenyei, The Hermite-Hadamard inequality on simplices, *Amer. Math. Monthly* **115** (2008), 339–345.

[2] A. Farissi, Simple proof and refinement of Hermite-Hadamard inequality, *J. Math. Inequal.* **4** (2010), 365–369.

[3] J. Hadamard, Étude sur les propriétés des fonctions entières et en particulier d'une fonction considerée par Riemann, *J. Math. Pures Appl.*, **58** (1893), 171–215.

[4] Ch. Hermite, Sur deux limites d'une intégrale définie, *Mathesis*, **3** (1883), 82.

[5] O. Hölder, Uber einen Mittelwertsatz, *Nachr. Ges. Wiss. Goettingen* (1889), 38–47.

[6] J. L. W. V. Jensen, Om konvekse Funktioner og Uligheder mellem Middelværdier, *Nyt Tidsskr. Math. B* **16** (1905), 49–68.

[7] J. L. W. V. Jensen, Sur les fonctions convexes et les inégalités entre les valeurs moyennes, *Acta Math.* **30** (1906), 175–193.

[8] E. J. McShane, Jensen's inequality, *Bulletin of the American Mathematical Society*, **43** (1937), 521–527.

[9] H. Minkowski, Theorie der Konvexen Körper, *Insbesondere Begründung ihres Oberflächenbegriffs,* Gesammelte Abhandlungen II, Leipzig, (1911).

[10] F.-C. Mitroi and C. I. Spiridon, Refinements of Hermite-Hadamard inequality on simplices, *Math. Rep. (Bucur.)***15** (2013), arXiv:1105.5043.

[11] E. Neuman, Inequalities involving multivariate convex functions II, *Proc. Amer. Math. Soc.* **109** (1990), 965–974.

[12] C. P. Niculescu and L. E. Persson, *Convex Functions and Their Applications,* Canadian Mathematical Society, Springer, New York, (2006).

[13] Z. Pavić, Extension of Jensen's inequality to affine combinations, *J. Inequal. Appl.* **2014** (2014), Article 298.

[14] Z. Pavić, Geometric and analytic connections of the Jensen and Hermite-Hadamard inequality, *Math. Sci. Appl. E-Notes* **4** (2016), 69–76.

[15] Z. Pavić, Improvements of the Hermite-Hadamard inequality for the simplex, *J. Inequal. Appl.* **2017** (2017), Article 3.

[16] Z. Pavić, J. Pečarić and I. Perić, Integral, discrete and functional variants of Jensen's inequality, *J. Math. Inequal.* **5** (2011), 253–264.

[17] Z. Pavić, The Jensen and Hermite-Hadamard inequality on the triangle, *J. Math. Inequal.* **11** (2017), 1099–1112.

[18] A. W. Roberts and D. E. Varberg, *Convex Functions,* Academic Press, New York and London, (1973).

[19] L. J. Rogers, An extension of a certain theorem in inequalities, *Messenger of Math.* **17** (1888), 145–150.

[20] W. H. Young, On classes of summable functions and their Fourier series, *Proceedings of the Royal Society A* **87** (1912), 225–229.

8 Refinements of Young's Integral Inequality via Fundamental Inequalities and Mean Value Theorems for Derivatives[1]

Feng Qi
Henan Polytechnic University
Inner Mongolia University for Nationalities
Tianjin Polytechnic University

Wen-Hui Li
Zhengzhou University of Science and Technology

Guo-Sheng Wu
Sichuan Technology and Business University

Bai-Ni Guo
Henan Polytechnic University

CONTENTS

[1] Dedicated to people facing and fighting COVID-19.

8.1 YOUNG'S INTEGRAL INEQUALITY AND SEVERAL REFINEMENTS

In the first part of this paper, we mainly review several refinements of Young's integral inequality via several mean value theorems, such as Lagrange's and Taylor's mean value theorems of Lagrange's and Cauchy's type remainders, and via several fundamental inequalities, such as Čebyšev's integral inequality, Hermite-Hadamard's type integral inequalities, Hölder's integral inequality, and Jensen's discrete and integral inequalities, in terms of higher-order derivatives and their norms, and simply survey several applications of several refinements of Young's integral inequality.

8.1.1 YOUNG'S INTEGRAL INEQUALITY

One of the fundamental and general inequalities in mathematics is Young's integral inequality below.

Theorem 8.1 ([55]). *Let $h(x)$ be a real-valued, continuous, and strictly increasing function on $[0,c]$ with $c>0$. If $h(0)=0$, $a\in[0,c]$, and $b\in[0,h(c)]$, then*

$$\int_0^a h(x)\,\mathrm{d}x+\int_0^b h^{-1}(x)\,\mathrm{d}x\ge ab, \tag{8.1}$$

where h^{-1} denotes the inverse function of h. The equality in (8.1) is valid if and only if $b=h(a)$.

Proof. This proof is adapted from the proof of [25, Section 2.7, Theorem 1].

Set

$$f(a)=ab-\int_0^a h(x)\,\mathrm{d}x \tag{8.2}$$

and consider $b>0$ as a parameter. Since $f'(a)=b-h(a)$ and h is strictly increasing, one obtains

$$f'(a)\begin{cases}>0, & 0<a<h^{-1}(b);\\ =0, & a=h^{-1}(b);\\ <0, & a>h^{-1}(b).\end{cases}$$

This means that $f(a)$ has a maximum of f at $a=h^{-1}(b)$. Therefore, it follows that

$$f(a)\le\max\{f(x)\}=f\big(h^{-1}(b)\big). \tag{8.3}$$

Integrating by parts gives

$$f\big(h^{-1}(b)\big)=bh^{-1}(b)-\int_0^{h^{-1}(b)}h(x)\,\mathrm{d}x=\int_0^{h^{-1}(b)}xh'(x)\,\mathrm{d}x.$$

Substituting $y=h(x)$ into the above integral yields

$$f\big(h^{-1}(b)\big)=\int_0^b h^{-1}(y)\,\mathrm{d}y. \tag{8.4}$$

Putting (8.2) and (8.4) into (8.3) results in (8.1). The proof of Theorem 8.1 is complete. □

Remark 8.1. *The geometric interpretation of Young's integral inequality* (8.1) *can be demonstrated by Figures 8.1 and 8.2.*

In Figure 8.1, we have

$$A+C=\int_0^a h(x)\,\mathrm{d}x,\quad A+B=ab,\quad B=\int_0^b h^{-1}(x)\,\mathrm{d}x,$$
$$A+B+C=\int_0^a h(x)\,\mathrm{d}x+\int_0^b h^{-1}(x)\,\mathrm{d}x\geq ab=A+B.$$

Therefore, the inequality (8.1) *means that the area*

$$C=\int_{h^{-1}(b)}^a h(x)\,\mathrm{d}x-b\big[a-h^{-1}(b)\big]\geq 0. \tag{8.5}$$

In Figure 8.2, we have

$$A=\int_0^a h(x)\,\mathrm{d}x,\quad A+B=ab,\quad B+C=\int_0^b h^{-1}(x)\,\mathrm{d}x,$$
$$A+B+C=\int_0^a h(x)\,\mathrm{d}x+\int_0^b h^{-1}(x)\,\mathrm{d}x\geq ab=A+B.$$

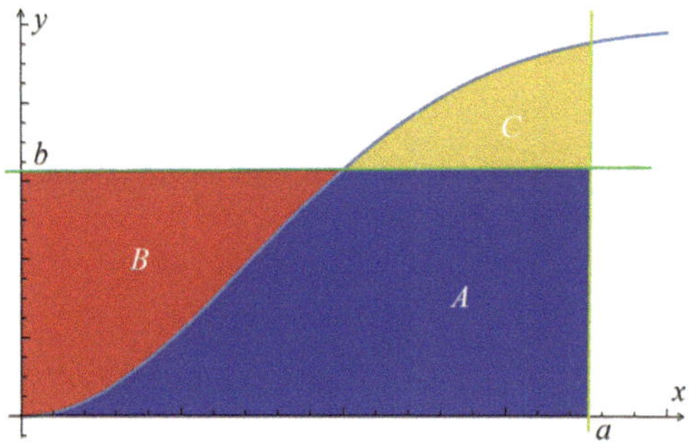

Figure 8.1 Geometric interpretation of the inequality (8.1).

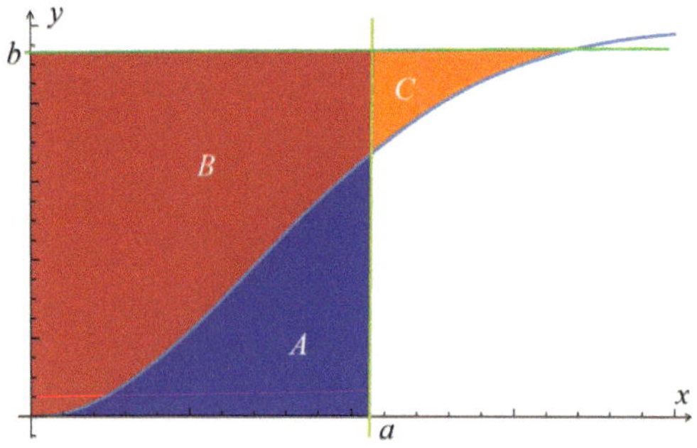

Figure 8.2 Geometric interpretation of the inequality (8.1).

Therefore, the inequality (8.1) *means that the area*

$$C=b\left[h^{-1}(b)-a\right]-\int_{a}^{h^{-1}(b)}h(x)\,\mathrm{d}x\geq 0. \tag{8.6}$$

Remark 8.2. *We notice that two expressions* (8.5) *and* (8.6) *are of the same form*

$$C=\int_{h^{-1}(b)}^{a}h(x)\,\mathrm{d}x-ab+bh^{-1}(b)\geq 0, \tag{8.7}$$

no matter which of a and $h^{-1}(b)$ is smaller or bigger.

Remark 8.3. *When $p>1$, taking $h(x)=x^{p-1}$ in* (8.1) *derives*

$$\frac{1}{p}a^{p}+\frac{1}{q}b^{q}\geq ab$$

for $a,b\geq 0$ and $p,q>1$ satisfying $\frac{1}{p}+\frac{1}{q}=1$. Further replacing a^p and b^q by x and y, respectively, leads to

$$x^{1/p}y^{1/q}\leq\frac{x}{p}+\frac{y}{q} \tag{8.8}$$

for $x,y\geq 0$ and $a,q>1$ satisfying $\frac{1}{p}+\frac{1}{q}=1$. Perhaps this is why the weighted arithmetic-geometric inequality (8.8) *is also called Young's inequality in [13,14,21] and closely related references therein.*

Remark 8.4. *The inequality*

$$\sum_{k=1}^{n}\frac{\cos(k\theta)}{k}>-1,\quad n\geq 2,\quad \theta\in[0,\pi]$$

is also called Young's inequality in [2,3] and closely related references therein.

Remark 8.5. *In [25, Secton 2.7] and [26, Chapter XIV], a plenty of refinements, extensions, generalizations, and applications of Young's integral inequality* (8.1) *were collected, reviewed, and surveyed. For some new and recent development on this topic after the year 1990, please refer to the papers [4,43,47,51,56] and closely related references therein.*

8.1.2 REFINEMENTS OF YOUNG'S INTEGRAL INEQUALITY VIA LAGRANGE'S MEAN VALUE THEOREM

In 2008, Hoorfar and Qi refined Young's integral inequality (8.1) via Lagrange's mean value theorem for derivatives.

Theorem 8.2 ([18, Theorem 1])**.** *Let $h(x)$ be a differentiable and strictly increasing function on $[0,c]$ for $c>0$, and let h^{-1} be the inverse function of h. If $h(0)=0$, $a\in[0,c]$, $b\in[0,h(c)]$, and $h'(x)$ is strictly monotonic on $[0,c]$, then*

$$\frac{m}{2}\left[a-h^{-1}(b)\right]^{2}\leq\int_{0}^{a}h(x)\,\mathrm{d}x+\int_{0}^{b}h^{-1}(x)\,\mathrm{d}x-ab\leq\frac{M}{2}\left[a-h^{-1}(b)\right]^{2}, \tag{8.9}$$

where

$$m = \min\{h'(a), h'(h^{-1}(b))\}$$

and

$$M = \max\{h'(a), h'(h^{-1}(b))\}.$$

The equalities in (8.9) *are valid if and only if* $b = h(a)$.

Proof. This is a modification of the proof of [18, Theorem 1] in [18, Section 2].

Changing the variable of integration by $x = h(y)$ and integrating by parts yield

$$\begin{aligned}
\int_0^a h(x)\,\mathrm{d}x + \int_0^b h^{-1}(x)\,\mathrm{d}x &= \int_0^a h(x)\,\mathrm{d}x + \int_0^{h^{-1}(b)} yh'(y)\,\mathrm{d}y \\
&= \int_0^a h(x)\,\mathrm{d}x + bh^{-1}(b) - \int_0^{h^{-1}(b)} h(x)\,\mathrm{d}x \\
&= bh^{-1}(b) + \int_{h^{-1}(b)}^a h(x)\,\mathrm{d}x \\
&= ab + \int_{h^{-1}(b)}^a [h(x) - b]\,\mathrm{d}x. \qquad (8.10)
\end{aligned}$$

From the last line in (8.10), we can see that if $h^{-1}(b) = a$, then those equalities in (8.9) hold.

If $h^{-1}(b) < a$, since $h(x)$ is strictly increasing, then $h(x) - b > 0$ for $x \in (h^{-1}(b), a)$. By Lagrange's mean value theorem for derivatives, we can see that there exists $\xi = \xi(x)$, satisfying $h^{-1}(b) < \xi < x \le a$, such that

$$0 < h(x) - b = [x - h^{-1}(b)]h'(\xi).$$

By virtue of monotonicity of $h'(x)$ on $[0, c]$, we reveal that

$$0 < m = \min\{h'(a), h'(h^{-1}(b))\} < h'(\xi) < \max\{h'(a), h'(h^{-1}(b))\} = M.$$

Consequently, we have

$$0 < m[x - h^{-1}(b)] < h(x) - b < M[x - h^{-1}(b)].$$

As a result, we have

$$m\int_{h^{-1}(b)}^a [x - h^{-1}(b)]\,\mathrm{d}x < \int_{h^{-1}(b)}^a [h(x) - b]\,\mathrm{d}x < M\int_{h^{-1}(b)}^a [x - h^{-1}(b)]\,\mathrm{d}x$$

which is equivalent to

$$\frac{m}{2}[a - h^{-1}(b)]^2 < \int_{h^{-1}(b)}^a [h(x) - b]\,\mathrm{d}x < \frac{M}{2}[a - h^{-1}(b)]^2. \qquad (8.11)$$

If $h^{-1}(b) > a$, we can derive inequalities in (8.11) by a similar argument as above.

Substituting the double inequality (8.11) into the equality (8.10) leads to the double inequality (8.9). The proof of Theorem 8.2 is complete. □

Remark 8.6. *The geometric interpretation of the double inequality* (8.9) *is that the areas C in Figures 8.3–8.6 satisfy*

$$\frac{m}{2}\left[a-h^{-1}(b)\right]^2 \le C \le \frac{M}{2}\left[a-h^{-1}(b)\right]^2. \tag{8.12}$$

When $h'(x)$ is strictly increasing, the double inequality (8.12) *can be equivalently written as*

$$\frac{h'(a)}{2}\left[a-h^{-1}(b)\right] \le \frac{\int_{h^{-1}(b)}^{a} h(x)\,\mathrm{d}x}{a-h^{-1}(b)} \le \frac{h'(h^{-1}(b))}{2}\left[a-h^{-1}(b)\right]$$

and

$$\frac{h'(a)}{2}\left[h^{-1}(b)-a\right] \le \frac{\int_{a}^{h^{-1}(b)} h(x)\,\mathrm{d}x}{h^{-1}(b)-a} \le \frac{h'(h^{-1}(b))}{2}\left[h^{-1}(b)-a\right]$$

corresponding to Figures 8.3 and 8.4, respectively.

Remark 8.7. *If Q is a convex function on J, then*

$$Q\left(\frac{\tau+\mu}{2}\right) \le \frac{1}{\mu-\tau}\int_{\tau}^{\mu} Q(x)\,\mathrm{d}x \le \frac{Q(\tau)+Q(\mu)}{2}; \tag{8.13}$$

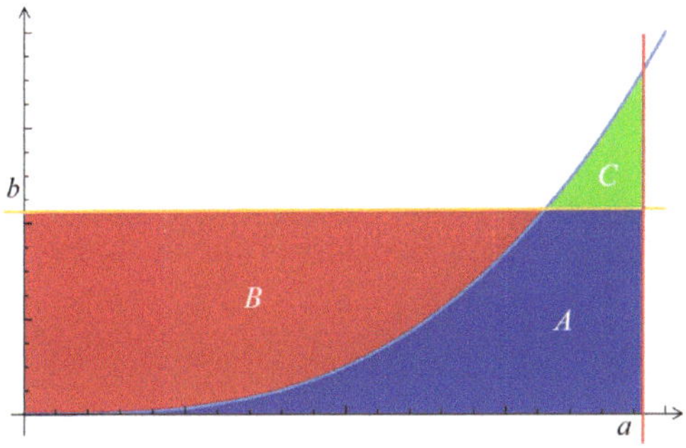

Figure 8.3 Geometric interpretation of the double inequality (8.9).

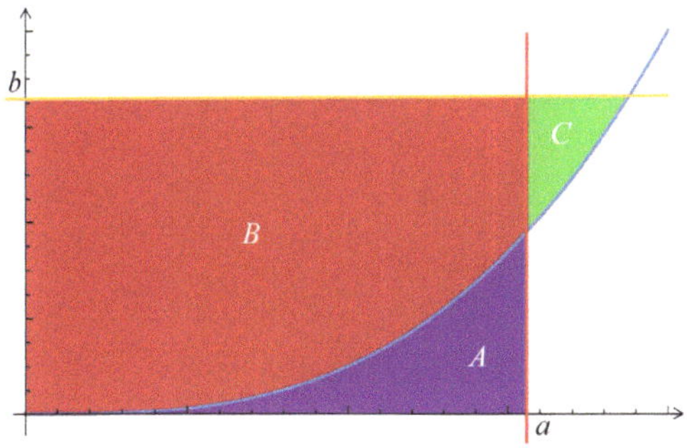

Figure 8.4 Geometric interpretation of the double inequality (8.9).

if Q is a concave function on J, then the double inequality (8.13) *is reversed, where $J \subseteq \mathbb{R}$ is a nonempty interval and $\tau, \mu \in J$ with $\tau < \mu$. The double inequality* (8.13) *is called Hermite-Hadamard's integral inequality for convex functions [7,38,45]. When $a > h^{-1}(b)$, as shown in Figures 8.3 and 8.5, and $h'(x)$ is strictly increasing, i.e., the function $h(x)$ is convex, as shown in Figures 8.3 and 8.4, applying the double inequality* (8.13) *yields*

$$h\left(\frac{a+h^{-1}(b)}{2}\right) \le \frac{\int_{h^{-1}(b)}^{a} h(x)\,\mathrm{d}x}{a-h^{-1}(b)} \le \frac{h(a)+b}{2}.$$

Substituting this into the third line in (8.10) *gives*

$$\int_0^a h(x)\,\mathrm{d}x + \int_0^b h^{-1}(x)\,\mathrm{d}x \le ab + \frac{h(a)-b}{2}\left[a-h^{-1}(b)\right]$$

and

$$\begin{aligned}\int_0^a h(x)\,\mathrm{d}x + \int_0^b h^{-1}(x)\,\mathrm{d}x &\ge bh^{-1}(b) + h\left(\frac{a+h^{-1}(b)}{2}\right)\left[a-h^{-1}(b)\right]\\ &= ab + \left[h\left(\frac{a+h^{-1}(b)}{2}\right) - b\right]\left[a-h^{-1}(b)\right].\end{aligned}$$

Equivalently speaking, it follows that the area C satisfies

$$\left[h\left(\frac{a+h^{-1}(b)}{2}\right) - b\right]\left[a-h^{-1}(b)\right] \le C \le \frac{h(a)-b}{2}\left[a-h^{-1}(b)\right].$$

Similarly, we can discuss other cases, corresponding to Figures 8.5 and 8.6, that the derivative $h'(x)$ is strictly decreasing.

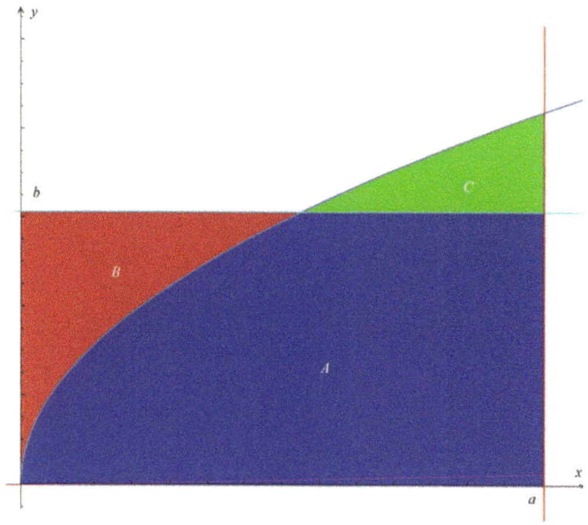

Figure 8.5 Geometric interpretation of the double inequality (8.9).

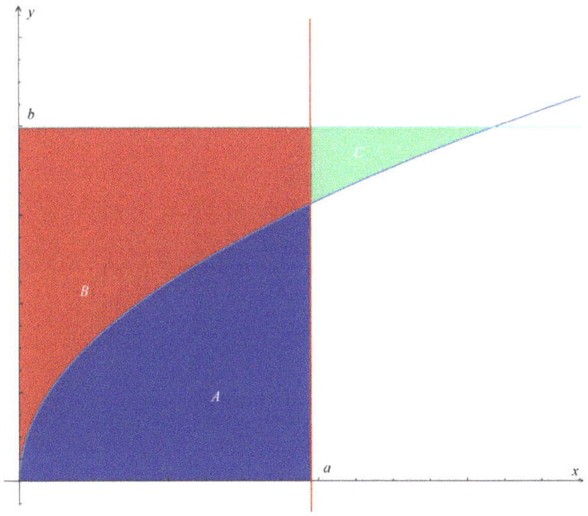

Figure 8.6 Geometric interpretation of the double inequality (8.9).

Remark 8.8. *Mercer has applied and employed the double inequality* (8.9) *in the paper [23] and in the Undergraduate Texts in Mathematics [24].*

8.1.3 REFINEMENTS OF YOUNG'S INTEGRAL INEQUALITY VIA HERMITE-HADAMARD'S AND ČEBYŠEV'S INTEGRAL INEQUALITIES

In 2009 and 2010, among other things, Jakšetić and Pečarić refined Young's integral inequality (8.1) and Hoorfar–Qi's double inequality (8.9) in [19,20].

Theorem 8.3 ([19, Theorem 2.1] and [20, Theorem 2.3]). *Let $h(x)$ be a differentiable and strictly increasing function on $[0,c]$ for $c>0$, $h(0)=0$, $a\in[0,c]$, $b\in[0,h(c)]$, and h^{-1} be the inverse function of h. Denote*

$$\alpha=\min\{a,h^{-1}(b)\} \quad \text{and} \quad \beta=\max\{a,h^{-1}(b)\}. \tag{8.14}$$

1. *If $h'(x)$ is increasing on $[\alpha,\beta]$ and $b<h(a)$, or if $h'(x)$ is decreasing on $[\alpha,\beta]$ and $b>h(a)$, then*

$$\begin{aligned}[a-h^{-1}(b)]\left[h\left(\frac{a+h^{-1}(b)}{2}\right)-b\right] &\le \int_0^a h(x)\,\mathrm{d}x+\int_0^b h^{-1}(x)\,\mathrm{d}x-ab\\ &\le \frac{1}{2}[a-h^{-1}(b)][h(a)-b].\end{aligned} \tag{8.15}$$

2. *If $h'(x)$ is increasing on $[\alpha,\beta]$ and $b>h(a)$, or if $h'(x)$ is decreasing on $[\alpha,\beta]$ and $b<h(a)$, then the inequality* (8.15) *is reversed.*
3. *The equality in* (8.15) *is valid if and only if $h(x)=\lambda x$ for $\lambda>0$ or $b=h(a)$.*

Proof. This is the outline of proofs of [19, Theorem 2.1] and [20, Theorem 2.3].

From the third line in (8.10), it follows that

$$\int_0^a h(x)\,\mathrm{d}x+\int_0^b h^{-1}(x)\,\mathrm{d}x-ab=b\big[h^{-1}(b)-a\big]+\int_{h^{-1}(b)}^a h(x)\,\mathrm{d}x. \tag{8.16}$$

Considering monotonicity of $h'(x)$ and applying the double inequality (8.13) to the integrand in the last term of (8.16), we can derive the double inequality (8.15).

The last term in (8.10) can be rewritten as

$$\begin{aligned}\int_{h^{-1}(b)}^a [h(x)-b]\,\mathrm{d}x&=\int_{h^{-1}(b)}^a \big[h(x)-h\big(h^{-1}(b)\big)\big]\,\mathrm{d}x\\&=\int_{h^{-1}(b)}^a\int_{h^{-1}(b)}^x h'(u)\,\mathrm{d}u\,\mathrm{d}x=\int_{h^{-1}(b)}^a (a-u)h'(u)\,\mathrm{d}u. \end{aligned}\tag{8.17}$$

Let $f,g:[\mu,\nu]\to\mathbb{R}$ be the integrable functions satisfying that they are both increasing or both decreasing. Then

$$\int_\mu^\nu f(x)\,\mathrm{d}x\int_\mu^\nu g(x)\,\mathrm{d}x\le(\nu-\mu)\int_\mu^\nu f(x)g(x)\,\mathrm{d}x. \tag{8.18}$$

If one of the function f or g is nonincreasing and the other nondecreasing, then the inequality in (8.18) is reversed. The inequality (8.18) is called Čebyšev's integral inequality in the literature [26, Chapter IX] and [35,39]. Applying (8.18) to the last term in (8.17) leads to the right-hand side of the inequality (8.15). The proof of Theorem 8.3 is complete. □

Remark 8.9. *The double inequality* (8.15) *can be geometrically interpreted as*

$$\big[a-h^{-1}(b)\big]\left[h\left(\frac{a+h^{-1}(b)}{2}\right)-b\right]\le C\le\frac{1}{2}\big[a-h^{-1}(b)\big]\big[h(a)-b\big],$$

where C denotes the area shown in Figures 8.1–8.6.

8.1.4 REFINEMENTS OF YOUNG'S INTEGRAL INEQUALITY VIA JENSEN'S DISCRETE AND INTEGRAL INEQUALITIES

In [20, Theorem 2.6], Jensen's discrete and integral inequalities were employed to establish the following inequalities which refine Young's integral inequality (8.1) and Hoorfar–Qi's double inequality (8.9).

Theorem 8.4 ([20, Theorem 2.6]). *Let $h(x)$ be a differentiable and strictly increasing function on $[0,c]$ for $c>0$, and let h^{-1} be the inverse function of h. If $h(0)=0$, $a\in[0,c]$, $b\in[0,h(c)]$, and $h'(x)$ is convex on $[\alpha,\beta]$, then*

$$\begin{aligned}\frac{\big[a-h^{-1}(b)\big]^2}{2}h'\left(\frac{a+2h^{-1}(b)}{3}\right)&\le\int_0^a h(x)\,\mathrm{d}x+\int_0^b h^{-1}(x)\,\mathrm{d}x-ab\\&\le\frac{\big[a-h^{-1}(b)\big]^2}{3}\left[\frac{h'(a)}{2}+h'\big(h^{-1}(b)\big)\right].\end{aligned}\tag{8.19}$$

If $h'(x)$ is concave, then the double inequality (8.19) *is reversed.*

Proof. This is the outline of the proof of [20, Theorem 2.6].

Changing the variable of the last term in (8.17) results in

$$\int_{h^{-1}(b)}^{a}(a-u)h'(u)\,\mathrm{d}u=\int_0^1\left[a-h^{-1}(b)\right]^2(1-x)h'\big(xa+(1-x)h^{-1}(b)\big)\,\mathrm{d}x. \quad (8.20)$$

If f is a convex function on an interval $I\subseteq\mathbb{R}$ and if $n\geq 2$ and $x_k\in I$ for $1\leq k\leq n$, then

$$f\left(\frac{1}{\sum_{k=1}^n p_k}\sum_{k=1}^n p_k x_k\right)\leq\frac{1}{\sum_{k=1}^n p_k}\sum_{k=1}^n p_k f(x_k), \quad (8.21)$$

where $p_k>0$ for $1\leq k\leq n$. If f is concave, the inequality (8.21) is reversed. The inequality (8.21) is called Jensen's discrete inequality for convex functions in the literature [25, Section 1.4] and [26, Chapter I]. Applying (8.21) to the third factor in the integrand of the right-hand side in (8.20) arrives at the right inequality in (8.19).

Let ϕ be a convex function on $[\mu,\nu]$, $f\in L_1(\mu,\nu)$, and σ be a nonnegative measure. Then,

$$\phi\left(\frac{\int_\mu^\nu f(x)\,\mathrm{d}\sigma}{\int_\mu^\nu\mathrm{d}\sigma}\right)\leq\frac{\int_\mu^\nu \phi(f(x))\,\mathrm{d}\sigma}{\int_\mu^\nu\mathrm{d}\sigma}. \quad (8.22)$$

If ϕ is a concave function, then the inequality (8.22) is reversed. The inequality (8.22) is called Jensen's integral inequality for convex functions in the literature [26, p. 10, (7.15)]. Applying (8.22) yields

$$\begin{aligned}\int_{h^{-1}(b)}^{a}(a-x)h'(x)\,\mathrm{d}x&\geq\frac{[1-h^{-1}(b)]^2}{2}h'\left(\frac{\int_{h^{-1}(b)}^{a}(a-x)x\,\mathrm{d}x}{\int_{h^{-1}(b)}^{a}(a-x)\,\mathrm{d}x}\right)\\&=\frac{[1-h^{-1}(b)]^2}{2}h'\left(\frac{a+2h^{-1}(b)}{3}\right).\end{aligned}$$

The proof of Theorem 8.4 is complete. □

Remark 8.10. *The double inequality* (8.19) *can be geometrically interpreted as*

$$\frac{\left[a-h^{-1}(b)\right]^2}{2}h'\left(\frac{a+2h^{-1}(b)}{3}\right)\leq C\leq\frac{\left[a-h^{-1}(b)\right]^2}{3}\left[\frac{h'(a)}{2}+h'\big(h^{-1}(b)\big)\right],$$

where C denotes the area shown in Figures 8.1–8.6.

8.1.5 REFINEMENTS OF YOUNG'S INTEGRAL INEQUALITY VIA HÖLDER'S INTEGRAL INEQUALITY

In [20, Theorem 2.1], Hölder's integral inequality was utilized to present the following inequalities, which refine Young's integral inequality (8.1) and Hoorfar–Qi's double inequality (8.9), for the normed spaces.

Theorem 8.5 ([20, Theorem 2.1]). *Let $h(x)$ be a differentiable and strictly increasing function on $[0,c]$ for $c>0$, and let h^{-1} be the inverse function of h. If $h(0)=0$, $a\in[0,c]$, $b\in[0,h(c)]$, and $h'(x)$ is almost everywhere continuous with respect to Lebesgue measure on $[\alpha,\beta]$, then the double inequality*

$$C_u\|h'\|_v \le \int_0^a h(x)\,\mathrm{d}x + \int_0^b h^{-1}(x)\,\mathrm{d}x - ab \le C_p\|h'\|_q \tag{8.23}$$

is valid for all u,v and p,q satisfying

1. $\frac{1}{u}+\frac{1}{v}=1$ *for* $u,v\in(-\infty,0)\cup(0,1)$, *or* $(u,v)=(1,-\infty)$, *or* $(u,v)=(-\infty,1)$;
2. $\frac{1}{p}+\frac{1}{q}=1$ *for* $1<p,q<\infty$, *or* $(p,q)=(+\infty,1)$, *or* $(p,q)=(1,+\infty)$;

where

$$C_r=\begin{cases}\left[\dfrac{\left|a-h^{-1}(b)\right|^{r+1}}{r+1}\right]^{1/r}, & r\ne 0,\pm\infty;\\ \left|a-h^{-1}(b)\right|, & r=+\infty;\\ 0, & r=-\infty\end{cases}$$

and

$$\|h'\|_r=\begin{cases}\left[\int_\alpha^\beta [h'(t)]^r\,\mathrm{d}t\right]^{1/r}, & r\ne 0,\pm\infty;\\ \sup\{h'(t),t\in[\alpha,\beta]\}, & r=+\infty;\\ \inf\{h'(t),t\in[\alpha,\beta]\}, & r=-\infty.\end{cases}$$

Proof. This is the outline of the proof of [20, Theorem 2.1].

Let $\frac{1}{p}+\frac{1}{q}=1$ with $p>0$ and $p\ne 1$, let f and g be the real functions on $[\mu,\nu]$, and let $|f|^p$ and $|g|^q$ be integrable on $[\mu,\nu]$.

1. If $p>1$, then

$$\int_\mu^\nu |f(x)g(x)|\,\mathrm{d}x \le \left[\int_\mu^\nu |f(x)|^p\,\mathrm{d}x\right]^{1/p}\left[\int_\mu^\nu |g(x)|^q\,\mathrm{d}x\right]^{1/q}. \tag{8.24}$$

   The equality in (8.24) holds if and only if $A|f(x)|^p=B|g(x)|^q$ almost everywhere for two constants A and B.
2. If $0<p<1$, then the inequality (8.24) is reversed.

The inequality (8.24) is called Hölder's integral inequality in the lierature [26, Chapter V] and [44,48,49].

From (8.17), it follows that,

1. by a property of definite integrals, we have

$$\int_{h^{-1}(b)}^a (a-u)h'(u)\,\mathrm{d}u=\int_\beta^\alpha |a-u|h'(u)\,\mathrm{d}u$$
$$\le \left|h^{-1}(b)-a\right|\int_\beta^\alpha h'(u)\,\mathrm{d}u=C_\infty\|h'\|_1;$$

2. by a property of definite integrals, we have

$$\int_{h^{-1}(b)}^{a}(a-u)h'(u)\,\mathrm{d}u=\int_{\beta}^{\alpha}|a-u|h'(u)\,\mathrm{d}u\le C_1\|h'\|_\infty;$$

3. by Hölder's integral inequality (8.24), we have

$$\begin{aligned}\int_{h^{-1}(b)}^{a}(a-u)h'(u)\,\mathrm{d}u&=\int_{\beta}^{\alpha}|a-u|h'(u)\,\mathrm{d}u\\&\le\left(\int_{\beta}^{\alpha}|a-u|^q\,\mathrm{d}u\right)^{1/q}\left(\int_{\beta}^{\alpha}[h'(u)]^p\,\mathrm{d}u\right)^{1/p}=C_q\|h'\|_p.\end{aligned}$$

The rest proofs are straightforward. The proofs of the double inequality (8.23) and Theorem 8.5 are thus complete. □

Remark 8.11. *The double inequality* (8.23) *can be geometrically interpreted as*

$$C_u\|h'\|_v\le C\le C_p\|h'\|_q,$$

where C denotes the area shown in Figures 8.1–8.6.

8.1.6 REFINEMENTS OF YOUNG'S INTEGRAL INEQUALITY VIA TAYLOR'S MEAN VALUE THEOREM OF LAGRANGE'S TYPE REMAINDER

In [50, Theorem 3.1], making use of Taylor's mean value theorem of Lagrange's type remainder, Wang, Guo, and Qi refined the above inequalities of Young's type via higher-order derivatives.

Theorem 8.6 ([50, Theorem 3.1]). *Let $h(0)=0$ and $h(x)$ be strictly increasing on $[0,c]$ for $c>0$, let $h^{(n)}(x)$ for $n\ge 0$ be continuous on $[0,c]$, let $h^{(n+1)}(x)$ be finite and strictly monotonic on $(0,c)$, and let h^{-1} be the inverse function of h. For $a\in[0,c]$ and $b\in[0,h(c)]$,*

1. *if $b<h(a)$, then*

$$\begin{aligned}&\sum_{k=1}^{n}h^{(k)}\left(h^{-1}(b)\right)\frac{\left[a-h^{-1}(b)\right]^{k+1}}{(k+1)!}+m_n(a,b)\frac{\left[a-h^{-1}(b)\right]^{n+2}}{(n+2)!}\\&\le\int_0^a h(x)\,\mathrm{d}x+\int_0^b h^{-1}(x)\,\mathrm{d}x-ab\\&\le\sum_{k=1}^{n}h^{(k)}\left(h^{-1}(b)\right)\frac{\left[a-h^{-1}(b)\right]^{k+1}}{(k+1)!}+M_n(a,b)\frac{\left[a-h^{-1}(b)\right]^{n+2}}{(n+2)!},\end{aligned}\tag{8.25}$$

where

$$m_n(a,b)=\min\left\{h^{(n+1)}\left(h^{-1}(b)\right),h^{(n+1)}(a)\right\}$$

and

$$M_n(a,b)=\max\left\{h^{(n+1)}\left(h^{-1}(b)\right),h^{(n+1)}(a)\right\};$$

2. *if $b > h(a)$, then*
   a. *when $n = 2\ell$ for $\ell \geq 0$, the double inequality* (8.25) *is valid;*
   b. *when $n = 2\ell + 1$ for $\ell \geq 0$, we have*

$$\begin{aligned}
&\sum_{k=1}^{n} h^{(k)}\left(h^{-1}(b)\right)\frac{\left[a-h^{-1}(b)\right]^{k+1}}{(k+1)!} - M_n(a,b)\frac{\left[a-h^{-1}(b)\right]^{n+2}}{(n+2)!} \\
&\leq \int_0^a h(x)\,\mathrm{d}x + \int_0^b h^{-1}(x)\,\mathrm{d}x - ab \\
&\leq \sum_{k=1}^{n} h^{(k)}\left(h^{-1}(b)\right)\frac{\left[a-h^{-1}(b)\right]^{k+1}}{(k+1)!} - m_n(a,b)\frac{\left[a-h^{-1}(b)\right]^{n+2}}{(n+2)!};
\end{aligned} \tag{8.26}$$

3. *if, and only if, $b = h(a)$, those equalities in* (8.25) *and* (8.26) *hold.*

Proof. This is the outline of the proof of [50, Theorem 3.1].

Let $f(x)$ be a function having finite nth derivative $f^{(n)}(x)$ everywhere in an open interval (μ, ν) and assume that $f^{(n-1)}(x)$ is continuous on the closed interval $[\mu, \nu]$. Then, for a fixed point $x_0 \in [\mu, \nu]$ and every $x \in [\mu, \nu]$ with $x \neq x_0$, there exists a point x_1 interior to the interval joining x and x_0 such that

$$f(x) = f(x_0) + \sum_{k=1}^{n-1} \frac{f^{(k)}(x_0)}{k!}(x - x_0)^k + \frac{f^{(n)}(x_1)}{n!}(x - x_0)^n. \tag{8.27}$$

Formula (8.27) is called Taylor's mean value theorem of Lagrange's type remainder in the literature [6, p. 113, Theorem 5.19]. Applying (8.27) in the last term of (8.10) reveals

$$\begin{aligned}
\int_{h^{-1}(b)}^{a} [h(x) - b]\,\mathrm{d}x &= \int_{h^{-1}(b)}^{a} \left[h(x) - h\left(h^{-1}(b)\right)\right]\mathrm{d}x \\
&= \sum_{k=1}^{n} \frac{h^{(k)}\left(h^{-1}(b)\right)}{k!} \int_{h^{-1}(b)}^{a} \left[x - h^{-1}(b)\right]^k \mathrm{d}x \\
&\quad + \frac{1}{(n+1)!} \int_{h^{-1}(b)}^{a} h^{(n+1)}(\xi)\left[x - h^{-1}(b)\right]^{n+1} \mathrm{d}x \\
&= \sum_{k=1}^{n} h^{(k)}\left(h^{-1}(b)\right)\frac{\left[a - h^{-1}(b)\right]^{k+1}}{(k+1)!} \\
&\quad + \int_{h^{-1}(b)}^{a} h^{(n+1)}(\xi)\frac{\left[x - h^{-1}(b)\right]^{n+1}}{(n+1)!}\,\mathrm{d}x,
\end{aligned}$$

where ξ is a point interior to the interval joining x and $h^{-1}(b)$. The rest proofs are straightforward discussions on various cases of the factor $h^{(n+1)}(\xi)$. The proof of Theorem 8.6 is complete. □

Remark 8.12. *The double inequalities* (8.25) *and* (8.26) *can be geometrically interpreted as*

$$\sum_{k=1}^{n} h^{(k)}\big(h^{-1}(b)\big)\frac{\left[a-h^{-1}(b)\right]^{k+1}}{(k+1)!}+m_n(a,b)\frac{\left[a-h^{-1}(b)\right]^{n+2}}{(n+2)!}\le C$$
$$\le \sum_{k=1}^{n} h^{(k)}\big(h^{-1}(b)\big)\frac{\left[a-h^{-1}(b)\right]^{k+1}}{(k+1)!}+M_n(a,b)\frac{\left[a-h^{-1}(b)\right]^{n+2}}{(n+2)!}$$

and

$$\sum_{k=1}^{n} h^{(k)}\big(h^{-1}(b)\big)\frac{\left[a-h^{-1}(b)\right]^{k+1}}{(k+1)!}-M_n(a,b)\frac{\left[a-h^{-1}(b)\right]^{n+2}}{(n+2)!}\le C$$
$$\le \sum_{k=1}^{n} h^{(k)}\big(h^{-1}(b)\big)\frac{\left[a-h^{-1}(b)\right]^{k+1}}{(k+1)!}-m_n(a,b)\frac{\left[a-h^{-1}(b)\right]^{n+2}}{(n+2)!},$$

where C denotes the area shown in Figures 8.1–8.6.

8.1.7 REFINEMENTS OF YOUNG'S INTEGRAL INEQUALITY VIA TAYLOR'S MEAN VALUE THEOREM OF CAUCHY'S TYPE REMAINDER AND HÖLDER'S INTEGRAL INEQUALITY

In [50, Theorem 3.2], employing Taylor's mean value theorem of Cauchy's type remainder and Hölder's integral inequality, Wang, Guo, and Qi refined the above inequalities of Young's type via norms of higher-order derivatives.

Theorem 8.7 ([50, Theorem 3.2]). *Let $n \ge 0$ and $h(x) \in C^{n+1}[0,c]$ such that $h(0) = 0$, $h^{(n+1)}(x) \ge 0$ on $[\alpha,\beta]$, and $h(x)$ is strictly increasing on $[0,c]$ for $c > 0$, let h^{-1} be the inverse function of h, and let $a \in [0,c]$ and $b \in [0,h(c)]$. Then*

1. *when $b > h(a)$ and $n = 2\ell$ for $\ell \ge 0$ or when $b < h(a)$, we have*

$$\frac{C_{u,n}}{(n+1)!}\left\|h^{(n+1)}\right\|_v \le \int_0^a h(x)\,\mathrm{d}x+\int_0^b h^{-1}(x)\,\mathrm{d}x-ab$$
$$-\sum_{k=1}^{n} h^{(k)}\big(h^{-1}(b)\big)\frac{\left[a-h^{-1}(b)\right]^{k+1}}{(k+1)!}$$
$$\le \frac{C_{p,n}}{(n+1)!}\left\|h^{(n+1)}\right\|_q;$$

2. *when $b > h(a)$ and $n = 2\ell+1$ for $\ell \ge 0$, we have*

$$-\frac{C_{p,n}}{(n+1)!}\left\|h^{(n+1)}\right\|_q \le \int_0^a h(x)\,\mathrm{d}x+\int_0^b h^{-1}(x)\,\mathrm{d}x-ab$$
$$-\sum_{k=1}^{n} h^{(k)}\big(h^{-1}(b)\big)\frac{\left[a-h^{-1}(b)\right]^{k+1}}{(k+1)!}$$
$$\le -\frac{C_{u,n}}{(n+1)!}\left\|h^{(n+1)}\right\|_v;$$

where α, β are defined as in (8.14),

$$C_{r,n} = \begin{cases} \left[\dfrac{\left|a-h^{-1}(b)\right|^{r(n+1)+1}}{r(n+1)+1} \right]^{1/r}, & r \neq 0, \pm\infty; \\ \left|a-h^{-1}(b)\right|^{n+1}, & r = +\infty; \\ 0, & r = -\infty, \end{cases}$$

$$\left\|h^{(n+1)}\right\|_r = \begin{cases} \left[\int_\alpha^\beta \left[h^{(n+1)}(t)\right]^r \mathrm{d}t \right]^{1/r}, & r \neq 0, \pm\infty; \\ \sup\{h^{(n+1)}(t), t \in [\alpha, \beta]\}, & r = +\infty; \\ \inf\{h^{(n+1)}(t), t \in [\alpha, \beta]\}, & r = -\infty, \end{cases}$$

and u, v, p, q satisfy

1. $u < 1$ *and* $u \neq 0$ *with* $\frac{1}{u} + \frac{1}{v} = 1$, *or* $(u, v) = (-\infty, 1)$, *or* $(u, v) = (1, -\infty)$;
2. $1 < p, q < \infty$ *with* $\frac{1}{p} + \frac{1}{q} = 1$, *or* $(p, q) = (+\infty, 1)$, *or* $(p, q) = (1, +\infty)$.

Proof. This is the outline of the proof of [50, Theorem 3.2].

If $f(x) \in C^{n+1}[\mu, \nu]$ and $x_0 \in [\mu, \nu]$, then

$$f(x) = \sum_{k=0}^{n} \frac{f^{(k)}(x_0)}{k!}(x - x_0)^k + \frac{1}{n!}\int_{x_0}^{x} (x-t)^n f^{(n+1)}(t)\,\mathrm{d}t. \tag{8.28}$$

Formula (8.28) is called Taylor's mean value theorem of Cauchy's type remainder in the literature [5, p. 279, Theorem 7.6] and [27, p. 6, 1.4.37]. Applying formula (8.28) to the integrand in the last term of (8.10) yields

$$\begin{aligned} \int_{h^{-1}(b)}^{a} [h(x) - b]\,\mathrm{d}x &= \int_{h^{-1}(b)}^{a} \left[h(x) - h(h^{-1}(b))\right]\mathrm{d}x \\ &= \sum_{k=1}^{n} h^{(k)}(h^{-1}(b)) \frac{\left[a - h^{-1}(b)\right]^{k+1}}{(k+1)!} \\ &\quad + \int_{h^{-1}(b)}^{a} \frac{1}{n!} \int_{h^{-1}(b)}^{x} (x-t)^n h^{(n+1)}(t)\,\mathrm{d}t\,\mathrm{d}x \\ &= \sum_{k=1}^{n} h^{(k)}(h^{-1}(b)) \frac{\left[a - h^{-1}(b)\right]^{k+1}}{(k+1)!} \\ &\quad + \int_{h^{-1}(b)}^{a} \frac{1}{n!} \int_{t}^{a} (x-t)^n h^{(n+1)}(t)\,\mathrm{d}x\,\mathrm{d}t \\ &= \sum_{k=1}^{n} h^{(k)}(h^{-1}(b)) \frac{\left[a - h^{-1}(b)\right]^{k+1}}{(k+1)!} \\ &\quad + \frac{1}{(n+1)!} \int_{h^{-1}(b)}^{a} (a-t)^{n+1} h^{(n+1)}(t)\,\mathrm{d}t \end{aligned}$$

$$= \sum_{k=1}^{n} h^{(k)}\left(h^{-1}(b)\right)\frac{\left[a-h^{-1}(b)\right]^{k+1}}{(k+1)!}$$
$$+\begin{cases} \frac{1}{(n+1)!}\int_\alpha^\beta |a-t|^{n+1}h^{(n+1)}(t)\,\mathrm{d}t, & b<h(a); \\ \frac{(-1)^n}{(n+1)!}\int_\alpha^\beta |a-t|^{n+1}h^{(n+1)}(t)\,\mathrm{d}t, & b>h(a). \end{cases}$$

Discussing and making use of Hölder's integral inequality (8.24) as in the proof of Theorem 8.5, we can complete the proof of Theorem 8.7. □

Remark 8.13. *Two double inequalities in Theorem 8.7 can be geometrically interpreted as*

$$\frac{C_{u,n}}{(n+1)!}\left\|h^{(n+1)}\right\|_v \le C-\sum_{k=1}^{n} h^{(k)}\left(h^{-1}(b)\right)\frac{\left[a-h^{-1}(b)\right]^{k+1}}{(k+1)!}$$
$$\le \frac{C_{p,n}}{(n+1)!}\left\|h^{(n+1)}\right\|_q$$

and

$$-\frac{C_{p,n}}{(n+1)!}\left\|h^{(n+1)}\right\|_q \le C-\sum_{k=1}^{n} h^{(k)}\left(h^{-1}(b)\right)\frac{\left[a-h^{-1}(b)\right]^{k+1}}{(k+1)!}$$
$$\le -\frac{C_{u,n}}{(n+1)!}\left\|h^{(n+1)}\right\|_v,$$

where C denotes the area shown in Figures 8.1–8.6.

8.1.8 REFINEMENTS OF YOUNG'S INTEGRAL INEQUALITY VIA TAYLOR'S MEAN VALUE THEOREM OF CAUCHY'S TYPE REMAINDER AND ČEBYŠEV'S INTEGRAL INEQUALITY

Theorem 8.8 ([50, Theorem 3.3]). *Let $n\ge 0$ and $h(x)\in C^{n+1}[0,c]$ such that $h(0)=0$ and $h(x)$ is strictly increasing on $[0,c]$ for $c>0$, let h^{-1} be the inverse function of h, let $a\in[0,c]$ and $b\in[0,h(c)]$, and let $\ell\ge 0$ be an integer. Then*

1. *when*
   a. *either $h(a)>b$ and $h^{(n+1)}(x)$ is increasing on $[\alpha,\beta]$;*
   b. *or $h(a)<b$, $h^{(n+1)}(x)$ is increasing on $[\alpha,\beta]$, and $n=2\ell+1$;*
   c. *or $h(a)<b$, $h^{(n+1)}(x)$ is decreasing on $[\alpha,\beta]$, and $n=2\ell$;*

   the inequality

$$\int_0^a h(x)\,\mathrm{d}x+\int_0^b h^{-1}(x)\,\mathrm{d}x-ab-\sum_{k=1}^{n} h^{(k)}\left(h^{-1}(b)\right)\frac{\left[a-h^{-1}(b)\right]^{k+1}}{(k+1)!}$$
$$\le \frac{\left[a-h^{-1}(b)\right]^{n+1}}{(n+2)!}\left[h^{(n)}(a)-h^{(n)}\left(h^{-1}(b)\right)\right] \tag{8.29}$$

   is valid;

2. *when*
   a. *either* $h(a) > b$ *and* $h^{(n+1)}(x)$ *is decreasing on* $[\alpha, \beta]$*;*
   b. *or* $h(a) < b$*,* $h^{(n+1)}(x)$ *is increasing on* $[\alpha, \beta]$*, and* $n = 2\ell$*;*
   c. *or* $h(a) < b$*,* $h^{(n+1)}(x)$ *is decreasing on* $[\alpha, \beta]$*, and* $n = 2\ell + 1$*;*

   the inequality (8.29) *is reversed;*

where α, β *are defined as in* (8.14).

Proof. This is the outline of the proof of [50, Theorem 3.3].

This follows from applying formula (8.28) as in the proof of Theorem 8.7 and applying Čebyšev's integral inequality (8.18) to the integral

$$\int_{h^{-1}(b)}^{a} (a-t)^{n+1} h^{(n+1)}(t)\,\mathrm{d}t \tag{8.30}$$

in the proof of Theorem 8.7. The proof of Theorem 8.8 is complete. □

Remark 8.14. *The inequality* (8.29) *can be geometrically interpreted as*

$$C - \sum_{k=1}^{n} h^{(k)}\left(h^{-1}(b)\right) \frac{\left[a-h^{-1}(b)\right]^{k+1}}{(k+1)!} \le \frac{\left[a-h^{-1}(b)\right]^{n+1}}{(n+2)!} \left[h^{(n)}(a) - h^{(n)}\left(h^{-1}(b)\right)\right],$$

where C *denotes the area shown in Figures 8.1–8.6.*

8.1.9 REFINEMENTS OF YOUNG'S INTEGRAL INEQUALITY VIA TAYLOR'S MEAN VALUE THEOREM OF CAUCHY'S TYPE REMAINDER AND JENSEN'S INEQUALITIES

Theorem 8.9 ([50, Theorem 3.4])**.** *Let* $h(x) \in C^{n+1}[0,c]$ *such that* $h(0) = 0$ *and* $h(x)$ *is strictly increasing on* $[0,c]$ *for* $c > 0$*, let* h^{-1} *be the inverse function of* h*, and let* $a \in [0,c]$ *and* $b \in [0, h(c)]$*. If* $h^{(n+1)}(x)$ *is convex on* $[\alpha, \beta]$*, where* α, β *are defined as in* (8.14)*, then*

1. *when* $h(a) > b$ *or when* $h(a) < b$ *and* $n = 2\ell$*, we have*

$$\begin{aligned} &\frac{\left[a-h^{-1}(b)\right]^{n+2}}{n+2} h^{(n+1)}\left(\frac{a+(n+2)h^{-1}(b)}{n+3}\right) \\ &\le \int_0^a h(x)\,\mathrm{d}x + \int_0^b h^{-1}(x)\,\mathrm{d}x - ab \quad - \sum_{k=1}^{n} h^{(k)}\left(h^{-1}(b)\right) \frac{\left[a-h^{-1}(b)\right]^{k+1}}{(k+1)!} \\ &\le \left[a-h^{-1}(b)\right]^{n+2} \frac{h^{(n+1)}(a) + (n+2)h^{(n+1)}\left(h^{-1}(b)\right)}{(n+3)!}; \end{aligned} \tag{8.31}$$

2. *when $h(a) < b$ and $n = 2\ell + 1$, the double inequality* (8.31) *is reversed,*

where $\ell \geq 0$ is an integer. If $h^{(n+1)}(x)$ is concave on $[\alpha, \beta]$, all the above inequalities are reversed for all corresponding cases.

Proof. This is the outline of the proof of [50, Theorem 3.4].

Considering the integral (8.30) and substituting integral variables give

$$\int_{h^{-1}(b)}^{a} (a-t)^{n+1} h^{(n+1)}(t)\,\mathrm{d}t = \left[a - h^{-1}(b)\right]^{n+2} \times \int_0^1 (1-s)^{n+1} h^{(n+1)}\left(sa + (1-s)h^{-1}(b)\right)\mathrm{d}s.$$

Applying Jensen's inequalities (8.21) and (8.22) to $h^{(n+1)}\left(sa + (1-s)h^{-1}(b)\right)$ in the above equation yield the double inequality (8.31) and its reversed version. The proof of Theorem 8.9 is complete. □

Remark 8.15. *The double inequality* (8.31) *can be geometrically interpreted as*

$$\begin{aligned}\frac{\left[a-h^{-1}(b)\right]^{n+2}}{n+2} h^{(n+1)}\left(\frac{a+(n+2)h^{-1}(b)}{n+3}\right) &\leq C - \sum_{k=1}^{n} h^{(k)}\left(h^{-1}(b)\right)\frac{\left[a-h^{-1}(b)\right]^{k+1}}{(k+1)!} \\ &\leq \left[a-h^{-1}(b)\right]^{n+2}\frac{h^{(n+1)}(a)+(n+2)h^{(n+1)}\left(h^{-1}(b)\right)}{(n+3)!},\end{aligned}$$

where C denotes the area shown in Figures 8.1–8.6.

8.1.10 REFINEMENTS OF YOUNG'S INTEGRAL INEQUALITY VIA TAYLOR'S MEAN VALUE THEOREM OF CAUCHY'S TYPE REMAINDER AND INTEGRAL INEQUALITIES OF HERMITE-HADAMARD TYPE FOR THE PRODUCT OF TWO CONVEX FUNCTIONS

Theorem 8.10 ([50, Theorem 3.5]). *Let $n \geq 0$ and $h(x) \in C^{n+1}[0,c]$ such that $h(0) = 0$ and $h(x)$ is strictly increasing on $[0,c]$ for $c > 0$, let h^{-1} be the inverse function of h, let $a \in [0,c]$ and $b \in [0,h(c)]$, and let $h^{(n+1)}(x)$ be nonnegative and convex on $[\alpha,\beta]$, where α, β are defined as in* (8.14). *If $h(a) > b$, then*

$$\begin{aligned}&\frac{\left[a-h^{-1}(b)\right]^{n+2}}{(n+1)!}\left[\frac{1}{2^n} h^{(n+1)}\left(\frac{a+h^{-1}(b)}{2}\right) - \frac{2h^{(n+1)}(a)+h^{(n+1)}\left(h^{-1}(b)\right)}{6}\right] \\ &\leq \int_0^a h(x)\,\mathrm{d}x + \int_0^b h^{-1}(x)\,\mathrm{d}x - ab - \sum_{k=1}^{n} h^{(k)}\left(h^{-1}(b)\right)\frac{\left[a-h^{-1}(b)\right]^{k+1}}{(k+1)!} \\ &\leq \frac{\left[a-h^{-1}(b)\right]^{n+2}}{(n+1)!}\,\frac{h^{(n+1)}(a)+2h^{(n+1)}\left(h^{-1}(b)\right)}{6}. \qquad (8.32)\end{aligned}$$

If $h(a) < b$ and $n = 2\ell$ for $\ell \geq 0$, then

$$\begin{aligned}
&\frac{\left[h^{-1}(b)-a\right]^{n+2}}{(n+1)!}\left[\frac{1}{2^n}h^{(n+1)}\left(\frac{a+h^{-1}(b)}{2}\right)-\frac{2h^{(n+1)}(a)+h^{(n+1)}\left(h^{-1}(b)\right)}{6}\right]\\
&\leq \int_0^a h(x)\,\mathrm{d}x+\int_0^b h^{-1}(x)\,\mathrm{d}x-ab-\sum_{k=1}^{n} h^{(k)}\left(h^{-1}(b)\right)\frac{\left[a-h^{-1}(b)\right]^{k+1}}{(k+1)!}\\
&\leq \frac{\left[h^{-1}(b)-a\right]^{n+2}}{(n+1)!}\frac{h^{(n+1)}(a)+2h^{(n+1)}\left(h^{-1}(b)\right)}{6}.
\end{aligned} \tag{8.33}$$

If $a < h^{-1}(b)$ and $n = 2\ell+1$ for $\ell \geq 0$, the double inequality (8.33) *is reversed.*

Proof. This is the outline of the proof of [50, Theorem 3.5].

Let $f(x)$ and $g(x)$ be nonnegative and convex functions on $[\mu,\nu]$. Then,

$$\begin{aligned}
&2f\left(\frac{\mu+\nu}{2}\right)g\left(\frac{\mu+\nu}{2}\right)-\frac{1}{6}M(\mu,\nu)-\frac{1}{3}N(\mu,\nu)\\
&\qquad\leq \frac{1}{\nu-\mu}\int_\mu^\nu f(x)g(x)\,\mathrm{d}x \leq \frac{1}{3}M(\mu,\nu)+\frac{1}{6}N(\mu,\nu),
\end{aligned} \tag{8.34}$$

where

$$M(\mu,\nu)=f(\mu)g(\mu)+f(\nu)g(\nu) \quad\text{and}\quad N(\mu,\nu)=f(\mu)g(\nu)+f(\nu)g(\mu).$$

The double inequality (8.34) can be found in [28,52–54] and closely related references therein. Applying (8.34) in the integral (8.30) arrives at the double inequalities in (8.32) and (8.33). The proof of Theorem 8.10 is complete. □

Remark 8.16. *The double inequalities* (8.32) *and* (8.33) *can be geometrically interpreted as*

$$\begin{aligned}
&\frac{\left[a-h^{-1}(b)\right]^{n+2}}{(n+1)!}\left[\frac{1}{2^n}h^{(n+1)}\left(\frac{a+h^{-1}(b)}{2}\right)-\frac{2h^{(n+1)}(a)+h^{(n+1)}\left(h^{-1}(b)\right)}{6}\right]\\
&\leq C-\sum_{k=1}^{n} h^{(k)}\left(h^{-1}(b)\right)\frac{\left[a-h^{-1}(b)\right]^{k+1}}{(k+1)!}\leq \frac{\left[a-h^{-1}(b)\right]^{n+2}}{(n+1)!}\frac{h^{(n+1)}(a)+2h^{(n+1)}\left(h^{-1}(b)\right)}{6}
\end{aligned}$$

and

$$\begin{aligned}
&\frac{\left[h^{-1}(b)-a\right]^{n+2}}{(n+1)!}\left[\frac{1}{2^n}h^{(n+1)}\left(\frac{a+h^{-1}(b)}{2}\right)-\frac{2h^{(n+1)}(a)+h^{(n+1)}\left(h^{-1}(b)\right)}{6}\right]\\
&\leq C-\sum_{k=1}^{n} h^{(k)}\left(h^{-1}(b)\right)\frac{\left[a-h^{-1}(b)\right]^{k+1}}{(k+1)!}\leq \frac{\left[h^{-1}(b)-a\right]^{n+2}}{(n+1)!}\frac{h^{(n+1)}(a)+2h^{(n+1)}\left(h^{-1}(b)\right)}{6},
\end{aligned}$$

where C denotes the area shown in Figures 8.1–8.6.

8.1.11 THREE EXAMPLES SHOWING REFINEMENTS OF YOUNG'S INTEGRAL INEQUALITY

8.1.11.1 First Example

In [18, Section 3], the double inequality (8.9) was applied to obtain the estimate

$$\begin{aligned}
9.000042866\ldots &= \frac{4\sqrt[4]{125}}{27}\left(3-2\sqrt[4]{5}\right)^2 \\
&< \int_0^3 \sqrt[4]{x^4+1}\,\mathrm{d}x + \int_1^3 \sqrt[4]{x^4-1}\,\mathrm{d}x - 9 \\
&< \frac{27}{2\sqrt[4]{82^3}}\left(3-2\sqrt[4]{5}\right)^2 \\
&= 9.000042871\ldots
\end{aligned}$$

whose gap between the upper and lower bounds is 0.000000005... and which refines a known result

$$9 < \int_0^3 \sqrt[4]{x^4+1}\,\mathrm{d}x + \int_1^3 \sqrt[4]{x^4-1}\,\mathrm{d}x < 9.0001$$

In [20, Example 2.5] and [20, Remark 2.7], it was obtained that

$$9.000042866 < \int_0^3 \sqrt[4]{x^4+1}\,\mathrm{d}x + \int_1^3 \sqrt[4]{x^4-1}\,\mathrm{d}x < 9.000042868880$$

and

$$9.000042868058 < \int_0^3 \sqrt[4]{x^4+1}\,\mathrm{d}x + \int_1^3 \sqrt[4]{x^4-1}\,\mathrm{d}x < 9.000042868066.$$

whose gaps between the upper and lower bounds are

$$0.0000000028\ldots \quad \text{and} \quad 0.000000000008\ldots$$

respectively.

In [19, Example 2.1], it was estimated that

$$9.00004286765564 < \int_0^3 \sqrt[4]{x^4+1}\,\mathrm{d}x + \int_1^3 \sqrt[4]{x^4-1}\,\mathrm{d}x < 9.00004286805781.$$

whose gap between the upper and lower bounds is 0.0000000004021....

In [50, Example 4.1], by virtue of the double inequality (8.31), the above double inequality was refined as

$$\begin{aligned}
9.0000428983186013\ldots &= \frac{\left(3-80^{1/4}\right)^3}{3}\,\frac{3072\left(\sqrt[4]{95}\sqrt{2}+3\right)^2}{\left[\left(\sqrt[4]{95}\sqrt{2}+3\right)^4+256\right]^{7/4}} \\
&\quad + 9 + \frac{8\times 5^{3/4}}{27}\,\frac{\left(3-80^{1/4}\right)^2}{2!}
\end{aligned}$$

$$
\begin{aligned}
&\geq \int_0^3 \sqrt[4]{x^4+1}\,\mathrm{d}x + \int_1^3 \sqrt[4]{x^4-1}\,\mathrm{d}x \\
&\geq \frac{\left(3-80^{1/4}\right)^3}{4!}\left(\frac{27}{82^{7/4}} + 3\times\frac{4\sqrt{5}}{729}\right) \\
&\quad + 9 + \frac{8\times 5^{3/4}}{27}\frac{\left(3-80^{1/4}\right)^2}{2!} \\
&= 9.0000428680640760\ldots
\end{aligned}
$$

whose gap between the upper and lower bounds is 0.00000003025452....

8.1.11.2 Second Example

In [50, Example 4.2], by virtue of the double inequality (8.15), it follows that

$$
\begin{aligned}
0.364469045537996606\ldots &= \frac{1}{4} + \left(\frac{1}{2} - \frac{1}{\ln 2}\right)\left[\frac{1}{\exp[\frac{1}{2}(\frac{1}{2}+\frac{1}{\ln 2})]} - \frac{1}{2}\right] \\
&\leq \int_0^{1/2} \frac{1}{e^{1/x}}\,\mathrm{d}x - \int_0^{1/2}\frac{1}{\ln x}\,\mathrm{d}x \\
&\leq \frac{1}{4} + \frac{1}{2}\left(\frac{1}{2}-\frac{1}{\ln 2}\right)\left(\frac{1}{e^2}-\frac{1}{2}\right) \\
&= 0.421883810040011829\ldots.
\end{aligned}
\tag{8.35}
$$

The gap between the upper and lower bounds in the double inequality (8.35) is 0.057414764502015....

8.1.11.3 Third Example

In [50, Example 4.3], by virtue of the double inequality (8.32), we can obtain the estimate

$$
2.044751320\ldots \leq \int_0^1 e^{t^2}\,\mathrm{d}t + \int_0^1 \sqrt{\ln(1+t)}\,\mathrm{d}t \leq 2.060536019\ldots. \tag{8.36}
$$

The gap between the upper and lower bounds in the double inequality (8.36) is 0.01578469....

8.2 NEW REFINEMENTS OF YOUNG'S INTEGRAL INEQUALITY VIA PÓLYA'S TYPE INTEGRAL INEQUALITIES

In this section, by virtue of Pólya's type integral inequalities [33,46], we establish some new refinements in terms of higher-order derivatives.

8.2.1 REFINEMENTS OF YOUNG'S INTEGRAL INEQUALITY IN TERMS OF BOUNDS OF THE FIRST DERIVATIVE

Theorem 8.11. *Let $h(x)$ be a strictly increasing function on $[0,c]$ for $c>0$ and let h^{-1} be the inverse function of h. If $h(0)=0$, $a\in[0,c]$, $b\in[0,h(c)]$, L and U are the real constants, and $L\leq h'(x)\leq U$ on (α,β), then*

$$\begin{aligned}&\frac{LU\left[a-h^{-1}(b)\right]^2-2\left[a-h^{-1}(b)\right][Lh(a)-Ub]+[h(a)-b]^2}{2(U-L)}\\&\le\int_0^a h(x)\,\mathrm{d}x+\int_0^b h^{-1}(x)\,\mathrm{d}x-bh^{-1}(b)\\&\le-\frac{LU\left[a-h^{-1}(b)\right]^2-2\left[a-h^{-1}(b)\right][Uh(a)-Lb]+[h(a)-b]^2}{2(U-L)}.\end{aligned}\tag{8.37}$$

Proof. Let $f(x)$ be continuous on $[a,b]$ and differentiable on (a,b). If $f(x)$ is not identically a constant and $m\le f'(x)\le M$ in (a,b), then

$$\begin{aligned}&\left|\frac{1}{b-a}\int_a^b f(x)\,\mathrm{d}x-\frac{f(a)+f(b)}{2}\right|\\&\qquad\le\frac{(M-m)(b-a)}{2}\left[\frac{1}{4}-\frac{\left(\frac{f(b)-f(a)}{b-a}-\frac{M+m}{2}\right)^2}{(M-m)^2}\right].\end{aligned}\tag{8.38}$$

The inequality (8.38) can be rearranged as a double inequality

$$\begin{aligned}&\frac{mM(b-a)^2-2(b-a)[mf(b)-Mf(a)]+[f(b)-f(a)]^2}{2(M-m)}\le\int_a^b f(x)\,\mathrm{d}x\\&\qquad\le-\frac{mM(b-a)^2-2(b-a)[Mf(b)-mf(a)]+[f(b)-f(a)]^2}{2(M-m)}.\end{aligned}\tag{8.39}$$

These inequalities can be found in [1, Theorem 2], the papers [8–12], [32, Proposition 2], [33, Section 5], and closely related references therein.

The area C can be computed by (8.7) in Remark 8.2, which can be estimated, by applying the double inequality (8.39), as

$$\begin{aligned}&\frac{LU\left[a-h^{-1}(b)\right]^2-2\left[a-h^{-1}(b)\right][Lh(a)-Ub]+[h(a)-b]^2}{2(U-L)}\le\int_{h^{-1}(b)}^a h(x)\,\mathrm{d}x\\&\qquad\le-\frac{LU\left[a-h^{-1}(b)\right]^2-2\left[a-h^{-1}(b)\right][Uh(a)-Lb]+[h(a)-b]^2}{2(U-L)}.\end{aligned}$$

Since

$$\int_{h^{-1}(b)}^a h(x)\,\mathrm{d}x-b\left[a-h^{-1}(b)\right]=\int_0^a h(x)\,\mathrm{d}x+\int_0^b h^{-1}(x)\,\mathrm{d}x-ab,$$

i.e.,

$$\int_{h^{-1}(b)}^a h(x)\,\mathrm{d}x=\int_0^a h(x)\,\mathrm{d}x+\int_0^b h^{-1}(x)\,\mathrm{d}x-bh^{-1}(b),\tag{8.40}$$

the double inequality (8.37) follows straightforwardly. The proof of Theorem 8.11 is complete. □

8.2.2 REFINEMENTS OF YOUNG'S INTEGRAL INEQUALITY IN TERMS OF BOUNDS OF THE SECOND DERIVATIVE

Theorem 8.12. *Let $h(x)$ be a strictly increasing function on $[0,c]$ for $c>0$, let h^{-1} be the inverse function of h, let $h(0)=0$, $a\in[0,c]$, and $b\in[0,h(c)]$, and let L and U be the real constants such that $L\le h''(x)\le U$ on (α,β). Then,*

$$\begin{aligned}
&\frac{L\left[a^3-\left(h^{-1}(b)\right)^3\right]}{6}+\frac{\begin{pmatrix}b-h(a)+ah'(a)-h^{-1}(b)h'\left(h^{-1}(b)\right)\\ +L\left[\left(h^{-1}(b)\right)^2-a^2\right]/2\end{pmatrix}^2}{2\left[\left(h^{-1}(b)-a\right)L-h'\left(h^{-1}(b)\right)+h'(a)\right]}\\
&\le\int_0^a h(x)\,\mathrm{d}x+\int_0^b h^{-1}(x)\,\mathrm{d}x-ah(a)+\frac{a^2h'(a)-\left[h^{-1}(b)\right]^2h'\left(h^{-1}(b)\right)}{2}\\
&\le\frac{U\left[a^3-\left(h^{-1}(b)\right)^3\right]}{6}+\frac{\begin{pmatrix}b-h(a)+ah'(a)-h^{-1}(b)h'\left(h^{-1}(b)\right)\\ +U\left[\left(h^{-1}(b)\right)^2-a^2\right]/2\end{pmatrix}^2}{2\left[\left(h^{-1}(b)-a\right)U-h'\left(h^{-1}(b)\right)+h'(a)\right]}.
\end{aligned}\tag{8.41}$$

Proof. In [29, Corollary] and [42, Corollary 1.2], it was acquired that if $f(x)\in C([a,b])$ satisfying $N\le f''(x)\le M$ on (a,b), then

$$\begin{aligned}
&\frac{N(b^3-a^3)}{6}+\frac{\left[f(a)-f(b)+bf'(b)-af'(a)+N\left(a^2-b^2\right)/2\right]^2}{2[(a-b)N-f'(a)+f'(b)]}\\
&\le\int_a^b f(x)\,\mathrm{d}x-bf(b)+af(a)+\frac{b^2f'(b)-a^2f'(a)}{2}\\
&\le\frac{M(b^3-a^3)}{6}+\frac{\left[f(a)-f(b)+bf'(b)-af'(a)+M\left(a^2-b^2\right)/2\right]^2}{2[(a-b)M-f'(a)+f'(b)]}.
\end{aligned}\tag{8.42}$$

Applying the double inequality (8.42) to the integral $\int_{h^{-1}(b)}^a h(x)\,\mathrm{d}x$ and considering Remark 8.2 yield

$$\begin{aligned}
&\frac{L\left[a^3-\left(h^{-1}(b)\right)^3\right]}{6}+\frac{\begin{pmatrix}b-h(a)+ah'(a)-h^{-1}(b)h'\left(h^{-1}(b)\right)\\ +L\left[\left(h^{-1}(b)\right)^2-a^2\right]/2\end{pmatrix}^2}{2\left[\left(h^{-1}(b)-a\right)L-h'\left(h^{-1}(b)\right)+h'(a)\right]}\\
&\le\int_{h^{-1}(b)}^a h(x)\,\mathrm{d}x-ah(a)+bh^{-1}(b)+\frac{a^2h'(a)-\left[h^{-1}(b)\right]^2h'\left(h^{-1}(b)\right)}{2}\\
&\le\frac{U\left[a^3-\left(h^{-1}(b)\right)^3\right]}{6}+\frac{\begin{pmatrix}b-h(a)+ah'(a)-h^{-1}(b)h'\left(h^{-1}(b)\right)\\ +U\left[\left(h^{-1}(b)\right)^2-a^2\right]/2\end{pmatrix}^2}{2\left[\left(h^{-1}(b)-a\right)U-h'\left(h^{-1}(b)\right)+h'(a)\right]}.
\end{aligned}\tag{8.43}$$

Substituting (8.40) into (8.43) results in the double inequality (8.41). The proof of Theorem 8.12 is complete. □

8.2.3 REFINEMENTS OF YOUNG'S INTEGRAL INEQUALITY IN TERMS OF BOUNDS OF HIGHER-ORDER DERIVATIVES

Theorem 8.13. *Let $h(x)$ be a strictly increasing function on $[0,c]$ for $c>0$, let h^{-1} be the inverse of h, let $h(0)=0$, $a\in[0,c]$, and $b\in[0,h(c)]$, and let $h(x)$ have the $(n+1)$-th derivative on $[0,c]$ such that $L\le h^{(n+1)}(x)\le U$ on (α,β). Then, for all t between a and $h^{-1}(b)$,*

1. *when n is a nonnegative odd integer,*

$$\sum_{i=0}^{n+2}\frac{(-1)^i}{i!}\Big[S_{n+2}^{(i)}\big(h;h^{-1}(b),h^{-1}(b),L\big)-S_{n+2}^{(i)}(h;a,a,L)\Big]t^i \le \int_0^a h(x)\,\mathrm{d}x+\int_0^b h^{-1}(x)\,\mathrm{d}x-bh^{-1}(b) \le \sum_{i=0}^{n+2}\frac{(-1)^i}{i!}\Big[S_{n+2}^{(i)}\big(h;h^{-1}(b),h^{-1}(b),U\big)-S_{n+2}^{(i)}(h;a,a,U)\Big]t^i; \tag{8.44}$$

2. *when n is a nonnegative even integer,*

$$\sum_{i=0}^{n+2}\frac{(-1)^i}{i!}\Big[S_{n+2}^{(i)}\big(h;h^{-1}(b),h^{-1}(b),L\big)-S_{n+2}^{(i)}(h;a,a,U)\Big]t^i \le \int_0^a h(x)\,\mathrm{d}x+\int_0^b h^{-1}(x)\,\mathrm{d}x-bh^{-1}(b) \le \sum_{i=0}^{n+2}\frac{(-1)^i}{i!}\Big[S_{n+2}^{(i)}\big(h;h^{-1}(b),h^{-1}(b),U\big)-S_{n+2}^{(i)}(h;a,a,L)\Big]t^i; \tag{8.45}$$

where L and U are the real constants,

$$S_n(h;u,v,w)=\sum_{k=1}^{n-1}\frac{(-1)^k}{k!}u^k h^{(k-1)}(v)+(-1)^n\frac{w}{n!}u^n,$$

and

$$S_n^{(k)}(h;u,v,w)=\frac{\partial^k S_n(h;u,v,w)}{\partial u^k}.$$

Proof. In [29, Theorem], it was discovered that if $f\in C^n([a,b])$ has derivative of $(n+1)$-th order satisfying $N\le f^{(n+1)}(x)\le M$ on (a,b), then, for all $t\in(a,b)$,

1. when n is a nonnegative odd integer,

$$\sum_{i=0}^{n+2}\frac{(-1)^i}{i!}\Big[S_{n+2}^{(i)}(f;a,a,N)-S_{n+2}^{(i)}(f;b,b,N)\Big]t^i\le\int_a^b f(x)\,\mathrm{d}x \le\sum_{i=0}^{n+2}\frac{(-1)^i}{i!}\Big[S_{n+2}^{(i)}(f;a,a,M)-S_{n+2}^{(i)}(f;b,b,M)\Big]t^i; \tag{8.46}$$

2. when n is a nonnegative even integer,

$$\sum_{i=0}^{n+2}\frac{(-1)^i}{i!}\Big[S_{n+2}^{(i)}(f;a,a,N)-S_{n+2}^{(i)}(f;b,b,M)\Big]t^i\le\int_a^b f(x)\,\mathrm{d}x$$
$$\le\sum_{i=0}^{n+2}\frac{(-1)^i}{i!}\Big[S_{n+2}^{(i)}(f;a,a,M)-S_{n+2}^{(i)}(f;b,b,N)\Big]t^i. \quad (8.47)$$

These inequalities can also be found in [30,31,34,41,46] and closely related references therein.

Applying (8.46) and (8.47) to the integral $\int_{h^{-1}(b)}^{a}h(x)\,\mathrm{d}x$ and considering Remark 8.2 yield

1. when n is a nonnegative odd integer,

$$\sum_{i=0}^{n+2}\frac{(-1)^i}{i!}\Big[S_{n+2}^{(i)}(h;h^{-1}(b),h^{-1}(b),L)-S_{n+2}^{(i)}(h;a,a,L)\Big]t^i\le\int_{h^{-1}(b)}^{a}h(x)\,\mathrm{d}x$$
$$\le\sum_{i=0}^{n+2}\frac{(-1)^i}{i!}\Big[S_{n+2}^{(i)}(h;h^{-1}(b),h^{-1}(b),U)-S_{n+2}^{(i)}(h;a,a,U)\Big]t^i; \quad (8.48)$$

2. when n is a nonnegative even integer,

$$\sum_{i=0}^{n+2}\frac{(-1)^i}{i!}\Big[S_{n+2}^{(i)}(h;h^{-1}(b),h^{-1}(b),L)-S_{n+2}^{(i)}(h;a,a,U)\Big]t^i\le\int_{h^{-1}(b)}^{a}h(x)\,\mathrm{d}x$$
$$\le\sum_{i=0}^{n+2}\frac{(-1)^i}{i!}\Big[S_{n+2}^{(i)}(h;h^{-1}(b),h^{-1}(b),U)-S_{n+2}^{(i)}(h;a,a,L)\Big]t^i. \quad (8.49)$$

Substituting (8.40) into (8.48) and (8.49) results in (8.44) and (8.45). The proof of Theorem 8.13 is complete. □

8.2.4 REFINEMENTS OF YOUNG'S INTEGRAL INEQUALITY IN TERMS OF L^p-NORMS

Theorem 8.14. *Let $h(x)$ be a strictly increasing function on $[0,c]$ for $c>0$, let h^{-1} be the inverse of h, let $h(0)=0$, $a\in[0,c]$, and $b\in[0,h(c)]$, and let $h(x)$ have the $(n+1)$-th derivative on $[\alpha,\beta]$ such that $h^{(n+1)}\in L^p([\alpha,\beta])$ for $p,q>0$ with $\frac{1}{p}+\frac{1}{q}=1$. Then, for all $t\in[\alpha,\beta]$,*

1. *when $p,q>1$, we have*

$$\left|\int_{h^{-1}(b)}^{a}h(x)\,\mathrm{d}x-\sum_{i=0}^{n}\frac{h^{(i)}(h^{-1}(b))}{(i+1)!}\left(t-h^{-1}(b)\right)^{i+1}+\sum_{i=0}^{n}\frac{h^{(i)}(a)}{(i+1)!}(t-a)^{i+1}\right|$$

$$\leq \frac{\left(t-h^{-1}(b)\right)^{n+1+1/q}+(a-t)^{n+1+1/q}}{(n+1)!\sqrt[q]{nq+q+1}}\left\|h^{(n+1)}\right\|_{L^p([h^{-1}(b),a])}$$
$$\leq \frac{2\left(a-h^{-1}(b)\right)^{n+2}}{(n+1)!}\left\|h^{(n+1)}\right\|_{L^p([h^{-1}(b),a])}; \tag{8.50}$$

2. *when $p=\infty$, we have*

$$\left|\int_{h^{-1}(b)}^{a} h(x)\,\mathrm{d}x-\sum_{i=0}^{n}\frac{h^{(i)}\left(h^{-1}(b)\right)}{(i+1)!}\left(t-h^{-1}(b)\right)^{i+1}+\sum_{i=0}^{n}\frac{h^{(i)}(a)}{(i+1)!}(t-a)^{i+1}\right|$$
$$\leq \frac{\left(t-h^{-1}(b)\right)^{n+2}+(a-t)^{n+2}}{(n+2)!}\left\|h^{(n+1)}\right\|_{L^\infty([h^{-1}(b),a])}$$
$$\leq \frac{2\left(a-h^{-1}(b)\right)^{n+2}}{(n+2)!}\left\|h^{(n+1)}\right\|_{L^\infty([h^{-1}(b),a])}; \tag{8.51}$$

3. *when $p=1$, we have*

$$\left|\int_{h^{-1}(b)}^{a} h(x)\,\mathrm{d}x-\sum_{i=0}^{n}\frac{h^{(i)}\left(h^{-1}(b)\right)}{(i+1)!}\left(t-h^{-1}(b)\right)^{i+1}+\sum_{i=0}^{n}\frac{h^{(i)}(a)}{(i+1)!}(t-a)^{i+1}\right|$$
$$\leq \frac{\left(t-h^{-1}(b)\right)^{n+1}+(a-t)^{n+1}}{(n+1)!}\left\|h^{(n+1)}\right\|_{L([h^{-1}(b),a])}$$
$$\leq \frac{2\left(a-h^{-1}(b)\right)^{n+1}}{(n+1)!}\left\|h^{(n+1)}\right\|_{L([h^{-1}(b),a])}. \tag{8.52}$$

Proof. Let $f\in C^n([a,b])$ have derivative of $(n+1)$-th order on (a,b) and $f^{(n+1)}\in L^p([a,b])$ for positive numbers p and q satisfying $\frac{1}{p}+\frac{1}{q}=1$. In [16] and [17, Theorem 2], it was established that, for any $t\in(a,b)$,

1. when $p,q>1$, we have

$$\left|\int_{a}^{b} f(x)\,\mathrm{d}x-\sum_{i=0}^{n}\frac{f^{(i)}(a)}{(i+1)!}(t-a)^{i+1}+\sum_{i=0}^{n}\frac{f^{(i)}(b)}{(i+1)!}(t-b)^{i+1}\right|$$
$$\leq \frac{(t-a)^{n+1+1/q}+(b-t)^{n+1+1/q}}{(n+1)!\sqrt[q]{nq+q+1}}\left\|f^{(n+1)}\right\|_{L^p([a,b])}$$
$$\leq \frac{2(b-a)^{n+2}}{(n+1)!}\left\|f^{(n+1)}\right\|_{L^p([a,b])}; \tag{8.53}$$

2. when $p = \infty$, we have

$$\left| \int_a^b f(x)\,\mathrm{d}x - \sum_{i=0}^{n} \frac{f^{(i)}(a)}{(i+1)!}(t-a)^{i+1} + \sum_{i=0}^{n} \frac{f^{(i)}(b)}{(i+1)!}(t-b)^{i+1} \right|$$
$$\leq \frac{(t-a)^{n+2} + (b-t)^{n+2}}{(n+2)!} \|f^{(n+1)}\|_{L^\infty([a,b])}$$
$$\leq \frac{2(b-a)^{n+2}}{(n+2)!} \|f^{(n+1)}\|_{L^\infty([a,b])}; \tag{8.54}$$

3. when $p = 1$, we have

$$\left| \int_a^b f(x)\,\mathrm{d}x - \sum_{i=0}^{n} \frac{f^{(i)}(a)}{(i+1)!}(t-a)^{i+1} + \sum_{i=0}^{n} \frac{f^{(i)}(b)}{(i+1)!}(t-b)^{i+1} \right|$$
$$\leq \frac{(t-a)^{n+1} + (b-t)^{n+1}}{(n+1)!} \|f^{(n+1)}\|_{L([a,b])}$$
$$\leq \frac{2(b-a)^{n+1}}{(n+1)!} \|f^{(n+1)}\|_{L([a,b])}. \tag{8.55}$$

Applying three inequalities (8.53), (8.54), and (8.55) to the integral $\int_{h^{-1}(b)}^{a} h(x)\,\mathrm{d}x$ and considering Remark 8.2 lead to the following conclusions:

1. when $p, q > 1$, we have

$$\left| \int_{h^{-1}(b)}^{a} h(x)\,\mathrm{d}x - \sum_{i=0}^{n} \frac{h^{(i)}(h^{-1}(b))}{(i+1)!}\left(t - h^{-1}(b)\right)^{i+1} + \sum_{i=0}^{n} \frac{h^{(i)}(a)}{(i+1)!}(t-a)^{i+1} \right|$$
$$\leq \frac{\left(t-h^{-1}(b)\right)^{n+1+1/q} + (a-t)^{n+1+1/q}}{(n+1)!\sqrt[q]{nq+q+1}} \|h^{(n+1)}\|_{L^p([h^{-1}(b),a])}$$
$$\leq \frac{2\left(a-h^{-1}(b)\right)^{n+2}}{(n+1)!} \|h^{(n+1)}\|_{L^p([h^{-1}(b),a])}; \tag{8.56}$$

2. when $p = \infty$, we have

$$\left| \int_{h^{-1}(b)}^{a} h(x)\,\mathrm{d}x - \sum_{i=0}^{n} \frac{h^{(i)}(h^{-1}(b))}{(i+1)!}\left(t - h^{-1}(b)\right)^{i+1} + \sum_{i=0}^{n} \frac{h^{(i)}(a)}{(i+1)!}(t-a)^{i+1} \right|$$
$$\leq \frac{\left(t-h^{-1}(b)\right)^{n+2} + (a-t)^{n+2}}{(n+2)!} \|h^{(n+1)}\|_{L^\infty([h^{-1}(b),a])}$$
$$\leq \frac{2\left(a-h^{-1}(b)\right)^{n+2}}{(n+2)!} \|h^{(n+1)}\|_{L^\infty([h^{-1}(b),a])}; \tag{8.57}$$

3. when $p = 1$, we have

$$\begin{aligned}
&\left| \int_{h^{-1}(b)}^{a} h(x)\,\mathrm{d}x - \sum_{i=0}^{n} \frac{h^{(i)}(h^{-1}(b))}{(i+1)!}\left(t-h^{-1}(b)\right)^{i+1} + \sum_{i=0}^{n} \frac{h^{(i)}(a)}{(i+1)!}(t-a)^{i+1} \right| \\
&\qquad \le \frac{\left(t-h^{-1}(b)\right)^{n+1} + (a-t)^{n+1}}{(n+1)!} \left\|h^{(n+1)}\right\|_{L([h^{-1}(b),a])} \\
&\qquad \le \frac{2\left(a-h^{-1}(b)\right)^{n+1}}{(n+1)!} \left\|h^{(n+1)}\right\|_{L([h^{-1}(b),a])}. \qquad (8.58)
\end{aligned}$$

Substituting (8.40) into (8.56), (8.57), and (8.58) results in (8.50), (8.51), and (8.52). The proof of Theorem 8.14 is complete. □

8.2.5 THREE EXAMPLES FOR NEW REFINEMENTS OF YOUNG'S INTEGRAL INEQUALITIES

8.2.5.1 First Example

Let $h(x) = \sqrt[4]{x^4+1} - 1$ and let $a = 3$ and $b = 2$ in Theorem 8.11. Then,

$$\begin{aligned}
h'(x) &= \frac{x^3}{(x^4+1)^{3/4}}, \qquad h''(x) = \frac{3x^2}{(x^4+1)^{7/4}} > 0, \\
h^{-1}(2) &= \left(3^4-1\right)^{1/4} = 2\sqrt[4]{5} = 2.990\ldots, \\
L = h'\left(2\sqrt[4]{5}\right) &= \frac{8\times 5^{3/4}}{27}, \qquad U = h'(3) = \frac{27}{82^{3/4}}, \\
h(3) = \sqrt[4]{82} - 1, &\qquad \int_0^3 h(x)\,\mathrm{d}x = \int_0^3 \sqrt[4]{x^4+1}\,\mathrm{d}x - 3, \\
\int_0^2 h^{-1}(x)\,\mathrm{d}x &= \int_0^2 \sqrt[4]{(x+1)^4-1} = \int_1^3 \sqrt[4]{x^4-1}\,\mathrm{d}x,
\end{aligned}$$

and

$$\begin{aligned}
&\frac{\begin{pmatrix} \dfrac{8\times 5^{3/4}}{27}\dfrac{27}{82^{3/4}}\left(3-2\sqrt[4]{5}\right)^2 + \left(\sqrt[4]{82}-3\right)^2 \\ -2\left(3-2\sqrt[4]{5}\right)\left[\dfrac{8\times 5^{3/4}}{27}\left(\sqrt[4]{82}-1\right) - \dfrac{2\times 27}{82^{3/4}}\right] \end{pmatrix}}{2\left(\frac{27}{82^{3/4}} - \frac{8\times 5^{3/4}}{27}\right)} \\
&\quad \le \int_0^3 \sqrt[4]{x^4+1}\,\mathrm{d}x + \int_1^3 \sqrt[4]{x^4-1}\,\mathrm{d}x - 3 - 4\sqrt[4]{5} \\
&\quad \le -\frac{\begin{pmatrix} \dfrac{8\times 5^{3/4}}{27}\dfrac{27}{82^{3/4}}\left(3-2\sqrt[4]{5}\right)^2 + \left(\sqrt[4]{82}-3\right)^2 \\ -2\left(3-2\sqrt[4]{5}\right)\left[\dfrac{27}{82^{3/4}}\left(\sqrt[4]{82}-1\right) - \dfrac{2\times 8\times 5^{3/4}}{27}\right] \end{pmatrix}}{2\left(\frac{27}{82^{3/4}} - \frac{8\times 5^{3/4}}{27}\right)}.
\end{aligned}$$

Consequently, we arrive at

$$9.00004286765564673\ldots < \int_0^3 \sqrt[4]{x^4+1}\,\mathrm{d}x + \int_1^3 \sqrt[4]{x^4-1}\,\mathrm{d}x < 9.00004287010602764\ldots \quad (8.59)$$

which is neither the best nor the weakest estimate among those in Section 8.1.11. The gap between the upper and lower bounds in the double inequality (8.59) is 0.0000000024506... which, comparing with those gaps in Section 8.1.11, is neither the smallest nor the biggest one.

8.2.5.2 Second Example

Let

$$h(x) = \begin{cases} e^{-1/x}, & x > 0; \\ 0, & x = 0. \end{cases}$$

Let $a = b = \frac{1}{2}$ in Theorem 8.11. Then,

$$h'(x) = \frac{e^{-1/x}}{x^2}, \quad h''(x) = \frac{e^{-1/x}(1-2x)}{x^4},$$

$$h^{-1}\left(\frac{1}{2}\right) = \frac{1}{\ln 2} = 1.44\ldots, \quad h\left(\frac{1}{2}\right) = \frac{1}{e^2},$$

$$U = h'\left(\frac{1}{2}\right) = \frac{4}{e^2} = 0.54134\ldots, \quad L = h'\left(\frac{1}{\ln 2}\right) = \frac{\ln^2 2}{2} = 0.24022\ldots,$$

and

$$\frac{\frac{\ln^2 2}{2}\frac{4}{e^2}\left(\frac{1}{2}-\frac{1}{\ln 2}\right)^2 - 2\left(\frac{1}{2}-\frac{1}{\ln 2}\right)\left(\frac{\ln^2 2}{2}\frac{1}{e^2}-\frac{4}{e^2}\frac{1}{2}\right) + \left(\frac{1}{e^2}-\frac{1}{2}\right)^2}{2\left(\frac{4}{e^2}-\frac{\ln^2 2}{2}\right)}$$
$$\le \int_0^{1/2} \frac{1}{e^{1/x}}\,\mathrm{d}x - \int_0^{1/2} \frac{1}{\ln x}\,\mathrm{d}x - \frac{1}{2\ln 2}$$
$$\le -\frac{\frac{\ln^2 2}{2}\frac{4}{e^2}\left(\frac{1}{2}-\frac{1}{\ln 2}\right)^2 - 2\left(\frac{1}{2}-\frac{1}{\ln 2}\right)\left(\frac{4}{e^2}\frac{1}{e^2}-\frac{\ln^2 2}{2}\frac{1}{2}\right) + \left(\frac{1}{e^2}-\frac{1}{2}\right)^2}{2\left(\frac{4}{e^2}-\frac{\ln^2 2}{2}\right)}.$$

Accordingly, it follows that

$$0.388457763460961578\ldots < \int_0^{1/2} \frac{1}{e^{1/x}}\,\mathrm{d}x - \int_0^{1/2} \frac{1}{\ln x}\,\mathrm{d}x < 0.455309856619062079\ldots \quad (8.60)$$

whose lower bound is better, but whose upper bound is worse, than the corresponding ones in (8.35). The gap between the upper and lower bounds in the double inequality (8.60) is 0.066852093209446... which is bigger than the gap 0.057414764502015... in the double inequality (8.35).

8.2.5.3 Third Example

Let $h(x) = e^{x^2} - 1$ for $x \geq 0$. Then, $h^{-1}(x) = \sqrt{\ln(1+x)}$ for $x \geq 0$. Let $a = b = 1$ in Theorem 8.11. Then,

$$h'(x) = 2xe^{x^2}, \quad h^{-1}(1) = \sqrt{\ln 2} = 0.83255\ldots, \quad h(1) = e - 1,$$
$$U = h'(1) = 2e = 5.4365\ldots, \quad L = h'\left(\sqrt{\ln 2}\right) = 4\sqrt{\ln 2} = 3.3302\ldots,$$

and

$$\frac{8e\sqrt{\ln 2}\left(1-\sqrt{\ln 2}\right)^2 - 2\left(1-\sqrt{\ln 2}\right)\left[4\sqrt{\ln 2}(e-1) - 2e\right] + (e-2)^2}{2\left(2e - 4\sqrt{\ln 2}\right)}$$
$$\leq \int_0^1 \left(e^{x^2} - 1\right) \mathrm{d}x + \int_0^1 \sqrt{\ln(1+x)}\, \mathrm{d}x - \sqrt{\ln 2}$$
$$\leq -\frac{8e\sqrt{\ln 2}\left(1-\sqrt{\ln 2}\right)^2 - 2\left(1-\sqrt{\ln 2}\right)\left[2e(e-1) - 4\sqrt{\ln 2}\right] + (e-2)^2}{2\left(2e - 4\sqrt{\ln 2}\right)}.$$

As a result, we have

$$2.05281277502489567\ldots \leq \int_0^1 e^{x^2}\, \mathrm{d}x + \int_0^1 \sqrt{\ln(1+x)}\, \mathrm{d}x \leq 2.06746020503978898\ldots \quad (8.61)$$

whose lower bound is better, but whose upper bound is worse, than the corresponding ones in (8.36). The gap between the upper and lower bounds in the double inequality (8.61) is 0.01464743001489... which is smaller than the corresponding gap 0.01578469... in the double inequality (8.36).

8.3 MORE REMARKS

Finally, we would like to list more remarks on our main results and possible developing directions.

Remark 8.17. *Theorems 8.11 and 8.12 are special cases of Theorem 8.13. In other words, Theorems 8.11 and 8.12 can be deduced from Theorem 8.13.*

Remark 8.18. *Some Taylor-like power expansions such as those in [15,22,37,40] and closely related references can be used to refine Young's integral inequality* (8.1).

Remark 8.19. *At the present position, we conclude that many estimates of definite integrals can be used to refine Young's integral inequality* (8.1).

Remark 8.20. *Essentially speaking, all refinements in this paper are estimates of the area C, which can be geometrically demonstrated in Figures 8.1–8.6 and analytically expressed by* (8.7) *in Remark 8.2.*

Remark 8.21. *This paper is a slightly revised version of the electronic preprint [36].*

ACKNOWLEDGMENTS

The authors are thankful to anonymous referees for their careful corrections, helpful suggestions, and valuable comments on the original version of this paper.

BIBLIOGRAPHY

[1] R. P. Agarwal and S. S. Dragomir, An application of Hayashi inequality for differentiable functions, *Computers Math. Appl.* **32** (1996), no. 6, 95–99; available online at https://doi.org/10.1016/0898-1221(96)00146-0.

[2] H. Alzer and M. K. Kwong, On Young's inequality, *J. Math. Anal. Appl.* **469** (2019), no. 2, 480–492; available online at https://doi.org/10.1016/j.jmaa.2018.06.061.

[3] H. Alzer and S. Koumandos, A new refinement of Young's inequality, *Proc. Edinb. Math. Soc.* (2) **50** (2007), no. 2, 255–262; available online at https://doi.org/10.1017/S0013091504000744.

[4] D. R. Anderson, Young's integral inequality on time scales revisited, *J. Inequal. Pure Appl. Math.* **8** (2007), no. 3, Art. 64; available online at http://www.emis.de/journals/JIPAM/article876.html.

[5] T. M. Apostol, *Calculus*, Vol. I: One-variable calculus, with an introduction to linear algebra; Second edition, Blaisdell Publishing Co. Ginn and Co., Waltham, Mass.-Toronto, Ont.-London, 1967.

[6] T. M. Apostol, *Mathematical Analysis*, Second edition, Addison-Wesley Publishing Co., Reading, Mass.-London-Don Mills, Ont., 1974.

[7] S.-P. Bai, S.-H. Wang, and F. Qi, On HT-convexity and Hadamard-type inequalities, *J. Inequal. Appl.* **2020**, Paper No. 3, 12 pages; available online at https://doi.org/10.1186/s13660-019-2276-3.

[8] P. Cerone, Generalised trapezoidal rules with error involving bounds of the n-th derivative, *Math. Inequal. Appl.* **5** (2002), no. 3, 451–462; available online at https://doi.org/10.7153/mia-05-44.

[9] P. Cerone, On Gini mean difference bounds via generalised Iyengar results, *Hacet. J. Math. Stat.* **44** (2015), no. 4, 789–799; available online at https://doi.org/10.15672/HJMS.2015449430.

[10] P. Cerone and S. S. Dragomir, Lobatto type quadrature rules for functions with bounded derivative, *Math. Inequal. Appl.* **3** (2000), no. 2, 197–209; available online at https://doi.org/10.7153/mia-03-23.

[11] P. Cerone and S. S. Dragomir, On a weighted generalization of Iyengar type inequalities involving bounded first derivative, *Math. Inequal. Appl.* **3** (2000), no. 1, 35–44; available online at https://doi.org/10.7153/mia-03-04.

[12] X.-L. Cheng, The Iyengar-type inequality, *Appl. Math. Lett.* **14** (2001), no. 8, 975–978; available online at https://doi.org/10.1016/S0893-9659(01)00074-X.

[13] S. S. Dragomir, A note on Young's inequality, *Rev. R. Acad. Cienc. Exactas Fís. Nat. Ser. A Mat. RACSAM* **111** (2017), no. 2, 349–354; available online at https://doi.org/10.1007/s13398-016-0300-8.

[14] S. S. Dragomir, Trace inequalities for positive operators via recent refinements and reverses of Young's inequality, *Spec. Matrices* **6** (2018), 180–192; available online at https://doi.org/10.1515/spma-2018-0015.

[15] S. S. Dragomir, F. Qi, G. Hanna, and P. Cerone, New Taylor-like expansions for functions of two variables and estimates of their remainders, *J. Korean Soc. Indust. Appl. Math.* **9** (2005), no. 2, 1–16.

[16] B.-N. Guo and F. Qi, Estimates for an integral in L^p norm of the $(n+1)$-th derivative of its integrand, *Inequality Theory and Applications,* Volume **3**, 127–131, Nova Science Publishers, Hauppauge, NY, 2003.

[17] B.-N. Guo and F. Qi, Some estimates of an integral in terms of the L^p-norm of the $(n+1)$st derivative of its integrand, *Anal. Math.* **29** (2003), no. 1, 1–6; available online at http://dx.doi.org/10.1023/A:1022894413541.

[18] A. Hoorfar and F. Qi, A new refinement of Young's inequality, *Math. Inequal. Appl.* **11** (2008), no. 4, 689–692; available online at https://doi.org/10.7153/mia-11-58.

[19] J. Jakšetić and J. Pečarić, An estimation of Young inequality, *Asian-Eur. J. Math.* **2** (2009), no. 4, 593–604; available online at https://doi.org/10.1142/S1793557109000509.

[20] J. Jakšetić and J. Pečarić, A note on Young inequality, *Math. Inequal. Appl.* **13** (2010), no. 1, 43–48; available online at https://doi.org/10.7153/mia-13-03.

[21] P. Kórus, A refinement of Young's inequality, *Acta Math. Hungar.* **153** (2017), no. 2, 430–435; available online at https://doi.org/10.1007/s10474-017-0735-1.

[22] Q.-M. Luo, F. Qi, and B.-N. Guo, K. Petr's formula of double integral and estimates of its remainder, *Int. J. Math. Sci.* **3** (2004), no. 1, 77–92.

[23] P. R. Mercer, Error terms for Steffensen's, Young's and Chebychev's inequalities, *J. Math. Inequal.* **2** (2008), no. 4, 479–486; available online at https://doi.org/10.7153/jmi-02-43.

[24] P. R. Mercer, Techniques of Integration, Chapter 11 in: *More Calculus of a Single Variable*, Undergraduate Texts in Mathematics, Springer, New York, 2014; available online at https://doi.org/10.1007/978-1-4939-1926-0_11.

[25] D. S. Mitrinović, *Analytic Inequalities*, In cooperation with P. M. Vasić, Die Grundlehren der mathematischen Wissenschaften, Band 165, Springer-Verlag, New York-Berlin, 1970.

[26] D. S. Mitrinović, J. E. Pečarić, and A. M. Fink, *Classical and New Inequalities in Analysis*, Kluwer Academic Publishers, 1993; available online at http://dx.doi.org/10.1007/978-94-017-1043-5.

[27] F. W. J. Olver, D. W. Lozier, R. F. Boisvert, and C. W. Clark (eds.), *NIST Handbook of Mathematical Functions*, Cambridge University Press, New York, 2010; available online at http://dlmf.nist.gov/.

[28] B. G. Pachpatte, On some inequalities for convex functions, *RGMIA Res. Rep. Coll.* **6** (2003), Suppl., Art. 1, 9 pages; available online at http://rgmia.org/v6(E).php.

[29] F. Qi, Further generalizations of inequalities for an integral, *Univ. Beograd. Publ. Elektrotehn. Fak. Ser. Mat.* **8** (1997), 79–83.

[30] F. Qi, Inequalities for a multiple integral, *Acta Math. Hungar.* **84** (1999), no. 1–2, 19–26; available online at https://doi.org/10.1023/A:1006642601341.

[31] F. Qi, Inequalities for a weighted multiple integral, *J. Math. Anal. Appl.* **253** (2001), no. 2, 381–388; available online at https://doi.org/10.1006/jmaa.2000.7138.

[32] F. Qi, Inequalities for an integral, *Math. Gaz.* **80** (1996), no. 488, 376–377; available online at https://doi.org/10.2307/3619581.

[33] F. Qi, Pólya type integral inequalities: origin, variants, proofs, refinements, generalizations, equivalences, and applications, *Math. Inequal. Appl.* **18** (2015), no. 1, 1–38; available online at http://dx.doi.org/10.7153/mia-18-01.

[34] F. Qi, P. Cerone, and S. S. Dragomir, Some new Iyengar type inequalities, *Rocky Mountain J. Math.* **35** (2005), no. 3, 997–1015; available online at https://doi.org/10.1216/rmjm/1181069718.

[35] F. Qi, L.-H. Cui, and S.-L. Xu, Some inequalities constructed by Tchebysheff's integral inequality, *Math. Inequal. Appl.* **2** (1999), no. 4, 517–528; available online at http://dx.doi.org/10.7153/mia-02-42.

[36] F. Qi, W.-H. Li, G.-S. Wu, and B.-N. Guo, Refinements of Young's integral inequality via fundamental inequalities and mean value theorems for derivatives, *arXiv preprint* (2020), available online at https://arxiv.org/abs/2002.04428.

[37] F. Qi, Q.-M. Luo, and B.-N. Guo, Darboux's formula with integral remainder of functions with two independent variables, *Appl. Math. Comput.* **199** (2008), no. 2, 691–703; available online at https://doi.org/10.1016/j.amc.2007.10.028.

[38] F. Qi, P. O. Mohammed, J.-C. Yao, and Y.-H. Yao, Generalized fractional integral inequalities of Hermite–Hadamard type for (α,m)-convex functions, *J. Inequal. Appl.* **2019**, Paper No. 135, 17 pages; available online at https://doi.org/10.1186/s13660-019-2079-6.

[39] F. Qi, G. Rahman, S. M. Hussain, W.-S. Du, and K. S. Nisar, Some inequalities of Čebyšev type for conformable k-fractional integral operators, *Symmetry* **10** (2018), no. 11, Article 614, 8 pages; available online at https://doi.org/10.3390/sym10110614.

[40] F. Qi and W. Ul-Haq, Some integral inequalities involving the expectation and variance via Darboux's expansion, *Adv. Appl. Math. Sci.* **18** (2019), no. 7, 545–552.

[41] F. Qi, Z.-L. Wei, and Q. Yang, Generalizations and refinements of Hermite–Hadamard's inequality, *Rocky Mountain J. Math.* **35** (2005), no. 1, 235–251; available online at http://dx.doi.org/10.1216/rmjm/1181069779.

[42] F. Qi and Y.-J. Zhang, Inequalities for a weighted integral, *Adv. Stud. Contemp. Math. (Kyungshang)* **4** (2002), no. 2, 93–101.

[43] D. Ruthing, On Young's inequality, *Internat. J. Math. Ed. Sci. Techn.* **25** (1994), no. 2, 161–164; available online at https://doi.org/10.1080/0020739940250201.

[44] J. Sándor and V. E. S. Szabó, On an inequality for the sum of infimums of functions, *J. Math. Anal. Appl.* **204** (1996), no. 3, 646–654; available online at https://doi.org/10.1006/jmaa.1996.0459.

[45] Y. Shuang and F. Qi, Integral inequalities of Hermite–Hadamard type for extended s-convex functions and applications, *Mathematics* **6** (2018), no. 11, Article 223, 12 pages; available online at https://doi.org/10.3390/math6110223.

[46] Y. Sun, H.-T. Yang, and F. Qi, Some inequalities for multiple integrals on the n-dimensional ellipsoid, spherical shell, and ball, *Abstr. Appl. Anal.* **2013** (2013), Article ID 904721, 8 pages; available online at https://doi.org/10.1155/2013/904721.

[47] T. Takahashi, Remarks on some inequalities, *Tôhoku Math. J.* **36** (1932), 99–106.

[48] J.-F. Tian, Extension of Hu Ke's inequality and its applications, *J. Inequal. Appl.* **2011**, 2011:77, 14 pages; available online at https://doi.org/10.1186/1029-242X-2011-77.

[49] J.-F. Tian and M.-H. Ha, Properties of generalized sharp Hölder's inequalities, *J. Math. Inequal.* **11** (2017), no. 2, 511–525; available online at https://doi.org/10.7153/jmi-11-42.

[50] J.-Q. Wang, B.-N. Guo, and F. Qi, Generalizations and applications of Young's integral inequality by higher order derivatives, *J. Inequal. Appl.* **2019**, Paper No. 243, 18 pages; available online at https://doi.org/10.1186/s13660-019-2196-2.

[51] A. Witkowski, On Young inequality, *J. Inequal. Pure Appl. Math.* **7** (2006), no. 5, Art. 164; available online at http://www.emis.de/journals/JIPAM/article782.html.

[52] Y. Wu, F. Qi, and D.-W. Niu, Integral inequalities of Hermite–Hadamard type for the product of strongly logarithmically convex and other convex functions, *Maejo Int. J. Sci. Technol.* **9** (2015), no. 3, 394–402.

[53] H.-P. Yin and F. Qi, Hermite–Hadamard type inequalities for the product of (α,m)-convex functions, *J. Nonlinear Sci. Appl.* **8** (2015), no. 3, 231–236; available online at https://doi.org/10.22436/jnsa.008.03.07.
[54] H.-P. Yin and F. Qi, Hermite-Hadamard type inequalities for the product of (α,m)-convex functions, *Missouri J. Math. Sci.* **27** (2015), no. 1, 71–79; available online at http://projecteuclid.org/euclid.mjms/1449161369.
[55] W. H. Young, On classes of summable functions and their Fourier series, *Proc. Roy. Soc. London Ser. A* **87** (1912), 225–229; available online at https://doi.org/10.1098/rspa.1912.0076.
[56] L. Zhu, On Young's inequality, *Internat. J. Math. Ed. Sci. Tech.* **35** (2004), no. 4, 601–603; available online at https://doi.org/10.1080/00207390410001686698.

9 On the Coefficient Estimates for New Subclasses of Bi-univalent Functions Associated with Subordination and Fibonacci Numbers

Şahsene Altınkaya
Bursa Uludag University

CONTENTS

9.1 THE DEFINITION AND ELEMENTARY PROPERTIES OF UNIVALENT FUNCTIONS

Let $\mathbb{R} = (-\infty, \infty)$ be the set of real numbers, $\mathbb{C}$ be the set of complex numbers, and

$$\mathbb{N} := \{1, 2, 3, \ldots\} = \mathbb{N}_0 \setminus \{0\}$$

be the set of positive integers. Let $\mathbb{D}(z_0,r)$ be the open unit disk of radius $r>0$ centered at $z_0 \in \mathbb{C}$,

$$\mathbb{D}(z_0,r)=\{z\in\mathbb{C}:|z-z_0|<r\}.$$

The open disk $\mathbb{D}(0,r)$ will be indicated by $\mathbb{D}_r$, and the unit disk $\mathbb{D}_1$ will be indicated by $\mathbb{D}$.

A complex-valued function $f: B\to\mathbb{C}$ of a complex variable is differentiable at a point $z_0\in B\subset\mathbb{C}$ if it has a derivative at z_0; i.e.,

$$f'(z_0)=\lim_{z\to z_0}\frac{f(z)-f(z_0)}{z-z_0}.$$

A function f is said to be analytic at a point $z_0\in B$ if it is differentiable in some neighborhood of z_0, and it is analytic in a domain B if it is analytic at all points in domain B. We can say that f is an entire function if it is analytic on the whole complex plane.

Definition 9.1. *An analytic function f is said to be univalent in a domain B if the conditions*

$$f(z_1)=f(z_2)\quad (z_1,z_2\in B)$$

imply that $z_1=z_2$.

Geometrically, this means that different points in the domain will be mapped into different points on the image domain ([25], p. 26). The theory of univalent functions is so vast and complicated that certain simplifying assumptions are necessary. The most obvious one is to replace the arbitrary domain B by one that is convenient, and the most attractive selection is the open unit disk $\mathbb{D}$.

For example, consider the function $f(z)=(1+z)^2$ in the open unit disk $\mathbb{D}$. The univalence of this function in $\mathbb{D}$ is easy to see on geometric grounds. Indeed, $1+z$ shifts the open unit disk to the right, and the effect of squaring $1+z$ is easy to visualize. The same type of argument shows that $w=(1+z)^3$ is not univalent in $\mathbb{D}$ (see [31]).

One of the most basic results in the theory of univalent functions in one variable is the Riemann mapping theorem. Its failure in several variables is one of the key differences between complex analysis in one variable and higher dimensions.

Theorem 9.1 (Riemann Mapping Theorem). *Every simply connected domain B, which is a proper subset of $\mathbb{C}$, can be mapped conformally onto the unit disk. Moreover, if $z_0\in B$, there is a unique conformal map of B onto $\mathbb{D}$ such that $f(z_0)=0$ and $f'(z_0)>0$.*

Let $\mathcal{A}$ represent the class of functions f of the form

$$f(z)=z+a_2z^2+a_3z^3+\cdots=z+\sum_{n=2}^{\infty}a_nz^n, \tag{9.1}$$

which are analytic in $\mathbb{D}$ and normalized by $f(0)=f'(0)-1=0$.

The subclass of $\mathcal{A}$ consisting of univalent functions is indicated by $\mathcal{S}$. The leading example of a function of the class $\mathcal{S}$ is the *Koebe function*

$$k(z) = \frac{z}{(1-z)^2} = \sum_{n=1}^{\infty} n z^n \quad (z \in \mathbb{D}).$$

The Koebe function maps $\mathbb{D}$ onto the complex plane except for a slit along the half-line $\left(-\infty, -\frac{1}{4}\right]$ and is univalent. This is the best seen by writing

$$k(z) = \frac{1}{4}\left(\frac{1+z}{1-z}\right)^2 - \frac{1}{4}$$

and observing that the function

$$w(z) = \frac{1+z}{1-z}$$

maps $\mathbb{D}$ conformally onto the right half-plane $\Re(w) > 0$. The rotation of the Koebe function, i.e., the function given by

$$k_\theta(z) = \frac{z}{(1-e^{i\theta}z)^2} \quad (z \in \mathbb{D}),$$

belongs to the class $\mathcal{S}$ for each $\theta \in \mathbb{R}$. This image of the unit disk is in the complex plane except for a radial slit from ∞ to $-\frac{e^{i\theta}}{4}$. The Koebe function and its rotations are the only extremal functions for various problems in the class $\mathcal{S}$.

Other simple examples of functions in $\mathcal{S}$ are as follows:

i. $f(z) = z$, the identity mapping;
ii. $f(z) = \frac{z}{1-z}$, which maps $\mathbb{D}$ conformally onto the half-plane $\Re(w) > -\frac{1}{2}$;
iii. $f(z) = \frac{z}{1-z^2}$, which maps $\mathbb{D}$ onto the entire plane minus the two half-lines $\frac{1}{2} \leq y < \infty$ and $-\infty < y \leq -\frac{1}{2}$.

Among the first important papers that discuss topics from this area are Koebe [42], Alexander [5], and Bieberbach [17]. Koebe initiated in 1907 the study about univalent functions, while Bieberbach presented in 1916 would soon become a famous conjecture. In 1916, Bieberbach [17] conjectured that for $f \in \mathcal{S}$,

$$|a_n| \leq n \quad (n \geq 2).$$

He proved only for the case when $n = 2$. For many years, this conjecture has stood as a challenge to all mathematicians and has inspired the development of important new methods in complex analysis. For the cases $n = 3$ and $n = 4$, the conjecture was proved by Lowner [48], Garabedian, and Schiffer [30], respectively. Later, Pederson and Schiffer [58] proved the conjecture for $n = 5$; for $n = 6$, it was proved by Pederson [57] and Ozawa [56], independently. In 1985, Louis de Branges [24] proved the Bieberbach's conjecture for all the coefficients n. Although almost 70 years had passed until the Bieberbach conjecture was finally proved in this paper, bounds for the Taylor coefficients were obtained in the meantime for some subclasses of univalent functions. After the proof of the Bieberbach conjecture, the study of different subclasses of analytic and univalent functions has began to take shape, still remaining an interesting subject. Nowadays, there are many books dedicated to the study of univalent functions, of which we mention those of Conway [23], Duren [25], Goodman [31], Miller and Mocanu [51], and Pommerenke [60]. Further reading and some additional results on this subject can also be found in the wide variety of classical and modern textbooks devoted to the univalent function theory and related topics, including [2,16,21,22,37,44,52,62,63,71].

9.1.1 INTEGRAL OPERATORS

The study of operators plays an important role in geometric function theory in complex analysis and its related fields. Hence, in this part, we consider a few of the classic integral operators defined on analytic functions.

We recall the definition of the Komatu integral operator of a complex-valued function $f(z)$:

Definition 9.2. *(See [43]) The Komatu integral operator of $f \in \mathcal{A}$ is denoted by $\mathfrak{L}_t^\mu f(z)$ and defined by*

$$\mathfrak{L}_t^\mu f(z) = z + \sum_{n=2}^{\infty} \left(\frac{t}{t+n-1} \right)^\mu a_n z^n \quad (t > 0,\ \mu \geq 0,\ z \in \mathbb{D})$$

$$= \frac{t^\mu}{\Gamma(\mu)} \int_0^1 \xi^{t-2} \left(\log \frac{1}{\xi} \right)^{\mu-1} f(z\xi) d\xi.$$

It is easy to verify that

$$\mathfrak{L}_t^\mu \left(z f'(z) \right) = z \left(\mathfrak{L}_t^\mu f(z) \right)'.$$

Many subclasses of analytic univalent functions involving the Komatu integral operator have been studied by various authors (see, e.g., [14,15,20]). Further, by suitably specializing the parameters μ and t, we obtain the following operators studied by various authors:

i. $\mathfrak{L}_t^0 f(z) = f(z)$;
ii. $\mathfrak{L}_2^1 f(z) = A[f](z)$, called Libera operator [46];
iii. $\mathfrak{L}_1^{-k} f(z) = D^k f(z)$, $(k \in \mathbb{N}_0)$, called Sălăgean differential operator [61].

9.2 SUBCLASSES OF ANALYTIC AND UNIVALENT FUNCTIONS

In this part, we briefly discuss some of the well-known subclasses of the analytic univalent function class $\mathcal{S}$, including starlike and convex functions (see [31]).

Definition 9.3. *A set D in the plane is called convex if for every pair of points w_1 and w_2 in the interior of D, the line segment joining w_1 and w_2 is also in the interior of D. If a function $f(z)$ maps $\mathbb{D}$ onto a convex domain, then $f(z)$ is called a convex function.*

Definition 9.4. *A set D in the plane is said to be starlike with respect to w_0 an interior point of D if each ray with initial point w_0 intersects the interior of D in a set that is either a line segment or a ray. If a function $f(z)$ maps $\mathbb{D}$ onto a domain that is starlike with respect to w_0, then we say that $f(z)$ is starlike with respect to w_0. In the special case $w_0 = 0$, we say that $f(z)$ is a starlike function.*

Examples of convex and starlike domains are shown in Figures 9.1 and 9.2, respectively. The domain shown in Figure 9.2 is starlike with respect to w_0 but is not

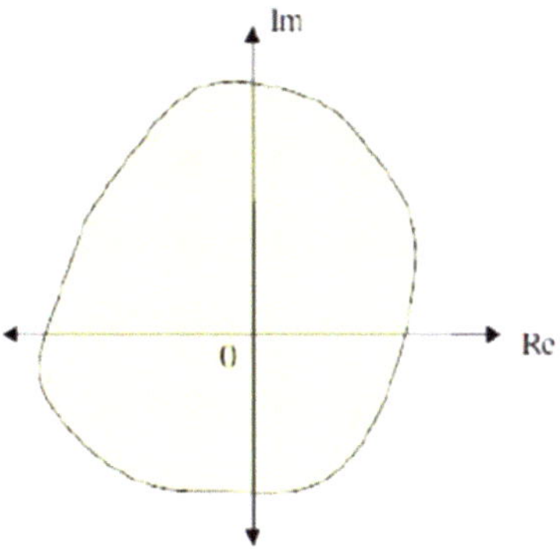

Figure 9.1 Convex domain.

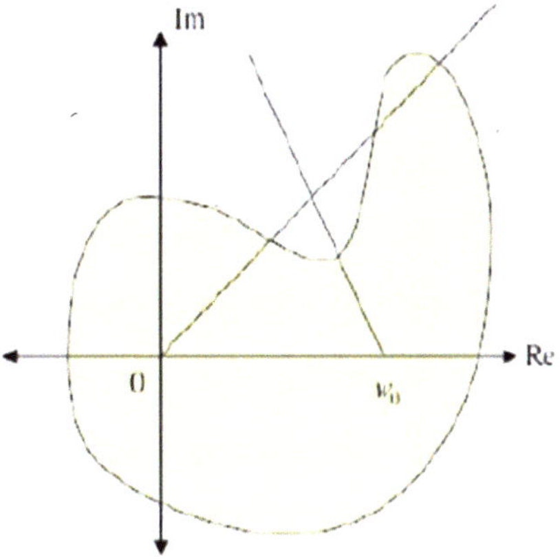

Figure 9.2 Starlike domain.

starlike with respect to the origin. The special function $w(z) = \frac{1+z}{1-z}$ is a convex function because it maps $\mathbb{D}$ onto a half-plane. The Koebe function is a starlike function. In fact, the domain $k(\mathbb{D})$ is starlike with respect to each $w_0 > -\frac{1}{4}$.

Further, two of the important and well-investigated subclasses of the analytic and univalent function class $\mathcal{S}$ are the class $\mathcal{S}^*(\beta)$ of starlike functions of order β in $\mathbb{D}$ and the class $\mathcal{K}(\beta)$ of convex functions of order β in $\mathbb{D}$, respectively. By definition, we have

$$\mathcal{S}^*(\alpha) = \left\{ f : f \in \mathcal{S} \text{ and } \Re\left(\frac{zf'(z)}{f(z)}\right) > \beta, \quad (z \in \mathbb{D}; 0 \leq \beta < 1) \right\} \tag{9.2}$$

and

$$\mathcal{K}(\alpha) = \left\{ f : f \in \mathcal{S} \text{ and } \Re\left(1 + \frac{zf''(z)}{f'(z)}\right) > \beta, \quad (z \in \mathbb{D}; 0 \leq \beta < 1) \right\}. \tag{9.3}$$

It is clear from definitions (9.2) and (9.3) that $\mathcal{K}(\beta) \subset \mathcal{S}^*(\beta)$. Also, we have

$$f(z) \in \mathcal{K}(\beta) \Leftrightarrow zf'(z) \in \mathcal{S}^*(\beta).$$

9.3 THE CLASS Σ

The *Koebe-One Quarter Theorem* [25] provides that the image of $\mathbb{D}$ under every univalent function $f \in \mathcal{A}$ contains a disk of radius $1/4$. Thus, every univalent function $f \in \mathcal{A}$ has an inverse f^{-1} satisfying

$$f^{-1}(f(z)) = z,$$

and

$$f\left(f^{-1}(w)\right) = w \quad \left(|w| < r_0(f),\ r_0(f) \geq \frac{1}{4}\right),$$

where

$$g(w) = f^{-1}(w) = w - a_2 w^2 + \left(2a_2^2 - a_3\right) w^3 - \left(5a_2^3 - 5a_2 a_3 + a_4\right) w^4 + \cdots. \tag{9.4}$$

A function $f \in \mathcal{A}$ is said to be bi-univalent in $\mathbb{D}$ if both f and f^{-1} are univalent in $\mathbb{D}$. Let Σ represent the class of bi-univalent functions in $\mathbb{D}$ given by (9.1). Examples of functions in the class Σ are

$$\frac{z}{1-z}, \ -\log(1-z), \ \frac{1}{2}\log\left(\frac{1+z}{1-z}\right)$$

and so on. However, the familiar Koebe function is not a member of Σ. Other common examples of functions in $\mathcal{S}$ such as

$$z - \frac{z^2}{2}, \ \frac{z}{1-z^2}$$

are also not the members of Σ.

Historically, Lewin [45] studied the class of bi-univalent functions, obtaining the bound 1.51 for the modulus of the second coefficient $|a_2|$. Subsequently, Brannan and Clunie [18] conjectured that $|a_2| \leqq \sqrt{2}$ for $f \in \Sigma$. Later on, Netanyahu [53] showed that $\max|a_2| = \frac{4}{3}$ if $f \in \Sigma$. Brannan and Taha [19] introduced certain subclasses of the bi-univalent function class Σ similar to the familiar subclasses $\mathcal{S}^{\star}(\beta)$ and $\mathcal{K}(\beta)$ of starlike and convex functions of order β $(0 \leqq \beta < 1)$ in $\mathbb{D}$, respectively (see [53]). The classes $\mathcal{S}_{\Sigma}^{\star}(\beta)$ and $\mathcal{K}_{\Sigma}(\beta)$ of bi-starlike functions of order β in $\mathbb{D}$ and bi-convex functions of order β in $\mathbb{D}$, corresponding to the function classes $\mathcal{S}^{\star}(\beta)$ and $\mathcal{K}(\beta)$, were also introduced analogously. For each of the function classes $\mathcal{S}_{\Sigma}^{\star}(\beta)$ and $\mathcal{K}_{\Sigma}(\beta)$, they found non-sharp estimates for the initial coefficients. Recently, motivated substantially by the aforementioned pioneering work on this subject by Srivastava *et al.* [69], many authors investigated the coefficient bounds for various subclasses of bi-univalent functions (see, for example, [3,9,12,13,38,50,68,74,75]). Not much is known about the bounds on the general coefficient $|a_n|$ for $n \geqq 4$. In the literature, there are only a few works determining the general coefficient bounds for $|a_n|$ for the analytic bi-univalent functions (see, for example, [7,10,35,36,70,72,73]). The coefficient estimate problem for each of the coefficients

$$|a_n| \qquad (n \in \mathbb{N} \setminus \{1,2\})$$

is presumably still an open problem for a number of subclasses of the bi-univalent function calss Σ.

Furthermore, the classical Fekete-Szegö inequality, presented by means of Loewner's method, for the coefficients of $f \in \mathcal{S}$ is

$$\left|a_3 - \rho a_2^2\right| \leq 1 + 2\exp(-2\rho/(1-\vartheta)) \;\text{ for } \rho \in [0,1).$$

As $\rho \to 1^{-}$, we have the elementary inequality $\left|a_3 - a_2^2\right| \leq 1$. Moreover, the coefficient functional

$$\mathcal{F}_{\rho}(f) = a_3 - \rho a_2^2$$

on the normalized analytic functions f in the unit disk $\mathbb{D}$ plays an important role in the function theory. The problem of maximizing the absolute value of the functional $\mathcal{F}_{\vartheta}(f)$ is called the Fekete-Szegö problem (see [28]). The Fekete-Szegö problem has continued to receive attention of researches in geometric function theory (see, for example, [8,11,29,39,40,54,59,67,76]). Various interesting developments involving the Fekete-Szegö problem can be found in Abdel-Gawad and Thomas [1], Keogh and Merkes [41], and London [47].

9.4 FUNCTIONS WITH POSITIVE REAL PART

The well-known class of functions with positive real part, consisting of all functions p analytic in $\mathbb{D}$ satisfying $p(0) = 1$ and $\Re p(z) > 0$, is usually denoted by $\mathcal{P}$ and called the Carathéodory class. For example, the function

$$p(z) = \frac{1+z}{1-z} \qquad (z \in \mathbb{D})$$

belongs to $\mathcal{P}$. This function gives a conformal map of $\mathbb{D}$ onto the right-half-plane, and consequently, it plays a fundamental role in the class $\mathcal{P}$, similar to the Koebe function for the class $\mathcal{S}$. It should be noted that $p(z)$ is not required to be univalent. Thus, $p(z) = 1 + z^n$ is in $\mathcal{P}$ for any integer $n \geq 0$, but if $n \geq 2$, this function is not univalent.

Each $p \in \mathcal{P}$ has a Taylor series expansion

$$p(z) = 1 + x_1 z + x_2 z^2 + x_3 z^3 + \cdots \quad (x_1 > 0)$$

with coefficients satisfying $|x_n| \leq 2$ for $n \in \mathbb{N}$ (see [60]). More refinement coefficient bounds in the Carathéodory class were obtained by Grenander and Szegö [32].

9.4.1 SUBORDINATION

With a view to remaining the rule of subordination between analytic functions, let the functions f, g be analytic in $\mathbb{D}$, we say that the function f is subordinate to g, indicated as $f \prec g$ (or $f(z) \prec g(z)$) $(z \in \mathbb{D})$, if there exists a Schwarz function $\mathfrak{w} \in \Lambda$, where

$$\Lambda = \{\mathfrak{w} : \mathfrak{w}(0) = 0, \ |\mathfrak{w}(z)| < 1, \ z \in \mathbb{D}\},$$

such that

$$f(z) = g(\mathfrak{w}(z)) \qquad (z \in \mathbb{D}).$$

Furthermore, if the function g is univalent in $\mathbb{D}$, then we have the following equivalence that holds (see [51]):

$$f(z) \prec g(z) \Leftrightarrow f(0) = g(0) \text{ and } f(\mathbb{D}) \subset g(\mathbb{D}).$$

Ma and Minda [49] unified various subclasses of starlike and convex functions for which either of the quantities

$$\frac{zf'(z)}{f(z)} \quad \text{and} \quad 1 + \frac{zf''(z)}{f'(z)}$$

is subordinate to a more general superordinate function. For this purpose, they considered an analytic function φ with positive real part in the open unit disk $\mathbb{D}$, $\varphi(0) = 1, \varphi'(0) = 1$, and φ maps $\mathbb{D}$ onto a region starlike with respect to 1 and symmetric with respect to the real axis. The class of Ma-Minda starlike functions consists of functions $f \in \mathcal{A}$ satisfying the following subordination condition:

$$\frac{zf'(z)}{f(z)} \prec \varphi(z) \qquad (z \in \mathbb{D}).$$

Similarly, the class of Ma-Minda convex functions consists of functions $f \in \mathcal{A}$ satisfying the following subordination condition:

$$1 + \frac{zf''(z)}{f'(z)} \prec \varphi(z) \qquad (z \in \mathbb{D}).$$

A function f is said to be bi-starlike of Ma-Minda type or bi-convex of Ma-Minda type if both f and f^{-1} are, respectively Ma-Minda starlike or convex. These classes are denoted, respectively, by $\mathcal{S}^{\star}_{\Sigma}(\varphi)$ and $\mathcal{K}_{\Sigma}(\varphi)$ (see [6]).

9.5 BI-UNIVALENT FUNCTION CLASSES $\mathcal{S}^{\mu}_{t,\Sigma}(\widetilde{\mathfrak{P}})$ AND $\mathcal{K}^{\mu}_{t,\Sigma}(\widetilde{\mathfrak{P}})$

In this section, we can formulate the definition of the classes $\mathcal{S}^{\mu}_{t,\Sigma}(\widetilde{\mathfrak{p}})$ and $\mathcal{K}^{\mu}_{t,\Sigma}(\widetilde{\mathfrak{p}})$ by using subordination and the Komatu integral operator mentioned above.

Definition 9.5. *A function $f \in \Sigma$ is said to be in the class*

$$\mathcal{S}^{\mu}_{t,\Sigma}(\widetilde{\mathfrak{p}}) \quad (0 \leq \varepsilon \leq 1,\ t > 0,\ \mu \geq 0,\ z, w \in \mathbb{D})$$

if the following subordinations are satisfied:

$$\frac{z\left(\mathfrak{L}^{\mu}_{t} f(z)\right)'}{(1-\varepsilon)z + \varepsilon \mathfrak{L}^{\mu}_{t} f(z)} \prec \widetilde{\mathfrak{p}}(z) = \frac{1+\tau^2 z^2}{1-\tau z-\tau^2 z^2}$$

and

$$\frac{w\left(\mathfrak{L}^{\mu}_{t} g(w)\right)'}{(1-\varepsilon)w + \varepsilon \mathfrak{L}^{\mu}_{t} g(w)} \prec \widetilde{\mathfrak{p}}(w) = \frac{1+\tau^2 w^2}{1-\tau w-\tau^2 w^2},$$

where the function $g = f^{-1}$ and $\tau = \frac{1-\sqrt{5}}{2} \approx -0.618$.

Definition 9.6. *A function $f \in \Sigma$ is said to be in the class*

$$\mathcal{K}^{\mu}_{t,\Sigma}(\widetilde{\mathfrak{p}}) \quad (0 \leq \varepsilon \leq 1,\ t > 0,\ \mu \geq 0,\ z, w \in \mathbb{D})$$

if the following conditions are satisfied:

$$\frac{z\left(\mathfrak{L}^{\mu}_{t} f(z)\right)' + z^2\left(\mathfrak{L}^{\mu}_{t} f(z)\right)''}{(1-\varepsilon)z + \varepsilon z\left(\mathfrak{L}^{\mu}_{t} f(z)\right)'} \prec \widetilde{\mathfrak{p}}(z) = \frac{1+\tau^2 z^2}{1-\tau z-\tau^2 z^2}$$

and

$$\frac{w\left(\mathfrak{L}^{\mu}_{t} g(w)\right)' + w^2\left(\mathfrak{L}^{\mu}_{t} g(w)\right)''}{(1-\varepsilon)w + \varepsilon w\left(\mathfrak{L}^{\mu}_{t} g(w)\right)'} \prec \widetilde{\mathfrak{p}}(w) = \frac{1+\tau^2 w^2}{1-\tau w-\tau^2 w^2},$$

where the function $g = f^{-1}$ and $\tau = \frac{1-\sqrt{5}}{2} \approx -0.618$.

If we can take the parameters $\mu = 0$ and $\varepsilon = 1$ in the above definitions, we have the following function classes $\mathcal{SL}_{\Sigma}(\widetilde{\mathfrak{p}}(z))$ and $\mathcal{KL}_{\Sigma}(\widetilde{\mathfrak{p}}(z))$, respectively.

Definition 9.7. *(See [33]) A function $f \in \Sigma$ is said to be in the class $\mathcal{SL}_{\Sigma}(\widetilde{\mathfrak{p}}(z))$ if the following subordination holds:*

$$\frac{zf'(z)}{f(z)} \prec \widetilde{\mathfrak{p}}(z) = \frac{1+\tau^2 z^2}{1-\tau z-\tau^2 z^2}$$

and

$$\frac{wg'(w)}{g(w)} \prec \widetilde{\mathfrak{p}}(w) = \frac{1+\tau^2 w^2}{1-\tau w-\tau^2 w^2},$$

where the function $g = f^{-1}$ and $\tau = \frac{1-\sqrt{5}}{2} \approx -0.618$.

Definition 9.8. *(See [33]) A function $f \in \Sigma$ is said to be in the class $\mathcal{KL}_{\Sigma}(\widetilde{\mathfrak{p}}(z))$ if the following subordination holds:*

$$1+\frac{zf''(z)}{f'(z)} \prec \widetilde{\mathfrak{p}}(z) = \frac{1+\tau^2z^2}{1-\tau z-\tau^2z^2}$$

and

$$1+\frac{wg''(w)}{g'(w)} \prec \widetilde{\mathfrak{p}}(w) = \frac{1+\tau^2w^2}{1-\tau w-\tau^2w^2},$$

where the function $g = f^{-1}$ and $\tau = \frac{1-\sqrt{5}}{2} \approx -0.618$.

Remark 9.1. *The function $\widetilde{\mathfrak{p}}(z)$ is not univalent in $\mathbb{D}$, but it is univalent in the disk $|z| < \frac{3-\sqrt{5}}{2} \approx 0.38$. For example, $\widetilde{\mathfrak{p}}(0) = \widetilde{\mathfrak{p}}\left(-\frac{1}{2\tau}\right)$ and $\widetilde{\mathfrak{p}}\left(e^{\pm i\arccos(1/4)}\right) = \frac{\sqrt{5}}{5}$. Also, it can be written as*

$$\frac{1}{|\tau|} = \frac{|\tau|}{1-|\tau|}$$

which indicates that the number $|\tau|$ divides $[0,1]$ such that it fulfills the golden section (see for details Dziok et al. [26]).

Additionally, Dziok et al. [26] indicate a useful connection between the function $\widetilde{\mathfrak{p}}(z)$ and the Fibonacci numbers. Let $\{\Lambda_n\}$ be the sequence of Fibonacci numbers

$$\Lambda_0 = 0,\ \Lambda_1 = 1,\ \Lambda_{n+2} = \Lambda_n + \Lambda_{n+1}\ (n \in \mathbb{N}_0),$$

then

$$\Lambda_n = \frac{(1-\tau)^n - \tau^n}{\sqrt{5}},\quad \tau = \frac{1-\sqrt{5}}{2}.$$

If we set

$$\widetilde{\mathfrak{p}}(z) = 1+\sum_{n=1}^{\infty}\widetilde{\mathfrak{p}}_n z^n = 1+(\Lambda_0+\Lambda_2)\tau z+(\Lambda_1+\Lambda_3)\tau^2z^2$$

$$+\sum_{n=3}^{\infty}(\Lambda_{n-3}+\Lambda_{n-2}+\Lambda_{n-1}+\Lambda_n)\tau^n z^n,$$

then the coefficients $\widetilde{\mathfrak{p}}_n$ satisfy

$$\widetilde{\mathfrak{p}}_n = \begin{cases} \tau & (n=1) \\ 3\tau^2 & (n=2) \\ \tau\widetilde{\mathfrak{p}}_{n-1}+\tau^2\widetilde{\mathfrak{p}}_{n-2} & (n=3,4,\ldots) \end{cases}. \tag{9.5}$$

9.6 INEQUALITIES FOR THE TAYLOR-MACLAURIN COEFFICIENTS

In this part, we offer to get the estimates on the Taylor-Maclaurin coefficients and derive the Fekete-Szegö inequalities for functions in the classes $\mathcal{S}_{t,\Sigma}^{\mu}(\widetilde{\mathfrak{p}})$ and $\mathcal{K}_{t,\Sigma}^{\mu}(\widetilde{\mathfrak{p}})$.

Theorem 9.2. *Let the function f given by (9.1) be in the class $\mathcal{S}_{t,\Sigma}^{\mu}(\widetilde{\mathfrak{p}})$.Then,*

$$|a_2| \leq \frac{|\tau|}{\sqrt{\left|(2-\varepsilon)^2\left(\frac{t}{t+1}\right)^{2\mu}+(3-\varepsilon)\left[\left(\frac{t}{t+2}\right)^{\mu}-2(2-\varepsilon)\left(\frac{t}{t+1}\right)^{2\mu}\right]\tau\right|}},$$

$$|a_3| \leq \frac{|\tau|}{(3-\varepsilon)\left(\frac{t}{t+2}\right)^{\mu}}+\frac{\tau^2}{(2-\varepsilon)^2\left(\frac{t}{t+1}\right)^{2\mu}},$$

for any real number ρ,

$$\left|a_3-\rho a_2^2\right| \leq$$

$$\begin{cases} \dfrac{|\tau|}{(3-\varepsilon)\left(\frac{t}{t+2}\right)^{\mu}}, & |\rho-1| \leq T \\[2ex] \dfrac{|1-\rho|\tau^2}{\left|(2-\varepsilon)^2\left(\frac{t}{t+1}\right)^{2\mu}+(3-\varepsilon)\left[\left(\frac{t}{t+2}\right)^{\mu}-2(2-\varepsilon)\left(\frac{t}{t+1}\right)^{2\mu}\right]\tau\right|}, & |\rho-1| \geq T \end{cases},$$

where $T = \dfrac{\left|(2-\varepsilon)^2\left(\frac{t}{t+1}\right)^{2\mu}+(3-\varepsilon)\left[\left(\frac{t}{t+2}\right)^{\mu}-2(2-\varepsilon)\left(\frac{t}{t+1}\right)^{2\mu}\right]\tau\right|}{(3-\varepsilon)\left(\frac{t}{t+2}\right)^{\mu}|\tau|}.$

Proof. Suppose that $f \in \mathcal{S}_{t,\Sigma}^{\mu}(\widetilde{\mathfrak{p}})$. First, let $p \prec \widetilde{\mathfrak{p}}$. Then, by the definition of subordination, for two analytic functions $\mathfrak{u}, \mathfrak{v}$ such that $\mathfrak{u}(0)=\mathfrak{v}(0)=0$, $|\mathfrak{u}(z)|<1, |\mathfrak{v}(w)|<1$ $(z, w \in \mathbb{D})$, we can write

$$\frac{z\left(\mathfrak{L}_t^{\mu} f(z)\right)'}{(1-\varepsilon)z+\varepsilon\mathfrak{L}_t^{\mu} f(z)} = \widetilde{\mathfrak{p}}(\mathfrak{u}(z)) \tag{9.6}$$

and

$$\frac{w\left(\mathfrak{L}_t^{\mu} g(w)\right)'}{(1-\varepsilon)w+\varepsilon\mathfrak{L}_t^{\mu} g(w)} = \widetilde{\mathfrak{p}}(\mathfrak{v}(w)). \tag{9.7}$$

Next, define the functions p_1 and p_2 by

$$p_1(z) = \frac{1+\mathfrak{u}(z)}{1-\mathfrak{u}(z)} = 1+x_1 z+x_2 z^2+\cdots,$$

$$p_2(w) = \frac{1+\mathfrak{v}(w)}{1-\mathfrak{v}(w)} = 1 + y_1 w + y_2 w^2 + \cdots .$$

Since $\mathfrak{u}$ and $\mathfrak{v}$ are the Schwarz functions, p_1 and p_2 are the analytic functions in $\mathbb{D}$, with $p_1(0) = p_2(0) = 1$ and which have a positive real part in $\mathbb{D}$, we obtain the equations

$$\mathfrak{u}(z) = \frac{p_1(z)-1}{p_1(z)+1} = \frac{1}{2}\left[x_1 z + \left(x_2 - \frac{x_1^2}{2}\right) z^2\right] + \cdots,$$

$$\mathfrak{v}(w) = \frac{p_2(w)-1}{p_2(w)+1} = \frac{1}{2}\left[y_1 w + \left(y_2 - \frac{y_1^2}{2}\right) w^2\right] + \cdots$$

leading to

$$\widetilde{\mathfrak{p}}(\mathfrak{u}(z)) = 1 + \frac{\widetilde{\mathfrak{p}}_1 x_1}{2} z + \left[\frac{1}{2}\left(x_2 - \frac{x_1^2}{2}\right)\widetilde{\mathfrak{p}}_1 + \frac{x_1^2}{4}\widetilde{\mathfrak{p}}_2\right] z^2 + \cdots,$$

$$\widetilde{\mathfrak{p}}(\mathfrak{v}(w)) = 1 + \frac{\widetilde{\mathfrak{p}}_1 y_1}{2} w + \left[\frac{1}{2}\left(y_2 - \frac{y_1^2}{2}\right)\widetilde{\mathfrak{p}}_1 + \frac{y_1^2}{4}\widetilde{\mathfrak{p}}_2\right] w^2 + \cdots .$$

Now, upon comparing the corresponding coefficients in (9.6) and (9.7), we get

$$(2-\varepsilon)\left(\frac{t}{t+1}\right)^{\mu} a_2 = \frac{\widetilde{\mathfrak{p}}_1 x_1}{2}, \tag{9.8}$$

$$(3-\varepsilon)\left(\frac{t}{t+2}\right)^{\mu} a_3 - (2\varepsilon - \varepsilon^2)\left(\frac{t}{t+1}\right)^{2\mu} a_2^2 = \frac{1}{2}\left(x_2 - \frac{x_1^2}{2}\right)\widetilde{\mathfrak{p}}_1 + \frac{x_1^2}{4}\widetilde{\mathfrak{p}}_2, \tag{9.9}$$

$$-(2-\varepsilon)\left(\frac{t}{t+1}\right)^{\mu} a_2 = \frac{\widetilde{\mathfrak{p}}_1 y_1}{2}, \tag{9.10}$$

$$(3-\varepsilon)\left(\frac{t}{t+2}\right)^{\mu} (2a_2^2 - a_3) - (2\varepsilon - \varepsilon^2)\left(\frac{t}{t+1}\right)^{2\mu} a_2^2 = \frac{1}{2}\left(y_2 - \frac{y_1^2}{2}\right)\widetilde{\mathfrak{p}}_1 + \frac{y_1^2}{4}\widetilde{\mathfrak{p}}_2. \tag{9.11}$$

From equations (9.8) and (9.10), one can easily find that

$$x_1 = -y_1, \tag{9.12}$$

$$2(2-\varepsilon)^2\left(\frac{t}{t+1}\right)^{2\mu} a_2^2 = \frac{\widetilde{\mathfrak{p}}_1^2}{4}(x_1^2 + y_1^2). \tag{9.13}$$

If we add (9.9) to (9.11), we obtain

$$2\left[(3-\varepsilon)\left(\frac{t}{t+2}\right)^{\mu} - (2\varepsilon - \varepsilon^2)\left(\frac{t}{t+1}\right)^{2\mu}\right] a_2^2 = \frac{\widetilde{\mathfrak{p}}_1}{2}(x_2 + y_2) + \frac{(\widetilde{\mathfrak{p}}_2 - \widetilde{\mathfrak{p}}_1)}{4}(x_1^2 + y_1^2). \tag{9.14}$$

By making the use of (9.13) in (9.14), we have

$$a_2^2 = \frac{\widetilde{\mathfrak{p}}_1^3(x_2+y_2)}{4\left\{\left[(3-\varepsilon)\left(\frac{t}{t+2}\right)^{\mu}-(2\varepsilon-\varepsilon^2)\left(\frac{t}{t+1}\right)^{2\mu}\right]\widetilde{\mathfrak{p}}_1^2-(2-\varepsilon)^2\left(\frac{t}{t+1}\right)^{2\mu}(\widetilde{\mathfrak{p}}_2-\widetilde{\mathfrak{p}}_1)\right\}} \tag{9.15}$$

which yields

$$|a_2| \leq \frac{|\tau|}{\sqrt{\left|(2-\varepsilon)^2\left(\frac{t}{t+1}\right)^{2\mu}+(3-\varepsilon)\left[\left(\frac{t}{t+2}\right)^{\mu}-2(2-\varepsilon)\left(\frac{t}{t+1}\right)^{2\mu}\right]\tau\right|}}.$$

Next, if we subtract (9.11) from (9.9), we obtain

$$2(3-\varepsilon)\left(\frac{t}{t+2}\right)^{\mu}\left(a_3-a_2^2\right) = \frac{\widetilde{\mathfrak{p}}_1}{2}\left(x_2-y_2\right). \tag{9.16}$$

Then, in view of (9.13), the equation (9.16) becomes

$$a_3 = \frac{\widetilde{\mathfrak{p}}_1^2(x_1^2+y_1^2)}{8(2-\varepsilon)^2\left(\frac{t}{t+1}\right)^{2\mu}} + \frac{\widetilde{\mathfrak{p}}_1\left(x_2-y_2\right)}{4(3-\varepsilon)\left(\frac{t}{t+2}\right)^{\mu}}.$$

Notice that from (9.5), we get

$$|a_3| \leq \frac{|\tau|}{(3-\varepsilon)\left(\frac{t}{t+2}\right)^{\mu}} + \frac{\tau^2}{(2-\varepsilon)^2\left(\frac{t}{t+1}\right)^{2\mu}}.$$

From (9.15) and (9.16), we find that

$$\begin{aligned} a_3-\rho a_2^2 &= \frac{(1-\rho)\widetilde{\mathfrak{p}}_1^3\left(x_2+y_2\right)}{4\left\{\left[(3-\varepsilon)\left(\frac{t}{t+2}\right)^{\mu}-(2\varepsilon-\varepsilon^2)\left(\frac{t}{t+1}\right)^{2\mu}\right]\widetilde{\mathfrak{p}}_1^2-(2-\varepsilon)^2\left(\frac{t}{t+1}\right)^{2\mu}(\widetilde{\mathfrak{p}}_2-\widetilde{\mathfrak{p}}_1)\right\}} \\ &\quad + \frac{\widetilde{\mathfrak{p}}_1\left(x_2-y_2\right)}{4(3-\varepsilon)\left(\frac{t}{t+2}\right)^{\mu}} \\ &= \frac{\widetilde{\mathfrak{p}}_1}{4}\left[\left(h(\rho)+\frac{1}{(3-\varepsilon)\left(\frac{t}{t+2}\right)^{\mu}}\right)x_2+\left(h(\rho)-\frac{1}{(3-\varepsilon)\left(\frac{t}{t+2}\right)^{\mu}}\right)y_2\right], \end{aligned}$$

where

$$h(\rho) = \frac{(1-\rho)\widetilde{\mathfrak{p}}_1^2}{\left[(3-\varepsilon)\left(\frac{t}{t+2}\right)^{\mu}-(2\varepsilon-\varepsilon^2)\left(\frac{t}{t+1}\right)^{2\mu}\right]\widetilde{\mathfrak{p}}_1^2-(2-\varepsilon)^2\left(\frac{t}{t+1}\right)^{2\mu}(\widetilde{\mathfrak{p}}_2-\widetilde{\mathfrak{p}}_1)}.$$

Thus, in view of (9.5), we get

$$\left|a_3-\rho a_2^2\right| \leq \begin{cases} \dfrac{|\widetilde{\mathfrak{p}}_1|}{(3-\varepsilon)\left(\dfrac{t}{t+2}\right)^{\mu}}, & 0 \leq |h(\rho)| \leq \dfrac{1}{(3-\varepsilon)\left(\frac{t}{t+2}\right)^{\mu}} \\ |h(\rho)|\,|\widetilde{\mathfrak{p}}_1|, & |h(\rho)| \geq \dfrac{1}{(3-\varepsilon)\left(\frac{t}{t+2}\right)^{\mu}} \end{cases},$$

which evidently completes the proof of Theorem 9.2. □

Analysis similar to that in the proof of the previous theorem shows that

Theorem 9.3. *Let the function f given by (9.1) be in the class $\mathcal{K}^{\mu}_{t,\Sigma}(\widetilde{\mathfrak{p}})$.Then,*

$$|a_2| \leq \frac{|\tau|}{\sqrt{\left|4(2-\varepsilon)^2\left(\dfrac{t}{t+1}\right)^{2\mu}+(3-\varepsilon)\left[\left(\dfrac{t}{t+2}\right)^{\mu}-8(2-\varepsilon)\left(\dfrac{t}{t+1}\right)^{2\mu}\right]\tau\right|}},$$

$$|a_3| \leq \frac{|\tau|}{3(3-\varepsilon)\left(\dfrac{t}{t+2}\right)^{\mu}}+\frac{\tau^2}{4(2-\varepsilon)^2\left(\dfrac{t}{t+1}\right)^{2\mu}},$$

for any real number ρ,

$$\left|a_3-\rho a_2^2\right| \leq$$

$$\begin{cases} \dfrac{|\tau|}{3(3-\varepsilon)\left(\dfrac{t}{t+2}\right)^{\mu}}, & |\rho-1| \leq Y \\ \dfrac{|1-\rho|\tau^2}{\left|4(2-\varepsilon)^2\left(\dfrac{t}{t+1}\right)^{2\mu}+(3-\varepsilon)\left[3\left(\dfrac{t}{t+2}\right)^{\mu}-8(2-\varepsilon)\left(\dfrac{t}{t+1}\right)^{2\mu}\right]\tau\right|}, & |\rho-1| \geq Y \end{cases},$$

where $Y = \dfrac{\left|4(2-\varepsilon)^2\left(\dfrac{t}{t+1}\right)^{2\mu}+(3-\varepsilon)\left[3\left(\dfrac{t}{t+2}\right)^{\mu}-8(2-\varepsilon)\left(\dfrac{t}{t+1}\right)^{2\mu}\right]\tau\right|}{3(3-\varepsilon)\left(\dfrac{t}{t+2}\right)^{\mu}|\tau|}.$

Taking $\mu = 0$ and $\varepsilon = 1$ in Theorems 9.2 and 9.3, we have the following corollaries.

Corollary 9.1. *(See [33]) Let the function f given by (9.1) be in the class $\mathcal{SL}_{\Sigma}(\widetilde{\mathfrak{p}}(z))$.Then*

$$|a_2| \leq \frac{|\tau|}{\sqrt{1-2\tau}},$$

$$|a_3| \leq \frac{|\tau|(1-4\tau)}{2(1-2\tau)},$$

for any real number ρ,

$$|a_3 - \rho a_2^2| \leq \begin{cases} \dfrac{|\tau|}{2}, & |\rho - 1| \leq \dfrac{1-2\tau}{2|\tau|} \\ \dfrac{|1-\rho|\tau^2}{1-2\tau}, & |\rho - 1| \geq \dfrac{1-2\tau}{2|\tau|} \end{cases}.$$

Corollary 9.2. *(See [33]) Let the function* f *given by (9.1) be in the class* $\mathcal{KL}_\Sigma(\widetilde{\mathfrak{p}}(z))$*.Then*

$$|a_2| \leq \frac{|\tau|}{\sqrt{4-10\tau}},$$

$$|a_3| \leq \frac{|\tau|(1-4\tau)}{3(2-5\tau)},$$

for any real number ρ,

$$|a_3 - \rho a_2^2| \leq \begin{cases} \dfrac{|\tau|}{6}, & |\rho - 1| \leq \dfrac{2-5\tau}{3|\tau|} \\ \dfrac{|1-\rho|\tau^2}{2(2-5\tau)}, & |\rho - 1| \geq \dfrac{2-5\tau}{3|\tau|} \end{cases}.$$

9.7 CONCLUDING REMARKS AND OBSERVATIONS

In our present investigation, we have introduced and studied the coefficient problems associated with the following new subclasses

$$\mathcal{S}_{t,\Sigma}^{\mu}(\widetilde{\mathfrak{p}}) \text{ and } \mathcal{K}_{t,\Sigma}^{\mu}(\widetilde{\mathfrak{p}}) \quad (t > 0,\ \mu \geq 0)$$

of the class of normalized bi-univalent functions in the open unit disk $\mathbb{D}$. For functions belonging to this bi-univalent function class, we have derived Taylor-Maclaurin coefficient inequalities and we have considered the celebrated Fekete-Szegö problem in Section 9.6. For the motivation and validity of our results, we have also pointed out relevant connections with those that were given in earlier works. Moreover, with a view to potentially motivate the interested reader, we choose to include a citation of a very recent survey-cum-expository article [64], which also provides a review of many other related recent works in geometric function theory of complex analysis.

The geometric properties of the function classes $\mathcal{S}_{t,\Sigma}^{\mu}(\widetilde{\mathfrak{p}})$, $\mathcal{K}_{t,\Sigma}^{\mu}(\widetilde{\mathfrak{p}})$ vary according to the values assigned to the parameters involved. Nevertheless, some results for the special cases of the parameters involved could be presented as illustrative examples.

If, on the other hand, we restrict our considerations for a given univalent function $\widetilde{\mathfrak{p}}(z)$ in $\mathbb{D}$, we can investigate the corresponding mapping problems for other regions of the complex z-plane. In this way, one can introduce many other subclasses of the function classes which we have studied in this paper.

Determination of extremal functions for bi-univalent functions (in general) and for bi-subordinate functions (in particular) remains a challenge.

We conclude our present investigation by observing that the interested reader will find several related recent developments concerning geometric function theory of complex analysis (see, for example, [4,27,34,55,65,66]) to be potentially useful for motivating further researches in this subject and on other related topics.

ACKNOWLEDGMENT

This work is supported by the Scientific and Technological Research Council of Turkey (TUBITAK 1002-Short Term R&D Funding Program) Project Number: 118F543.

BIBLIOGRAPHY

[1] H. R. Abdel-Gawad, D. K. Thomas, The Fekete-Szegö problem for strongly close-to-convex functions, *Proc. Amer. Math. Soc.,* 114 (1992) 345–349.

[2] L. V. Ahlfors, *Complex Analysis,* 2nd edn, McGraw-Hill, New York, 1966.

[3] A. Akgül, Ş. Altınkaya, Coefficient estimates associated with a new subclass of bi-univalent functions, *Acta Universitatis Apulensis,* 52 (2017) 121–128.

[4] O. Al-Refai, M. Ali, General coefficient estimates for bi-univalent functions: a new approach, *Turk. J. Math.,* 44 (2020) 240–251.

[5] J. W. Alexander, Functions which map the interior of the unit circle upon simple regions, *Ann. Math.,* 17 (1915) 12–22.

[6] R. M. Ali, S. K. Lee, V. Ravichandran, S. Supramanian, Coefficient estimates for bi-univalent Ma-Minda starlike and convex functions, *Appl. Math. Lett.,* 25 (2012) 344–351.

[7] Ş. Altınkaya, S. Yalçın, Coefficient bounds for a subclass of bi-univalent functions, *TWMS J. Pure Appl. Math.,* 6 (2015) 180–185.

[8] Ş. Altınkaya, S. Yalçın, Fekete-Szegö inequalities for certain classes of bi-univalent functions, Internat. *Scholar. Res. Notices,* 2014 (2014) Article ID 327962, 1–6.

[9] Ş. Altınkaya, S. Yalçın, Coefficient estimates for two new subclasses of bi-univalent functions with respect to symmetric points, *J. Funct. Spaces,* 2015 (2015) Article ID 145242, 1–5.

[10] Ş. Altınkaya, S. Yalçın, Faber polynomial coefficient bounds for a subclass of bi-univalent functions, *C. R. Acad. Sci. Paris Sér. I,* 353 (2015) 1075–1080.

[11] Ş. Altınkaya, S. Yalçın, The Fekete-Szegö problem for a general class of bi-univalent functions satisfying subordinate conditions, *Sahand Commun. Math. Anal.,* 5 (2017) 1–7.

[12] Ş. Altınkaya, S. Yalçın, Faber polynomial coefficient estimates for bi-univalent functions of complex order based on subordinate conditions involving of the Jackson (p,q)-derivative operator, *Miskolc Mathematical Notes,* 18 (2017) 555–572.

[13] Ş. Altınkaya, S. Yalçın, S. Çakmak, A subclass of bi-univalent functions based on the Faber polynomial expansions and the Fibonacci numbers, *Mathematics,* 160 (2019) 1–9.

[14] Ş. Altınkaya, S. Yalçın, Chebyshev polynomial bounds for a certain subclass of univalent functions defined by Komatu integral operator, *Afrika Matematika,* 30 (2019) 563–570.
[15] M. K. Aouf, Some inclusion relationships associated with the Komatu integral operator, *Mathe. Comput. Modell.* 50 (2009) 1360–1366.
[16] S. D. Bernardi, A survey of the development ofthe theory of schlicht functions, *Duke Math. J.,* 19 (1952) 263–287.
[17] L. Bieberbach, Uber die Koe zienten derjenigen Potenzreihen, welche eine schlichte Abbildung des Einheitskreises vernitteln, Sitzungsber. Preuss. *Akad. Wiss. Phys-Math.,* (1916) 940–955.
[18] D. A. Brannan, J. G. Clunie, Aspects of contemporary complex analysis, Proceedings of the NATO Advanced Study Instute Held at University of Durham, New York: Academic Press, 1979.
[19] D. A. Brannan, T. S. Taha, On some classes of bi-univalent functions, *Studia Universitatis Babeş-Bolyai Mathematica,* 31 (2) (1986) 70–77.
[20] S. Bulut, Fekete–Szegö problem for subclasses of analytic functions defined by Komatu integral operator, *Arab. J. Math.,* 2 (2013) 177–183.
[21] J. Clunie, On schlicht functions, *Ann. Math.,* 69 (1959) 511–519.
[22] J. Clunie, Ch. Pommerenke, On the coefficients of univalent functions, *Michigan Math. J.,* 14 (1967) 71–78.
[23] J. B. Conway, *Functions of one complex variable,* 2nd edition, Springer-Verlag, 1978.
[24] L. De Branges, A proof of the Bieberbach conjecture, *Acta Math.,* 154 (1985) 137–152.
[25] P. L. Duren, *Univalent Functions, Grundlehren der Mathematischen Wissenschaften,* Springer, New York, 259, 1983.
[26] J. Dziok, R. K. Raina, J. Sokół, On α-convex functions related to shell-like functions connected with Fibonacci numbers, *Applied Mathematics and Computation,* 218 (2011) 996–1002.
[27] S. M. El-Deeb, T. Bulboaca, B. M. El-Matary, Maclaurin coefficient estimates of bi-univalent functions connected with the q-derivative, *Mathematics,* 8 (2020) 1–14.
[28] M. Fekete, G. Szegö, Eine Bemerkung Über Ungerade Schlichte Funktionen, *J. London Math. Soc.,* (1933) [s1-8 (2)] 85–89.
[29] B. A. Frasin, M. Darus, On the Fekete-Szegö problem, *Int. J. Math. Math. Sci.,* 24 (2000) 577–581.
[30] P. R. Garabedian, M. Schiffer, A proof of the Bieberbach conjecture for the fourth coeffcient, *J. Rational Mech. Anal.,* 4 (1955) 427–465.
[31] A. W. Goodman, *Univalent Functions,* vols. I, II. Polygonal Publishing House, Washington, NJ, 1983.
[32] U. Grenander, G. Szegö, Toeplitz forms and their applications, California Monographs in Mathematical Sciences University, California Press, Berkeley, CA, 1958.
[33] H. Ö. Güney, G. Murugusundaramoorthy, J. Sokol, Subclasses of bi-univalent functions related to shell-like curves connected with Fibonacci numbers, *Acta Universitatis Sapientiae Mathematica,* 10 (2018) 70–84.
[34] H. Ö.Güney, G. Murugusundaramoorthy, New classes of pseudo-type bi-univalent functions, Revista de la Real Academia de Ciencias Exactas, *Físicas y Naturales. Serie A. Matemática,* 114 (2020) 1–8.
[35] S. G. Hamidi, J. M. Jahangiri, Faber polynomial coefficient estimates for analytic bi-close-to-convex functions, *C. R. Acad. Sci. Paris Sér. I,* 352 (2014) 17–20.
[36] S. G. Hamidi, J. M. Jahangiri, Faber polynomial coefficients of bi-subordinate functions, *C. R. Acad. Sci. Paris Sér. I,* 354 (2016) 365–370.

[37] W.K. Hayman, On successive coefficients of univalent functions, *J. London Math. Soc.*, 38 (1963) 228–243.
[38] P. Kamble, M. Shrigan, Ş. Altınkaya, On λ-pseudo q-bi-starlike functions, *Turkish J. Math.*, 43 (2019) 751–758.
[39] S. Kanas, An unified approach to the Fekete-Szegö problem, *Appl. Math, Comput.*, 218 (2012) 8453–8461.
[40] S. Kanas, H. E. Darwish, Fekete-Szegö problem for starlike and convex functions of complex order, *Appl. Math. Lett.* 23 (2010) 777–782.
[41] F. R. Keogh, E. P. Merkes, A coefficient inequality for certain classes of analytic functions, *Proc. Amer. Math. Soc.*, 20 (1969) 8–12.
[42] P. Koebe, Uber die uniformisierung beliebeger analytischer kurven, *Nach. Ges. Wiss. Gottingen,* (1907) 191–210.
[43] Y. Komatu, On analytic prolongation of a family of operators, *Math. (Cluj)* 32 (1990) 141–145.
[44] S. G. Krantz, *Goemtric Function Theory, Explorations in Complex Analysis,* Brikhäuser, Boston, MA, 2006.
[45] M. Lewin, On a coefficient problem for bi-univalent functions, *Proc. Amer. Math. Soc.*, 18 (1967) 63-68.
[46] R. J. Libera, Some classes of regular univalent functions, *Proc. Amer. Math. Soc.,* 16 (1965) 755–758.
[47] R. R. London, Fekete-Szegö inequalities for close-to convex functions, *Proc. Amer. Math. Soc.,* 117 (1993) 947–950.
[48] K. Lowner, Uniersuchungen uber schlichte konforme Abbildungen des Einheitskreises. *I., Math. Ann.,* 89 (1923) 103–121.
[49] W. C. Ma, D. Minda, A unified treatment of some special classes of univalent functions, in: *Proceedings of the Conference on Complex Analysis*, Tianjin, 1992, 157–169, Conference of Proceedings, Lecture Notes Analysis I, Int. Press, Cambridge, MA, 1994.
[50] N. Magesh, V. K. Balaji, Certain subclasses of bi-starlike and bi-convex functions of complex order, *Kyungpook Math. J.,* 55 (2015) 705–714.
[51] S. S. Miller, P. T. Mocanu, *Differential Subordinations: Theory and Applications,* Series on Monographs and Textbooks in Pure and Applied Mathematics, Vol. 225, Marcel Dekker, New York and Basel, 2000.
[52] Z. Nehari, *Conformal Mapping,* Mc. Grraw-Hill Book Comp., New York, 1952.
[53] E. Netanyahu, The minimal distance of the image boundary from the origin and the second coefficient of a univalent function in $|z| < 1$, *Arch. Ration. Mech. Anal.,* 32 (1969) 100–112.
[54] S. O. Olatunji, H. Dutta, Coefficient inequalities for pseudo subclasses of analytical functions related to Petal type domains defined by error function, *AIMS Math.,* 5 (2020) 2526–2538.
[55] H. Orhan, N. Magesh, V. K. Balaji, Fekete–Szegö problem for certain classes of Ma-Minda bi-univalent functions, *Afrika Matematika,* 27 (2016) 889–897.
[56] M. Ozawa, On the Bieberbach conjecture for the sixth coefficient, *Kodai Math. Sem. Rep.,* 21 (1969) 97–128.
[57] R. W. Pederson, A proof of the Bieberbach conjecture for the sixth coefficient, *Arch. Rational Mech. Anal.,* 31 (1968) 331–351.
[58] R. W. Pederson, M. Schiffer, A proof of the Bieberbach conjecture for the fifth coefficient, *Arch. Rational Mech. Anal.,* 45 (1972) 161–193.
[59] A. Pfluger, Fekete-Szegö inequality for complex parameters, *Complex Var. Theory Appl.,* 7 (1986) 149–160.
[60] C. Pommerenke, *Univalent Functions,* Vandenhoeck & Ruprecht, Göttingen. 1975.

[61] G. S. Sălăgean, *Subclasses of univalent functions,* in: Complex Analysis - Fifth Romanian Finish Seminar, Bucharest, 1 (1983) 362–372.

[62] A. C. Schaeffer, D. C. Spencer, The coefficients of schlicht functions, *Duke Math. J.,* 12 (1945) 107–125.

[63] G. Schober, *Univalent functions-selected topics,* Berlin-Heidelberg-New York: Springer, 1975.

[64] H. M. Srivastava, Operators of basic (or q-) calculus and fractional q-calculus and their applications in geometric function theory of complex analysis, *Iran. J. Sci. Technol. Trans. A Sci.,* 44 (2020) 327–344.

[65] H. M. Srivastava, Some general families of the Hurwitz-Lerch Zeta functions and their applications: Recent developments and directions for further researches, *Proc. Inst. Math. Mech. Nat. Acad. Sci Azerbaijan,* 45 (2019) 234–269.

[66] H. M. Srivastava, Ş. Altınkaya, S. Yalçın, Certain subclasses of bi-univalent functions associated with the Horadam polynomials, *Iran. J. Sci. Technol. Trans. A Sci.,* 43 (2019) 1873–1879.

[67] H. M. Srivastava, A. K. Mishra, M. K. Das, The Fekete-Szegö problem for a subclass of close-to-convex functions, *Complex Var. Theory Appl.,* 44 (2001) 145–163.

[68] H. M. Srivastava, S. B. Joshi, S. S. Joshi, H. Pawar, Coefficient estimates for certain subclasses of meromorphically bi-univalent functions, *Palest. J. Math.,* 5 (2016) 250–258.

[69] H. M. Srivastava, A. K. Mishra, P. Gochhayat, Certain subclasses of analytic and bi-univalent functions, *Appl. Math. Lett.,* 23 (2010) 1188–1192.

[70] H. M. Srivastava, F. M. Sakar, H. Ö. Güney, Some general coefficient estimates for a new class of analytic and bi-univalent functions defined by a linear combination, *Filomat,* 32 (2018) 1313–1322.

[71] H. M. Srivastava, S. Owa (Eds.), *Current Topics in Analytic Function Theory,* World Scientific Publishing Company, Singapore, New Jersey, London, and Hong Kong, 1992.

[72] H. M. Srivastava, S. Sümer Eker, S. G. Hamidi, J. M. Jahangiri, Faber polynomial coefficient estimates for bi-univalent functions defined by the Tremblay fractional derivative operator, *Bull. Iran. Math. Soc.,* 44 (2018) 149–157.

[73] H. M. Srivastava, S. Sümer Eker, R. M. Ali, Coefficient bounds for a certain class of analytic and bi-univalent functions, *Filomat,* 29 (2015) 1839–1845.

[74] Q.-H. Xu, Y.-C. Gui, H. M. Srivastava, Coefficient estimates for a certain subclass of analytic and bi-univalent functions, *Appl. Math. Lett.,* 25 (2012) 990–994.

[75] Q.-H. Xu, H.-G. Xiao, H. M. Srivastava, A certain general subclass of analytic and bi-univalent functions and associated coefficient estimate problems, *Appl. Math. Comput.,* 218 (2012) 11461–11465.

[76] Z. Zaprawa, On Fekete-Szegö problem for classes of bi-univalent functions, *Bull. Belg. Math. Soc. Simon Stevin,* 21 (2014) 169–178.

10 Fixed Point of Multivalued Cyclic Contractions

Talat Nazir
University of South Africa
COMSATS University Islamabad

Mujahid Abbas
Government College University Lahore

CONTENTS

10.1 MULTIVALUED MAPPINGS IN METRIC SPACES

The theory of multivalued mappings (also called set-valued mappings) has been extended by many researchers in different ways. The basic tool for generalization is Banach contraction principle [6] which has been used in different ways, either by considering generalized contractive conditions of mappings or extending the area of mappings. Following the Banach contraction principle, the hypothesis of multivalued maps has different applications in convex optimization, dynamical frameworks, commutative polynomial math, differential conditions, and economics. Nadler [14] gave the idea of set-valued contraction and established that a set-valued contraction has fixed point in complete metric space. Thus,the Nadler principle has been used by many researchers [1,2,4,5,9,11,13,19].

All through this work, $P(X)$, $P_{Cl}(X)$, $P_{CB}(X)$, $\mathbb{R}$, $\mathbb{C}$, $\mathbb{R}_+$, $\mathbb{R}^n_+$ and $\mathbb{N}$ signify the family of nonempty subsets of X, non-unfilled closed subsets of X, nonempty closed and bounded subsets of X, the set of real numbers, complex numbers, non-negative real numbers, n-tuples of non-negative real numbers, and natural numbers, respectively.

In this section, we examine some important definitions and major results from existing writing.

Definition 10.1. *For a multivalued mapping $T : X \to P(X)$, fixed point of T is defined as a point u in X if and only if $u \in Tu$. And if $Tu = \{u\}$, then it is called end point.*

Definition 10.2. *Let d be a metric space on X. The Hausdorff–Pompeiu metric on $P_{CB}(X)$ is represented by H, that is,*

$$H(A,B) = \max\{\sup_{u\in A}\{d(u,B)\}, \sup_{v\in B}\{d(v,A)\}\},$$

where A, $B \in P_{CB}(X)$ and

$$d(u,A) = \inf_{v\in B}\{d(u,v)\}.$$

If (X,d) is complete, then $(P_{CB}(X),H)$ is also complete metric space.

Lemma 10.1. *[3,14] Let d be a metric space on X, A, $B \in P_{CB}(X)$. For any $a \in A$, there exists $b = b(a) \in B$ such that*

$$d(a,b) \leq \lambda H(A,B),$$

where $\lambda \geq 1$.

10.2 MULTIVALUED CYCLIC *F*-CONTRACTIVE MAPPINGS

In 2003, Kirk et al. [10] extended the Banach contraction principle to cyclic contractive mappings, studied the cyclical contractive condition for self-mappings, and proved some fixed point results. They introduced cyclic representation and cyclic contractions. A mapping T such that $T : A_1 \cup A_2 \to A_1 \cup A_2$ is called cyclic if $T(A_1) \subset A_2$ and $T(A_2) \subset A_1$, while A_1 and A_2 are non-unfilled subsets of (X,d). And representation of T is cyclic if there exists $\alpha \in (0,1)$ such that $d(Tu,Tv) \leq \alpha d(u,v)$ where $u \in A$ and $v \in B$. It is important worth of cyclic contraction mappings that a map satisfying the Banach contraction is always continuous, but a map satisfying a cyclic contractive condition needs not to be continuous. Pacurar and Rus [16] obtained some fixed point results for maps satisfying cyclic weak contractive conditions. Petric [17] studied some results on cyclic Meir–Keeler contractions in metric spaces. Using fixed point result for weakly contractive map, Karapinar [7] gave some interesting fixed point results for cyclic $\phi-$weak contractive mappings.

Definition 10.3. *For a metric space (X,d), nonempty and closed subsets of X are $A_1, A_2, \ldots, A_p$, where p is a positive integer and $Y = \cup_{i=1}^{p} A_i$ and $T : Y \to P_{CB}(X)$. Then, cyclic representation of Y with respect to T is*

$$T(A_1) \subset A_2, T(A_2) \subset A_3, \ldots, T(A_{p-1}) \subset A_p, T(A_p) \subset A_1.$$

Wardowski [21] gave the following definition for class of mappings.

Definition 10.4. *Suppose $\digamma$ be the set of all continuous mappings $F : \mathbb{R}_+ \to \mathbb{R}$ satisfying the following conditions:*

F_1) *F is strictly increasing, and for all $\gamma, \delta \in \mathbb{R}_+$ such that $\gamma < \delta$ implies that $F(\gamma) < F(\delta)$.*

F_2) *For every sequence $\{\gamma_n\}$ of positive real numbers, $\lim_{n\to\infty} \gamma_n = 0$ and $\lim_{n\to\infty} F(\gamma_n) = -\infty$ are equivalent.*

F_3) *There exists $\eta \in (0,1)$ such that $\lim_{\gamma\to 0^+} \gamma^\eta F(\gamma) = 0$.*

Definition 10.5. *Suppose (X,d) be a metric space, let $A_1, A_2, \ldots, A_p$ be nonempty closed subsets of X, where p is a positive integer, $Y = \cup_{i=1}^{p} A_i$. A multivalued mapping $T : Y \to P_{CB}(X)$ is called*

1. *cyclic $F-$contraction mapping if:*
   (a) *Y has cyclic representation with respect to T.*
   (b) *For every $(u,v) \in A_i \times A_{i+1}$, $i = 1,2,\ldots,p$ and $A_{p+1} = A_1$, with $H(Tu,Tv) > 0$ implies*

$$F(H(Tu,Tv)) + \tau(M_T(u,v)) \leq F(M_T(u,v)),$$

   where $F \in \digamma$, $\tau : \mathbb{R}_+ \to \mathbb{R}_+$ is a continuous function such that $\liminf_{s\to t^+} \tau(s) \geq 0$ for all $t \geq 0$, and

$$M_T(u,v) = \max\{d(u,v), d(u,Tu), d(v,Tv), \frac{d(u,Tv)+d(v,Tu)}{2}\}.$$

2. *Hardy Roger-type-cyclic contractive mapping if*
   (i) *Y has cyclic representation with respect to T.*
   (ii) *For every $(u,v) \in A_i \times A_{i+1}$, $i = 1,2,\ldots,p$ and $A_{p+1} = A_1$,*

$$H(Tu,Tv) \leq a_1 d(u,v) + a_2 d(u,Tu) + a_3 d(v,Tv) + a_4 d(u,Tv) + a_5 d(v,Tu)$$

   holds, where $a_1, \ldots, a_5 \geq 0$ and $a_1 + a_2 + a_3 + 2a_4 + a_5 < 1$.
3. *Reich-type-cyclic contractive mapping if*
   (i) *Y has cyclic representation with respect to T.*
   (ii) *For every $(u,v) \in A_i \times A_{i+1}$, $i = 1,2,\ldots,p$ and $A_{p+1} = A_1$,*

$$H(Tu,Tv) \leq ad(u,v) + bd(u,Tu) + cd(v,Tv)$$

   holds, where a, b, and $c \geq 0$ with $a+b+c < 1$.
4. *Kannan-type-cyclic contractive mapping if*
   (i) *Y has cyclic representation with respect to T.*
   (ii) *For every $(u,v) \in A_i \times A_{i+1}$, $i = 1,2,\ldots,p$ and $A_{p+1} = A_1$,*

$$H(Tu,Tv) \leq \alpha[d(u,Tu) + d(v,Tv)]$$

   holds, where $0 \leq \alpha < \frac{1}{2}$.

5. *Chatterjee-type-cyclic contractive mapping if*
   (i) Y has cyclic representation with respect to T.
   (ii) For every $(u,v) \in A_i \times A_{i+1}$, $i = 1,2,\ldots,p$ *and* $A_{p+1} = A_1$,

$$H(Tu,Tv) \leq \eta[d(u,Tv)+d(v,Tu)],$$

   holds, where $0 \leq \eta < \frac{1}{2}$.

Example 10.1. *Let* $X = \mathbb{R}$ *and d be a usual metric on* X. *Let* $A_1 = [-10,5]$ *and* $A_2 = [-5,10]$ *be any two closed subsets of* X, *such that* $Y = A_1 \cup A_2$ *and* $A_1 \cap A_2 = [-5,5]$. *Let* $T : Y \to P_{CB}(X)$ *be cyclic multivalued mapping such that*

$$T(x) = \begin{cases} [0, -\frac{x}{20}] & if\ x \leq 0, \\ [0, \frac{x}{20}] & if\ x > 0. \end{cases}$$

Note that the set Y has cyclic representation with respect to T, that is, $T(A_1) \subseteq A_2$ *and* $T(A_2) \subseteq A_1$.

1. *Now let us take* $F(x) = \ln x + x$ *for* $x > 0$ *and* $\tau : \mathbb{R}_+ \to \mathbb{R}_+$ *is a function defined as*

$$\tau(r) = \begin{cases} \frac{1}{30}\ if\ r = 0, \\ \frac{y}{30}\ if\ r > 0. \end{cases}$$

   Then for every $(u,v) \in A_i \times A_{i+1}$, $i = 1,2$ *with* $H(Tu,Tv) > 0$ *implies*

$$F(H(Tu,Tv)) + \tau(M_T(u,v)) \leq F(M_T(u,v)),$$

   where

$$M_T(u,v) = \max\{d(u,v), d(u,Tu), d(v,Tv), \frac{d(u,Tv)+d(v,Tu)}{2}\}.$$

   Thus, T is the cyclic F−contraction mapping.
2. *If we take* $a_1 = \frac{1}{4}$, $a_2 = a_3 = \frac{1}{8}, a_4 = \frac{1}{6}, a_5 = \frac{1}{4}$, *then for every* $(u,v) \in A_i \times A_{i+1}$, $i = 1,2$,

$$H(Tu,Tv) \leq a_1 d(u,v) + a_2 d(u,Tu) + a_3 d(v,Tv) + a_4 d(u,Tv) + a_5 d(v,Tu)$$

   holds with $a_1 + a_2 + a_3 + 2a_4 + a_5 < 1$. *Thus, T is the Hardy Roger-type-cyclic contractive mapping.*
3. *If we take* $a = \frac{1}{2}, b = \frac{1}{4}$, *and* $c = \frac{1}{5}$, *then for every* $(u,v) \in A_i \times A_{i+1}$, $i = 1,2$,

$$H(Tu,Tv) \leq ad(u,v) + bd(u,Tu) + cd(v,Tv)$$

   holds with $a + b + c < 1$. *Thus, T is the Reich-type-cyclic contractive mapping.*

4. *If we take* $\alpha = \frac{9}{20}$, *then for every* $(u,v) \in A_i \times A_{i+1}$ *for* $i = 1,2$,

$$H(Tu,Tv) \leq \alpha[d(u,Tu)+d(v,Tv)]$$

holds, where $0 \leq \alpha < \dfrac{1}{2}$. *Thus,* T *is the Kannan-type-cyclic contractive mapping.*

5. *If we take* $\eta = \frac{7}{15}$, *then for every* $(u,v) \in A_i \times A_{i+1}$ *for* $i = 1,2$,

$$H(Tu,Tv) \leq \eta[d(u,Tv)+d(v,Tu)],$$

holds, where $0 \leq \eta < \dfrac{1}{2}$. *Thus,* T *is the Chatterjee-type-cyclic contractive mapping.*

10.3 FIXED POINT RESULTS OF MULTIVALUED CYCLIC *F*-CONTRACTIVE MAPPINGS

In this section, we obtain the fixed point results for multivalued cyclic $F-$contractive mappings. We start with the following result:

Theorem 10.1. *Let* d *be a complete metric on* X, $p \in \mathbb{N}$, $A_1, A_2, \ldots, A_p$ *be nonempty closed subsets of* X *with* $\cap_{i=1}^{p} A_i \neq \emptyset$ *and* $Y = \cup_{i=1}^{p} A_i$. *If* $T : Y \to P_{CB}(X)$ *be a cyclic multivalued* $F-$*contraction mapping, then* T *has a fixed point in* $\cap_{i=1}^{p} A_i$.

Proof. Let $x_0 \in A_1$ and $x_1 \in T(x_0) \subset A_2$. Then, there exists $x_2 \in T(x_1) \subset A_3$, and then, by Lemma 10.1, we have

$$d(x_1,x_2) \leq \lambda H(Tx_0,Tx_1). \tag{10.1}$$

Similarly, there exists $x_3 \in T(x_2) \subset A_4$ such that

$$d(x_2,x_3) \leq \lambda H(Tx_1,Tx_2), \tag{10.2}$$

and there exists $x_4 \in T(x_3) \subset A_5$ such that

$$d(x_3,x_4) \quad \leq \quad \lambda H(Tx_2,Tx_3), \tag{10.3}$$

$$\vdots$$

and there exists $x_{p-2} \in T(x_{p-3}) \subset A_{p-1}$ and $x_{p-1} \in T(x_{p-2}) \subset A_p$ such that

$$d(x_{p-2},x_{p-1}) \leq \lambda H(Tx_{p-3},Tx_{p-2}). \tag{10.4}$$

Similarly, there exists $x_{n+1} \in T(x_n) \subset A_{n+2}$ such that

$$d(x_n,x_{n+1}) \leq \lambda H(Tx_{n-1},Tx_n). \tag{10.5}$$

Suppose that $d(x_n,x_{n+1}) > 0$, for all $n \in \mathbb{N}$. If not, then for some $k \in \mathbb{N}$, we have

$$d(x_k,x_{k+1}) = 0,$$

which implies $x_k = x_{k+1} \in Tx_k$. The proof is finished. Therefore, we assume that $d(x_n, x_{n+1}) > 0$, for all $n \in \mathbb{N}$. So we have

$$0 < d(x_n, x_{n+1}) \leq H(Tx_{n-1}, Tx_n). \tag{10.6}$$

As $\lambda \geq 1$, we have $H(Tx_{n-1}, Tx_n) > 0$.
This implies

$$F(H(Tx_{n-1}, Tx_n)) + \tau(M_T(x_{n-1}, x_n)) \leq F(M_T(x_{n-1}, x_n)),$$

that is,

$$\begin{aligned} F(H(Tx_{n-1}, Tx_n)) &\leq F(M_T(x_{n-1}, x_n)) - \tau(M_T(x_{n-1}, x_n)) \\ &< F(M_T(x_{n-1}, x_n)). \end{aligned}$$

As F is strictly increasing, so we get

$$H(Tx_{n-1}, Tx_n) < M_T(x_{n-1}, x_n), \tag{10.7}$$

where

$$\begin{aligned} M_T(x_{n-1}, x_n) &= \max\{d(x_{n-1}, x_n), d(x_{n-1}, Tx_{n-1}), d(x_n, Tx_n), \\ &\quad \frac{d(x_{n-1}, Tx_n) + d(x_n, Tx_{n-1})}{2}\} \\ &\leq \max\{d(x_{n-1}, x_n), d(x_{n-1}, x_n), d(x_n, x_{n+1}), \\ &\quad \frac{d(x_{n-1}, x_{n+1}) + d(x_n, x_n)}{2}\} \\ &= \max\{d(x_{n-1}, x_n), d(x_n, x_{n+1})\}. \end{aligned}$$

Now, if $M_T(x_{n-1}, x_n) = d(x_n, x_{n+1})$, then from (10.6), we have

$$d(x_n, x_{n+1}) < d(x_n, x_{n+1})$$

a contradiction. Therefore, $M_T(x_{n-1}, x_n) = d(x_{n-1}, x_n)$ and

$$d(x_n, x_{n+1}) < d(x_{n-1}, x_n)$$

for all $n = 0, 1, 2, \ldots$. Thus, the sequence $\{d(x_n, x_{n+1})\}$ is monotonically decreasing and consequently,

$$\tau(d(x_{n-1}, x_n)) + F(d(x_n, x_{n+1})) \leq F(d(x_{n-1}, x_n)) \text{ for all } n = 0, 1, 2, \ldots.$$

By the given assumption on τ, there exists $c > 0$ and $n \in \mathbb{N}$ such that $\tau(d(x_n, x_{n+1})) > c$ for all $n > n_0$. Thus, we obtain that

$$\begin{aligned} F(d(x_n, x_{n+1})) &\leq F(d(x_{n-1}, x_n)) - \tau(d(x_{n-1}, x_n)) \\ &\leq F(d(x_{n-2}, x_{n-1})) - \tau(d(x_{n-2}, x_{n-1})) - \tau(d(x_{n-1}, x_n)) \end{aligned}$$

$$
\begin{aligned}
&\leq \cdots \leq F(d(x_0,x_1)) - \{\tau(d(x_0,x_1)) + \cdots + \tau(d(x_{n_0-1},x_{n_0}))\\
&- \{\tau(d(x_{n_0},x_{n_0+1}) + \cdots + \tau(d(x_{n-1},x_n)\}\\
&= F(d(x_0,x_1)) - n_0.
\end{aligned}
$$

On taking limit as $n \to \infty$, we obtain that

$$\lim_{n\to\infty} F(d(x_n,x_{n+1})) = -\infty.$$

Together with F_2, we have

$$\lim_{n\to\infty} d(x_n,x_{n+1}) = 0.$$

By F_3, there exists $r \in (0,1)$ such that

$$\lim_{n\to\infty} \{d(x_n,x_{n+1})\}^r F(d(x_n,x_{n+1})) = 0.$$

Hence, it follows that

$$
\begin{aligned}
&[d(x_n,x_{n+1})]^r F(d(x_n,x_{n+1}) - [d(x_n,x_{n+1})]^r F(d(x_0,x_1))\\
&\leq [d(x_n,x_{n+1})]^r \{F(d(x_0,x_1)) - n_0 - F(d(x_0,x_1))\}\\
&\leq -n_0[d(x_n,x_{n+1})]^r \leq 0,
\end{aligned}
$$

by applying limit as $n \to \infty$, we have

$$\lim_{n\to\infty} n[d(x_n,x_{n+1})]^r = 0,$$

that is

$$\lim_{n\to\infty} n^{\frac{1}{r}} d(x_n,x_{n+1}) = 0.$$

Now, let us consider that there exists $n_1 \in \mathbb{N}$ such that $n^{\frac{1}{r}} d(x_n,x_{n+1}) \leq 1$ for all $n \geq n_1$. Consequently, we have

$$d(x_n,x_{n+1}) \leq \frac{1}{n^{\frac{1}{r}}} \text{ for all } n \geq n_1.$$

In order to show that $\{x_n\}$ is a Cauchy sequence, consider $m,n \in \mathbb{N}$ such that $m > n$,

$$
\begin{aligned}
d(x_m,x_n) &\leq d(x_m,x_{m-1}) + d(x_{m-1},x_{m-2}) + \cdots + d(x_{n+1},x_n)\\
&< \sum_{i=n}^{\infty} d(x_{i+1},x_i) \leq \sum_{i=n}^{\infty} \frac{1}{i^{\frac{1}{r}}}.
\end{aligned}
$$

If series $\sum_{i=1}^{\infty} \frac{1}{i^{\frac{1}{r}}}$ is convergent, then $\{x_n\}$ is a Cauchy sequence in X. Also d is complete metric on X, then there exists $x^* \in X$ such that $x_n \to x^*$ as $n \to \infty$. Thus, T has a fixed point in X. Since $A_1,A_2,\ldots,A_p$ are closed subsets in X, then $x^* \in A_i$ for $i = 1,2,\ldots,p$, which implies that $x^* \in \cap_{i=1}^{p} A_i$. □

Example 10.2. *Let $X = \mathbb{R}$ and d be a usual metric on X. Let $A_1 = (-\infty, 0]$ and $A_2 = [0, \infty)$ be any two closed subsets of X, such that $Y = A_1 \cup A_2$ and $A_1 \cap A_2 \neq \emptyset$. Let $T : Y \to P_{CB}(X)$ be cyclic multivalued mapping such that*

$$T(x) = \begin{cases} [0, \frac{-x}{40}] \text{ if } x \leq 0 \\ [\frac{-x}{40}, 0] \text{ if } x > 0. \end{cases}$$

Clearly $T(A_1) \subseteq A_2$ and $T(A_2) \subseteq A_1$.
Consider a mapping $F : \mathbb{R}_+ \to \mathbb{R}$ defined as $F(x) = \ln x + x$ for $x > 0$ and $\tau : \mathbb{R}_+ \to \mathbb{R}_+$ is a function defined as

$$\tau(r) = \begin{cases} \frac{1}{20} \text{ if } r = 0, \\ \frac{y}{20} \text{ if } r > 0. \end{cases}$$

To consider the contractive condition

$$H(Tx,Ty)e^{H(Tx,Ty) - M_T(x,y) + \tau(M_T(x,y))} \leq M_T(x,y)$$

for $H(Tx,Ty) > 0$, we have the following two cases:
Case (i): For $x \in A_1$, $y \in A_2$, $T(x) = [0, \frac{-x}{40}]$ and $T(y) = [\frac{-y}{40}, 0]$. Then

$$\begin{aligned} H(Tx,Ty) &= \max\left\{ \sup_{u \in [0, \frac{-x}{40}]} d\left(u, \left[\frac{-y}{40}, 0\right]\right), \sup_{v \in [\frac{-y}{40}, 0]} d\left(v, [0, \frac{-x}{40}]\right) \right\} \\ &= \max\left\{ \frac{-x}{40}, \frac{y}{40} \right\} = \frac{1}{40} \max\{-x, y\} \end{aligned}$$

and

$$\begin{aligned} M_T(x,y) &= \max\left\{ d(x,y), d(x,Tx), d(y,Ty), \frac{d(x,Ty) + d(y,Tx)}{2} \right\} \\ &= \max\left\{ 0, |x|, y, \frac{1}{80}(|x + 40y| + |40x + y|) \right\} \\ &= \max\{|x|, y\}. \end{aligned}$$

So we get

$$\begin{aligned} H(Tx,Ty)e^{H(Tx,Ty) - M_T(x,y) + \tau(M_T(x,y))} &= \frac{1}{40} \max\{-x, y\} e^{\frac{1}{40} \max\{-x,y\} - \frac{19}{20} \max\{|x|,y\}} \\ &= \frac{1}{40} \max\{-x, y\} e^{\frac{-37}{40} \max\{-x,y\}} \\ &\leq \max\{|x|, y\} \\ &= M_T(x,y). \end{aligned}$$

Case (ii): When $x \in A_2$ and $y \in A_1$, $T(x) = [\frac{-x}{40}, 0]$ and $T(y) = [0, \frac{-y}{40}]$. Then,

$$H(Tx,Ty) = \max\left\{ \sup_{u\in[0,\frac{-y}{40}]} d\left(u, \left[\frac{-x}{40}, 0\right]\right), \sup_{v\in[\frac{-x}{40},0]} d\left(v, \left[0, \frac{-y}{40}\right]\right) \right\}$$
$$= \max\left\{\frac{x}{40}, \frac{-y}{40}\right\} = \frac{1}{40}\max\{x, -y\}$$

and

$$M_T(x,y) = \max\left\{d(x,y), d(x,Tx), d(y,Ty), \frac{d(x,Ty)+d(y,Tx)}{2}\right\}$$
$$= \max\left\{0, x, \frac{1}{80}(|40x+y| + |x+40y|)\right\}$$
$$= \max\{x, |y|\}.$$

So we get

$$H(Tx,Ty)e^{H(Tx,Ty)-M_T(x,y)+\tau(M_T(x,y))} = \frac{1}{40}\max\{x,-y\}e^{\frac{1}{40}\max\{x,-y\}-\frac{19}{20}\max\{|x|,y\}}$$
$$= \frac{1}{40}\max\{x,-y\}e^{\frac{-37}{40}\max\{x,-y\}}$$
$$\leq \max\{x, |y|\}$$
$$= M_T(x,y).$$

Therefore, T is cyclic $F-$contraction mapping. Thus, all the conditions of Theorem 10.1 are satisfied. Moreover, $\frac{1}{2}$ is the fixed point of T.

Theorem 10.2. *Let (X,d) be a complete metric space, $p \in \mathbb{N}$, $A_1, A_2, \ldots, A_p$ be nonempty closed subsets of X with $\cap_{i=1}^{p} A_i \neq \emptyset$ and $Y = \cup_{i=1}^{p} A_i$. If $T : Y \to P_{CB}(X)$ be a mapping such that*
(a) $Y = \cup_{i=1}^{p} A_i$ has cyclic representation with respect to T.
(b) For any $(x,y) \in A_i \times A_{i+1}$, $i = 1,2,\ldots,p$ and $A_{p+1} = A_1$ where $H(Tx,Ty) > 0$ implies

$$\tau\left(\overline{M}_T(x,y)\right) + F(H(Tx,Ty)) \leq F\left(\overline{M}_T(x,y)\right), \tag{10.8}$$

where $F \in \digamma$, $\tau : \mathbb{R}_+ \to \mathbb{R}_+$ is a continuous function such that $\liminf_{s\to t^+} \tau(s) \geq 0$ for all $t \geq 0$, and

$$\overline{M}_T(x,y) = \alpha d(x,y) + \beta d(x,Tx) + \gamma d(y,Ty) + \delta_1 d(x,Ty) + \delta_2 d(y,Tx),$$

where $\alpha, \beta, \gamma, \delta_1, \delta_2 \geq 0$, $\delta_1 \leq \delta_2$ with $\alpha+\beta+\gamma+\delta_1+\delta_2 \leq 1$.
Then, T has a fixed point in $\cap_{i=1}^{p} A_i$.

Proof. Let $x_0 \in A_1$ and $x_1 \in T(x_0) \subset A_2$. Then, there exists $x_2 \in T(x_1) \subset A_3$, and then, by Lemma 10.1, we have

$$d(x_1,x_2) \leq \lambda H(Tx_0,Tx_1). \tag{10.9}$$

Similarly, there exists $x_3 \in T(x_2) \subset A_4$ such that

$$d(x_2,x_3) \leq \lambda H(Tx_1,Tx_2), \tag{10.10}$$

and there exists $x_4 \in T(x_3) \subset A_5$ such that

$$d(x_3,x_4) \leq \lambda H(Tx_2,Tx_3), \tag{10.11}$$

$$\vdots$$

and there exists $x_{p-2} \in T(x_{p-3}) \subset A_{p-1}$ and $x_{p-1} \in T(x_{p-2}) \subset A_p$ such that

$$d(x_{p-2},x_{p-1}) \leq \lambda H(Tx_{p-3},Tx_{p-2}). \tag{10.12}$$

Similarly, there exists $x_{n+1} \in T(x_n) \subset A_{n+2}$ such that

$$d(x_n,x_{n+1}) \leq \lambda H(Tx_{n-1},Tx_n). \tag{10.13}$$

Since $d(x_n,x_{n+1}) > 0$, for all $n \in \mathbb{N}$.
If not, then for some $k \in \mathbb{N}$, we have

$$d(x_k,x_{k+1}) = 0,$$

which implies $x_k = x_{k+1} \in Tx_k$. Thus, proof is finished. Therefore, we assume that $d(x_n,x_{n+1}) > 0$, for all $n \in \mathbb{N}$. So, we have

$$0 < d(x_n,x_{n+1}) \leq \lambda H(Tx_{n-1},Tx_n),$$

As $\lambda \geq 1$, so $H(Tx_{n-1},Tx_n) > 0$. Therefore,

$$d(x_n,x_{n+1}) \leq H(Tx_{n-1},Tx_n).$$

This implies that

$$\begin{aligned} F(H(Tx_{n-1},Tx_n)) &\leq F(\overline{M}_T(x_{n-1},x_n)) - \tau(\overline{M}_T(x_{n-1},x_n)) \\ &< F(\overline{M}_T(x_{n-1},x_n)). \end{aligned}$$

As F is strictly increasing, this implies

$$H(Tx_{n-1},Tx_n) < \overline{M}_T(x_{n-1},x_n),$$

where

$$\begin{aligned} \overline{M}_T(x_{n-1},x_n) &= \alpha d(x_{n-1},x_n) + \beta d(x_{n-1},Tx_{n-1}) + \gamma d(x_n,Tx_n) \\ &\quad + \delta_1 d(x_{n-1},Tx_n) + \delta_2 d(x_n,Tx_{n-1}) \\ &\leq \alpha d(x_{n-1},x_n) + \beta d(x_{n-1},x_n) + \gamma d(x_n,x_{n+1}) \\ &\quad + \delta_1 d(x_{n-1},x_{n+1}) + \delta_2 d(x_n,x_n) \\ &\leq (\alpha+\beta+\delta_1)d(x_{n-1},x_n) + (\gamma+\delta_1)d(x_n,x_{n+1}). \end{aligned}$$

Now if $d(x_{n-1},x_n) < d(x_n,x_{n+1})$, then

$$\begin{aligned} d(x_n,x_{n+1}) &< (\alpha+\beta+\gamma+2\delta_1)d(x_n,x_{n+1}) \\ &< d(x_n,x_{n+1}), \end{aligned}$$

a contradiction. Therefore, $d(x_n, x_{n+1}) < d(x_{n-1}, x_n)$, and this implies

$$
\begin{aligned}
d(x_n, x_{n+1}) &< (\alpha+\beta+\gamma+2\delta_1)d(x_{n-1}, x_n) \\
&< d(x_{n-1}, x_n).
\end{aligned}
$$

Thus, the sequence $\{d(x_n, x_{n+1})\}$ is monotonically decreasing. Consequently,

$$
F(d(x_n, x_{n+1})) \leq F(d(x_{n-1}, x_n)) - \tau(d(x_{n-1}, x_n)) \text{ for all } n = 0, 1, 2, \ldots,
$$

and by the given assumption on τ, there exists $c > 0$ such that $\tau(d(x_n, x_{n+1})) > c$ for all $n \geq n_0$. Now

$$
\begin{aligned}
F(d(x_n, x_{n+1})) &\leq F(d(x_{n-1}, x_n)) - \tau(d(x_{n-1}, x_n)) \\
&\leq F(d(x_{n-2}, x_{n-1})) - \tau(d(x_{n-2}, x_{n-1})) - \tau(d(x_{n-1}, x_n)) \\
&\leq \cdots \leq F(d(x_0, x_1)) - \{\tau(d(x_0, x_1)) + \cdots + \tau(d(x_{n_0-1}, x_{n_0})) \\
&+ \tau(d(x_{n_0}, x_{n_0+1}) + \cdots + \tau(d(x_{n-1}, x_n)\} \\
&\leq F(d(x_0, x_1)) - n_0.
\end{aligned}
$$

By taking limit as $n \to \infty$, we get

$$
\lim_{n\to\infty} F(d(x_n, x_{n+1})) = -\infty,
$$

and together with F_2, it gives

$$
\lim_{n\to\infty} d(x_n, x_{n+1}) = 0.
$$

Now by F_3, there exists $r \in (0,1)$ such that

$$
\begin{aligned}
\lim_{n\to\infty} [d(x_n, x_{n+1})]^r F(d(x_n, x_{n+1})) &= 0 \\
\lim_{n\to\infty} n[d(x_n, x_{n+1})]^r &= 0.
\end{aligned}
$$

This implies

$$
\lim_{n\to\infty} n^{\frac{1}{r}} [d(x_n, x_{n+1})] = 0.
$$

Now, let us consider that there exists $n_1 \in \mathbb{N}$ such that $n^{\frac{1}{r}} d(x_n, x_{n+1}) \leq 1$ for all $n \geq n_1$. Consequently, we have

$$
d(x_n, x_{n+1}) \leq \frac{1}{n^{\frac{1}{r}}} \text{ for all } n \geq n_1.
$$

In order to show that $\{x_n\}$ is a Cauchy sequence, consider $m, n \in \mathbb{N}$ such that $m > n$,

$$
\begin{aligned}
d(x_m, x_n) &\leq d(x_m, x_{m-1}) + d(x_{m-1}, x_{m-2}) + \cdots + d(x_{n+1}, x_n) \\
&< \sum_{i=n}^{\infty} d(x_{i+1}, x_i) \leq \sum_{i=n}^{\infty} \frac{1}{i^{\frac{1}{r}}}.
\end{aligned}
$$

If series $\sum_{i=1}^{\infty} \frac{1}{i^{\frac{1}{r}}}$ is convergent, then $\{x_n\}$ is a Cauchy sequence in X. Since (X,d) is complete, there exists $x^* \in X$ such that $x_n \to x^*$ as $n \to \infty$. Thus, T has a fixed point in X. Since $A_1, A_2, \ldots, A_p$ are closed subsets in X, $x^* \in A_i$, $i = 1,2,\ldots,p$ which implies that $x^* \in \cap_{i=1}^{p} A_i$. □

Remark 10.1. *Let (X,d) be a complete metric space, $p \in \mathbb{N}$, $A_1, A_2, \ldots, A_p$ be nonempty closed subsets of X with $\cap_{i=1}^{p} A_i \neq \emptyset$ and $Y = \cup_{i=1}^{p} A_i$. If a map $T : Y \to P_{CB}(X)$ is satisfying either one of the following:*

1. *Hardy Roger-type-cyclic contractive mapping.*
2. *Reich-type-cyclic contractive mapping.*
3. *Kannan-type-cyclic contractive mapping.*
4. *Chatterjee-type-cyclic contractive mapping.*
   Then T has a fixed point in $\cap_{i=1}^{p} A_i$.

10.4 STABILITY OF FIXED POINT SETS OF CYCLIC *F*-CONTRACTIONS

Stability is a concept associated with limiting behaviors of a system. It has been studied in the contexts of both discrete and continuous dynamical systems. The study of the relationship between the convergence of a sequence of mappings and their fixed points, known as the stability of fixed points, has also been widely studied in various settings. The fixed point sets of a sequence of mappings are said to be stable if they converge to the set of fixed points of the limit mapping in the Hausdorff metric. Multivalued mappings often have more fixed points than their single-valued mappings. Therefore, the set of fixed points of multivalued mappings becomes larger and hence more interesting for the study of stability.

Definition 10.6. *The stability of fixed point sets is defined as in the Hausdorff metric the fixed point sets of a sequence of mappings $\{T_n\}$ converges to the fixed point sets of the limit mapping T, that is, $\lim_{n\to\infty} H(F(T_n), F(T)) = 0$.*

We investigate the stability of fixed point sets of multivalued mappings that are satisfying cyclic $F-$contraction condition.

Theorem 10.3. *Let (X,d) be a complete metric space, p be a positive integer, $A_1, A_2, \ldots, A_p$ be nonempty closed subsets of X with $\cap_{i=1}^{p} A_i \neq \emptyset$ such that $Y = \cup_{i=1}^{p} A_i$ and $\{T_i\}_{i=1}^{m} : Y \to P_{CB}(X)$ be family of multivalued mappings satisfying cyclic $F-$contraction condition.*

(i) *$Y = \cup_{i=1}^{p} A_i$ has cyclic representation of with respect to T_i for $i \in \{1,2,\ldots,m\}$.*
(ii) *For any $(x,y) \in A_i \times A_{i+1}$, $i = 1,2,\ldots,p$ and $A_{p+1} = A_1$ such that $H(Tx,Ty) > 0$ implies*

$$F(H(T_i x, T_i y)) + \tau(M_{T_i}(x,y)) \leq F(M_{T_i}(x,y)), \tag{10.14}$$

where $F \in \digamma$, $\tau : \mathbb{R}_+ \to \mathbb{R}_+$ *is a continuous function such that* $\liminf_{s \to t^+} \tau(s) \geq 0$ *for all* $t \geq 0$, *and*

$$M_{T_i}(x,y) = \max\{d(x,y), d(x,T_ix), d(y,T_iy), \frac{d(x,T_iy)+d(y,T_ix)}{2}\}.$$

Then,

$$H(F(T_i), F(T_{i+1})) \leq k,$$

where $k = \sup_{x \in X} H(T_ix, T_{i+1}x)$.

Proof. From Theorem 10.1, the set of fixed points of T_i $(i = 1,2,\ldots,m)$ is nonempty, that is, $F(T_i) \neq \emptyset$, for $i = 1,2,\ldots,m$. Let $y_0 \in A_1$, and $y_1 \in F(T_1)$ that is $y_1 \in T_1y_1 \subset A_2$. Then, by Lemma 10.1, there exists $y_2 \in T_2y_1 \subset A_3$ such that

$$d(y_1,y_2) \leq H(T_1y_1, T_2y_1). \tag{10.15}$$

Since $y_2 \in T_2y_1 \subset A_3$, again by Lemma 10.1, there exists $y_3 \in T_2y_2 \subset A_4$ such that

$$d(y_2,y_3) \leq H(T_2y_1, T_2y_2).$$

By continuing in this way, we obtain a sequence $y_{n+1} \in T_2y_n \subset A_{n+2}$ such that

$$d(y_n,y_{n+1}) \leq H(T_2y_{n-1}, T_2y_n). \tag{10.16}$$

Since $d(y_n,y_{n+1}) > 0$ for all $n \in \mathbb{N}$, $H(T_2y_{n-1}, T_2y_n) > 0$.
This implies that

$$\begin{aligned} F(H(T_2y_{n-1},T_2y_n)) &\leq F(M_T(y_{n-1},y_n)) - \tau(M_T(y_{n-1},y_n)) \\ &< F(M_T(y_{n-1},y_n)), \end{aligned}$$

since F is monotonically increasing, we get

$$\begin{aligned} H(T_2y_{n-1},T_2y_n) &< M_T(y_{n-1},y_n) \\ &= \max\{d(y_{n-1},y_n), d(y_{n-1},Ty_{n-1}), d(y_n,Ty_n), \\ &\quad \frac{d(y_{n-1},Ty_n)+d(y_n,Ty_{n-1})}{2}\} \\ &\leq \max\{d(y_{n-1},y_n), d(y_{n-1},y_n), d(y_n,y_{n+1}), \\ &\quad \frac{d(y_{n-1},y_{n+1})+d(y_n,y_n)}{2}\} \\ &\leq \max\{d(y_{n-1},y_n), d(y_n,y_{n+1})\}. \end{aligned}$$

Now, if $M_T(y_{n-1},y_n) = d(y_n,y_{n+1})$, then it implies

$$H(T_2y_{n-1},T_2y_n) < d(y_n,y_{n+1}), \tag{10.17}$$

and from (10.16) and (10.17), we obtain

$$d(y_n,y_{n+1}) < d(y_n,y_{n+1}),$$

a contradiction.
Also if $M_T(y_{n-1}, y_n) = d(y_{n-1}, y_n)$, then we obtain

$$H(T_2 y_{n-1}, T_2 y_n) < d(y_{n-1}, y_n). \tag{10.18}$$

From (10.17) and (10.18), we get

$$d(y_n, y_{n+1}) < d(y_{n-1}, y_n).$$

Thus, the sequence $\{d(y_n, y_{n+1})\}$ is monotonically decreasing. Consequently, we have

$$\begin{aligned} F(d(y_n, y_{n+1})) &\leq F(d(y_{n-1}, y_n)) - \tau(d(y_{n-1}, y_n)) \\ &< F(d(y_{n-1}, y_n)). \end{aligned}$$

By the given assumption on τ, there exists $c > 0$ and $n \in \mathbb{N}$ such that $\tau(d(y_n, y_{n+1})) > c$ for all $n > n_0$.

$$\tau(d(y_n, y_{n+1})) > c \text{ for all } n > n_0.$$

Thus, we obtain that

$$\begin{aligned} F(d(y_n, y_{n+1})) &\leq F(d(y_{n-1}, y_n)) - \tau(d(y_{n-1}, y_n)) \\ &\leq F(d(y_{n-2}, y_{n-1})) - \tau(d(y_{n-2}, y_{n-1})) - \tau(d(y_{n-1}, y_n)) \\ &\leq \cdots \\ &\leq F(d(y_0, y_1)) - \{\tau(d(y_0, y_1)) + \cdots + \tau(d(y_{n_0-1}, y_{n_0})) \\ &\tau(d(y_{n_0}, y_{n_0+1})) + \cdots + \tau(d(y_{n-1}, y_n))\} \\ &= F(d(y_0, y_1)) - n_0. \end{aligned}$$

On taking limit as $n \to \infty$, we obtain that

$$\lim_{n\to\infty} F(d(y_n, y_{n+1})) = -\infty.$$

And together with F_2, we have

$$\lim_{n\to\infty} d(y_n, y_{n+1}) = 0.$$

By F_3, there exists $r \in (0,1)$ such that

$$\lim_{n\to\infty} \{d(y_n, y_{n+1})\}^r F(d(y_n, y_{n+1})) = 0.$$

Hence, it follows that

$$\begin{aligned} &[d(y_n, y_{n+1})]^r F(d(y_n, y_{n+1})) - [d(y_n, y_{n+1})]^r F(d(y_0, y_1)) \\ &\leq -n_0 [d(y_n, y_{n+1})]^r \leq 0, \end{aligned}$$

by taking limit $n \to \infty$, we get

$$\lim_{n\to\infty} n[d(y_n, y_{n+1})]^r = 0.$$

Now, let us consider that there exists $n_1 \in \mathbb{N}$, such that $n^{\frac{1}{r}} d(y_n, y_{n+1}) \leq 1$ for all $n \geq n_1$. Consequently, we have

$$d(y_n, y_{n+1}) \leq \frac{1}{n^{\frac{1}{r}}} \text{ for all } n \geq n_1.$$

In order to show that $\{y_n\}$ is a Cauchy sequence, consider $m, n \in \mathbb{N}$ such that $m > n > n_1$.

$$\begin{aligned} d(y_m, y_n) &\leq d(y_m, y_{m-1}) + d(y_{m-1}, y_{m-2}) + \cdots + d(y_{n+1}, y_n) \\ &\leq \sum_{i=n}^{\infty} d(y_{i+1}, y_i) \\ &\leq \sum_{i=n}^{\infty} \frac{1}{i^{\frac{1}{r}}}. \end{aligned}$$

Thus, from the convergence of the series $\sum_{i=1}^{\infty} \frac{1}{i^{\frac{1}{r}}}$, we obtain that $\{y_n\}$ is a Cauchy sequence in X. Since (X, d) is complete, there exists $u \in X$ such that $y_n \to u$ as $n \to \infty$. Also u is a fixed point of T_2 that is $u \in T_2(u)$. Then by definition of k and (10.15), we have

$$d(y_1, y_2) \leq H(T_1 y_1, T_2 y_1) \leq k = \sup_{x \in X} H(T_i x, T_{i+1} x).$$

Again by the triangle inequality, we have

$$\begin{aligned} d(y_1, u) &\leq \sum_{i=1}^{n} d(y_i, y_{i+1}) + d(y_{n+1}, u) \\ &\leq \sum_{i=1}^{n} \frac{1}{i^{\frac{1}{r}}} + d(y_{n+1}, u), \end{aligned}$$

Taking the limit as $n \to \infty$, we obtain that

$$d(y_1, u) \leq \sum_{i=1}^{\infty} \frac{1}{i^{\frac{1}{r}}} \leq k,$$

that is, for $y_1 \in F(T_1)$ and $u \in F(T_2)$, we have

$$d(y_1, u) \leq k.$$

Similarly, for an arbitrary $z_0 \in F(T_2)$, we can find $v \in F(T_1)$ such that

$$d(z_0, v) \leq k.$$

Thus, we conclude that

$$H(F(T_1), F(T_2)) \leq k.$$

□

Lemma 10.2. *Let (X,d) be a complete metric space and $\{T_n : X \to P_{CB}(X) : n \in \mathbb{N}\}$ be a sequence of multivalued mappings uniformly convergent to a multivalued mapping $T : X \to P_{CB}(X)$. If T_n satisfies the condition (10.14) of Theorem 10.3 for every $n \in \mathbb{N}$, then T also satisfies the condition (10.14).*

Proof. As T_n satisfies the axiom (10.14) of Theorem 10.3 for every $n \in \mathbb{N}$, we have for $(x,y) \in A_i \times A_{i+1}$, $i = 1,2,\ldots,p$ and $A_{p+1} = A_1$ such that $H(T_nx, T_ny) > 0$ implies

$$F(H(T_nx,T_ny)) + \tau(M_{T_n}(x,y)) \leq F(M_{T_n}(x,y)),$$

where $F \in \digamma$, $\tau : \mathbb{R}_+ \to \mathbb{R}_+$ is a continuous function such that $\liminf_{s\to t^+} \tau(s) \geq 0$ for all $t \geq 0$, and

$$M_{T_n}(x,y) = \max\{d(x,y), d(x,T_nx), d(y,T_ny), \frac{d(y,T_nx)+d(x,T_ny)}{2}\}.$$

Since the sequence $\{T_n\}$ is uniformly convergent to T, taking the limit $n \to \infty$ we get for $H(Tx,Ty) > 0$

$$F(H(Tx,Ty)) + \tau(M_T(x,y)) \leq F(M_T(x,y)),$$

where $F \in \digamma$, $\tau : \mathbb{R}_+ \to \mathbb{R}_+$ is a continuous function such that $\liminf_{s\to t^+} \tau(s) \geq 0$ for all $t \geq 0$, and

$$M_T(Tx,Ty) = \max\{d(x,y), d(x,Tx), d(y,Ty), \frac{d(y,Tx)+d(x,Ty)}{2}\}.$$

which shows that T also satisfies the (10.14). □

Theorem 10.4. *Let (X,d) be a complete metric space and $\{T_n : X \to P_{CB}(X) : n \in \mathbb{N}\}$ be a sequence of multivalued mappings uniformly convergent to $T : X \to P_{CB}(X)$. If T_n satisfies (10.14) for every $n \in \mathbb{N}$, then*

$$\lim_{n\to\infty} H(F(T_n), F(T)) = 0,$$

that is, the fixed point sets of T_n are stable.

Proof. By the above Lemma 10.2, T_n satisfies (10.14). Let $k_n = \sup_{x\in X} H(T_nx, Tx)$. Since the sequence $\{T_n\}$ is uniformly convergent to T on X,

$$\lim_{n\to\infty} k_n = \lim_{n\to\infty} \sup_{x\in X} H(T_nx, Tx) = 0.$$

By using Theorem 10.3, we have

$$H(F(T_n), F(T)) \leq k_n \text{ for every } n \in \mathbb{N}.$$

Taking limit on the above inequality implies

$$\lim_{n\to\infty} H(F(T_n), F(T)) \leq \lim_{n\to\infty} k_n = 0.$$

Thus, the fixed point sets of T_n are stable. □

10.5 MULTIVALUED MAPPINGS UNDER CYCLIC SIMULATION FUNCTION

In this section, we present the idea of fixed points for multivalued mappings under the cyclic simulation function. The surely understood Banach contraction principle empowers the existence and uniqueness of fixed point of contraction in complete metric space. Because of this principle, numerous authors generalized this principle by presenting distinctive contractions on a metric space. Thus in this manner in this work, the mapping $\zeta : [0,\infty) \times [0,\infty) \to \mathbb{R}$ called the simulation function, and the idea of $Z-$contraction concerning ζ. $Z-$contraction sums up the Banach contraction principle and bring together few known types of contractions including the combination of $d(Tx,Ty)$ and $d(x,y)$. We create a connection amongst cyclic and simulation function.

Recently, the authors in [8] introduced the class of simulation functions as follows.

Definition 10.7. *A mapping $\zeta : [0,\infty) \times [0,\infty) \to \mathbb{R}$ is said to be simulation function if*

ζ_1) $\zeta(0,0) = 0$.
ζ_2) $\zeta(t,s) < s - t$ *for all* $t,s > 0$.
ζ_3) *if* $\{t_n\}$, $\{s_n\}$ *are sequences in* $(0,\infty)$ *such that* $\lim_{n\to\infty} t_n = \lim_{n\to\infty} s_n > 0$ *then*

$$\lim_{n\to\infty} \sup \zeta(t_n, s_n) < 0.$$

We denote the set of all simulation functions by Z.

Definition 10.8. *For a metric space (X,d), let $A_1, A_2, \ldots, A_p$ be nonempty closed subsets of X, where p be a positive integer, $Y = \cup_{i=1}^{p} A_i$. A multivalued mapping $T : Y \to P_{CB}(X)$ is called*

1. *cyclic $Z-$contractive mapping if:*
   (a) *Y has cyclic representation with respect to T.*
   (b) *For every $(w,v) \in A_i \times A_{i+1}$, $i = 1,2,\ldots,p$ and $A_{p+1} = A_1$, with $H(Tw,Tv) > 0$ implies*

$$\zeta(H(Tw,Tv), M_1(w,v)) \geq 0, \tag{10.19}$$

   where

$$M_1(w,v) = \max\{d(w,v), d(w,Tw), d(v,Tv), \frac{d(w,Tv) + d(v,Tw)}{2}\}.$$

2. *Hardy Roger-type-cyclic $Z-$contractive mapping if*
   (a) *Y has cyclic representation with respect to T.*
   (b) *For every $(w,v) \in A_i \times A_{i+1}$, $i = 1,2,\ldots,p$ and $A_{p+1} = A_1$, with $H(Tw,Tv) > 0$ implies*

$$\zeta(H(Tw,Tv),M_2(w,v)) \geq 0, \tag{10.20}$$

where

$$M_2(w,v) = a_1 d(w,v) + a_2 d(w,Tw) + a_3 d(v,Tv) + a_4 d(w,Tv) + a_5 d(w,Tv)$$

and $a_1,\ldots,a_5 \geq 0$ *with* $a_1 + a_2 + a_3 + 2a_4 + a_5 < 1$.

Example 10.3. *Let* $X = \mathbb{R}$ *and* d *be a usual metric on* X. *Let* $A_1 = [-20,10]$ *and* $A_2 = [-10,30]$ *be any two closed subsets of* X, *such that* $Y = A_1 \cup A_2$ *and* $A_1 \cap A_2 = [-10,10]$. *Let* $T : Y \to P_{CB}(X)$ *be cyclic multivalued mapping such that*

$$T(x) = \begin{cases} [0, \frac{1-x}{40}] & \text{if } x \leq 1, \\ [0, \frac{1+x}{40}] & \text{if } x > 1. \end{cases}$$

Note that the set Y *has cyclic representation with respect to* T, *that is,* $T(A_1) \subseteq A_2$ *and* $T(A_2) \subseteq A_1$.
Let $\zeta : [0,\infty) \times [0,\infty) \to \mathbb{R}$ *be a simulation function in [8] defined by*

$$\zeta(t_1,t_2) = ct_2 - t_1 \text{ for all } t_1,t_2 \in [0,\infty),$$

where $c = \frac{9}{10} \in [0,1)$.

1. *Then for every* $(w,v) \in A_i \times A_{i+1}$, $i = 1,2$ *with* $H(Tw,Tv) > 0$ *implies*

   $$\zeta(H(Tw,Tv),M_1(w,v)) \geq 0,$$

   where

   $$M_1(w,v) = \max\{d(w,v), d(w,Tw), d(v,Tv), \frac{d(w,Tv)+d(v,Tw)}{2}\}.$$

   Thus, T *is cyclic* $Z-$*contractive mapping.*
2. *If we take* $a_1 = \frac{1}{4}$, $a_2 = a_3 = \frac{1}{8}, a_4 = \frac{1}{6}, a_5 = \frac{1}{4}$, *then for every* $(w,v) \in A_i \times A_{i+1}$, $i = 1,2$, *with* $H(Tw,Tv) > 0$ *implies*

   $$\zeta(H(Tw,Tv),M_2(w,v)) \geq 0,$$

   where

   $$M_2(w,v) = a_1 d(w,v) + a_2 d(w,Tw) + a_3 d(v,Tv) + a_4 d(w,Tv) + a_5 d(w,Tv)$$

   with $a_1 + a_2 + a_3 + 2a_4 + a_5 < 1$. *Thus,* T *is Hardy Roger-type-cyclic* $Z-$*contractive mapping.*

10.6 FIXED POINT THEOREMS UNDER CYCLIC SIMULATION FUNCTION

In this section, we present fixed point results under cyclic simulation function. We start with the following result:

Theorem 10.5. *Let (X,d) be a complete metric space, $p \in \mathbb{N}$, $A_1, A_2, \ldots, A_p$ be nonempty closed subsets of X with $\cap_{i=1}^{p} A_i \neq \emptyset$ and $Y = \cup_{i=1}^{p} A_i$. If $T : Y \to P_{CB}(X)$ be a cyclic $Z-$contractive mapping with $\zeta \in Z$. Then, T has a fixed point in $\cap_{i=1}^{p} A_i$.*

Proof. Let $x_0 \in A_1$ and $x_1 \in T(x_0) \subset A_2$. Then, by Lemma 10.1, there exists $x_2 \in T(x_1) \subset A_3$, such that

$$d(x_1,x_2) \leq \lambda H(Tx_0,Tx_1). \tag{10.21}$$

Since $x_2 \in T(x_1) \subset A_3$. Then, again by Lemma 10.1, there exists $x_3 \in T(x_2) \subset A_4$ such that

$$d(x_2,x_3) \leq \lambda H(Tx_1,Tx_2). \tag{10.22}$$

And there exists $x_4 \in T(x_3) \subset A_5$ such that

$$d(x_3,x_4) \leq \lambda H(Tx_2,Tx_3), \tag{10.23}$$

$$\vdots$$

and there exists $x_{p-2} \in T(x_{p-3}) \subset A_{p-1}$ and $x_{p-1} \in T(x_{p-2}) \subset A_p$ such that

$$d(x_{p-2},x_{p-1}) \leq \lambda H(Tx_{p-3},Tx_{p-2}). \tag{10.24}$$

Similarly, there exists $x_{n+1} \in T(x_n) \subset A_{n+2}$ such that

$$d(x_n,x_{n+1}) \leq \lambda H(Tx_{n-1},Tx_n). \tag{10.25}$$

We assume that $d(x_n,x_{n+1}) > 0$, for all $n \in \mathbb{N}$.
If not, then for some $k \in \mathbb{N}$, we have

$$d(x_k,x_{k+1}) = 0,$$

which implies $x_k = x_{k+1} \in Tx_k$, and the proof is finished. Therefore, we assume that $d(x_n,x_{n+1}) > 0$ for all $n \in \mathbb{N}$. Now

$$0 < d(x_{n+1},x_{n+2}) \leq \lambda H(Tx_n,Tx_{n+1}),$$

where $\lambda \geq 1$, implies

$$H(Tx_n,Tx_{n+1}) > 0.$$

This implies that

$$\begin{aligned} 0 &\leq \zeta(H(Tx_n,Tx_{n+1}),M_1(x_n,x_{n+1})) \\ &< M_1(x_n,x_{n+1}) - H(Tx_n,Tx_{n+1}), \end{aligned}$$

which implies

$$\begin{aligned} H(Tx_n, Tx_{n+1}) &< M_1(x_n, x_{n+1}), \\ d(x_{n+1}, x_{n+2}) &< M_1(x_n, x_{n+1}), \end{aligned} \tag{10.26}$$

where

$$\begin{aligned} M_1(x_n, x_{n+1}) &= \max\{d(x_n, x_{n+1}), d(x_n, Tx_n), d(x_{n+1}, Tx_{n+1}), \\ &\quad \frac{d(x_n, Tx_{n+1}) + d(x_{n+1}, Tx_n)}{2}\} \\ &\leq \max\{d(x_n, x_{n+1}), d(x_n, x_{n+1}), d(x_{n+1}, x_{n+2}), \\ &\quad \frac{d(x_n, x_{n+2}) + d(x_{n+1}, x_{n+1})}{2}\} \\ &= \max\{d(x_n, x_{n+1}), d(x_{n+1}, x_{n+2})\}. \end{aligned}$$

Now, if $M_1(x_n, x_{n+1}) = d(x_{n+1}, x_{n+2})$, then (10.26) implies

$$d(x_{n+1}, x_{n+2}) < d(x_{n+1}, x_{n+2}),$$

a contradiction. Therefore, $M_1(x_n, x_{n+1}) = d(x_n, x_{n+1})$, which implies

$$d(x_{n+1}, x_{n+2}) < d(x_n, x_{n+1}) \text{ for all } n \in \mathbb{N}.$$

Thus, $\{d(x_{n+1}, x_{n+2})\}$ is a monotonically decreasing sequence of non-negative real numbers which is bounded below, and then, there exists $r \geq 0$ such that $\{d(x_{n+1}, x_{n+2})\}$ converges to r. we claim that $r = 0$. Assume on contrary $r > 0$. Obviously,

$$\lim_{n\to\infty} d(x_{n+1}, x_{n+2}) = \lim_{n\to\infty} d(x_n, x_{n+1}) = r.$$

It follows from the property (δ_3) of a simulation function that

$$0 \leq \limsup_{n\to\infty} \zeta(d(x_{n+1}, x_{n+2}), d(x_n, x_{n+1})) < 0.$$

Implies a contradiction, this shows that $r = 0$. Hence,

$$\lim_{n\to\infty} d(x_{n+1}, x_{n+2}) = 0.$$

Now to show $\{x_n\}$ is a Cauchy sequence in X, it is sufficient to show for Cauchyness that its subsequence $\{x_{2n}\}$ is also Cauchy in X. If it doesn't hold, then there exists $\varepsilon > 0$ such that we can find subsequences $\{x_{2m_k}\}$ and $\{x_{2n_k}\}$ of $\{x_{2n}\}$ with $n_k > m_k \geq k$ such that

$$d(x_{2m_k}, x_{2n_k}) \geq \varepsilon \text{ for all } k \in \mathbb{N}. \tag{10.27}$$

Without any loss of generality, we assume that for all $k \in \mathbb{N}$, n_k is the smallest positive integer greater than m_k for which this inequality holds, then

$$d(x_{2m_k}, x_{2n_k-2}) < \varepsilon \text{ for all } k \in \mathbb{N}. \tag{10.28}$$

Now by (10.27) and (10.28), we have

$$\begin{aligned}\varepsilon &\le d(x_{2m_k}, x_{2n_k}) \\ &\le d(x_{2m_k}, x_{2n_k-2}) + d(x_{2n_k-2}, x_{2n_k-1}) + d(x_{2n_k-1}, x_{2n_k}) \\ &< \varepsilon + d(x_{2n_k-2}, x_{2n_k-1}) + d(x_{2n_k-1}, x_{2n_k}),\end{aligned} \tag{10.29}$$

and by taking limit as $k \to \infty$ in the above inequality and using (10.28), we get that

$$\lim_{k\to\infty} d(x_{2m_k}, x_{2n_k}) = \varepsilon.$$

Similarly, we have

$$\begin{aligned}\varepsilon &\le d(x_{2m_k}, x_{2n_k}) \\ &\le d(x_{2m_k}, x_{2m_k+1}) + d(x_{2m_k+1}, x_{2n_k+1}) + d(x_{2n_k+1}, x_{2n_k}).\end{aligned} \tag{10.30}$$

Also,

$$d(x_{2m_{k+1}}, x_{2n_k+1}) \le d(x_{2m_{k+1}}, x_{2m_k}) + d(x_{2m_k}, x_{2n_k}) + d(x_{2n_k}, x_{2n_k+1}). \tag{10.31}$$

By taking limit as $k \to \infty$ on both sides of (10.30) and (10.31), we have

$$\lim_{k\to\infty} d(x_{2m_{k+1}}, x_{2n_k+1}) = \varepsilon.$$

As $\{x_{2m_k}\}$ and $\{x_{2n_k}\}$ are subsequences of $\{x_{2n}\}$ with $n_k > m_k \ge k$ and the property δ_3 of simulation function that

$$0 \le \limsup_{n\to\infty} \zeta(d(x_{2m_{k+1}}, x_{2n_k+1}), d(x_{2m_k}, x_{2n_k})) < 0,$$

a contradiction arises and hence $\{x_n\}$ is a Cauchy sequence in X. As A is a closed subset of a complete metric space X, there exists $x \in A$ such that $\lim_{n\to\infty} x_n = x$. Hence, x is a fixed point of T in $\cap_{i=1}^{p} A_i$. □

Example 10.4. *Let $X = \mathbb{R}$ and d be a usual metric on X. Let $A_1 = [-10, 0]$ and $A_2 = [0, 20]$ be any two closed subsets of X, such that $Y = A_1 \cup A_2$ and $A_1 \cap A_2 \neq \emptyset$. Consider a mapping $T : Y \to P_{CB}(X)$ defined as*

$$T(x) = \begin{cases} [0, \frac{-x}{15}] & \text{if } x \le 0 \\ [\frac{-x}{15}, 0] & \text{if } x > 0. \end{cases}$$

Clearly, $T(A_1) \subseteq A_2$ and $T(A_2) \subseteq A_1$, so T is cyclic multivalued mapping. Let $\zeta : [0,\infty) \times [0,\infty) \to \mathbb{R}$ be a simulation function in [8] defined by

$$\zeta(t_1, t_2) = \kappa t_2 - t_1 \text{ for all } t_1, t_2 \in [0, \infty),$$

where $\kappa = \frac{4}{5} \in [0, 1)$.

To consider the contractive condition that for every $(w,v) \in A_i \times A_{i+1}$, $i = 1,2$ with $H(Tw,Tv) > 0$ such that

$$\zeta(H(Tw,Tv), M_1(w,v)) \geq 0,$$

where

$$M_1(w,v) = \max\{d(w,v), d(w,Tw), d(v,Tv), \frac{d(w,Tv)+d(v,Tw)}{2}\},$$

we have the following two cases:
Case (i): For $w \in A_1$, $v \in A_2$, $T(w) = [0, \frac{-w}{15}]$ and $T(v) = [\frac{-v}{15}, 0]$. Then

$$\begin{aligned} H(Tw,Tv) &= \max\{\sup_{u\in[0,\frac{-w}{15}]} d(u,[\frac{-v}{15},0]), \sup_{k\in[\frac{-v}{15},0]} d(k,[0,\frac{-w}{15}])\} \\ &= \max\{\frac{|w|}{15}, \frac{v}{15}\} = \frac{1}{15}\max\{|w|,v\} \end{aligned}$$

and

$$\begin{aligned} M_1(w,v) &= \max\{d(w,v), d(w,Tw), d(v,Tv), \frac{d(w,Tv)+d(v,Tw)}{2}\} \\ &= \max\{0, |w|, v, \frac{1}{30}(|w+15v| + |15w+v|)\} \\ &= \max\{|w|, v\}. \end{aligned}$$

So we have

$$\begin{aligned} \zeta(H(Tw,Tv), M_1(w,v)) &= \frac{4}{5}\max\{|w|,v\} - \frac{1}{15}\max\{|w|,v\} \\ &= \frac{11}{15}\max\{|w|,v\} \geq 0. \end{aligned}$$

Case (ii): When $w \in A_2$ and $v \in A_1$, $T(w) = [\frac{-w}{15}, 0]$ and $T(v) = [0, \frac{-v}{15}]$,

$$\begin{aligned} H(Tw,Tv) &= \max\{\sup_{u\in[0,\frac{-y}{15}]} d(u,[\frac{-w}{15},0]), \sup_{r\in[\frac{-x}{15},0]} d(r,[0,\frac{-y}{15}])\} \\ &= \max\{\frac{w}{15}, \frac{|v|}{15}\} = \frac{1}{15}\max\{w,-v\} \end{aligned}$$

and

$$\begin{aligned} M_1(w,v) &= \max\{d(w,v), d(w,Tw), d(v,Tv), \frac{d(w,Tv)+d(v,Tw)}{2}\} \\ &= \max\{0, w, |v|, \frac{1}{30}(|15w+v| + |w+15v|)\} \\ &= \max\{|w|, v\}. \end{aligned}$$

So we get

$$\begin{aligned}\zeta(H(Tw,Tv),M_1(w,v)) &= \frac{4}{5}\max\{|w|,v\} - \frac{1}{15}\max\{|w|,v\}\\ &= \frac{11}{15}\max\{|w|,v\} \geq 0.\end{aligned}$$

Therefore, T is cyclic $Z-$contractive mapping. Thus, all the conditions of Theorem 10.5 are satisfied. Moreover, 0 is the fixed point of T.

Example 10.5. *Let $X = [0,10]$ and d be a usual metric on X. Let $A_1 = [0,5]$, $A_2 = [5,10]$ be any two nonempty closed subsets of X such that $X = A_1 \cup A_2$ and $A_1 \cap A_2 = \{5\}$. Let $T : X \to P_{CB}(X)$ be cyclic multivalued mapping defined by*

$$T(x) = \begin{cases} \{5\} & \text{if } x \in A_1,\\ \\ \{0,5\} & \text{if } x \in A_2.\end{cases}$$

Let $\zeta : [0,\infty) \times [0,\infty) \to \mathbb{R}$ be a simulation function in [8] defined by

$$\zeta(t,s) = \begin{cases} 2(s-t) < s-t & \text{if } s < t,\\ ks - t < s - t & \text{otherwise where } k < 1.\end{cases}$$

Now, we consider the following cases:
Case (i): *If $x \in A_1$, $y \in A_2$ implies*

$$\begin{aligned}H(Tx,Ty) &= H(\{5\},\{0,5\})\\ &= \max(\{5\},\{5\}) = 5\end{aligned}$$

and

$$M_1(x,y) = \max\left\{d(x,y), d(x,Tx), d(y,Ty), \frac{d(x,Ty)+d(y,Tx)}{2}\right\},$$

where

$$\begin{aligned}&d(x,Tx) = \inf d([0,5],\{5\}) = \inf d(0,\{5\}) = 0\\ &d(y,Ty) = \inf d([5,10],\{0,5\}) = \inf d(\{5\},0) = 0\\ &\frac{d(x,Ty)+d(y,Tx)}{2} = \frac{5}{2}\end{aligned}$$

implies that

$$\zeta(H(Tx,Ty),d(x,y)) = \zeta(5,d(x,y)) \geq 0.$$

Case (ii): *If $x \in A_2$, $y \in A_1$ implies*

$$\begin{aligned}H(Tx,Ty) &= H(\{0,5\},\{5\})\\ &= \max(\{5\},\{5\}) = 5\end{aligned}$$

and

$$M_T(x,y) = \max\{d(x,y), d(x,Tx), d(y,Ty), \frac{d(x,Ty)+d(y,Tx)}{2}\},$$

where

$$d(x,Tx) = \inf d([5,10],\{0,5\}) = \inf d(\{5\}.0) = 0$$
$$d(y,Ty) = \inf d([0,5],\{5\}) = \inf d(0,\{5\}) = 0$$
$$\frac{d(x,Ty)+d(y,Tx)}{2} = \frac{5}{2}$$

implies that

$$\zeta(H(Tx,Ty), d(x,y)) = \zeta(5, d(x,y)) \geq 0.$$

Thus, mapping T satisfies the cyclic $Z-$contractive condition. Moreover, 5 is the fixed point of T in $A_1 \cap A_2$.

Theorem 10.6. *Let (X,d) be a complete metric space, $p \in \mathbb{N}$, $A_1, A_2, \ldots, A_p$ be nonempty closed subsets of X with $\cap_{i=1}^{p} A_i \neq \emptyset$ and $Y = \cup_{i=1}^{p} A_i$. If $T : Y \to P_{CB}(X)$ is Hardy Roger-type-cyclic $Z-$contractive mapping. Then, T has a fixed point in $\cap_{i=1}^{p} A_i$.*

Proof. Let $x_0 \in A_1$ and $x_1 \in T(x_0) \subset A_2$. Then, there exists $x_2 \in T(x_1) \subset A_3$, and by Lemma 10.1, we have

$$d(x_1, x_2) \leq \lambda H(Tx_0, Tx_1). \tag{10.32}$$

Since $x_2 \in T(x_1) \subset A_3$, again by Lemma 10.1, there exists $x_3 \in T(x_2) \subset A_4$ such that

$$d(x_2, x_3) \leq \lambda H(Tx_1, Tx_2). \tag{10.33}$$

And there exists $x_4 \in T(x_3) \subset A_5$ such that

$$d(x_3, x_4) \leq \lambda H(Tx_2, Tx_3). \tag{10.34}$$

And there exists $x_{p-2} \in T(x_{p-3}) \subset A_{p-1}$ and $x_{p-1} \in T(x_{p-2}) \subset A_p$ such that

$$d(x_{p-2}, x_{p-1}) \leq \lambda H(Tx_{p-3}, Tx_{p-2}). \tag{10.35}$$

By continuing in this way, we obtain a sequence $x_{n+1} \in T(x_n) \subset A_{n+2}$ such that

$$d(x_n, x_{n+1}) \leq \lambda H(Tx_{n-1}, Tx_n). \tag{10.36}$$

We assume that $d(x_n, x_{n+1}) > 0$, for all $n \in \mathbb{N}$. If not, then for some $k \in \mathbb{N}$, we have

$$d(x_k, x_{k+1}) = 0,$$

which implies $x_k = x_{k+1} \in Tx_k$. The proof is finished. Therefore, $d(x_n, x_{n+1}) > 0$, for all $n \in \mathbb{N}$.

$$0 < d(x_{n+1}, x_{n+2}) \leq \lambda H(Tx_n, Tx_{n+1}).$$

As $\lambda \geq 1$, so we have $H(Tx_n, Tx_{n+1}) > 0$, which implies

$$\begin{aligned} 0 &\leq \zeta(H(Tx_n, Tx_{n+1}), M_2(x_n, x_{n+1})) \\ &< M_2(x_n, x_{n+1}) - H(Tx_n, Tx_{n+1}), \end{aligned}$$

which implies

$$H(Tx_n, Tx_{n+1}) < M_2(x_n, x_{n+1}), \tag{10.37}$$

where

$$\begin{aligned} M_2(x_n, x_{n+1}) &= \alpha d(x_n, x_{n+1}) + \beta d(x_n, Tx_n) + \gamma d(x_{n+1}, Tx_{n+1}) \\ &\quad + \delta_1 d(x_n, Tx_{n+1}) + \delta_2 d(x_{n+1}, Tx_n) \\ &\leq \alpha d(x_n, x_{n+1}) + \beta d(x_n, x_{n+1}) + \gamma d(x_{n+1}, x_{n+2}) \\ &\quad + \delta_1 d(x_n, x_{n+2}) + \delta_2 d(x_{n+1}, x_{n+1}) \\ &\leq (\alpha + \beta + \delta_1) d(x_n, x_{n+1}) + (\gamma + \delta_1) d(x_{n+1}, x_{n+2}). \end{aligned}$$

Now, if $d(x_n, x_{n+1}) < d(x_{n+1}, x_{n+2})$, then

$$\begin{aligned} M_2(x_n, x_{n+1}) &\leq (\alpha + \beta + \gamma + 2\delta_1) d(x_{n+1}, x_{n+2}) \\ &< d(x_{n+1}, x_{n+2}) \end{aligned}$$

and (10.37) implies

$$H(Tx_n, Tx_{n+1}) < d(x_{n+1}, x_{n+2}),$$

that is,

$$d(x_{n+1}, x_{n+2}) < d(x_{n+1}, x_{n+2}),$$

a contradiction.

Therefore, $d(x_{n+1}, x_{n+2}) < d(x_n, x_{n+1})$ for all $n \in \mathbb{N}$. Thus, $\{d(x_{n+1}, x_{n+2})\}$ is a monotonically decreasing sequence of non-negative real numbers, bounded from below; then, there exists $r \geq 0$ such that $\{d(x_{n+1}, x_{n+2})\}$ converges to r. If we take $r = 0$. Assume on contrary that $r > 0$. Obviously,

$$\lim_{n \to \infty} d(x_{n+1}, x_{n+2}) = \lim_{n \to \infty} d(x_n, x_{n+1}) = r.$$

It follows from the property (δ_3) of a simulation function that

$$0 \leq \limsup_{n \to \infty} \zeta(d(x_{n+1}, x_{n+2}), d(x_n, x_{n+1})) < 0.$$

This shows that $r = 0$. Hence,

$$\lim_{n \to \infty} d(x_{n+1}, x_{n+2}) = 0.$$

Now to show $\{x_n\}$ is a Cauchy sequence in X, it suffices to show that $\{x_{2n}\}$ is a Cauchy sequence in X. If not, then there exists $\varepsilon > 0$ such that we can find subsequences $\{x_{2m_k}\}$ and $\{x_{2n_k}\}$ of $\{x_{2n}\}$ with $n_k > m_k \geq k$ such that

$$d(x_{2m_k}, x_{2n_k}) \geq \varepsilon \text{ for all } k \in \mathbb{N}. \tag{10.38}$$

Without any loss of generality, we assume that for all $k \in \mathbb{N}$, n_k is the smallest positive integer greater than m_k for which this inequality holds, then

$$d(x_{2m_k}, x_{2n_k-2}) < \varepsilon \text{ for all } k \in \mathbb{N}. \tag{10.39}$$

Now by (10.38) and (10.39), we have

$$\begin{aligned}\varepsilon &\leq d(x_{2m_k}, x_{2n_k}) \\ &\leq d(x_{2m_k}, x_{2n_k-2}) + d(x_{2n_k-2}, x_{2n_k-1}) + d(x_{2n_k-1}, x_{2n_k}) \\ &< \varepsilon + d(x_{2n_k-2}, x_{2n_k-1}) + d(x_{2n_k-1}, x_{2n_k}).\end{aligned} \tag{10.40}$$

By taking limit as $k \to \infty$ in the above inequality and using (10.39), we obtain that

$$\lim_{k\to\infty} d(x_{2m_k}, x_{2n_k}) = \varepsilon.$$

Similarly, we have

$$\begin{aligned}\varepsilon &\leq d(x_{2m_k}, x_{2n_k}) \\ &\leq d(x_{2m_k}, x_{2m_k+1}) + d(x_{2m_k+1}, x_{2n_k+1}) + d(x_{2n_k+1}, x_{2n_k}).\end{aligned} \tag{10.41}$$

Also,

$$d(x_{2m_{k+1}}, x_{2n_k+1}) \leq d(x_{2m_{k+1}}, x_{2m_k}) + d(x_{2m_k}, x_{2n_k}) + d(x_{2n_k}, x_{2n_k+1}). \tag{10.42}$$

By taking limit as $k \to \infty$ on both sides of (10.41) and (10.42), we have

$$\lim_{k\to\infty} d(x_{2m_{k+1}}, x_{2n_k+1}) = \varepsilon.$$

As $\{x_{2m_k}\}$ and $\{x_{2n_k}\}$ are subsequences of $\{x_{2n}\}$ with $n_k > m_k \geq k$, and the property δ_3 of simulation function that

$$0 \leq \limsup_{n\to\infty} \zeta(d(x_{2m_{k+1}}, x_{2n_k+1}), d(x_{2m_k}, x_{2n_k})) < 0,$$

a contradiction arises, and hence, Cauchyness of sequence is proved. As A is a closed subset of a complete metric space X, then there exists $x \in A$ such that x_n converges to x as $n \to \infty$. Hence x is a fixed point of T in $\cap_{i=1}^{p} A_i$. □

10.7 STABILITY OF FIXED POINT SETS UNDER CYCLIC SIMULATION FUNCTION

In this section, we present the stability results of cyclic simulation function.

Theorem 10.7. *Let (X,d) be a complete metric space, $p \in \mathbb{N}$ be a positive integer, $A_1, A_2, \ldots, A_p$ be nonempty closed subsets of X with $\cap_{i=1}^{p} A_i \neq \emptyset$ such that $Y = \cup_{i=1}^{p} A_i$ and $\{T_i\}_{i=1}^{m} : Y \to P_{CB}(X)$, $i = 1, 2, \ldots, m$ be family of multivalued mappings satisfying cyclic simulation function such that* *(i)* $Y = \cup_{i=1}^{p} A_i$ *has cyclic representation of with respect to* T.

(ii) *For any* $(x,y) \in A_i \times A_{i+1}$, $i = 1,2,\ldots,p$ *and* $A_{p+1} = A_1$ *such that* $H(T_i x, T_i y) > 0$ *implies*

$$\zeta(H(T_i x, T_i y), M_{T_i}(x,y)) \geq 0, \tag{10.43}$$

where

$$M_{T_i}(x,y) = \max\{d(x,y), d(x,T_i x), d(y,T_i y), \frac{d(x,T_i y) + d(y,T_i x)}{2}\}.$$

Then,

$$H(F(T_i), F(T_{i+1})) \leq k,$$

where $k = \sup_{x \in X} H(T_i x, T_{i+1} x)$.

Proof. From Theorem 10.5, the fixed point set of T_i is nonempty, that is, $F(T_i) \neq \emptyset$ for $i = 1,2,\ldots,m$. Let $y_0 \in A_1$, then for any $y_1 \in F(T_1)$, that is, $y_1 \in T_1 y_1 \subset A_2$. By Lemma 10.1, there exists $y_2 \in T_2 y_1 \subset A_3$ such that

$$d(y_1, y_2) \leq H(T_1 y_1, T_2 y_1). \tag{10.44}$$

Since $y_2 \in T_2 y_1 \subset A_3$, again by Lemma 10.1 there exists $y_3 \in T_2 y_2 \subset A_4$ such that

$$d(y_2, y_3) \leq H(T_2 y_1, T_2 y_2). \tag{10.45}$$

By continuing in this way, we obtain a sequence $y_{n+1} \in T_2 y_n \subset A_{n+2}$ such that

$$d(y_n, y_{n+1}) \leq H(T_2 y_{n-1}, T_2 y_n). \tag{10.46}$$

Since $d(y_n, y_{n+1}) > 0$ for all $n \in \mathbb{N}$. Therefore, $H(T_2 y_{n-1}, T_2 y_n) > 0$ for all $n \in \mathbb{N}$. This implies that

$$\begin{aligned} 0 &\leq \zeta(H(T_2 y_{n-1},\ T_2 y_n), M_{T_2}(y_{n-1}, y_n) \\ &< M_{T_2}(y_{n-1}, y_n) - H(T_2 y_{n-1}, T_2 y_n), \end{aligned}$$

that is,

$$H(T_2 y_{n-1}, T_2 y_n) < M_{T_2}(y_{n-1}, y_n), \tag{10.47}$$

where

$$\begin{aligned} M_{T_2}(y_{n-1}, y_n) &= \max\{d(y_{n-1}, y_n), d(y_{n-1}, T_2 y_{n-1}), d(y_n, T_2 y_n), \\ &\quad \frac{d(y_{n-1}, T_2 y_n) + d(y_n, T_2 y_{n-1})}{2}\} \\ &\leq \max\{d(y_{n-1}, y_n), d(y_{n-1}, y_n), d(y_{n-1}, y_{n+1}), \\ &\quad \frac{d(y_{n-1}, y_{n+1}) + d(y_n, y_n)}{2}\} \\ &\leq \max\{d(y_{n-1}, y_n), d(y_n, y_{n+1})\}. \end{aligned}$$

As $\frac{d(y_{n-1},y_{n+1})}{2} \leq \frac{d(y_{n-1},y_n)+d(y_n,y_{n+1})}{2} \leq \max\{d(y_{n-1},y_n),d(y_n,y_{n+1})\}$.
If $M_{T_2}(y_{n-1},y_n) = d(y_n,y_{n+1})$, then (10.46) and (10.47) implies

$$d(y_n,y_{n+1}) < d(y_n,y_{n+1}),$$

a contradiction. Therefore, $M_{T_2}(y_{n-1},y_n) = d(y_{n-1},y_n)$, which implies

$$d(y_n,y_{n+1}) < d(y_{n-1},y_n).$$

Thus, $\{d(y_n,y_{n+1})\}$ is a monotonically decreasing sequence of non-negative real numbers bounded from below, and then, there exists $r \geq 0$ such that $\{d(y_n,y_{n+1})\}$ converges to r. We claim that $r = 0$. Assume on contrary that $r > 0$.

$$\lim_{n\to\infty} d(y_n,y_{n+1}) = \lim_{n\to\infty} d(y_{n-1},y_n) = r.$$

It follows from the property (δ_3) of a simulation function that

$$0 \leq \limsup_{n\to\infty} \zeta(d(y_n,y_{n+1}),d(y_{n-1},y_n)) < 0.$$

This shows that $r = 0$. Hence,

$$\lim_{n\to\infty} d(y_n,y_{n+1}) = 0.$$

Now to show $\{y_n\}$ is a Cauchy sequence in X, it suffices to show that $\{y_{2n}\}$ is a Cauchy sequence in X. If not, then there exists $\varepsilon > 0$ such that we can find subsequences $\{y_{2m_k}\}$ and $\{y_{2n_k}\}$ of $\{y_{2n}\}$ with $n_k > m_k \geq k$ such that

$$d(y_{2m_k},y_{2n_k}) \geq \varepsilon \text{ for all } k \in \mathbb{N}. \tag{10.48}$$

Without any loss of generality, we assume that for all $k \in \mathbb{N}$, n_k is the smallest positive integer greater than m_k for which this inequality holds, then

$$d(y_{2m_k},y_{2n_k-2}) < \varepsilon \text{ for all } k \in \mathbb{N}. \tag{10.49}$$

Now by (10.48) and (10.49), we have

$$\begin{aligned}
\varepsilon &\leq d(y_{2m_k},y_{2n_k}) \\
&\leq d(y_{2m_k},y_{2n_k-2}) + d(y_{2n_k-2},y_{2n_k-1}) + d(y_{2n_k-1},y_{2n_k}) \\
&< \varepsilon + d(y_{2n_k-2},y_{2n_k-1}) + d(y_{2n_k-1},y_{2n_k})
\end{aligned} \tag{10.50}$$

and by taking limit as $k \to \infty$ on both sides of (10.50) and using (10.49), we have

$$\lim_{k\to\infty} d(y_{2m_k},y_{2n_k}) = \varepsilon. \tag{10.51}$$

Similarly, we have

$$\begin{aligned}
\varepsilon &\leq d(y_{2m_k},y_{2n_k}) \\
&\leq d(y_{2m_k},y_{2m_k+1}) + d(y_{2m_k+1},y_{2n_k+1}) + d(y_{2n_k+1},y_{2n_k}).
\end{aligned} \tag{10.52}$$

Also,

$$d(y_{2m_{k+1}}, y_{2n_k+1}) \leq d(y_{2m_{k+1}}, y_{2m_k}) + d(y_{2m_k}, y_{2n_k}) + d(y_{2n_k}, y_{2n_k+1}). \qquad (10.53)$$

By taking limit as $k \to \infty$ in the above inequality and using (10.51), we obtain that

$$\lim_{k\to\infty} d(y_{2m_{k+1}}, y_{2n_k+1}) = \varepsilon.$$

Since $\{y_{2m_k}\}$ and $\{y_{2n_k}\}$ are subsequences of $\{y_{2n}\}$ with $n_k > m_k \geq k$, and the property δ_3 of simulation function that

$$0 \leq \lim_{k\to\infty} \sup \zeta(d(y_{2m_{k+1}}, y_{2n_k+1}), d(y_{2m_k}, y_{2n_k})) < 0,$$

a contradiction and hence $\{y_n\}$ is a Cauchy sequence in X and there exists a $u \in X$ such that $y_n \to u$ as $n \to \infty$. Also u is a fixed point of T_2; that is, $u \in T_2u$.
From (10.44) and the definition of k, it follows that

$$\begin{aligned} d(y_1, y_2) &\leq H(T_1y_1,\ T_2y_1) \\ &\leq k = \sup_{x\in X} H(T_1x,\ T_2x). \end{aligned}$$

Again by the triangle inequality and using the above inequality, we have

$$d(y_1, u) \leq \sum_{i=1}^{n} d(y_i, y_{i+1}) + d(y_{n+1}, u),$$

on taking limit as $n \to \infty$ we have

$$\begin{aligned} d(y_1, u) &\leq \sum_{i=1}^{\infty} d(y_i, y_{i+1}) \\ &\leq \varepsilon. \end{aligned}$$

Thus, given an arbitrary $y_1 \in F(T_1)$, we can find $u \in F(T_2)$ for which

$$d(y_1, u) \leq k.$$

Similarly for an arbitrary $z_0 \in F(T_2)$, there exists $w \in F(T_1)$ such that

$$d(z_0, w) \leq k.$$

Hence, we conclude that

$$H(F(T_1), F(T_2)) \leq k.$$

□

Lemma 10.3. *Let (X,d) be a complete metric space. Let $\{T_n : X \to P_{CB}(X) : n \in \mathbb{N}\}$ be a sequence of multivalued mappings uniformly convergent to a multivalued mapping $T : X \to P_{CB}(X)$. If T_n satisfies condition (10.43) of Theorem 10.7 for every $n \in \mathbb{N}$, then T also satisfies condition (10.43).*

Proof. As T_n satisfies axiom (10.43) of Theorem 10.7 for every $n \in \mathbb{N}$, we have for $(x,y) \in A_i \times A_{i+1}$, $i = 1,2,\dots,p$ and $A_{p+1} = A_1$ such that $H(T_n x, T_n y) > 0$ implies

$$\zeta(H(T_n x, T_n y), M_{T_n}(x,y)) \geq 0,$$

where

$$M_{T_n}(x,y) = \max\{d(x,y), d(x,T_n x), d(y,T_n y), \frac{d(y,T_n x) + d(x,T_n y)}{2}\}.$$

Since the sequence $\{T_n\}$ is uniformly convergent to T, taking the limit $n \to \infty$ in the above inequality, we get for $H(Tx,Ty) > 0$

$$\zeta(H(Tx,Ty), M_T(x,y)) \geq 0,$$

where

$$M_T(Tx,Ty) = \max\{d(x,y), d(x,Tx), d(y,Ty), \frac{d(y,Tx) + d(x,Ty)}{2}\},$$

which shows that T also satisfies the (10.43). □

We now present the stability result of fixed point.

Theorem 10.8. *Let (X,d) be a complete metric space. Let $\{T_n : X \to P_{CB}(X) : n \in \mathbb{N}\}$ be a sequence of multivalued mappings uniformly convergent to $T : X \to P_{CB}(X)$. If T_n satisfies (10.43) for every $n \in \mathbb{N}$, then*

$$\lim_{n\to\infty} H(F(T_n), F(T)) = 0;$$

that is, the fixed point sets of T_n are stable.

Proof. By Lemma 10.3, T satisfies (10.43). Let $k_n = \sup_{x\in X} H(T_n x, Tx)$. Since the sequence $\{T_n\}$ is uniformly convergent to T on X, by taking limit as $n \to \infty$, we have

$$\lim_{n\to\infty} k_n = \lim_{n\to\infty} \sup_{x\in X} H(T_n x, Tx) = 0.$$

From Theorem 10.7, we have

$$H(F(T_n), F(T)) \leq k_n, \text{ for every } n \in \mathbb{N}.$$

By taking limit as $n \to \infty$, we have

$$\lim_{n\to\infty} H(F(T_n), F(T)) \leq \lim_{n\to\infty} k_n = 0,$$

that is,

$$\lim_{n\to\infty} H(F(T_n), F(T)) = 0.$$

Thus, the fixed point sets of T_n are stable. □

BIBLIOGRAPHY

[1] Abbas, M. & Rhoades B. E. (2009). Fixed point theorems for two new classes of multivalued mappings. *Appl. Math.* Lett. 22, 1364–1368.

[2] Acar, O., Durmaz & Minak G. (2014). Generalized multivalued F-contractions on complete metric spaces. *Bulletin of the Iranian Mathematical Society.* 40 (6), 1469–1478.

[3] Aubin, J.P. & Frankowska, H. (1990). Set-valued Analysis, Systems and Control. BirkhR auser, Basel.

[4] Beg, I. & Butt A. R. (2013). Fixed point of set-valued graph contractive mappings. *Journal of Inequalities and Applications.* 1–7.

[5] Berinde, M. & Berinde V. (2007). On a general class of multi-valued weakly Picard mappings. *Journal of Mathematical Analysis and Applications.* 326(2):772–782.

[6] Banach S. (1922). Sur les opérations dans les ensembles abstraits et leur application aux équations intégrales. *Fund. Math.* 3 (1), 133–181.

[7] Karapinar, E. (2011). Fixed point theory for cyclic weak Φ-contraction. *Appl. Math.* Lett. 24 (6), 822 825.

[8] Khojasteh, F., Shukla, S. & Radenovic, S. (2015). A new approach to the study of fixed point theory for simulation functions. *Filomat* 29 (6), 1189–1194.

[9] Khojasteh, F. & Rakočević V. (2012). Some new common fixed point results for generalized contractive multi-valued non-self-mappings. *Applied Mathematics Letters* 25 (3), 287–293.

[10] Kirk, W. A., Srinivasan, P. S. & Veeramani P. (2003). Fixed points for mappings satisfying cyclical contractive conditions. *Fixed Point Theory* 4 (1), 79–89.

[11] Klim, D. & Wardowsk, D. (2015). Fixed points of dynamic processes of set-valued F-contractions and application to functional equations. *Fixed Point Theory and Appl.* 22.

[12] Minak, G. Helvasi, A. & Altun I. Ciric type generalized F-contractions on complete metric spaces and fixed point results. *Filomat* 28 (6) (2014), 1143–1151.

[13] Mizoguchi, N. & Takahashi W. (1989). Fixed point theorems for multivalued mappings on complete metric spaces, *Journal of Mathematical Analysis and Applications*, 141 (1), 177–188.

[14] Nadler, S.B. (1969). Multivalued contraction mappings, *Pacific J. Math.* 20 (2), 457–488.

[15] Păcurar, M. (2011). Fixed point theory for cyclic Berinde operators, *Fixed Point Theory* 12 (2), 419–428.

[16] Păcurar, M. & Rus I. A. (2010). Fixed point theory for cyclic weak-contractions. *Nonlinear Anal.* 72, 1181–1187.

[17] Petric, M. A. (2010). Some results concerning cyclical contractive mappings. *Gen. Math.* 18 (4), 213–226.

[18] Rhoades, B. E.(1977). A comparison of various definitions of contractive mappings. *Transactions of the American Mathematical Society* 226, 257–290.

[19] Rus, I. A., Petruşel, A. & Sîntămărian A. (2003). Data dependence of the fixed point set of some multivalued weakly Picard operators. *Nonlinear Analysis: Theory, Methods & Applications.* 52 (8), 1947–1959.

[20] Sintunavarat W. & Kumam P. (2012). Common fixed point theorem for cyclic generalized multivalued mappings. *Appl. Math. Lett.* 25, 1849–1855.

[21] Wardowski, D. (2012). Fixed points of new type of contractive mappings in complete metric spaces. *Fixed Point Theory Appl.* 94, 6.

11 Significance and Relevances of Functional Equations in Various Fields

B. V. Senthil Kumar
Nizwa College of Technology

Hemen Dutta
Gauhati University

CONTENTS

11.1 INTRODUCTION

An equation that indicates a function in hidden type is a functional equation. A functional equation communicates the value of a function at a particular point with its values at other points. Since a function is a solution of a functional equation, we can determine the properties of such function which satisfies the equation. It is not so easy to reduce a functional equation to an algebraic equation.

The significant role of functional equations in other fields of mathematics such as abstract algebra, number theory, differential geometry, differential equations, iterations, and analytic functional equations shows the importance of application of functional equations. Hence, this theory of functional equations has gained its own behavior. By the motivation of outdated analytic methods to some level in many areas of mathematics, this theory of functional equations has attracted many mathematicians. This theory comprises simple elementary methods which are very easy when compared with the classical methods of mathematical analysis.

There are many noteworthy applications of functional equations in various branches of mathematics, such as measure theory, group theory, geometry, mechanics, statistics, and algebraic geometry. There are some other important applications of functional equations in various other fields such as economics, classical mechanics, game theory, dynamic programming, computer graphics, statistics, wireless sensor networks, astronomy, stochastic processes, cognitive science, fuzzy set theory, artificial intelligence, information theory, neural networks, coding theory, digital image processing, cluster analysis, interest formulae, Gaussian functions, population ethics, multivalued logic, electric circuits, financial management, iteration, psychometry, probability theory, scalar products, Gaussian functions, determinants and sum of powers, nondifferentiable functions, the Cobb–Douglas production function and quasilinearity, binomial expansion, and Chebyshev polynomials. The usage of functional equations is increasing day-by-day vigorously in the above mentioned fields to investigate many problems. Hence, it is not so easy to provide an explanatory survey of all the applications of functional equations. We mention some interesting and remarkable applications of functional equations.

1. The communication and networks systems consider the ensuing functional equation involving two variables of the form:

   $$K_1(u,v)P(u,v) = K_2(u,v)P(u,0) + K_3(u,v)P(0,v) + K_4(u,v)P(0,0)$$

   where $K_i(u,v); i = 1,2,3,4$ are given polynomials in two complex variables u,v to study the nature of the systems [5].
2. The Cauchy additive equation $\phi(u+v) = \phi(u) + \phi(v)$ arises in genetics to determine the combinatorial function $g_r(n) =$ the number of possible ways of choosing r objects at a time from n objects allowing repetitions, since this function produces the number of possibilities from a gene pool. For detailed information, one can refer [7].
3. By the application of logarithmic Cauchy equation $\ell(ab) = \ell(a) + \ell(b)$, we can show that $\int_1^y \frac{1}{u}du = \ln y$ [17].

Let us define $\ell : \mathbb{R}_+ \to \mathbb{R}$ by

$$\ell(a) = \int_1^y \frac{1}{u} du, \qquad a > 0.$$

Hence, in the case $a, b \in (1, \infty)$, we have

$$\begin{aligned}
\ell(a) + \ell(b) &= \int_1^a \frac{1}{u} du + \int_1^b \frac{1}{u} du \\
&= \int_1^a \frac{1}{u} du + \int_a^{ab} \frac{1}{v} dv, \qquad \text{where} \quad v = ua \\
&= \int_1^{ab} \frac{1}{v} dv \quad \text{(additive property of the integral)} \\
&= \ell(ab). \qquad (11.1)
\end{aligned}$$

4. Murali et al. [10] employed the generalized additive functional equation

$$k[f(kx+y) + f(kx-y)] + f(x+ky) + f(x-ky) = f(x+y) + f(x-y) + 2k^2 g(x)$$

with $k \neq 0, \pm 1$ to encrypt and decrypt the digital spatial image, and investigated its modular stability in [11].

Here, we illustrate some examples how functional equations are applied to solve some interesting problems in geometry, finance, information theory, wireless sensor networks, and electric circuits with parallel resistances.

11.2 APPLICATION OF FUNCTIONAL EQUATION IN GEOMETRY

Legendre used functional equations to find the area of a rectangle [17]. He considered a rectangle whose length is ℓ and breadth is b. Then, the area of the rectangle is $\phi(\ell, b)$.

Then, he divided the rectangle horizontally so that the rectangle is divided into two subrectangles with breadths b_1 and b_2 and the same length ℓ as in Figure 11.1. Then, the areas of subrectangles are $\phi(\ell, b_1)$ and $\phi(\ell, b_2)$, and the area of the full rectangle is $\phi(\ell, b_1 + b_2)$. Then, he arrived at

$$\phi(\ell, b_1 + b_2) = \phi(\ell, b_1) + \phi(\ell, b_2). \qquad (11.2)$$

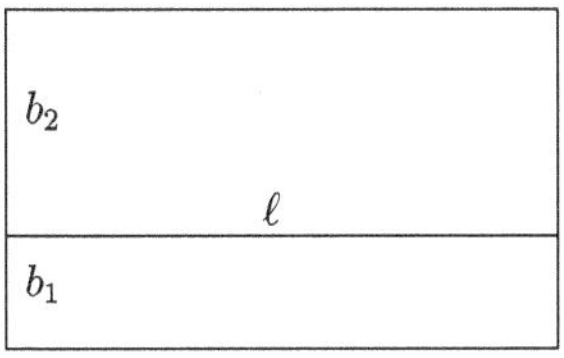

Figure 11.1 Rectnagle divided into two subrectangles along the breadth.

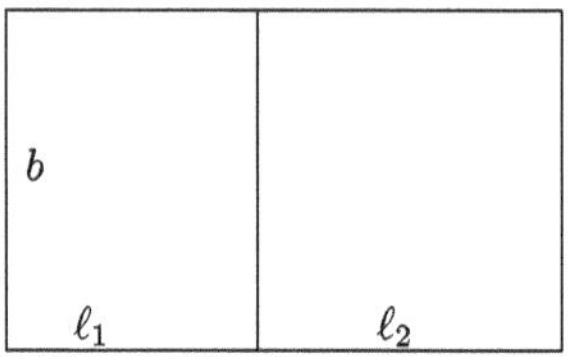

Figure 11.2 Rectangle divided into two subrectangles along the length.

In a similar manner, he divided the rectangle vertically with breadths ℓ_1 and ℓ_2 and the same length b as in Figure 11.2. Then, the resulting areas are $\phi(\ell_1,b)$ and $\phi(\ell_2,b)$ and $\phi(\ell_1+\ell_2,b)$. In the latter division of the rectangle, he obtained

$$\phi(\ell_1+\ell_2,b)=\phi(\ell_1,b)+\phi(\ell_2,b). \tag{11.3}$$

In equation (11.2), ℓ is a constant, and whereas in equation (11.3), b is a constant. Both the equations are similar to Cauchy's equation $\phi(u+v)=\phi(u)+\phi(v)$ whose solution is $\phi(u)=ku$. Therefore, he obtained the solution of (11.2) and (11.3) as

$$\phi(\ell,b)=k_2(\ell)b=k_1(b)\ell. \tag{11.4}$$

From (11.4)

$$\frac{k_1(b)}{b}=\frac{k_2(\ell)}{\ell}=k. \tag{11.5}$$

From (11.5)

$$k_1(b)=kb, \qquad k_2(\ell)=k\ell. \tag{11.6}$$

Substituting (11.6) in (11.4), he obtained

$$\phi(\ell,b)=k\ell b$$

where k is an arbitrary positive constant. He assumed the initial conditions, that is, when $\ell=1$, $b=1$, the area of the rectangle $=1$, to get the value of k as 1. Therefore, he proved $\phi(\ell,b)=\ell b$ which is the area of the rectangle.

11.3 APPLICATION OF FUNCTIONAL EQUATION IN FINANCIAL MANAGEMENT

In this section, the role of functional equation in calculating compound interest is explained in [17]. Suppose a person invests a principal of Rs.p at the rate of interest $r\%$ for the period of q years. Then, the final amount after q years is a function of p and q, that is, $C(p,q)$. Now, we have two cases:

i. The final amount will be the same, if we invest the principal amount p_1+p_2 together or principals p_1,p_2 are invested separately for q years. This can be expressed in the following functional equation:

$$g(p_1+p_2,q)=g(p_1,q)+g(p_2,q) \tag{11.7}$$

whose solution is

$$g(p,q)=K(q)p. \tag{11.8}$$

ii. The final amount is same, whether we invest the amount p for a period of q_1+q_2 years or p invested for q_1 years and then invest the resultant amount in q_2 years. It is expressed as

$$g(p,q_1+q_2) = g(g(p,q_1),q_2). \tag{11.9}$$

Applying (11.8) in (11.9), we get

$$\begin{aligned} K(q_1+q_2)p &= g(K(q_1)p,q_2) \\ K(q_1+q_2)p &= K(q_2)K(q_1)p \\ K(q_1+q_2) &= K(q_2)K(q_1). \end{aligned}$$

It is a multiplicative functional equation whose solution is

$$K(q) = a^q. \tag{11.10}$$

Substituting (11.10) in (11.8), we get

$$g(p,q) = a^q p.$$

For one year, $g(p,1) = p + \text{interest}$. Hence,

$$\begin{aligned} ap &= p + \frac{p\times 1\times r}{100} \\ ap &= p\left(1+\frac{r}{100}\right) \\ a &= \left(1+\frac{r}{100}\right). \end{aligned}$$

Therefore, $$g(p,q) = p\left(1+\frac{r}{100}\right)^q.$$

So, we arrive the compound interest formula $= p\left(1+\frac{r}{100}\right)^q$.

11.4 APPLICATION OF FUNCTIONAL EQUATION IN INFORMATION THEORY

Some functional equations of the following forms:

i. $h(u)+(1-u)^{\alpha}h\left(\frac{v}{1-u}\right) = h(v)+(1-v)^{\alpha}h\left(\frac{u}{1-v}\right)$
ii. $g(uv)+g((1-u)v) = g(v)\{m(u)+m(1-u)\}+m(v)\{g(u)+g(1-u)\}$
iii. $\sum_{\ell=1}^{n}\sum_{k=1}^{m} h(u_\ell v_k) = \sum_{\ell=1}^{n} h(u_\ell)+\sum_{k=1}^{m} h(v_k)$
iv. $\sum_{\ell=1}^{n}\sum_{k=1}^{m} s_{\ell k}(u_\ell v_k) = \sum_{\ell=1}^{n} p_\ell(u_\ell)+\sum_{k=1}^{m} q_k(v_k)+\sum_{\ell=1}^{n} r_\ell(u_\ell)\sum_{k=1}^{m} l_k(v_k)$

are applied in the information theory.

Definition 11.1. *Let $\Delta_m = \{p=(p_1,p_2,\ldots,p_m) | p_i \geq 0, \sum_j p_j = 1\}$ be the set of all finite complete discrete probability distribution on a given partition of the sure event E into m events $E_1,E_2,\ldots,E_m$. In 1948, Shannon, in his paper [C.E. Shannon, A*

Mathematical theory of Communication, Bell System Tech. J. 27 (1948), 378-423 and 632-656], introduced the measure of information

$$H_m(p) = -\sum_{j=1}^{m} p_j log p_j, \qquad p \in \Delta_m$$

known as **Shannon's entropy**.

We have multiplicative functional equation

$$M(uv) = M(u) + M(v)$$

whose solution is $M(u) = \log u$, which is a function whose value on the product of probabilities of events is equal to the sum of its values on the probabilities of the individual events. Shannon used the above functional equation, in the information theory since with an intuitive notion that the information content of two independent events should be the sum of the information in each event.

In particular, the functional equation

$$f_1(u) + \alpha(1-u)f_2\left(\frac{v}{1-u}\right) = f_3(v) + \alpha(1-v)f_4\left(\frac{u}{1-v}\right)$$

for all $u, v \in [0,1]$ with $u+v \in [0,1]$. When $f_1 = f_2 = f_3 = f_4$ and $\alpha =$ the identity map, it is known as the fundamental equation of information. It has been extensively investigated by many authors. The general solution of the above equation is dealt by P.L. Kannappan [*Can. J. Math. Vol. XXXV, No. 5, 1983, pp. 862–872*].

The effect of the information communicated in a message can be measured by the changes in the probability concerning the receiver of the message. The effect of information will depend upon the expectation of receiver before and after receiving the message. Naturally, the information received can be taken as the ratio of the logarithm of two probabilities. Thus, the information received about the event E is given by

$$I(E) = \frac{\text{Probability concerning the receiver after receiving the information}}{\text{Probability concerning the receiver before receiving the information}}. \tag{11.11}$$

In case of noiseless channel, probability concerning the receiver after receiving the information equals to 1, as there will be no distortion of information during the process. The above equation becomes

$$\begin{aligned} I(E) &= \log\left[\frac{1}{\text{Probability concerning the receiver before receiving the information}}\right] \\ &= -\log[\text{Probability concerning the receiver before receiving the information}]. \end{aligned} \tag{11.12}$$

Shannon, with his intuitive idea, proposed a decreasing function $h(p)$, as a measure of the amount of information satisfying

$$h(p) = -\log p, \qquad 0 < p \leq 1. \tag{11.13}$$

The function $h(p)$ is called the information function, and it satisfies the additive property. Let A and B be any two events with $p(A) > 0$, $p(B) > 0$. Suppose that first we are informed that A has occurred and next that we are informed that B has occurred and if A and B are independent, then

$$-\log[p(A)] - \log[p(B)] = -\log[p(AB)].$$

If $p(A) = p_1$, $p(B) = p_2$ and $p(AB) = p_1 p_2$, then

$$-\log(p_1) - \log(p_2) = -\log(p_1 p_2).$$

Hence, $h(p_1) + h(p_2) = h(p_1 p_2)$, which shows that the information function h satisfies the Cauchy's functional equation:

$$f(xy) = f(x) + f(y). \tag{11.14}$$

11.5 APPLICATION OF FUNCTIONAL EQUATION IN WIRELESS SENSOR NETWORKS

The applications of functional equation in wireless sensor networks are discussed in [14]. Wireless sensor networks (WSNs) consist of small nodes with sensing, computation, and wireless communications capabilities. Many routing, power management, and data dissemination protocols have been specifically designed for WSNs where energy awareness is an essential design issue.

Due to recent technological advances, the manufacturing of small and low-cost sensors became technically and economically feasible. The sensing electronics measure ambient conditions related to the environment surrounding the sensor and transforms them into an electric signal. Processing such a signal reveals some properties about objects located and/or events happening in the vicinity of the sensor. A large number of these disposable sensors can be networked in many applications that require unattended operations. A WSN contains hundreds or thousands of these sensor nodes. These sensors have the ability to communicate either among each other or directly to an external base station (BS). A greater number of sensors allow for sensing over larger geographical regions with greater accuracy. Basically, each sensor node comprises sensing, processing, transmission, mobilizer, position finding system, and power units (some of these components are optional like the mobilizer). Sensor nodes are usually scattered in a sensor field, which is an area where the sensor nodes are deployed. Sensor nodes coordinate among themselves to produce high-quality information about the physical environment. Each sensor node bases its decisions on its mission, the information it currently has, and its knowledge of its computing, communication, and energy resources. Each of these scattered sensor nodes has the capability to collect and route data either to other sensors or back to an external base station(s).

Networking unattended sensor nodes may have profound effect on the efficiency of many military and civil applications such as target field imaging, intrusion detection, weather monitoring, security and tactical surveillance, distributed computing, detecting ambient conditions such as temperature, movement, sound, light, or the presence of certain objects, inventory control, and disaster management. Deployment of a sensor network in these applications can be in random fashion (e.g., dropped from an airplane) or can be planted manually (e.g., fire alarm sensors in a facility). For example, in a disaster management application, a large number of sensors can be dropped from a helicopter. Networking these sensors can assist rescue operations by locating survivors, identifying risky areas, and making the rescue team more aware of the overall situation in the disaster area.

Routing is the process of selecting path in a network along which to send network traffic. Routing trees are typical structures used in WSN to deliver data to sink. To ensure robust data communication, efficient methods are required to choose routes across a network that can react quickly to communication link changes. Many algorithms have been proposed in literature to support the routing protocols of the network. In 1958, Richard Bellman [*Dynamic Programming, Princeton University Press, 1957*] applied the functional equation approach to devise an algorithm which converges to the solution at atmost $N-1$ steps for a network with N nodes.

It is stated as follows:

"Given a set of N cities, with every two cities linked by a road. The time required to travel from i to j is not directly proportional to the distance between i and j, due to road conditions and traffic. Given the matrix $T = (t_{ij})$ not necessarily symmetric, where t_{ij} is the time required to travel from i to j. We wish to determine the path from one given city to another given city which minimizes the travel time."

The functional equation technique of dynamic programming, combined with approximation in policy space, yields an iterative algorithm which converges after at most $(N-1)$ iterations.

Let us now introduce the functional equation technique of dynamic programming. Let $f_i =$ the time required to travel from i to N, $i = 1,2,\ldots,N-1$, using an optimal policy with $f_n = 0$.

Employing the principle of optimality, we see that the f_i satisfies the non-linear system of equations

$$\begin{aligned} f_i &= \min[t_{ij} + f_i], \qquad i = 1,2,\ldots,N-1 \\ f_N &= 0. \end{aligned} \tag{11.15}$$

The equation (11.15) is a functional equation because functions appear on both sides. We try to obtain the solution of the system (11.15) by using method of successive approximations. Choose an initial sequence $\left\{f_i^{(0)}\right\}$, and then, proceed iteratively, setting

$$f_i^{(k+1)} = \min_{i \neq j} \left(t_{ij} + f_i^{(k)} \right), \qquad i = 1, 2, \ldots, N-1$$

$$f_N^{(k+1)} = 0, \text{ for } k = 0, 1, 2, \ldots \tag{11.16}$$

The sequence in (11.16) converges to the solution after $(N-1)$ iterations by suitable algorithm. In this way, we can solve routing problem by functional equation.

11.6 APPLICATION OF RATIONAL FUNCTIONAL EQUATION

In this section, we deal with the following new rational functional equation:

$$r(m+n) = \frac{r(m)r(n)}{r(m)+r(n)}. \tag{11.17}$$

It is easy to see the function $r(m) = \frac{k}{m}$ is a solution of the equation (11.17), and hence, it is said to be a reciprocal functional equation. For additional facts of (11.17), one can refer [12,13].

11.6.1 GEOMETRICAL INTERPRETATION OF EQUATION (11.17)

Consider a right-angled triangle ABC with sides "a" and "b" as shown in Figure 11.3.

Construct a square BDEF inside the triangle ABC as shown in Figure 11.3 with side "p". Then, AD $= a - p$, FC $= b - p$. Now,

$$\text{Area of triangle ABC} = \frac{1}{2}ab. \tag{11.18}$$

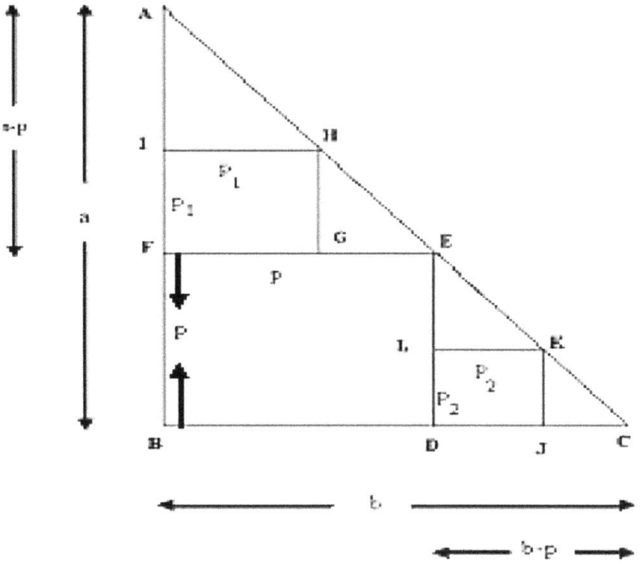

Figure 11.3 Geometrical interpretation of (11.17).

From the equation (11.18), it is easy to show that $p = \frac{ab}{a+b}$. Now, construct another two squares FGHI and DJKL with sides "p_1" and "p_2", respectively, as shown in Figure 11.3. Then $p_1 = \frac{p(a-p)}{a} = \frac{a^2b}{(a+b)^2}$ and $p_2 = \frac{p(b-p)}{b} = \frac{ab^2}{(a+b)^2}$. Now, $p_1 + p_2 = \frac{ab}{(a+b)^2}(a+b) = \frac{ab}{a+b} = p$. Therefore,

$$p_1 + p_2 = p. \tag{11.19}$$

In this construction, if we take $a = \frac{1}{m}$, $b = \frac{1}{n}$, then

$$p_1 = \frac{n}{(m+n)^2}, \tag{11.20}$$

$$p_2 = \frac{m}{(m+n)^2} \tag{11.21}$$

and

$$p = \frac{\frac{1}{m}\frac{1}{n}}{\frac{1}{m}+\frac{1}{n}} \tag{11.22}$$

Substituting the relations (11.20), (11.21), and (11.22) in (11.19), we get

$$\frac{1}{m+n} = \frac{\frac{1}{m}\frac{1}{n}}{\frac{1}{m}+\frac{1}{n}}.$$

Since $r(m) = \frac{k}{m}$ is a solution of the functional equation (11.17), the property (11.19) is satisfied by the functional equation (11.17). Hence, the functional equation (11.17) holds good in the above geometric construction.

11.6.2 AN APPLICATION OF EQUATION (11.17) TO RESISTANCES CONNECTED IN PARALLEL

We know the conductance of any material is reciprocal of its resistance. Consider two resistors R_1 and R_2 with resistances $\frac{1}{x}$ and $\frac{1}{y}$, respectively, connected in parallel as shown in Figure 11.4. Then, x and y are the conductances of the resistors R_1 and R_2, respectively, and hence, $x+y$ is the total circuit conductance. To find the equivalent resistance of loads wired in parallel, we use a mathematical formula known as the **"reciprocal formula"** which is given by

$$\frac{1}{\text{Total circuit conductance}} = \text{Total equivalent resistance of the parallel circuit.} \tag{11.23}$$

The reciprocal formula (11.23) satisfies the following algebraic identity:

$$\frac{1}{x+y} = \frac{\frac{1}{x}\frac{1}{y}}{\frac{1}{x}+\frac{1}{y}}$$

and hence, the functional equation (11.17) holds good in the above circuit.

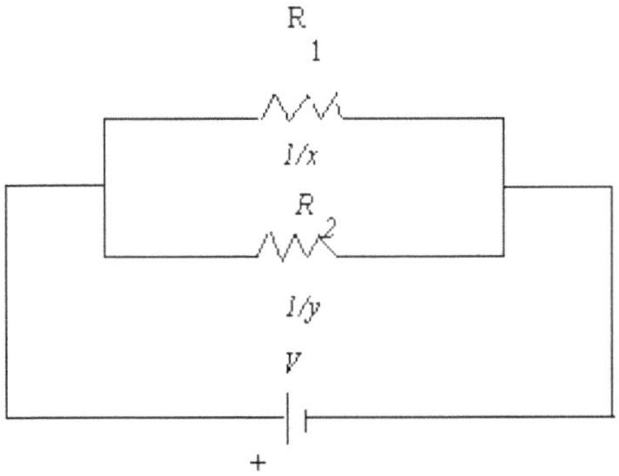

Figure 11.4 Couple of resistors connected in parallel.

11.7 APPLICATION OF RQD AND RQA FUNCTIONAL EQUATIONS

In this section, we introduce the following functional equation in several variables:

$$F\left(\frac{r_1+r_2}{2}\right)-F(r_1+r_2)=\frac{3F(r_1)F(r_2)}{F(r_1)+F(r_2)+2\sqrt{F(r_1)F(r_2)}}. \tag{11.24}$$

and

$$F\left(\frac{r_1+r_2}{2}\right)+F(r_1+r_2)=\frac{5F(r_1)F(r_2)}{F(r_1)+F(r_2)+2\sqrt{F(r_1)F(r_2)}}. \tag{11.25}$$

We establish the geometrical descriptions of functional equations (11.24) and (11.25) using Newton's law of gravitation.

Newton's law of universal gravitation states that a particle attracts every other particle in the universe with a force which is directly proportional to the product of their masses and inversely proportional to the square of the distance between their centers.

Let F be the force between the masses m_1 and m_2 denoted in Figure 11.5. Let G be the gravitational constant and r be the distance between the centres of the masses m_1 and m_2. Then, the force of attraction F between m_1 and m_2 is

$$F=G\frac{m_1m_2}{r^2}.$$

Suppose both the above two objects are of unit mass, then the force of attraction between them is

$$F=\frac{G}{r^2}.$$

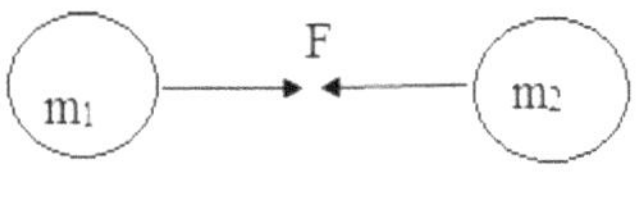

Figure 11.5 Force between two masses m_1 and m_2.

Now, consider three objects of unit mass with the following situation. Let r_1 be the distance between the objects 1 and 2. Let r_2 be the distance between the objects 2 and 3 (Figure 11.6).

The force of attraction between the objects 1 and 2 is

$$F(r_1) = \frac{G}{r_1^2}. \tag{11.26}$$

The force of attraction between the objects 2 and 3 is

$$F(r_2) = \frac{G}{r_2^2}. \tag{11.27}$$

The force of attraction between the objects 1 and 3 is

$$F(r_1+r_2) = \frac{G}{(r_1+r_2)^2}. \tag{11.28}$$

Using (11.26), (11.27), and (11.28), we have a relation as follows:

$$\begin{aligned} F(r_1+r_2) &= \frac{G}{r_1^2+r_2^2+2r_1r_2} \\ &= \frac{G}{r_1^2r_2^2\left(\frac{1}{r_1^2}+\frac{1}{r_2^2}+\frac{2}{r_1r_2}\right)} \\ &= \frac{\frac{G}{r_1^2r_2^2}}{\frac{1}{r_1^2}+\frac{1}{r_2^2}+\frac{2}{r_1r_2}} \\ &= \frac{F(r_1)F(r_2)}{F(r_1)+F(r_2)+2\sqrt{F(r_1)F(r_2)}}. \end{aligned} \tag{11.29}$$

It is not hard to verify that the reciprocal-quadratic function $F(r) = \frac{k}{r^2}$, where k is a constant, is a solution of (11.29). Thus, the reciprocal-quadratic functional equation (11.29) arises in the above physical phenomena.

If the distance between object 1 and object 3 is halved, that is, $\frac{r_1+r_2}{2}$, then the force of attraction between them becomes

$$F\left(\frac{r_1+r_2}{2}\right) = \frac{G}{\left(\frac{r_1+r_2}{2}\right)^2} = 4\frac{G}{(r_1+r_2)^2}.$$

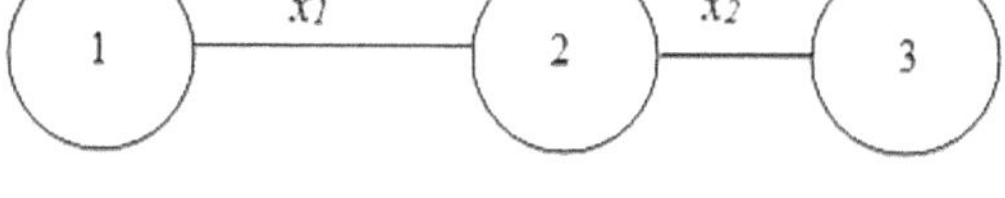

Figure 11.6 Forces when three unit masses in the same line.

The relation between the difference of the forces $F\left(\frac{r_1+r_2}{2}\right)$ and $F(r_1+r_2)$ and the forces between object 1 and object 2; and object 2 and object 3 can be modeled as a functional equation as follows:

$$F\left(\frac{r_1+r_2}{2}\right)-F(r_1+r_2)=\frac{3G}{(r_1+r_2)^2}$$
$$=\frac{3F(r_1)F(r_2)}{F(r_1)+F(r_2)+2\sqrt{F(r_1)F(r_2)}}. \quad (11.30)$$

We call the above functional equation (11.30) as reciprocal-quadratic difference functional (RQDF) equation in two variables r_1 and r_2.

Similarly, the relation between the sum of the forces $F\left(\frac{r_1+r_2}{2}\right)$ and $F(r_1+r_2)$ and the forces between the objects 1 and 2, and the objects 2 and 3 can be modeled as a functional equation as follows:

$$F\left(\frac{r_1+r_2}{2}\right)+F(r_1+r_2)=\frac{5G}{(r_1+r_2)^2}$$
$$=\frac{5F(r_1)F(r_2)}{F(r_1)+F(r_2)+2\sqrt{F(r_1)F(r_2)}}. \quad (11.31)$$

The above functional equation (11.31) is said to be reciprocal-quadratic adjoint functional (RQAF) Equation with a couple of variables r_1 and r_2.

11.8 APPLICATION OF OTHER MULTIPLICATIVE INVERSE FUNCTIONAL EQUATIONS

In this section, we discuss about various other multiplicative inverse functional equations and their applications.

11.8.1 MULTIPLICATIVE INVERSE SECOND POWER DIFFERENCE AND ADJOINT FUNCTIONAL EQUATIONS

Here, we deal with the following multiplicative inverse second power difference functional equation in several variables

$$m_i\left(\frac{1}{p}\sum_{\ell=1}^{p}v_\ell\right)-m_i\left(\sum_{\ell=1}^{p}v_\ell\right)=\frac{(p^2-1)\prod_{\ell=1}^{p}m_i(v_\ell)}{\left[\sqrt{\sum_{\ell=1}^{p}m_i(v_\ell)\prod_{m=1,j\neq\ell}^{p}m_i(v_m)}\right]^2} \quad (11.32)$$

and multiplicative inverse second power adjoint functional equation in several variables

$$m_i\left(\frac{1}{p}\sum_{\ell=1}^{p}v_\ell\right)+m_i\left(\sum_{\ell=1}^{p}v_\ell\right)=\frac{(p^2+1)\prod_{\ell=1}^{p}m_i(v_i)}{\left[\sqrt{\sum_{\ell=1}^{p}m_i(v_\ell)\prod_{m=1,m\neq\ell}^{p}r(v_m)}\right]^2}. \quad (11.33)$$

When $p=2$, the above equations (11.32) and (11.33) are interpreted using Newton's law of gravitation. The left-hand side of (11.32) represents the difference of forces of attraction between two objects O_1 and O_2 and the force of attraction between the those objects when the distance is halved with an object in between them. The right-hand side of (11.32) relates with the force of attraction between the first two objects and second two objects. For detailed information, one can refer [3]. Other forms of multiplicative inverse second power functional equations are dealt in [1,16].

11.8.2 MULTIPLICATIVE INVERSE THIRD POWER FUNCTIONAL EQUATION

We consider the following multiplicative inverse third power functional equation:

$$R_c(u_1+u_2)=\frac{R_c(u_1)R_c(u_2)}{\left(R_c(u_1)^{\frac{1}{3}}+R_c(u_2)^{\frac{1}{3}}\right)^3}. \tag{11.34}$$

It is easy to check that the multiplicative inverse third power function $R_c(u)=\frac{c}{u^3}$ is a solution of (11.34). Equation (11.34) is associated with the well-known inverse cube law occuring in electromagnetism. The left-hand side of (11.34) denotes the magnetic field strength due to a dipole at a distance u_1+u_2. The right-hand side of (11.34) involves the magnetic fields strengths at the distances u_1 and u_2.

11.8.3 MULTIPLICATIVE INVERSE FOURTH POWER FUNCTIONAL EQUATION

We consider the following multiplicative inverse fourth power functional equation:

$$m_q(u+v)=\frac{m_q(u)m_q(v)}{\left[m_q(u)^{\frac{1}{4}}+m_q(v)^{\frac{1}{4}}\right]^4}. \tag{11.35}$$

One can easily verify that the multiplicative inverse fourth power function $m_q(u)=\frac{1}{u^4}$ is a solution of (11.35). The solution of (11.35) is associated with the intensity of scattered light and decay of radar energy in physics. According to Rayleigh's law of scattering, the intensity of scattered light is inversely proportional to the fourth power of its wavelength, that is, $I\propto\frac{1}{\lambda^4}$ or $I=\frac{c}{\lambda^4}$, where I is the intensity, λ is wavelength of the scattered light, and c is a constant. The energy of radar decays in inverse proportion to the fourth power of the distances to the targets. Hence, the intensity of scattered light and decay of radar energy could be studied through modeling equation (11.2).

11.8.4 MULTIPLICATIVE INVERSE QUINTIC FUNCTIONAL EQUATION

Now, we introduce a new multiplicative inverse quintic functional equation:

$$m_Q(x_1+x_2) = \frac{m_Q(x_1)m_Q(x_2)}{\left[m_Q(x_1)^{\frac{1}{5}} + m_Q(x_2)^{\frac{1}{5}}\right]^5}. \tag{11.36}$$

It is easy to substantiate that the multiplicative inverse quintic function $m_Q(x) = \frac{1}{x^5}$ is a solution of (11.36). The solution of (11.36) is linked with various hypotheses arising in physics, chemistry, and mechanics.

1. If an object moves on a circular path under the impact of an attractive central force which is directing the object towards a point on the circle, then this central force is inversely proportional to the fifth power of distance. Hence, the central force is a function of reciprocal fifth power of the distance.
2. In wave spectra theory, the rate of energy decay for the high-frequency part is inversely proportional to the fifth power of frequency. In this case, the rate of energy decay is a function of reciprocal fifth power of frequency.
3. In kinetic theory of gases, molecules are conceived as portions of matter moving as single bodies, repelling by a force inversely proportional to the fifth power of the distance between their centres of gravity. The inverse fifth power law is consistent with gas viscosity in terms of the time relaxation of stresses in the gas, a concept related to the macroscopic elastic properties of the gas.
4. Turbulent flow occurs in the aortic arch and in the large airways of the tracheobronchial tree down to the fifth bronchial division. The pressure drop is inversely proportional to the fifth power of radius of the airway.

11.8.5 MULTIPLICATIVE INVERSE FUNCTIONAL EQUATION INVOLVING TWO VARIABLES

We study about a multiplicative inverse functional equation involving two variables of the form:

$$r(u_1+u_2, v_1+v_2) = \frac{\prod_{j=1}^{2}\prod_{k=1}^{2} r(u_j, v_k)}{\sum_{j=1}^{2}\sum_{k=1}^{2}\left(\frac{1}{r(u_j,v_k)}\prod_{m=1}^{2}\prod_{n=1}^{2} r(u_m, v_n)\right)}. \tag{11.37}$$

It can be verified that the function $r(u,v) = \frac{1}{uv}$ is a solution of (11.37). Some system designs occurring in physics, such as to find the rigidity moduli in several situations and pressures of material in various occasions, are interpreted through (11.37). More details about (11.37) are available in [21].

11.8.6 SYSTEM OF MULTIPLICATIVE INVERSE FUNCTIONAL EQUATIONS WITH THREE VARIABLES

We discuss about the following system of multiplicative inverse functional equations involving three variables:

$$\left.\begin{aligned} T_r(u_1+u_2,v,w) &= \frac{T_r(u_1,v,w)T_r(u_2,v,w)}{T_r(u_1,v,w)+T_r(u_2,v,w)},\\ T_r(u,v_1+v_2,w) &= \frac{T_r(u,v_1,w)T_r(u,v_2,w)}{T_r(u,v_1,w)+T_r(u,v_2,w)},\\ T_r(u,v,w_1+w_2) &= \frac{T_r(u,v,w_1)T_r(u,v,w_2)}{T_r(u,v,w_1)+T_r(u,v,w_2)}. \end{aligned}\right\} \tag{11.38}$$

It can be verified that the multiplicative inverse function $T_r(u,v,w) = \frac{c}{uvw}$ is a solution of the system (11.38), where c is a constant. The basic properties like density and volume of a cuboid shaped sponge are studied through this system (11.38). The density of a cuboid shaped sponge represents left hand side of any member of the system (11.38) which is equal the half of the harmonic mean of the volumes of the two sub cuboid shaped sponges when original sponge is divided along its length. Further features of (11.38) are dealt in [20].

11.9 APPLICATIONS OF FUNCTIONAL EQUATIONS IN OTHER FIELDS

- The parallelogram law of forces is obtained using the functional equation $h(u+v)+h(u-v) = 2h(u)h(v)$. Further, this equation is used to describe circular functions and to illustrate their relation to spherical trigonometry.
- Functional equations are used by Einstein in the theory of relativity to demonstrate the light signaling process in the space-time coordinates. [Bulletin of the American Mathematical Society Vol. XXVI, Oct 1919 to July 1920, pp. 26–34].
- Ramanujan adopted functional equations to describe Bernoulli's number of negative index.
- The system of functional equations

$$f(u+v) = \frac{f(u)+\{[g(u)]^2-[f(u)]^2\}f(v)}{1-f(u)f(v)}; \qquad f(u+v) = \frac{f(u)f(v)}{1-g(u)g(v)}$$

  has significant role in the optics and in the probability theory.
- The system of functional equations
  i. $\phi(u) = \sup\limits_{v\in D} H(x,y,f(T(u,v)))$, for all $u \in S$;
  ii. $\phi(u) = \sup\limits_{v\in D}\{h(u,v)+G(u,v,g(T(u,v)))\}$, for all $u \in S$;
  iii. $\varphi(u) = \sup\limits_{v\in D}\{h(u,v)+F(u,v,\phi(T(u,v)))\}$, for all $u \in S$

  is used in dynamic programming of multistage decision processes.

- Several other types of multiplicative inverse functional equations were considered to obtain their solution, to prove their fundamental stability results associated with Ulam stability theory and their role in various fields. More information are available in [2,4,6,8,9,15,18,19,22–26].

11.10 OPEN PROBLEMS

1. Is it possible to form a mixed-type functional equation arising from additive and multiplicative inverse functions? If possible, form such an equation.
2. Form a functional equation whose solution is a rational function of the form $\frac{x}{x^2+1}$.
3. Find the solution of $f(x)f(y) = f(xy) + f\left(\frac{x}{y}\right)$.

BIBLIOGRAPHY

[1] A. Bodaghi, P. Narasimman, J. M. Rassias and K. Ravi, Ulam stability of the reciprocal functional equation in non-Archimedean fields, *Acta Mathematica Universitatis Comenianae,* LXXXV, 1 (2016), 113–124.

[2] A. Bodaghi and B. V. Senthil Kumar, Estimation of inexact reciprocal-quintic and reciprocal-sextic functional equations, *Mathematica,* 59 (82), No 1–2 (2017), 3–14.

[3] H. Dutta and B. V. Senthil Kumar, Geometrical elucidations and approximation of some functional equations in numerous variables, *Proc. Indian Natn. Sci. Acad.* 85, No. 3, (2019), 603–611.

[4] H. Dutta and B. V. Senthil Kumar, Classical stabilities of an inverse fourth power functional equation, *J. Interdisciplinary Math.* 22 (7) (2019), 1061–1070.

[5] E.-S. El-Hady, W. Forg-Rob and M. Mahmoudi, On a two-variable functional equation arising from databases, *WSEAS Transactions on Mathematics,* 14 (2015), 265–270.

[6] E. Gupta, R. Chugh and B. V. Senthil Kumar, Non-Archimedean approximation of MIQD and MIQA functional equations, *Int. J. Appl. Engg. Research,* 14(6) (2019), 1313–1318.

[7] P. Kannappan, Application of Cauchy's equation in combinatorics and genetics, *Mathware & Soft Computing,* 8 (2001), 61–64.

[8] S. O. Kim, B. V. Senthil Kumar and A. Bodaghi, Approximation on the reciprocal-cubic and reciprocal-quartic functional equations in non-Archimedean fields, *Advances in Difference Equ.* 77 (2017), 1–12.

[9] S. Merlin and B. V. Senthil Kumar, Approximations and applications of a reciprocal fifth power mapping, *Int. J. Engg. Advanced Tech.* 9(1S4) (2019), 983–986.

[10] R. Murali, P. Divyakumari and Sandra Pinelas, Generalized additive functional equation in digital spatial image crypto techniques system, *IOSR J. Math.,* 15 (4) (2019), 69–76.

[11] R. Murali, P. Divyakumari and H. Dutta, Functional equation and its modular stability with and without Δ_p-condition, *Filomat,* 34(3) (2020), 1–12.

[12] P. Narasimman, K. Ravi and S. Pinelas, Stability of Pythagorean mean functional equation, *Global J. Math.* 4 (1) (2015), 398–411.

[13] K. Ravi and B. V. Senthil Kumar, Stability and geometrical interpretation of reciprocal type functional equation, *Asian Journal of Current Engineering and Maths,* 1 (2012), 300–304.

[14] K. Ravi, R. Jamuna and R. Dhinesh Kumar, Functional equations in wireless sensor networks, *Bull. Marathwada Math. Soc.* 14 (2) (2013), 86–93.

[15] K. Ravi, J. M. Rassias and B. V. Senthil Kumar, Stability of reciprocal difference and adjoint functional equations in paranormed spaces: Direct and fixed point methods, *Functional Anal. Approx. Comp.* 5(1) (2013), 57–72.

[16] K. Ravi, J. M.Rassias, S. Pinelas and P. Narasimman, The Stability of a generalized radical reciprocal quadratic functional equation in Felbin's space, *PanAmerican Math. J.* 24 (1) (2014), 75–92.

[17] P. K. Sahoo and P. Kannappan, *Introduction to Functional Equations*, CRC Press, Taylor & Francis Group, 2011.

[18] B. V. Senthil Kumar, Ashish Kumar and G. Suresh, Functional equations related to spatial filtering in image enhancement, *Int. J. Control Theory Appl.* 9(28) (2016), 555–564.

[19] B. V. Senthil Kumar and H. Dutta, Non-Archimedean stability of a generalized reciprocal-quadratic functional equation in several variables by direct and fixed point methods, *Filomat,* 32(9) (2018), 3199–3209.

[20] B. V. Senthil Kumar, H. Dutta and S. Sabarinathan, Approximation of a system of rational functional equations of three variables, *Int. J. Appl. Comput. Math.* 5 (2019),1–16.

[21] B. V. Senthil Kumar and H. Dutta, Fuzzy stability of a rational functional equation and its relevance to system design, *Int. J. General Syst.,* 48, No. 2 (2019), 157–169.

[22] B. V. Senthil Kumar and H. Dutta, Approximation of multiplicative inverse undecic and duodecic functional equations, *Math. Meth. Appl. Sci.* 42 (2019), 1073–1081.

[23] B. V. Senthil Kumar, J. M. Rassias and S. Sabarinathan, Stabilities of various multiplicative inverse functional equations, *Tbilisi Math. J.* 12(4) (2019), 15–28.

[24] B. V. Senthil Kumar, H. Dutta and K. Al-Shaqsi, On a functional equation arising from subcontrary mean and its pertinences, *Advances in Intelligent Systems and Computing 1111, 4th International Conference on Computational Mathematics and Engineering Sciences (CMES2019)*, 2020, 241–247.

[25] B. V. Senthil Kumar, H. Dutta and S. Sabarinathan, Fuzzy approximations of a multiplicative inverse cubic functional equation, *Soft Comput.,* 24 (2020), 13285–13292, https://doi.org/10.1007/s00500-020-04741-x.

[26] B.V. Senthil Kumar and A. Bodaghi, A fixed point approach to generalized Hyers-Ulam stability of Jensen type reciprocal functional equation, *Boletim da Sociedade Paranaense de Matematica,* 38(3) (2020), 125–132.

12 Unified-Type Nondifferentiable Second-Order Symmetric Duality Results over Arbitrary Cones

Ramu Dubey
J.C. Bose University of Science and Technology

Vishnu Narayan Mishra
Indira Gandhi National Tribal University

CONTENTS

12.1 INTRODUCTION

Multiobjective-type programming problems are common in mathematical modeling of realistic phenomenon for a greatly spectrum of utilization. Optimality conditions given by Pareto that noticeable to be the physical evolvement of the optimization of a single purpose to the contemplation of several purposes. In his perusal, Hanson [9] has mentioned an illustration which exhibits the application of the second-order duality in certain apart frame of mind. Mathematical programming is the branch of operational research, which deals with the method of solving problems by findings the extrema of functions (defined by linear or nonlinear constraints) in finite dimensional vector space. In the development of mathematical programming, concept of optimality and concept of duality are very important for solving the problems. It has found its way into all branches of science and engineering due to its wide range of applications.

Duality plays an important role in nonlinear programming. Indeed, when the solution of a problem poses some difficulties, we shall see the solution of its dual problem provides some valuable information about the original problem. Symmetric duality in nonlinear programming deals with the situation where dual of the dual is primal duality in mathematical programming, which is not only used in many theoretical and computational developments in mathematical programming itself but also used in economics, control theory, business problems, and other diverse fields. Mangasarian [17] introduced the concept of second- and higher-order dualities for nonlinear problems. The study of higher-order duality is significant due to the computational advantage over the first-order duality as it provides tighter bounds for the value of the objective function when approximations are used.

In recent past, several definitions such as nonsmooth univex, nonsmooth quasiunivex, and nonsmooth pseudoinvex functions have been introduced by Xianjun [29]. By introducing these new concepts, sufficient optimality conditions for a nonsmooth multiobjective problem were obtained, and, a fortiori, weak and strong duality results were established for a Mond–Weir-type multiobjective dual program. Mond and Zhang [18] obtained duality results for various higher-order dual problems under higher-order invexity assumptions. Chandra et al. [2] and Yang et al. [30] discussed a mixed symmetric dual formulation for a nonlinear programming problem and for a class of nondifferentiable nonlinear programming problems, respectively. Later on, Chen [5] studied duality relations for Mond–Weir-type multiobjective higher-order symmetric dual programs under F-convexity assumptions.

In this chapter, we have formulated a new mixed-type second-order nondifferentiable symmetric duality in scalar-objective programming problem. In literature, we have discussed the results either Wolfe- or Mond–Weir-type dual or separately, whereas in this, we have combined result over one model over arbitrary cones. The duality theorems are proved for these programs over arbitrary cones under bonvexity and pseudobonvexity with respect to η assumptions.

12.2 LITERATURE REVIEW

The following convention for vector inequalities will be used: If a, b $\in R^n$, then
$a \geqq b \Leftrightarrow a_i \geqq b_i, i = 1,2,...,n;$
$a \geqslant b \Leftrightarrow a \geqq b$ and $a \neq b;$
$a > b \Leftrightarrow a_i > b_i, i = 1,2,...,n.$

A problem in which the dual of the dual is again the primal problem is called symmetric problem. Linear programming problems are always symmetric, but it is not in general true for nonlinear problems. This concept in nonlinear problems was first introduced by Dorn [8] for quadratic functions. Later on, Dantzig et al. [6] extended this notion for a general nonlinear problem and derived duality results under convexity/concavity assumptions. The problem considered in Dantzig et al. [6] is as follows:

(PP1) Minimize $F = k(x,y) - y^T \nabla_y k(x,y)$
subject to $\nabla_y k(x,y) \leqq 0,$
$x \geqq 0,\ y \geqq 0.$

(DP1) Minimize $G = k(x,y) - x^T \nabla_x k(x,y)$
subject to $\nabla_x k(x,y) \geqq 0,$
$x \geqq 0,\ y \geqq 0.$

Mond and Weir [19] considered the following primal-dual pair and established duality theorems under pseudoconvexity/pseudoconcavity assumptions:

(PP2) Minimize $H = k(x,y)$
subject to $\nabla_y k(x,y) \leqq 0,$
$y^T \nabla_y k(x,y) \geqq 0,$
$x \geqq 0.$

(DP2) Minimize $T = k(x,y)$
subject to $\nabla_x k(x,y) \geqq 0,$
$x^T \nabla_x k(x,y) \leqq 0,$
$y \geqq 0.$

Bazaraa and Goode [1] further extended the problem of Dantzig et al. [6] over arbitrary cones and proved duality relations under convexity assumptions. Later on, Chandra et al. [3] constructed a pair of nondifferentiable symmetric dual problems and discussed duality theorems. After that, Mond and Schecter [20] studied the following nondifferentiable symmetric dual programs:

(PP3) Minimize $\varphi(x,y) + S(x|C) - y^T \nabla_y \varphi(x,y)$
subject to $\nabla_y \varphi(x,y) - z \leqq 0,$
$x \geqq 0,\ z \in D.$

(DP3) Maximize $\varphi(u,v) - S(v|D) - u^T \nabla_x \varphi(u,v)$
subject to $\nabla_x \varphi(u,v) + \omega \geqq 0,$
$v \geqq 0,\ \omega \in C,$

where $\varphi : R^n \times R^m \to R$ is a differentiable function, and C and D are compact convex sets in R^n and R^m, respectively. Further, they obtained the following duality results:

Theorem 12.1 (Weak duality). Suppose that φ is convex in x for fixed y and is concave in y for fixed x. Then, inf (PP3)$\geqq$ sup (DP3).

Theorem 12.2 (Strong duality). Suppose that φ is twice continuously differentiable and that $(\bar{x},\bar{y},\bar{z})$ is optimal for problem (PP3). Suppose also that the Hessian

$(\nabla_{xx})\varphi(\bar{x},\bar{y})$ is nonsingular. Then, $\exists\ \alpha$ such that $(u,v,w) = (\bar{x},\bar{y},\alpha)$ is feasible for problem (DP3), and the objective function of problem (DP3) has the value min (PP3) at this feasible solution.

Motivated by [1,19], Chandra and Kumar [4] considered the following Mond–Weir-type symmetric model over arbitrary cones:

(PP4) Minimize $\Psi = \psi(x,y)$

$$\text{subject to} \quad \nabla_y \psi(x,y) \in C_2^*, \quad y^T \nabla_y \psi(x,y) \geqq 0, \quad x \in C_1,$$

(DP4) Maximize $\Omega = \psi(u,v)$

$$\text{subject to} \quad -\nabla_x \psi(u,v) \in C_1^*, \quad u^T \nabla_x \psi(u,v) \leqq 0, \quad v \in C_2,$$

where $\phi \neq C_i \subseteq R^n$ and $\phi \neq C_2 \subseteq R^m$ are closed convex cones. For $i = 1,2$, C_i^* is the positive polar of C_i. $S_1 \subseteq R^n$ and $S_2 \subseteq R^m$ are open sets such that $C_1 \times C_2 \subset S_1 \times S_2$ and $H : S_1 \times S_2 \to R$ is a twice differentiable function.

Further, they derived duality results under generalized convexity assumptions. Recently, Mandal and Nahak [15] introduced a new type of invex functions called $(p,r)-\rho-(\eta,\theta)$-invex and proved weak, strong, and converse duality relations for the following multiobjective symmetric primal-dual problems:

(PP5) Minimize $f(x,y)$

$$\text{subject to} \quad \nabla_y f(x,y) \in C_2^*, \quad y^T \nabla_y f(x,y) \geqq 0, \quad x \in C_1.$$

(DP5) Minimize $f(u,v)$

$$\text{subject to} \quad -\nabla_x f(u,v) \in C_1^*, \quad u^T \nabla_x f(u,v) \leqq 0, \quad v \in C_2,$$

where f is a twice differentiable function. Further, they also established duality results for multiobjective symmetric programming problem over arbitrary cones under $(p,r)-\rho-(\eta,\theta)$-invexity assumptions. Many researchers have worked related to the symmetric problems over arbitrary cones [23,25,27]. Recently, Gulati et al. [14] considered the multiobjective nondifferentiable symmetric dual problems over arbitrary cones and derived duality results under K-preinvexity/K- convexity/K-pseudoinvexity assumptions.

The main importance of the second-order duality over the first-order duality is that it gives more closer bounds whenever numerical calculations/approximations are involved. This will also help to provide suitable stopping technique for a numerical algorithm. Mangasarian [16] was the first who has formulated the second-order dual for a general nonlinear program and then obtained duality theorems under generalized convexity assumptions. Kim and Yun [24] considered the following Wolfe-type multiobjective symmetric dual pair:

Primal Problem (PP6)
minimize $\Psi_P(x,y,\lambda,p) = \phi(x,y) - (y^T\nabla_y(\lambda^T\phi)(x,y))e - (y^T\nabla_{yy}(\lambda^T\phi)(x,y)p)e$

subject to

$$\nabla_y(\lambda^T\phi)(x,y) + \nabla_{yy}(\lambda^T\phi)(x,y)p \leqq 0,\ x,p \geqq 0,$$
$$\lambda > 0,\ \lambda^T e = 1.$$

Dual Problem (DP6)
maximize $\Psi_D(u,v,\lambda,q) = \phi(u,v) - (u^T\nabla_x(\lambda^T\phi)(u,v))e - (u^T\nabla_{xx}(\lambda^T\phi)(u,v)p)e$

subject to

$$-\nabla_x(\lambda^T\phi)(u,v) - \nabla_{xx}(\lambda^T\phi)(u,v)p \geqq 0,\ v,q \geqq 0,$$
$$\lambda > 0,\ \lambda^T e = 1,$$

and established duality theorems under convexity/concavity assumptions. Later on, Devi [7] constructed a pair of second-order symmetric dual, and corresponding duality results are established under η-bonvexity/η-pseudobonvexity conditions. Hou and Yang [10] formulated a nondifferentiable Mond–Weir-type symmetric model. After that, Suneja et al. [28] constructed a pair of Mond–Weir-type multiobjective second-order symmetric dual program and established duality theorems under η-bonvexity/η-pseudobonvexity assumptions. After that, Yang et al. [32] formulated a pair of Mond–Weir-type nondifferentiable second-order symmetric dual program and proved appropriate duality theorems under F-convexity assumptions. The work in Ref. [10] was further extended to multiobjective in Yang et al. [31] under generalized convexity assumptions. Kim et al. [27] constructed and proved usual duality theorems under second-order invexity assumptions for the following two multiobjective nondifferentiable symmetric pairs over arbitrary cones $C_1 \subseteq R^n$ and $C_2 \subseteq R^m$:

Primal Problem (PP7)
minimize $\Phi(x,y,\lambda,z,p) = \phi(x,y) + S(x|D) - (y^Tw)e - \frac{1}{2}(p^T\nabla_{yy}(\lambda^T\phi)(x,y)p)e$

subject to

$$-[\nabla_y(\lambda^T\phi)(x,y) - w + \nabla_{yy}(\lambda^T\phi)(x,y)p] \in C_2^*,$$
$$y^T[\nabla_y(\lambda^T\phi)(x,y) - w + \nabla_{yy}(\lambda^T\phi)(x,y)p] \leqq 0,$$
$$x \in C_1,\ w \in E_i,\ \lambda \in K^*,\ \lambda^T e = 1,\ e \in \text{int}K.$$

Dual Problem (DP7)
minimize $\Psi(u,v,\lambda,z,r) = \phi(u,v) - S(v|E) + (u^Tz)e - \frac{1}{2}(r^T\nabla_{xx}(\lambda^T\phi)(u,v)r)e$

subject to

$$[\nabla_x(\lambda^T\phi)(x,y) + z + \nabla_{xx}(\lambda^T\phi)(u,v)r] \in C_1^*,$$
$$u^T[\nabla_x(\lambda^T\phi)(u,v) + z + \nabla_{xx}(\lambda^T\phi)(u,v)r] \geqq 0,$$
$$v \in C_2,\ z \in D_i,\ \lambda \in K^*,\ \lambda^T e = 1,\ e \in \text{int}K.$$

Primal Problem (PP8)

minimize $\Psi_P(x,y,\lambda,z,p) = \phi(x,y) - (y^T\nabla_x(\lambda^T\phi)(x,y))e - (y^T\nabla_x(\lambda^T\phi)(x,y)p)e$

$$-\frac{1}{2}(p^T\nabla_{yy}(\lambda^T\phi)(x,y)p)e$$

subject to

$$-[\nabla_y(\lambda^T\phi)(x,y) - w + \nabla_{yy}(\lambda^T\phi)(x,y)p] \in C_2^*,$$

$$x \in C_1,\ w \in E_i,\ \lambda \in K^*,\ \lambda^T e = 1,\ e \in \text{int}K.$$

Dual Problem (DP8)

maximize $\Psi_D(u,v,\lambda,z,r) = \phi(u,v) - (u^T\nabla_x(\lambda^T\phi)(u,v))e - (u^T\nabla_x(\lambda^T\phi)(x,y)r)e$

$$-\frac{1}{2}(u^T\nabla_{xx}(\lambda^T\phi)(u,v)r)e$$

subject to

$$[\nabla_x(\lambda^T\phi)(u,v) + z + \nabla_{xx}(\lambda^T\phi)(u,v)r] \in C_1^*,$$

$$v \in C_2,\ z \in D_i,\ \lambda \in K^*,\ \lambda^T e = 1,\ e \in \text{int}K,$$

where $\phi : R^n \times R^m \to R^k$ is a thrice differentiable function. K is a closed convex cone in R^k such that $\text{int}K \neq \phi$ and $R^k_+ \subseteq K$. $r,z \in R^n$, $p,w \in R^m$, $e = (1,...,1)^T \in R^k$, D_i, and E_i, $i \in K$ are compact and convex sets in R^n and R^m, respectively.

Gulati et al. [11] formulated the second-order multiobjective Mond–Weir-type second-order symmetric duality model over arbitrary cones and discussed duality theorems under η-bonvexity/η-pseudobonvexity assumptions. Gulati and Geeta [14] studied nondifferentiable multiobjective Mond–Weir-type symmetric duality model in which the objective function is optimized over cones and derived duality relations under second-order K-F-convexity/K-η-bonvexity/K-η-pseudobonvexity assumptions.

The concept of higher-order duality was first introduced by Mangasarian [16]. Higher-order duality is more significant over second-order duality since it gives more tighter bounds due to the presence of more parameters. It may provide a lower bound to the infimum of a primal optimization problem when it is difficult to find a feasible solution for the first-order dual. This makes the study of second- and higher-order dual interesting and useful. Chen [5] presented the Mond–Weir-type higher-order symmetric duality for multiobjective nondifferentiable programming problems and derived duality results under higher-order F-convexity. Further, Gulati and Gupta [12] formulated and discussed the results for the following Wolfe-type nondifferentiable symmetric dual pair:

Primal Problem (PP9)

Minimize $\Omega(x,y,p) = f(x,y) + S(x|C) + h(x,y,p) - p^T\nabla_p h(x,y,p) - y^T\nabla_y f(x,y)$
$\qquad - y^T\nabla_p h(x,y,p)$

subject to

$$\nabla_y f(x,y) - z + \nabla_p h(x,y,p) \leq 0.$$

$$z \in D.$$

Dual Problem (DP9)

Maximize $\Upsilon(u,v,r) = f(u,v) - S(v|D) + g(u,v,r) - r^T\nabla_r g(u,v,r) - u^T\nabla_x f(u,v) - u^T\nabla_r g(u,v,r)$

subject to

$$\nabla_x f(u,v) + w + \nabla_r g(u,v,r) \geq 0,$$
$$w \in C,$$

where $f : R^n \times R^m \mapsto R$, $g : R^n \times R^m \times R^n \mapsto R$ and $h : R^n \times R^m \times R^m \to R$ are differentiable functions.

Gulati and Gupta [13] proved duality results for Mond–Weir- and Wolfe-type models under generalized existing convexity assumptions over arbitrary cones constraints. After that, Kassem [21] formulated a higher-order symmetric primal-dual problem and discussed duality results under cone-invexity assumptions. Later on, Kassem [22] considered the symmetric dual problems over arbitrary cones and established duality relations under pseudoinvexity assumptions. Ying [33] introduced the following new class of higher-order multiobjective Mond–Weir-type dual pair over arbitrary cones:

(PP10) K-minimize $\left(f(x,y) + h(x,y,p) - p^T\nabla_p h(x,y,p)\right)$

subject to

$$-\sum_{i=1}^{k} \lambda_i[\nabla_y f_i(x,y) + \nabla_p h_i(x,y,p)] \in C_2^*,$$

$$y^T\sum_{i=1}^{k} \lambda_i[\nabla_y f_i(x,y) + \nabla_p h_i(x,y,p)] \geqq 0,$$

$$\lambda \in \text{int}K^*,\ x \in C_1.$$

(DP10) K-maximize $\left(f(u,v) + g(u,v,q) - q^T\nabla_q g(u,v,q)\right)$

subject to

$$\sum_{i=1}^{k} \lambda_i[\nabla_x f_i(u,v) + \nabla_q g_i(u,v,q)] \in C_1^*,$$

$$u^T\sum_{i=1}^{k} \lambda_i[\nabla_x f_i(u,v) + w_i + \nabla_q g_i(u,v,q)] \leqq 0,$$

$$\lambda \in \text{int}K^*,\ v \in C_2,$$

where $f : R^n \times R^m \to R^k$, $h : R^n \times R^m \times R^m \to R^k$ and $g : R^n \times R^m \times R^n \to R^k$ are twice differentiable functions and established duality theorems under K-pseudoinvex/strongly K-pseudoinvex. Recently, Padhan and Nahak [26] discussed a higher-order symmetric duality programming problem and derived duality results under higher-order generalized invexity assumptions.

12.3 PRELIMINARIES AND DEFINITIONS

We consider the following scalar-objective programming problem:

(P) Minimize $F(x)$,

$$x \in X$$

where $X \subseteq R^{n+m}$ and $F : X \to R$.

12.3.1 DEFINITION

Let C be a nonempty compact convex set in R^n. The support function $s(x|C)$ of C is defined by

$$s(x|C) = \max\{x^T y : y \in C\}.$$

The subdifferential of $s(x|C)$ is given by

$$\partial s(x|C) = \{z \in C : z^T x = s(x|C)\}.$$

For any convex set $S \subset R^n$, the normal cone to S at a point $x \in S$ is defined by

$$N_S(x) = \{y \in R^n : y^T (z - x) \leqq 0 \text{ for all } z \in S\}.$$

It is readily verified that for a compact convex set E, y is in $N_E(x)$ if and only if

$$s(y|E) = x^T y.$$

Remark 12.1. A support function $\pi_A : R^n \mapsto R$ of a nonempty closed convex set A in R^n is given by

$$\pi_A(x) = \sup\{x \,.\, a : a \in A\}, \quad x \in R^n.$$

Its interpretation is most intuitive when x is a unit vector: by definition, A is contained in the closed half space

$$\{y \in R^n : y \,.\, x \leqq \pi_A(x)\},$$

and there is at least one point of A in the boundary

$$H(x) = \{y \in R^n : y \,.\, x = \pi_A(x)\}$$

of this half space. The hyperplane $H(x)$ is therefore called a supporting hyperplane with exterior (or outer) unit normal vector x. The word exterior is important here, as the orientation of x plays a role and the set $H(x)$ is in general different from $H(-x)$. Now π_A is the (signed) distance of $H(x)$ from the origin.

Example 12.1. If A is a line segment through the origin with end points $-\alpha$ and α, then $\pi_A(x) = |x \,.\, \alpha|$.

12.3.2 DEFINITION

The positive polar cone P^* of a cone P is defined by

$$P^* = \{y \in R^p : x^T y \geqq 0, \forall x \in P\}$$

12.3.3 DEFINITION

A function $\Phi : R^n \mapsto R$ is said to be bonvex at $u \in R^n$ with respect to $\eta : R^n \times R^n \mapsto R^n$, if for all $(x,p) \in R^n \times R^n$,

$$\Phi(x) - \Phi(u) + \frac{1}{2}p^T \nabla_{xx}\Phi(x)p \geqq \eta^T(x,u)\{\nabla_x\Phi(u) + \nabla_{xx}\Phi(x)p\}.$$

Example 12.2 Let $X = [0,2] \subseteq R$, $n = m = 1$ and $k = 1$. Consider the function $\Phi : X \to R$, which is given by

$$\Phi(x) = \left(\frac{e^x - e^{-x}}{2}\right)^3$$

and $\eta(x,u) = x^2u^2 + u$.
We have to claim that Φ is bonvex at $u \in X$ with respect to η. For this, it is sufficient to prove that the following expression is nonnegative, i.e.,

$$\Upsilon = \Phi(x) - \Phi(u) + \frac{1}{2}\nabla_{xx}p^T\Phi(x)p - \eta^T(x,u)\{\nabla_x\Phi(u) + \nabla_{xx}\Phi(x)p\}. \geqq 0.$$

Substituting the values of Φ and η in the above expression, we have

$$\begin{aligned}\Upsilon = {} & \left(\frac{e^x - e^{-x}}{2}\right)^3 - \left(\frac{e^u - e^{-u}}{2}\right)^3 + \frac{1}{2}p^T\left\{6\left(\frac{e^u - e^{-u}}{2}\right)\left(\frac{e^u + e^{-u}}{2}\right)^2\right.\\ & \left. +3\left(\frac{e^u - e^{-u}}{2}\right)^3\right\}p - (x^2u^2 + u)\left[3\left(\frac{e^u - e^{-u}}{2}\right)^2\left(\frac{e^u + e^{-u}}{2}\right)\right.\\ & \left. +\left\{6\left(\frac{e^u - e^{-u}}{2}\right)\left(\frac{e^u + e^{-u}}{2}\right)^2 + 3\left(\frac{e^u - e^{-u}}{2}\right)^3\right\}p\right].\end{aligned}$$

Simplifying the above equation at the point $u = 0 \in X$, we obtain

$$\Upsilon = \left(\frac{e^x - e^{-x}}{2}\right)^3 \quad \forall\, x \in X.$$

It is clear that $\Upsilon \geqq 0$, $\forall\, x \in X$. Therefore, Φ is bonvex at $u = 0 \in X$ with respect to η.

12.3.4 DEFINITION

A function $\Phi : R^n \mapsto R$ is pseudobonvex at $u \in R^n$ with respect to $\eta : R^n \times R^n \mapsto R^n$, if for all $(x,p) \in R^n \times R^n$,

$$\eta^T(x,u)\{\nabla_x\Phi(u) + \nabla_{xx}\Phi(x)p\} \geqq 0 \Rightarrow \Phi(x) - \Phi(u) + \frac{1}{2}p^T\nabla_{xx}\Phi(x)p \geqq 0.$$

12.4 NONDIFFERENTIABLE SECOND-ORDER MIXED-TYPE SYMMETRIC DUALITY MODEL OVER ARBITRARY CONES

For N = $\{1,2,3, \ldots,n\}$ and M = $\{1,2,3, \ldots,m\}$, let us assume $J_1 \subset N$, $K_1 \subset M$ and $J_2 = N \setminus J_1$ and $K_2 = M \setminus K_1$, where $|J_1|$ denotes the number of elements in the set J_1. The other numbers $|J_2|$, $|K_1|$ and $|K_2|$ are defined similarly. Notice that if $J_1 = \varnothing$, then $J_2 = N$, then $R^{|J_1|}$ is zero-dimensional Euclidean space and $R^{|J_2|}$ is n-dimensional Euclidean space. It is clear that any $x \in R^n$ can be written as $x = \{x_1,\ x_2\}$, $x_1 \in R^{|J_1|}$, $x_2 \in R^{|J_2|}$. Similarly, any $y \in R^m$ can be written as $y = \{y_1,\ y_2\}$, $y_1 \in R^{|K_1|}$, $y_2 \in R^{|K_2|}$. Let

i. $f_1 : R^{|J_1|} \times R^{|K_1|} \to R,$
ii $f_2 : R^{|J_2|} \times R^{|K_2|} \to R.$

In this section, we introduce the following pair of nondifferentiable second-order symmetric duality model over arbitrary cones and derive duality theorems.

Primal Problem (MNHP):
Minimize $L(x,y,z,p) = f_1(x_1,y_1) + s(x_1|E_1) + f_2(x_2,y_2) + s(x_2|E_2) - y_1^T z_1$

$$-\frac{1}{2}p_1^T \nabla_{y_1y_1} f_1(x_1,y_1)p_1 - \frac{1}{2}p_2^T \nabla_{y_2y_2} f_2(x_2,y_2)p_2 - y_2^T [\nabla_{y_2} f_2(x_2,y_2) + \nabla_{y_2y_2} f_2(x_2,y_2)p_2]$$

subject to

$$-\left(\nabla_{y_1} f_1(x_1,y_1) - z_1 + \nabla_{y_1y_1} f_1(x_1,y_1)p_1\right) \in C_1^*, \tag{12.1}$$

$$-\left(\nabla_{y_2} f_2(x_2,y_2) - z_2 + \nabla_{y_2y_2} f_2(x_2,y_2)p_2\right) \in C_2^*, \tag{12.2}$$

$$y_1^T [\nabla_{y_1} f_1(x_1,y_1) - z_1 + \nabla_{y_1y_1} f_1(x_1,y_1)p_1] \geqq 0, \tag{12.3}$$

$$p_1^T [\nabla_{y_1} f_1(x_1,y_1) - z_1 + \nabla_{y_1y_1} f_1(x_1,y_1)p_1] \geqq 0, \tag{12.4}$$

$$p_2^T [\nabla_{y_2} f_2(x_2,y_2) - z_2 + \nabla_{y_2y_2} f_2(x_2,y_2)p_2] \geqq 0, \tag{12.5}$$

$$x_1, x_2, y_2 \geqq 0, \tag{12.6}$$

$$z_1 \in D_1, z_2 \in D_2, x_1 \in C_3, x_2 \in C_4. \tag{12.7}$$

Dual Problem (MNHD):
Minimize $M(u,v,w,r) = f_1(u_1,v_1) - s(v_1|D_1) + f_2(u_2,v_2) - s(v_2|D_2) + u_1^T w_1$

$$-\frac{1}{2}r_1 \nabla_{u_1u_1} f_1(u_1,v_1)r_1 - \frac{1}{2}r_2 \nabla_{u_2u_2} f_2(u_2,v_2)r_2 - u_2^T [\nabla_{u_2} f_2(u_2,v_2) + \nabla_{u_2u_2} f_2(u_2,v_2)r_2]$$

subject to

$$\left(\nabla_{u_1} f_1(u_1,v_1)+w_1+\nabla_{u_1u_1} f_1(u_1,v_1)r_1\right)\in C_3^*, \tag{12.8}$$

$$\left(\nabla_{u_2} f_2(u_2,v_2)+w_2+\nabla_{u_2u_2} f_2(u_2,v_2)r_2\right)\in C_4^*, \tag{12.9}$$

$$u_1^T[\nabla_{u_1} f_1(u_1,v_1)+w_1+\nabla_{u_1u_1} f_1(u_1,v_1)r_1]\leqq 0, \tag{12.10}$$

$$r_1^T[\nabla_{u_1} f_1(u_1,v_1)+w_1+\nabla_{u_1u_1} f_1(u_1,v_1)r_1]\leqq 0, \tag{12.11}$$

$$r_2^T[\nabla_{u_2} f_2(u_2,v_2)+w_2+\nabla_{u_2u_2} f_2(u_2,v_2)r_2]\leqq 0, \tag{12.12}$$

$$v_1,v_2,u_2\geqq 0, \tag{12.13}$$

$$w_1\in E_1,w_2\in E_2,v_1\in C_1,v_2\in C_2, \tag{12.14}$$

where $p_1\in R^{|K_1|}$, $p_2\in R^{|K_2|}$, $r_1\in R^{|J_1|}$ and $r_2\in R^{|J_2|}$ and E_1,E_2,D_1 and D_2 are compact convex sets in $R^{|J_1|},R^{|J_2|},R^{|K_1|}$ and $R^{|K_2|}$, respectively.

12.4.1 REMARKS

For $C_i=R_+$, $i=1,2,3,4$.

i. If $|K_1|=0$ and $|J_1|=0$, then our model becomes Wolfe-type dual model.
ii. If $|K_2|=0$ and $|J_2|=0$, then our model reduces to Mond–Weir-type dual model.

In the next section, we have discussed the duality theorems under generalized assumptions. Let P^0 and Q^0 be the set of feasible solution of primal problem (MNHP) and dual problem (MNHD), respectively.

12.5 DUALITY THEOREMS

Theorem 12.1. *(Weak Duality) Let $(x_1,x_2,y_1,y_2,z_1,z_2,p_1,p_2)\in P^0$ and $(u_1,u_2,v_1,v_2,w_1,w_2,r_1,r_2)\in Q^0$. Let*

i. $f_1(.,v_1)+(.)^T w_1$ *be pseudobonvex at u_1 with respect to η_1,*
ii. $-f_1(x_1,.)+(.)^T z_1$ *be pseudobonvex at y_1 with respect to η_2,*
iii. $f_2(.,v_2)+(.)^T w_2$ *be bonvex at u_2 with respect to η_3,*
iv. $-f_2(x_2,.)+(.)^T z_2$ *be bonvex at y_2 with respect to η_4,*
v. $\eta_1(x_1,u_1)+u_1+r_1\in C_1$,
vi. $\eta_2(v_1,y_1)+y_1+p_1\in C_2$,
vii. $\eta_3(x_2,u_2)+u_2+r_2\in C_3$,
viii. $\eta_4(v_2,y_2)+y_2+p_2\in C_4$.

Then,

$$L(x_1,x_2,y_1,y_2,z_1,p_1,p_2)\nless M(u_1,u_2,v_1,v_2,w_1,r_1,r_2). \tag{12.15}$$

Proof: By hypotheses (iii) and (iv), we get

$$f_2(x_2,v_2)+x_2^T w_2 - f_2(u_2,v_2) - u_2^T w_2 + \frac{1}{2} r_2^T \nabla_{u_2u_2} f_2(u_2,v_2) r_2$$
$$\geqq \eta_3(x_2,u_2)[\nabla_{x_2} f_2(u_2,v_2) + w_2 + \nabla_{u_2u_2} f_2(u_2,v_2) r_2], \tag{12.16}$$

and

$$f_2(x_2,y_2) - y_2^T z_2 - f_2(x_2,v_2) + v_2^T z_2 + \frac{1}{2} p_2^T \nabla_{x_2x_2} f_2(x_2,v_2) p_2$$
$$\geqq \eta_4(v_2,y_2)[-\nabla_{y_2} f_2(x_2,y_2) + z_2 - \nabla_{x_2x_2} f_2(x_2,v_2) p_2]. \tag{12.17}$$

Using hypotheses $(vii) and$ $(viii)$ and dual constraints (12.2) and (12.9), we have

$$(\eta_3(x_2,u_2)+u_2+r_2)[\nabla_{x_2} f_2(u_2,v_2)+w_2+\nabla_{u_2u_2} f_2(u_2,v_2)r_2] \geqq 0,$$

and

$$(\eta_4(v_2,y_2)+y_2+p_2)[-\nabla_{y_2} f_2(x_2,y_2)+z_2-\nabla_{x_2x_2} f_2(x_2,v_2)p_2] \geqq 0.$$

Above inequalities follows that

$$\eta_3(x_2,u_2)[\nabla_{x_2} f_2(u_2,v_2)+w_2+\nabla_{u_2u_2} f_2(u_2,v_2)p_2] + u_2[\nabla_{x_2} f_2(u_2,v_2)+w_2$$
$$+\nabla_{u_2u_2} f_2(u_2,v_2)r_2] \geqq -r_2[\nabla_{x_2} f_2(u_2,v_2)+w_2+\nabla_{u_2u_2} f_2(u_2,v_2)r_2],$$

and

$$\eta_4(v_2,y_2)[-\nabla_{y_2} f_2(x_2,y_2)+z_2-\nabla_{y_2y_2} f_2(x_2,y_2)p_2] + y_2[-\nabla_{y_2} f(x_2,y_2)+z_2$$
$$-\nabla_{p_2} h_2(x_2,y_2,p_2)] \geqq p_2[\nabla_{y_2} f_2(x_2,y_2)-z_2+\nabla_{y_2y_2} f_2(x_2,y_2)p_2].$$

Using inequalities (12.5) and (12.12) gives that

$$\eta_3(x_2,u_2)[\nabla_{x_2} f_2(u_2,v_2)+w_2+\nabla_{u_2u_2} f_2(u_2,v_2)r_2]$$
$$\geqq -u_2[\nabla_{x_2} f_2(u_2,v_2)+w_2+\nabla_{u_2u_2} f_2(u_2,v_2)r_2],$$

$$\eta_4(v_2,y_2)[-\nabla_{y_2} f_2(x_2,y_2)+z_2-\nabla_{y_2y_2} h_2(x_2,y_2)p_2]$$
$$\geqq y_2[\nabla_{y_2} f_2(x_2,y_2)+z_2+\nabla_{y_2y_2} f_2(x_2,y_2)p_2].$$

Further, from inequalities (12.16) and (12.17), we obtain

$$f_2(x_2,v_2)+x_2^T w_2 - f_2(u_2,v_2) - u_2^T w_2 + r_2^T \nabla_{u_2u_2} f_2(u_2,v_2) p_2$$
$$\geqq -u_2[\nabla_{x_2} f_2(u_2,v_2)+w_2+\nabla_{u_2u_2} f_2(u_2,v_2)r_2],$$

$$f_2(x_2,y_2) - y_2^T z_2 - f_2(x_2,v_2) + v_2^T z_2 + p_2^T \nabla_{y_2y_2} f_2(x_2,v_2) p_2$$
$$\geqq y_2[\nabla_{y_2} f_2(x_2,y_2) + z_2 + \nabla_{y_2y_2} f_2(x_2,y_2) p_2].$$

Adding the above inequalities, we have

$$f_2(x_2,y_2) + x_2^T w_2 - y_2^T z_2 - \tfrac{1}{2} p_2^T \nabla_{y_2y_2} f_2(x_2,y_2) p_2$$
$$-y_2[\nabla_{y_2} f_2(x_2,y_2) - z_2 + \nabla_{y_2y_2} f_2(x_2,y_2) p_2]$$
$$\geqq f_2(u_2,v_2) + u_2^T w_2 - v_2^T z_2 - r_2^T \nabla_{u_2u_2} f_2(u_2,v_2) p_2$$
$$-u_2[\nabla_{x_2} f_2(u_2,v_2) + w_2 + \nabla_{u_2u_2} f_2(u_2,v_2) r_2].$$

Now, using $x_2^T w_2 \leqq s(x_2|E_2)$ and $v_2^T z_2 \leqq s(v_2|D_2)$, we obtain

$$f_2(x_2,y_2) + s(x_2|E_2) - \tfrac{1}{2} p_2^T \nabla_{y_2y_2} f_2(x_2,y_2) p_2$$
$$-y_2[\nabla_{y_2} f(x_2,y_2) + \nabla_{x_2x_2} f_2(x_2,y_2) p_2]$$
$$\geqq f_2(u_2,v_2) - s(v_2|D_2) - \tfrac{1}{2} r_2^T \nabla_{u_2u_2} f_2(u_2,v_2) p_2$$
$$-u_2[\nabla_{x_2} f_2(u_2,v_2) + \nabla_{u_2u_2} f_2(u_2,v_2) r_2]. \tag{12.18}$$

Similarly, using hypotheses $(v) - (vi)$, primal-dual constraints and the fact that $x_1^T w_1 \leqq s(x_1|E_1)$ and $v_1^T z_1 \leqq s(v_1|D_1)$, we get

$$\eta_1(x_1,u_1)[\nabla_{u_1} f_1(u_1,v_1) + w_1 + \nabla_{u_1u_1} f_1(u_1,v_1) r_1]$$
$$\geqq -(u_1 + r_1)[\nabla_{u_1} f_1(u_1,v_1) + w_1 + \nabla_{u_1u_1} f_1(u_1,v_1) r_1],$$

and

$$\eta_2(v_1,y_1)[-\nabla_{y_1} f_1(x_1,y_1) + z_1 - \nabla_{y_1y_1} f_1(x_1,y_1) p_1]$$
$$\geqq (y_1 + p_1)[\nabla_{y_1} f_1(x_1,y_1) - z_1 + \nabla_{y_1y_1} f_1(x_1,y_1) p_1].$$

Now inequalities (12.3), (12.4), (12.10), and (12.11) give

$$\eta_1(x_1,u_1)[\nabla_{u_1} f_1(u_1,v_1) + w_1 + \nabla_{u_1u_1} f_1(u_1,v_1) r_1] \geqq 0,$$

and

$$\eta_2(v_1,y_1)[-\nabla_{y_1} f_1(x_1,y_1) + z_1 - \nabla_{y_1y_1} f_1(x_1,y_1) p_1] \geqq 0,$$

which by hypothesis (i) and (ii) implies

$$f_1(x_1,v_1)+x_1^T w_1 - f_1(u_1,v_1) - v_1^T w_1 + \frac{1}{2} r_1^T \nabla_{u_1u_1} f_1(u_1,v_1) p_1 \geqq 0,$$

and

$$f_1(x_1,y_1)+v_1^T z_1 - f_1(x_1,v_1) - y_1^T z_1 - \frac{1}{2} p_1^T \nabla_{x_1x_1} f_1(x_1,v_1) p_1 \geqq 0.$$

Adding the above two inequalities, we get

$$\begin{aligned} & f_1(x_1,y_1) - y_1^T z_1 + x_1^T w_1 - \tfrac{1}{2} p_1^T \nabla_{y_1y_1} f_1(x_1,y_1) p_1 \\ & \geqq f_1(u_1,v_1) + v_1^T w_1 - v_1^T z_1 - \tfrac{1}{2} r_1^T \nabla_{u_1u_1} f_1(u_1,v_1) p_1. \end{aligned}$$

Using $x_1^T w_1 \leqq s(x_1|E_1)$ and $v_1^T z_1 \leqq s(v_1|D_1)$, we have

$$\begin{aligned} & f_1(x_1,y_1) - y_1^T (y_1)^T z_1 + s(x_1|E_1) - \tfrac{1}{2} p_1^T \nabla_{y_1y_1} f_1(x_1,y_1) p_1 \\ & \quad \geqq f_1(u_1,v_1) + v_1^T w_1 - s(v_1|D_1) + g_1(u_1,v_1,p_1) - r_1^T \nabla_{r_1} g_1(u_1,v_1,p_1). \end{aligned} \tag{12.19}$$

Combining inequalities (12.18) and (12.19), we obtain

$$L(x_1,x_2,y_1,y_2,z_1,p_1,p_2) \geqq M(u_1,u_2,v_1,v_2,w_1,r_1,r_2).$$

This completes the proof.

Theorem 12.2. *(Strong Duality) Let $(\bar{x_1},\bar{x_2},\bar{y_1},\bar{y_2},\bar{z_1},\bar{z_2},\bar{p_1},\bar{p_2})$ be an optimal solution of (MNHP). Suppose that*

i. $\nabla_{y_1y_1} f_1(\bar{x_1},\bar{y_1})$ *is positive or negative definite and* $\nabla_{y_2y_2} f_2(\bar{x_2},\bar{y_2})$ *is negative definite,*
ii. $\nabla_{y_1} f_1(\bar{x_1},\bar{y_1}) - \bar{z_1} + \nabla_{y_1y_1} f_1(\bar{x_1},\bar{y_1}) p_1 \neq 0$ *and* $\nabla_{y_2} f_2(\bar{x_2},\bar{y_2}) - \bar{z_2} + \nabla_{y_2y_2} f_2(\bar{x_2},\bar{y_2}) \bar{p_2} \neq 0,$
iii. $(\bar{p_1})^T [\nabla_{y_1} f_1(\bar{x_1},\bar{y_1}) - \bar{z_1} + \nabla_{y_1y_1} f_1(\bar{x_1},\bar{y_1}) \bar{p_1}] = 0 \Rightarrow \bar{p_1} = 0$ *and* $y_2[\nabla_{y_2} h_2(\bar{x_2},\bar{y_2},\bar{p_2}) - \nabla_{p_2} h_2(\bar{x_2},\bar{y_2},\bar{p_2}) + \nabla_{y_2y_2} f_2(\bar{x_2},\bar{y_2}) \bar{p_2}] = 0 \Rightarrow \bar{p_2} = 0.$

Then, their exist $\xi_1 \in E_1$, $\xi_2 \in E_2$ such that

i. $(\bar{x_1},\bar{x_2},\bar{y_1},\bar{y_2},\xi_1,\xi_2,\bar{r_1}=0,\bar{r_2}=0)$ *is feasible for (MNHD) and*

ii. $L(\bar{x_1},\bar{x_2},\bar{y_1},\bar{y_2},\bar{p_1},\bar{p_2}) = M(\bar{x_1},\bar{x_2},\bar{y_1},\bar{y_2},\bar{r_1},\bar{r_2}).$

Furthermore, if the hypotheses of Theorem 12.1 are satisfied for all feasible solutions of (MNHP) and (MNHD), then $(\bar{x_1},\bar{x_2},\bar{y_1},\bar{y_2},\xi_1,\xi_2,\bar{r_1}=0,\bar{r_2}=0)$ is an optimal solution for (MNHD).

Proof:

Since $(\bar{x}_1, \bar{x}_2, \bar{y}_1, \bar{y}_2, \bar{p}_1, \bar{p}_2)$ is a n optimal solution of (MNHP), by the Fritz John necessary optimality conditions [17], there exist $\alpha, \gamma \in R_+, \delta_1 \in C_3, \delta_2 \in C_4$, $\beta_1 \in R^{|K_1|}$, $\beta_2, \zeta \in R^{|K_2|}$, $\xi_1 \in R^{|J_1|}$, $\xi_2 \in R^{|J_2|}$ such that the following conditions are satisfied at $(\bar{x}_1, \bar{x}_2, \bar{y}_1, \bar{y}_2, \bar{p}_1, \bar{p}_2)$:

$$(x_1 - \bar{x}_1)^T \Big(\alpha[\nabla_{x_1} f_1(\bar{x}_1, \bar{y}_1) + \xi_1 - \tfrac{1}{2}\nabla_{x_1}\{\bar{p}_1 \nabla_{yy} f_1(\bar{x}_1, \bar{y}_1)\bar{p}_1\} + [\nabla_{y_1 x_1} f_1(\bar{x}_1, \bar{y}_1)$$

$$+\nabla_{x_1}\{\nabla_{y_1 y_1} f_1(\bar{x}_1, \bar{y}_1)\bar{p}_1\}(\beta_1 - \gamma\bar{y}_1 - \delta_1\bar{p}_1)\Big) \geqq 0, \ \forall\, x_1 \in C_1, \tag{12.20}$$

$$(x_2 - \bar{x}_2)^T \Big(\alpha[\nabla_{x_2} f_2(\bar{x}_2, \bar{y}_2) + \xi_2 - \tfrac{1}{2}\nabla_{x_2}\{\bar{p}_2 \nabla_{y_2 y_2} f_2(\bar{x}_2, \bar{y}_2)\bar{p}_2](\beta_2 - \alpha\bar{y}_2$$

$$-\alpha\bar{p}_2 - \delta_2\bar{p}_2) + \{\nabla_{y_2 x_2} f_2(\bar{x}_2, \bar{y}_2)\}(\beta_2 - \alpha\bar{y}_2 - \delta_2\bar{p}_2) \geqq 0, \ \forall\, x_2 \in C_2, \tag{12.21}$$

$$\alpha[\nabla_{y_1} f_1(\bar{x}_1, \bar{y}_1) - \bar{z}_1 - \tfrac{1}{2}\nabla_{y_1}(\nabla_{y_1 y_1} f_1(\bar{x}_1, \bar{y}_1)\bar{p}_1)] + (\nabla_{y_1 y_1} f_1(\bar{x}_1, \bar{y}_1)$$

$$+\nabla_{y_1}(\nabla_{y_1 y_1} h_1(\bar{x}_1, \bar{y}_1)\bar{p}_1)(\beta_1 - \gamma\bar{y}_1 - \delta_1\bar{p}_1)$$

$$-\gamma[\nabla_{y_1} f_1(\bar{x}_1, \bar{y}_1) - \bar{z}_1 + \nabla_{y_1 y_1} f_1(\bar{x}_1, \bar{y}_1)\bar{p}_1] = 0, \tag{12.22}$$

$$\{\nabla_{y_2}(\nabla_{y_2 y_2} f_2(\bar{x}_2, \bar{y}_2)\bar{p}_2)\}(\beta_2 - \alpha\bar{y}_2 - \alpha\bar{p}_2 - \delta_2\bar{p}_2) - \tfrac{1}{2}\alpha[\nabla_{y_2}(\nabla_{y_2 y_2} f_2(\bar{x}_2, \bar{y}_2)\bar{p}_2)]$$

$$+\{\nabla_{y_2 y_2} f_2(\bar{x}_2, \bar{y}_2)\}(\beta_2 - \alpha\bar{y}_2 - \delta_2\bar{p}_2) - \zeta = 0, \tag{12.23}$$

$$\{\nabla_{y_1 y_1} f_1(\bar{x}_1, \bar{y}_1)\}(\beta_1 - \alpha\bar{p}_1 - \gamma\bar{y}_1 - \delta_1\bar{p}_1)$$

$$-\delta_1[\nabla_{y_1} f_1(\bar{x}_1, \bar{y}_1) - \bar{z}_1 + \nabla_{y_1 y_1} f_1(\bar{x}_1, \bar{y}_1)\bar{p}_1] = 0, \tag{12.24}$$

$$\{\nabla_{y_2 y_2} f_2(\bar{x}_2, \bar{y}_2)\}(\beta_2 - \alpha\bar{y}_2 - \alpha\bar{p}_2 - \delta_2\bar{p}_2)$$

$$-\delta_2[\nabla_{y_2} f_2(\bar{x}_2, \bar{y}_2) - \bar{z}_2 + \nabla_{y_2 y_2} f_2(\bar{x}_2, \bar{y}_2)\bar{p}_2] = 0, \tag{12.25}$$

$$\beta_1[\nabla_{y_1} f_1(\bar{x}_1, \bar{y}_1) - \bar{z}_1 + \nabla_{y_1 y_1} h_1(\bar{x}_1, \bar{y}_1)\bar{p}_1] = 0, \tag{12.26}$$

$$\beta_2[\nabla_{y_2} f_2(\bar{x}_2, \bar{y}_2) - \bar{z}_2 + \nabla_{y_2 y_2} f_2(\bar{x}_2, \bar{y}_2)\bar{p}_2] = 0, \tag{12.27}$$

$$\gamma\bar{y}_1[\nabla_{y_1} f_1(\bar{x}_1, \bar{y}_1) - \bar{z}_1 + \nabla_{y_1 y_1} f_1(\bar{x}_1, \bar{y}_1)\bar{p}_1] = 0, \tag{12.28}$$

$$\delta_1\bar{p}_1[\nabla_{y_1} f_1(\bar{x}_1, \bar{y}_1) - \bar{z}_1 + \nabla_{y_1 y_1} f_1(\bar{x}_1, \bar{y}_1)\bar{p}_1] = 0, \tag{12.29}$$

$$\delta_2\bar{p}_2[\nabla_{y_2} f_2(\bar{x}_2, \bar{y}_2) - \bar{z}_2 + \nabla_{y_2 y_2} f_2(\bar{x}_2, \bar{y}_2)\bar{p}_2] = 0, \tag{12.30}$$

$$(\alpha - \gamma^1)y_1 + \beta_1 - \delta_1 p_1 \in N_{D_1}(\bar{z}_1), \tag{12.31}$$

$$\beta_2 - \delta_2 p_2 \in N_{D_2}(\bar{z}_2), \tag{12.32}$$

$$\xi_1{}^T\bar{x}_1 = s(x_1|E_1), \xi_1 \in E_1, \tag{12.33}$$

$$\xi_2{}^T\bar{x}_2 = s(x_2|E_2), \xi_2 \in E_2, \tag{12.34}$$

$$\mu_1\bar{x}_1 = 0, \tag{12.35}$$

$$\mu_2\bar{x}_2 = 0, \tag{12.36}$$

$$\eta^1\bar{y}_1 = 0, \tag{12.37}$$

$$\zeta\bar{y}_2 = 0, \tag{12.38}$$

$$(\alpha, \beta_1, \beta_2, \gamma, \delta_1, \delta_2, \zeta) \neq 0, \tag{12.39}$$

$$(\alpha, \beta_1, \beta_2, \gamma, \delta_1, \delta_2, \zeta) \geqq 0, \tag{12.40}$$

Premultiplying equations (12.24) and (12.25) by $(\beta_1 - \alpha\bar{p}_1 - \gamma\bar{y}_1 - \delta_1\bar{p}_1)$ and $(\beta_2 - \alpha\bar{p}_2 - \alpha\bar{y}_2 - \delta_2\bar{p}_2)$, respectively, and then, using equations (12.26)–(12.30), we get

$$(\beta_1 - \alpha\bar{p}_1 - \gamma\bar{y}_1 - \delta_1\bar{p}_1)^T \nabla_{y_1y_1} h(\bar{x}_1, \bar{y}_1)(\beta_1 - \alpha\bar{p}_1 - \gamma\bar{y}_1 - \delta_1\bar{p}_1) = 0,$$

and

$$(\beta_2 - \alpha\bar{p}_2 - \alpha\bar{y}_2 - \delta_2\bar{p}_2)\nabla_{y_2y_2} f_2(\bar{x}_2, \bar{y}_2)(\beta_2 - \alpha\bar{p}_2 - \alpha\bar{y}_2 - \delta_2\bar{p}_2)$$
$$= -\alpha\delta\bar{y}_2[\nabla_{y_2} f_2(\bar{x}_2, \bar{y}_2) + \nabla_{y_2y_2} f_2(\bar{x}_2, \bar{y}_2)\bar{p}_2].$$

Using hypothesis (i), we get

$$\beta_1 = \alpha\bar{p}_1 + \gamma\bar{y}_1 + \delta_1\bar{p}_1. \tag{12.41}$$

Further using inequality (12.1), (12.6), and (12.40), we obtain

$$(\beta_2 - \alpha\bar{p}_2 - \alpha\bar{y}_2 - \delta_2\bar{p}_2)\nabla_{y_2y_2} f_2(\bar{x}_2, \bar{y}_2)(\beta_2 - \alpha\bar{p}_2 - \alpha\bar{y}_2 - \delta_2\bar{p}_2) \geqq 0,$$

which on using hypothesis (i)

$$\beta_2 = \alpha\bar{p}_2 + \alpha\bar{y}_2 + \delta_2\bar{p}_2. \tag{12.42}$$

From equations (12.24) and (12.25), and hypothesis (ii), we obtain

$$\delta_1 = 0, \tag{12.43}$$

and

$$\delta_2 = 0. \tag{12.44}$$

Now suppose, $\alpha = 0$. Then, equations (12.42) and (12.44) imply $\beta_2 = 0$ and (12.23), (12.42), (12.44) gives $\zeta = 0$. From equation (12.22) and hypothesis (ii)

yield $\gamma = 0$, which along with equations (12.41) and (12.43) gives $\beta_1 = 0$. Thus, $(\alpha, \beta_1, \beta_2, \gamma, \delta_1, \delta_2, \zeta) = 0$, a contradiction to equation (12.39). Hence, from (12.40),

$$\alpha > 0. \tag{12.45}$$

Using equations (12.26), (12.28), and (12.29), we have

$$(\beta_1 - \gamma\bar{y}_1 - \delta_1\bar{p}_1)^T[\nabla_{y_1} f_1(\bar{x}_1, \bar{y}_1) - \bar{z}_1 + \nabla_{y_1 y_1} f_1(\bar{x}_1, \bar{y}_1)\bar{p}_1] = 0,$$

and now using equation (12.41) in the above equation gives

$$\alpha\bar{p}_1{}^T[\nabla_{y_1} f_1(\bar{x}_1, \bar{y}_1) - \bar{z}_1 + \nabla_{y_1 y_1} f_1(\bar{x}_1, \bar{y}_1)\bar{p}_1] = 0. \tag{12.46}$$

which along with hypothesis (iii) yields

$$\bar{p}_1 = 0. \tag{12.47}$$

Further, from equations (12.23) and (12.42), we get

$$\alpha[\nabla_{y_2}(\nabla_{y_2 y_2} f_2(\bar{x}_2, \bar{y}_2)\bar{p}_2) - \nabla_{y_2 y_2} f_2(\bar{x}_2, \bar{y}_2)\bar{p}_2 + \nabla_{y_2 y_2} f_2(\bar{x}_2, \bar{y}_2)\bar{p}_2] = 0. \tag{12.48}$$

Now from hypothesis (iii), we obtain

$$\bar{p}_2 = 0. \tag{12.49}$$

Therefore, equations (12.41) and (12.42) reduce to

$$\beta_1 = \gamma\bar{y}_1, \tag{12.50}$$

and

$$\beta_2 = \alpha\bar{y}_2. \tag{12.51}$$

Also, it follows from equations (12.22), (12.41), (12.47) and hypothesis (ii) that

$$\alpha - \gamma = 0$$

As $\alpha > 0$, we get

$$\alpha = \gamma > 0. \tag{12.52}$$

So equation (12.50) implies

$$\bar{y}_1 = \frac{\beta_1}{\gamma} \geqq 0. \tag{12.53}$$

Similarly,

$$\bar{y}_2 = \frac{\beta_2}{\alpha} \geqq 0. \tag{12.54}$$

Moreover, equations (12.20) and (12.21) along with (12.41), (12.42), and (12.49) yield

$$(x_1-\bar{x}_1)^T\left(\nabla_{x_1}f_1(\bar{x}_1,\bar{y}_1)-\bar{z}_1+\nabla_{x_1x_1}f_1(\bar{x}_1,\bar{y}_1)r_1\right)\geqq 0,\ x_1\in C_1, \tag{12.55}$$

$$(x_2-\bar{x}_2)^T\left(\nabla_{x_2}f_2(\bar{x}_2,\bar{y}_2)-\bar{z}_2+\nabla_{x_2x_2}f_2(\bar{x}_2,\bar{y}_2)r_2\right)\geqq 0,\ \ x_2\in C_2. \tag{12.56}$$

Let $x_1\in C_1$. Then, $x_1+\bar{x}_1\in C_1$, as C_1 is a closed convex cone. By substituting $x_1+\bar{x}_1$ in place of x_1 in (12.55), we get

$$x_1^T[\nabla_{x_1}f_1(\bar{x}_1,\bar{y}_1)-\bar{z}_1+\nabla_{x_1x_1}f_1(\bar{x}_1,\bar{y}_1)r_1]\geqq 0, \tag{12.57}$$

which in turn implies that for all $x_1\in C_1$, we have

$$[\nabla_{x_1}f_1(\bar{x}_1,\bar{y}_1)-\bar{z}_1+\nabla_{x_1x_1}f_1(\bar{x}_1,\bar{y}_1)r_1]\in C_1^*, \tag{12.58}$$

Also, substituting $x_1=0$ and $x_1=2\bar{x}_1$ simultaneously in (12.55) yields

$$\bar{x}_1^T[\nabla_{x_1}f_1(\bar{x}_1,\bar{y}_1)-\bar{z}_1+\nabla_{x_1x_1}f_1(\bar{x}_1,\bar{y}_1)r_1]\geqq 0. \tag{12.59}$$

Using (12.53), we get

$$\bar{y}_1=\frac{\beta_1}{\gamma}\in C_3. \tag{12.60}$$

Let $x_2\in C_2$. Then, $x_2+\bar{x}_2\in C_2$, as C_2 is a closed convex cone. By substituting $x_2+\bar{x}_2$ in place of x_2 in (12.56), we obtain

$$x_2^T[\nabla_{x_2}f_2(\bar{x}_2,\bar{y}_2)-\bar{z}_2+\nabla_{x_2x_2}f_2(\bar{x}_2,\bar{y}_2)r_2]\geqq 0, \tag{12.61}$$

which in turn implies that for all $x_2\in C_2$, we have

$$[\nabla_{x_2}f_2(\bar{x}_2,\bar{y}_2)-\bar{z}_2+\nabla_{x_2x_2}f_2(\bar{x}_2,\bar{y}_2)r_2]\in C_2^*. \tag{12.62}$$

Also, substituting $x_2=0$ and $x_2=2\bar{x}_2$, simultaneously, in (12.56) yields

$$\bar{x}_2^T[\nabla_{x_2}f_1(\bar{x}_2,\bar{y}_2)-\bar{z}_2+\nabla_{x_2x_2}f_2(\bar{x}_2,\bar{y}_2)r_2]\geqq 0. \tag{12.63}$$

Using (12.54), we get

$$\bar{y}_2=\frac{\beta_2}{\gamma}\in C_4. \tag{12.64}$$

$$\bar{x}_2^T[\nabla_{x_2}f_2(\bar{x}_2,\bar{y}_2)-\bar{z}_2+\nabla_{x_2x_2}f_2(\bar{x}_2,\bar{y}_2)r_2]\geqq 0\ \text{(using equation (12.36))}. \tag{12.65}$$

Thus, $(\bar{x}_1,\bar{x}_2,\bar{y}_1,\bar{y}_2,\bar{r}_1=0,\bar{r}_2=0)$ satisfies the dual constraints (12.8)–(12.13). Now using equations (12.27), (12.50), and (12.52), we obtain

$$\bar{y}_1^T\nabla_{y_1}f_1(\bar{x}_1,\bar{y}_1)=\bar{y}_1^T\bar{z}_1, \tag{12.66}$$

and from (12.30), (12.47), (12.50), and (12.52), we get

$$\bar{y}_2^T \bar{z}_2 = s(\bar{y}_2|D_2). \tag{12.67}$$

Moreover, since $\beta_2 = \alpha \bar{y}_2$ and $\alpha > 0$ then from (12.35) and (12.49), we obtain $\bar{y}_1 \in N_{D_1}(\bar{z}_1)$. Also D_1 is a compact convex set in $R^{|K_1|}$:

$$\bar{y}_1^T \bar{z}_1 = s(\bar{y}_1|D_1). \tag{12.68}$$

Thus, after using (12.33), (12.34), (12.47), (12.49), (12.66)–(12.68), the values of the objective functions of (MNHP) and (MNHD) at $(\bar{x}_1, \bar{x}_2, \bar{y}_1, \bar{y}_2, \bar{p}_1 = 0, \bar{p}_2 = 0)$ and $(\bar{x}_1, \bar{x}_2, \bar{y}_1, \bar{y}_2, \bar{r}_1 = 0, \bar{r}_2 = 0)$ are equal. Using weak duality, it has easily shown that $(\bar{x}_1, \bar{x}_2, \bar{y}_1, \bar{y}_2, \bar{r}_1 = 0, \bar{r}_2 = 0)$ is an optimal solution for (MNHD).

Theorem 12.3. *(Converse Duality) Let $(\bar{u}_1, \bar{u}_2, \bar{v}_1, \bar{v}_2, \bar{w}_1, \bar{w}_2, \bar{r}_1, \bar{r}_2)$ be an optimal solution of (MNHD). Suppose that*

i. $\nabla_{u_1u_1} f_1(\bar{u}_1, \bar{v}_1)$ *is positive or negative definite, and* $\nabla_{r_2r_2} g_2(\bar{u}_2, \bar{v}_2, \bar{r}_2)$ *is negative definite,*
ii. $\nabla_{u_1} f_1(\bar{u}_1, \bar{v}_1) + \bar{w}_1 + \nabla_{u_1u_1} f_1(\bar{u}_1, \bar{v}_1) \neq 0$ *and* $v_2[\nabla_{y_2} f_2(\bar{x}_2, \bar{y}_2) + \bar{w}_2 + \nabla_{y_2y_2} f_2(\bar{x}_2, \bar{y}_2)] \neq 0,$
iii. $\bar{r}_1^T [\nabla_{u_1} f_1(\bar{u}_1, \bar{v}_1) + \bar{w}_1 + \nabla_{u_1u_1} f_1(\bar{u}_1, \bar{v}_1)] = 0 \Rightarrow \bar{r}_1 = 0$ *and* $u_2[\nabla_{u_2} g_2(\bar{u}_2, \bar{v}_2, \bar{r}_2) - \nabla_{r_2} g_2(\bar{u}_2, \bar{v}_2, \bar{r}_2) + \nabla_{u_2u_2} f_2(\bar{u}_2, \bar{v}_2)\bar{r}_2] = 0 \Rightarrow \bar{r}_2 = 0,$

Then, their exist $\vartheta_1 \in D_1$, $\vartheta_2 \in D_2$ such that

i. $(\bar{u}_1, \bar{u}_2, \bar{v}_1, \bar{v}_2, \vartheta_1, \vartheta_2, \bar{r}_1 = 0, \bar{r}_2 = 0)$ *is feasible for (MNHP)*
ii. $L(\bar{u}_1, \bar{u}_2, \bar{v}_1, \bar{v}_2, \bar{p}_1, \bar{p}_2) = M(\bar{u}_1, \bar{u}_2, \bar{v}_1, \bar{v}_2, \bar{r}_1, \bar{r}_2).$

Furthermore, if the hypothesis of Theorem 12.1 is satisfied for all feasible solutions of (MNHP) and (MNHD), then $(\bar{x}_1, \bar{x}_2, \bar{y}_1, \bar{y}_2, \bar{r}_1 = 0, \bar{r}_2 = 0)$ is an optimal solution for (MNHP).

Proof. Follows on the line of Theorem 12.2.

12.6 SELF-DUALITY

In general, $(MNHP)$ and (MNHD) are not self-duals without some added restrictions on f. If we assume $D_1 = D_2, E_1 = E_2, C_1 = C_2 = C_3 = C_4 = C$, $f_1 : R^{|J_1|} \times R^{|K_1|} \to R$, $f_2 : R^{|J_2|} \times R^{|K_2|} \to R$ are skew symmetric, that is,

$$f_i(u_1, v_1) = -f_i(v_1, u_1), i = 1, 2, ...k,$$

then, we shall show that (MNHP) and (MNHD) are self-duals. By recasting the dual problem (MNHD) as a minimization problem, we have

Minimize $M(u,v,r) =$
$-\{f_1(u_1,v_1) - s(v_1|D_1) + f_2(u_2,v_2) - s(v_2|D_2) + u_1^T w_1$

$-\frac{1}{2} r_1^T \nabla_{u_1u_1} f_1(u_1,v_1,r_1) - \frac{1}{2} r_2^T \nabla_{u_2u_2} f_2(u_2,v_2,r_2) - u_2^T [\nabla_{u_2} f_2(u_2,v_2) + \nabla_{u_2u_2} f_2(u_2,v_2) r_2]\}$
subject to

$$\nabla_{u_1} f_1(u_1,v_1) + w_1 + \nabla_{u_1u_1} f_1(u_1,v_1) r_1 \in C_3^*,$$
$$\nabla_{u_2} f_2(u_2,v_2) + w_2 + \nabla_{u_2u_2} f_2(u_2,v_2) r_2 \in C_4^*,$$
$$u_1^T [\nabla_{u_1} f_1(u_1,v_1) + w_1 + \nabla_{u_1u_1} f_1(u_1,v_1) r_1] \leqq 0,$$
$$r_1^T [\nabla_{u_1} f_1(u_1,v_1) + w_1 + \nabla_{u_1u_1} f_1(u_1,v_1) r_1] \leqq 0,$$
$$r_2^T [\nabla_{u_2} f_2(u_2,v_2) + w_2 + \nabla_{u_2u_2} f_2(u_2,v_2) r_2] \leqq 0,$$
$$v_1, v_2, u_2 \geqq 0.$$

Since f are skew symmetric,
$\nabla_{u_1} f_1(u_1,v_1) = -\nabla_{u_1} f_1(v_1,u_1)$ and $\nabla_{u_1} f_2(u_2,v_2) = -\nabla_{u_1} f_2(v_2,u_2)$,

now the above problem becomes
Minimize $M(u,v,r) =$
$f_1(v_1,u_1) + s(v_1|D_1) + f_2(v_2,u_2) + s(v_2|D_2) - u_1^T w_1$

$-\frac{1}{2} r_1^T \nabla_{u_1u_1} f_1(v_1,u_1) r_1 - \frac{1}{2} r_2^T \nabla_{u_2u_2} f_2(u_2,v_2) r_2 - u_2^T [\nabla_{u_2} f_2(v_2,u_2) + \nabla_{u_2u_2} f_2(v_2,u_2) r_2]$
subject to

$$-\left(\nabla_{u_1} f_1(v_1,u_1) + w_1 + \nabla_{u_1u_1} f_1(v_1,u_1) r_1\right) \in C_1^*,$$
$$-\left(\nabla_{u_2} f_2(v_2,u_2) + w_2 + \nabla_{u_2u_2} f_2(v_2,u_2) r_2\right) \in C_2^*,$$
$$u_1^T [\nabla_{u_1} f_1(v_1,u_1) + w_1 + \nabla_{u_1u_1} f_1(v_1,u_1) r_1] \geqq 0,$$
$$r_1^T [\nabla_{u_1} f_1(v_1,u_1) + w_1 + \nabla_{u_1u_1} f_1(v_1,u_1) r_1] \geqq 0,$$
$$r_2^T [\nabla_{u_2} f_2(v_2,u_2) + w_2 + \nabla_{u_2u_2} f_2(v_2,u_2) r_2] \geqq 0,$$
$$v_1, v_2, u_2 \geqq 0,$$

which shows that $M(u,v,p)$ is identical to $L(x,y,p)$; that is, the objective and the constraint functions are equal. Thus, the problem $L(x,y,p)$ becomes self-dual.

It is obvious that the feasibility of $(x_1,x_2,y_1,y_2,p_1,p_2)$ for $L(x,y,p)$ implies the feasibility of $(y_1,y_2,x_1,x_2,p_1,p_2)$ $(MNHP)$ implies the feasibility of for $(MNHD)$ and conversely.

12.7 CONCLUSION

A pair of nondifferentiable mixed-type second-order symmetric dual programs has been formulated over arbitrary constraints by considering the optimization under the assumptions of bonvexity and pseudobonvexity with respect to η assumptions. While discussing the result of Wolfe-type higher-order dual model over arbitrary cones, we can see the result of duality over Mond–Weir also. It may be noted that the symmetric duality between $(MNHP)$ and $(MNHD)$ can be utilized to establish mixed symmetric duality in integer for scalar and multiobjective programming over cone and other related programming problems. The question arises as to whether the duality results developed in this chapter hold for Wolfe-type higher-order nondifferentiable multiobjective optimization problems under arbitrary cones. This may be the future direction for the researchers working in this area.

BIBLIOGRAPHY

[1] Bazaraa, M. S. and Goode, J. J.: On symmetric duality in nonlinear programming, *Operations Research,* 21 (1973), 1–9.

[2] Chandra, S., Husain, I. and Abha, On mixed symmetric duality in mathematical programming, *Opsearch,* 36 (1999), 165–171. View at Zentralblatt MATH.

[3] Chandra, S., Craven, B. D. and Mond, B.: Generalized concavity and duality with a square root term, *Optimization,* 16 (1985), 653–662.

[4] Chandra, S. and Kumar, V.: A note on pseudoinvexity and symmetric duality, *European Journal of Operational Research,* 105 (1998), 626–629.

[5] Chen, X.: Higher-order symmetric duality in nondifferentiable multiobjective programming problems, *Journal of Mathematical Analysis and Applications,* 290 (2004), 423–435.

[6] Dantzig, G. B., Eisenberg E. and Cottle R. W.: Symmetric dual nonlinear programming, *Pacific Journal of Mathematics,* 15 (1965), 809–812.

[7] Devi, G.: Symmetric duality for nonlinear programming problems involving η-bonvex functions, *European Journal of Operational Research,* 104 (1998), 615–621.

[8] Dorn, W. S.: A symmetric dual theorems for quadratic programs, *Journal of the Operations Research Society of Japan,* 2 (1960), 93–97.

[9] Hanson, M.A.: Second-order invexity and duality in mathematical programming, *Opsearch,* 30 (1989), 313–320.

[10] Hou, S. H. and Yang, X. M.: On second-order symmetric duality in nondifferentiable programming, *Journal of Mathematical Analysis and Applications,* 255 (2001), 491–498.

[11] Gulati, T. R., Himani, S. and Gupta, S. K.: 2010, Second-order multiobjective symmetric duality with cone constraints, *European Journal of Operational Research,* 205 (2005), 247–252.

[12] Gulati, T. R. and Gupta, S. K.: Higher-order nondifferentiable symmetric duality with generalized F-convexity, *Journal of Mathematical Analysis and Applications,* 329 (2007), 229–237.

[13] Gulati, T. R. and Gupta, S. K.: Higher-order symmetric duality with cone constraints, *Applied Mathematics Letters,* 22 (2009), 776–781.

[14] Gulati, T. R. and Mehndiratta, G.: Nondifferentiable multiobjective Mond-Weir type second-order symmetric duality over cones, *Optimization Letters,* 4 (2010), 293–309.

[15] Mandal, P. and Nahak, C.: Symmetric duality with $(p,r)-\rho-(\eta,\theta)$-invexity, *International Journal of Pure and Applied Mathematics,* 217 (2011), 8141–8148.
[16] Mangasarian, O. L.: *Nonlinear Programming,* McGraw-Hill, New York, (1969).
[17] Mangasarian, O. L.: Second and higher-order duality in nonlinear programming, *Journal of Mathematical Analysis and Applications,* 51 (1975), 607–620.
[18] Mond, B. and Zhang, J.: Higher-order invexity and duality in mathematical programming, in: J. P. Crouzeix, et al. (Eds.), *Generalized Convexity, Generalized Monotonicity: Recent Results,* Kluwer Academic, Dordrecht, (1998), 357–372.
[19] Mond, B. and Weir, T.: Generalized concavity and duality in Generalized Concavity in Optimization and Economics (S. Schaible and W. T. Ziemba Eds.), Academic Press, New York, (1981), 263–280.
[20] Mond, B. and Schechter, M.: Nondifferentiable symmetric duality, *Bulletin of the Australian Mathematical Society,* 53 (1996), 177–188.
[21] Kassem, M.: Higher-order symmetric duality in vector optimization problem involving generalized cone-invex functions, *Applied Mathematics and Computation,* 209 (2009), 405–409.
[22] Kassem, M.: Multiobjective nonlinear symmetric duality involving generalized pseudoconvexity, *Applied Mathematics and Computation,* 2 (2011), 1236–1242.
[23] Khurana, S.: Symmetric duality in multiobjective programming involving generalized cone-invex functions, *European Journal of Operational Research,* 165 (2005), 592–597.
[24] Kim, D. S. and Yun, Y. B.: Second-order symmetric and self duality in multiobjective programming, *Applied Mathematics Letters,* 10 (1997), 17–22.
[25] Kim, D. S., Kang, H. S. and Lee, Y. J.: Second-order symmetric duality for nondifferentiable multiobjective programming involving cones, *Taiwanese Journal of Mathematics,* 12 (2008), 1347–1363.
[26] Padhan, S. K. and Nahak, C.: Higher-order symmetric duality with higherorder generalized invexity, *Journal of Applied Mathematics and Computing,* 48 (2015), 407–420.
[27] Suneja, S. K., Sunila, A. and Sonia, D.: Multiobjective symmetric duality involving cones, *European Journal of Operational Research,* 141 (2002), 471–479.
[28] Suneja, S. K., Lalitha, C. S. and Khurana, S.: Second order symmetric duality in multiobjective programming, *European Journal of Operational Research,* 144 (2003), 492–500.
[29] Xianjun, L.: Sufficiency and duality for nonsmooth multiobjective programming problems involving generalized univex functions, *Journal of Systems Science and Complexity,* 26 (2013), 1002–1018.
[30] Yang, X. M., Teo, K. L. and Yang, X. Q.: Mixed symmetric duality in nondifferentiable mathematical programming, *Indian Journal of Pure and Applied Mathematics,* 34 (2003), 805–815. View at Zentralblatt MATH.
[31] Yang, X. M., Yang, X. Q., Teo, K. L. and Hou, S. H.: Second order symmetric duality in non-differentiable multiobjective programming with F -convexity, *European Journal of Operational Research,* 164 (2005), 406–416.
[32] Yang, X. M., Yang, X. Q., Teo, K. L. and Hou, S. H.: Multiobjective second-order symmetric duality with F-convexity, *European Journal of Operational Research,* 165 (2005), 585–591.
[33] Ying, G.: Higher-order symmetric duality in multiobjective programming problems, *Acta Mathematicae Applicatae Sinica, English Series,* 32 (2016), 485–494.

Index